Patent Prosecution

2001 Case Digest

Patent Prosecution

2001 Case Digest

Irah H. Donner

Hale and Dorr LLP
Washington, D.C.

The Bureau of National Affairs, Inc., Washington, D.C.

Library of Congress Cataloging-in-Publication Data

Donner, Irah H.
   Patent prosecution case digest / Irah H. Donner.
    p. cm.
   ISBN 1-57018-038-5
   1. Patent laws and legislation--United States--Digests.
I. Title.
KF3105.3.D66   1996
346.7304´86--dc21

                                              96-39218
                                                 CIP

Published by BNA Books
1231 25th St., N.W., Washington, D.C. 20037
http://www.bnabooks.com

International Standard Book Number: 1-57018-312-0
Printed in the United States of America

To Zachary, Tali, J.J. and Loni

Preface and Suggestions for How to Use
Patent Prosecution Case Digest with CD-ROM

When prosecuting U.S. patent applications, oftentimes an Examiner refuses to allow a patent for reasons not supported by current law. If the patent attorney can in turn cite a relevant decision favorable to the applicant, the Examiner is then forced to review the cited decision and determine whether, in fact, the cited decision governs the grant of a patent.

Of course, there is no guarantee that the Examiner will in fact follow the cited decision(s). Nevertheless, citing legal opinions to an Examiner will also assist the patent attorney or patent agent in defining the appropriate issues that might be required to be appealed to the Board of Patent Appeals and Interferences (the Board).

This *Case Digest* with CD-ROM is organized in accordance with the common rejections received from the U.S. Patent Office. To assist the patent attorney or patent agent in overcoming these common rejections—and to permit easy insertion into Amendments or Responses to Official Actions—the book and CD-ROM include self-explanatory quotes from important decisions from the Supreme Court, the Federal Circuit, the Court of Customs and Patent Appeals, and the Board.

To use these products, I recommend that you first familiarize yourself with the *Case Digest* workbook and its layout. You may then choose to use the *Digest* without the CD-ROM by using the table of contents and perusing relevant quotes. Or, you can aid your search and save keystrokes by calling up the CD-ROM's file in your word processor.

The file is in Corel® WordPerfect® 6/7/8/9 for Windows. (Corel® and WordPerfect® are registered trademarks of Corel Corporation or Corel Corporation Limited.) WordPerfect® 6/7/8/9 can be read by MicroSoft Word, although the file may take several minutes to convert because of its size. The file can then be saved as a Word file, but it must be saved to a hard drive because it will be too large for a diskette.

To use the CD-ROM most efficiently (and avoid "false hits"), I suggest that you first use the printed table of contents to identify and locate the basic legal issue. Note the outline number associated with that issue (*e.g.,* "Anticipation of Ranges in a Claim" would be "III.M."), and use your word processor's search function to find that number.

Once at the beginning of the legal issue, you can simply browse through all quotes in that section, or you can use your word processor to search for a specific word or phrase.

Because of the dynamic nature of patent law, regular updates to this *Case*

Digest are planned. However, this product can only improve with feedback from those who use it. I therefore ask for your help as a reader. If there are any quotes that you think should be included herein, please send them to my attention. Suggestions regarding improvements to this book and CD-ROM would also be greatly appreciated. Please send comments to me c/o BNA Books Editorial Offices, 1231 25th St. NW, Washington, DC 20037-1197; or e-mail: books@bna.com.

Irah H. Donner
October 2001

Summary Contents

Statutory Subject Matter Issues

Prior Art Issues

Disclosure/Claim Requirement Issues

Claim Interpretation Issues

Priority and Related Application Issues

Other Issues

Post Issuance Issues

Detailed Contents

Statutory Subject Matter Issues

Prior Art Issues

Disclosure/Claim Requirement Issues

Claim Interpretation Issues

Priority and Related Application Issues

Other Issues

Post Issuance Issues

I. Inventorship/Ownership

1. ***In re Facius***, 161 USPQ 294, 301 (C.C.P.A. 1969)

   However, the existence of combination claims does *not* evidence inventorship by the patentee of the individual elements or sub-combinations thereof if the latter are not separately claimed apart from the combination. It is clear that the inventor of a combination may not have invented *any* element of that combination, much less each of the elements. . . .

2. ***Regents of Univ. of Cal. v. Synbiotics Corp.***, 29 USPQ 2d 1463, 1466–67 (S.D. Cal. 1993)

   Joint invention connotes collaboration of effort to produce a complete and operative invention. *Garrett Corp. v. United States*, 422 F.2d 874, 881 [164 USPQ 521] (Ct. Cl. 1970). One who merely suggests an idea of a result to be accomplished, rather than the means of accomplishing it, is not a joint inventor. *Id. See also Amgen, Inc. v. Chugai Pharmaceutical Co.*, 927 F.2d 1200, 1206 [18 USPQ 2d 1016] (Fed. Cir. 1991). In *Garrett*, the Court held that a person who only suggests a broad idea (wherein the idea is obvious in view of prior art) without further participation or responsibility for making the invention complete and operable is not a joint inventor. *Garrett*, 422 F.2d at 881. In *Amgen*, the Court held that conception requires both the idea of the invention's structure and possession of an operative method of making it. *Amgen*, 927 F.2d at 1206. In some instances the inventor is unable to establish a conception until he or she has reduced the invention to practice through a successful experiment. *Id.*

3. ***Kimberly-Clark Corp. v. Procter & Gamble Distrib. Co.***, 23 USPQ 2d 1921, 1925 (Fed. Cir. 1992)

   The "Section by Section Analysis" in the Congressional Record indicates that Congress intended to codify the principles of *Monsanto*:

   > Subsection (a) of section 105 amends section 116 of the patent law to allow inventors to apply for a patent jointly even though (i) they did not physically work together or at

the same time, (ii) each did not make the same type or amount of contribution, or (iii) each did not make a contribution to the subject matter of every claim of the patent. Items (i) and (ii) adopt the rationale of decisions such as *Monsanto* []

4. ***Kimberly-Clark Corp. v. Procter & Gamble Distrib. Co.***, 23 USPQ 2d 1921, 1925 (Fed. Cir. 1992)

The court in *Monsanto* [] stated the pertinent principles as follows:

A joint invention is the product of collaboration of the inventive endeavors of two or more persons working toward the same end and producing an invention by their aggregate efforts. To constitute a joint invention, it is necessary that each of the inventors work on the same subject matter and make some contribution of the inventive thought and to the final result. Each needs to perform but a part of the task if an invention emerges from all of the steps taken together. It is not necessary that the entire inventive concept should occur to each of the joint inventors, or that the two should physically work on the project together. One may take a step at one time, the other an approach at different times. One may do more of the experimental work while the other makes suggestions from time to time. The fact that each of the inventors plays a different role and that the contribution of one may not be as great as that of another does not detract from the fact that the invention is joint if each makes some original contribution, though partial, to the final solution of the problem.

5. ***Kimberly-Clark Corp. v. Procter & Gamble Distrib. Co.***, 23 USPQ 2d 1921, 1926 (Fed. Cir. 1992)

What is clear is that the statutory word "jointly" is not mere surplusage. For persons to be joint inventors under Section 116, there must be some element of joint behavior, such as collaboration or working under common direction, one inventor seeing a relevant report, and building upon it or hearing another's suggestion at a meeting. Here there was nothing of that nature. Individuals can not be joint inventors if they are completely ignorant of what each other has done until years after their individual independent efforts. They can not be totally independent of each other and be joint inventors.

We therefore hold that joint inventorship under Section 116 requires at least some quantum of collaboration or connection.

6. ***Regents of Univ. of Cal. v. Synbiotics Corp.***, 29 USPQ 2d 2032, 2033 (S.D. Cal. 1994)

In some instances, such as the discovery of genes or chemicals, an inventor is unable to establish a conception until he has reduced the invention to practice through a successful experiment. This situation results in what is termed "simultaneous conception and reduction to practice." In *Amgen*, the Court held that, with respect to the discovery of a gene which is considered a chemical compound, conception has not been achieved until reduction to practice has occurred, or until after the gene is isolated.

Brown admits in her deposition that she made no contribution to the isolation of the virus or to the determination of its structure, name, or chemical or physical properties. In essence, Brown's sole contribution to the discovery of FIV is that she brought her sick cats, along with her written observations of the cats' symptoms, to UC Davis with a suspicion that the cats may have a virus similar to the human AIDS virus. These facts do not support a claim that Brown is a co-inventor for the '753 or '602 patent.

7. ***Credle v. Bond***, 30 USPQ 2d 1911, 1917–18 (Fed. Cir. 1994)

Credle's original preliminary statement clearly asserted two entirely separate, non-overlapping sets of dates for both Credle and Boone. Such allegations do not compel a conclusion that both are joint inventors, a status that necessarily requires some degree of collaboration. . . . On the contrary, where the sets of dates alleged define distinct, non-overlapping periods, the allegation that the inventors are joint is facially inconsistent with the two distinct periods, because a person who first conceived and first reduced the subject matter of the invention to practice cannot, under the law, be a joint inventor with a person who allegedly did not even conceive the invention until after the former's reduction to practice. Collaboration under such circumstances simply is not possible. Consequently, Credle and Boone cannot be joint inventors of the subject matter of the count.

8. ***Burroughs Wellcome Co. v. Barr Labs., Inc.***, 32 USPQ 2d 1915, 1919 (Fed. Cir. 1994), ***cert. denied***, 515 U.S. 1130 (1995)

A joint invention is the product of a collaboration between two or more persons working together to solve the problem addressed. . . . People may be joint inventors even though they do not physically work on the invention together or at the same time, and even though each does not make the same type or amount of contribution. 35 U.S.C. § 116. The statute does not set forth the minimum quality or quantity of contribution required for joint inventorship.

9. ***Sewall v. Walters***, 30 USPQ 2d 1356, 1359 (Fed. Cir. 1994)

Sewall has failed to persuade us that the Board clearly erred in finding that Sewall's design of circuits to carry out Walters' idea was simply the exercise of the normal skill expected of an ordinary chip designer, which did not involve any inventive acts on the part of Sewall. . . . The specification thus renders the presence of Sewall's alleged coinventive contributions, namely, the circuits that he designed, completely optional to the apparatus of the count. It also explicitly states that the design of those circuits is self-evident from their function. Thus, the specification itself indicates that one of ordinary skill in the art could construct the back projecting apparatus functionally described therein without unduly extensive research or experimentation.

10. ***Stark v. Advanced Magnetics Inc.***, 31 USPQ 2d 1290, 1294 (Fed. Cir. 1994)

[W]e clarify and reinforce that the governing principle is as stated in the statute and regulations. Neither 35 U.S.C. §256 nor 37 C.F.R. §1.324 requires that an omitted inventor of an issued patent must diligently bring a lawsuit to correct inventorship or be forever barred from doing so.

11. ***Hess v. Advanced Cardiovascular Sys., Inc.***, 41 USPQ 2d 1782, 1785–86 (Fed. Cir.), ***cert. denied***, 520 U.S. 1277 (1997)

"The inventors as named in an issued patent are presumed to be correct." *Amax Fly Ash Corp. v. United States*, 514 F.2d 1041, 1047, 182 USPQ 210, 215 (Ct. Cl. 1975). As the court there stated, in holding that one claiming that the inventor listed in the patent derived the invention from the claimant's work must show derivation by clear and convincing evidence, "the temptation for even honest witnesses to reconstruct, in a manner favorable to their own position, what their state of mind may have been years earlier, is simply too great to permit a lower standard." *Id.* at 1047, 182 USPQ at 215 (footnote omitted). This language is similarly applicable to claims of co-inventorship made after a patent has been issued—particularly where, as here, the patent has been outstanding for a considerable time and the patented device has been successful. In that situation, too, there is an equally strong temptation for persons who consulted with the inventor and provided him with materials and advice, to reconstruct, so as to further their own position, the extent of their contribution to the conception of the invention. In these circumstances, it would be inappropriate to permit a lower standard than clear and convincing evidence.

12. ***Hess v. Advanced Cardiovascular Sys., Inc.***, 41 USPQ 2d 1782, 1786 (Fed. Cir.), ***cert. denied***, 117 S. Ct. 2459 (1997) (quoting ***O'Reilly v. Morse***, 56 U.S. 62, 111 (1853); ***Shatterproof Glass Corp. v. Libbey-Owens Ford Co.***, 225 USPQ 634, 641 (Fed. Cir. 1985))

    More than 140 years ago the Supreme Court, in holding that Samuel Morse's discussions with scientists in connection with his invention of the telegraph did not alter his status of the sole inventor of that device, stated:

    > No invention can possibly be made, consisting of a combination of different elements . . . without a thorough knowledge of the properties of each of them, and the mode in which they operate on each other. And it can make no difference, in this respect, whether [the inventor] derives his information from books, or from conversation with men skilled in the science. If it were otherwise, no patent, in which a combination of different elements is used, could ever be obtained.

    Similarly, . . . this court stated that

    > [a]n inventor may use the services, ideas, and aid of others in the process of perfecting his invention without losing his right to a patent.

13. ***Final Oil & Chemical Co. v. Ewen***, 43 USPQ 2d 1935, 1941 (Fed. Cir. 1997) (quoting ***Burroughs Wellcome Co. v. Barr Labs., Inc.***, 32 USPQ 2d 1915, 1921 (Fed. Cir. 1994))

    [A] joint invention is simply the product of a collaboration between two or more persons working together to solve the problem addressed. . . . The determination of whether a person is a joint inventor is fact specific, and no bright-line standard will suffice in every case.

    Nonetheless, our precedent provides guidance as to what types of acts are, or are not, sufficient in quantum and quality to establish joint inventorship. One need not alone conceive of the entire invention, for this would obviate the concept of joint inventorship. However, a joint inventor must contribute in some significant manner to the conception of the invention. . . . As such, "each inventor must contribute to the joint arrival at a definite and permanent idea of the invention as it will be used in practice."

14. ***Final Oil & Chem. Co. v. Ewen***, 43 USPQ 2d 1935, 1941 (Fed. Cir. 1997)

If a person supplies the required quantum of inventive contribution, that person does not lose his or her status as a joint inventor just because he or she used the services, ideas, and aid of others in the process of perfecting the invention. . . . However, those others may also in appropriate circumstances become joint inventors by their contributions. In addition, a person is not precluded from being a joint inventor simply because his or her contribution to a collaborative effort is experimental.

15. ***Final Oil & Chem. Co. v. Ewen***, 43 USPQ 2d 1935, 1941 (Fed. Cir. 1997)

The basic exercise of the normal skill expected of one skilled in the art, without an inventive act, also does not make one a joint inventor. . . . Therefore, a person will not be a co-inventor if he or she does no more than explain to the real inventors concepts that are well known and the current state of the art. . . . The case law thus indicates that to be a joint inventor, an individual must make a contribution to the conception of the claimed invention that is not insignificant in quality, when that contribution is measured against the dimension of the full invention.

16. ***Schering Corp. v. Roussel-UCLAF SA***, 41 USPQ 2d 1359, 1362 (Fed. Cir. 1997)

There is no dispute as to the principles that provide the backdrop for this case. Each co-owner of a United States patent is ordinarily free to make, use, offer to sell, and sell the patented invention without regard to the wishes of any other co-owner. 35 U.S.C. § 262. Each co-owner's ownership rights carry with them the right to license others, a right that also does not require the consent of any other co-owner. *See, e.g., Willingham v. Lawton*, 555 F.2d 1340, 1344, 194 USPQ 249, 253 (6th Cir. 1977) ("a co-owner of a patent can even grant a license to a third party without consent of the other owners"); *Talbot v. Quaker State Oil Ref. Co.*, 28 F. Supp. 544, 548, 37 USPQ 453, 456 (W.D. Pa. 1938) (a co-owner "may make use of and sell specimens of the patented invention and may license others to do so; and neither he nor his licensees can be enjoined from a continuance in so doing"), *aff'd*, 104 F.2d 967, 41 USPQ 1 (3d Cir. 1939). Thus, unless the co-owner has given up these rights through an "agreement to the contrary," 35 U.S.C. § 262, the co-owner may not be prohibited from exploiting its rights in the patent, including the right to grant licenses to third parties on whatever conditions the co-owner chooses.

17. ***Schering Corp. v. Roussel-UCLAF SA***, 41 USPQ 2d 1359, 1362 (Fed. Cir. 1997)

It is true that by granting a license to a prospective infringement defendant, or to a defendant that has already been sued for infringement, a patent co-owner can effectively deprive its fellow co-owner of the right to sue for and collect any infringement damages that accrue after the date of the license. It is also true that the suing co-owner may not obtain an injunction against future acts of infringement by the licensee, since the license grants full protection against a claim of future infringement. But the grant of a license by one co-owner cannot deprive the other co-owner of the right to sue for accrued damages for past infringement. That would require a release, not a license, and the rights of a patent co-owner, absent agreement to the contrary, do not extend to granting a release that would defeat an action by other co-owners to recover damages for past infringement.

18. ***Final Oil & Chem. Co. v. Ewen***, 43 USPQ 2d 1935, 1941 (Fed. Cir. 1997)

Conception is the touchstone to determining inventorship. . . . Conception of a chemical substance requires knowledge of both the specific chemical structure of the compound and an operative method of making it.

19. ***Minco, Inc. v. Combustion Eng'g, Inc.***, 40 USPQ 2d 1001, 1006 (Fed. Cir. 1996)

Patentees include not only the one to whom the patent issued but also any successors in title. 35 U.S.C. § 100(d) (1994). Parties may transfer patent rights by a legal agreement. *CMS Indus., Inc. v. L.P.S. Int'l, Ltd.*, 643 F.2d 289, 294, 217 USPQ 20, 23 (5th Cir. 1981). A conveyance of interests in a patent typically constitutes either an assignment or a mere license. An assignment of patent rights operates to transfer title to the patent, while a license leaves title in the patent owner. *Waterman v. Mackenzie*, 138 U.S. 252, 255, 34 L. Ed. 923, 11 S. Ct. 334 (1891). Thus, an assignee holds title to a patent and may sue for infringement without further permission or clearance. A licensee, however, cannot sue without joinder of the patent owner. *Id.* To create an assignment, a contract must transfer: (1) the entire exclusive patent right, (2) an undivided interest in the patent rights, or (3) the entire exclusive right within any geographical region of the United States. *Waterman*, 138 U.S. at 255. An agreement that does not transfer one of these three interests is merely a license. *Id.*

An assignee may bring an action to redress any violations of the exclusive rights conferred by the patent. 35 U.S.C. § 271 (1994). Infringement, however, harms only the owner of the patent at the time of the infringing acts. *See United States v. Loughrey*, 172 U.S. 206, 211–12, 43 L. Ed. 420, 19 S. Ct. 153 (1898). Thus, the conveyance of the patent does not normally include the right to recover for injury occurring to the prior owner. *Crown Die & Tool Co. v. Nye Tool & Mach. Works*, 261 U.S. 24, 43, 67 L. Ed. 516, 43 S. Ct. 254 (1923) (the assignee may sue for past infringement if the "owner assigns the patent and also the claim for past infringements to the same person") . . . As the Supreme Court stated, it is a "great mistake" to "suppose" that the assignment of the patent carries with it the right to sue for past infringement. *Moore v. Marsh*, 74 U.S. (7 Wall.) 515, 522, 19 L. Ed. 37 (1868). These cases establish a general rule that the right to sue for prior infringement is not transferred unless the assignment agreement manifests an intent to transfer this right. Neither statute nor common law precedent, however, requires a particular formula or set prescription of words to express that conveyance.

20. ***Dynamic Mfg, Inc. v. Craze***, 46 USPQ 2d 1548, 1552 & n.9 (E.D. Va. 1998)

The Patent Act, 35 U.S.C. § 261 (1994), states that "applications for patent, patents, or any interest therein, shall be assignable in law by an instrument in writing." . . . The statute further states that "an assignment, grant or conveyance shall be void as against any subsequent purchaser or mortgagee for a value consideration, without notice, unless it is recorded in the Patent and Trademark Office within three months from its date or prior to the date of such subsequent purchase or mortgage." 35 U.S.C. § 261 (1994). . . . Furthermore, courts have repeatedly upheld [that] except in limited circumstances, an assignment of a patent right must be in writing. . . . [T]he Federal Circuit considered a case where there was a clear agreement to assign a patent, however there was no written assignment of the rights to the patent. . . . The court in that case found that even where there is a clear oral agreement to assign a patent, to establish standing in case under the Patent Act, the party must have an actual assignment in writing.

21. ***Enzo APA & Son, Inc. v. Geapag A.G.***, 45 USPQ 2d 1368, 1370–71 (Fed. Cir. 1998)

Accordingly, an assignee is the patentee and has standing to bring suit for infringement in its own name. See 35 U.S.C. § 100(d) (1994). The assignment of legal title in a patent can be conveyed in the form of the entire patent, an undivided part or share of the entire patent, or all rights under the patent in a specified geographical region of the United States (a so called "grant"). . . . Any less than a complete transfer of these rights is merely a license, in which case the title remains with the owner of the patent and the suit must be brought in its name. Id.

We have accorded standing, in certain limited circumstances, where all substantial rights under the patent have been transferred in the form of an exclusive license, rendering the licensee the virtual assignee. . . . While we acknowledge that a license may be written, verbal, or implied, if the license is to be considered a virtual assignment to assert standing, it must be in writing. The limited exception we have provided conferring standing on licensees is restricted to virtual assignees. As such, the licensing arrangement conferring such must, logically, resemble an assignment in both form and substance. Under the 35 U.S.C. § 261 (1994), "applications for patent, patents, or any interest therein, shall be assignable in law by an instrument in writing." If we were to expand the exception to include verbal licenses, the exception would swallow the rule. Parties would be free to engage in revisionist history, circumventing the certainty provided by the writing requirement of section 261 by claiming to be patentee by virtue of a verbal licensing arrangement.

22. ***Canon Computer Sys., Inc. v. Nu-Kote Int'l, Inc.***, 45 USPQ 2d 1355, 1358–59 (Fed. Cir. 1998)

Nu-Kote argues that the sheer number of named inventors is evidence of the patent's invalidity. We disagree. Improper inventorship is not presumed simply because a large number of individuals are listed on the patent as joint inventors. On the contrary, the "inventors as named in an issued patent are presumed to be correct." *Hess v. Advanced Cardiovascular Sys., Inc.*, 106 F.3d 976, 980, 41 USPQ 2d 1782, 1785–86 (Fed. Cir.) (citation omitted), *cert. denied*, 138 L. Ed. 2d 216, 117 S. Ct. 2459 (1997). . . . Although the inventors were incapable of recalling each individual's specific contribution, they all generally recalled collaborating together in a series of meetings to produce the patented invention. As any member of a large discussion group well knows, it is often difficult to remember who first said what. Significantly, none of the inventors testified that any named inventor was not involved in that collaborative effort. We note in passing that the patent has 66 figures and 19 embodiments, indicating the plausibility of contributions by multiple inventors.

23. ***Canon Computer Sys., Inc. v. Nu-Kote Int'l, Inc.***, 45 USPQ 2d 1355, 1359 (Fed. Cir. 1998)

Nu-Kote also argues that misjoinder has been established with regard to two of the named inventors because they are not listed on any of the foreign priority documents. Canon responds that the two inventors were properly absent from the priority documents because their only contribution was to dependent claim 6, the subject matter of which Canon asserts is not described in the priority documents. . . . Incorrect inventorship is a technical defect in a patent that may be easily curable. . . . In this case, the patentee has introduced evidence showing that all of the inventors believed they jointly collaborated to produce the invention. Furthermore, Canon has identified the specific contributions of the two inventors who are not listed on the priority documents.

24. ***Ethicon, Inc. v. United States Surgical Corp.***, 45 USPQ 2d 1545, 1547–48 (Fed. Cir.), ***cert. denied***, 525 U.S. 923 (1998)

Patent issuance creates a presumption that the named inventors are the true and only inventors. . . . A patented invention may be the work of two or more joint inventors. . . . Because "conception is the touchstone of inventorship," each joint inventor must generally contribute to the conception of the invention. *Burroughs Wellcome Co. v. Barr Lab., Inc.*, 40 F.3d 1223, 1227–28, 32 USPQ 2d 1915, 1919 (Fed. Cir. 1994). "Conception is the 'formation in the mind of the inventor, of a definite and permanent idea of the complete and operative invention, as it is hereafter to be applied in practice.'" *Hybritech, Inc. v. Monoclonal Antibodies, Inc.*, 802 F.2d 1367, 1376, 231 USPQ 81, 87 (Fed. Cir. 1986) (quoting 1 Robinson on Patents 532 (1890)). An idea is sufficiently "definite and permanent" when "only ordinary skill would be necessary to reduce the invention to practice, without extensive research or experimentation." *Burroughs Wellcome*, 40 F.3d at 1228.

The conceived invention must include every feature of the subject matter claimed in the patent. . . . Nevertheless, for the conception of a joint invention, each of the joint inventors need not "make the same type or amount of contribution" to the invention. . . . Rather, each needs to perform only a part of the task which produces the invention. On the other hand, one does not qualify as a joint inventor by merely assisting the actual inventor after conception of the claimed invention. . . . One who simply provides the inventor with well-known principles or explains the state of the art without ever having "a firm and definite idea" of the claimed combination as a whole does not qualify as a joint inventor. . . . Moreover, depending on the scope of a patent's claims, one of ordinary skill in the art who simply reduced the inventor's idea to practice is not necessarily a joint inventor, even if the specification discloses that embodiment to satisfy the best mode requirement. . . . Furthermore, a co-inventor need not make a contribution to every claim of a patent. . . . A contribution to one claim is enough.

25. ***Ethicon, Inc. v. United States Surgical Corp.***, 45 USPQ 2d 1545, 1550–51 (Fed. Cir.), ***cert. denied,*** 525 U.S. 923 (1998)

To determine whether Choi made a contribution to the conception of the subject matter of claim 47, this court must determine what Choi's contribution was and then construe the claim language to determine if Choi's contribution found its way into the defined invention. . . . [C]laim 47 recites a "means . . . for [detaining]." The use of the word "means" gives rise to "a presumption that the inventor used the term advisedly to invoke the statutory mandates for means-plus-function clauses." *York Prods., Inc. v. Central Tractor Farm & Family Ctr.*, 99 F.3d 1568, 1574, 40 USPQ 2d 1619, 1623 (Fed. Cir. 1996). Although the presumption is not conclusive, . . . the means language here invokes the interpretation regimens of section 112, paragraph 6. Thus applying section 112, paragraph 6 to interpret this claim, the language adopted the two structures in the specification to define the means for detaining.

Choi showed contribution to one of these alternative structures. The contributor of any disclosed means of a means-plus-function claim element is a joint inventor as to that claim, unless one asserting sole inventorship can show that the contribution of that means was simply a reduction to practice of the sole inventor's broader concept.

26. ***Ethicon, Inc. v. United States Surgical Corp.***, 45 USPQ 2d 1545, 1552 (Fed. Cir.), ***cert. denied***, 525 U.S. 923 (1998)

Questions of patent ownership are distinct from questions of inventorship. See *Beech Aircraft Corp. v. EDO Corp.*, 990 F.2d 1237, 1248, 26 U.S.P.Q.2D (BNA) 1572, 1582 (Fed. Cir. 1993). In accordance with this principle, this court has nonetheless noted that "an invention presumptively belongs to its creator." *Teets v. Chromalloy Gas Turbine Corp.*, 83 F.3d 403, 406, 38 U.S.P.Q.2D (BNA) 1695, 1697 (Fed. Cir.), cert. denied, 136 L. Ed. 2d 402, 117 S. Ct. 513 (1996).

Indeed, in the context of joint inventorship, each co-inventor presumptively owns a pro rata undivided interest in the entire patent, no matter what their respective contributions. Several provisions of the Patent Act combine to dictate this rule. 35 U.S.C. § 116, as amended in 1984, states that a joint inventor need not make a contribution "to the subject matter of every claim of the patent." In amending section 116 as to joint inventorship, Congress did not make corresponding modifications as to joint ownership. For example, section 261 continues to provide that "patents shall have the attributes of personal property." This provision suggests that property rights, including ownership, attach to patents as a whole, not individual claims. Moreover, section 262 continues to speak of "joint owners of a patent," not joint owners of a claim. Thus, a joint inventor as to even one claim enjoys a presumption of ownership in the entire patent.

This rule presents the prospect that a co-inventor of only one claim might gain entitlement to ownership of a patent with dozens of claims. . . . Thus, where inventors choose to cooperate in the inventive process, their joint inventions may become joint property without some express agreement to the contrary.

27. ***Ethicon, Inc. v. United States Surgical Corp.***, 45 USPQ 2d 1545, 1554 & n.9 (Fed. Cir.), ***cert. denied,*** 525 U.S. 923 (1998)

One more settled principle governs this case, however. An action for infringement must join as plaintiffs all co-owners. *See Waterman v. Mackenzie*, 138 U.S. 252, 255, 34 L. Ed. 923, 11 S. Ct. 334 (1891) ("The patentee or his assigns may, by instrument in writing, assign, grant, and convey, either (1) the whole patent . . .; or (2) an undivided part or share of that exclusive right; or (3) the exclusive right under the patent within and throughout a specified part of the United States. A transfer of either of these three kinds of interests is an assignment, properly speaking, and vests in the assignee a title in so much of the patent itself, with a right to sue infringers. In the second case, *jointly with the assignor.* In the first and third cases, in the name of the assignee alone." (emphasis added)) . . .

Further, as a matter of substantive patent law, all co-owners must ordinarily consent to join as plaintiffs in an infringement suit. . . . Two established exceptions exist. First, when any patent owner has granted an exclusive license, he stands in a relationship of trust to his licensee and must permit the licensee to sue in his name. *See Independent Wireless Telegraph Co. v. Radio Corp. of Am.*, 269 U.S. 459, 469, 70 L. Ed. 357, 46 S. Ct. 166 (1926). Second, the obligation may arise by contract among co-owners. If, by agreement, a co-owner waives his right to refuse to join suit, his co-owners may subsequently force him to join in a suit against infringers. *See Willingham v. Lawton*, 555 F.2d 1340, 1344–45, 194 USPQ (BNA) 249, 252 (6th Cir. 1977). . . . Consequently, "one co-owner has the right to impede the other co-owner's ability to sue infringers by refusing to voluntarily join in such a suit." *Schering*, 104 F.3d [341,] 345 [, 41 USPQ 2d 1359 (Fed. Cir. 1997)].

This rule finds support in section 262 of the Patent Act:

> In the absence of any agreement to the contrary, each of the joint owners of a patent may make, use, offer to sell, or sell the patented invention within the United States, or import the patented invention into the United States, without the consent of and without accounting to the other owners.

This freedom to exploit the patent without a duty to account to other co-owners also allows co-owners to freely license others to exploit the patent without the consent of other co-owners.

28. ***Pannu v. Iolab Corp.***, 47 USPQ 2d 1657, 1661–62 & n.4 (Fed. Cir. 1998)

Section 102, which is within Part II of Title 35, is entitled "Conditions for patentability; novelty and loss of right to patent"; section 102(f) provides that "[a] person shall be entitled to a patent unless he did not himself invent the subject matter sought to be patented." Since the word "he" refers to the specific inventive entity named on the patent, . . . this subsection mandates that a patent accurately list the correct inventors of a claimed invention . . . . Thus, section 102(f) still makes the naming of the correct inventor or inventors a condition of patentability; failure to name them renders a patent invalid.

However, in cases of misjoinder and nonjoinder the operation of section 102(f) is ameliorated by section 256. . . . If a patentee demonstrates that inventorship can be corrected as provided for in section 256, a district court must order correction of the patent, thus saving it from being rendered invalid.

When a party asserts invalidity under § 102(f) due to nonjoinder, a district court should first determine whether there exists clear and convincing proof that the alleged unnamed inventor was in fact a co-inventor. Upon such a finding of incorrect inventorship, a patentee may invoke section 256 to save the patent from invalidity. Accordingly, the patentee must then be given an opportunity to correct inventorship pursuant to that section. Nonjoinder may be corrected "on notice and hearing of all parties concerned" and upon a showing that the error occurred without any deceptive intent on the part of the unnamed inventor. . . . While lack of deceptive intent, as a negative, may be hard for a patentee to prove when it claims relief under the statute, good faith is presumed in the absence of a persuasive showing of deceptive intent. . . . Finally, a patent with improper inventorship does not avoid invalidation simply because it might be corrected under section 256. Rather, the patentee must claim entitlement to relief under the statute and the court must give the patentee an opportunity to correct the inventorship. If the inventorship is successfully corrected, section 102(f) will not render the patent invalid. On the other hand, if the patentee does not claim relief under the statute and a party asserting invalidity proves incorrect inventorship, the court should hold the patent invalid for failure to comply with section 102(f).

29. ***C.R. Bard, Inc. v. M3 Sys., Inc.***, 48 USPQ 2d 1225, 1232 (Fed. Cir. 1998)

The "inventor," in patent law, is the person or persons who conceived the patented invention. *Collar Co. v. Van Dusen*, 90 U.S. (23 Wall.) 530, 563–64, 23 L. Ed. 128 (1874); *Burroughs Wellcome Co. v. Barr Lab., Inc.*, 40 F.3d 1223, 1227–28, 32 USPQ 2d 1915, 1919 (Fed. Cir. 1994) ("Conception is the touchstone of inventorship.") Thus facts relevant to inventorship are those showing the conception of the invention, for others may provide services in perfecting the invention conceived by another without becoming an "inventor" by operation of law. *Id.*; *Agawam Co. v. Jordan*, 74 U.S. (7 Wall.) 583, 602–04, 19 L. Ed. 177 (1868); *Hess*, 106 F.3d at 980–81, 41 USPQ 2d at 1786–87. As explained in *Shatterproof Glass Corp. v. Libbey-Owens Ford Co.*, 758 F.2d 613, 624, 225 USPQ 634, 641 (Fed. Cir. 1985), "an inventor may use the services, ideas, and aid of others in the process of perfecting his invention without losing his right to a patent."

30. ***University of Colorado Found., Inc. v. American Cyanamid Co.***, 52 USPQ 2d 1801, 1806–07 (Fed. Cir. 1999) (quoting ***Stark v. Advanced Magnetics, Inc.***, 43 USPQ 2d 1321, 1324 (Fed. Cir. 1997))

Section 256 allows deletion of a misjoined inventor whether that error occurred by deception or by innocent mistake. As well, the section allows addition of an unnamed actual inventor, but this error of nonjoinder cannot betray any deceptive intent by that inventor. In other words, the statute allows correction in all misjoinder cases featuring an error and in those nonjoinder cases where the unnamed inventor is free of deceptive intent. . . . Thus, the district court's premise—that the actual inventors could not be substituted for a fraudulently-named inventor in a patent without thereby invalidating the patent—was incorrect.

31. ***Virginia Electronic & Lighting Corp. v. National Service Industries, Inc.,*** Civ. App. No. 99-1226, slip op. at 9 (Fed. Cir. Jan. 6, 2000) (unpublished), ***cert. denied***, 530 U.S. 1275 (2000)

    Section 256 of Title 35 of the United States Code authorizes judicial and Patent and Trademark Commissioner resolution of inventorship contests involving issued patents. . . . Section 256 allows not only the addition of an inventor, but the complete substitution of one inventor for another, provided that the true inventor acted without deceptive intent. . . . The inventor named on an issued patent, however, is presumed to be the true inventor.

32. ***Solomon v. Kimberly-Clark Corp.***, 55 USPQ 2d 1279, 1284 (Fed. Cir. 2000)

    As for the suggestion that Solomon's attorney might be the true inventor, we regard that argument as misguided. An attorney's professional responsibility is to assist his or her client in defining her invention to obtain, if possible, a valid patent with maximum coverage. An attorney performing that role should not be a competitor of the client, asserting inventorship as a result of representing his client. Cf. Patent and Trademark Office, U.S. Dep't of Commerce, Manual of Patent Examining Procedure app. R Section 10.64 (7th ed. 1998) ("Avoiding acquisition of interest in litigation or proceeding before the [Patent and Trademark] Office"). Thus, to assert that proper performance of the attorney's role is a ground for invalidating the patent constitutes a failure to understand the proper role of a patent attorney.

I.A. *Ownership and Government Related Inventions*

1. ***Fretheim v. Department of the Air Force***, 49 USPQ 2d 1316, 1318 (U.S. Dep't Comm. 1998)

   Paragraph 1(a) of EO 10096, as amended, provides that the Government shall obtain the entire right, title, and interest in and to all inventions made by any Government employee with a contribution by the Government of facilities, equipment, materials, funds or information or of time or services of other Government employees on official duty. See also 37 CFR 501.6(a)(1). However, the contribution may be insufficient equitably to justify an assignment. 37 CFR 501.6(a)(2).

2. ***Fretheim v. Department of the Air Force***, 49 USPQ 2d 1316, 1319 (U.S. Dep't Comm. 1998)

   Fretheim argues in his notice of appeal that the AF [Air Force] determination is contrary to the requirements of the Federal Technology Transfer Act (FTTA) because the AF was not actively pursuing commercialization of all the embodiments of the patented invention. Although Fretheim does not identify the particular requirement in the FTTA, we believe that it is found in 15 U.S.C. Section 3710d(a). That section requires that an agency having the right of ownership to an invention, but which does not intend to file a patent application or otherwise commercialize the invention, shall allow the inventor to retain title subject to a royalty free license to the Government. Since AFLSA [Air Force Legal Services Agency] filed two patent applications thereby complying with at least one of the above alternate conditions, it has not violated FTTA.

3. *Freund v. Department of the Navy*, 49 USPQ 2d 1700, 1702 (U.S. Dep't Comm. 1998)

Paragraph 1(a) of Executive Order 10096, as amended, provides that the Government shall obtain the entire right, title, and interest in and to all inventions made by any Government employee (1) during working hours, or (2) with a contribution by the Government of facilities, equipment, materials, funds or information or of time or services of other Government employees on official duty, or (3) which bear a direct relation to or are made in consequence of the official duties of the inventor. See also 37 CFR 501.6(a) (1).

Paragraph 1(c) of the Executive Order provides that an invention made by an employee hired to (i) invent, (ii) conduct research, (iii) supervise Government financed or conducted research, or (iv) act as liaison among Government or non-government agencies conducting such research, shall be presumed to be made under Paragraph 1(a). See also 37 CFR 501.6(a) (3). Inventions made by other employees are presumed to fall under the scope of Paragraph 1(b). Either presumption may be overcome by the facts and circumstances of a given case. . . . Since the three categories are connected by the disjunctive ("or"), any one of them would give rise to the presumption of title.

4. *Goldberg v. Department of the Army*, 49 USPQ 2d 1382, 1383 (U.S. Dep't Comm. 1998)

Paragraph 1(a) of Executive Order 10096, as amended, provides that the Government shall obtain the entire right, title, and interest in and to all inventions made by any Government employee (1) during working hours, or (2) with a contribution by the Government of facilities, equipment, materials, funds or information or of time or services of other Government employees on official duty, or (3) which bear a direct relation to or are made in consequence of the official duties of the inventor. See also 37 CFR 501.6(a)(1).

Paragraph 1(c) of the Executive Order provides that an invention made by an employee hired to (i) invent, (ii) conduct research, (iii) supervise Government financed or conducted research, or (iv) act as liaison among Government or nongovernment agencies conducting such research, shall be presumed to be made under Paragraph 1(a). See also 37 CFR 501.6(a)(3). Inventions made by other employees are presumed to fall under the scope of Paragraph 1(b). Either presumption may be overcome by the facts and circumstances of a given case.

I.B. Assignment of Intellectual Property/Patents

1. ***Filmtec Corp. v. Allied-Signal Inc.***, 19 USPQ 2d 1508, 1511 (Fed. Cir. 1991)

   Since property rights in an invention itself could not, under any conventional meaning of the term, be considered real property, they are by definition personal property. While early cases have pointed to the myriad ways in which patent rights—that is, property in patents—are closer in analogy to real than to personal property, the statutes establish as a matter of law that patents today have the attributes of personal property. And 35 U.S.C. § 261 makes clear that an application for patent as well as the patent itself may be assigned. Further, it is settled law that between the time of an invention and the issuance of a patent, rights in an invention may be assigned and legal title to the ensuing patent will pass to the assignee upon grant of the patent.

2. ***Filmtec Corp. v. Allied-Signal Inc.***, 19 USPQ 2d 1508, 1511 n.5 (Fed. Cir. 1991) (quoting ***A.S. Solomons v. United States***, 21 Ct. Cl. 479, 483 (1886), ***aff'd***, 137 U.S. 342 (1890))

   Intellectual property is

   > the most intangible form of property, it still, in many characteristics, is closer in analogy to real than to personal estate. Unlike personal property, it cannot be lost or found; it is not liable to casualty or destruction; it cannot pass by manual delivery. Like real property, it may be disposed of, territorially, by metes or bounds; it has its system of conveyancing by deed and registration; estates may be created in it, such as for years and in remainder; and the statutory action for infringement bears a much closer relation to an action of trespass than to an action in trover and replevin. It has, too, what the law of real property has, a system of user by license.

3. ***Filmtec Corp. v. Allied-Signal Inc.***, 19 USPQ 2d 1508, 1511 (Fed. Cir. 1991)

   If an assignment of rights in an invention is made prior to the existence of the invention, this may be viewed as an assignment of an expectant interest. n8 An assignment of an expectant interest can be a valid assignment. . . . In such a situation, the assignee holds at most an equitable title.

4. ***Filmtec Corp. v. Allied-Signal Inc.***, 19 USPQ 2d 1508, 1511 (Fed. Cir. 1991)

Once the invention is made and an application for patent is filed, however, legal title to the rights accruing thereunder would be in the assignee (subject to the rights of a subsequent purchaser under § 261), and the assignor-inventor would have nothing remaining to assign.

5. ***Filmtec Corp. v. Allied-Signal Inc.***, 19 USPQ 2d 1508, 1512 (Fed. Cir. 1991)

It is well established that when a legal title holder of a patent transfers his or her title to a third party purchaser for value without notice of an outstanding equitable claim or title, the purchaser takes the entire ownership of the patent, free of any prior equitable encumbrance. . . . This is an application of the common law bona fide purchaser for value rule.

Section 261 of Title 35 goes a step further. It adopts the principle of the real property recording acts, and provides that the bona fide purchaser for value cuts off the rights of a prior assignee who has failed to record the prior assignment in the Patent and Trademark Office by the dates specified in the statute. Although the statute does not expressly so say, it is clear that the statute is intended to cut off prior legal interests, which the common law rule did not.

Both the common law rule and the statute contemplate that the subsequent purchaser be exactly that—a transferee who pays valuable consideration, and is without notice of the prior transfer.

6. ***Prima Tek II, L.L.C. v. A-Roo Co.***, 222 F.3d 1372, 55 USPQ 2d 1742, 1745 (Fed. Cir. 2000)

As defined in section 100(d), the term "patentee" includes "not only the patentee to whom the patent was issued but also the successors in title to the patentee." 35 U.S.C. § 100(d) (1994). A transfer of "title" to a patent—also called an assignment—is governed by 35 U.S.C. § 261, which states that:

> Applications for patent, patents, or any interest therein, shall be assignable in law by an instrument in writing. The applicant, patentee, or his assigns or legal representatives may in like manner grant and convey an exclusive right under his application for patent, or patents, to the whole or any specified part of the United States.

35 U.S.C. § 261 (1994). Section 261 recognizes, and courts have long held, that an exclusive, territorial license is equivalent to an assignment and may therefore confer standing upon the licensee to sue for patent infringement. . . . Conversely, a "bare licensee"—one who enjoys only a nonexclusive license—has no standing to sue for infringement under the Patent Act.

7. ***Prima Tek II, L.L.C. v. A-Roo Co.***, 222 F.3d 1372, 55 USPQ 2d 1742, 1747 & n.2 (Fed. Cir. 2000)

A patent represents the legal right to exclude others from making, using, selling, or offering to sell a patented invention in the United States, and from importing the invention into the United States. See 38 U.S.C. § 154 (1994). Implicit in the right to exclude is the ability to waive that right, i.e., to license activities that would otherwise be excluded, such as making, using and selling the patented invention in the United States. Those activities, of course, may be subject to further limitations such as governmental restrictions or "blocking" patents. . . . A "blocking patent" is an earlier patent that must be licensed in order to practice a later patent. This often occurs, for instance, between a pioneer patent and an improvement patent.

8. ***Scott System, Inc. v. Scott***, 53 USPQ 2d 1692, 1693-94 (Colo. App. 2000)

Generally, an invention is the property of the inventor who conceived, developed, and perfected it. Hence, the mere fact that the inventor was employed by another at the time of the invention does not mean that that inventor is required to assign the patent rights to the employer. The right, if any, of an employer to inventions of its employee is determined primarily by the contract of employment. If, as here, the contract of employment does not contain an express provision respecting the subject, an employer is, nonetheless, not necessarily precluded from claiming a right to the invention.

If an employee's job duties include the responsibility for inventing or for solving a particular problem that requires invention, any invention created by that employee during the performance of those responsibilities belongs to the employer. Hence, such an employee is bound to assign to the employer all rights to the invention. This is so because, under these circumstances, the employee has produced only that which he was employed to produce, and the courts will find an implied contract obligation to assign any rights to the employer. . . .

On the other hand, if an employee is not employed to invent or to solve a particular problem, that employee owns the right to any invention made by the employee during the term of employment. However, under such circumstances, if the employer has contributed to the development of the invention, such as by paying for the employee's efforts, the employer has a "shop right" to use it free of charge and without liability for infringement.

9. ***Scott System, Inc. v. Scott***, 53 USPQ 2d 1692, 1695 (Colo. App. 2000)

All officers and directors of a corporation owe a fiduciary duty to the corporation and to its stockholders. They are required to act in good faith and in a reasonable manner in the best interests of those parties. *Michaelson v. Michaelson*, 939 P.2d 835 (Colo. 1997). Such a fiduciary duty obligates an officer or director to assign a patent to the corporation if the invention was developed while he or she was employed by the corporation and it is related to the corporation's business. *Lacy v. Rotating Productions Systems, Inc.*, 961 P.2d 1144 (Colo. App. 1998).

Contrary to defendants' assertion, the decision in *Lacy* was not based upon the nature of the particular responsibilities of the officer or director; it was based upon the general fiduciary responsibility owed by all who occupy such positions. Indeed, we know of no rule that states that a distinction in the degree of fiduciary obligation may be recognized based upon the degree of corporate involvement. It is the nature of the position, itself, and not the nature of the specific responsibilities that may be assumed, that gives rise to the obligation.

10. ***Banks v. Unisys Corp.***, 56 USPQ 2d 1222, 1224 (Fed. Cir. 2000)

The general rule is that an individual owns the patent rights to the subject matter of which he is an inventor, even though he conceived it or reduced it to practice in the course of his employment. There are two exceptions to this rule: first, an employer owns an employee's invention if the employee is a party to an express contract to that effect; second, where an employee is hired to invent something or solve a particular problem, the property of the invention related to this effort may belong to the employer. Both exceptions are firmly grounded in the principles of contract law that allow parties to freely structure their transactions and obtain the benefit of any bargains reached. See *Teets*, 83 F.3d at 407, 38 USPQ 2d at 1697; *Melin v. United States*, 201 Ct. Cl. 748, 478 F.2d 1210, 1213 (Ct. Cl. 1973).

"An implied-in-fact contract is an agreement 'founded upon a meeting of the minds, which, although not embodied in an express contract, is inferred, as a fact from conduct of the parties showing, in the light of the surrounding circumstances, their tacit understanding.'" *Id.* at 407, 38 USPQ 2d at 1698 (quoting *Baltimore & Ohio R.R. v. United States*, 261 U.S. 592, 597, 67 L. Ed. 816, 43 S. Ct. 425 (1923)). When applying the "employed to invent" exception, "a court must examine the employment relationship at the time of the inventive work to determine if the parties entered an implied-in-fact contract to assign patent rights." *Id.* "State contract principles provide the rules for identifying and enforcing implied-in-fact contracts." *Id.* (citing *Erie R.R. v. Tompkins*, 304 U.S. 64, 82 L. Ed. 1188, 58 S. Ct. 817 (1938)).

11. ***Messagephone, Inc. v. SVI Systems, Inc.***, Civ. App. No. 99-1471, slip op. at 8–9 (Fed. Cir. Aug. 11, 2000) (unpublished)

As a general rule, only a party that possessed legal title to a patent at the time the infringement occurred can bring suit to recover damages for such infringement. . . . A narrow exception to the foregoing rule is that a party may sue for infringement transpiring before it acquired legal title if a written assignment expressly grants the party a right to do so; that right, however, must be articulated explicitly in the assignment and will not be inferred by the court.

12. ***Prima Tek II, L.L.C. v. A-Roo Co.***, 55 USPQ 2d 1742, 1747 & n.2 (Fed. Cir. 2000)

A patent represents the legal right to exclude others from making, using, selling, or offering to sell a patented invention in the United States, and from importing the invention into the United States. See 38 U.S.C. § 154 (1994). Implicit in the right to exclude is the ability to waive that right, i.e., to license activities that would otherwise be excluded, such as making, using and selling the patented invention in the United States. Those activities, of course, may be subject to further limitations such as governmental restrictions or "blocking" patents. . . . A "blocking patent" is an earlier patent that must be licensed in order to practice a later patent. This often occurs, for instance, between a pioneer patent and an improvement patent.

13. ***Solomon v. Kimberly-Clark Corp.***, 55 USPQ 2d 1279, 1283–84 (Fed. Cir. 2000)

[A]n inventor is not competent to construe patent claims for the following reasons:

> [C]ommonly the claims are drafted by the inventor's patent solicitor and they may even be drafted by the patent examiner in an examiner's amendment (subject to the ap-

proval of the inventor's solicitor). While presumably the inventor has approved any changes to the claim scope that have occurred via amendment during the prosecution process, it is not unusual for there to be a significant difference between what an inventor thinks his patented invention is and what the ultimate scope of the claims is after allowance by the PTO.

Markman, 52 F.3d at 985, 34 USPQ 2d at 1335 (citation omitted).

II. Statutory Subject Matter Under Section 101

1. ***Pioneer Hi-Bred Int'l, Inc. v. J.E.M. Ag Supply, Inc.***, 53 USPQ 2d 1440, 1441 (Fed. Cir. 2000), ***cert. granted***, 121 S. Ct. 1077 (Feb 20, 2001) (No. 99-1996)

   Although there remain the traditional categories that have never been viewed as patentable subject matter, viz., laws of nature, natural phenomena, and abstract ideas, the policy underlying the patent system fosters its application to all areas of technology-based commerce.

II.A. *Mathematical Algorithm Rejections*

1. ***Ex parte Akamatsu***, 22 USPQ 2d 1915, 1922 (B.P.A.I. 1992)

   The recitation of three distinct "means" whose outputs are used by the "means for generating" provides some semblance of structure and interconnection.

2. ***Ex parte Akamatsu***, 22 USPQ 2d 1915, 1922 (B.P.A.I. 1992)

   That the apparatus distinguishes over a general purpose digital computer is considered to be a key factor in cases involving mathematical algorithms.

3. Denny, Notice Interpreting ***In re Iwahashi*** (Fed. Cir. 1989), 1112 TMOG 18 (1990)

   Because the Court determined a ROM to be a specific apparatus for implementing a table look-up function, and not as broad as a means-plus-function recitation, appellants carried their burden of demonstrating that the claim is 'truly drawn to specific apparatus distinct from other apparatus capable of performing the identical functions.' . . . Once it is determined that the claim is truly drawn to a specific apparatus, it necessarily follows that the apparatus is statutory subject matter under 35 USC §101.

4. ***Arrhythmia Research Tech., Inc. v. Corazonix Corp.***, 22 USPQ 2d 1033, 1037 (Fed. Cir. 1992)

   [M]athematics may also be used to describe steps of a statutory method or elements of a statutory apparatus. . . . [T]he emphasis is "on *what* the claimed method steps do rather than *how* the steps are performed."

5. ***In re Walter***, 205 USPQ 397, 408 (C.C.P.A. 1980)

In such cases the burden must be placed on the applicant to demonstrate that the claims are truly drawn to specific apparatus distinct from other apparatus capable of performing the identical functions.

6. ***In re Pardo***, 214 USPQ 673, 677 (C.C.P.A. 1982)

Appellants' method claims are directed to executing programs in a computer. The method operates on any program and any formula which may be input, regardless of mathematical content. That a computer controlled according to the invention is capable of handling mathematics is irrelevant to the question of whether a mathematical algorithm is recited by the claims.

7. ***In re Taner***, 214 USPQ 678, 681 (C.C.P.A. 1982)

Appellants' claimed process involves the taking of substantially spherical seismic signals obtained in conventional seismic exploration and converting ("simulating from") those signals into another form, i.e., to a form representing the earth's response to cylindrical or plane waves. Thus the claims set forth a process and are statutory within §101.

Though the board conceded that appellants' process includes conversion of seismic signals into a different form, it took the position that "there is nothing necessarily physical about 'signals'" and that the "end product of [appellants' invention] is a mathematical result in the form of a pure number." That characterization is contrary to the views expressed by this court in *In re Sherwood*, . . . and *In re Johnson*, . . . where signals were viewed as physical and the processes were viewed as transforming them to a different state. . . . In both cases, this court found that, though appellants' claims recited a mathematical algorithm for manipulating seismic data, the claims were, as a whole, drawn not to a method of solving that algorithm but to a process of converting one physical thing into another physical thing, and in *Sherwood* expressly recognized that "seismic traces are * * * physical apparitions."

8. ***In re Chatfield***, 191 USPQ 730, 735 (C.C.P.A. 1976), ***cert. denied sub nom. Dann v. Noll***, 434 U.S. 875 (1977)

Chatfield's inventive contribution, as set forth in the appealed claims and described above, is a unique method for improving the operating efficiency of a system of electro-mechanical machines, i.e., a computing system. No formula or algorithm appears in Chatfield's independent claims.

9. ***In re Chatfield***, 191 USPQ 730, 735 (C.C.P.A. 1976), ***cert. denied sub nom. Dann v. Noll***, 434 U.S. 875 (1977) (quoting ***In re Bernhart***, 417 F.2d 1395, 1399–1400, 163 USPQ 611, 616 (C.C.P.A. 1969))

Accordingly, no rule of law should be announced which would impress a monopoly upon all uses of the equations disclosed by appellants here in their patent application. To allow the claims in issue here would not prohibit all uses of those equations. As we have pointed out above, a member of the public would have to do much more than use the equations to infringe any of these claims. He would have to use them in the physical equipment recited in the claim. Moreover, all machines function according to laws of physics which can be mathematically set forth if known. We cannot deny patents on machines merely because their novelty may be explained in terms of such laws if we are to obey the mandate of Congress that a machine is subject matter for a patent. We should not penalize the inventor who makes his invention by discovering new and unobvious mathematical relationships which he then utilizes in a machine, as against the inventor who makes the same machine by trial and error and does not disclose the laws by which it operates.

10. ***In re Prater***, 162 USPQ 541, 549–50 n.29 (C.C.P.A. 1969)

But once a program has been introduced, the general-purpose digital computer becomes a special-purpose digital computer (i.e., a specific electrical circuit with or without electro-mechanical components) which, along with the process by which it operates, may be patented subject, of course, to the requirements of novelty, utility, and non-obviousness. Based on the present law, we see no other reasonable conclusion.

11. ***In re Chatfield***, 191 USPQ 730, 733 (C.C.P.A. 1976), ***cert. denied sub nom. Dann v. Noll***, 434 U.S. 875 (1977)

[T]he fundamental rationale we glean from Benson is that a patent containing Benson's claims would have preempted all practical use of both the underlying mathematical formula and the involved algorithm.

12. ***Arrhythmia Research Tech., Inc. v. Corazonix Corp.***, 22 USPQ 2d 1033, 1038 (Fed. Cir. 1992)

[T]he claimed steps of "converting", "applying", "determining", and "comparing" are physical process steps . . . [which] comprise statutory subject matter.

13. ***Arrhythmia Research Tech., Inc. v. Corazonix Corp.***, 22 USPQ 2d 1033, 1038 (Fed. Cir. 1992) (quoting ***In re Taner***, 681 F.2d 787, 790, 214 USPQ 678, 681 (C.C.P.A. 1982))

[T]he view that "there is nothing necessarily physical about signals" is incorrect.

14. ***Ex parte Cordova***, 10 USPQ 2d 1949, 1950 (B.P.A.I. 1987)

We recognize that under certain circumstances a preambular recitation indicating intended use may impose sufficient structural limitations upon a claimed article to differentiate it over a prior art article.

15. ***In re Deutsch***, 193 USPQ 645, 649 (C.C.P.A. 1977)

A determination of the presence or absence of statutory subject matter must rest upon the claimed invention considered as a whole, not upon selected unclaimed portions of the specification. It was error, therefore, for the board to focus upon one of Deutsch's disclosed optimization techniques and to transpose it from the specification to the claims as though the optimization technique were being claimed and preempted.

16. ***In re Abele***, 214 USPQ 682, 688 (C.C.P.A. 1982)

We are faced simply with an improved CAT-scan process comparable to the improved process for curing synthetic-rubber in *Diehr*, supra. The improvement in either case resides in the application of a mathematical formula within the context of a process which encompasses significantly more than the algorithm alone.

17. ***Diamond v. Diehr***, 209 USPQ 1, 8, 450 U.S. 175 (1981)

In contrast, the respondents here do not seek to patent a mathematical formula. Instead, they seek patent protection for a process of curing synthetic rubber. Their process admittedly employs a well known mathematical equation, but they do not seek to pre-empt the use of that equation. Rather, they seek only to foreclose from others the use of that equation in conjunction with all of the other steps in their claimed process. These include installing rubber in a press, closing the mold, constantly determining the temperature of the mold, constantly recalculating the appropriate cure time through the use of the formula and a digital computer, and automatically opening the press at the proper time. Obviously, one does not need a "computer" to cure natural or synthetic rubber, but if the computer use incorporated in the process patent significantly lessens the possibility of "overcuring" or "undercuring", the process as a whole does not thereby become unpatentable subject matter.

18. ***Diamond v. Diehr***, 209 USPQ 1, 9, 450 U.S. 175 (1981)

In determining the eligibility of respondents' claimed process for patent protection under §101, their claims must be considered as a whole. It is inappropriate to dissect the claims into old and new elements and then ignore the presence of the old elements in the analysis. This is particularly true in a process claim because a new combination of steps in a process may be patentable even though all the constituents of the combination were well known and in common use before the combination was made. The "novelty" of any element or steps in a process, or even the process itself, is of no relevance in determining whether the subject matter of a claim falls within the §101 categories of possibly patentable subject matter.

19. *In re de Castelet*, 195 USPQ 439, 443 (C.C.P.A. 1977)

Absent contrary directions, no basis exists for a moratorium on protection of inventions embodying or using computer programs. Such broad prohibition could subject meritorious statutory inventions to unabatable piracy, and could forestall invention disclosure, the hallmark of the patent system, until Congress chooses to act.

20. *Ex parte Head*, 214 USPQ 551, 554 (B.P.A.I. 1981)

Considering the claimed invention as a whole, it is our view that the function specified in clause (a), although involving mathematical calculations, nevertheless is implemented in a specific manner to define structural relationships between the physical elements of the claim. That is, the particular physical positioning of the measuring means on a plurality of chords in turn dictates the structural make-up of a data processing means coupled thereto that would appear to be simpler in nature, vis-a-vis such data processing means specified in the prior art of record. Under these circumstances, we find that the claims pass muster under the rationale presented by the court in Walter. The fact that activity subsequent to the solution activity recited in clause (a) is also mathematical in nature, would not justify ignoring the definition of structural relationships discussed supra, or justify considering the function of clause (a) to be a mere data gathering function dictated by the equation solved in clause (b). Although the equation specified in clause (b) would dictate a determination of velocity values and weight factors, it would not dictate the positioning of measuring means as specified in clause (a) of the claim. Accordingly, under these circumstances, we cannot sustain a rejection of the claims at bar as being directed to nonstatutory subject matter under Section 101 of the Statute.

21. *In re Abele*, 214 USPQ 682, 686 (C.C.P.A. 1982)

[T]he *Walter* analysis . . . does not limit patentable subject matter only to claims in which structural relationships or process steps are defined, limited or refined by the application of the algorithm.

Rather, *Walter* should be read as requiring no more than that the algorithm be "applied in any manner to physical elements or process steps," provided that its application is circumscribed by more than a field of use limitation or non-essential post-solution activity. Thus if the claim would be "otherwise statutory," *id.*, albeit inoperative or less useful without the algorithm, the claim likewise presents statutory subject matter when the algorithm is included. This broad reading of *Walter*, we conclude, is in accord with the Supreme Court decisions.

22. ***Ex parte Logan***, 20 USPQ 2d 1465, 1468 (B.P.A.I. 1991)

[A] claim should be considered as reciting a mathematical algorithm only if it *essentially* recites, . . . a method of computing one or more numbers from a different set of numbers by performing a series of mathematical computations.

23. ***Arrhythmia Research Tech., Inc. v. Corazonix Corp.***, 22 USPQ 2d 1033, 1039 (Fed. Cir. 1992) (quoting ***In re Sherwood***, 204 USPQ 537, 546 (C.C.P.A. 1980), ***cert. denied***, 450 U.S. 994 (1981))

The computer-performed operations transform a particular input signal to a different output signal, in accordance with the internal structure of the computer as configured by electronic instructions. "The claimed invention . . . converts one physical thing into another physical thing just as any other electrical circuitry would do."

24. ***In re Alappat***, 31 USPQ 2d 1545, 1558 (Fed. Cir. 1994) (en banc)

Alappat admits that claim 15 would read on a general purpose computer programmed to carry out the claimed invention, but argues that this alone also does not justify holding claim 15 unpatentable as directed to nonstatutory subject matter. We agree. We have held that such programming creates a new machine, because a general purpose computer in effect becomes a special purpose computer once it is programmed to perform particular functions pursuant to instructions from program software. . . . The Supreme Court has never held that a programmed computer may never be entitled to patent protection. . . . Consequently, a computer operating pursuant to software may represent patentable subject matter, provided, of course, that the claimed subject matter meets all of the other requirements of Title 35.

25. ***In re Lowry***, 32 USPQ 2d 1031, 1035 (Fed. Cir. 1994)

More than a mere abstraction, the data structures are specific electrical or magnetic structural elements in a memory. . . . In short, Lowry's data structures are physical entities that provide increased efficiency in computer operation. They are not analogous to printed matter. The Board is not at liberty to ignore such limitations.

26. ***In re Pardo***, 214 USPQ 673, 676 (C.C.P.A. 1982)

Applying the first part of the *Freeman* analysis to the appealed claims, we are unable to find any mathematical formula, calculation or algorithm either directly or indirectly recited in the claimed steps of examining, compiling, storing, and executing. Indeed, the examiner acknowledged that "[t]he 'algorithm' of the present application is not 'mathematical' (although it deals with the proper sequence for performing mathematics), but it does establish the rules which are to be followed by a data processor . . . ."

27. ***In re Iwahashi***, 12 USPQ 2d 1908, 1911–12 (Fed. Cir. 1989)

Appellants emphasize that they specify a ROM in clause [d] to which is fed an input from an adder specified in clause [c]. The Solicitor states that [c] and [d] are connected together by a signal path. Next are means in the form of disclosed electronic circuitry which take from the ROM its output in the form of squares of numbers supplied as ROM input and feed them to a calculating circuit [h]. The claim as a whole certainly defines apparatus in the form of a combination of interrelated means and we cannot discern any logical reason why it should not be deemed statutory subject matter as either a machine or a manufacture as specified in Section 101. . . . We point out that the claim is a combination of means all but one of which is a means-plus-function limitation, the one exception being the ROM, clause [d], which is a specific piece of apparatus.

28. ***In re Noll***, 191 USPQ 721, 726 (C.C.P.A. 1976), ***cert. denied***, 434 U.S. 875 (1977)

[T]he instant claims are limited to a particular technology (computer graphics systems and scan-conversion of graphic information). Furthermore, not all machines for achieving appellant's results are included within the scope of appellant's claims; non-program-controlled machines are clearly excluded.

29. ***In re Alappat***, 31 USPQ 2d 1545, 1558 (Fed. Cir. 1994) (en banc)

[T]he claim preamble's recitation that the subject matter for which Alappat seeks patent protection is a rasterizer for creating a smooth waveform is not a mere field-of-use label having no significance. Indeed, the preamble specifically recites that the claimed rasterizer converts waveform data into output illumination data for a display, and the means elements recited in the body of the claim make reference not only to the inputted waveform data recited in the preamble but also to the output illumination data also recited in the preamble. Claim 15 thus defines a combination of elements constituting a machine for producing an anti-aliased waveform.

30. ***In re Deutsch***, 193 USPQ 645, 648 (C.C.P.A. 1977)

Nothing in the methods claimed by Deutsch preempts a mathematical formula, an algorithm, or any specific computer program. Assuming eventual issue of the claims on appeal, the formulae, algorithms, and programs disclosed in Deutsch's specification would be freely available to all and could be used for any purpose other than the operation of a system of plants or their equivalents, as spelled out in the appealed claims.

31. ***In re Beauregard***, 35 USPQ 2d 1383, 1384 (Fed. Cir. 1995)

The Commissioner now states "that computer programs embodied in a tangible medium, such as floppy diskettes, are patentable subject matter under 35 U.S.C. § 101 and must be examined under 35 U.S.C. §§ 102 and 103." The Commissioner states that he agrees with Beauregard's position on appeal that the printed matter doctrine is not applicable.

32. ***Schlafly v. Caro-Kann Corp.***, Civ. App. 98-1005, slip op. at 12 (Fed. Cir. Apr. 29, 1998) (unpublished)

We therefore address whether the apparatus claims of the '829 patent recite non-statutory subject matter under section 101. Each of the apparatus claims of the '829 patent contains limitations drafted in means-plus-function format. Those limitations are therefore limited according to 35 U.S.C. § 112, ¶ 6 to structure disclosed in the specification and equivalent structures.

This court, *in banc*, has determined that claims written in means-plus-function format contain statutory subject matter even if functional phrases of the means limitations recite mathematical calculations. See Alappat, 33 F.3d at 1544, 31 U.S.P.Q.2D (BNA) at 1558. Therefore, the claims of the '829 patent do not wholly preempt the use of mathematical calculations because the claims are limited to the structure disclosed in the specification and equivalent structures for performing the claimed functions.

33. ***Ex parte Nassim***, Appeal No. 91-2486 (B.P.A.I. 1991) (unpublished)

Just because the court in Prater held, in the particular fact situation there involved, that the method claimed therein was drawn to statutory subject matter because all the steps recited therein could be performed by a machine, it does not follow that a method is drawn to non-statutory subject matter simply because one or more of the method steps recited therein are "mental" steps which cannot be performed by a machine. . . . It is not important whether the claims contain mental steps or not if the process is within the technological or useful arts. *See In re Foster*, 438 F.2d 1011, 169 USPQ 99 (C.C.P.A. 1971). Here, the process defined by independent claim 30 which includes the steps of "supplying . . .," "testing . . ." "storing . . ." and "reading . . ." clearly set forth a process that is within the technological arts and, therefore, the claims here involved are clearly drawn to statutory subject matter under §101. . . .

Thus, even if we were to agree with the examiner that a mental step was inherent in step (e) of independent claim 30, we cannot agree that the mere presence of any such step would render this claim unpatentable under §101. Accordingly, we will not sustain the examiner's rejection of claims 30–38 under 35 U.S.C. 101.

34. ***In re Bergy***, 596 F.2d 952, 960, 201 USPQ 352, 360 (C.C.P.A. 1979)

The first door which must be opened on the difficult path to patentability is § 101. . . . The person approaching that door is an inventor, whether his invention is patentable or not. . . . Being an inventor or having an invention, however, is no guarantee of opening even the first door. What kind of an invention or discovery is it? In dealing with the question of kind, as distinguished from the qualitative conditions which make the invention patentable, § 101 is broad and general; its language is: "any * * * process, machine, manufacture, or composition of matter, or any * * * improvement thereof." Section 100(b) further expands "process" to include "art or method, and * * * a new use of a known process, machine, manufacture, composition of matter, or material." If the invention, as the inventor defines it in his claims (pursuant to § 112, second paragraph), falls into any one of the named categories, he is allowed to pass through to the second door, which is § 102; "novelty and loss of right to patent" is the sign on it. Notwithstanding the words "new and useful" in § 101, the invention is not examined under that statute for novelty because that is not the statutory scheme of things or the long-established administrative practice.

35. ***State Street Bank & Trust Co. v. Signature Fin. Group, Inc.***, 47 USPQ 2d 1596, 1601 (Fed. Cir.), ***cert. denied***, 119 S. Ct. 336 (1998)

Unpatentable mathematical algorithms are identifiable by

showing they are merely abstract ideas constituting disem-
bodied concepts or truths that are not "useful." From a practical standpoint, this means that to be patentable an algorithm
must be applied in a "useful" way.

36. ***State Street Bank & Trust Co. v. Signature Fin. Group,
    Inc.***, 47 USPQ 2d 1596, 1601 (Fed. Cir.), ***cert. denied***, 525
    U.S. 1093 (1999)

    Today, we hold that the transformation of data, represent-
    ing discrete dollar amounts, by a machine through a series
    of mathematical calculations into a final share price, consti-
    tutes a practical application of a mathematical algorithm,
    formula, or calculation, because it produces "a useful, con-
    crete and tangible result"—a final share price momentarily
    fixed for recording and reporting purposes and even ac-
    cepted and relied upon by regulatory authorities and in sub-
    sequent trades.

37. ***State Street Bank & Trust Co. v. Signature Fin. Group,
    Inc.***, 47 USPQ 2d 1596, 1602 (Fed. Cir.), ***cert. denied***, 525
    U.S. 1093 (1999)

    However, after Diehr and Alappat, the mere fact that a
    claimed invention involves inputting numbers, calculating
    numbers, outputting numbers, and storing numbers, in and
    of itself, would not render it nonstatutory subject matter,
    unless, of course, its operation does not produce a "useful,
    concrete and tangible result." *Alappat*, 33 F.3d at 1544, 31
    USPQ 2d at 1557.

38. ***State Street Bank & Trust Co. v. Signature Fin. Group,
    Inc.***, 47 USPQ 2d 1596, 1602 (Fed. Cir.), ***cert. denied***, 525
    U.S. 1093 (1999)

    The question of whether a claim encompasses statutory
    subject matter should not focus on which of the four catego-
    ries of subject matter a claim is directed to—process, ma-
    chine, manufacture, or composition of matter—but rather on
    the essential characteristics of the subject matter, in partic-
    ular, its practical utility. Section 101 specifies that statutory
    subject matter must also satisfy the other "conditions and
    requirements" of Title 35, including novelty, nonobvious-
    ness, and adequacy of disclosure and notice.

39. ***State Street Bank & Trust Co. v. Signature Fin. Group,
    Inc.***, 47 USPQ 2d 1596, 1602 (Fed. Cir.), ***cert. denied***, 525
    U.S. 1093 (1999)

    For purpose of our analysis, as noted above, claim 1 is di-
    rected to a machine programmed with the Hub and Spoke
    software and admittedly produces a "useful, concrete, and

tangible result." *Alappat*, 33 F.3d at 1544, 31 USPQ 2d at 1557. This renders it statutory subject matter, even if the useful result is expressed in numbers, such as price, profit, percentage, cost, or loss.

40. **AT&T Corp. v. Excel Communications, Inc.**, 50 USPQ 2d 1447, 1450 (Fed. Cir. 1999)

This court recently pointed out that any step-by-step process, be it electronic, chemical, or mechanical, involves an "algorithm" in the broad sense of the term. . . . Because § 101 includes processes as a category of patentable subject matter, the judicially-defined proscription against patenting of a "mathematical algorithm," to the extent such a proscription still exists, is narrowly limited to mathematical algorithms in the abstract.

41. **AT&T Corp. v. Excel Communications, Inc.**, 50 USPQ 2d 1447, 1451 (Fed. Cir. 1999)

Whether stated implicitly or explicitly, we consider the scope of § 101 to be the same regardless of the form—machine or process—in which a particular claim is drafted.

42. **AT&T Corp. v. Excel Communications, Inc.**, 50 USPQ 2d 1447, 1452 (Fed. Cir. 1999) (quoting **Diamond v. Diehr**, 450 U.S. 175, 192 (1981))

The notion of "physical transformation" can be misunderstood. In the first place, it is not an invariable requirement, but merely one example of how a mathematical algorithm may bring about a useful application. As the Supreme Court itself noted, "when [a claimed invention] is performing a function which the patent laws were designed to protect (e.g., transforming or reducing an article to a different state or thing), then the claim satisfies the requirements of § 101." . . . The "e.g." signal denotes an example, not an exclusive requirement.

43. **AT&T Corp. v. Excel Communications, Inc.**, 50 USPQ 2d 1447, 1453 (Fed. Cir. 1999)

In contrast, our inquiry here focuses on whether the mathematical algorithm is applied in a practical manner to produce a useful result.

44. **AT&T Corp. v. Excel Communications, Inc.**, 50 USPQ 2d 1447, 1454 (Fed. Cir. 1999)

[I]t is now clear that computer-based programming constitutes patentable subject matter so long as the basic requirements of § 101 are met. . . . [T]he focus is understood to be not on whether there is a mathematical algorithm at work, but on whether the algorithm-containing invention, as a whole, produces a tangible, useful, result.

II.B. Utility Rejections

1. ***Carl Zeiss Stiftung v. Renishaw plc***, 20 USPQ 2d 1094, 1100 (Fed. Cir. 1991)

   When a properly claimed invention meets at least one stated objective, utility under §101 is clearly shown. . . . An invention need not be the best or the only way to accomplish a certain result, and it need only be useful to some extent and in certain applications.

2. ***Raytheon Co. v. Roper Corp.***, 220 USPQ 592, 596, 598–99 (Fed. Cir. 1983), ***cert. denied***, 469 U.S. 835 (1984)

   A correct finding of infringement of otherwise valid claims mandates as a matter of law a finding of utility under §101. . . . The rule relates to the time of decision not to the time of trial, and is but a common sense approach to the law. If a party has made, sold, or used a properly claimed device, and has thus infringed, proof of that device's utility is thereby established. People rarely, if ever, appropriate useless inventions.

3. ***In re Ziegler***, 26 USPQ 2d 1600, 1605 (Fed. Cir. 1993)

   The utility of a chemical compound may not reside in its "potential role as an object of use-testing." *Brenner v. Manson*, 383 U.S. 519, 535, 148 USPQ 689, 696 (1966). To satisfy 35 U.S.C. § 101, to be able to serve as a predicate for a section 119 claim, the disclosure must assert a "specific benefit . . . in currently available form." *See id.* at 534–35, 148 USPQ at 695. . . . [We] must nevertheless abide by the principle underlying 35 U.S.C. § 101 that a patent "is not a reward for the search, but compensation for its successful conclusion." *Id.* at 536, 148 USPQ at 696.

4. ***Moleculon Research Corp. v. CBS, Inc.***, 229 USPQ 805, 810–11 (Fed. Cir. 1986), ***cert. denied***, 479 U.S. 1030 (1987)

   CBS also argues that the subject matter of the claims are not "useful" because the claims do not "teach" anyone the complicated method of solving Nichols' or Rubik's puzzle. The argument misperceives the purpose of a claim. The claims are directed to "a method for restoring a preselected pattern." They claim a general *approach* for solving the puzzle. As the district court correctly observed, neither the claims nor the disclosure need set forth a *particular* series of moves to solve the puzzle.

5. ***In re Slocombe***, 184 USPQ 740, 743 (C.C.P.A. 1975)

There is no requirement that superiority over prior art be disclosed in the application; it is enough if the basic property or utility in which the advantage resides is disclosed.

6. ***In re Nelson***, 126 USPQ 242, 253 (C.C.P.A. 1960), ***overruled in part on other grounds by In re Kirk***, 153 USPQ 48 (C.C.P.A. 1967)

[Section 112] requires as a minimum, that the inventor "indicate" a use for a new composition . . . . [T]he test is what the application as a whole communicates to one skilled in the art. In some cases an applicant may, merely by naming his new instrument or material, have indicated what its use is, as, for example, by saying he has invented a "match," "hammer," "paint," "adhesive," or "detergent."

7. ***In re Brana***, 34 USPQ 2d 1436, 1440 (Fed. Cir. 1995)

Since one of the tested compounds, NSC 308847, was found to be highly effective against these two lymphocytic leukemia tumor models, applicants' favorable comparison implicitly asserts that their claimed compounds are highly effective (i.e. useful) against lymphocytic leukemia. . . . We conclude that these tumor models represent a specific disease against which the claimed compounds are alleged to be effective. Accordingly, in light of the explicit reference to Paull, applicants' specification alleges a sufficiently specific use.

8. ***In re Brana***, 34 USPQ 2d 1436, 1441 (Fed. Cir. 1995)

[T]he PTO has the initial burden of challenging a presumptively correct assertion of utility in the disclosure. . . . Only after the PTO provides evidence showing that one of ordinary skill in the art would reasonably doubt the asserted utility does the burden shift to the applicant to provide rebuttal evidence sufficient to convince such a person of the invention's asserted utility.

9. ***In re Brana***, 34 USPQ 2d 1436, 1441 (Fed. Cir. 1995)

The purpose of treating cancer with chemical compounds does not suggest an inherently unbelievable undertaking or involve implausible scientific principles. . . . Modern science has previously identified numerous successful chemotherapeutic agents. In addition, the prior art, specifically Zee Cheng et al., discloses structurally similar compounds to those claimed by the applicants which have been proven in vivo to be effective as chemotherapeutic agents against various tumor models.

10. ***In re Brana***, 34 USPQ 2d 1436, 1442 (Fed. Cir. 1995)

Our court's predecessor has determined that proof of an alleged pharmaceutical property for a compound by statistically significant tests with standard experimental animals is sufficient to establish utility.

11. ***In re Brana***, 34 USPQ 2d 1436, 1442 (Fed. Cir. 1995)

FDA approval, however, is not a prerequisite for finding a compound useful within the meaning of the patent laws. . . . Usefulness in patent law, and in particular in the context of pharmaceutical inventions, necessarily includes the expectation of further research and development. The stage at which an invention in this field becomes useful is well before it is ready to be administered to humans.

12. ***Fujikawa v. Wattanasin***, 39 USPQ 2d 1895, 1899 (Fed. Cir. 1996)

In the pharmaceutical arts, our court has long held that practical utility may be shown by adequate evidence of any pharmacological activity. *See, e.g., Nelson v. Bowler*, 626 F.2d 853, 856, 206 USPQ 881, 883 (CCPA 1980); *In re Krimmel*, 292 F.2d 948, 952–53, 130 USPQ 215, 219 (CCPA 1961) ". . . . Accordingly, under well-established precedent, evidence establishing substantial utility for any purpose is sufficient to show reduction to practice." . . . Such activity constitutes a practical utility because "[i]t is inherently faster and easier to combat illnesses and alleviate symptoms when the medical profession is armed with an arsenal of chemicals having known pharmacological activities. Since it is crucial to provide researchers with an incentive to disclose pharmacological activities in as many compounds as possible, we conclude that adequate proof of any such activity constitutes a showing of practical utility." *Nelson*, 626 F.2d at 856, 206 USPQ at 883; *see also Krimmel*, 292 F.2d at 952–53, 130 USPQ at 219.

13. ***Fujikawa v. Wattanasin***, 39 USPQ 2d 1895, 1899 n.4 (Fed. Cir. 1996)

Strictly speaking, this articulation of the standard (i.e. evidence of *any* pharmacological activity) applies only when the count does not recite a particular utility. *See Rey-Bellet v. Engelhardt*, 493 F.2d 1380, 1383, 181 USPQ 453, 454 (CCPA 1974). In contrast, when the count recites a particular utility, practical utility requires an adequate showing of the recited utility.

14. ***Fujikawa v. Wattanasin***, 39 USPQ 2d 1895, 1899 (Fed. Cir. 1996)

It may be difficult to predict, however, whether a novel compound will exhibit pharmacological activity, even when the behavior of analogous compounds is known to those skilled in the art. Consequently, testing is often required to establish practical utility. *See, e.g., Blicke*, 241 F.2d at 720, 112 USPQ at 475. But the test results need not absolutely prove that the compound is pharmacologically active. All that is required is that the tests be "*reasonably* indicative of the desired [pharmacological] response." *Nelson*, 626 F.2d at 856, 206 USPQ at 884 (emphasis added). In other words, there must be a sufficient correlation between the tests and an asserted pharmacological activity so as to convince those skilled in the art, to a reasonable probability, that the novel compound will exhibit the asserted pharmacological behavior.

15. ***Fujikawa v. Wattanasin***, 39 USPQ 2d 1895, 1899–1900 (Fed. Cir. 1996)

The facts in this case are substantially similar to those in *Cross v. Iizuka*, 753 F.2d 1040, 224 USPQ 739 (Fed. Cir. 1985). There, we expressly held that, in appropriate circumstances, evidence of *in vitro* testing could adequately establish a practical utility. As we there explained:

> We perceive no insurmountable difficulty, under appropriate circumstances, in finding that the first link in the screening chain, *in vitro* testing, may establish a practical utility for the compound in question. . . . [U]nder the circumstances of the instant case, where [an application] discloses an *in vitro* utility, . . . and where the disclosed *in vitro* utility is supplemented by the similar *in vitro* and *in vivo* pharmacological activity of structurally similar compounds, . . . we agree with the Board that this *in vitro* utility is sufficient to [establish utility].

Id. at 1051, 224 USPQ at 748. Thus, *Cross* holds that positive *in vitro* results, in combination with a known correlation between such *in vitro* results and *in vivo* activity, may be sufficient to establish practical utility.

16. ***Ex parte Bhide***, 42 USPQ 2d 1441, 1447 (B.P.A.I. 1996)

Whatever might have been the case earlier in the 20th Century, in 1992 when applicants filed their application, the notion that a chemical compound may be useful in treating cancer is not inherently incredible.

17. ***Ex parte Bhide***, 42 USPQ 2d 1441, 1447 (B.P.A.I. 1996)

A claim is not unpatentable under 35 U.S.C. Section 101 or 35 U.S.C. Section 112, first paragraph, merely because compounds within its scope have different reactivities.

18. ***Juicy Whip, Inc. v. Orange Bang, Inc.***, 51 USPQ 2d 1700, 1702 (Fed. Cir. 1999)

Section 101 of the Patent Act of 1952, 35 U.S.C. § 101, provides that "whoever invents or discovers any new and useful process, machine, manufacture, or composition of matter, or any new and useful improvement thereof," may obtain a patent on the invention or discovery. The threshold of utility is not high: An invention is "useful" under section 101 if it is capable of providing some identifiable benefit.

19. ***Juicy Whip, Inc. v. Orange Bang, Inc.***, 51 USPQ 2d 1700, 1702 (Fed. Cir. 1999) (quoting ***Lowell v. Lewis***, 15 F. Cas. 1018, 1019 (C.C.D. Mass. 1817))

[S]ince Justice Story's opinion in *Lowell v. Lewis*, it has been stated that inventions that are "injurious to the well-being, good policy, or sound morals of society" are unpatentable. As examples of such inventions, Justice Story listed "a new invention to poison people, or to promote debauchery, or to facilitate private assassination." . . . Courts have continued to recite Justice Story's formulation, . . . but the principle that inventions are invalid if they are principally designed to serve immoral or illegal purposes has not been applied broadly in recent years. For example, years ago courts invalidated patents on gambling devices on the ground that they were immoral, . . . but that is no longer the law.

20. ***Juicy Whip, Inc. v. Orange Bang, Inc.***, 51 USPQ 2d 1700, 1703 (Fed. Cir. 1999)

The fact that one product can be altered to make it look like another is in itself a specific benefit sufficient to satisfy the statutory requirement of utility.

It is not at all unusual for a product to be designed to appear to viewers to be something it is not. For example, cubic zirconium is designed to simulate a diamond, imitation gold leaf is designed to imitate real gold leaf, synthetic fabrics are designed to simulate expensive natural fabrics, and imitation leather is designed to look like real leather. In each case, the invention of the product or process that makes such imitation possible has "utility" within the meaning of the patent statute, and indeed there are numerous patents directed toward making one product imitate another. . . . Much of the value of such products resides in the fact that they appear to be something they are not. Thus, in this case the claimed post-mix dispenser meets the statutory requirement of utility by embodying the features of a post-mix dispenser while imitating the visual appearance of a pre-mix dispenser.

21. ***Juicy Whip, Inc. v. Orange Bang, Inc.***, 51 USPQ 2d 1700, 1703 (Fed. Cir. 1999)

The requirement of "utility" in patent law is not a directive to the Patent and Trademark Office or the courts to serve as arbiters of deceptive trade practices. Other agencies, such as the Federal Trade Commission and the Food and Drug Administration, are assigned the task of protecting consumers from fraud and deception in the sale of food products. . . . As the Supreme Court put the point more generally, "Congress never intended that the patent laws should displace the police powers of the States, meaning by that term those powers by which the health, good order, peace and general welfare of the community are promoted." Of course, Congress is free to declare particular types of inventions unpatentable for a variety of reasons, including deceptiveness. . . . Until such time as Congress does so, however, we find no basis in section 101 to hold that inventions can be ruled unpatentable for lack of utility simply because they have the capacity to fool some members of the public.

22. ***Process Control Corp. v. HydReclaim Corp.***, 52 USPQ 2d 1029, 1034–35 (Fed. Cir. 1999)

Lack of enablement and absence of utility are closely related grounds of unpatentability. . . . The enablement requirement of 35 U.S.C. § 112, ¶ 1 requires that the specification adequately discloses to one skilled in the relevant art how to make, or in the case of a process, how to carry out, the claimed invention without undue experimentation. . . . The utility requirement of 35 U.S.C. § 101 mandates that any patentable invention be useful and, accordingly, the subject matter of the claim must be operable. . . . If a patent claim fails to meet the utility requirement because it is not useful or operative, then it also fails to meet the how-to-use aspect of the enablement requirement.

23. ***Process Control Corp. v. HydReclaim Corp.***, 52 USPQ 2d 1029, 1035 (Fed. Cir. 1999) (quoting ***Brooktree Corp. v. Advanced Micro Devices, Inc.***, 24 USPQ 2d 1401, 1412 (Fed. Cir. 1992))

[W]hen an impossible limitation, such as a nonsensical method of operation, is clearly embodied within the claim, the claimed invention must be held invalid. While an otherwise valid patent covering a meritorious invention should not be struck down simply because of the patentee's misconceptions about scientific principles concerning the invention, . . . when "the claimed subject matter is inoperable, the patent may indeed be invalid for failure to meet the utility requirement of § 101 and the enablement requirement of § 112."

24. ***Process Control Corp. v. HydReclaim Corp.***, 52 USPQ 2d 1029, 1035 (Fed. Cir. 1999)

In the present case, it is undisputed by both HydReclaim and Process Control that a consistent definition of "discharge rate" in clauses [b] and [d] of claim 1 leads to a nonsensical conclusion. . . . In other words, clause [d] requires determining a quantity from the sum of that exact same quantity and something else, or symbolically, $A = A + B$, which is impossible, where, as here, B is not equal to zero. Accordingly, we hold that the correctly construed claims are invalid because they are inoperative, and thus the claims fail to comply with the utility and enablement requirements of 35 U.S.C. §§ 101 and 112, ¶ 1, respectively.

25. ***In re Cortright***, 49 USPQ 2d 1464, 1466 (Fed. Cir. 1999) (quotations omitted)

A lack of enablement rejection under section 112, ¶ 1 is appropriate where the written description fails to teach those in the art to make and use the invention as broadly as it is claimed without undue experimentation. . . .

This rejection takes several forms. The PTO will make a scope of enablement rejection where the written description enables something within the scope of the claims, but the claims are not limited to that scope. . . . This type of rejection is marked by language stating that the specification does not enable one of ordinary skill to use the invention commensurate with the scope of the claims. On the other hand, if the written description does not enable any subject matter within the scope of the claims, the PTO will make a general enablement rejection, stating that the specification does not teach how to make or use the invention. . . .

If the written description fails to illuminate a credible utility, the PTO will make both a section 112, ¶ 1 rejection for failure to teach how to use the invention and a section 101 rejection for lack of utility. . . . This dual rejection occurs because "the how to use prong of section 112 incorporates as a matter of law the requirement of 35 U.S.C. § 101 that the specification disclose as a matter of fact a practical utility for the invention." . . . Thus, an applicant's failure to disclose how to use an invention may support a rejection under either section 112, ¶ 1 for lack of enablement as a result of "the specification's . . . failure to disclose adequately to one ordinarily skilled in the art 'how to use' the invention without undue experimentation," or section 101 for lack of utility "when there is a complete absence of data supporting the statements which set forth the desired results of the claimed invention." . . .

The PTO cannot make this type of rejection, however, unless it has reason to doubt the objective truth of the statements contained in the written description. . . . The PTO may establish a reason to doubt an invention's asserted utility when the written description "suggests an inherently unbelievable undertaking or involves implausible scientific principles."

26. ***In re Cortright***, 49 USPQ 2d 1464, 1469 (Fed. Cir. 1999) (quoting ***Newman v. Quigg***, 11 USPQ 2d 1340, 1345 (Fed. Cir. 1989))

"It is not a requirement of patentability that an inventor correctly set forth, or even know, how or why the invention works." . . . Furthermore, statements that a physiological phenomenon was observed are not inherently suspect simply because the underlying basis for the observation cannot be predicted or explained. Therefore, the board erred in suggesting that Cortright was required to prove the cause of the resultant hair growth.

II.C. Printed Matter Rejections

1. ***In re Sterling***, 21 USPQ 519, 521 (C.C.P.A. 1934)

The foregoing cases and numerous cases cited therein are authorities for holding that patentable novelty cannot be predicated upon printing alone but must reside in physical structure.

The street railroad transfer ticket there [*Cincinnati Traction v. Pope*] involved had printed matter upon it arranged so as to adapt it readily and conveniently to the definite uses described in the opinion, but the court did not rest its decision upholding the validity of the patent upon the printing, or the arrangement thereof, but stated specifically:

The device of the patent clearly involves physical structure. The claims themselves are, in a proper sense, limited to such structure.

If the check and stub structure here involved presented some new and useful physical form with the printed matter adjusted to such form, as was the situation with reference to the transfer ticket, a different question would confront us in view of the doctrine of the Traction Co. case. . . .

2. ***In re Royka***, 180 USPQ 580, 583 (C.C.P.A. 1974)

Printed matter may very well constitute structural limitations upon which patentability can be predicated.

3. ***Ex parte Gwinn***, 112 USPQ 439, 446 (Pat. Off. Bd. App. 1955)

We have carefully reviewed many decisions, which will be enumerated below, and it is our view that they are controlling and that they hold: (A) that where the sole distinction set out in the claims over the prior art is in the printed matter, there being no new feature of physical structure and no new relation of printed matter to physical structure, such claims may not be allowed; with the further holding (B) that it is only where the claims define either new features of structure or new relations of printed matter to structure, or both, which new features or new relations give rise to some new and useful function or effect or result that claims may properly be allowed.

4. ***In re Miller***, 164 USPQ 46, 49 (C.C.P.A. 1969)

The fact that printed matter by itself is not patentable subject matter, because non-statutory, is no reason for ignoring it when the claim is directed to a combination. Here there is a new and unobvious functional relationship between a measuring receptacle, volumetric indicia thereon indicating volume in a certain ratio to actual volume, and a legend indicating the ratio, and in our judgment the appealed claims properly define this relationship.

5. ***In re Jones***, 153 USPQ 77, 80–81 (C.C.P.A. 1967)

By doubling its length, and then electrically compensating for the error thus deliberately introduced, appellant has solved a problem by what seems to us to be a structural change in the disc, which also brings about a new dimensional and hence functional relationship between the shortest segment in the outer track and the transition point in the innermost track, allowing greater latitude in positioning the latter. . . . That claim, and the others likewise, do not, in our opinion, define "printed matter" in the sense in which that term has heretofore been used to indicate various sorts of indicia whose primary purpose is the conveying of intelligence to a reader. What we find on the disc we would not characterize as indicia or printing but as structure, albeit the "pattern areas" of claim 1 are not necessarily transparent and opaque, respectively, and might be produced by some sort of printing technique. A dark area on a light base can be an element of structure.

6. ***In re Jones***, 153 USPQ 77, 82 (C.C.P.A. 1967)

The disc is devised, made and used as a component part of a machine utilizing optics and electronics to perform functions of which we are not fully apprised by the record. We think it is error to confuse the lines on a patent drawing, which may have the appearance of "printed matter," with functional elements of a mechanism which in use actuate other mechanisms or electrical circuits or devices intended to be illustrated by the drawing.

7. *In re Gulack*, 217 USPQ 401, 403 (Fed. Cir. 1983)

Differences between an invention and the prior art cited against it cannot be ignored merely because those differences reside in the content of the printed matter. Under section 103, the board cannot dissect a claim, excise the printed matter from it, and declare the remaining portion of the mutilated claim to be unpatentable. The claim must be read as a whole.

8. *In re Gulack*, 217 USPQ 401, 403 n.8 (Fed. Cir. 1983)

The CCPA has considered all of the limitations of the claims including the printed matter limitations, in determining whether the invention would have been obvious. . . . In *Royka*, . . . the CCPA, notably weary of reiterating this point, clearly stated that printed matter may well constitute structural limitations upon which patentability can be predicated.

9. *In re Gulack*, 217 USPQ 401, 404 (Fed. Cir. 1983)

Where the printed matter is not functionally related to the substrate, the printed matter will not distinguish the invention from the prior art in terms of patentability.

Similarly, in examining Gulack's invention, we find that a functional relationship does exist between the printed matter and the substrate. A functional relationship of the precise type found by the CCPA in *Miller*—to size or to type of substrate, or conveying information about substrate—is not required. What is required is the existence of differences between the appealed claims and the prior art sufficient to establish patentability. The bare presence or absence of a specific functional relationship, without further analysis, is not dispositive of obviousness. Rather, the critical question is whether there exists any new and unobvious functional relationship between the printed matter and the substrate.

10. *In re Gulack*, 217 USPQ 401, 405 (Fed. Cir. 1983)

The appealed claims, on the other hand, require a particular sequence of digits to be displayed on the outside surface of a band. These digits *are related* to the band in two ways: (1) the band supports the digits; and (2) there is an endless sequence of digits—each digit residing in a unique position with respect to every other digit in an endless loop. Thus, the digits exploit the endless nature of the band.

11. *Flood v. Coe*, 45 USPQ 72, 72–73 (D.D.C. 1940)

The ticket is like prior tickets in that it is formed in two parts with a line of perforations between the two parts and in that each part carries a series of identification indicia and also a price mark, the marking on the two parts being the same. When a garment is sold one part of the ticket is torn off and retained by the store while the other part is left attached to the garment taken by the customer.

The applicant's ticket, however, differs from the prior art in that the line of perforations extends lengthwise of the ticket instead of crosswise; in that the series of identification indicia is arranged in a row extending lengthwise of the line of perforation instead of being tabulated in a column extending perpendicularly to the line of perforations; in that the price marks of the two sections are printed in alignment crosswise of the line of perforations at one end of the ticket instead of merely being included in the columns of other indicia. . . . The invention here is more than an arrangement of printed matter on a piece of paper. There is definite and decided relationship between the physical structure and the printed matter. The one depends upon the other. In other words, there is cooperative relationship between the printed indicia and the structural features of the ticket.

12. ***Ex parte Whittlesey***, 65 USPQ 43, 44 (Pat. Off. Bd. App. 1943)

Briefly the card as disclosed is an elongated one capable of being cut apart along a line between the two ends. It has around the main section both perforations and notches on one or all three of the free edges. The supplemental section has perforations and notches along its short edge opposite the severance line between the two sections. . . . Upon separating the two sections along the severance line the quadrilateral perforations become notches which are utilized in machine-sorting of the cards.

Under the law applicable it becomes necessary to find actual structure recited in the claims to distinguish from the references rather than merely the presence of different printed matter. Claim 20 recites two features of a structural nature not found in the references. First, is a correspondence in position between (referring to elements of the drawing, Fig. 2) notches 34' and 33' on the main section and the notches 34 and 33 on the edge of the supplemental section; and second, the fact that the perforations (34' and 33') extend to the line of severance so that upon severance they become notches.

13. ***Ex parte Lang***, 56 USPQ 423, 424–25 (Pat. Off. Bd. App. 1942)

The examiner has rejected the claims as covering printed matter which is not patentable within the patent Statutes. The claims, 8 to 11, recite the card, the printed matter and the perforations, and specify the relation between them. Claims 12 to 14 do not recite perforations but recite columns of spaced digit identifying positions, with only one position for each digit and a special identifying position for receiving a distinguishing designation. They also state the relation between the different positions.

Appellant has cited a long list of patents and quoted claims from them. These claims cover merely controlling cards having printed matter and perforations on them or only printed matter on them. They, however, state the relationship between the various parts of the printed matter as well as between the perforations and the printed matter. Hence patents have been granted covering controlling cards. It is clear that the present claims are drawn to actually cover physical structure and are not in our opinion rejectable as merely covering printed matter.

14. ***Ex parte Anderson***, 52 USPQ 185, 186 (Pat. Off. Bd. App. 1941)

Applicant has provided a special flat map in the form of a developed surface of a cone and indicated various geographical points on it. . . . When a proper template is selected and placed on the map a grate circle can be marked between two selected points by following the straight and stepped portions. . . .

Claims 18, 19 and 20 are drawn to cover the template. The examiner has rejected these claims on the ground that they merely cover printed matter. We do not agree with this rejection of these claims because they involve structural features with which the printed matter cooperates. It is quite well established that claims of this character involve more than mere printed matter and are not rejected on this ground. . . . We think that there is a good combination between the parts set out in these claims. The different parts carry indicia which cooperate to achieve the result desired. If the parts did not contain the cooperating indicia and if the parts were not used together the result desired could not be achieved.

15. ***Ex parte Harrington***, 51 USPQ 235, 236 (Pat. Off. Bd. App. 1941)

The examiner takes the position that the particular shapes of the characters employed by applicant amount to a non-patentable difference in design. We are not satisfied that this is a correct statement of the case where the design is given definite mechanical characteristics such as uniform area of each mark and uniform enclosing areas. These features have distinct mechanical advantages in the detection of forgery and the examiner does not contend that the references show these features.

The examiner has rejected the claims also on the ground that they are directed to mere printed matter. We believe the mechanical advantages of applicant's arrangement are such as to take this case out of the class of cases condemning patents on mere printed matter.

16. ***Ex parte Johnson***, 45 USPQ 621, 622 (Pat. Off. Bd. App. 1940)

The claims also stand rejected on the ground that they are directed to subject matter which is unpatentable under various decisions relating to printed matter, . . .

None of the decisions cited by the Primary Examiner relate particularly to sets of game pieces. Obviously, the application of the doctrine now urged by the Primary Examiner would invalidate all the references on which he relies in rejecting the claims. It seems to us that, while games in the form of printed cards do differentiate from each other solely by reason of the indicia printed on the cards, there is sufficient coordination between the various pieces to constitute patentable subject matter despite this fact. . . . We are not satisfied that the Courts in the various decisions to which the examiner has called attention intended to go so far as to preclude the obtaining of patents for sets of cards which, because of certain indicia borne by them, are capable of use in a new and [un-]obvious way.

17. ***In re Lowry***, 32 USPQ 2d 1031, 1034 (Fed. Cir. 1994)

The printed matter cases "dealt with claims defining as the invention certain novel arrangements of printed lines or characters, useful and intelligible only to the human mind." *In re Bernhart*, 417 F.2d 1395, 1399, 163 USPQ 611, 615 (C.C.P.A. 1969). The printed matter cases have no factual relevance where "the invention as defined by the claims *requires* that the information be processed not by the mind but by a machine, the computer." *Id.* (emphasis in original). Lowry's data structures, which according to Lowry greatly facilitate data management by data processing systems, are processed by a machine. Indeed, they are not accessible other than through sophisticated software systems. The printed matter cases have no factual relevance here.

18. ***In re Lowry***, 32 USPQ 2d 1031, 1035 (Fed. Cir. 1994)

More than mere abstraction, the data structures are specific electrical or magnetic structural elements in a memory. According to Lowry, the data structures provide tangible benefits: data stored in accordance with the claimed data structures are more easily accessed, stored, and erased. Lowry further notes that, unlike prior art data structures, Lowry's data structures simultaneously represent complex data accurately and enable powerful nested operations. In short, Lowry's data structures are physical entities that provide increased efficiency in computer operation. They are not analogous to printed matter.

19. ***In re Levin***, slip. op. at 4, Civ. App. 96-1180 (Fed. Cir. Feb. 3, 1997) (unpublished)

The only requirement that 35 U.S.C. § 101 imposes as set forth in *In re Miller* is that a new and unobvious functional relationship must exist between the claimed combination of printed matter and other claimed elements. . . . For instance, as we stated in *In re Gulack*, "the critical question is whether there exists any new and unobvious functional relationship between the printed matter and the substrate." . . . We hold that the relationship between the expiration date indicia on the container or pharmaceutical product is a functional relationship. The color coded expiration date indicia provides information about the substrate or what is contained in the substrate.

II.D. *Method of Doing Business Rejections*

1. ***Ex parte Murray***, 9 USPQ 2d 1819, 1821 (B.P.A.I. 1988)

However, in deciding the validity of the Musmanno patent under §101, it is noteworthy that the district court had before it patent claims directed to a "system" for managing a cash account which combined three financial services offered by financial institutions and brokerage houses. The patent contained no "method" claims. Consequently, the court was not presented, as we are, with a "method of doing business." Whereas an apparatus or system capable of performing a business function may comprise patentable subject matter, a method of doing business generated by the apparatus or system is not.

2. ***Paine, Webber, Jackson & Curtis, Inc. v. Merrill Lynch, Pierce, Fenner & Smith, Inc.***, 218 USPQ 212, 220 (D. Del. 1983)

The CCPA, however, has made clear that if no Benson algorithm exists, the product of a computer program is irrelevant, and the focus of analysis should be on the operation of the program on the computer. The Court finds that the '442 patent claims statutory subject matter because the claims allegedly teach a method of operation on a computer to effectuate a business activity. Accordingly, the '442 patent passes the threshold requirement of Section 101.

3. ***Loew's Drive-In Theatres, Inc. v. Park-In Theatres, Inc.***, 81 USPQ 149, 153 (1st Cir.), ***cert. denied***, 338 U.S. 822 (1949)

Thus a system for the transaction of business, such, for example, as the cafeteria system for transacting the restaurant business, or similarly the open-air drive-in system for conducting the motion picture theater business, however novel, useful, or commercially successful is not patentable apart from the means for making the system practically useful, or carrying it out.

4. ***In re Patton***, 53 USPQ 376, 379 (C.C.P.A. 1942)

In this connection it is sufficient to say that a system of transacting business, apart from the means for carrying out such system, is not within the purview of section 4886, supra, nor is an abstract idea or theory, regardless of its importance or the ingenuity with which it was conceived, apart from the means for carrying such idea or theory into effect, patentable subject matter.

5. ***In re Johnston***, 183 USPQ 172, 177 (C.C.P.A. 1974), ***rev'd on other grounds sub nom. Dann v. Johnston***, 425 U.S. 219 (1976)

The board's reluctance to "grant a monopoly to appellant on a method of conducting the banking business" is misplaced. The appealed apparatus claims are not drawn to cover either a method of doing business or even a method of bookkeeping. Nor would banks "be restricted to the use of their data processing equipment only for their own bookkeeping and not * * * [be] allowed to freely expand into the business of keeping books for their customers." Obviously, banks would be free to so expand their services and use any apparatus they may desire except the apparatus set forth in appellant's claims.

6. ***In re Deutsch***, 193 USPQ 645, 648 n.5 (C.C.P.A. 1977)

Methods of doing business and mental steps were discussed at oral argument. Deutsch's methods are not methods of doing business. . . . They do not merely facilitate business dealings. That translation of business data into mathematical language intelligible to computers is employed in carrying them out does not make a method of automatically controlling a system of manufacturing plants a method of "doing business." For that reason, also, the doctrine of mental steps is inapposite.

7. ***Rand, McNally & Co. v. Exchange Scrip-Book Co.***, 187 F. 984, 986 (7th Cir. 1911)

Nor do we think that this patented concept is nothing more than a business method. Its use is a part of a business method. The ticket patented is not a method at all, but a physical tangible facility, without which the method would have been impracticable, and with which it is practicable. And this is the status of thousands of like facilities that, once designed and put into use, have become the first of a new business method; and patents on such facilities have been sustained.

8. ***State Street Bank & Trust Co. v. Signature Fin. Group, Inc.***, 47 USPQ 2d 1596, 1601 (Fed. Cir.), ***cert. denied***, 525 U.S. 1093 (1999)

Today, we hold that the transformation of data, representing discrete dollar amounts, by a machine through a series of mathematical calculations into a final share price, constitutes a practical application of a mathematical algorithm, formula, or calculation, because it produces "a useful, concrete and tangible result"—a final share price momentarily fixed for recording and reporting purposes and even accepted and relied upon by regulatory authorities and in subsequent trades.

9. ***State Street Bank & Trust Co. v. Signature Fin. Group, Inc.***, 47 USPQ 2d 1596, 1602 (Fed. Cir.), ***cert. denied***, 525 U.S. 1093 (1999)

However, after Diehr and Alappat, the mere fact that a claimed invention involves inputting numbers, calculating numbers, outputting numbers, and storing numbers, in and of itself, would not render it nonstatutory subject matter, unless, of course, its operation does not produce a "useful, concrete and tangible result." *Alappat*, 33 F.3d at 1544, 31 USPQ 2d at 1557.

10. ***State Street Bank & Trust Co. v. Signature Fin. Group, Inc.***, 47 USPQ 2d 1596, 1602 (Fed. Cir.), ***cert. denied***, 525 U.S. 1093 (1999)

The question of whether a claim encompasses statutory subject matter should not focus on which of the four categories of subject matter a claim is directed to —process, machine, manufacture, or composition of matter—but rather on the essential characteristics of the subject matter, in particular, its practical utility. Section 101 specifies that statutory subject matter must also satisfy the other "conditions and requirements" of Title 35, including novelty, nonobviousness, and adequacy of disclosure and notice.

11. ***State Street Bank & Trust Co. v. Signature Fin. Group, Inc.***, 47 USPQ 2d 1596, 1602 (Fed. Cir.), ***cert. denied***, 525 U.S. 1093 (1999)

For purpose of our analysis, as noted above, claim 1 is directed to a machine programmed with the Hub and Spoke software and admittedly produces a "useful, concrete, and tangible result." *Alappat*, 33 F.3d at 1544, 31 USPQ 2d at 1557. This renders it statutory subject matter, even if the useful result is expressed in numbers, such as price, profit, percentage, cost, or loss.

12. ***State Street Bank & Trust Co. v. Signature Fin. Group, Inc.***, 47 USPQ 2d 1603–04 (Fed. Cir.), ***cert. denied***, 525 U.S. 1093 (1999)

Since its inception, the "business method" exception has merely represented the application of some general, but no longer applicable legal principle, perhaps arising out of the "requirement for invention"—which was eliminated by § 103. Since the 1952 Patent Act, business methods have been, and should have been, subject to the same legal requirements for patentability as applied to any other process or method. . . . This acknowledgment is buttressed by the U.S. Patent and Trademark 1996 Examination Guidelines for Computer Related Inventions which now read:

> Office personnel have had difficulty in properly treating claims directed to methods of doing business. Claims should not be categorized as methods of doing business. Instead such claims should be treated like any other process claims.

Examination Guidelines, 61 Fed. Reg. 7478, 7479 (1996). We agree that this is precisely the manner in which this type of claim should be treated. Whether the claims are directed to subject matter within § 101 should not turn on whether the claimed subject matter does "business" instead of something else.

13. ***AT&T Corp. v. Excel Communications, Inc.***, 50 USPQ 2d 1447, 1450 (Fed. Cir. 1999)

Since the process of manipulation of numbers is a fundamental part of computer technology, we have had to reexamine the rules that govern the patentability of such technology. The sea-changes in both law and technology stand as a testament to the ability of law to adapt to new and innovative concepts, while remaining true to basic principles. In an earlier era, the PTO published guidelines essentially rejecting the notion that computer programs were patentable. As the technology progressed, our predecessor court disagreed, and, overturning some of the earlier limiting principles regarding § 101, announced more expansive principles formulated with computer technology in mind. n3 In our recent decision in *State Street*, this court discarded the so-called "business method" exception and reassessed the "mathematical algorithm" exception, . . . both judicially-created "exceptions" to the statutory categories of § 101. As this brief review suggests, this court (and its predecessor) has struggled to make our understanding of the scope of § 101 responsive to the needs of the modern world.

14. ***AT&T Corp. v. Excel Communications, Inc.***, 50 USPQ 2d 1447, 1452 (Fed. Cir. 1999)

In *State Street*, we held that the processing system there was patentable subject matter because the system takes data representing discrete dollar amounts through a series of mathematical calculations to determine a final share price—a useful, concrete, and tangible result.

II.E. Plants and Statutory Subject Matter Issues

1. ***Pioneer Hi-Bred Int'l, Inc. v. J.E.M. Ag Supply, Inc.***, 53 USPQ 2d 1440, 1441–43 (Fed. Cir. 2000), ***cert. granted***, 121 S.Ct. 1077 (Feb 20, 2001) (No. 99-1996)

The district court held that the Supreme Court in *Diamond v. Chakrabarty*, 447 U.S. 303, 309, 206 USPQ 193, 197, 65 L. Ed. 2d 144, 100 S. Ct. 2204 (1980), in stating that "Congress intended statutory subject matter to 'include anything under the sun that is made by man,'" (quoting S. Rep. No. 1979 at 5 (1952)), confirmed that there is no basis in law for excluding living things, in this case seeds and seed-grown plants and parts thereof, from the subject matter included in §101. . . . Although there remain the traditional categories that have never been viewed as patentable subject matter, viz., laws of nature, natural phenomena, and abstract ideas, the policy underlying the patent system fosters its application to all areas of technology-based commerce. . . . We conclude that patentable subject matter under 35 U.S.C. §101 includes seeds and seed-grown plants.

III. Anticipation Under Section 102

1. ***Akzo N.V. v. United States Int'l Trade Comm'n***, 1 USPQ 2d 1241, 1245 (Fed. Cir. 1986), ***cert. denied***, 482 U.S. 909 (1987)

Under 35 U.S.C. §102, anticipation requires that each and every element of the claimed invention be disclosed in the prior art. . . . In addition, the prior art reference must be enabling, thus placing the allegedly disclosed matter in the possession of the public.

2. ***W.L. Gore & Assocs. v. Garlock, Inc.***, 220 USPQ 303, 313 (Fed. Cir. 1983), ***cert. denied***, 469 U.S. 851 (1984)

Anticipation requires the disclosure in a single prior art reference of each element of the claim under consideration.

3. ***Continental Can Co. USA v. Monsanto Co.***, 20 USPQ 2d 1746, 1748 (Fed. Cir. 1991)

   When more than one reference is required to establish unpatentability of the claimed invention anticipation under § 102 can not be found, and validity is determined in terms of § 103.

4. ***Lindemann Maschinenfabrik GmbH v. American Hoist & Derrick Co.***, 221 USPQ 481, 485 (Fed. Cir. 1984) (emphasis added)

   Anticipation requires the presence in a single prior art reference disclosure of each and every element of the claimed invention, *arranged as in the claim.*

5. ***In re Sun***, 31 USPQ 2d 1451, 1453 (Fed. Cir. 1993) (unpublished)

   Under section 102(b), anticipation requires that the prior art reference disclose, either expressly or under the principles of inherency, every limitation of the claim. . . .

   But to be prior art under section 102(b), a reference must be enabling. . . . That is, it must put the claimed invention in the hand of one skilled in the art. . . . The examiner bears the burden of presenting at least a prima facie case of anticipation.

6. ***Scripps Clinic & Research Found. v. Genentech Inc.***, 18 USPQ 2d 1001, 1010 (Fed. Cir. 1991)

   Invalidity for anticipation requires that all of the elements and limitations of the claim are found within a single prior art reference. . . . There must be no difference between the claimed invention and the reference disclosure, as viewed by a person of ordinary skill in the field of the invention.

7. ***In re Warner***, 154 USPQ 173, 177 (C.C.P.A. 1967), ***cert. denied***, 389 U.S. 1057 (1968)

   We think the precise language of 35 U.S.C. 102 that "a person shall be entitled to a patent unless," concerning novelty and unobviousness, clearly places a burden of proof on the Patent Office which requires it to produce the factual basis for its rejection of an application under sections 102 and 103. . . .

8. ***In re Bass***, 177 USPQ 178, 186 (C.C.P.A. 1973)

   From the evidence available to it, the initial burden of making out a prima facie case of prior invention is on the Patent Office. . . . When the Patent Office has made out a prima facie case of priority the burden would then shift to the applicant to rebut it.

   The evidence of priority in the record consists of filing dates, the contents of the application and reference patents, statements in affidavits filed and accepted under Rule 131, and statements by appellant's attorneys during prosecution.

9. *In re Schreiber*, 44 USPQ 2d 1429, 1431–32 (Fed. Cir. 1997)

It is well settled that the recitation of a new intended use for an old product does not make a claim to that old product patentable. *See In re Spada*, 911 F.2d 705, 708, 15 USPQ 2d 1655, 1657 (Fed. Cir. 1990) ("The discovery of a new property or use of a previously known composition, even when that property and use are unobvious from prior art, can not impart patentability to claims to the known composition."); . . . Accordingly, Schreiber's contention that his structure will be used to dispense popcorn does not have patentable weight if the structure is already known, regardless of whether it has ever been used in any way in connection with popcorn.

10. *In re Schreiber*, 44 USPQ 2d 1429, 1432 (Fed. Cir. 1997)

[T]he question whether a reference is analogous art is irrelevant to whether that reference anticipates. . . . A reference may be from an entirely different field of endeavor than that of the claimed invention or may be directed to an entirely different problem from the one addressed by the inventor, yet the reference will still anticipate if it explicitly or inherently discloses every limitation recited in the claims.

11. *Motorola, Inc. v. Interdigital Tech. Corp.*, 43 USPQ 2d 1481, 1490 (Fed. Cir. 1997)

For a prior art reference to anticipate a claim, the reference must disclose each and every element of the claim with sufficient clarity to prove its existence in the prior art. *See In re Spada*, 911 F.2d 705, 708, 15 USPQ 2d 1655, 1657 (Fed. Cir. 1990) ("[T]he [prior art] reference must describe the applicant's claimed invention sufficiently to have placed a person of ordinary skill in the field of the invention in possession of it." (citations omitted)). Although this disclosure requirement presupposes the knowledge of one skilled in the art of the claimed invention, that presumed knowledge does not grant a license to read into the prior art reference teachings that are not there.

12. *Row v. Dror*, 42 USPQ 2d 1550, 1553 (Fed. Cir. 1997) (quoting *Kloster Speedsteel AB v. Crucible, Inc.*, 230 USPQ 81, 84 (Fed. Cir. 1986))

A prior art reference anticipates a claim only if the reference discloses, either expressly or inherently, every limitation of the claim. . . . "[A]bsence from the reference of any claimed element negates anticipation."

13. ***Woodland Trust v. Flowertree Nursery, Inc.***, 47 USPQ 2d 1363, 1365–66 (Fed. Cir. 1998)

Section 102(a) establishes that a person can not patent what was already known to others. If the invention was known to or used by others in this country before the date of the patentee's invention, the later inventor has not contributed to the store of knowledge, and has no entitlement to a patent. Accordingly, in order to invalidate a patent based on prior knowledge or use, that knowledge or use must have been available to the public. . . . Therefore, notwithstanding abandonment of the prior use—which may preclude a challenge under § 102(g)—prior knowledge or use by others may invalidate a patent under § 102(a) if the prior knowledge or use was accessible to the public. . . . Section 102(b), unlike § 102(a), is primarily concerned with the policy that encourages an inventor to enter the patent system promptly, while recognizing a one year period of public knowledge or use or commercial exploitation before the patent application must be filed. Thus an inventor's own prior commercial use, albeit kept secret, may constitute a public use or sale under § 102(b), barring him from obtaining a patent. . . . However, when an asserted prior use is not that of the applicant, § 102(b) is not a bar when that prior use or knowledge is not available to the public.

14. ***Celeritas Techs., Ltd. v. Rockwell Int'l Corp.***, 47 USPQ 2d 1516, 1522 (Fed. Cir 1998), ***cert. denied***, 525 U.S. 1106 (1999)

It is well settled that a claim is anticipated if each and every limitation is found either expressly or inherently in a single prior art reference. *See Structural Rubber Prods. Co. v. Park Rubber Co.*, 749 F.2d 707, 715, 223 USPQ 1264, 1270 (Fed. Cir. 1984). A reference is no less anticipatory if, after disclosing the invention, the reference then disparages it. Thus, the question whether a reference "teaches away" from the invention is inapplicable to an anticipation analysis.

15. ***ATD Corp. v. Lydall, Inc.***, 48 USPQ 2d 1321, 1328 (Fed. Cir. 1998)

An anticipating reference must describe the patented subject matter with sufficient clarity and detail to establish that the subject matter existed and that its existence was recognized by persons of ordinary skill in the field of the invention.

16. ***Ecolochem, Inc. v. Southern California Edison Co.***, 56 USPQ 2d 1065, 1071 (Fed. Cir. 2000)

A presentation indicative of the state of knowledge and use in this country therefore qualifies as prior art for anticipation purposes under § 102.

17. ***Helifix Ltd. v. Blok-Lok, Ltd.***, 54 USPQ 2d 1299, 1304 (Fed. Cir. 2000)

"[E]ven if the claimed invention is disclosed in a printed publication, that disclosure will not suffice as prior art if it was not enabling." *Donohoe*, 766 F.2d at 533, 226 USPQ at 621.

18. ***In re Ductmate Industries, Inc.***, Reexamination Control Number 90/004,369, U.S. Patent 4,584,756, p.4 (Comm'r Feb. 12, 1997)

While catalogs may, by their nature, be intended to be widely disseminated, the documents submitted as Exhibits 1 and 2 do not, on their face, show such dissemination. They do not show that access to these documents was unrestricted. They do not even clearly and unequivocally show publication dates. And they do not show that in the absence of distribution, they were so indexed and catalogued that a person of ordinary skill in the art interested in obtaining a copy, could have done so. *In re Hall*, 228 USPQ 453 (Fed. Cir. 1986); *In re Cronym*, 13 USPQ 2d 1070 (Fed. Cir. 1989).

19. ***Hockerson-Halberstadt, Inc. v. Avia Group Int'l, Inc.***, 55 USPQ 2d 1487, 1491 (Fed. Cir. 2000)

Under our precedent, however, it is well established that patent drawings do not define the precise proportions of the elements and may not be relied on to show particular sizes if the specification is completely silent on the issue. *See In re Wright*, 569 F.2d 1124, 1127, 193 USPQ 332, 335 (CCPA 1977) ("Absent any written description in the specification of quantitative values, arguments based on measurement of a drawing are of little value."); *In re Olson*, 212 F.2d 590, 592, 101 USPQ 401, 402 (CCPA 1954); cf. Manual of Patent Examining Procedure Section 2125 (1998). Thus, in the present case, a reasonable competitor, being aware that figures in a patent are not drawn to scale unless otherwise indicated, would understand the arguments in the prosecution history as clearly disclaiming a groove having a width greater than the combined width of the fins.

III.A.   *Section 102(a)—Prior to Applicant's Date of Invention*

1. ***Innovative Scuba Concepts Inc. v. Feder Indus. Inc.***, 27 USPQ 2d 1254, 1263 (D. Colo. 1993), ***rev'd, remanded on other grounds***, 31 USPQ 2d 1132 (Fed. Cir. 1994)

A patent is barred if the invention was "patented or described in a printed publication in this or a foreign country" prior to the applicant's date of invention. 35 U.S.C. § 102(a). Description by a prior publication occurs where the work adequately describes the invention in question and the work qualifies as a "printed publication." The description must enable a person with ordinary skill in the art not only to comprehend the invention but also to make it. . . .

The concept of a publication requires that a work be circulated to some extent. Publication includes a book, periodical, or newspaper of general circulation. 1 W. Robinson, *The Law of Patents for Useful Inventions*, §§ 325–27 (1890). Works of less general circulation, such as trade catalogs and conference papers may also constitute publications. . . . Very little circulation or permanency is required if the work is specially directed to those skilled in the art or trade to which the patent in question relates.

2. ***Mahurkar v. C.R. Bard, Inc.***, 38 USPQ 2d 1288, 1290 (Fed. Cir. 1996)

In ex parte patent prosecution, an examiner may refer to a document published within one year before the filing date of a patent application as prior art. However, this label only applies until the inventor comes forward with evidence showing an earlier date of invention. Once the inventor shows an earlier date of invention, the document is no longer prior art under section 102(a).

Any suggestion that a document is prior art because it appears before the filing date of a patent ignores the requirements of section 102(a). Section 102(a) explicitly refers to invention dates, not filing dates. Thus, under section 102(a), a document is prior art only when published before the invention date.

III.A.i. Prior Art of "Another"

1. ***De Graffenried v. United States***, 16 USPQ 2d 1321, 1328 (Cl. Ct. 1990)

But as explained in *In re DeBaun*, 687 F.2d 459, 214 USPQ 933 (C.C.P.A. 1982), simply because a patent is issued to joint inventors does not mean that everything disclosed in that patent is necessarily joint work which would constitute prior art against a subsequent patent application by one of the two joint inventors. In *DeBaun*, . . . [t]he court rejected the argument that all information disclosed in a joint patent was necessarily the product of a joint invention. The court stated: "The [joint] patent is silent with respect to who invented the [cross] section itself, and we do not presume that it is the invention of DeBaun and Noll jointly or of either of them." *Id.* at 463, 214 USPQ at 936. The *DeBaun* court explained that in such a case "the proper subject of inquiry was . . . what the *evidence* showed as [to] *who* invented the [cross section disclosed in the patent]." *Id.* at 462, 214 USPQ at 935 (emphasis added).

Thus, *DeBaun* requires a factual determination as to which parts of the indicator patent were the product of joint work and, hence, would constitute prior art, and as to which parts were the product of plaintiff's independent work and, hence, would not constitute prior art.

III.A.ii.　Publicly Available Prior Art

1. ***In re Lund***, 153 USPQ 625, 633 (C.C.P.A. 1967)

   Consistent with those rulings, we think the disclosure in Example 2 of the abandoned Margerison application becomes available as evidence of prior knowledge, if at all, only as of the issue date of the Margerison patent, as public access to the abandoned application is then provided for by Patent Office Rule 14 (b).

2. ***Lockwood v. American Airlines, Inc.***, 41 USPQ 2d 1961, 1965 (Fed. Cir. 1997)

   If a device was "known or used by others" in this country before the date of invention or if it was "in public use" in this country more than one year before the date of application, it qualifies as prior art. *See* 35 U.S.C. § 102(a) and (b) (1994). Lockwood attempts to preclude summary judgment by pointing to record testimony that one skilled in the art would not be able to build and practice the claimed invention without access to the secret aspects of SABRE. However, it is the claims that define a patented invention. . . . As we have concluded earlier in this opinion, American's public use of the high-level aspects of the SABRE system was enough to place the *claimed* features of the '359 patent in the public's possession. . . . Lockwood cannot negate this by evidence showing that other, *unclaimed* aspects of the SABRE system were not publicly available.

3. ***Giora Georger Angres, Ltd. v. Tinny Beauty and Figure, Inc.***, Civ. App. 96-1507, slip op. 16–17 (Fed. Cir. June 26, 1997) (unpublished)

   Pavlik's practicing the invention is prior art under section 102(a) since she testified she was performing the procedure in public before 1982, the year Angres established he invented the subject matter of the patent. As discussed above, her activities anticipate claim 1 of the patent. Angres makes no allegation that they were not "public," but argues that an ordinary artisan would not have known of Pavlik's work. Under section 102(a), however, all that is required is that the use be "public." Pavlik stated she had practiced the invention in her salon which was open to the public. Angres introduced no evidence to show that an individual in Laguna, California, would not have been able to have the procedure performed or observe the procedure. While obviousness is judged from the perspective of the hypothetical person of ordinary skill in the art, once something is determined to be prior art under section 102(a), knowledge of it is imputed to the hypothetical person.

4. ***Systemation, Inc. v. Engel Indus., Inc.***, Civ. App. No. 98-1489, slip op. at 10 (Fed. Cir. Mar. 10, 1999) (unpublished)

Systemation is also likely to withstand Engel's validity challenges to claim 1 of the '880 patent. The only prior art relevant to claim 1 of the '880 patent is long public use of the manual method of inserting angle plates. Engel argues that the manual method anticipates claim 1 of the '880 patent. Systemation, however, argues that the manual method cannot anticipate claim 1 which is clearly directed toward an automatic method. The district court agreed. So do we.

It is clear, at least when claim 1 is read in light of the written description and the other claims, that the claim is directed to an automated method of inserting plates. . . . Such a method cannot be anticipated by a manual method for doing the same. The steps of the former are necessarily more in number. Further, the district court's factual findings that the claimed invention enjoyed significant commercial success and met a long-felt need are not clearly erroneous, and support a conclusion that the claimed invention was nonobvious.

5. ***Ecolochem, Inc. v. Southern Cal. Edison Co.***, 56 USPQ 2d 1065, 1071 (Fed. Cir. 2000)

A presentation indicative of the state of knowledge and use in this country therefore qualifies as prior art for anticipation purposes under § 102.

6. ***Helifix Ltd. v. Blok-Lok, Ltd.***, 54 USPQ 2d 1299, 1304 (Fed. Cir. 2000)

"[E]ven if the claimed invention is disclosed in a printed publication, that disclosure will not suffice as prior art if it was not enabling." *Donohoe*, 766 F.2d at 533, 226 USPQ at 621.

7. ***In re Ductmate Indus., Inc.***, Reexamination Control Number 90/004,369, U.S. Patent 4,584,756, p.4 (Comm'r Feb. 12, 1997)

While catalogs may, by their nature, be intended to be widely disseminated, the documents submitted as Exhibits 1 and 2 do not, on their face, show such dissemination. They do not show that access to these documents was unrestricted. They do not even clearly and unequivocally show publication dates. And they do not show that in the absence of distribution, they were so indexed and catalogued that a person of ordinary skill in the art interested in obtaining a copy, could have done so. *In re Hall*, 228 USPQ 453 (Fed. Cir. 1986); *In re Cronym*, 13 USPQ 2d 1070 (Fed. Cir. 1989).

III.B. Section 102(b)—On Sale/Public Use Bar

1. ***Keystone Retaining Wall Sys., Inc. v. Westrock, Inc.***, 27 USPQ 2d 1297, 1303 (Fed. Cir. 1993)

An invention may be found to have been on sale if there was a sale or offer to sell prior to the critical date. . . . An on sale bar determination requires that the claimed invention asserted to be on sale was operable, the complete invention claimed was embodied in or obvious in view of the device offered for sale, and the sale or offer was primarily for profit rather than for experimental purposes. "Section 102(b) may create a bar to patentability either alone, if the device placed on sale is an anticipation of the later claimed invention or, in conjunction with 35 U.S.C. § 103 (1988), if the claimed invention would have been obvious from the on-sale device in conjunction with the prior art." *LaBounty Mfg., Inc. v. United States Int'l Trade Comm'n*, 958 F.2d 1066, 1071, 22 USPQ 2d 1025, 1028 (Fed. Cir. 1992).

2. ***Moleculon Research Corp. v. CBS, Inc.***, 229 USPQ 805, 807–08 (Fed. Cir. 1986), ***cert. denied***, 479 U.S. 1030 (1987) (quoting district court with approval)

The essence of "public use" is the free and unrestricted giving over of an invention to a member of the public or the public in general. What I see here, by contrast, is the inventor's private use of his own invention for his own enjoyment. "Private use of one's own invention is permissible." . . . While it is true that Nichols explained his puzzle to a few close colleagues who inquired about it and allowed Obermayer to in fact use it, the personal relationships and other surrounding circumstances were such that Nichols at all times retained control over its use as well as over the distribution of information concerning it. He never used the puzzle or permitted it used in a place or at a time when he did not have a legitimate expectation of privacy and of confidentiality.

3. ***Ex parte C***, 27 USPQ 2d 1492, 1499 (B.P.A.I. 1992)

"Publication use" of a claimed invention under section 102(b) has been defined as any use of that invention by a person other than the inventor who is under no limitation, restriction or obligation of secrecy to the inventor. . . . The public use proscription in 35 U.S.C. § 102(b) prohibits "commercial activity", i.e., the competitive exploitation of the invention by the inventor or his assigns after it is ready for patenting; the reason being that "it is part of the consideration for a patent that the public shall as soon as possible begin to enjoy the disclosure." *See Metallizing Engineering Co., Inc. v. Kenyon Bearing Auto Parts, Inc.*, 153 F.2d 516, 68 USPQ 54, 58 (2d Cir.), *cert. denied*, 328 U.S. 840 (1946).

4. ***National Research Dev. Corp. v. Varian Assocs.***, 30 USPQ 2d 1537, 1538–39 (Fed. Cir. 1994) (unpublished)

This court in *In re Smith*, 714 F.2d 1127, 218 USPQ 976 (Fed. Cir. 1983), defined the public use of a claimed invention under section 102(b) as including "any use of that invention by a person other than the inventor who is under no limitation, restriction or obligation of secrecy to the inventor." *Id.* at 1134, 218 USPQ at 983

. . . .

Moreover, use by only one member of the public, without that use informing other members of the public as to the true nature of the invention, is sufficient under Supreme Court jurisprudence to invalidate a patent under section 102(b) for prior public use. *See, e.g., Egbert v. Lippmann*, 104 U.S. (14 Otto) 333, 336 (1881) ("If an inventor . . . gives or sells [the invention] to another, to be used by the donee or vendee, without limitation or restriction, or injunction of secrecy and it is so used, such use is public, even though the use and knowledge of the use may be confined to one person.").

5. ***Allied Colloids, Inc. v. American Cyanamid Co.***, 35 USPQ 2d 1840, 1842 (Fed. Cir. 1995)

Thus the public use bar of §102(b) requires that (1) the invention was used in public and (2) the use was not primarily experimental in purpose. The determination of these aspects requires considering and weighing such factors as the nature of the activity that occurred in public; the public access to and knowledge of the public use; whether there was any confidentiality obligation imposed on persons who observed the use; whether progress records or other indicia of experimental activity were kept; whether persons other than the inventor or acting for the inventor conducted the experiments; how many tests were conducted; the scale of the tests compared with commercial conditions; the length of the test period in comparison with tests of similar products; and whether payment was made for the product of the tests.

6. ***Allied Colloids, Inc. v. American Cyanamid Co.***, 35 USPQ 2d 1840, 1843 (Fed. Cir. 1995)

The district court held that the April 16–17 tests in the Detroit sewage treatment laboratory were an invalidating public use even if the tests were for purposes of experimentation, for the reason that they were "commercially motivated." This was an error of law. *See Manville Sales*, 917 F.2d at 551, 16 USPQ2d at 1592 (testing to determine whether the invention performs as intended negates §102(b) bar). As illustrated in precedent, public acts may range from experimentation where there are many unknowns, to simply using an already proven product in an unrestricted public location. Commercial purpose underlies virtually every contact between inventor and potential customer. When testing an invention entails customer contact, that does not convert an otherwise experimental purpose into a public use.

7. ***Allied Colloids, Inc. v. American Cyanamid Co.***, 35 USPQ 2d 1840, 1844 (Fed. Cir. 1995)

The district court referred to the absence of a written confidentiality agreement between Colloids and the City of Detroit. Although a written promise of confidentiality is a factor to be considered in appropriate circumstances, such as when persons other than the patentee conduct the experiments, *see Hycor*, 740 F.2d at 1535, 222 USPQ at 558; *TP Labs.*, 724 F.2d at 971–72, 220 USPQ at 583, the absence of such a promise does not make a use "public" as a matter of law. . . .

8. ***Allied Colloids, Inc. v. American Cyanamid Co.***, 35 USPQ 2d 1840, 1844 (Fed. Cir. 1995)

That Colloids hoped to obtain Detroit's business is not dispositive of the §102(b) analysis. Undoubtedly the Detroit tests were conducted in order to determine whether Colloids had or could make products that would satisfactorily treat Detroit sewage. Such testing at the potential customer's site does not raise a public use bar as a matter of law.

9. ***Allied Colloids, Inc. v. American Cyanamid Co.***, 35 USPQ 2d 1840, 1844 (Fed. Cir. 1995)

The court referred to a letter from Colloids' British patent attorney, written in March 1985, stating that the patent application should be filed before a "commercial sampling" in Detroit "the end of April." Colloids argues that this letter does not establish the nature of the April 16–17 tests. We agree that this letter was inadequate ground for the grant of judgment as a matter of law. Cautionary advice from a foreign patent attorney, advice that was not implemented, is not an admission of United States law or fact.

10. ***Allied Colloids, Inc. v. American Cyanamid Co.***, 35 USPQ 2d 1840, 1844 (Fed. Cir. 1995)

A public use under §102(b) does not start the one-year period until the invention has left the experimental stage. *See*

Manville Sales, 917 F.2d at 551, 16 USPQ2d at 1592 (determining when tests were completed and invention was found to work as intended, in order to determine when grace period began and ended).

11. ***Allied Colloids, Inc. v. American Cyanamid Co.***, 35 USPQ 2d 1840, 1844 (Fed. Cir. 1995)

    [The law recognizes] an inventor's need to test the invention, to ascertain whether the work is complete or further changes should be made, and to show that the invention will work for its intended purpose. . . . [S]uch testing and development may encompass or even require disclosure to the public, without barring the inventor's access to the patent system. . . . That the testing leads to and is followed by commercial success does not convert the test activity into an invalidating public use. The dispositive consideration is whether the inventor was in fact testing the invention.

12. ***City of Elizabeth v. American Nicholson Pavement Co.***, 97 U.S. 126, 135 (1878)

    [It is not necessary] that the machine should be put up and used only in the inventor's own shop or premises. He may have it put up and used in the premises of another, and the use may inure to the benefit of the owner of the establishment. Still, if used under the surveillance of the inventor, and for the purpose of enabling him to test the machine, and ascertain whether it will answer the purpose intended, and make such alterations and improvements as experience demonstrates to be necessary, it will still be a mere experimental use, and not a public use, within the meaning of the statute.

13. ***Seal-Flex, Inc. v. Athletic Track & Court Constr.***, 40 USPQ 2d 1450, 1453–54 (Fed. Cir. 1996)

    Thus the statute limits the period of commercial sale or offers of sale of an invention to one year, before the patent application must be filed or be forever barred. However, the policy embodied in §102(b) does not require that the one-year period start to accrue on an invention that is not yet known to work satisfactorily for its intended purpose. Precedent illustrates a variety of factual situations wherein contacts with potential customers before an invention was completed did not start the accrual of the on-sale bar period.

14. ***Lough v. Brunswick Corp.***, 39 USPQ 2d 1100, 1105 (Fed. Cir. 1996), ***cert. denied,*** 522 U.S. 806 (1997)

    [I]f the inventor has no control over the alleged experiments, he is not experimenting. If he does not inquire about the testing or receive reports concerning the results, similarly, he is not experimenting.

15. ***Lough v. Brunswick Corp.***, 39 USPQ 2d 1100, 1105 (Fed. Cir. 1996), ***cert. denied,*** 522 U.S. 806 (1997)

In order to justify a determination that legally sufficient experimentation has occurred, there must be present certain minimal indicia. The framework might be quite formal, as may be expected when large corporations conduct experiments, governed by contracts and explicit written obligations. When individual inventors or small business units are involved, however, less formal and seemingly casual experiments can be expected. Such less formal experiments may be deemed legally sufficient to avoid the public use bar, but only if they demonstrate the presence of the same basic elements that are required to validate any experimental program.

16. ***Mahurkar v. Impra, Inc.***, 37 USPQ 2d 1138, 1141 (Fed. Cir. 1995) (quoting 35 U.S.C. 102(b))

An inventor loses the right to a patent if he placed the claimed invention "in public use or on sale in this country, more than one year prior to the date of the application for patent in the United States."

17. ***Baxter Int'l, Inc. v. Cobe Labs., Inc.***, 39 USPQ 2d 1437, 1441 (Fed. Cir. 1996)

Experimental use negates public use; when proved, it may show that particular acts, even if apparently public in a colloquial sense, do not constitute a public use within the meaning of section 102. *TP Lab., Inc. v. Professional Positioners, Inc.*, 724 F.2d 965, 971, 220 USPQ 577, 582 (Fed. Cir.), *cert. denied*, 469 U.S. 826 (1984).

18. ***Baxter Int'l, Inc. v. Cobe Labs., Inc.***, 39 USPQ 2d 1437, 1442 (Fed. Cir. 1996)

Accordingly, we hold that public testing before the critical date by a third party for his own unique purposes of an invention previously reduced to practice and obtained from someone other than the patentee, when such testing is independent of and not controlled by the patentee, is an invalidating public use, not an experimental use.

19. ***W.L. Gore Assocs., Inc. v. Garlock, Inc.***, 220 USPQ 303, 310 (Fed. Cir. 1983), ***cert. denied,*** 469 U.S. 851 (1984)

There is no evidence that Budd's secret use of the Cropper machine made knowledge of the claimed process accessible to the public. The district court held all claims of the '566 patent invalid under 102(b), . . . because "the invention" was "in public use [and] on sale" by Budd more than one year before Gore's application for patent. . . . [I]t was error to hold that Budd's activity with the Cropper machine, as above indicated, was a "public" use of the processes claimed in the '566 patent, that activity having been secret, not public.

Assuming, arguendo, that Budd sold tape produced on the Cropper machine before October 1969, and that tape was made by a process set forth in a claim of the '566 patent, the issue under §102(b) is whether that sale would defeat Dr. Gore's right to a patent on the process inventions set forth in the claims. . . . If Budd and Cropper commercialized the tape, that could result in a forfeiture of a patent granted them for their process on an application filed by them more than a year later. . . . There is no reason or statutory basis, however, on which Budd's and Cropper's secret commercialization of a process, if established, could be held a bar to the grant of a patent to Gore on that process.

20. ***In re Caveney***, 226 USPQ 1, 3–4 (Fed. Cir. 1985)

An exception to this rule exists where a patented method is kept secret and remains secret after a sale of the unpatented product of the method. Such a sale prior to the critical date is a bar if engaged in by the patentee or patent applicant, but not if engaged in by another.

21. ***In re Caveney***, 226 USPQ 1, 3–4 (Fed. Cir. 1985)

It is well settled that a sale is a contract between parties to give and to pass rights of property for consideration which the buyer pays or promises to pay the seller for the thing bought or sold. . . . Further, one cannot make a contract with himself. . . . Accordingly, a sale or offer to sell under 35 U.S.C. §102(b) must be between two separate entities.

22. ***PPG Indus., Inc. v. Guardian Indus. Corp.***, 37 USPQ 2d 1618, 1623 (Fed. Cir. 1996) (quoting ***Ex parte Jackson***, 217 USPQ 804, 807 (1982))

The Patent and Trademark Office Board of Appeals summarized the point well when it stated:

> The test is not merely quantitative, since a considerable amount of experimentation is permissible, if it is merely routine, or if the specification in question provides a reasonable amount of guidance with respect to the direction in which the experimentation should proceed to enable the determination of how to practice a desired embodiment of the invention claimed.

23. ***Ex parte Kuklo***, 25 USPQ 2d 1387, 1390 (B.P.A.I. 1992)

With respect to appellant's argument that the public did not see the inner workings of the dye laser amplifier, we are not aware of any requirement that the person to which an invention is publicly disclosed has to understand the significance and the technical complexities of the invention.

24. *Estee Lauder Inc. v. L'Oreal, S.A.*, 44 USPQ 2d 1610, 1613–14 (Fed. Cir. 1997)

[W]e are left to answer a single question of law: where testing is required to establish utility, must there be some recognition of successful testing prior to the critical date for an invention to be reduced to practice, or is it only necessary that the testing be completed before the critical date and ultimately prove successful, regardless of when that success is appreciated or recognized? We hold that the law requires the former.

25. *Evans Cooling Sys., Inc. v. General Motors Corp.*, 44 USPQ 2d 1037, 1040, 1042 (Fed. Cir. 1997), *cert. denied,* 522 U.S. 1115 (1998)

Evans urges this court to create a new exception to the on sale bar. Specifically, Evans asks us to rule that an otherwise invalidating offer for sale does not invalidate a patent "where a third party surreptitiously steals an invention while it is a trade secret and then, unbeknownst to the inventor, allegedly puts the invention on sale [more than one year] before the inventor files a patent application covering the stolen invention." . . . [W]e decline to create the suggested new exception to the 102(b) bar which has no basis in the language of the statute.

26. *Pfaff v. Wells Elecs., Inc.*, 43 USPQ 2d 1928 (Fed. Cir. 1997), *rev'd on other grounds,* 525 U.S. 55, 48 USPQ 2d 1641 (1998)

The on-sale bar is not limited solely to a sale of, or an offer to sell, a product that anticipates the later patented invention. It also applies if the subject matter of the sale or offer to sell . . . would have rendered the claimed invention obvious by its addition to the prior art. . . . In effect, what was offered for sale before the critical date becomes "a [prior art] reference under section 103 against the claimed invention." *Baker Oil Tools v. Geo Vann, Inc.*, 828 F.2d 1558, 1563, 4 USPQ 2d 1210, 1213 (Fed. Cir. 1987). Because of the conjunctive use of sections 102(b) and 103, this bar has been called the § 102(b)/103 bar.

27. *Robotic Vision Sys., Inc. v. View Eng'g, Inc.*, 42 USPQ 2d 1619, 1623 (Fed. Cir. 1997)

The claimed invention in this case is a method. What Robotic is accused of putting on sale in March 1991 is a device for carrying out that method. Thus, an offer to sell the device (or otherwise provide it in a commercial context), if it met the requirements for an on-sale bar, would constitute a bar to the patentability of the claimed method. However, an alleged offer to sell the device is not an on-sale bar to the patentability of the method unless the activities involving the device meet the criteria for the on-sale bar. In this case the software program, even though not recited in the claims, was necessary for the operation of the invention. Without workable software, there was no device that could have been on sale, and the method of using such a device therefore could not have been on sale.

28. ***Robotic Vision Sys., Inc. v. View Eng'g, Inc.***, 42 USPQ 2d 1619, 1623–24 (Fed. Cir. 1997)

[S]ubsequent completion of an invention after the critical date does not relate back to the date of an earlier alleged offer of sale. . . . If mere discussions prior to the critical date, or even an agreement to develop and provide a device that had not yet been invented, developed, or completed were to be held to be a bar to patentability, then collaboration between inventors and customers would be greatly impeded. Patent applications would be required to be filed prematurely, before an invention was completed. The on-sale bar was not intended to prevent discussions between potential inventor-suppliers and customers concerning inventions not yet completed. Thus, the later completion of an invention concerning which an alleged offer to sell had been made earlier does not relate back to the date of that offer.

29. ***Robotic Vision Sys., Inc. v. View Eng'g, Inc.***, 42 USPQ 2d 1619, 1624 (Fed. Cir. 1997)

This case presents the interesting situation in which the use of software was sufficiently within the skill of the art so as to not run afoul of the best mode requirement, but it may not have been sufficiently developed by the critical date to cause an offer of the product to constitute an on-sale bar. The reason for this apparent inconsistency is that the relevant statutory provisions have different purposes, one to promote prompt filing of patent applications after commercialization has begun, and the other to compel full disclosure of an invention. Knowledge of one skilled in the art is relevant to satisfaction of the best mode requirement, but such knowledge does not create a completed invention in an on-sale context when the invention at the time of the offer is nothing more than a concept for improving a method of using a prior art machine.

30. ***Hupp v. Siroflex of Am., Inc.***, 43 USPQ 2d 1887, 1891 (Fed. Cir. 1997)

[O]rganizations that invite inventors to submit their ideas in order to obtain patent services and assistance in development and marketing are not ordinarily "customers" whereby contact with such an organization raises the on-sale bar. An inventor's quest for aid and advice in developing and patenting an invention is not an on-sale event as contemplated by 35 U.S.C. §102(b).

31. *C.R. Bard, Inc. v. M3 Sys., Inc.*, 48 USPQ 2d 1225, 1235–36 (Fed. Cir. 1998) (Newman, J., dissenting)

Generally cost defrayal arrangements between collaborators are not deemed to be invalidating sales, nor are payments for use substantially for test purposes. *See In re Mahurkar*, 71 F.3d 1573, 1577, 37 USPQ 2d 1138, 1142 (Fed. Cir. 1995) (actual sale of two prototype catheters "did not place the invention in the public domain or lead the public to believe that the device was freely available"); *Ethicon, Inc. v. United States Surgical Corp.*, 762 F. Supp. 480, 506–07, 19 USPQ 2d 1721, 1740 (D. Conn. 1991) (clinical tests by surgeon not a public use under § 102(b)), *aff'd*, 965 F.2d 1065 (Fed. Cir. 1992); *Baker Oil Tools*, 828 F.2d at 1564, 4 USPQ 2d at 1214 (discussing factors in deciding whether the purpose of testing was primarily experimental).

32. *C.R. Bard, Inc. v. M3 Sys., Inc.*, 48 USPQ 2d 1225, 1236 (Fed. Cir. 1998) (Newman, J., dissenting)

Quotation of a sales price to a potential distributor of a product that is not available for sale and distribution does not of itself establish an on-sale bar. See Continental Can, 948 F.2d at 1270, 20 USPQ 2d at 1750 (price terms set between collaborators in joint research not an on-sale bar). . . . Although exceptions have arisen on particular facts, normally the on-sale bar does not accrue based on customer contacts made while the product is still being developed or tested. . . . To satisfy the on-sale requirement of section 102(b) there must be more than an informational exchange of price information, when there is no reasonable contemplation that the quotation will be followed by purchase and sale as a commercial transaction.

33. *C.R. Bard, Inc. v. M3 Sys., Inc.*, 48 USPQ 2d 1225, 1237 (Fed. Cir. 1998) (Newman, J., dissenting)

An offer of sale originating in a foreign country, directed to a consumer in the United States, can establish an on-sale bar as to what was offered. *In re Caveney*, 761 F.2d 671, 676–77, 226 USPQ 1, 4 (Fed. Cir. 1985).

34. *C.R. Bard, Inc. v. M3 Sys., Inc.*, 48 USPQ 2d 1225, 1252 (Fed. Cir. 1998) (Mayer, C.J., concurring in part and dissenting in part)

Clinical testing is not required before a sale can bar patent rights. Nor can subsequent clinical testing excuse a prior sale, if what was offered for sale was the claimed invention. Clinical testing is merely one possible policy reason why a particular sale might be excused from the bar. Since Radiplast did not contemplate sales to Engstrom for testing purposes, the possibility of subsequent clinical testing is of no moment. Likewise, FDA approval is not required before a sale can bar patent rights. Even an illegal sale of the claimed invention before the critical date can bar patent rights. Nor is a domestic distributor relevant to the on sale bar inquiry; a sale by a foreign distributor, from a foreign country to the United States can bar patent rights. *See, e.g., In re Caveney,* 761 F.2d 671, 676–77, 226 USPQ 1, 4 (Fed. Cir. 1985).

The first of Bard's two remaining arguments—that no operable device had been made—is a feint because manufacture of an operable device is not a prerequisite for application of the on sale bar. *See, e.g., Barmag Barmer Maschinenfabrik AG v. Murata Machinery, Ltd.,* 731 F.2d 831, 837, 221 USPQ 561, 565 (Fed. Cir. 1984). While operability may or may not be relevant, *see, e.g., UMC,* 816 F.2d at 656, 2 USPQ 2d at 1472 (reduction to practice is not a requirement for application of the on sale bar), manufacture of an operable device alone is not . . . Operability is relevant only to the extent it demonstrates that a claimed element of the invention had not yet been invented, or the inventors did not know they had a workable invention and thus had nothing to offer for sale.

35. ***C.R. Bard, Inc. v. M3 Sys., Inc.,*** 48 USPQ 2d 1225, 1255 (Fed. Cir. 1998) (Bryson, J., concurring in part and dissenting in part)

The so-called "experimental testing" exception to the on-sale bar applies only if commercial exploitation is "merely incidental to the primary purpose of experimentation to perfect the invention." *Barmag Barmer Maschinenfabrik AG v. Murata Mach., Ltd.,* 731 F.2d 831, 839, 221 USPQ 561, 567 (Fed. Cir. 1984). In determining whether the inventor made the sale in question for purposes of determining whether the invention would work for its intended purpose, a court must consider various factors, such as the amount of control the inventor exercised over the testing; the length of the test period; whether any payment was made; whether there was a secrecy obligation; whether progress records were kept; whether someone other than the inventor conducted the experiments; and the degree of commercial exploitation during the tests in relation to the purpose of the experimentation. *Baker Oil Tools, Inc. v. Geo Vann, Inc.,* 828 F.2d 1558, 1564, 4 USPQ 2d 1210, 1214 (Fed. Cir. 1987). Certain factors, such as the requirement that the inventor control the testing,

that detailed progress records be kept, and that the pur-
ported testers know that testing is occurring, are critical to
proving experimental purpose. *Lough v. Brunswick Corp.*,
86 F.3d 1113, 1120, 39 USPQ 2d 1100, 1105 (Fed. Cir. 1996)
("if the inventor has no control over the alleged experiments,
he is not experimenting")

36. ***C.R. Bard, Inc. v. M3 Sys., Inc.***, 48 USPQ 2d 1225, 1256
(Fed. Cir. 1998) (Bryson, J., concurring in part and dissenting in part)

"A patent owner may have created an on-sale bar despite
losing money on a sale." *U.S. Envtl. Prods., Inc. v. Westall*,
911 F.2d 713, 717, 15 USPQ 2d 1898, 1902 (Fed. Cir. 1990).

37. ***Scaltech Inc. v. Retec/Tetra, L.L.C.***, 48 USPQ 2d 1037,
1040 (Fed. Cir. 1998)

The "invention" which has been offered for sale must, of
course, be something circumscribed by metes and bounds of
the claim. . . . Hence, the first determination in the section
102(b) analysis must be whether the subject of the barring
activity met each of the limitations of the claim, and thus
was an embodiment of the invention. . . . We note that there
is no requirement that the offer specifically identify these
limitations.

38. ***Scaltech Inc. v. Retec/Tetra, L.L.C.***, 48 USPQ 2d 1037,
1040–41 (Fed. Cir. 1998)

In *UMC Elec. Co. v. United States*, we indicated that

> we do not intend to sanction attacks on patents on the
> ground that the inventor or another offered for sale, before
> the critical date, the mere concept of the invention. Nor
> should inventors be forced to rush into the Patent and
> Trademark Office prematurely.

> If the inventor had merely a conception or was working to-
> wards development of that conception, it can be said that
> there [was not] . . . any "invention" which could [have
> been] placed on sale.

816 F.2d 647, 656–57, 2 USPQ 2d 1465, 1471–72 (Fed. Cir.
1987). This is consistent with the policy of preventing delay
in the expiration of patent protection by delaying the filing
of the application more than a year after substantial completion of the invention. Both the reasonable expectation that
the claimed invention will work for its intended purpose and
the prevention of the delay require that the inventor understand the nature of the invention in order to contemplate its
sale. In other words, in order to have a reasonable expectation that he can reduce the invention to practice he must
have conceived of the invention.

39. ***Scaltech Inc. v. Retec/Tetra, L.L.C.***, 48 USPQ 2d 1037, 1041 (Fed. Cir. 1998)

In the case before us, Scaltech offered to treat the waste prior to injecting it into the coker unit. It believed that de-oiling the waste would increase the amount of waste which could be consumed by the coke bed. It is only in hindsight that Scaltech recognized that two claim limitations, the particle size and the solid concentration, were critical to achieve this purpose and that those limitations might be met by practicing some of the process apparently offered in 1987–1991. Accordingly, on the record before us, the inventor was working toward the development of a conception, and there was not yet an "invention" which could have been offered on sale. *See UMC Elec. Co.*, 816 F.2d at 656–57, 2 USPQ 2d at 1471–72. We further note that an accidental or unwitting duplication of an invention cannot constitute an anticipation. *See Tilghman v. Proctor*, 102 U.S. 707, 26 L. Ed. 279 (1880); *Eibel Process Co. v. Minnesota & Ontario Paper Co.*, 261 U.S. 45, 67 L. Ed. 523, 43 S. Ct. 322 (1923).

40. ***Brasseler, U.S.A. I, L.P. v. Stryker Sales Corp.***, 51 USPQ 2d 1470, 1472 (Fed. Cir. 1999) (quoting ***Pfaff v. Wells Elecs., Inc.***, 525 U.S. 55, 119 S. Ct. 304, 311–12 & n.11, 48 USPQ 2d 1641 (1998))

In arguing that these facts establish that there was no § 102(b) sale, Brasseler places heavy reliance on our previously used "totality of the circumstances" test under which all of the circumstances surrounding the sale are considered and weighed against the "policies" underlying § 102(b). . . . Recently, the Supreme Court rejected this test, indicating a preference for "a definite standard for determining when a patent application must be filed." . . . The Court in Pfaff concluded that the on-sale bar of § 102(b) applies if, prior to the critical date, a product embodying the patented invention was "the subject of a commercial offer for sale . . . . [, and] the invention [was] ready for patenting."

41. ***Brasseler, U.S.A. I, L.P. v. Stryker Sales Corp.***, 51 USPQ 2d 1470, 1472 (Fed. Cir. 1999) (quoting ***Buildex Inc. v. Kason Indus., Inc.***, 7 USPQ 2d 1325, 1328 (Fed. Cir. 1988))

The fact that Brasseler may have retained control over the manufacturing of the patented invention as a result of the alleged exclusive relationship between the two companies says nothing about the basic corporate relationships.

We decline Brasseler's invitation to establish a new exception based on the fact (alleged) that it and DS Manufacturing were joint developers and as such a sale between the two of them should not be considered a § 102(b) sale. It is true that Brasseler and DS Manufacturing both employed one or

more of the named inventors. However, we have "never recognized a 'joint development' exception to the 'on sale' bar."

42. ***Brasseler, U.S.A. I, L.P. v. Stryker Sales Corp.***, 51 USPQ
2d 1470, 1473 (Fed. Cir. 1999)

This is not a case in which an individual inventor takes a
design to a fabricator and pays the fabricator for its services
in fabricating a few sample products. Here DS Manufacturing made a large number of the agreed-upon product for general marketing by Brasseler. The transaction was invoiced
as a sale of product, and the parties understood the transaction to be such.

43. ***Brasseler, U.S.A. I, L.P. v. Stryker Sales Corp.***, 51 USPQ
2d 1470, 1473 (Fed. Cir. 1999)

Lastly, we are not persuaded by the fact that Brasseler
may have taken certain additional processing steps (i.e.,
marking, packaging, and sterilization) prior to selling the
saw blades to hospitals. This alleged fact is immaterial because the saw blades sold by DS Manufacturing to Brasseler
undisputedly included all of the limitations of the patent
claims; the additional steps allegedly performed by Brasseler are not recited in the claims. Thus the additional steps
undertaken for marketing of the product do not change the
basic transaction—a sale of completed product in quantity,
constituting a commercial sale of a product ready for patenting, and for marketing by Brasseler.

44. ***IGT v. Global Gaming Tech., Inc.***, Civ. App. 98-1246, slip
op. at 7 (Fed. Cir. June 17, 1999) (unpublished)

Global argues that the on-sale bar is not applicable in this
case, because the sales agreement was not for commercial
purposes but was intended to further the settlement of a dispute. That argument is not persuasive. Global has not demonstrated that the transaction was a sham, ... The transaction in this case, by contrast, was a bona fide commercial
sale. Global's arguments do not suggest that the transaction
was of the same sort of noncommercial character as the
transaction in Mahurkar. That the agreement may have
been instrumental in settling a dispute between related parties is of no moment. It is enough that the parties were separate entities and that the agreement was an arm's-length
transaction that bore all the earmarks of a commercial sale.

45. ***Systemation, Inc. v. Engel Indus., Inc.***, Civ. App. No.
98-1489, slip op. at 10 (Fed. Cir. Mar. 10, 1999) (unpublished)

Systemation is also likely to withstand Engel's validity
challenges to claim 1 of the '880 patent. The only prior art

relevant to claim 1 of the '880 patent is long public use of the manual method of inserting angle plates. Engel argues that the manual method anticipates claim 1 of the '880 patent. Systemation, however, argues that the manual method cannot anticipate claim 1 which is clearly directed toward an automatic method. The district court agreed. So do we.

It is clear, at least when claim 1 is read in light of the written description and the other claims, that the claim is directed to an automated method of inserting plates. . . . Such a method cannot be anticipated by a manual method for doing the same. The steps of the former are necessarily more in number. Further, the district court's factual findings that the claimed invention enjoyed significant commercial success and met a long-felt need are not clearly erroneous, and support a conclusion that the claimed invention was nonobvious.

46. ***Scaltech Inc. v. Retec/Tetra, L.L.C.***, 51 USPQ 2d 1055, 1058 (Fed. Cir. 1999)

A claimed invention is considered to be on sale within the meaning of § 102(b) if, more than one year before the filing date to which the claim is entitled (the critical date), two conditions are satisfied. First, the product must be the subject of a commercial offer for sale. . . . Second, the invention must be ready for patenting. . . . One way to satisfy the second condition is by proof of reduction to practice before the critical date.

47. ***Scaltech Inc. v. Retec/Tetra, L.L.C.***, 51 USPQ 2d 1055, 1058 (Fed. Cir. 1999)

The "invention" which has been offered for sale must, of course, be something within the scope of the claim. . . . Hence, the first determination in the § 102(b) analysis must be whether the subject of the barring activity met each of the limitations of the claim, and thus was an embodiment of the claimed invention.

48. ***Scaltech Inc. v. Retec/Tetra, L.L.C.***, 51 USPQ 2d 1055, 1059 (Fed. Cir. 1999)

We note that there is no requirement that the offer specifically identify these [claim] limitations. . . . Nor is there a requirement that Scaltech must have recognized the significance of these limitations at the time of offer. . . . If the process that was offered for sale inherently possessed each of the claim limitations, then the process was on sale, whether or not the seller recognized that his process possessed the claimed characteristics.

49. ***Scaltech Inc. v. Retec/Tetra, L.L.C.***, 51 USPQ 2d 1055, 1059 n.1 (Fed. Cir. 1999)

Scaltech argues that its invention was still experimental at the time Scaltech was soliciting an opportunity to practice the invention. This argument fails because it is premised on the "experimental stage" doctrine which has been rejected by both this court and the Supreme Court. . . . Commercial exploitation, if not incidental to the primary purpose of experimentation, will result in an on sale bar, even if the invention was still in its experimental stage.

50. ***Abbott Labs. v. Geneva Pharms., Inc.***, 51 USPQ 2d 1307, 1309 (Fed. Cir. 1999)

Abbott argues that claim 4 is not invalid under the on-sale bar because the "invention" was not on sale. For an "invention" to be on sale, Abbott submits, the parties must "conceive," [**7] or know precisely, the nature of the subject matter with which they are dealing. Since the parties did not know that they were dealing with Form IV, Abbott reasons, they did not "conceive" the subject matter sold and therefore there was no "invention" on sale. The defendants respond that we need only apply the two-part test for the on-sale bar recently set forth by the Supreme Court in *Pfaff v. Wells Electronics, Inc.*, and that, under this test, it is irrelevant that the parties to the sales did not know that they were dealing with Form IV rather than with another anhydrous terazosin hydrochloride crystalline form.

We agree with defendants that claim 4 is invalid and that the parties' ignorance that they were dealing with Form IV is irrelevant. . . . Even though the parties did not know it at the time, it is undisputed that Form IV was the subject matter of at least three commercial sales in the United States before the critical date. It is also clear that the invention was "ready for patenting" because at least two foreign manufacturers had already reduced it to practice. . . . Furthermore, the statutory on-sale bar is not subject to exceptions for sales made by third parties either innocently or fraudulently.

51. ***Abbott Labs. v. Geneva Pharms., Inc.***, 51 USPQ 2d 1307, 1309–10 (Fed. Cir. 1999)

Abbott argues that the invention was not on sale because those who sold the claimed product did not know all of its characteristics. We disagree. It is well settled in the law that there is no requirement that a sales offer specifically identify all the characteristics of an invention offered for sale or that the parties recognize the significance of all of these characteristics at the time of the offer. . . . If a product that is offered for sale inherently possesses each of the limitations of the claims, then the invention is on sale, whether or not the parties to the transaction recognize that the product possesses the claimed characteristics.

52. ***Weatherchem Corporation v. J. L. Clark, Inc.***, 49 USPQ 2d 1001, 1006 (Fed. Cir. 1998) (quoting from ***Pfaff v. Wells Elecs., Inc.***, 525 U.S. 55, 119 S. Ct. 304, 48 USPQ 2d 1641 (1998))

The Supreme Court has recently addressed the standards for application of the on-sale bar. . . . In *Pfaff* [*v. Wells Electronics, Inc.*], the inventor showed detailed engineering drawings of his computer chip socket invention to Texas Instruments. Before the critical date, Texas Instruments provided the inventor with a written order for over 30,000 of his new sockets. In accord with the inventor's normal practice, he had not made any prototypes before offering his invention for commercial sale. After receiving Texas Instruments' purchase order, the inventor set out to make the device in commercial quantities. The inventor did not reduce his invention to practice or fill Texas Instruments' order until after the critical date. The Supreme Court determined that "the invention had been on sale for more than one year in this country before [the inventor] . . . filed his patent application." . . .

The facts of *Pfaff* required the Supreme Court to address "whether the commercial marketing of a newly invented product may mark the beginning of the 1-year period even though the invention has not yet been reduced to practice." . . . In addressing this question, the Supreme Court first examined precedents governing the completion of an invention. Then the Court stated:

> We conclude, therefore, that the on-sale bar applies when two conditions are satisfied before the critical date.
> First, the product must be the subject of a commercial offer for sale . . . .
> Second, the invention must be ready for patenting. That condition may be satisfied in at least two ways: by proof of reduction to practice before the critical date; or by proof that prior to the critical date the inventor had prepared drawings or other descriptions of the invention that were sufficiently specific to enable a person skilled in the art to practice the invention. . . .

Applying the first part of the test, the Supreme Court found:

> In this case the acceptance of the [Texas Instrument] purchase order . . . makes it clear that such an offer had been made, and there is no question that the sale was commercial rather than experimental in character. . . .

Applying the second part of the test, the Supreme Court found:

> In this case the second condition of the on-sale bar is satisfied because the drawings [the inventor] sent to the

manufacturer before the critical date fully disclosed the invention.

53. ***Weatherchem Corporation v. J. L. Clark, Inc.***, 49 USPQ 2d 1001, 1007 (Fed. Cir. 1998)

It is immaterial that the record shows no delivery of the later patented caps and no exchange of money until after the critical date. Record evidence of a signed purchase agreement before the critical date establishes an offer for sale sufficient to invoke the on-sale bar.

54. ***Tec Air, Inc. v. Denso Manufacturing Michigan Inc.***, 52 USPQ 2d 1294, 1297 (Fed. Cir. 1999) (quoting ***Scaltech Inc. v. Retec/Tetra, L.L.C.***, 51 USPQ 2d 1055, 1058 (Fed. Cir. 1999))

[B]ecause the offer for sale did not involve subject matter that either anticipates the invention or would have rendered it obvious, Pfaff's second prong is irrelevant. Pfaff did not remove the requirement that the subject matter of the commercial offer for sale "be something within the scope of the claim." . . . Accordingly, Denso's reliance on Pfaff does not have the talismanic effect it desires.

55. ***STX LLC v. Brine Inc.***, 54 USPQ 2d 1347, 1349 (Fed. Cir. 2000)

The fact that delivery was set for dates after the critical date is irrelevant to the finding of a commercial offer to sell. See Pfaff, 525 U.S. at 67, 48 USPQ 2d at 1647.

56. ***STX LLC v. Brine Inc.***, 54 USPQ 2d 1347, 1349 (Fed. Cir. 2000)

STX argues that there could not have been a sale of the invention because it did not know by September 18, 1984, the date of the Bart's transaction, whether the Excalibur head would have "improved playing and handling" characteristics while retaining the strength and durability exhibited by the prior solid sidewall design. That assumes that the preamble language STX added to Claim 1 of the '947 patent is a limitation on that claim.

But we have said that "where a patentee defines a structurally complete invention in the claim body and uses the preamble only to state a purpose or intended use for the invention, the preamble is not a claim limitation." *Rowe v. Dror,* 112 F.3d 473, 478, 42 USPQ 2d 1550, 1553 (Fed. Cir. 1997). Here, the trial court properly held that Claim 1, following the preamble phrase, "which provides improved playing and handling characteristics," was a self-contained description that could stand alone, with or without the preamble. In fact, the patent examiner's rejection of the claim for obviousness even after the preamble language was added, suggests that the phrase was not essential in distinguishing it over the prior art, and was not decisive in securing allowance of the claim during prosecution. We agree with the district court's conclusion that the preamble phrase is not a limitation, and therefore its holding that the first prong of Pfaff, requiring an offer to sell, is satisfied.

57. **STX LLC v. Brine Inc.**, 54 USPQ 2d 1347, 1350 (Fed. Cir. 2000)

The fact that the first squeezes that formed the basis of the commercial offer to sell might not have exhibited the desired degree of "improved playing and handling" characteristics, including the desired strength and durability, is irrelevant, not least because the preamble to Claim 1 is not a limitation. In any event, any "fine tuning" the Excalibur heads may have required after the Bart's sale does not undermine the conclusion that the invention was ready for patenting. See *Weatherchem*, 163 F.3d at 1332–34, 49 USPQ 2d at 1006–7. And none of the "material" changes STX alleges remained to be made at the time of the barring activity are reflected in either the claims or specification of the patent that eventually issued. STX's confidence that its invention was complete and operative is reflected in the fact that the Bart's sale was for a commercial quantity. See *Id.* at 1334, 49 USPQ 2d at 1007. Subjective qualities inherent in a product, such as "improved playing and handling," cannot serve as an escape hatch to circumvent the on-sale bar.

58. **Vanmoor v. Wal-Mart Stores, Inc.**, 53 USPQ 2d 1377, 1379 (Fed. Cir.), **cert. denied**, 531 U.S. 821 (2000)

Although Wal-Mart and the manufacturers bore the burden of proving that the cartridges that were the subject of the pre-critical date sales anticipated the '331 patent, that burden was satisfied by Vanmoor's allegation that the accused cartridges infringe the '331 patent. See *Id.* (holding patent invalid under on-sale bar where accused product was offered for sale prior to the critical date of the patented invention). . . . Here the pre-critical date sales were of completed cartridges made to specifications that remain unchanged to the present day, showing that any invention embodied in the accused cartridges was reduced to practice before the critical date. The Pfaff ready for patenting condition is also satisfied because the specification drawings, available prior to the critical date, were actually used to produce the accused cartridges.

59. ***Zacharin v. United States,*** 55 USPQ 2d 1047, 1049 (Fed. Cir. 2000)

In *Pfaff v. Wells Electronics, Inc.*, 525 U.S. 55, 142 L. Ed. 2d 261, 119 S. Ct. 304 (1998), the Supreme Court held that a patent claim is invalid under the on-sale bar if two conditions are met: first, the invention must have been the subject of a commercial offer for sale more than one year before the patent application was filed; second, the invention must have been ready for patenting more than one year before the filing of the application. Reduction of the invention to practice is sufficient to satisfy the second condition. See *Id.* at 67; *Weatherchem Corp. v. J.L. Clark, Inc.*, 163 F.3d 1326, 1332, 49 USPQ 2d 1001, 1006 (Fed. Cir. 1998).

60. ***Zacharin v. United States***, 55 USPQ 2d 1047, 1049 (Fed. Cir. 2000)

A sale is "a contract between parties to give and pass rights of property for consideration which the buyer pays or promises to pay the seller for the thing bought or sold." *In re Caveney*, 761 F.2d 671, 676, 226 USPQ 1, 4 (Fed. Cir. 1985). In this case, Breed contracted to fabricate 6000 t-RADs and deliver them to the Army. In fact, Mr. Zacharin inspected and accepted the t-RADs for the Army, implying that he could have rejected any of unacceptable quality. Thus, under the contract Breed manufactured the t-RADs and transferred all its rights in the fabricated t-RADs to the Army in exchange for a payment that guaranteed Breed that its costs would be covered in addition to some amount of profit.

This case is not one in which the inventor took his design to a fabricator "and paid the fabricator for its services in fabricating a few sample products." *See Brasseler, U.S.A. I, L.P. v. Stryker Sales Corp.*, 182 F.3d 888, 891, 51 USPQ 2d 1470, 1473 (Fed. Cir. 1999). Rather, Mr. Zacharin disclosed his invention to a third party, the Army, with the hope and expectation that his t-RAD design would be used in the MPSM program, and the Army entered into a contract for the production of a large number of products embodying the invention. Mr. Zacharin placed no restrictions on the Army's use or disclosure of the design. He cannot now argue that this court should view the 0095 contract as a collaborative offer between him and the Army, after having earlier argued to the PTO in the rights determination that the Army had no rights to the invention of the '341 patent. Moreover, because Mr. Zacharin stipulated that the t-RAD had been reduced to practice before the 0095 contract was entered into, he cannot now argue that the purpose of the 0095 contract was testing of the t-RAD design.

61. ***Zacharin v. United States,*** 55 USPQ 2d 1047, 1049–50 (Fed. Cir. 2000)

The fact that the sale in question was made in the context of a research and development contract and that there was no fixed price set for the t-RADs does not suffice to avoid the on-sale bar. This court held in *RCA Corp. v. Data General Corp.*, 887 F.2d at 1062–63, 12 USPQ 2d at 1454–55, that a cost-plus contract to supply experimental systems incorporating an invention that was reduced to practice constituted an invalidating offer for sale, and that precedent is equally applicable to the contract at issue in this case. Likewise, the fact that the products sold to the Army were to be used for testing rather than as routine production units, is not sufficient to avoid the effect of the on-sale bar, as our predecessor court held in *General Electric Co. v. United States*, 228 Ct. Cl. 192, 654 F.2d 55, 59 & n.6, 211 USPQ 867, 871 & n.6 (Ct. Cl. 1981). A contract to supply goods is a sales contract, regardless of the means used to calculate payment and regardless of whether the goods are to be used for testing in a laboratory or for deployment in the field.

62. ***Zacharin v. United States,*** 55 USPQ 2d 1047, 1051 (Fed. Cir. 2000)

[U]nder this court's precedents, it is of no consequence that the sale was made by a third party, not by the inventor, see *Abbott Lab. v. Geneva Pharms., Inc.*, 182 F.3d 1315, 1318, 51 USPQ 2d 1307, 1309 (Fed. Cir. 1999), or that the product was constructed and the sale made pursuant to the buyer's directions, see *Brasseler*, 182 F.3d at 891, 51 USPQ 2d at 1473.

63. ***Helifix Ltd. v. Blok-Lok, Ltd.***, 54 USPQ 2d 1299, 1305 (Fed. Cir. 2000)

In *Pfaff v. Wells Electronics., Inc.*, 525 U.S. 55, 119 S.Ct. 304 [48 USPQ 2d 1641] (1998), the Supreme Court held that the on-sale bar applies when two conditions are met before the critical date, which in this case is February 28, 1994. First, "the product must be the subject of a commercial offer for sale." *Id.* at __, 119 S.Ct. at 311. Second, "the invention must be ready for patenting." *Id.* at__, 119 S.Ct. at 312. The Court explained that the second condition may be satisfied in at least two ways: "by proof of reduction to practice before the critical date; or by proof that prior to the critical date the inventor had prepared drawings or other descriptions of the invention that were sufficiently specific to enable a person skilled in the art to practice the invention." *Id.* at __, 119 S.Ct. at 312.

III.C. Section 102(c)—Abandonment

1. ***Ex parte Dunne***, 20 USPQ 2d 1479, 1480 (B.P.A.I. 1991)

   Actual abandonment under 35 U.S.C. 102(c) requires that the inventor intend to abandon the invention, and intent can be implied from the inventor's conduct with respect to the invention. . . . Such intent to abandon an invention will not be imputed, and every reasonable doubt should be resolved in favor of the inventor. . . . Delay in filing alone is not a sufficient basis from which to infer the requisite intent to abandon under 35 U.S.C. 102(c).

2. ***Douglas v. Manbeck***, 21 USPQ 2d 1697, 1700 (E.D. Pa. 1991)

   The negligence of the attorney does not discharge the duty of the plaintiff to exercise due diligence. . . . The applicant has the duty to make sure his application is being prosecuted. . . . The applicant here did nothing for two and one-half years to determine whether his application was being prosecuted. During that time period the lack of due diligence by the plaintiff overcame and superseded any negligence by the attorney.

III.D. Section 102(d)—Foreign Patent Filed More Than One Year Before U.S. Filing

1. ***In re Kathawala***, 28 USPQ 2d 1785, 1787 (Fed. Cir. 1993)

   When a foreign patent issues with claims directed to the same invention as the U.S. application, the invention is "patented" within the meaning of section 102(d); validity of the foreign claims is irrelevant to the section 102(d) inquiry. This is true irrespective of whether the applicant asserts that the claims in the foreign patent are invalid on grounds of non-statutory subject matter or more conventional patentability reasons such as prior art or inadequate disclosure.

2. ***In re Kathawala***, 28 USPQ 2d 1785, 1787–88 (Fed. Cir. 1993)

   Kathawala nevertheless asserts that the effective date of a foreign patent for purposes of § 102(d), the date on which an invention is "patented," is not the date the foreign patent issues and becomes enforceable, but the date on which it becomes publicly available. . . . The import of the decisions in *Monks* and *Talbott* is that, contrary to Kathawala's argument, it is irrelevant under section 102(d) whether the Spanish patent was publicly available prior to the U.S. filing date. Rather, the Board correctly concluded that an invention is "patented" in a foreign country under section 102(d) when the patentee's rights under the patent become fixed.

3. ***In re Kathawala***, 28 USPQ 2d 1785, 1788–89 (Fed. Cir. 1993)

We thus hold that when an applicant files a foreign application fully disclosing his invention and having the potential to claim his invention in a number of different ways, the reference in section 102(d) to "invention . . . patented" necessarily includes all disclosed aspects of the invention. Thus, the section 102(d) bar applies regardless of whether the foreign patent contains claims to less than all aspects of the invention.

III.E. Section 102(e)—Prior Art From Less Than One Year Before Filing

1. ***In re Land***, 151 USPQ 621, 630–32 (C.C.P.A. 1966)

A U.S. patent is a "prior art reference" under 102(e) as of its filing date; a "reference" can be overcome only by "swearing back" of it under Rule 131. . . .

[A] patent to the same applicant or applicants is recognized as incapable of being such a reference because it does not show knowledge by "others" but a sole applicant or patentee and joint applicants or patentees are separate or different "legal entities" and either is treated as "another" relative to the other (until *Blout and Rogers* raised a question about it). Therefore, joint applicants A and B must "overcome" a reference patent to A or to B and the only way one can overcome a "reference" is by complying with all of the requirements of Rule 131.

2. ***In re Bayer***, 196 USPQ 670, 675 (C.C.P.A. 1978)

The concept underlying 35 USC 102(e) is that a complete description of an applicant's invention in an earlier filed application of another, which subsequently matures into a patent, constitutes prima facie evidence that the applicant is not the first inventor of the invention in controversy. The Supreme Court in *Milburn* was of the opinion that administrative delays in the Patent Office should not detract from the anticipatory effect of such evidence.

III.F. Section 102(f)—Invention of Another

1. ***Ex parte Billottet***, 192 USPQ 413, 415 (B.P.A.I. 1976)

The mere fact that a claim recites the use of various components, each of which can be argumentatively assumed to be old, does not provide a proper basis for a rejection under 35 U.S.C. 102(f). The particular arrangement of components called for in the claims here presented is not shown in any single reference. For a rejection under this paragraph, use of a plurality of references is normally not proper.

2. ***Gambro Lundia AB v. Baxter Health Care Corp.***, 42
   USPQ 2d 1378, 1381–82 (Fed. Cir. 1997)

   To show derivation, the party asserting invalidity must
   prove both prior conception of the invention by another and
   communication of that conception to the patentee. . . . The
   Supreme Court announced the standard for finding communication of a prior conception over 125 years ago in *Agawam
   Woolen v. Jordan*, 74 U.S. (7 Wall.) 583 (1868). The Court required a showing that the communication "*enabled* an ordinary mechanic, without the exercise of any ingenuity and
   special skill on his part, to construct and put the improvement in successful operation." *Id.* at 602–03 (emphasis
   added).

3. ***The F.B. Leopold Co. v. Roberts Filter Mfg Co.***, Civ. App.
   96-1218, slip op. at 6 (Fed. Cir. July 2, 1997) (unpublished)

   Leopold first asserts that the district court erroneously instructed the jury on the issue of derivation. Under 35 U.S.C.
   § 102, "[a] person shall be entitled to a patent unless— . . .
   (f) he did not himself invent the subject matter sought to be
   patented." The jury was instructed that it could find derivation by Brown if he "derived the invention from other
   sources." This instruction implicitly allowed the jury to find
   derivation from multiple sources, *i.e.*, without anticipation.
   This was error. This court recently made clear . . . that a determination of obviousness should not be incorporated into
   section 102(f). Thus, it was error to permit the jury to combine multiple references in finding derivation.

4. ***Oddzon Prods., Inc. v. Just Toys, Inc.***, 43 USPQ 2d 1641,
   1644 (Fed. Cir. 1997)

   Section 102(f) provides that a person shall be entitled to a
   patent unless "he did not himself invent the subject matter
   sought to be patented." This is a derivation provision, which
   provides that one may not obtain a patent on that which is
   obtained from someone else whose possession of the subject
   matter is inherently "prior." It does not pertain only to public knowledge, but also applies to private communications
   between the inventor and another which may never become
   public. Subsections (a), (b), (e), and (g), on the other hand,
   are clearly prior art provisions. They relate to knowledge
   manifested by acts that are essentially public.

5. ***Oddzon Prods., Inc. v. Just Toys, Inc.***, 43 USPQ 2d 1641,
   1646 (Fed. Cir. 1997)

   We therefore hold that subject matter derived from another
   not only is itself unpatentable to the party who derived it
   under § 102(f), but, when combined with other prior art, may

make a resulting obvious invention unpatentable to that party under a combination of §§ 102(f) and 103. Accordingly, the district court did not err by considering the two design disclosures known to the inventor to be prior art under the combination of §§ 102(f) and 103. . . . It means that an invention, A', that is obvious in view of subject matter A, derived from another, is also unpatentable. The obvious invention, A', may not be unpatentable to the inventor of A, and it may not be unpatentable to a third party who did not receive the disclosure of A, but it is unpatentable to the party who did receive the disclosure.

6. ***Pannu v. Iolab Corp.***, 47 USPQ 2d 1657, 1661–62 & n.4 (Fed. Cir. 1998)

Section 102, which is within Part II of Title 35, is entitled "Conditions for patentability; novelty and loss of right to patent"; section 102(f) provides that "[a] person shall be entitled to a patent unless he did not himself invent the subject matter sought to be patented." Since the word "he" refers to the specific inventive entity named on the patent, . . . this subsection mandates that a patent accurately list the correct inventors of a claimed invention . . . Thus, section 102(f) still makes the naming of the correct inventor or inventors a condition of patentability; failure to name them renders a patent invalid.

However, in cases of misjoinder and nonjoinder the operation of section 102(f) is ameliorated by section 256. . . . If a patentee demonstrates that inventorship can be corrected as provided for in section 256, a district court must order correction of the patent, thus saving it from being rendered invalid.

When a party asserts invalidity under § 102(f) due to nonjoinder, a district court should first determine whether there exists clear and convincing proof that the alleged unnamed inventor was in fact a co-inventor. Upon such a finding of incorrect inventorship, a patentee may invoke section 256 to save the patent from invalidity. Accordingly, the patentee must then be given an opportunity to correct inventorship pursuant to that section. Nonjoinder may be corrected "on notice and hearing of all parties concerned" and upon a showing that the error occurred without any deceptive intent on the part of the unnamed inventor. . . . While lack of deceptive intent, as a negative, may be hard for a patentee to prove when it claims relief under the statute, good faith is presumed in the absence of a persuasive showing of deceptive intent. . . . Finally, a patent with improper inventorship does not avoid invalidation simply because it might be corrected under section 256. Rather, the patentee must claim entitlement to relief under the statute and the court must give the patentee an opportunity to correct the inventorship. If the inventorship is successfully corrected, section 102(f) will not render the patent invalid. On the other hand, if the patentee does not claim relief under the statute and a party asserting invalidity proves incorrect inventorship, the court should hold the patent invalid for failure to comply with section 102(f).

III.G.   Section 102(g)—Priority, Abandonment, Suppression, Concealment

1. *E.I. du Pont de Nemours & Co. v. Phillips Petroleum Co.*, 7 USPQ 2d 1129, 1134 (Fed. Cir.), *cert. denied*, 488 U.S. 986 (1988)

   Also, Phillips is entitled to rely not only on the Witt and Leatherman patent application and its corresponding foreign patent applications, but also on the notebook data presented by Phillips. The district court did not allow Phillips to use that data regarding the two improper claim limitations discussed above in Part I, A, because it determined that the data on stress crack resistance was "abandoned, suppressed, or concealed." . . . That was legally incorrect if 35 U.S.C. § 102(g), as opposed to the Federal Rules of Evidence, was used as the basis of excluding the data. The inquiry under § 102(g) allows Phillips to use any relevant data to prove its defense unless the information is otherwise untimely produced.

2. *Fujikawa v. Wattanasin*, 39 USPQ 2d 1895, 1901 (Fed. Cir. 1996)

   Our case law distinguishes between two types of suppression and concealment: cases in which the inventor deliberately suppresses or conceals his invention, and cases in which a legal inference of suppression or concealment is drawn based on "too long" a delay in filing a patent application. *Paulik v. Rizkalla*, 760 F.2d 1270, 1273, 226 USPQ 224, 226 (Fed. Cir. 1985) (en banc). . . . Intentional suppression refers to situations in which an inventor "designedly, and with the view of applying it indefinitely and exclusively for his own profit, withholds his invention from the public." *Id.* (quoting *Kendall v. Winsor*, 62 U.S. (21 How.) 322, 328 (1858)).

3. *Fujikawa v. Wattanasin*, 39 USPQ 2d 1895, 1903 (Fed. Cir. 1996)

   In *Paulik*, we held that a suppression or concealment could be negated by renewed activity prior to an opposing party's effective date. There, inventor Paulik reduced his invention to practice and submitted an invention disclosure to his employer's patent department. For four years the patent department did nothing with the disclosure. Then, just two months before Rizkalla's effective date, the patent department allegedly picked up Paulik's disclosure and worked diligently to prepare a patent application which it ultimately filed. *See id.* at 1271–72, 226 USPQ at 224–25. We held that although Paulik could not rely on his original date of reduction to practice to establish priority, he could rely on the date of renewed activity in his priority contest with Rizkalla.

4. ***Mahurkar v. C.R. Bard, Inc.***, 38 USPQ 2d 1288, 1290 (Fed. Cir. 1996)

Section 102(g) of title 35 contains the basic rule for determining priority. 35 U.S.C. § 102(g) (1994). Section 102(g) also provides basic protection for the inventive process, shielding in particular the creative steps of conception and reduction to practice. In the United States, the person who first reduces an invention to practice is "prima facie the first and true inventor." *Christie v. Seybold*, 55 F. 69, 76 (6th Cir. 1893) (Taft, J.). However, the person "who first conceives, and, in a mental sense, first invents . . . may date his patentable invention back to the time of its conception, if he connects the conception with its reduction to practice by reasonable diligence on his part, so that they are substantially one continuous act." *Id.* Stated otherwise, priority of invention "goes to the first party to reduce an invention to practice unless the other party can show that it was the first to conceive the invention and that it exercised reasonable diligence in later reducing that invention to practice." *Price v. Symsek*, 988 F.2d 1187, 1190, 26 USPQ2d 1031, 1033 (Fed. Cir. 1993).

5. ***Oddzon Prods., Inc. v. Just Toys, Inc.***, 43 USPQ 2d 1641, 1645 (Fed. Cir. 1997)

[A] prior invention of another that was not abandoned, suppressed, or concealed (102(g) prior art) [may] be combined with other prior art to support rejection of a claim for obviousness under § 103.

6. ***Thomson S.A. v. Quixote Corp.***, 49 USPQ 2d 1530, 1532 (Fed. Cir. 1999)

We have interpreted the first sentence of subsection 102(g) to permit qualifying art to invalidate a patent claim even if the same art may not qualify as prior art under other subsections of § 102.

7. ***Thomson S.A. v. Quixote Corp.***, 49 USPQ 2d 1530, 1532 n.3 (Fed. Cir. 1999)

As the second sentence in the subsection indicates, 102(g) was written merely to provide a statutory basis for determining priority of invention in the context of interference proceedings before what was then the United States Patent Office. . . . Nevertheless, the first sentence is clear and, as the cases show, has been taken to have independent significance as a basis for prior art outside of the interference context.

This result makes sense. The first to invent who has invested time and labor in making and using the invention—but who might have opted not to apply for a patent—will not be liable for infringing another's patent on that same invention, while the public will have benefited because the invention was not abandoned, suppressed or concealed. However, in view of these and other related policy concerns, and amendment of the statute, we have made clear that art qualifying only under subsection 102(g) may not be used under § 103 to invalidate other patents of fellow employees engaged in team research.

III.H. *Functional Language*

1. ***Ex parte Malcom***, 47 USPQ 395, 396 (Pat. Off. Bd. App. 1940)

   The examiner states that if the functional statements as to the manner in which the strip is adapted for use be ignored and the claims considered as being directed to a strip per se, it will be found that the claims are substantially readable on metal strips having rectangular offsets, such as shown in certain figures of the two Fischer patents, the Mensch patent and the patent to Robertson.

   Taking the first Fischer patent No. 1,735,270, the form of the strip shown in Figs. 5 and 6 thereof is not located between the joint strip and the concrete strip nor does it seem that the plates shown in Figs. 5 and 6 of this patent are adapted to be so located. While the plates shown in Fig. 3 of the other Fischer patent are somewhat of the form of the plate claimed by applicant, it is used in an entirely different manner and it is believed that it is not a proper anticipation of a claim to a plate adapted to be used in the manner claimed.

2. ***In re Mills***, 16 USPQ 2d 1430, 1432 (Fed. Cir. 1990)

   The Board found that the difference between the claimed subject matter and the prior art resided solely in functional language and that appellant had to show that the prior art device lacked the functional characteristics of the claimed device citing *In re Ludtke* . . . . *Ludtke*, however, dealt with a rejection for lack of novelty [§102] . . . it was proper to require that a prior art reference cited as anticipating a claimed invention be shown to lack the [functional] characteristics of the claimed invention.

3. ***In re Mills***, 16 USPQ 2d 1430, 1432 (Fed. Cir. 1990)

It is not pertinent whether the prior art device possesses the functional characteristics of the claimed invention if the reference does not describe or suggest its structure.

4. ***RCA Corp. v. Applied Digital Data Sys., Inc.***, 221 USPQ 385, 389 n.5 (Fed. Cir. 1984)

The limitations which must be met by an anticipatory reference are those set forth in each statement of function. . . . Such a limitation cannot be met by an element in a reference that performs a different function, even though it may be part of a device embodying the same general overall concept.

5. ***In re Chiang***, Civ. App. No. 94-1144, slip op. at 5 (Fed. Cir. Nov. 23, 1994) (unpublished)

Chiang's "calculating" claim limitation cannot reasonably be interpreted to read on a reference that does not show such a calculation. . . . Unlike Chiang's calculated interval, Bray's preset interval is not "a function of on-line fault conditions." The cited prior art does not disclose Chiang's "calculating" claim limitation. The Board committed clear error by finding that this prior art anticipates Chiang claims 2 and 4.

6. ***In re Tholen***, Civ. App. 96-1445, slip op. 4 (Fed. Cir. July 16, 1997) (unpublished) (emphasis in original)

Tholen gave precise meaning to the phrase "edit data" as used in the specification (written description and claims combined). In view of the specification, "edit data" is a term meaning a certain type of data—data that has an editing function. The phrase as used in the specification does not mean data that is edited; nor does it mean the editing of data. According to the Tholen application, edit data is the subsequently-recorded, supplemental data that instructs a CD reader which of the previously-recorded songs (information signals) are to be skipped, or which of the previously-recorded edit data is to be skipped. In the Tholen application, the edit data does not amend or replace the table of contents but merely supplements it.

Ando [prior art], however, does not teach the use of *edit data* but merely teaches one way *to edit* data. There is no supplemental edit data in *Ando*. There is only the editing and replacing of an entire table of contents. . . . Because the cited prior art does not contain each and every limitation of the claims in the Tholen application, we reverse the decision of the Board that the claimed invention is not patentable over the cited prior art.

7. ***In re Schreiber***, 44 USPQ 2d 1429, 1432 (Fed. Cir. 1997)

A patent applicant is free to recite features of an apparatus either structurally or functionally. *See In re Swinehart*, 439

F.2d 210, 212, 169 USPQ 226, 228 (CCPA 1971) ("[T]here is nothing intrinsically wrong with [defining something by what it does rather than what it is] in drafting patent claims."). Yet, choosing to define an element functionally, *i.e.*, by what it does, carries with it a risk. As our predecessor court stated in *Swinehart*, 439 F.2d at 213, 169 USPQ at 228:

> where the Patent Office has reason to believe that a functional limitation asserted to be critical for establishing novelty in the claimed subject matter may, in fact, be an inherent characteristic of the prior art, it possesses the authority to require the applicant to prove that the subject matter shown to be in the prior art does not possess the characteristic relied on.

8. ***Ultradent Prods., Inc. v. Life-Like Cosmetics, Inc.***, 44 USPQ 2d 1336, 1341 (Fed. Cir. 1997)

The parties do not dispute the district court's claim interpretation, nor does Life-Like take issue with the patent's purely functional method of claiming the bleaching composition.

9. ***Rodime PLC v. Seagate Tech., Inc.***, 50 USPQ 2d 1429, 1435 (Fed. Cir. 1999)

A claim need not claim every function of a working device. Rather, a claim may specify improvements in one function without claiming the entire machine with its many functions.

10. ***K-2 Corp. v. Salomon S.A.***, 52 USPQ 2d 1001, 1004 (Fed. Cir. 1999) (citing ***Wright Med. Tech., Inc. v. Osteonics Corp.***, 43 USPQ 2d 1837, 1840 (Fed. Cir. 1997))

The functional language is, of course, an additional limitation in the claim.

11. ***WMS Gaming Inc. v. International Game Tech.***, 51 USPQ 2d 1385, 1393 (Fed. Cir. 1999)

Because the structure recited in the Telnaes patent is limited by the disclosed algorithm, our analysis of structural equivalence necessarily discusses the disclosed algorithm, which includes functional-type elements.

III.I. *Priority of Invention: Conception, Diligence, Reduction to Practice*

1. ***Hull v. Davenport***, 33 USPQ 506, 508 (C.C.P.A. 1937)

Clearly it was the intent of Congress to assure the first inventor who had completed the mental act of invention that he should not be deprived of his reward by reasons of delays which he could not reasonably avoid in giving his invention to the public. But we must bear in mind that it was not alone to reward the inventor that the patent monopoly was granted. The public was to get its reward and have the advantage of the inventor's discovery as early as was reasonably possible. See Robinson on Patents, Sec. 385. It will be noticed that the act of 1836 which is the genesis of the rule of diligence as applied in Patent Office practice, said: "who was using reasonable diligence in adapting and perfecting the same." As applied by the Patent Office and the courts in most instances, the rule has finally crystallized to be that the first conceiver who is last to reduce to practice must couple his conception to his reduction to practice with reasonable diligence. . . . The weight of authority, however, regards his diligence sufficiently shown if it be found that he was diligent from a time just prior to the second conceiver's entrance into the field to the first conceiver's reduction to practice either actually or constructively. . . .

His lack of diligence from the time of conception to the time immediately preceding the conception date of the second conceiver is not regarded as of importance except as it may have a bearing upon his subsequent acts, for the reason that he has not forfeited his right to a patent by his delay when no adverse interests are involved, and it follows that his adversary should only be concerned with what happened immediately prior to and after his entry into the field. Evidence of diligence during the critical period may be shown either by affirmative acts or acceptable excuses or reasons for failure of action. . . .

2. ***Hull v. Davenport***, 33 USPQ 506, 508–09 (C.C.P.A. 1937)

It is also well settled that the first conceiver cannot account for his failure to reduce his invention to practice for an unreasonable time after his conception by showing that he merely turned the matter over to his attorney if in fact the attorney in preparing the application and getting it into the Patent Office showed inexcusable lack of diligence. . . . Of course, in determining the diligence or the lack of diligence on the part of the attorney, considerations are involved unlike those in many respects which appertain to the inventor. Courts have been liberal in their holdings with respect to the length of time a busy patent attorney may take in the preparation and filing of patent applications. . . .

We cannot presume under the facts in this case that appellant's attorneys were diligent at the time appellee entered the field nor are there any facts proven from which we may conclude that they were diligent at any particular time during the entire eight months period. Of course, they were using diligence when they were engaged in preparing the application, but when the preparation of it began has not been shown. It is not shown that the several hundred cases in the attorneys' hands were taken up in their regular order or that appellant's case was not put to one side and others preferred over it.

3. *Sewall v. Walters*, 30 USPQ 2d 1356, 1358–59 (Fed. Cir. 1994)

Conception exists when a definite and permanent idea of an operative invention, including every feature of the subject matter sought to be patented, is known. . . . Conception is complete when one of ordinary skill in the art could construct the apparatus without unduly extensive research or experimentation.

4. *Regents of University of California v. Synbiotics Corp.*, 29 USPQ 2d 2032, 2033 (S.D. Cal. 1994)

Conception is defined as the "formation in the mind of the inventor, of a definite and permanent idea of the complete and operative invention, as it is hereafter to be applied in practice." *Hybritech Inc. v. Monoclonal Antibodies, Inc.*, 802 F.2d 1367, 1376 [231 USPQ 81] (Fed. Cir. 1986) [*cert. denied*, 480 U.S. 947 (1987)]. Actual reduction to practice requires that the claimed invention work for its intended purposes. Accordingly, conception requires both the idea of the invention's structure and possession of an operative method of making it. . . .

In some instances, such as the discovery of genes or chemicals, an inventor is unable to establish a conception until he has reduced the invention to practice through a successful experiment. This situation results in what is termed "simultaneous conception and reduction to practice." In *Amgen*, the Court held that, with respect to the discovery of a gene which is considered a chemical compound, conception has not been achieved until reduction to practice has occurred, or until after the gene is isolated.

5. *Staehelin v. Secher*, 24 USPQ 2d 1513, 1522–33 (B.P.A.I. 1992)

As the court in *Shurie* noted at 699 F.2d at 1158, 216 USPQ at 1044 [(Fed. Cir. 1983)], "An actual reduction to practice in Canada is irrelevant in an interference proceeding concerning priority of invention." . . . Activities abroad *will not* be considered for the purposes of establishing diligence in reducing an invention to practice. *But see* 35 U.S.C. §104 (Supp. 1995).

6. ***In re Bass***, 177 USPQ 178, 187 (C.C.P.A. 1973)

[P]rior conception and simultaneous reduction to practice makes diligence irrelevant.

7. ***Kawai v. Metlesics***, 178 USPQ 158, 163 (C.C.P.A. 1973)

[A] constructive reduction to practice, as opposed to an actual reduction to practice, is not proven unless the specification relied upon discloses a practical utility for the invention where one would not be obvious. We also think that proof of a constructive reduction to practice would also require that there be sufficient disclosure in the specification to enable any person skilled in the art to take advantage of that utility where it would not be obvious how this is done. This latter requirement is, of course, the so-called "how to use" requirement of section 112. It goes without saying that proof of a constructive reduction to practice would also require that the specification be sufficient to enable anyone skilled in the art to make the invention, i.e., the "how to make" requirement of section 112 should also be met by the specification.

8. ***Kawai v. Metlesics***, 178 USPQ 158, 162 (C.C.P.A. 1973)

Under our law, an applicant for a patent, with one exception not relevant here, cannot establish a date of invention by proving acts done in a foreign country except as provided for in section 119. This prohibition is found in 35 U.S.C. 104. The only act done abroad that is referred to in section 119 is the filing of an application for patent in a foreign country. Therefore, the net effect of sections 104 and 119 is to restrict a foreign inventor, for purposes of United States law, to a date of invention which corresponds to the date when his United States application was filed unless there was an earlier filing of a foreign application. In this respect, the act of filing the United States application has the legal effect of being, constructively at least, a simultaneous conception and reduction to practice of the invention.

9. ***Burroughs Wellcome Co. v. Barr Labs., Inc.***, 32 USPQ 2d 1915, 1919 (Fed. Cir. 1994), ***cert. denied***, 515 U.S. 1130 (1995)

Conception is the touchstone of inventorship, the completion of the mental part of invention. . . . It is "the formation in the mind of the inventor, of a definite and permanent idea of the complete and operative invention, as it is hereafter to be applied in practice." *Hybritech Inc. v. Monoclonal Antibodies, Inc.*, 802 F.2d 1367, 1376, 231 USPQ 81, 87 (Fed. Cir. 1986) [*cert. denied*, 480 U.S. 947 (1987)] (citation omitted). Conception is complete only when the idea is so clearly de-

fined in the inventor's mind that only ordinary skill would
be necessary to reduce the invention to practice, without extensive research or experimentation. . . . An idea is definite
and permanent when the inventor has a specific, settled
idea, a particular solution to the problem at hand, not just a
general goal or research plan he hopes to pursue. . . . But an
inventor need not know that his invention will work for conception to be complete. . . . He need only show that he had
the idea; the discovery that an invention actually works is
part of its reduction to practice.

10. ***Innovative Scuba Concepts, Inc. v. Feder Indus.***, 31
    USPQ 2d 1132, 1134 (Fed. Cir. 1994)

    In determining that Mr. Feder was the first to invent de-
    spite these facts, the court erred by according controlling
    weight to non-dispositive evidence. Specifically, the court fo-
    cused on the fact that the patent attorney responsible for fil-
    ing Innovative's patent application did not have Innovative's
    prototype strap in his possession when he drafted and filed
    the patent application, but instead had seen only Feder's ac-
    cused infringing straps. However, what a patent attorney
    does or does not have in his possession when he drafts and
    files a patent application is not relevant in evaluating dates
    of invention. The dispositive facts are those that establish
    which party was first to invent the subject matter of a claim.
    The failure of the attorney drafting the Baker patent appli-
    cation to see the prototype strap does not vitiate or disqual-
    ify from consideration the controlling fact that Baker in-
    vented that strap prior to Feder's earliest date of invention.

11. ***Sewall v. Walters***, 30 USPQ 2d 1356, 1358–59 (Fed. Cir.
    1994)

    Conception exists when a definite and permanent idea of an
    operative invention, including every feature of the subject
    matter sought to be patented, is known. . . . Conception is
    generally complete when one of ordinary skill in the art
    could construct the apparatus without unduly extensive re-
    search or experimentation.

12. ***Scott v. Finney***, 32 USPQ 2d 1115, 1119 (Fed. Cir. 1994)

    All cases deciding the sufficiency of testing to show reduc-
    tion to practice share a common theme. In each case, the
    court examined the record to discern whether the testing in
    fact demonstrated a solution to the problem intended to be
    solved by the invention. *See, e.g., Farrand Optical Co. v.
    United States*, 325 F.2d 328, 333, 139 USPQ 249, 253 (2d Cir.
    1963) ("The essential inquiry here is whether the *advance in
    the art* represented by the invention . . . was embodied in a

workable device that demonstrated that it could do what it was claimed to be capable of doing.") (emphasis added). In tests showing the invention's solution of a problem, the courts have not required commercial perfection nor absolute replication of the circumstances of the invention's ultimate use. Rather, they have instead adopted a common sense assessment. This common sense approach prescribes more scrupulous testing under circumstances approaching actual use conditions when the problem includes many uncertainties. On the other hand, when the problem to be solved does not present myriad variables, common sense similarly permits little or no testing to show the soundness of the principles of operation of the invention.

13. ***Scott v. Finney***, 32 USPQ 2d 1115, 1119 (Fed. Cir. 1994)

Reduction to practice, however, does not require actual use, but only a reasonable showing that the invention will work to overcome the problem it addresses.

14. ***Scott v. Finney***, 32 USPQ 2d 1115, 1120 (Fed. Cir. 1994)

Testing for the full safety and effectiveness of a prosthetic device is more properly left to the Food and Drug Administration (FDA). Title 35 does not demand that such human testing occur within the confines of Patent and Trademark Office (PTO) proceedings.

15. ***Fujikawa v. Wattanasin***, 39 USPQ 2d 1895, 1901 n.7 (Fed. Cir. 1996)

Before the Board, Fujikawa additionally argued that *in vivo* testing cannot establish reduction to practice of the method count because it does not fulfill every limitation of the count. In particular, Fujikawa argued that only human beings can be considered "patients in need of" cholesterol biosynthesis inhibition, as required by the count. As noted above, the Board rejected this argument and held that the term "patient" in the count is broad enough to encompass mammals, such as the laboratory rats tested *in vivo*.

16. ***Mahurkar v. C.R. Bard, Inc.***, 38 USPQ 2d 1288, 1290–91 (Fed. Cir. 1996)

To have conceived of an invention, an inventor must have formed in his or her mind "a definite and permanent idea of the complete and operative invention, as it is hereafter to be applied in practice." *Burroughs Wellcome Co. v. Barr Labs., Inc.*, 40 F.3d 1223, 1228, 32 USPQ2d 1915, 1919 (Fed. Cir. 1994), *cert. denied*, 116 S. Ct. 771 (1996) (citations omitted). The idea must be "so clearly defined in the inventor's mind that only ordinary skill would be necessary to reduce the invention to practice, without extensive research or experimentation." *Id.*

17. ***Mahurkar v. C.R. Bard, Inc.***, 38 USPQ 2d 1288, 1291 (Fed. Cir. 1996)

Reduction to practice follows conception. To show actual reduction to practice, an inventor must demonstrate that the invention is suitable for its intended purpose. *Scott v. Finney*, 34 F.3d 1058, 1061, 32 USPQ2d 1115, 1118 (Fed. Cir. 1994). Depending on the character of the invention and the problem it solves, this showing may require test results. *Id.* at 1062; *Manville Sales Corp. v. Paramount Sys., Inc.*, 917 F.2d 544, 550, 16 USPQ2d 1587, 1592 (Fed. Cir. 1990). Less complicated inventions and problems do not demand stringent testing. *Scott*, 34 F.3d at 1062. In fact, some inventions are so simple and their purpose and efficacy so obvious that their complete construction is sufficient to demonstrate workability. *Id.*; *King Instrument Corp. v. Otari Corp.*, 767 F.2d 853, 861, 226 USPQ 402, 407 (Fed. Cir. 1985), *cert. denied*, 475 U.S. 1016 (1986).

18. ***Estee Lauder Inc. v. L'Oreal, S.A.***, 44 USPQ 2d 1610, 1614 (Fed. Cir. 1997)

[A] reduction to practice does not occur until an inventor, or perhaps his agent, knows that the invention will work for its intended purpose. Indeed, we agree with *Standard Oil* that the "utility requirement is satisfied when an inventor has learned enough about the product to justify the conclusion that it is useful for a specific purpose." 494 F. Supp. at 381, 206 USPQ at 691. But until he learns that threshold information, there can be no reduction to practice. Moreover, *Burroughs Wellcome* states that a reduction to practice requires "the discovery that an invention actually works." . . . This suggests that until that "discovery" is actually made, there is no reduction to practice. These cases trumpet, therefore, the principle that a reduction to practice does not occur until the inventor has determined that the invention will work for its intended purpose.

19. ***Estee Lauder Inc. v. L'Oreal, S.A.***, 44 USPQ 2d 1610, 1615 (Fed. Cir. 1997)

[W]hen the test results themselves show success, there is no requirement for further analysis. Nor is it necessary for the inventor to articulate, verbally or in writing, that the tests were successful because the results themselves say that. But we do not see . . . a rule that the successful testing date is the date of reduction to practice, even when success is not known until later. [W]hen testing is necessary to establish utility, there must be recognition and appreciation that the tests were successful for reduction to practice to occur.

20. ***Final Oil & Chemical Co. v. Ewen***, 43 USPQ 2d 1935, 1941 (Fed. Cir. 1997)

Conception is the touchstone to determining inventorship. . . . Conception of a chemical substance requires knowledge of both the specific chemical structure of the compound and an operative method of making it.

21. ***Hedgewick v. Akers***, 182 USPQ 167, 169 (C.C.P.A. 1974)

Communication of a complete conception must be sufficient to *enable* one of ordinary skill in the art to construct and successfully operate the invention.

22. ***Cooper v. Goldfarb***, 47 USPQ 2d 1896, 1900–01 (Fed. Cir. 1998)

In determining priority of invention, the Board must consider "not only the respective dates of conception and reduction to practice of the invention, but also the reasonable diligence of one who was first to conceive and last to reduce to practice, from a time prior to conception by the other." 35 U.S.C. § 102(g) (1994). Accordingly, priority of invention goes to the first party to reduce an invention to practice unless the other party can show that it was the first to conceive of the invention and that it exercised reasonable diligence in later reducing that invention to practice. . . . Priority therefore depends upon conception and reduction to practice. Priority, conception, and reduction to practice are questions of law which are based on subsidiary factual findings.

23. ***Cooper v. Goldfarb***, 47 USPQ 2d 1896, 1901 (Fed. Cir. 1998)

Conception is the formation, in the mind of the inventor, of a definite and permanent idea of the complete and operative invention, as it is thereafter to be applied in practice. . . . A reduction to practice can be either a constructive reduction to practice, which occurs when a patent application is filed, or an actual reduction to practice.

24. ***Cooper v. Goldfarb***, 47 USPQ 2d 1896, 1901 (Fed. Cir. 1998)

Depending on the character of the invention and the problem it solves, determining that the invention will work for its intended purpose may require testing. . . . When testing is necessary, the embodiment relied upon as evidence of priority must actually work for its intended purpose. . . . In addition, the inventor must contemporaneously appreciate that the embodiment worked and that it met all the limitations of the interference count [or claim].

25. ***Cooper v. Goldfarb***, 47 USPQ 2d 1896, 1904–05 (Fed. Cir. 1998)

Inurement involves a claim by an inventor that, as a matter of law, the acts of another person should accrue to the benefit of the inventor. . . . In particular, experiments conducted at the request of an inventor by another party may inure to the benefit of the inventor for purposes of establishing a reduction to practice. . . . As just noted, however, inurement involves the claim that, as a matter of law, another person's activities should accrue to the benefit of the inventor. In order to establish inurement, an inventor must show, among other things, that the other person was working either explicitly or implicitly at the inventor's request. . . . Communication of the conception by the inventor to the other party is not required to establish inurement.

26. ***Cooper v. Goldfarb***, 47 USPQ 2d 1896, 1905 (Fed. Cir. 1998)

In this case, depending on the exact nature of the relationship between Goldfarb and Cooper, Goldfarb's reduction to practice could inure to the benefit of Cooper even if Goldfarb independently conceived the invention in the course of performing experiments at Cooper's request.

27. ***Pfaff v. Wells Elecs., Inc.***, 525 U.S. 55, 48 USPQ 2d 1641, 1642 n.2 (1998)

"A process is reduced to practice when it is successfully performed. A machine is reduced to practice when it is assembled, adjusted and used. A manufacture is reduced to practice when it is completely manufactured. A composition of matter is reduced to practice when it is completely composed." *Corona Cord Tire Co. v. Dovan Chemical Corp.*, 276 U.S. 358, 383, 72 L. Ed. 610, 48 S. Ct. 380 (1928).

28. ***Pfaff v. Wells Elecs., Inc.***, 525 U.S. 55, 48 USPQ 2d 1641, 1644 (1998)

It is well settled that an invention may be patented before it is reduced to practice. In 1888, this Court upheld a patent issued to Alexander Graham Bell even though he had filed his application before constructing a working telephone. . . .

"The law does not require that a discoverer or inventor, in order to get a patent for a process, must have succeeded in bringing his art to the highest degree of perfection. It is enough if he describes his method with sufficient clearness and precision to enable those skilled in the matter to understand what the process is, and if he points out some practicable way of putting it into operation." *The Telephone Cases*, 126 U.S. 1, 31 L. Ed. 863, 8 S. Ct. 778 (1888).

29. ***Pfaff v. Wells Elecs., Inc.***, 525 U.S. 55, 48 USPQ 2d 1641, 1646–47 (1998)

A rule that makes the timeliness of an application depend on the date when an invention is "substantially complete" seriously undermines the interest in certainty. Moreover, such a rule finds no support in the text of the statute. . . .

The word "invention" must refer to a concept that is complete, rather than merely one that is "substantially complete." It is true that reduction to practice ordinarily provides the best evidence that an invention is complete. But just because reduction to practice is sufficient evidence of completion, it does not follow that proof of reduction to practice is necessary in every case. . . .

We conclude, therefore, that the on-sale bar applies when two conditions are satisfied before the critical date. First, the product must be the subject of a commercial offer for sale. An inventor can both understand and control the timing of the first commercial marketing of his invention. . . .

Second, the invention must be ready for patenting. That condition may be satisfied in at least two ways: by proof of reduction to practice before the critical date; or by proof that prior to the critical date the inventor had prepared drawings or other descriptions of the invention that were sufficiently specific to enable a person skilled in the art to practice the invention.

30. ***Hyatt v. Boone***, 47 USPQ 2d 1128, 1129 (Fed. Cir. 1998), ***cert. denied***, 525 U.S. 1141 (1999)

Determination of priority of invention invokes a complex body of procedural and substantive law, applied in the first instance in administrative proceedings in accordance with 35 U.S.C. § 135(a) ("The Board of Patent Appeals and Interferences shall determine questions of priority of the inventions and may determine questions of patentability.") . . .

The general rule is that the first person to conceive the invention is the first inventor, . . . provided that when the first to conceive the invention is the last to reduce it to practice, the person who was first to conceive must have exercised reasonable diligence to his own actual or constructive reduction to practice, "from a time prior to conception by the other." 35 U.S.C. § 102(g).

31. ***Hyatt v. Boone***, 47 USPQ 2d 1128, 1130 (Fed. Cir. 1998), ***cert. denied***, 525 U.S. 1141 (1999)

The filing of a patent application serves as conception and constructive reduction to practice of the subject matter described in the application. . . . Thus the inventor need not provide evidence of either conception or actual reduction to practice when relying on the content of the patent application.

32. ***Genentech, Inc. v. Chiron Corp.***, 55 USPQ 2d 1636, 1641–41 (Fed. Cir. 2000).

"In order to establish an actual reduction to practice, the inventor must prove that: (1) he constructed an embodiment . . . that met all the limitations of the interference count; and (2) he determined that the invention would work for its intended purpose." *Cooper v. Goldfarb*, 154 F.3d 1321, 1327, 47 USPQ 2d 1896, 1901 (Fed. Cir. 1998). "When testing is necessary to establish utility, there must be recognition and appreciation that the tests were successful for reduction to practice to occur." *Estee Lauder Inc. v. L'Oreal*, S.A., 129 F.3d 588, 594–95, 44 USPQ 2d 1610, 1615 (Fed. Cir. 1997).

33. ***Genentech, Inc. v. Chiron Corp.***, 55 USPQ 2d 1636, 1642–43 (Fed. Cir. 2000).

"Inurement involves a claim by an inventor that, as a matter of law, the acts of another person should accrue to the benefit of the inventor." *Cooper*, 154 F.3d at 1331, 47 USPQ 2d at 1904. In *Estee Lauder*, we suggested that the requirement that an inventor must know that the invention is useful might be satisfied when an agent of the inventor obtains such knowledge. See *Estee Lauder*, 129 F.3d at 593, 44 USPQ 2d at 1614. . . . [A]t least three requirements that must be met before a non-inventor's recognition of the utility of an invention can inure to the benefit of the inventor. First, the inventor must have conceived of the invention. Second, the inventor must have had an expectation that the embodiment tested would work for the intended purpose of the invention. Third, the inventor must have submitted the embodiment for testing for the intended purpose of the invention.

34. ***Helifix Ltd. v. Blok-Lok, Ltd.***, 54 USPQ 2d 1299, 1306 (Fed. Cir. 2000)

[R]eduction to practice of the claimed method does not require reduction to practice of the specific tool described in the . . . patent, but merely requires the development of any tool that meets the limitations recited in the claim.

III.J. *Anticipation and Means-Plus-Function Claim Language Under Section 112, Sixth Paragraph*

1. ***In re Runion***, Civ. App. No. 92-1401, slip op. at 4–5 (Fed. Cir. Feb. 1, 1993) (unpublished) (quoting ***In re Mott***, 557 F.2d 266, 269, 194 USPQ 305, 307 (C.C.P.A. 1977))

With respect to means-plus-function limitations in a claim,

the prior art reference cannot anticipate the claimed invention "[a]bsent structure [in the prior art reference] which is capable of performing the functional limitation of the 'means.'" . . . Thus, if the crucial property or characteristic of the reference is not *necessarily* implicit in the reference's disclosure, then the principles of inherency do not apply and a reference without either inherent or explicit disclosure of each and every element of the claim cannot anticipate the claim.

2. ***RCA Corp. v. Applied Digital Data Sys., Inc.***, 221 USPQ 385, 388 (Fed. Cir. 1984) (quoting ***In re Mott***, 194 USPQ 305, 307 (C.C.P.A. 1977))

[W]ith an element expressed in terms of a means plus function, absent structure in a prior art reference which is capable of performing the functional limitation of the 'means,' the prior art reference does not meet [or anticipate] the claim.

3. ***RCA Corp. v. Applied Digital Data Sys., Inc.***, 221 USPQ 385, 389 n.5 (Fed. Cir. 1984)

The claims here define the invention in terms of several specific "means-plus-function" elements. The limitations which must be met by an anticipatory reference are those set forth in each statement of function. . . . Such a limitation cannot be met by an element in a reference that performs a different function, even though it may be part of a device embodying the same general overall concept.

III.K. Anticipation and Inherency

1. ***In re Weiss***, 26 USPQ 2d 1885, 1888 (Fed. Cir. 1993) (unpublished)

The mere fact that a certain thing may result from a given set of circumstances is not sufficient [to establish inherency] . . . [which requires that] the disclosure is sufficient to show that the natural result flowing from the operation as taught would result in the performance of the questioned function.

2. ***Continental Can Co. USA v. Monsanto Co.***, 20 USPQ 2d 1746, 1749 (Fed. Cir. 1991)

To serve as an anticipation when the reference is silent about the asserted inherent characteristic, such gap in the reference may be filled with recourse to extrinsic evidence. Such evidence must make clear that the missing descriptive matter is necessarily present in the thing described in the reference and that it would be so recognized by persons of ordinary skill. *In re Oelrich*, 212 USPQ 323, 326 (C.C.P.A. 1981) (quoting *Hansgirg v. Kemmer*, 40 USPQ 665, 667 (C.C.P.A. 1939)) provides:

Inherency, however may not be established by probabilities or possibilities. The mere fact that a certain thing may result from a given set of circumstances is not sufficient.

3. ***Scripps Clinic & Research Found. v. Genentech Inc.***, 18 USPQ 2d 1001, 1010 (Fed. Cir. 1991)

Invalidity for anticipation requires that all of the elements and limitations of the claim are found within a single prior art reference. . . . There must be no difference between the claimed invention and the reference disclosure, as viewed by a person of ordinary skill in the field of the invention.

It is sometimes appropriate to consider extrinsic evidence to explain the disclosure of a reference. Such factual elaboration is necessarily of limited scope and probative value, for a finding of anticipation requires that all aspects of the claimed invention were already described in a single reference: a finding that is not supportable if it is necessary to prove facts beyond those disclosed in the reference in order to meet the claim limitations. The role of extrinsic evidence is to educate the decision-maker to what the reference meant to persons of ordinary skill in the field of the invention, not to fill gaps in the reference.

4. ***SGS-Thomson Microelectronics, Inc. v. International Rectifier Corp.***, 32 USPQ 2d 1496, 1503 (Fed. Cir.) (unpublished), ***cert. denied***, 513 U. S. 1052 (1994)

Before a reference can be found to disclose a feature by virtue of its inherency, one of ordinary skill in the art viewing the reference must understand that the unmentioned feature at issue is necessarily present in the reference. *Continental Can*, 948 F.2d at 1268–69, 20 USPQ 2d at 1749–50. The test of inherency is not satisfied by what a reference "may" teach. *Id.*, 20 USPQ 2d at 1749–50 ("Inherency . . . may not be established by probabilities or possibilities. The mere fact that a certain thing *may* result from a given set of circumstances is not sufficient.") (emphasis added).

5. ***Ex parte Levy***, 17 USPQ 2d 1461, 1464 (B.P.A.I. 1990)

[T]he examiner must provide a basis in fact and/or technical reasoning to reasonably support the determination that the allegedly inherent characteristic necessarily flows from the teachings of the applied prior art.

6. ***W.L. Gore & Assocs. v. Garlock, Inc.***, 220 USPQ 303, 314 (Fed. Cir. 1983), ***cert. denied***, 469 U.S. 851 (1984)

Given the unique nature of [the claimed product], we are not persuaded that the "effect" of the processes disclosed in

Smith and Sumitomo . . . would be always to inherently produce or be seen always to produce products meeting all of
the claim limitations. Anticipation . . . cannot be predicated
on mere conjecture respecting the characteristics of products
that might result from the practice of processes disclosed in
references.

7. ***In re Marshall***, 198 USPQ 344, 346 (C.C.P.A. 1978)
Nothing in the [reference] even remotely suggests taking ox-
ethazaine to lose weight. If anyone ever lost weight by following the [reference] teaching it was an unrecognized accident. An accidental or unwitting duplication of an invention
cannot constitute an anticipation.

8. ***In re Rinehart***, 189 USPQ 143, 148 (C.C.P.A. 1976)
The view that success would have been "inherent" cannot, in
this case, substitute for a showing of reasonable expectation
of success.

9. ***Ciba-Geigy Corp. v. Alza Corp.***, 37 USPQ 2d 1337,
1339–40 (Fed. Cir. 1995) (unpublished)
"Extrinsic evidence may be considered when it is used to
explain, but not expand, the meaning of a reference." *In re
Baxter Travenol Labs.*, 952 F.2d 388, 390, 21 U.S.P.Q.2D
(BNA) 1281, 1284 (Fed. Cir. 1991) . . . . Thus, although references cannot be combined for purposes of anticipation, additional references may be used to interpret the allegedly
anticipating reference and shed light on what it would have
meant to those skilled in the art at the time of the invention.
Studiengesellschaft Kohle, m.b.H. v. Dart Indus., Inc., 726
F.2d 724, 726–27, 220 USPQ 841, 842 (Fed. Cir. 1984). However, "such evidence must make clear that the missing descriptive matter is necessarily present in the thing described
in the reference, and that it would be so recognized by persons of ordinary skill." *Continental Can Co. USA Inc. v.
Monsanto Co.*, 948 F.2d 1264, 1268, 20 USPQ 2D 1746, 1749
(Fed. Cir. 1991).

10. ***In re Robertson***, 49 USPQ 2d 1949, 1950–51 (Fed. Cir.
1999) (quoting ***Continental Can Co. v. Monsanto Co.***, 20
USPQ 2d 1746, 1749 (Fed. Cir. 1991))
If the prior art reference does not expressly set forth a particular element of the claim, that reference still may anticipate if that element is "inherent" in its disclosure. To establish inherency, the extrinsic evidence "must make clear that
the missing descriptive matter is necessarily present in the
thing described in the reference, and that it would be so recognized by persons of ordinary skill." . . . "Inherency, how-

ever, may not be established by probabilities or possibilities. The mere fact that a certain thing may result from a given set of circumstances is not sufficient."

11. *In re Robertson*, 49 USPQ 2d 1949, 1951 (Fed. Cir. 1999)

In finding anticipation by inherency, the Board ignored the foregoing critical principles. The Board made no attempt to show that the fastening mechanisms of Wilson that were used to attach the diaper to the wearer also "necessarily" disclosed the third separate fastening mechanism of claim 76 used to close the diaper for disposal, or that an artisan of ordinary skill would so recognize. It cited no extrinsic evidence so indicating.

Instead, the Board ruled that one of the fastening means for attaching the diaper to the wearer also could operate as a third fastening means to close the diaper for disposal and that Wilson therefore inherently contained all the elements of claim 76. In doing so, the Board failed to recognize that the third mechanical fastening means in claim 76, used to secure the diaper for disposal, was separate from and independent of the two other mechanical means used to attach the diaper to the person. The Board's theory that these two fastening devices in Wilson were capable of being intermingled to perform the same function as the third and first fastening elements in claim 76 is insufficient to show that the latter device was inherent in Wilson. Indeed, the Board's analysis rests upon the very kind of probability or possibility—the odd use of fasteners with other than their mates—that this court has pointed out is insufficient to establish inherency.

12. *Continental Can Co., U.S.A. v. Monsanto Co.*, 20 USPQ 2d 1746, 1749–50 (Fed. Cir. 1991)

To serve as an anticipation when the reference is silent about the asserted inherent characteristic, such gap in the reference may be filled with recourse to extrinsic evidence. Such evidence must make clear that the missing descriptive matter is necessarily present in the thing described in the reference, and that it would be so recognized by persons of ordinary skill. *In re Oelrich*, 666 F.2d 578, 581, 212 USPQ 323, 326 (C.C.P.A. 1981) (quoting *Hansgirg v. Kemmer*, 102 F.2d 212, 214, 40 USPQ 665, 667 (C.C.P.A. 1939)) [states]:

> Inherency, however, may not be established by probabilities or possibilities. The mere fact that a certain thing may result from a given set of circumstances is not sufficient. If, however, the disclosure is sufficient to show that the natural result flowing from the operation as taught

would result in the performance of the questioned function, it seems to be well settled that the disclosure should be regarded as sufficient.

This modest flexibility in the rule that "anticipation" requires that every element of the claims appear in a single reference accommodates situations where the common knowledge of technologists is not recorded in the reference; that is, where technological facts are known to those in the field of the invention, albeit not known to judges.

13. ***Atlas Powder Co. v. IRECO Inc.***, 51 USPQ 2d 1943, 1945–46 (Fed. Cir. 1999) (quotations omitted)

To invalidate a patent by anticipation, a prior art reference normally needs to disclose each and every limitation of the claim. . . . However, a prior art reference may anticipate when the claim limitation or limitations not expressly found in that reference are nonetheless inherent in it. . . . Under the principles of inherency, if the prior art necessarily functions in accordance with, or includes, the claimed limitations, it anticipates. . . . Inherency is not necessarily coterminous with the knowledge of those of ordinary skill in the art. . . . Artisans of ordinary skill may not recognize the inherent characteristics or functioning of the prior art. . . . However, the discovery of a previously unappreciated property of a prior art composition, or of a scientific explanation for the prior art's functioning, does not render the old composition patentably new to the discoverer.

14. ***Atlas Powder Co. v. IRECO Inc.***, 51 USPQ 2d 1943, 1947 (Fed. Cir. 1999)

Insufficient prior understanding of the inherent properties of a known composition does not defeat a finding of anticipation.

15. ***Atlas Powder Co. v. IRECO Inc.***, 51 USPQ 2d 1943, 1948 (Fed. Cir. 1999)

[A]n insufficient scientific understanding does not defeat a showing of inherency.

16. ***Scaltech Inc. v. Retec/Tetra, L.L.C.***, 51 USPQ 2d 1055, 1059 (Fed. Cir. 1999)

Inherency may not be established by probabilities or possibilities. The mere fact that a certain thing may result from a given set of circumstances is not sufficient to establish inherency. . . . However, if the natural result flowing from the operation of the process offered for sale would necessarily result in achievement of each of the claim limitations, then claimed invention was offered for sale.

17. ***Mehl/Biophile Int'l Corp. v. Milgraum***, 192 F.3d 1362, 52 USPQ 2d 1303, 1306 (Fed. Cir. 1999)

Occasional results are not inherent.

18. ***Mehl/Biophile Int'l Corp. v. Milgraum***, 192 F.3d 1362, 52 USPQ 2d 1303, 1307 (Fed. Cir. 1999)

Where, as here, the result is a necessary consequence of what was deliberately intended, it is of no import that the article's authors did not appreciate the results.

19. ***Ex parte Schricker***, 56 USPQ 2d 1723, 1725 (B.P.A.I. 2000) (unpublished)

[T]he examiner talks in terms of inherency (which is really an anticipation rationale) while on the other hand the examiner talks in terms that it would have been obvious to experiment to divine optimum conditions.

Inherency and obviousness are somewhat like oil and water—they do not mix well. Claimed subject matter can be anticipated because a prior art reference describes a method which inherently meets the limitations of a claimed method. Claimed subject matter can be unpatentable for obviousness when, notwithstanding a difference between that subject matter and a prior art reference, the claimed subject matter, as a whole, would have been obvious. However, when an examiner relies on inherency, it is incumbent on the examiner to point to the "page and line" of the prior art which justifies an inherency theory. Compare *In re Rijckaert*, 9 F.3d 1531, 1533, 28 USPQ 2d 1955, 1957 (Fed. Cir. 1993) (when the PTO asserts that there is an explicit or implicit teaching or suggestion in the prior art, it must indicate where such a teaching or suggestion appears in the prior art) (citing *In re Yates*, 663 F.2d 1054, 1057, 211 USPQ 1149, 1151 (C.C.P.A. 1981).

III.L. *Anticipation Reference and Enablement Requirement*

1. ***In re Sun***, 31 USPQ 2d 1451, 1453 (Fed. Cir. 1993) (unpublished)

But to be prior art under section 102(b), a reference must be enabling. . . . That is, it must put the claimed invention in the hand of one skilled in the art.

2. ***Ex parte Humphreys***, 24 USPQ 2d 1255, 1261–62 (B.P.A.I. 1992)

As set forth in *In re Donohue*, 632 F.2d 123, 207 USPQ 196 (C.C.P.A. 1980):

For a publication to constitute an anticipation of an invention and, thus, to bar the grant of a patent under 35 USC 102, it must be capable, when taken in conjunction with the knowledge of those skilled in the art to which it pertains, of placing that invention in the possession of the public.

3. ***In re Wilder***, 166 USPQ 545, 548 (C.C.P.A. 1970)

Simply stated, a prior publication or patent description will be considered as anticipatory when its disclosure is at once specific and enabling with regard to the particular subject matter at issue. . . . However, such disclosure may yet be held not to legally anticipate the claimed subject matter if it is found not to be sufficiently enabling, in other words, if it does not place the subject matter of the claims within "the possession of the public."

4. ***Ciba-Geigy Corp. v. Alza Corp.***, 37 USPQ 2d 1337, 1341 n.3 (Fed. Cir. 1995) (unpublished)

An anticipatory reference must be enabling, *see Akzo N.V. v. United States Int'l Trade Comm'n*, 808 F.2d 1471, 1479, 1 U.S.P.Q.2D (BNA) 1241, 1245 (Fed. Cir. 1986), *cert. denied*, 482 U.S. 909, 96 L. Ed. 2d 382, 107 S. Ct. 2490 (1987), so as to place one of ordinary skill in possession of the claimed invention. *In re Spada*, 911 F.2d 705, 708, 15 U.S.P.Q.2D (BNA) 1655, 1657 (Fed. Cir. 1990); *see Seymour v. Osborne*, 78 U.S. 516, 555, 20 L. Ed. 33 (1870) ("The knowledge supposed to be derived from the publication must be sufficient to enable those skilled in the art or science to understand the nature and operation of the invention.").

5. ***F.B. Leopold Co. v. Roberts Filter Mfg. Co.***, Civ. App. 96-1218, slip op. at 5–6 (Fed. Cir. July 2, 1997) (unpublished)

[A]lthough our precedent states that a reference must be enabling to be prior art, that precedent simply means that a reference published before a patent's critical date is prior art only for that which the reference enables. The reference does not entirely lose its status as prior art simply because it fails to disclose a device that works as well as the patented device. Rather, if a prior art reference does not disclose or enable the entire claimed invention, we consider that as a factor in the obviousness determination, but we do not disqualify the reference entirely. *See Beckman Instruments, Inc. v. LKB Produkter AB*, 892 F.2d 1547, 1551, 13 USPQ 2d 1301, 1304 (Fed. Cir. 1989) ("Even if a reference discloses an inoperative device, it is prior art for all that it teaches.").

6. ***Ex parte Lemoine***, 46 USPQ 2d 1420, 1426 (B.P.A.I.), *reconsideration granted in part*, 46 USPQ 2d 1432 (B.P.A.I. 1998) (unpublished)

It is axiomatic that a reference must be considered in its entirety, and it is well established that the disclosure of a reference is not limited to specific working examples contained therein.

In re Fracalossi, 681 F.2d 792, 794 n.1, 215 USPQ 569, 570 n.1 (C.C.P.A. 1982). A reference must be considered for everything it teaches by way of technology. *EWP Corp. v. Reliance Universal Inc.*, 755 F.2d 898, 907, 225 USPQ 20, 25 (Fed. Cir.), *cert. denied*, 474 U.S. 843 (1985).

7. ***ATD Corp. v. Lydall, Inc.***, 48 USPQ 2d 1321, 1330–31 (Fed. Cir. 1998)

Although international search reports may contain information material to patentability if they contain closer prior art than that which was before the United States examiner, it is the reference itself, not the information generated in prosecuting foreign counterparts, that is material to prosecution in the United States. The details of foreign prosecution are not an additional category of material information.

8. ***Rockwell Int'l Corp. v. United States***, 47 USPQ 2d 1027, 1032 (Fed. Cir. 1998)

That prior art patents may have described failed attempts or attempts that used different elements is not enough. The prior art must be enabling. *See Motorola, Inc. v. Interdigital Tech. Corp.*, 121 F.3d 1461, 1471, 43 USPQ 2d 1481, 1489 (Fed. Cir. 1997) ("In order to render a claimed apparatus or method obvious, the prior art must enable one skilled in the art to make and use the apparatus or method." (quoting *Beckman Instruments, Inc. v. LKB Produkter AB*, 892 F.2d 1547, 1551, 13 USPQ 2d 1301, 1304 (Fed. Cir. 1989))).

III.M. *Anticipation of Ranges in a Claim*

1. ***In re Wertheim***, 191 USPQ 90, 100 (C.C.P.A. 1976)

Of course, the disclosure in the prior art of any value within a claimed range is an anticipation of the claimed range.

2. ***Atlas Powder Co. v. IRECO Inc.***, 51 USPQ 2d 1943, 1945–46 (Fed. Cir. 1999) (quotations omitted)

To anticipate a claim, a prior art reference must disclose every limitation of the claimed invention, either explicitly or inherently. . . . Anticipation of a patent claim requires a finding that the claim at issue "reads on" a prior art reference. . . . Specifically, when a patent claims a chemical composition in terms of ranges of elements, any single prior art reference that falls within each of the ranges anticipates the claim. . . . In chemical compounds, a single prior art species within the patent's claimed genus reads on the generic claim and anticipates.

3. ***Hockerson-Halberstadt, Inc. v. Avia Group Int'l, Inc.***, 55 USPQ 2d 1487, 1491 (Fed. Cir. 2000)

Under our precedent, however, it is well established that patent drawings do not define the precise proportions of the elements and may not be relied on to show particular sizes if the specification is completely silent on the issue. *See In re Wright*, 569 F.2d 1124, 1127, 193 USPQ 332, 335 (CCPA 1977) ("Absent any written description in the specification of quantitative values, arguments based on measurement of a drawing are of little value."); *In re Olson*, 212 F.2d 590, 592, 101 USPQ 401, 402 (CCPA 1954); cf. Manual of Patent Examining Procedure Section 2125 (1998). Thus, in the present case, a reasonable competitor, being aware that figures in a patent are not drawn to scale unless otherwise indicated, would understand the arguments in the prosecution history as clearly disclaiming a groove having a width greater than the combined width of the fins.

III.N. *Anticipation and Chemical/Biological Related Inventions*

1. ***Atlas Powder Co. v. IRECO Inc.***, 51 USPQ 2d 1943, 1945–46 (Fed. Cir. 1999) (quotations omitted)

To anticipate a claim, a prior art reference must disclose every limitation of the claimed invention, either explicitly or inherently. . . . Anticipation of a patent claim requires a finding that the claim at issue "reads on" a prior art reference. . . . Specifically, when a patent claims a chemical composition in terms of ranges of elements, any single prior art reference that falls within each of the ranges anticipates the claim. . . . In chemical compounds, a single prior art species within the patent's claimed genus reads on the generic claim and anticipates.

IV. Establishing Prima Facie Case of Obviousness Under Section 103

1. ***In re Lintner***, 173 USPQ 560, 562 (C.C.P.A. 1972)

In determining the propriety of the Patent Office case for obviousness in the first instance, it is necessary to ascertain whether or not the reference teachings would appear to be sufficient for one of ordinary skill in the relevant art having the references before him to make the proposed substitution, combination or other modification.

2. ***In re Fritch***, 23 USPQ 2d 1780, 1783 (Fed. Cir. 1992)

In proceedings before the Patent and Trademark Office, the Examiner bears the burden of establishing a prima facie case of obviousness based upon the prior art. . . . "[The Examiner] can satisfy this burden only by showing some objective teaching in the prior art or that knowledge generally available to one of ordinary skill in the art would lead that individual to combine the relevant teachings of the references." *In re Fine*, 837 F.2d 1071, 1074, 5 USPQ 2d 1596, 1598 (Fed. Cir. 1988).

3. *In re Oetiker*, 24 USPQ 2d 1443, 1446 (Fed. Cir. 1992)

The combination of elements from non-analogous sources, in a manner that reconstructs the applicant's invention only with the benefit of hindsight, is insufficient to present a prima facie case of obviousness. There must be some reason, suggestion, or motivation found in the prior art whereby a person of ordinary skill in the field of the invention would make the combination. That knowledge can not come from the applicant's invention itself.

4. *Panduit Corp. v. Dennison Mfg. Co.*, 1 USPQ 2d 1593, 1595–96 (Fed. Cir.), *cert. denied*, 481 U.S. 1052 (1987)

With the involved facts determined, the decision maker confronts a ghost, i.e., "a person having ordinary skill in the art," not unlike the "reasonable man" and other ghosts in the law. To reach a proper conclusion under §103, the decision maker must step backward in time and into the shoes worn by that "person" when the invention was unknown and just before it was made. In light of all the evidence, the decision maker must then determine whether the . . . claimed invention as a whole would have been obvious at that time to that person.

5. *In re O'Farrell*, 7 USPQ 2d 1673, 1681 (Fed. Cir. 1988)

For obviousness under §103, all that is required is a reasonable expectation of success.

6. *In re Oetiker*, 24 USPQ 2d 1443, 1444 (Fed. Cir. 1992)

If the examination at the initial stage does not produce a prima facie case of unpatentability, then without more the applicant is entitled to grant of the patent.

7. *In re Oetiker*, 24 USPQ 2d 1443, 1445 (Fed. Cir. 1992)

We think that the PTO is correct in treating the concept of the prima facie case as of broad applicability, for it places the initial burden on the examiner, the appropriate procedure whatever the technological class of invention.

8. *In re Fritch*, 23 USPQ 2d 1780, 1783 (Fed. Cir. 1992)

In proceedings before the Patent and Trademark Office, the Examiner bears the burden of establishing a prima facie case of obviousness based upon the prior art. . . . The patent applicant may then attack the Examiner's prima facie case determination as improperly made out, or the applicant may present objective evidence tending to support a conclusion of nonobviousness.

9. ***Comair Rotron Inc. v. Matsushita Elec. Corp. of Am.***, 33 USPQ 2d 1785, 1787 (Fed. Cir. 1994) (unpublished)

In determining obviousness, a court must (1) determine the scope and content of the prior art; (2) ascertain the differences between the prior art and the claimed invention; and (3) resolve the level of ordinary skill in the pertinent art. Secondary considerations such as commercial success, long felt but unsolved need, and failure of others are also considered. *Graham v. John Deere Co.*, 383 U.S. 1, 17–18, 148 USPQ 459, 467 (1966).

10. ***In re Deuel***, 34 USPQ 2d 1210, 1214 (Fed. Cir. 1995)

The examiner bears the burden of establishing a prima facie case of obviousness. . . . Only if this burden is met does the burden of coming forward with rebuttal argument or evidence shift to the applicant. . . . When the references cited by the examiner fail to establish a prima facie case of obviousness, the rejection is improper and will be overturned.

11. ***Allen Archery Inc. v. Browning Mfg. Co.***, 2 USPQ 2d 1490, 1493 (Fed. Cir. 1987)

Obviousness under 35 U.S.C. 103 (1982) & Supp. III (1985) is a legal issue, the determination of which involves factual inquiries into (1) the scope and content of the prior art, (2) the level of ordinary skill in the art, (3) the differences between the claimed invention and the prior art, and (4) any objective evidence of non obviousness, such as long-felt need, commercial success, failure of others.

12. ***Motorola, Inc. v. Interdigital Tech. Corp.***, 43 USPQ 2d 1481, 1489 (Fed. Cir. 1997) (quoting ***Beckman Instruments, Inc. v. LKB Produkter AB,*** 13 USPQ 2d 1301, 1304 (Fed. Cir. 1989))

In order to render a claimed apparatus or method obvious, the prior art must enable one skilled in the art to make and use the apparatus or method.

13. ***In re Mayne***, 41 USPQ 2d 1451, 1453 (Fed. Cir. 1997)

The legal determination under section 103 is whether the claimed invention as a whole would have been obvious to a person of ordinary skill in the art at the time the invention was made. . . . The foundational facts for the prima facie case of obviousness are: (1) the scope and content of the prior art; (2) the difference between the prior art and the claimed invention; and (3) the level of ordinary skill in the art. . . . More-

over, objective indicia such as commercial success and long
felt need are relevant to the determination of obviousness. . . .
Thus, each obviousness determination rests on its own facts.

14. ***Robotic Vision Sys., Inc. v. View Eng'g Inc.***, 51 USPQ 2d
1948, 1953 (Fed. Cir. 1999)

An obviousness determination is based on underlying factual inquiries including: (1) the scope and content of the
prior art; (2) the level of ordinary skill in the art; (3) the differences between the claimed invention and the prior art;
and (4) objective evidence of nonobviousness.

15. ***In re Wood***, 202 USPQ 171, 174 (C.C.P.A. 1979)

In resolving the question of obviousness under 35 U.S.C.
§ 103, we presume full knowledge by the inventor of all the
prior art in the field of his endeavor. However, with regard
to prior art outside the field of his endeavor, we only presume knowledge from those arts reasonably pertinent to the
particular problem with which the inventor was involved.
The rationale behind this rule precluding rejections based
on combination of teachings from references from non-analogous arts is the realization that an inventor could not possibly be aware of every teaching in every art. Thus, we attempt to more closely approximate the reality of the
circumstances surrounding the making of an invention by
only presuming knowledge by the inventor of prior art in the
field of his endeavor and in analogous arts.

The determination that a reference is from a nonanalogous art is therefore two-fold. First, we decide if the reference is within the field of the inventor's endeavor. If it is not,
we proceed to determine whether the reference is reasonably
pertinent to the particular problem with which the inventor
was involved.

16. ***Advanced Display Systems, Inc. v. Kent State University***, 54 USPQ 2d 1673, 1680 (Fed. Cir. 2000), **cert. denied**,
121 S. Ct. 1226 (Mar. 5, 2001)

Obviousness is ultimately a question of law that rests on
underlying factual inquiries including: (1) the scope and content of the prior art; (2) the level of ordinary skill in the art; (3)
the differences between the claimed invention and the prior
art; and (4) objective considerations of nonobviousness. . . .
Objective considerations such as failure by others to solve the
problem and copying, . . . may often be the most probative and
cogent evidence of nonobviousness.

17. ***In re Kotzab***, 55 USPQ 2d 1313, 1316 (Fed. Cir. 2000)

The ultimate determination of whether an invention would
have been obvious under 35 U.S.C. § 103(a) is a legal conclu-

sion based on underlying findings of fact. See *Dembiczak*, 175 F.3d at 998, 50 USPQ 2d at 1616. We review the Board's ultimate determination of obviousness de novo. See *Id.* However, we review the Board's underlying factual findings for substantial evidence. See *In re Gartside*, 203 F.3d 1305, 1316, 53 USPQ 2d 1769, 1776 (Fed. Cir. 2000).

Substantial evidence is something less than the weight of the evidence but more than a mere scintilla of evidence. See *Id.* at 1312, 53 USPQ 2d at 1773 (quoting *Consolidated Edison Co. v. NLRB*, 305 U.S. 197, 229–30, 83 L. Ed. 126, 59 S. Ct. 206 (1938)). In reviewing the record for substantial evidence, we must take into account evidence that both justifies and detracts from the factual determinations. See *Id.* (citing *Universal Camera Corp. v. NLRB*, 340 U.S. 474, 487–88, 95 L. Ed. 456, 71 S. Ct. 456 (1951)). We note that the possibility of drawing two inconsistent conclusions from the evidence does not prevent the Board's findings from being supported by substantial evidence. See *Id.* Indeed, if a reasonable mind might accept the evidence as adequate to support the factual conclusions drawn by the Board, then we must uphold the Board's determination.

18. ***Brown & Williamson Tobacco Corp. v. Philip Morris Inc.***, 56 USPQ 2d 1456, 1459 (Fed. Cir. 2000)

The statutory standard for the ultimate determination of obviousness provides that a claimed invention is unpatentable if the differences between it and the prior art "are such that the subject matter as a whole would have been obvious at the time the invention was made to a person having ordinary skill in the art." 35 U.S.C. § 103 (1994); *see also Graham*, 383 U.S. at 13. In line with this statutory standard, our case law provides that "the consistent criterion for determination of obviousness is whether the prior art would have suggested to one of ordinary skill in the art that this process should be carried out and would have a reasonable likelihood of success, viewed in the light of the prior art." *In re Dow Chem.*, 837 F.2d 469, 473, 5 USPQ 2d 1529, 1531 (Fed. Cir. 1988). Two requirements are contained in this criterion.

The first requirement is that a showing of a suggestion, teaching, or motivation to combine the prior art references is an "essential evidentiary component of an obviousness holding." *C.R. Bard, Inc. v. M3 Sys. Inc.*, 157 F.3d 1340, 1352, 48 USPQ 2d 1225, 1232 (Fed. Cir. 1998). This evidence may flow from the prior art references themselves, the knowledge of one of ordinary skill in the art, or, in some cases, from the nature of the problem to be solved. See *Pro-Mold & Tool Co. v. Great Lakes Plastics, Inc.*, 75 F.3d 1568,

1573, 37 USPQ 2d 1626, 1630 (Fed. Cir. 1996). However, the suggestion more often comes from the teachings of the pertinent references. See *In re Rouffet*, 149 F.3d 1350, 1359, 47 USPQ 2d 1453, 1459 (Fed. Cir. 1998). This showing must be clear and particular, and broad conclusory statements about the teaching of multiple references, standing alone, are not "evidence." See *Dembiczak*, 175 F.3d at 1000, 50 USPQ2d at 1617. However, the suggestion to combine need not be express and "may come from the prior art, as filtered through the knowledge of one skilled in the art." *Motorola, Inc. v. Interdigital Tech. Corp.*, 121 F.3d 1461, 1472, 43 USPQ 2d 1481, 1489 (Fed. Cir. 1997).

The second requirement is that the ultimate determination of obviousness "does not require absolute predictability of success. . . . All that is required is a reasonable expectation of success." *In re O'Farrell*, 853 F.2d 894, 903–904, 7 USPQ 2d 1673, 1681 (Fed. Cir. 1988); see also *In re Longi*, 759 F.2d 887, 897, 225 USPQ 645, 651–52 (Fed. Cir. 1985).

V. Overcoming Prima Facie Case of Obviousness

1. ***In re Rijckaert***, 28 USPQ 2d 1955, 1957 (Fed. Cir. 1993)
While the Commissioner criticizes Rijckaert's arguments regarding the § 103 rejections, the burden to rebut a rejection of obviousness does not arise until a prima facie case has been established. In the case before us, it was not.

V.A. *Nonanalogous Art—Suggestion for Combination or Modification*

1. ***In re Wood***, 202 USPQ 171, 174 (C.C.P.A. 1979)
The determination that a reference is from a nonanalogous art is . . . twofold. First, we decide if the reference is within the field of the inventor's endeavor. If it is not, we proceed to determine whether the reference is reasonably pertinent to the particular problem with which the inventor was involved.

2. ***In re Clay***, 23 USPQ 2d 1058, 1060–61 (Fed. Cir. 1992)
Two criteria have evolved for determining whether prior art is analogous: (1) whether the art is from the same field of endeavor, and (2) if the reference is not within the field of the inventor's endeavor, whether the reference still is reasonably pertinent to the particular problem with which the inventor is involved. . . . A reference is reasonably pertinent if . . . it is one which, because of the matter with which it deals, logically would have commended itself to the inventor's attention in considering his problem. . . . If a reference disclosure has the same purpose as the claimed invention, the reference

relates to the same problem, . . . [i]f it is directed to a different purpose, the inventor would accordingly have had less
motivation or occasion to consider it.

3. ***Lindemann Maschinenfabrik GmbH v. American
    Hoist & Derrick Co.***, 221 USPQ 481, 488 (Fed. Cir. 1984)

The '315 patent specifically stated that it disclosed and
claimed a combination of features previously used in two separate devices. That fact alone is not fatal to patentability.
The claimed invention must be considered as a whole, and
the question is whether there is something in the prior art as
a whole to suggest the desirability, and thus the obviousness,
of making the combination.

4. ***ACS Hosp. Sys., Inc. v. Montefiore Hosp.***, 221 USPQ 929,
    932, 933 (Fed. Cir. 1984)

Obviousness cannot be established by combining the
teaching of the prior art to produce the claimed invention,
absent some teaching or suggestion supporting the combination. Under section 103, teachings of references can be combined only if there is some suggestion or incentive to do so.
The prior art of record fails to provide any such suggestion or
incentive.

5. ***Ex parte Humphreys***, 24 USPQ 2d 1255, 1262 (B.P.A.I.
    1992)

We reverse this rejection. . . . The examiner's rejection is
not specific as to how one of ordinary skill in the art would
have found it obvious to practice any specific method within
the scope of these claims as of the filing date of this application. In this regard, we note that the examiner has not explained with any specificity on this record how Rose, either
as discussed on page 2 of the present specification or from a
consideration of the entire reference as supplied by appellants, would have suggested in combination with Malpartida
1984 the methods set forth by these claims.

6. ***In re Wood***, 202 USPQ 171, 174 (C.C.P.A. 1979)

In resolving the question of obviousness under 35 USC
103, we presume full knowledge by the inventor of all the
prior art in the field of his endeavor. However, with regard to
prior art outside the field of his endeavor, we only presume
knowledge from those arts reasonably pertinent to the particular problem with which the inventor was involved. . . .
The rationale behind this rule precluding rejections based on
combination of teachings of references from nonanalogous
arts is the realization that an inventor could not possibly be
aware of every teaching in every art.

7. ***Ex parte Clapp***, 227 USPQ 972, 973 (B.P.A.I. 1985)

In the instant application, the examiner has done little more than cite references to show that one or more elements or subcombinations thereof, when each is viewed in a vacuum, is known. The claimed invention, however, is clearly directed to a combination of elements. That is to say, appellant does not claim that he has invented one or more new elements but has presented claims to a new combination of elements. To support the conclusion that the claimed combination is directed to obvious subject matter, either the references must expressly or impliedly suggest the claimed combination or the examiner must present a convincing line of reasoning as to why the artisan would have found the claimed invention to have been obvious in light of the teachings of the references. . . . Based upon the record before us, we are convinced that the artisan would not have found it obvious to selectively pick and choose elements or concepts from the various references so as to arrive at the claimed invention without using the claims as a guide. It is to be noted that simplicity and hindsight are not proper criteria for resolving the issue of obviousness.

8. ***In re Oetiker***, 24 USPQ 2d 1443, 1446 (Fed. Cir. 1992)

We have reminded ourselves and the PTO that it is necessary to consider "the reality of the circumstances" . . . — in other words, common sense—in deciding in which fields a person of ordinary skill would reasonably be expected to look for a solution to the problem facing the inventor.

9. ***Wang Labs., Inc. v. Toshiba Corp.***, 26 USPQ 2d 1767, 1773 (Fed. Cir. 1993)

The Allen-Bradley art is not in the same field of endeavor as the claimed subject matter merely because it relates to memories. It involves memory circuits in which modules of varying sizes may be added or replaced; in contrast, the subject patents teach compact modular memories.

10. ***Wang Labs., Inc. v. Toshiba Corp.***, 26 USPQ 2d 1767, 1773 (Fed. Cir. 1993)

Wang's SIMMs were designed to provide compact computer memory with minimum size, low cost, easy repairability, and easy expandability. . . . In contrast, the Allen-Bradley patent relates to a memory circuit for a larger, more costly industrial controller. . . . Thus, there is substantial evidence in the record to support a finding that the Allen-Bradley prior art is not reasonably pertinent and is not analogous.

11. ***Ex parte Obukowicz***, 27 USPQ 2d 1063, 1065 (B.P.A.I. 1992)

[The] specific statement regarding combatting mosquitos using genetically engineered "natural pond microflora" is relied on by the examiner for the "suggestion" required by the aforementioned case law. However, the specific statement by Dean is not a suggestion to insert the gene into the chromosome of bacteria and apply that bacteria to the plant environment in order to protect the plant. At best, the Dean statement is but an invitation to scientists to explore a new technology that seems a promising field of experimentation. The Dean statement is of the type that gives only general guidance and is not at all specific as to the particular form of the claimed invention and how to achieve it. Such a suggestion may make an approach "obvious to try" but it does not make the invention obvious.

12. ***Ex parte Obukowicz***, 27 USPQ 2d 1063, 1065 (B.P.A.I. 1992)

In proceedings before the Patent and Trademark Office, the examiner bears the burden of establishing a prima facie case of obviousness based upon the prior art. . . . The examiner can satisfy this burden only by showing some objective teaching in the prior art or that knowledge generally available to one of ordinary skill in the art would lead that individual to combine the relevant teachings of the references.

13. ***In re Watter***, 64 USPQ 571, 573–74 (C.C.P.A. 1945)

Moreover, the problem of stretching a metal skin smoothly over the surface of an aeroplane part is not analogous to that encountered in the application of a string to a bow. The arts are remote from each other. The bow does not teach that the string shall lie smoothly against it. Accordingly, it does not seem likely that one seeking a solution to the problem confronting appellant would turn to the art of bows for suggestions. Similarly, the method of inserting a magazine in a wrapper, as described by the board, is too remote from appellant's method to be properly used in a rejection of the claims here involved.

14. ***Ex parte Re Qua***, 56 USPQ 279, 280 (Pat. Off. Bd. App. 1942)

The patent to Barnebl shows a filter drum against which a knife is fed continuously at a constant rate while the present claims call for the intermittent feeding. The patent to Trump does not appear to add anything of value for the reason that it is directed to a very different type of filter in which no filter aid is employed. There is no suggestion in either patent as to how the features of the two devices could be combined so as to meet the structure claimed. The decision of the examiner is reversed.

15. ***In re Fritch***, 23 USPQ 2d 1780, 1783–84 (Fed. Cir. 1992)

The mere fact that the prior art may be modified in the manner suggested by the Examiner does not make the modification obvious unless the prior art suggested the desirability of the modification.

16. ***In re Raleigh***, 16 USPQ 42, 43 (C.C.P.A. 1932)

It is argued, first, by appellant, that Sonneborn's patent is not in an analogous art. We are not able to agree with this contention. Both the appellant and Sonneborn are engaged in the art of making fluid-tight seams in metal of the same general character. As stated in *In re Schneider*, . . . the test is:

" . . . Is the patentable conception in Reich in an art so remote and nonanalogous to the concept in applicant's art as to require invention to make the necessary substitution?"

It is our opinion that no invention is involved in utilizing Schneider's seam and method in constructing appellant's thermostatic cell.

17. ***In re Greene***, Civ. App. No. 93-1446, slip op. at 3–4 (Fed. Cir. Mar. 17, 1994) (unpublished)

The Board erred in considering Dupuy analogous art. The test for analogous art outside an inventor's field of endeavor is whether the art pertains to the particular problem confronting the inventor. . . . In these situations, the law presumes knowledge only of those arts reasonably pertinent to the inventor's problem. Greene's problem involved protecting aircraft fuselages and engines from breaking away air vanes. A person of ordinary skill in the aircraft vane art simply would not find a 1919 reference about broken blades in a pugging mill reasonably pertinent to this problem.

18. ***Heidelberger Druckmaschinen AG v. Hantscho Commercial Prods., Inc.***, 30 USPQ 2d 1377, 1379–80 (Fed. Cir. 1994)

When the patented invention is made by combining known components to achieve a new system, the prior art must provide a suggestion or motivation to make such a combination.

19. ***SRI International, Inc. v. Advanced Tech. Labs., Inc.***, Civ. App. No. 93-1074, slip op. at 6 (Fed. Cir. Dec. 21, 1994) (unpublished)

The principle issue respecting the Minton patent is whether the reference is analogous art. . . . The claims in issue are directed to the ultrasonic imaging of the interior of body parts, such as for the purposes of medical diagnosis. Seismic prospecting, Minton's field of endeavor, is not the same. . . . The Minton reference, which related to seismic prospecting circa 1946, almost thirty years prior to Green's filing date, would not have logically commended itself to Green's attention in considering how to compensate for changes in the spectral distribution of a received ultrasonic signal in an object such as a body part.

20. *In re Schreiber*, 44 USPQ 2d 1429, 1432 (Fed. Cir. 1997)

[W]e note that Schreiber acknowledges in the specification that the prior art pertinent to his invention includes patents relating to dispensing fluids. Schreiber therefore may not now argue that such patents are non-analogous art.

21. *Motorola, Inc. v. Interdigital Tech. Corp.*, 43 USPQ 2d 1481, 1489 (Fed. Cir. 1997)

[T]here is no requirement that the prior art contain an express suggestion to combine known elements to achieve the claimed invention. Rather, the suggestion to combine may come *from* the prior art, as filtered through the knowledge of one skilled in the art. *See In re Jones*, 958 F.2d 347, 351, 21 USPQ 2d 1941, 1943–44 (Fed. Cir. 1992) ("there must be some suggestion for [combining prior art references], found either in the references themselves or in the knowledge generally available to one of ordinary skill in the art").

22. *Micro Chem., Inc. v. Great Plains Chem. Co.*, 41 USPQ 2d 1238, 1244–45 (Fed. Cir.), *cert. denied,* 521 U.S. 1122 (1997) (quoting *Pro-Mold and Tool Co. v. Great Lakes Plastics, Inc.*, 37 USPQ 2d 1626, 1630 (Fed. Cir. 1996))

A determination of obviousness must involve more than indiscriminately combining prior art; a motivation or suggestion to combine must exist. . . . As we recently stated:

> Such a suggestion may come expressly from the references themselves. . . . It may come from knowledge of those skilled in the art that certain references, or disclosures in the references, are known to be of special interest or importance in the particular field. . . . It may also come from the nature of a problem to be solved, leading inventors to look to references relating to possible solutions to that problem.

23. *C.R. Bard, Inc. v. M3 Sys., Inc.*, 48 USPQ 2d 1225, 1231–32 (Fed. Cir. 1998)

When a patent describes a new mechanical device that can be viewed as a new combination or arrangement of mechanical components, the legal conclusion of obviousness requires that there be some suggestion, motivation, or teaching in the prior art whereby the person of ordinary skill would have selected the components that the inventor selected and used them to make the new device. *See Heidelberger Druckmaschinen AG v. Hantscho Commercial Prods., Inc.*, 21 F.3d 1068, 1072, 30 USPQ 2d 1377, 1379 (Fed. Cir. 1993) ("When the patented invention is made by combining known components to achieve a new system, the prior art must provide a suggestion or motivation to make such a combination."); *Northern Telecom, Inc. v. Datapoint Corp.*, 908 F.2d 931, 934, 15 USPQ 2d 1321, 1323 (Fed. Cir. 1990) (it is insufficient that prior art shows similar components, unless it also contains some teaching, suggestion, or incentive for arriving at the claimed structure).

24. **C.R. Bard, Inc. v. M3 Sys., Inc.**, 48 USPQ 2d 1225, 1232 (Fed. Cir. 1998)

The invention that was made, however, does not make itself obvious; that suggestion or teaching must come from the prior art. *See, e.g., Uniroyal, Inc. v. Rudkin-Wiley Corp.*, 837 F.2d 1044, 1051–52, 5 USPQ 2d 1434, 1438 (Fed. Cir. 1988) (it is impermissible to reconstruct the claimed invention from selected pieces of prior art absent some suggestion, teaching, or motivation in the prior art to do so); *Interconnect Planning Corp. v. Feil*, 774 F.2d 1132, 1143, 227 USPQ 543, 551 (Fed. Cir. 1985) (it is insufficient to select from the prior art the separate components of the inventor's combination, using the blueprint supplied by the inventor); *Fromson v. Advance Offset Plate, Inc.*, 755 F.2d 1549, 1556, 225 USPQ 26, 31 (Fed. Cir. 1985) (the prior art must suggest to one of ordinary skill in the art the desirability of the claimed combination).

25. **ATD Corporation v. Lydall, Inc.**, 48 USPQ 2d 1321, 1329 (Fed. Cir. 1998)

Determination of obviousness can not be based on the hindsight combination of components selectively culled from the prior art to fit the parameters of the patented invention. There must be a teaching or suggestion within the prior art, or within the general knowledge of a person of ordinary skill in the field of the invention, to look to particular sources of information, to select particular elements, and to combine them in the way they were combined by the inventor.

26. **Rockwell Int'l Corp. v. United States**, 47 USPQ 2d 1027, 1033 (Fed. Cir. 1998)

Rather "the consistent criterion for determination of obviousness is whether the prior art would have suggested to one of ordinary skill in the art that this process should be carried out and would have a reasonable likelihood of success." *Dow*, 837 F.2d at 473, 5 USPQ 2d at 1531; *see also United States Surgical Corp. v. Ethicon, Inc.*, 103 F.3d 1554, 1564, 41 USPQ 2d 1225, 1233 (Fed. Cir. 1996).

27. ***Monarch Knitting Mach. Corp. v. Sulzer Morat GmbH***, 45 USPQ 2d 1977, 1981–82 (Fed. Cir. 1998)

The district court's formulation of the problem confronting the '053 inventors presumes the solution to the problem— modification of the stem segment. Defining the problem in terms of its solution reveals improper hindsight in the selection of the prior art relevant to obviousness. *See, e.g., In re Antle*, 58 C.C.P.A. 1382, 444 F.2d 1168, 1171–72, 170 USPQ 285, 287–88 (C.C.P.A. 1971) (warning against selection of prior art with hindsight). By importing the ultimate solution into the problem facing the inventor, the district court adopted an overly narrow view of the scope of the prior art. It also infected the district court's determinations about the content of the prior art. . . . By defining the inventor's problem in terms of its solution, the district court missed this necessary antecedent question, namely, whether the prior art contains a suggestion or motivation to combine references to form a trend.

28. ***In re Metz***, Civ. App. 97-1263, slip op. at 9 (Fed. Cir. Sept. 22, 1998) (unpublished)

Appellant argues that the board additionally erred in combining the Jannson article with the Metz admitted prior art, because the Jannson article concerns solar control films, a field and problem it maintains are not analogous to that of the Metz field or problem. The Metz admitted prior art discloses fluorescence-measuring apparatus including non-holographic beamsplitters and barrier filters. . . . We are persuaded that, while it may not be true in each and every case, there are certain overriding principles which would cross over the boundaries between the various subfields. The use of holographic filters would appear to be one of those overriding principles which would find such broad-based cross field applicability in the field of spectroscopy that it would be difficult to imagine that there would be no cross fertilization between the subfields.

29. ***In re Rouffet***, 47 USPQ 2d 1453, 1456 (Fed. Cir. 1998)

Therefore, "when determining the patentability of a claimed invention which combines two known elements, 'the question is whether there is something in the prior art as a whole to suggest the desirability, and thus the obviousness, of making the combination.'" *See In re Beattie*, 974 F.2d 1309, 1311–12, 24 USPQ 2d 1040, 1042 (Fed. Cir. 1992) (quoting *Lindemann Maschinenfabrik GmbH v. American Hoist & Derrick Co.*, 730 F.2d 1452, 1462, 221 USPQ 481, 488 (Fed. Cir. 1984)).

30. ***In re Rouffet***, 47 USPQ 2d 1453, 1457 (Fed. Cir. 1998)

As this court has stated, "virtually all [inventions] are combinations of old elements." *Environmental Designs, Ltd. v. Union Oil Co.*, 713 F.2d 693, 698, 218 USPQ 865, 870 (Fed. Cir. 1983); *see also Richdel, Inc. v. Sunspool Corp.*, 714 F.2d 1573, 1579–80, 219 USPQ 8, 12 (Fed. Cir. 1983) ("Most, if not all, inventions are combinations and mostly of old elements."). Therefore an examiner may often find every element of a claimed invention in the prior art. If identification of each claimed element in the prior art were sufficient to negate patentability, very few patents would ever issue. Furthermore, rejecting patents solely by finding prior art corollaries for the claimed elements would permit an examiner to use the claimed invention itself as a blueprint for piecing together elements in the prior art to defeat the patentability of the claimed invention. Such an approach would be "an illogical and inappropriate process by which to determine patentability." *Sensonics, Inc. v. Aerosonic Corp.*, 81 F.3d 1566, 1570, 38 USPQ 2d 1551, 1554 (Fed. Cir. 1996).

31. ***In re Rouffet***, 47 USPQ 2d 1453, 1457–58 (Fed. Cir. 1998)

To prevent the use of hindsight based on the invention to defeat patentability of the invention, this court requires the examiner to show a motivation to combine the references that create the case of obviousness. In other words, the examiner must show reasons that the skilled artisan, confronted with the same problems as the inventor and with no knowledge of the claimed invention, would select the elements from the cited prior art references for combination in the manner claimed.

This court has identified three possible sources for a motivation to combine references: the nature of the problem to be solved, the teachings of the prior art, and the knowledge of persons of ordinary skill in the art. In this case, the Board relied upon none of these. Rather, just as it relied on the high level of skill in the art to overcome the differences between the claimed invention and the selected elements in the references, it relied upon the high level of skill in the art to provide the necessary motivation. The Board did not, however, explain what specific understanding or technological principle within the knowledge of one of ordinary skill in the art would have suggested the combination. Instead, the Board merely invoked the high level of skill in the field of art. If such a rote invocation could suffice to supply a motivation to combine, the more sophisticated scientific fields would rarely, if ever, experience a patentable technical advance. Instead, in complex scientific fields, the Board could routinely identify the prior art elements in an application, invoke the lofty level of skill, and rest its case for rejection. To counter this potential weakness in the obviousness construct, the suggestion to combine requirement stands as a critical safeguard against hindsight analysis and rote application of the legal test for obviousness.

32. ***In re Rouffet***, 47 USPQ 2d 1453, 1458 (Fed. Cir. 1998)

Because the Board did not explain the specific understanding or principle within the knowledge of a skilled artisan that would motivate one with no knowledge of Rouffet's invention to make the combination, this court infers that the examiner selected these references with the assistance of hindsight. This court forbids the use of hindsight in the selection of references that comprise the case of obviousness. *See In re Gorman*, 933 F.2d 982, 986, 18 USPQ 2d 1885, 1888 (Fed. Cir. 1991). Lacking a motivation to combine references, the Board did not show a proper prima facie case of obviousness.

33. ***In re Alhamad***, Civ. App. 97-1345, slip op. at 3–4 (Fed. Cir. Dec. 18, 1997) (unpublished)

On appeal, Alhamad begins by noting that the term "expanded metal" has a specific meaning in the art that is operatively different from that of the claim element "expanded metal net." Citing *Stock*, one of the references relied upon by the examiner and the Board, Alhamad points out that expanded metal is well known in the industry to be a stiff and strength enhancing reinforcement for composite materials. Alhamad then points out that the claimed "expanded metal net" is specified in the claims to be "made from foil having a thickness in the range from about 0.028 to 0.5 mm." Citing *Schrenk*, another reference relied upon by the examiner and the Board, Alhamad points out that such a thin expanded metal net is known in the art to have "only limited dimensional stability" and is so flimsy that it will collapse under its own weight. *Schrenk* at Col. 1, lines 27–29. As a result, according to Alhamad, no reasonable artisan would even contemplate using a flimsy expanded metal net as a strength enhancing agent for reinforcing a wall board. Therefore, there is no motivation to combine these references for any reason, let alone for the claimed reason of promoting fire resistance. We agree with Alhamad and conclude that the Board has failed to make even a prima facie showing of obviousness.

34. ***Armament Sys. & Procedures, Inc. v. Monadnock Lifetime Prods., Inc.***, Civ. App. 97-1174, slip op. at 13 (Fed. Cir.
Aug. 7, 1998) (unpublished)

The pertinent field of art relating to the patented subject
matter is determined by the nature of the problem confronting the inventor. *See Orthopedic Equip. Co. v. United States*,
702 F.2d 1005, 1009, 217 USPQ 193, 196 (Fed. Cir. 1983).
Several factors may illuminate that inquiry, including an examination of the type of skills needed to understand the patent disclosure, the type of art applied to the application in
the Patent and Trademark Office, and the areas of expertise
of witnesses who are recruited to testify concerning the obviousness of the invention.

35. ***Armament Sys. & Procedures, Inc. v. Monadnock Lifetime Prods., Inc.***, Civ. App. 97-1174, slip op. at 13–15 (Fed.
Cir. Aug. 7, 1998) (unpublished)

Initially, it is clear that the problem that Parsons set out
to solve with his invention related specifically to baton manufacturing. Prior art expandable batons had suffered from
failures due to bending and distortion at the joints. The
record of prior art solutions and Parsons' own failed attempts demonstrate that metallurgy was not the exclusive
field to which baton designers looked in attempting to remedy the problem. Various tooling processes and mechanical
reinforcement techniques were also employed. That evidence supports the district court's conclusion that baton-
making is a discrete field of art rather than simply a field of
commercial application for metallurgical inventions. . . .

The type of art cited by the Patent and Trademark Office in
the prosecution of Parsons' application also argues against
defining the pertinent field as metallurgy. References cited
against Parsons included martial arts batons, police batons,
and expandable fish knockers, as well as the basic metallurgy texts that Monadnock relies on to support its position.

Monadnock argues that the use of metallurgy experts during patent prosecution and in the validity and infringement
trials demonstrates that metallurgy is the pertinent field of
art. While we agree that the use of experts in a certain field
to testify may be probative, the relevant inquiry for obviousness focuses on the time just before the invention was made.
In many cases, the post-invention use of experts simply reflects the field that provided a successful solution to the problem that confronted the inventor, without representing the
variety of available options before the invention was made.

Finally, the patent specification also suggests that the pertinent art is baton-making rather than metallurgy. The de-

scriptions of the invention and of the prior art are directed specifically at batons. The discussion of metallurgy is basic and functionally oriented. It reflects none of the subtlety and careful distinction between varying types of heat treatments that were the focus of attention at trial. The district court also found, based on ample evidence, that tactical police batons are designed by baton-makers, not metallurgists. As a result, the district court was justified in concluding that the relevant art was baton-making and that a person of ordinary skill in the art would be familiar with the rudiments of metallurgy and other techniques that had previously been applied to baton manufacture.

36. ***Fromson v. Anitec Printing Plates, Inc.***, 45 USPQ 2d 1269, 1276 (Fed. Cir. 1997), ***cert. denied,*** 525 U.S. 817 (1998)

That an inventor has probed the strengths and weaknesses of the prior art and discovered an improvement that escaped those who came before is indicative of unobviousness, not obviousness. The district court did not correctly apply the law of obviousness, for there is no suggestion or teaching in the prior art to select from the various known procedures and combine specific steps, along with a new electrical structure, in the way that is described and claimed by Fromson. The judgment of invalidity is reversed.

37. ***Union Carbide Corp. v. American Can Co.***, 220 USPQ 584, 591 & n.6 (Fed. Cir. 1984) (quotations omitted)

The starting place for determining the issue of obviousness is . . . with the inventor working in his shop with the prior art references—which he is presumed to know—hanging on the walls around him. No other evidence was in the Winslow case, and nothing more in the way of evidence was there to be considered in determining obviousness. Here, however, our inquiry cannot merely stop with the prior art . . . on the wall. Only after consideration of all evidence, including that with respect to "secondary considerations," can obviousness be judged. . . . [T]he prior art on the wall consists only of those patents one of ordinary skill in the art would have selected without the advantage of hindsight or knowledge of the invention.

38. ***In re Carroll***, 202 USPQ 571, 572 (C.C.P.A. 1979) (quoting ***Graham v. John Deere Co.***, 383 U.S. 1, 36 (1965))

One of the more difficult aspects of resolving questions of non-obviousness is the necessity "to guard against slipping into use of hindsight." . . . Many inventions may seem obvious to everyone after they have been made. However, 35 USC 103 instructs us to inquire into whether the claimed invention "would have been obvious at the time the invention was made to a person having ordinary skill in the art to which said subject matter pertains." Thus, in deciding the issue of obviousness, we must look at the prior art presented from a vantage point in time prior to when the invention was made, and through the eyes of a hypothetical person of ordinary skill in the art.

39. ***Al-Site Corp. v. VSI Int'l, Inc.***, 50 USPQ 2d 1161, 1171 (Fed. Cir. 1999)

VSI is unable, however, to point to any specific teaching or suggestion for making this combination. VSI instead relies on what it presumes is the level of knowledge of one of ordinary skill in the art at the time of the invention to supply the missing suggestion to combine. In the first place, the level of skill in the art is a prism or lens through which a judge or jury views the prior art and the claimed invention. This reference point prevents these deciders from using their own insight or, worse yet, hindsight, to gauge obviousness. Rarely, however, will the skill in the art component operate to supply missing knowledge or prior art to reach an obviousness judgment. . . . Skill in the art does not act as a bridge over gaps in substantive presentation of an obviousness case, but instead supplies the primary guarantee of objectivity in the process.

40. ***Smiths Indus. Med. Sys., Inc. v. Vital Signs, Inc.***, 51 USPQ 2d 1415, 1420–21 (Fed. Cir. 1999)

[T]here is no basis for concluding that an invention would have been obvious solely because it is a combination of elements that were known in the art at the time of the invention. . . . Instead, the relevant inquiry is whether there is a reason, suggestion, or motivation in the prior art that would lead one of ordinary skill in the art to combine the references, and that would also suggest a reasonable likelihood of success. . . . Such a suggestion or motivation may come from the references themselves, from knowledge by those skilled in the art that certain references are of special interest in a field, or even from the nature of the problem to be solved.

41. ***Interactive Techs., Inc. v. Pittway Corp.***, Civ. App. No. 98-1464, slip op. at 13 (Fed. Cir. June 1, 1999) (unpublished), ***cert. denied,*** 528 U.S. 1046 (1999).

[A] general relationship between the fields does not suggest a motivation to combine the particular references.

42. *In re Dembiczak*, 50 USPQ 2d 1614, 1616–17 (Fed. Cir. 1999) (quotations omitted)

Our analysis begins in the text of section 103 quoted above, with the phrase "at the time the invention was made." For it is this phrase that guards against entry into the tempting but forbidden zone of hindsight, . . . when analyzing the patentability of claims pursuant to that section. Measuring a claimed invention against the standard established by section 103 requires the oft-difficult but critical step of casting the mind back to the time of invention, to consider the thinking of one of ordinary skill in the art, guided only by the prior art references and the then-accepted wisdom in the field. . . . Close adherence to this methodology is especially important in the case of less technologically complex inventions, where the very ease with which the invention can be understood may prompt one to fall victim to the insidious effect of a hindsight syndrome wherein that which only the inventor taught is used against its teacher. . . . In this case, the Board fell into the hindsight trap. . . . The range of sources available, however, does not diminish the requirement for actual evidence. That is, the showing must be clear and particular.

Our case law makes clear that the best defense against the subtle but powerful attraction of a hindsight-based obviousness analysis is rigorous application of the requirement for a showing of the teaching or motivation to combine prior art references.

43. *Clearstream Wastewater Systems, Inc. v. Hydro-Action, Inc.*, 54 USPQ 2d 1185, 1189 (Fed. Cir. 2000)

In construing the disputed claim limitations, it must be kept in mind that the claims at issue in this case are combination claims. Combination claims can consist of new combinations of old elements or combinations of new and old elements. See *Intel Corp. v. U.S. Int'l Trade Comm.*, 946 F.2d 821, 842, 20 USPQ 2d 1161, 1179 (Fed. Cir. 1991); *Panduit Corp. v. Dennison Mfg.*, 810 F.2d 1561, 1575, 1 USPQ 2d 1593, 1603 (Fed. Cir. 1987). Because old elements are part of these combination claims, claim limitations may, and often do, read on the prior art. . . . It is well established in patent law that a claim may consist of all old elements, such as the rigid-conduit system, for it may be that the combination of the old elements is novel and patentable. Similarly, it is well established that a claim may consist of all old elements and one new element, thereby being patentable.

44. *In re Kotzab*, 55 USPQ 2d 1313, 1317–18 (Fed. Cir. 2000)

The United States Patent and Trademark Office argues that because Evans teaches that a single sensor may be used to provide "the temperature measurement at a selected part of the machine," it necessarily follows that the Evans "system" discussed later may have a single sensor—and that single sensor may control more than one valve. . . . While the test for establishing an implicit teaching, motivation, or suggestion is what the combination of these two statements of Evans would have suggested to those of ordinary skill in the art, the two statements cannot be viewed in the abstract. Rather, they must be considered in the context of the teaching of the entire reference. Further, a rejection cannot be predicated on the mere identification in Evans of individual components of claimed limitations. Rather, particular findings must be made as to the reason the skilled artisan, with no knowledge of the claimed invention, would have selected these components for combination in the manner claimed.

We do not take issue with the argument that Evans suggests the concept of using the historic temperature obtained by one temperature measurement to control coolant pulses. . . . However, there is not substantial evidence of record to extrapolate this teaching to the multiple zone system described later in Evans. . . . In the multiple zone system, Evans describes the use of a temperature sensor and an associated flow control valve in each zone. At most, the combined teachings suggest that the historic temperature of a mold zone may be measured by one sensor, and as part of a multiple zone system where multiple valves are controlled, that one sensor measurement can be used to control the valve for that zone. Thus, we cannot say that there is such relevant evidence as a reasonable mind might accept as adequate to support the conclusion that where there are a plurality of control valves in a multiple zone setting, only one temperature sensor provides the control for a plurality of valves.

45. *In re Kotzab*, 55 USPQ 2d 1313, 1318 (Fed. Cir. 2000)

In this case, the Examiner and the Board fell into the hindsight trap. The idea of a single sensor controlling multiple valves, as opposed to multiple sensors controlling multiple valves, is a technologically simple concept. With this simple concept in mind, the Patent and Trademark Office found prior art statements that in the abstract appeared to suggest the claimed limitation. But, there was no finding as to the specific understanding or principle within the knowledge of a skilled artisan that would have motivated one with no knowledge of Kotzab's invention to make the combination in the manner claimed. In light of our holding of the absence of a motivation to combine the teachings in Evans, we conclude that the Board did not make out a proper prima facie case of obviousness in rejecting claims 1, 2, and 4–9 under 35 U.S.C. § 103(a) over Evans. Moreover, because the rejections of claims 3 and 10 rely upon the foregoing, we also conclude that the Board did not make out a proper prima facie case of obviousness in rejecting those claims under 35 U.S.C. § 103(a).

46. ***Ecolochem, Inc. v. Southern California Edison Co.***, 56 USPQ 2d 1065, 1075 (Fed. Cir. 2000)

The absence of a convincing discussion of the specific sources of the motivation to combine the prior art references, particularly in light of the strength of prior art teaching away from the use of the Houghton process, is a critical omission in the district court's obviousness analysis, which mainly discusses the ways that the multiple prior art references can be combined to read on the claimed invention. . . . The opinion then lists each step and states where in the cited prior art references the step can be found. This reference-by-reference, limitation-by-limitation analysis wholly fails to demonstrate how the prior art teaches or suggests the combination claimed in the '411 patent.

With hindsight, we could perhaps agree that the Houghton article seems like an obvious place to start to address the need in the power plant industry for an improved carbon-catalyzed deoxygenation process employing hydrazine that can be used commercially in a variety of applications. But, "obvious to try" is not the standard.

47. ***Ecolochem, Inc. v. Southern California Edison Co.***, 56 USPQ 2d 1065, 1072–73 (Fed. Cir. 2000)

In *In re Dembiczak*, we noted that:

> Measuring a claimed invention against the standard established by section 103 requires the oft-difficult but critical step of casting the mind back to the time of invention, to consider the thinking of one of ordinary skill in the art, guided only by the prior art references and the then-accepted wisdom in the field.

In re Dembiczak, 175 F.3d 994, 999, 50 USPQ 2d 1614, 1617 (Fed. Cir. 1999). We "cannot use hindsight reconstruction to pick and choose among isolated disclosures in the prior art to deprecate the claimed invention." *In re Fine*, 837 F.2d 1071, 1075, 5 USPQ 2d 1596 (Fed. Cir. 1988). Our case law makes clear that the best defense against hindsight-based obviousness analysis is the rigorous application of the requirement for a showing of a teaching or motivation to combine the prior art references. See *Dembiczak*, 175 F.3d at 999, 50 USPQ 2d at 1617. "Combining prior art references without evidence of such a suggestion, teaching, or motivation simply takes the inventor's disclosure as a blueprint for piecing together the prior art to defeat patentability—the essence of hindsight." *Id.* . . . Although the suggestion to combine references may flow from the nature of the problem, see *Pro-Mold & Tool Co. v. Great Lakes Plastics, Inc.*, 75 F.3d 1568, 1573, 37 USPQ 2d 1626, 1630 (Fed. Cir. 1996), "defining the problem in terms of its solution reveals improper hindsight in the selection of the prior art relevant to obviousness," *Monarch Knitting Mach. Corp. v. Sulzer Morat Gmbh*, 139 F.3d 877, 880, 45 USPQ 2d 1977, 1981 (Fed. Cir. 1998). Therefore, "when determining the patentability of a claimed invention which combines two known elements, 'the question is whether there is something in the prior art as a whole to suggest the desirability, and thus the obviousness, of making the combination.'" *In re Beattie*, 974 F.2d 1309, 1311–12, 24 USPQ 2d 1040, 1042 (Fed. Cir. 1992) (quoting *Lindemann*, 730 F.2d at 1462, 221 USPQ at 488).

In this case, the district court used the '411 patent as a blueprint, with the Houghton process as the main structural diagram, and looked to other prior art for the elements present in the patent but missing from the Houghton process. The district court opinion does not discuss any specific evidence of motivation to combine, but only makes conclusory statements. "Broad conclusory statements regarding the teaching of multiple references, standing alone, are not 'evidence.'" *Dembiczak*, 175 F.3d at 999, 50 USPQ 2d at 1617. The district court provides no support for its broad conclusory statement that it was known in the art that a carbon bed, as used in the Houghton process, would produce water with high levels of conductivity caused by the presence of ionic contaminants. Nor does the district court then provide support for its implicit finding that given water so contaminated, it would be obvious to one of ordinary skill in the art to place a mixed bed ion exchange resin downstream of the carbon bed. In fact, nowhere does the district court particularly identify any suggestion, teaching, or motivation to combine the Houghton process with a mixed bed ion exchange resin to achieve the patented process.

48. ***Winner Int'l Royalty Corp. v. Wang***, 53 USPQ 2d 1580, 1587 & n.8 (Fed. Cir.), ***cert. denied***, 530 U.S. 1238 (2000)

[O]ne of ordinary skill in the art would not have reasonably elected trading the benefit of security for that of convenience. Trade-offs often concern what is feasible, not what is, on balance, desirable. Motivation to combine requires the latter. . . . The fact that the motivating benefit comes at the expense of another benefit, however, should not nullify its use as a basis to modify the disclosure of one reference with the teachings of another. Instead, the benefits, both lost and gained, should be weighed against one another.

V.B.   *Arguing Nonobviousness*

1. ***Ex parte Hiyamizu***, 10 USPQ 2d 1393, 1394–95 (B.P.A.I. 1988)

   Under 35 U.S.C. 103 where the examiner has relied on the teachings of several references, the test is whether or not the references viewed individually and collectively would have suggested the claimed invention to the person possessing ordinary skill in the art. It is to be noted, however, that citing references which merely indicate that isolated elements and/or features recited in the claims are known is not a sufficient basis for concluding that the combination of claimed elements would have been obvious. . . . Furthermore, it is well settled that where the claimed invention solves a problem, the discovery of the source of the problem and its solution are considered to be part of the "invention as a whole" under 35 U.S.C. 103.

2. ***In re Grasselli***, 218 USPQ 769, 779 (Fed. Cir. 1983)

   Accordingly, that comparison . . . which shows that the 15 catalyst outperformed the others . . . is evidence of unexpected superiority. This comparison, and the conclusion based thereon, is the ultimate extension of the "indirect showing of unexpected superiority" sanctioned by precedent.

3. ***Akzo N.V. v. United States Int'l Trade Comm'n***, 1 USPQ 2d 1241, 1246 (Fed. Cir. 1986), ***cert. denied***, 482 U.S. 909 (1987)

   [P]rior art references before the tribunal must be read as a whole and consideration must be given where the references diverge and teach away from the claimed invention. . . . Moreover, appellants cannot pick and choose among individual parts of assorted prior art references "as a mosaic to recreate a facsimile of the claimed invention."

4. ***Lear Siegler, Inc. v. Aeroquip Corp.***, 221 USPQ 1025, 1033 (Fed. Cir. 1984)

   [A]lthough *Graham v. John Deere Co.* . . . requires that certain factual inquiries, among them the differences between the prior art and the claimed invention, be conducted to support a determination of the issue of obviousness, the actual determination of the issue requires an evaluation in the light of the findings in those inquiries of the obviousness of the claimed invention as whole, not merely the differences between the claimed invention and the prior art.

5. ***W.L. Gore & Assocs., Inc. v. Garlock, Inc.***, 220 USPQ 303, 312–13 (Fed. Cir. 1983), ***cert. denied***, 469 U.S. 851 (1984)

To imbue one of ordinary skill in the art with knowledge of the invention in suit, when no prior art reference or references of record convey or suggest that knowledge, is to fall victim to the insidious effect of a hindsight syndrome wherein that which only the inventor taught is used against its teacher.

6. ***Ex parte Skinner***, 2 USPQ 2d 1788, 1790 (B.P.A.I. 1986)

When the incentive to combine the teachings of the references is not readily apparent, it is the duty of the examiner to explain why combination of the reference teachings is proper. . . . Absent such reasons or incentives, the teachings of the references are not combinable. We reverse the examiner's rejection.

7. ***In re Fritch***, 23 USPQ 2d 1780, 1783–84 (Fed. Cir. 1992)

"Obviousness cannot be established by combining the teachings of the prior art to produce the claimed invention, absent some teaching or suggestion supporting the combination. Under section 103, teachings of references can be combined *only* if there is some suggestion or incentive to do so." (quoting *ACS Hosp. Systems, Inc. v. Montefiore Hosp.*, 732 F.2d 1572, 1577, 221 USPQ 929, 933 (Fed. Cir. 1984)). . . . The mere fact that the prior art may be modified in the manner suggested by the Examiner does not make the modification obvious unless the prior art suggested the desirability of the modification.

8. ***In re Fritch***, 23 USPQ 2d 1780, 1784 (Fed. Cir. 1992)

It is impermissible to use the claimed invention as an instruction manual or "template" to piece together the teachings of the prior art so that the claimed invention is rendered obvious. This court has previously stated that "[o]ne cannot use hindsight reconstruction to pick and choose among isolated disclosures in the prior art to deprecate the claimed invention." (quoting *In re Fine*, 837 F.2d 1071, 1075, 5 USPQ 2d 1596, 1600 (Fed. Cir. 1988)).

9. ***Panduit Corp. v. Dennison Mfg. Co.***, 1 USPQ 2d 1593, 1600 (Fed. Cir.), ***cert. denied***, 481 U.S. 1052 (1987)

Though technology has burgeoned, the patent system is not limited to sophisticated technologies and powerful corporations. Nowhere in the statute or the Constitution is the patent system opened only to those who make complex inventions difficult for judges to understand and foreclosed to those who make less mysterious inventions a judge can understand after hearing, as here, the inventor's explanation of his invention and the engineering principles he employed. The constitutional purpose is to encourage disclosure of patentable contributions to "progress in the useful arts", all the useful arts, not just the esoteric. The statute requires utility, novelty and nonobviousness, not complexity.

10. ***In re Wright***, 6 USPQ 2d 1959, 1962 (Fed. Cir. 1988), ***overruled in part by In re Dillon***, 16 USPQ 2d 1897 (Fed. Cir. 1990), ***cert. denied***, 500 U.S. 904 (1991)

Applicant Wright agrees that he has combined old elements. The Commissioner agrees that Wright has achieved a new combination, and that the result obtained thereby is not suggested in the references. The patentability of such combinations is of ancient authority . . . ; see also H.T. Markey, *Why Not the Statute?*, 65 J. Pat. Off. Soc'y 331, 333–34 (1983) ("virtually all inventions are 'combinations', and . . . every invention is formed of 'old elements'. . . . Only God works from nothing. Man must work with old elements").

11. ***In re Mills***, 16 USPQ 2d 1430, 1432–33 (Fed. Cir. 1990)

We are here . . . facing an obviousness issue. It is not pertinent whether the prior art device possess the functional characteristics of the claimed invention if the reference does not describe or suggest its structure.

12. ***In re Kuehl***, 177 USPQ 250, 253 (C.C.P.A. 1973)

Assuming the existence, at the time of the invention, of general-purpose digital computers as well as typical programming techniques therefor, it is nevertheless plain that appellants' invention, as defined in apparatus claim 10, was not obvious under 35 U.S.C. 103 because one not having knowledge of appellants' discovery simply would not know what to program the computer to do.

13. ***Ex parte King***, 146 USPQ 590, 591 (Pat. Off. Bd. App. 1964)

From the examiner's detailed application of the reference to each of the claims on appeal to which reference is made it appears that apparatus operating on particular stored data through a particular stored program is regarded by him as patentably no different than a computer, absent such data and program. In other words, if the difference between a general purpose computer and the claims to a special purpose computer can be supplied by merely placing a suitable program in a general purpose machine then the examiner would deny a patent even though the art contained no suggestion for the preparation of such a program. We do not agree. To deny patent protection to a novel structure it must be shown that the same was obvious at the time the invention was made. A program for a computer which is not made obvious by the prior art but only by appellants' disclosure is not available to teach appellants' invention.

14. ***Fromson v. Advance Offset Plate, Inc.***, 225 USPQ 26, 31 (Fed. Cir. 1985)

That each "element" was old at the time the invention was made was undisputed in the PTO, at trial, and before this court. There is no basis in the law, however, for treating combinations of old elements differently in determining patentability. . . .

The critical inquiry is whether "there is something in the prior art as a whole to suggest the desirability, and thus the obviousness, of making the combination." *Lindemann Maschinenfabrik GmbH v. American Hoist & Derrick Co.*, 730 F.2d at 1462, 221 USPQ at 488.

15. ***In re Nomiya***, 184 USPQ 607, 612 (C.C.P.A. 1975)

It should not be necessary for this court to point out that a patentable invention may lie in the discovery of the source of a problem even though the remedy may be obvious once the source of the problem is identified. This is part of the "subject matter as a whole" which should always be considered in determining the obviousness of an invention under 35 U.S.C. 103.

16. ***In re Bisley***, 94 USPQ 80, 86–87 (C.C.P.A. 1952)

Moreover, the conception of a new and useful improvement must be considered along with the actual means of achieving it in determining the presence or absence of invention. . . . The discovery of a problem calling for an improvement is often a very essential element in an invention correcting such a problem; and though the problem, once realized, may be solved by use of old and known elements, this does not necessarily negative invention.

17. ***In re Ichihashi***, Civ. App. No. 93-1172, slip op. at 2–3 (Fed. Cir. Sept. 9, 1993) (unpublished)

No evidence, either of additional art, or supplementary evidence of what one of ordinary skill would have understood at the time the application was filed, was cited by the board in support of this assertion. . . . Nowhere in the board's opinion are there any findings as to the level of ordinary skill in the relevant art, or any examples, either from the single prior art reference or otherwise of an implementation of a route table. . . . [T]here remains no indication in the record that one of ordinary skill would find any motivation in the prior art to place the route table/switch unit in the position specified by the claims, thus allowing a communication device to function with a single transmitting-receiving unit.

At oral argument, the solicitor conceded that there was nothing in the board's opinion or the record before this court to support such motivation, other than the bald assertion by the board that it would have been obvious. In the absence of some evidence of the level of ordinary skill, including evidence tending to show what one of such ordinary skill would be motivated to accomplish in view of the cited prior art, the board may not rest a prima facie case only on its own unsupported assertions.

18. ***In re Blamer***, Civ. App. No. 93-1108, slip op. at 3–4 (Fed. Cir. Sept. 21, 1993) (unpublished)

The examiner concluded that applicant's invention would have been obvious in light of twelve references. The Board correctly stated that the examiner's reliance on so many references was "overkill" and concluded that applicant's invention would have been obvious in light of four of the references. We agree with the Board on the former statement, but disagree with the latter. What both the examiner and Board have done is to cite a number of references variously containing some of the limitations in applicant's claims. However, these references and the limitations for which they were cited were combined piecemeal without any suggestion or motivation for their combination and without regard to the purpose of applicant's invention. . . .

The problem addressed by applicant's invention is how to incorporate a microwave susceptor at a location in a bag structure which would be effective for cooking the contents without significantly adding to the cost or complexity of the overall bag manufacturing process. Applicant's solution to this problem was to print a metallized area on an unexposed surface of the bag as part of the overall bag printing process during the manufacture of the popcorn bags. . . .

What is lacking, given a fair reading of the references as a whole, is any teaching which would lead one skilled in the art to use the alternative teachings, either separately or in combination, to reduce the cost of manufacturing popcorn bags by printing a susceptor onto an unexposed surface of the bag during the manufacturing of the bags. In the absence of such teaching, we cannot agree that the claimed invention is rendered obvious by the cited combination of references.

19. ***Demaco Corp. v. F. Von Langsdorff Licensing Ltd.***, 7 USPQ 2d 1222, 1224–25 (Fed. Cir.), ***cert. denied***, 488 U.S. 956 (1988)

The patent statute does not require that a patentable invention be superior to all prior devices. . . . Nor does the patent statute require that an invention be complex in order to be nonobvious.

20. ***In re Debus***, Civ. App. No. 93-1320, slip op. at 3 (Fed. Cir. Dec. 10, 1993) (unpublished)

"The mere fact that the prior art may be modified in the manner suggested by the Examiner does not make the modification obvious unless the prior art suggested the desirability of the modification." *In re Fritch*, 972 F.2d 1260, 1266, 23 USPQ 2d 1780, 1783–84 (Fed. Cir. 1992) . . . .

The beveling on applicants' page holder is not merely ornamental; it is there because applicants have found that it makes page turning easier. Thus, this feature of applicants' invention, which is expressed both structurally and functionally in the claim, cannot be ignored. The claimed invention may in hindsight be a simple improvement but the test for obviousness is not the simplicity of the improvement.

21. ***In re Sponnoble***, 160 USPQ 237, 243 (C.C.P.A. 1969)

It should not be necessary for this court to point out that a patentable invention may lie in the discovery of the source of a problem even though the remedy may be obvious once the source of the problem is identified. This is part of the "subject matter as a whole" which should always be considered in determining the obviousness of an invention under 35 U.S.C. 103. . . . The court must be ever alert not to read obviousness into an invention on the basis of the applicant's own statements; that is, we must view the prior art without reading into that art appellant's teachings. . . . The issue, then, is whether the teachings of the prior art would, in and of themselves and without the benefits of appellant's disclosure, make the invention as a whole, obvious.

22. ***In re Nomiya***, 184 USPQ 607, 613 (C.C.P.A. 1975)

There must, however, be a reason apparent at the time the invention was made to the person of ordinary skill in the art for applying the teaching at hand, or the use of the teaching as evidence of obviousness will entail prohibited hindsight.

23. ***In re Lowry***, 32 USPQ 2d 1031, 1035 (Fed. Cir. 1994)

Kumpati does not, however, disclose Lowry's ADOs and their specific hierarchical and non-hierarchical relationships. More specifically, Kumpati does not disclose the claimed pyramidal arrangement of hierarchically arranged ADOs, complete with apex ADO. Kumpati's relationship sets are different from Lowry's relation data objects, having non-hierarchical relationships with other ADOs. Neither are Kumpati's "attributes," performing a mapping function, equivalent to Lowry's ADOs, containing information used by the application program as well as information regarding its interrelationships with other ADOs.

Lowry's claimed invention involves an organization of information and its interrelationships which Kumpati neither discloses nor suggests. Kumpati also does not render Lowry's claims obvious. The Board erred in holding otherwise. Claims 1 through 19 are, as a whole, not obvious in light of Kumpati.

24. ***In re Chu***, 36 USPQ 2d 1089, 1094–95 (Fed. Cir. 1995)

Additionally, the Board erred in apparently requiring Chu's evidence and arguments responsive to the obviousness rejection to be within his specification in order to be considered. To require Chu to include evidence and arguments in the specification . . . would be to require patent applicants to divine the rejections the PTO will proffer when patent applications are filed. . . . There is no logical support for such a proposition as well, given that obviousness is determined by the totality of the record including, in some instances most significantly, the evidence and arguments proffered during the give-and-take of ex parte patent prosecution.

25. ***In re Chu***, 36 USPQ 2d 1089, 1095 (Fed. Cir. 1995)

Chu's technical evidence relating to the frailty of fabric filters during pulse-jet cleaning clearly counters the assertion that placement of the catalyst in the baghouse is merely a "design choice." Specifically, Chu's evidence regarding the violent "snapping" action during pulse-jet cleaning, the difficulty in stitching compartments including the capacity to withstand high temperatures, and problems encountered from variable path lengths due to settling of the catalyst particles in each compartment militates against a conclusion that placement of the SCR catalyst is merely a "design choice." See *In re Gal*, 980 F.2d 717, 25 USPQ2d 1076 (Fed. Cir. 1992) (finding of "obvious design choice" precluded where the claimed structure and the function it performs are different from the prior art).

26. ***Micro Chem., Inc. v. Great Plains Chem. Co.***, 41 USPQ 2d 1238, 1245 (Fed. Cir.), ***cert. denied***, 521 U.S. 1122 (1997)

Pratt's extensive efforts to solve the problem of isolating the weighing system indicate the absence of a suggestion to combine the Brewster machine with the positive intermixing elements of the volume machines. See *In re Dow Chem. Co.*, 837 F.2d 469, 473, 5 USPQ 2d 1529, 1532 (Fed. Cir. 1988) (stating that the "five to six years of research that pre-

ceded the claimed invention" was entitled to fair evidentiary
weight in a determination of nonobviousness). These efforts
by Pratt tend to show that one skilled in the art would have
had no reasonable expectation of success in combining the
prior art machines in question.

27. ***In re Zurko***, 42 USPQ 2d 1476, 1479 (Fed. Cir.), ***rehearing
    in banc granted,*** 116 F.3d 874 (Fed. Cir. 1997), ***rev'd on
    other grounds***, ***Dickinson v. Zurko***, 50 USPQ 2d 1930,
    1931–32 (U.S. 1999)

[T]o say that the missing step comes from the nature of the
problem to be solved begs the question because the Board
has failed to show that this problem had been previously
identified anywhere in the prior art. *See In re Sponnable*,
405 F.2d 578, 585, 160 USPQ 237, 243 (CCPA 1969) ("[A]
patentable invention may lie in the discovery of the source
of a problem even though the remedy may be obvious once
the source of the problem is identified.").

28. ***Arkie Lures, Inc. v. Gene Larew Tackle, Inc.***, 43 USPQ
    2d 1294, 1296 (Fed. Cir. 1997)

It is insufficient to establish obviousness that the separate
elements of the invention existed in the prior art, absent
some teaching or suggestion, in the prior art, to combine the
elements. Indeed, the years of use of salty bait and of plastic
lures, without combining their properties, weighs on the side
of unobviousness of the combination. Mr. Larew persisted
against the accepted wisdom, and succeeded. The evidence
that the combination was not viewed as technically feasible
must be considered, for conventional wisdom that a combination should not be made is evidence of unobviousness.

29. ***In re Sponnoble***, 160 USPQ 237, 243–244 (C.C.P.A. 1969)

A patentable invention, within the ambit of 35 USC 103,
may result even if the inventor has, in effect, merely combined features, old in the art, for their known purpose, without producing anything beyond the results inherent in their
use.

It should not be necessary for this court to point out that
a patentable invention may lie in the discovery of the source
of a problem even though the remedy may be obvious once
the source of the problem is identified. This is part of the
"subject matter as a whole" which should always be considered in determining the obviousness of an invention under
35 USC 103. . . . The court must be ever alert not to read obviousness into an invention on the basis of the applicant's
own statements; that is, we must view the prior art without
reading into that art appellant's teachings.

30. ***Fromson v. Anitec Printing Plates, Inc.***, 45 USPQ 2d 1269, 1276 (Fed. Cir. 1997), ***cert. denied,*** 525 U.S. 817 (1998)

That an inventor has probed the strengths and weaknesses of the prior art and discovered an improvement that escaped those who came before is indicative of unobviousness, not obviousness. The district court did not correctly apply the law of obviousness . . . .

31. ***Union Carbide Corp. v. American Can Co.***, 220 USPQ 584, 591 & n.6 (Fed. Cir. 1984) (quotations omitted)

The starting place for determining the issue of obviousness is . . . with the inventor working in his shop with the prior art references—which he is presumed to know—hanging on the walls around him. No other evidence was in the Winslow case, and nothing more in the way of evidence was there to be considered in determining obviousness. Here, however, our inquiry cannot merely stop with the prior art . . . on the wall. Only after consideration of all evidence, including that with respect to "secondary considerations," can obviousness be judged. . . . [T]he prior art on the wall consists only of those patents one of ordinary skill in the art would have selected without the advantage of hindsight or knowledge of the invention.

32. ***In re Carroll***, 202 USPQ 571, 572 (C.C.P.A. 1979) (quoting ***Graham v. John Deere Co.,*** 383 U.S. 1, 36 (1965))

One of the more difficult aspects of resolving questions of non-obviousness is the necessity "to guard against slipping into use of hindsight." . . . Many inventions may seem obvious to everyone after they have been made. However, 35 USC 103 instructs us to inquire into whether the claimed invention "would have been obvious at the time the invention was made to a person having ordinary skill in the art to which said subject matter pertains." Thus, in deciding the issue of obviousness, we must look at the prior art presented from a vantage point in time prior to when the invention was made, and through the eyes of a hypothetical person of ordinary skill in the art.

33. ***Al-Site Corp. v. VSI Int'l, Inc.***, 50 USPQ 2d 1161, 1171 (Fed. Cir. 1999)

VSI is unable, however, to point to any specific teaching or suggestion for making this combination. VSI instead relies on what it presumes is the level of knowledge of one of ordinary skill in the art at the time of the invention to supply the missing suggestion to combine. In the first place, the level of skill in the art is a prism or lens through which a

judge or jury views the prior art and the claimed invention.
This reference point prevents these deciders from using
their own insight or, worse yet, hindsight, to gauge obviousness. Rarely, however, will the skill in the art component operate to supply missing knowledge or prior art to reach an
obviousness judgment. . . . Skill in the art does not act as a
bridge over gaps in substantive presentation of an obviousness case, but instead supplies the primary guarantee of objectivity in the process.

34. ***Smiths Indus. Med. Sys., Inc. v. Vital Signs, Inc.***, 51
    USPQ 2d 1415, 1420–21 (Fed. Cir. 1999)

    [T]here is no basis for concluding that an invention would
    have been obvious solely because it is a combination of ele-
    ments that were known in the art at the time of the inven-
    tion. . . . Instead, the relevant inquiry is whether there is a
    reason, suggestion, or motivation in the prior art that would
    lead one of ordinary skill in the art to combine the refer-
    ences, and that would also suggest a reasonable likelihood
    of success. . . . Such a suggestion or motivation may come
    from the references themselves, from knowledge by those
    skilled in the art that certain references are of special inter-
    est in a field, or even from the nature of the problem to be
    solved.

35. ***Interactive Techs., Inc. v. Pittway Corp.***, Civ. App. No.
    98-1464, slip op. at 13 (Fed. Cir. June 1, 1999) (unpublished),
    cert. denied, 528 U.S. 1046 (1999).

    [A] general relationship between the fields does not suggest
    a motivation to combine the particular references.

36. ***In re Dembiczak***, 50 USPQ 2d 1614, 1616–17 (Fed. Cir.
    1999) (quotations omitted)

    Our analysis begins in the text of section 103 quoted above,
    with the phrase "at the time the invention was made." For it
    is this phrase that guards against entry into the tempting
    but forbidden zone of hindsight, . . . when analyzing the pat-
    entability of claims pursuant to that section. Measuring a
    claimed invention against the standard established by sec-
    tion 103 requires the oft-difficult but critical step of casting
    the mind back to the time of invention, to consider the think-
    ing of one of ordinary skill in the art, guided only by the prior
    art references and the then-accepted wisdom in the field. . . .
    Close adherence to this methodology is especially important
    in the case of less technologically complex inventions, where
    the very ease with which the invention can be understood
    may prompt one to fall victim to the insidious effect of a hind-
    sight syndrome wherein that which only the inventor taught

is used against its teacher. . . . In this case, the Board fell into the hindsight trap. . . . The range of sources available, however, does not diminish the requirement for actual evidence. That is, the showing must be clear and particular.

Our case law makes clear that the best defense against the subtle but powerful attraction of a hindsight-based obviousness analysis is rigorous application of the requirement for a showing of the teaching or motivation to combine prior art references.

37. ***Hockerson-Halberstadt, Inc. v. Avia Group Int'l, Inc.***, 55 USPQ 2d 1487, 1491 (Fed. Cir. 2000)

Under our precedent, however, it is well established that patent drawings do not define the precise proportions of the elements and may not be relied on to show particular sizes if the specification is completely silent on the issue. *See In re Wright*, 569 F.2d 1124, 1127, 193 USPQ 332, 335 (CCPA 1977) ("Absent any written description in the specification of quantitative values, arguments based on measurement of a drawing are of little value."); *In re Olson*, 212 F.2d 590, 592, 101 USPQ 401, 402 (CCPA 1954); cf. Manual of Patent Examining Procedure Section 2125 (1998).

38. ***Ecolochem, Inc. v. Southern Cal. Edison Co.***, 56 USPQ 2d 1065, 1079 (Fed. Cir. 2000)

"The fact of near-simultaneous invention, though not determinative of statutory obviousness, is strong evidence of what constitutes the level of ordinary skill in the art." *The Int'l Glass Co. v. United States*, 187 Ct. Cl. 376, 408 F.2d 395, 405 (Ct. Cl. 1969). "The possibility of near simultaneous invention by two or more equally talented inventors working independently, . . . may or may not be an indication of obviousness when considered in light of all the circumstances." Lindemann, 730 F.2d at 1460, 221 USPQ at 487. . . . The issue of simultaneous invention is directly tied to the level of knowledge attributable to one of ordinary skill in the art.

39. ***Hockerson-Halberstadt, Inc. v. Avia Group Int'l, Inc.***, 55 USPQ 2d 1487, 1491 (Fed. Cir. 2000)

Under our precedent, however, it is well established that patent drawings do not define the precise proportions of the elements and may not be relied on to show particular sizes if the specification is completely silent on the issue. *See In re Wright*, 569 F.2d 1124, 1127, 193 USPQ 332, 335 (CCPA 1977) ("Absent any written description in the specification of quantitative values, arguments based on measurement of a drawing are of little value."); *In re Olson*, 212 F.2d 590, 592, 101 USPQ 401, 402 (CCPA 1954); cf. Manual of Patent Examining Procedure Section 2125 (1998). Thus, in the present case, a reasonable competitor, being aware that figures in a patent are not drawn to scale unless otherwise indicated,

40. ***Helifix Ltd. v. Blok-Lok, Ltd.***, 54 USPQ 2d 1299, 1304 (Fed. Cir. 2000)

"[E]ven if the claimed invention is disclosed in a printed publication, that disclosure will not suffice as prior art if it was not enabling." *Donohoe*, 766 F.2d at 533, 226 USPQ at 621.

41. ***In re Ductmate Industries, Inc.***, Reexamination Control Number 90/004,369, U.S. Patent 4,584,756, p.4 (Comm'r Feb. 12, 1997)

While catalogs may, by their nature, be intended to be widely disseminated, the documents submitted as Exhibits 1 and 2 do not, on their face, show such dissemination. They do not show that access to these documents was unrestricted. They do not even clearly and unequivocally show publication dates. And they do not show that in the absence of distribution, they were so indexed and catalogued that a person of ordinary skill in the art interested in obtaining a copy, could have done so. *In re Hall*, 228 USPQ 453 (Fed. Cir. 1986); *In re Cronym*, 13 USPQ 2d 1070 (Fed. Cir. 1989).

V.C. *Improper Standards*

1. ***In re Wood***, 202 USPQ 171, 174 (C.C.P.A. 1979)

The test for obviousness is not whether the features of one reference may be bodily incorporated into another reference. . . . Rather, we look to see whether combined teachings render the claimed subject matter obvious.

2. ***In re Lindell***, 155 USPQ 521, 523 (C.C.P.A. 1967)

Accordingly, we have criticized the "obvious to try" test on several recent occasions. . . .

Furthermore, application of the "obvious to try" test would often deny patent protection to inventions growing out of well-planned research which is, of course, guided into those areas in which success is deemed most likely. These are, perhaps, the obvious areas to try. But resulting inventions are not necessarily obvious. Serendipity is not a prerequisite to patentability. Our view is that "obvious to try" is not a sufficiently discriminatory test.

3. ***In re Geiger***, 2 USPQ 2d 1276, 1278 (Fed. Cir. 1987)

At best, in view of these disclosures, one skilled in the art might find it obvious to try various combinations of these known scale and corrosion prevention agents. However, this is not the standard of 35 U.S.C. §103.

4. **In re Spormann**, 150 USPQ 449, 452 (C.C.P.A. 1966)

[The] inherency of an advantage and its obviousness are entirely different questions. That which may be inherent is not necessarily known. Obviousness cannot be predicated on what is unknown.

5. **Ex parte Levengood**, 28 USPQ 2d 1300, 1301–02 (B.P.A.I. 1993)

The examiner notes that each reference discloses a different aspect of the claimed process. The examiner also notes that all aspects were "well known in the art." The examiner then indicates that because the various aspects of the claimed process were individually known in the art, the modifications of the electrophoretic process of Levengood by exposing Levengood's plant materials to cell-associated materials in order to "graft" or otherwise incorporate the cell associated material into the plants was "well within the ordinary skill of the art at the time the claimed invention was made."

We reverse the rejection because the examiner has used the wrong standard of obviousness. . . . At best, the examiner's comments regarding obviousness amount to an assertion that one of ordinary skill in the relevant art would have been able to arrive at appellant's invention because he had the necessary skills to carry out the requisite process steps. This is an inappropriate standard for obviousness. . . . That which is within the capabilities of one skilled in the art is not synonymous with obviousness. . . . That one can reconstruct and/or explain the theoretical mechanism of an invention by means of logic and sound scientific reasoning does not afford the basis for an obviousness conclusion unless that logic and reasoning also supplies sufficient impetus to have led one of ordinary skill in the art to combine the teachings of the references to make the claimed invention. . . .

Accordingly, an examiner cannot establish obviousness by locating references which describe various aspects of a patent applicant's invention without also providing evidence of the motivating force which would impel one skilled in the art to do what the patent applicant has done.

6. **Ex parte Goldgaber**, 41 USPQ 2d 1172, 1177 (B.P.A.I. 1996) (quoting **In re Eli Lilly and Co.**, 14 USPQ 2d 1741, 1743 (Fed. Cir. 1990))

In *Deuel*, . . . the court emphasizes that "obvious to try" is not the standard under 35 USC 103. As stated in *In re Eli Lilly and Co.*, . . .

An "obvious-to-try" situation exists when a general disclosure may pique the scientist's curiosity, such that further investigation might be done as a result of the disclosure, but the disclosure itself does not contain a sufficient teaching of how to obtain the desired result, or that the claimed result would be obtained if certain directions were pursued.

7. ***Monarch Knitting Mach. Corp. v. Sulzer Morat GmbH***, 45 USPQ 2d 1977, 1981 (Fed. Cir. 1998)

Given the occasional use of archaic terminology in the district court's opinion, this court also emphasizes that the standard for patentability is the statutory standard. The inquiry is not whether there was a "real discovery of merit" or whether the claimed invention offered a "new solution," but whether the claimed subject matter as a whole "would have been obvious at the time the invention was made to a person having ordinary skill in the art." 35 U.S.C. § 103(a) (Supp. I 1995).

V.D. *Level of Ordinary Skill*

1. ***In re Gentile***, Civ. App. No. 93-1086, slip op. at 5 n.1 (Fed. Cir. Oct. 5, 1993) (unpublished)

As the Board made no specific finding as to the level of ordinary skill in the art, we assume it to be that of a mechanic of ordinary skill. "[A]n invention may be held to have been either obvious (or nonobvious) without a specific finding of a particular level of skill . . . where, as here, the prior art itself reflects an appropriate level. . . ." *Chore-Time Equipment v. Cumberland*, 713 F.2d 774, 779, n.2, 218 USPQ 673, 676, n.2 (Fed. Cir. 1983).

2. ***In re Wertheim***, 191 USPQ 90, 98 (C.C.P.A. 1976)

The Pfluger patent-disclosure is also unavailable to appellants. The Swiss application was filed before Pfluger issued, which means that for the purposes of §112 the Pfluger disclosure is not evidence of what those skilled in the art considered conventional at the time the Swiss application was filed.

3. ***Ex parte Rodgers***, 27 USPQ 2d 1738, 1747 (B.P.A.I. 1992)

Although Mr. Colaianni's credentials as a patent expert are not open to question, there is nothing in his affidavit which establishes any expertise in the relevant art so as to render competent his opinions as to what one of ordinary skill in the art would know or do. The affidavit is, therefore, of no probative value on the question of obviousness.

4. ***Custom Accessories Inc. v. Jeffrey-Allan Indus.***, 1 USPQ 2d 1196, 1201 (Fed. Cir. 1986)

The person of ordinary skill is a hypothetical person who is presumed to be aware of all the pertinent prior art. The actual inventor's skill is not determinative. Factors that may be considered in determining level of skill include: type of problems encountered in art; prior art solutions to those problems; rapidity with which innovations are made; sophistication of the technology; and education level of active workers in the field. Not all such factors may be present in every case, and one or more of them may predominate. [Citations omitted.]

5. ***Ex parte Anderson***, 21 USPQ 2d 1241, 1254 (B.P.A.I. 1991)

In considering the issue of obviousness raised in each rejection, we find that the level of ordinary skill in this art is adequately represented by the disclosures of the various references relied upon in the rejections.

6. ***Standard Oil Co. v. American Cyanamid Co.***, 227 USPQ 293, 297 (Fed. Cir. 1985)

The issue of obviousness is determined entirely with reference to a hypothetical "person having ordinary skill in the art." It is only that hypothetical person who is presumed to be aware of all the pertinent prior art. The actual inventor's skill is irrelevant to the inquiry, and this is for a very important reason. The statutory emphasis is on a person of *ordinary* skill. Inventors, as a class, according to the concepts underlying the Constitution and the statues that have created the patent system, possess something—call it what you will—which sets them apart from the workers of *ordinary* skill, and one should not go about determining obviousness under §103 by inquiring into what *patentees* (i.e., inventors) would have known or would likely have done, faced with the revelations of references. A person of ordinary skill in the art is also presumed to be one who thinks along the line of conventional wisdom in the art and is not one who undertakes to innovate, whether by patient, and often expensive, systematic research or by extraordinary insights, it makes no difference which.

7. ***De Graffenried v. United States***, 16 USPQ 2d 1321, 1334 (Cl. Ct. 1990)

The parties disagree as to the level of ordinary skill in the art. Plaintiff argues that since the Arsenal is the sole manufacturer of large cannon barrels in the United States, the place to look when assessing the level of ordinary skill in the art is to Arsenal employees. Plaintiff notes that Arsenal employees with pertinent responsibility in cannon manufacture had no college education but significant practice experience with reamers used at the Arsenal for deep boring gun barrels. But it is incorrect to view the controller patent as narrowly involving the manufacture of large cannons. Rather, the controller patent is directed at the design of a machine tool employing a control system to control runout in deep boring operations. All relevant evidence considered . . . , defendant is correct that the pertinent level of ordinary skill in the art in early 1961 was an individual with a bachelor of science degree in electrical engineering with four years of machine tool design experience.

8. ***Endress + Hauser, Inc. v. Hawk Measurement Sys. Pty. Ltd.***, 43 USPQ 2d 1849, 1851 (Fed. Cir. 1997)

The "person of ordinary skill in the art" is a theoretical construct used in determining obviousness under § 103, and is not descriptive of some particular individual. . . . To suggest that the construct applies to particular individuals could mean that a person of *exceptional* skill in the art would be disqualified from testifying as an expert because not ordinary enough.

9. ***Arkie Lures, Inc. v. Gene Larew Tackle, Inc.***, 43 USPQ 2d 1294, 1296 (Fed. Cir. 1997)

The decision of obviousness *vel non* is made not from the viewpoint of the inventor, but from the viewpoint of a person of ordinary skill in the field of the invention. . . . The purpose is to assure an appropriate perspective of the decision-maker, and to focus on conditions as they existed when the invention was made. Good ideas may well appear "obvious" after they have been disclosed, despite having been previously unrecognized.

10. ***Ex parte Lemoine***, 46 USPQ 2d 1420, 1425 (B.P.A.I.), *reconsideration granted in part*, 46 USPQ 2d 1432 (B.P.A.I. 1998) (unpublished)

The person of ordinary skill in the art is presumed to know something about the art apart from what the references expressly disclose. *In re Jacoby*, 309 F.2d 513, 516, 135 USPQ 317, 319 (C.C.P.A. 1962).

11. ***In re Rouffet***, 47 USPQ 2d 1453, 1457 (Fed. Cir. 1998)

Obviousness is determined from the vantage point of a hypothetical person having ordinary skill in the art to which the patent pertains. *See* 35 U.S.C. § 103(a). This legal construct is akin to the "reasonable person" used as a reference in negligence determinations. The legal construct also presumes that all prior art references in the field of the invention are available to this hypothetical skilled artisan.

12. ***Multiform Desiccants, Inc. v. Medzam, Ltd.***, 45 USPQ 2d 1429, 1432 (Fed. Cir. 1998)

It is the person of ordinary skill in the field of the invention through whose eyes the claims are construed. Such person is deemed to read the words used in the patent documents with an understanding of their meaning in the field, and to have knowledge of any special meaning and usage in the field. The inventor's words that are used to describe the invention—the inventor's lexicography—must be understood and interpreted by the court as they would be understood and interpreted by a person in that field of technology. Thus the court starts the decisionmaking process by reviewing the same resources as would that person, *viz.*, the patent specification and the prosecution history. These documents have legal as well as technological content, for they show not only the framework of the invention as viewed by the inventor, but also the issues of patentability as viewed by the patent examiner.

13. ***Enzo Biochem, Inc. v. Calgene, Inc.***, 52 USPQ 2d 1129, 1137 (Fed. Cir. 1999) (quoting ***In re Naquin***, 158 USPQ 317, 319 (C.C.P.A. 1968))

We recognize that the field of genetics is highly specialized, and further acknowledge the well-established rule that "when an invention, in its different aspects, involves distinct arts, that specification is adequate which enables the adepts of each art, those who have the best chance of being enabled, to carry out the aspect proper to their specialty." . . . However, the "research associates" who conducted the failed experiments, all of whom possessed the requisite level of skill in the art, could hardly be characterized as mere laboratory technicians. We do not think it unreasonable that these highly trained researchers were found to have possessed a sufficient level of expertise to conduct experiments in organisms other than E. coli. Indeed, it defies common sense that Inouye would waste valuable resources conducting experiments in other organisms had he not believed that his research associates possessed sufficient skill to perform them.

14. ***Helifix Ltd. v. Blok-Lok, Ltd.***, 54 USPQ 2d 1299, 1304 (Fed. Cir. 2000)

The district court should not have constructed the hypothetical person of ordinary skill in the art by determining which persons working in the field of the invention are likely to be familiar with the relevant literature. Instead, the court should have considered the educational level of the inventor; the type of problems encountered in the art; the prior art solutions to those problems; the rapidity with which innovations are made; the sophistication of the technology, and the educational level of workers in the field.

15. ***Ecolochem, Inc. v. Southern Cal. Edison Co.***, 56 USPQ 2d 1065, 1079 (Fed. Cir. 2000)

"The fact of near-simultaneous invention, though not determinative of statutory obviousness, is strong evidence of what constitutes the level of ordinary skill in the art." The Int'l Glass Co. v. United States, 187 Ct. Cl. 376, 408 F.2d 395, 405 (Ct. Cl. 1969). "The possibility of near simultaneous invention by two or more equally talented inventors working independently, . . . may or may not be an indication of obviousness when considered in light of all the circumstances." Lindemann, 730 F.2d at 1460, 221 USPQ at 487. . . . The issue of simultaneous invention is directly tied to the level of knowledge attributable to one of ordinary skill in the art.

16. ***Brown & Williamson Tobacco Corp. v. Philip Morris Inc.***, 56 USPQ 2d 1456, 1460 (Fed. Cir. 2000)

[A] person of ordinary skill in the art of cigarette design in 1985 would have had a bachelor's degree in either engineering, chemistry, physics, or chemical engineering, and would have had at least five years experience in the field of cigarette design.

V.E. *Improper Prior Art/Teaching Away*

1. ***United States v. Adams***, 383 U.S. 39, 50 (1966)

An inoperable invention or one which fails to achieve its intended result does not negative novelty.

2. ***Fromson v. Advance Offset Plate, Inc.***, 225 USPQ 26, 33 (Fed. Cir. 1985)

The "failed" experiment reported in the prosecution history of the Mason patent renders that patent irrelevant as a prior art reference. As stated by Judge Learned Hand, "another's experiment, imperfect and never perfected will not serve either as an anticipation or as part of the prior art, for it has not served to enrich it." *Picard v. United Aircraft Corp.*, 128 F.2d 632, 635, 53 USPQ 563, 566 (2d Cir. 1942), *cert. denied*, 317 U.S. 651 (1942).

3. ***United States v. Adams***, 383 U.S. 39, 52 (1966)

We do say, however, that known disadvantages in old devices which would naturally discourage the search for new inventions may be taken into account in determining obviousness.

4. ***In re Worrest***, 96 USPQ 381, 384 (C.C.P.A. 1953)

Although it is a factor to be considered, the mere fact that a reference is 10 to 20 years old does not prevent it from being properly used as a reference, and that in itself is, as a rule, insufficient to indicate the state of the art or the presence of invention.

5. ***In re Van Der Bolt***, Civ. App. No. 92-1517, slip op. at 4–5 (Fed. Cir. Aug. 10, 1993) (unpublished)

Furthermore, Kautz shows that the mask to frame welds are disposed in a manner removed from the assembly corners to provide weld-free "floating" corner sectors. A respective pair of welds, including a terminal weld and a guard weld, are placed on either side of each corner sector in a predetermined manner to inhibit pivotal movement of the sector mask about the terminal points of affixation. The purpose of this configuration is to enhance thermal equilibrium of the floating corner regions to avoid restricting the expansive movement of the mask and frame relative to each other. Thus, Kautz is directed towards solving a completely different problem than Applicant's invention and teaches away from the limitation requiring that two adjacent sides be frictionally engaged by means of a resilient element in an arrangement that causes an asymmetrical load at the corner of the support frame.

6. ***In re Ruff***, 118 USPQ 340, 347 (C.C.P.A. 1958)

To rely on an equivalence known only to the applicant to establish obviousness is to assume that his disclosure is a part of the prior art. The mere statement of this proposition reveals its fallaciousness.

7. ***In re Wertheim***, 191 USPQ 90, 102 (C.C.P.A. 1976)

Applicant's own disclosures can not be used to support a rejection of the claims "absent some admission that matter disclosed in the specification is in the prior art."

8. ***In re Gurley***, 31 USPQ 2d 1130, 1131 (Fed. Cir. 1994)

A reference may be said to teach away when a person of ordinary skill, upon reading the reference, would be discouraged from following the path set out in the reference, or would be led in a direction divergent from the path that was taken by the applicant. The degree of teaching away will of course depend on the particular facts; in general, a reference will teach away if it suggests that the line of development flowing from the reference's disclosure is unlikely to be productive of the result sought by the applicant. *See United States v. Adams*, 383 U.S. 39, 52, 148 USPQ 479, 484 (1966) ("known disadvantages in old devices which would naturally discourage the search for new inventions may be taken into account in determining obviousness").

9. ***Monarch Knitting Mach. Corp. v. Sulzer Morat GmbH***, 45 USPQ 2d 1977, 1984 (Fed. Cir. 1998)

A prior art reference may be considered to teach away when "a person of ordinary skill, upon reading the reference, would be discouraged from following the path set out in the reference, or would be led in a direction divergent from the path that was taken by the applicant." *In re Gurley*, 27 F.3d 551, 553, 31 USPQ 2d 1130, 1131 (Fed. Cir. 1994). General skepticism of those in the art—not amounting to teaching away—is also "relevant and persuasive evidence" of nonobviousness. *Gillette Co. v. S.C. Johnson & Son, Inc.*, 919 F.2d 720, 726, 16 USPQ 2d 1923, 1929 (Fed. Cir. 1990). In effect, "teaching away" is a more pointed and probative form of skepticism expressed in the prior art. In any case, the presence of either of these indicia gives insight into the question of obviousness.

10. ***Tec Air, Inc. v. Denso Mfg. Mich. Inc.***, 52 USPQ 2d 1294, 1298 (Fed. Cir. 1999) (quoting ***In re Sponnoble***, 160 USPQ 237, 244 (C.C.P.A. 1969))

If when combined, the references "would produce a seemingly inoperative device," then they teach away from their combination.

11. ***Tec Air, Inc. v. Denso Mfg. Mich. Inc.***, 52 USPQ 2d 1294, 1298 (Fed. Cir. 1999)

Because, in the brass plug method, the operator drills the brass plugs from the cavity-side of the mold, combining this method with the teachings of the Gelbard patent results in cavity-side accessible screws. The Gelbard patent teaches, however, that each of its adjustable threaded members has "a non-threaded or smooth tip extending into a recess," which comes into contact with the molten plastic. . . . This teaching is consistent with the conventional wisdom as late as 1974, which counseled against arranging screw heads to face the cavity-side of the mold because molten plastic would (1) enter the screw slot, which would be difficult to remove, and (2) likely seep behind the screw head and jam the screw, according to Tec Air's expert, Dr. Williamson. Because the brass plugs-Gelbard patent combination would be inoperable for its intended purpose—no screw driver would be able to turn the smooth-headed screws from the cavity-side of the mold—the jury reasonably could have found that the Gelbard patent taught away from its combination with the brass plug method.

12. ***In re Rudko***, Civ. App. No. 98-1505, slip op. at 5–6 (Fed. Cir. May 14, 1999) (unpublished)

[W]e conclude that Sharon teaches away from a proposed combination with McFee. Whether a reference teaches away from a combination is also a question of fact. . . . Sharon discloses that previous laser surgical scalpels were difficult to manipulate and aim precisely, and Sharon's invention addresses this problem by providing the surgeon with "a clear unobstructed view of [the] working spot," that is, the point at which the laser beam is focused. . . . Sharon also discloses that this feature can be achieved by removing a portion of the laser device tip. . . . Consistent with Sharon's desire to provide a laser handpiece that is easily focused on a working spot, Sharon describes and illustrates numerous embodiments of the laser scalpel tip, all of which are tapered and end in a relatively small point. McFee's second embodiment, on the other hand, shows a flaring end that is significantly larger in diameter at the terminating end, rather than smaller as in Sharon. Such an enlarged end runs counter to Sharon's explicit recital of an unobstructed field of view and an easily manipulable and precisely aimed device. Accordingly, the Board's combination of Sharon with McFee to reject the disputed claims was clear error.

13. ***In re Gurley***, 31 USPQ 2d 1130, 1131 (Fed. Cir. 1994).

A reference will teach away if it suggests that the line of development flowing from the reference's disclosure is unlikely to be productive of the result sought by the applicant.

V.F. Formation of a Trend and Relationship to Obviousness

1. ***Monarch Knitting Mach. Corp. v. Sulzer Morat GmbH***, 45 USPQ 2d 1977, 1981–82 (Fed. Cir. 1998)

The district court based its conclusion of obviousness heavily on its determination that the prior art showed a "trend" towards increasingly lower stem segment heights. A "trend" might very well constitute a suggestion or teaching to one of ordinary skill in the art to make "minor" changes from the prior art in accordance with that trend to produce

the claimed invention. . . . The existence of a trend depends
on the content of the prior art, i.e., what the prior art would
have taught one of ordinary skill in this art at the time
of this invention. . . . By defining the inventor's problem
in terms of its solution, the district court missed this necessary antecedent question, namely, whether the prior art
contains a suggestion or motivation to combine references
to form a trend. . . . Thus, before proceeding to find a trend,
the trial court must discern whether one of ordinary skill
would have had a motivation to combine references to form
a trend.

2. ***Monarch Knitting Mach. Corp. v. Sulzer Morat GmbH***,
45 USPQ 2d 1977, 1982 (Fed. Cir. 1998)

Beyond the motivation to combine question, the trial court
must also determine whether the prior art forms a trend.
The record contains evidence calling into question whether,
even among needles employing a first segment configuration, the entire content of the prior art shows a trend towards decreasing first segment heights. The record shows
that the four needles selected by the district court were
made for four different knitting machines, not replacements
for the same machine over time. Given this evidence, a reasonable inference can—and on summary judgment must—
be drawn in favor of the patentee that the four examples
chosen by the trial court do not show a trend. Moreover, as
early as 1957, Groz-Beckert made a needle having a segment height of 1.5 mm. Because this 1957 needle "bucks the
trend" perceived in the four selected by the trial court, a reasonable fact finder could conclude that the entire body of
prior art does not evince a trend toward decreasing segment
heights.

V.G.   *Rebuttal Evidence Under Rule 132*

1. ***In re Reuter***, 210 USPQ 249, 257 (C.C.P.A. 1981)

Coming from a coinventor, the statements are probative
and, at a minimum, constitute expert opinion evidence which
supports the Poynter factual statement regarding the state
of the art.

2. ***Cable Electric Prods., Inc. v. Genmark, Inc.***, 226 USPQ
881, 888 (Fed. Cir. 1985)

[T]his court in *Stratoflex, Inc. v. Aeroquip Corp.* . . . has unequivocally stated that for commercial success of a product
embodying a claimed invention to have true relevance to the
issue of nonobviousness, that success must be shown to have

in some way been due to the nature of the claimed invention, as opposed to other economic and commercial factors unrelated to the technical quality of the patented subject matter. Thus, a "nexus is required between the merits of the claimed invention and the evidence offered, if that evidence is to be given substantial weight enroute to [a] conclusion on the obviousness issue."

3. ***In re Orfeo***, 169 USPQ 487, 489 (C.C.P.A. 1971)

As long as there is a question of obviousness, no matter how trivial that question may seem, we think appellants have the right to have considered the Rule 132 affidavit which allegedly shows new and unexpected results. If that affidavit is strong enough in its showing of new and unexpected results, the Patent Office's position that the claim invention is obvious may be found to be rebutted.

4. ***Continental Can Co. USA v. Monsanto Co.***, 20 USPQ 2d 1746, 1752 (Fed. Cir. 1991)

Thus when differences that may appear technologically minor nonetheless have a practical impact, particularly in a crowded field, the decision-maker must consider the obviousness of the new structure in this light. Such objective indicia as commercial success, or filling an existing need, illuminate the technological and commercial environment of the inventor, and aid in understanding the state of the art at the time the invention was made.

5. ***Stratoflex, Inc. v. Aeroquip Corp.***, 218 USPQ 871, 879 (Fed. Cir. 1983)

[E]vidence of secondary considerations may often be the most probative and cogent evidence in the record. It may often establish that an invention appearing to have been obvious in light of the prior art was not. It is to be considered as part of all the evidence, not just when the decision maker remains in doubt after reviewing the art.

6. ***In re Klosak***, 173 USPQ 14, 16 (C.C.P.A. 1972)

The fact that an invention provides results which would not have been expected by those skilled in the art is strong evidence in rebuttal of an assertion that the invention would have been obvious. However, the burden of showing unexpected results rests on he who asserts them. Thus it is not enough to show that results are obtained which differ from those obtained in the prior art: that difference must be shown to be an *unexpected* difference. . . . Nor is it enough to show that certain results would not have been expected by

those skilled in the art without establishing that those results are actually obtained through one's invention.

7. ***In re Zenitz***, 142 USPQ 158, 161 (C.C.P.A. 1964)

But the mere failure of a patentee to realize all the benefits
and possibilities of his invention is not fatal. The after-dis-
covery of unsuspected usefulness in a disclosed apparatus,
far from detracting from its value, may serve to enhance it.
It is the benefits which tests, use, and time unfold that really determine merit.

8. ***Merck & Co. v. Biocraft Labs., Inc.***, 10 USPQ 2d 1843,
1847 (Fed. Cir.), ***cert. denied***, 493 U.S. 975 (1989)

"Normally, it is to be expected that a change in temperature, or in concentration, or in both, would be an unpatentable modification." *In re Aller*, 220 F.2d 454, 456, 105 USPQ
233, 235 (C.C.P.A. 1955). Patentability may be imparted,
however, if the results achieved at the designated concentra-
tions are "unexpectedly good." *In re Antonie*, 559 F.2d 618,
620, 195 USPQ 6, 8 (C.C.P.A. 1977).

9. ***Kansas Jack, Inc. v. Kuhn***, 219 USPQ 857, 860 (Fed. Cir.
1983)

Facts determinable at a later time may serve to evidence
nonobviousness as of the time the invention was made. An
invention that did achieve "an effect greater" or that produced "unusual or surprising results" could of course be held
to have been nonobvious in light of those facts.

10. ***In re Wright***, 6 USPQ 2d 1959, 1962 (Fed. Cir. 1988), ***overruled in part by In re Dillon***, 16 USPQ 2d 1897 (Fed. Cir.
1990), ***cert. denied***, 500 U.S. 904 (1991)

In fact, various other factors may be considered in determining whether the prior art shows or suggests the claimed
invention. These other factors include, for instance, that the
invention provided over the prior art: unexpected results, a
solution to a different problem or novel properties. As stated
by the Federal Circuit, "[w]hen such factors are described in
the specification they are weighed in determining, in the
first instance, whether the prior art presents the prima facie
case of obviousness."

11. ***Demaco Corp. v. F. Von Langsdorff Licensing Ltd.***, 7
USPQ 2d 1222, 1226–27 (Fed. Cir.), ***cert. denied***, 488 U.S.
956 (1988)

When a patentee asserts that commercial success supports its contention of nonobviousness, there must of course

be a sufficient relationship between the commercial success and the patented invention. The term "nexus" is often used, in this context, to designate a legally and factually sufficient connection between the proven success and the patented invention, such that the objective evidence should be considered in the determination of nonobviousness. The burden of proof as to this connection or nexus resides with the patentee. . . .

A prima facie case of nexus is generally made out when the patentee shows both that there is commercial success, and that the thing (product or method) that is commercially successful is the invention disclosed and claimed in the patent. When the thing that is commercially successful is not coextensive with the patented invention—for example, if the patented invention is only a component of a commercially successful machine or process—the patentee must show prima facie a legally sufficient relationship between that which is patented and that which is sold. . . .

A patentee is not required to prove as part of its prima facie case that the commercial success of the patented invention is not due to factors other than the patented invention. It is sufficient to show that the commercial success was of the patented invention itself. A requirement for proof of the negative of all imaginable contributing factors would be unfairly burdensome, and contrary to the ordinary rules of evidence.

12. ***Goodyear Tire & Rubber Co. v. Ray-O-Vac Co.***, 321 U.S. 275, 60 USPQ 386, 388 (1944)

Viewed after the event, the means Anthony adopted seem simple and such as should have been obvious to those who worked in the field, but this is not enough to negative invention. During a period of a half a century, in which the use of flash light batteries increased enormously, and the manufacturers of flash light cells were conscious of the defects in them, no one devised a method of curing such defects. Once the method was discovered it commended itself to the public as evidenced by marked commercial success. These factors were entitled to weight in determining whether the improvement amounted to invention and should, in a close case, tip the scales in favor of patentability.

13. ***In re Quartz***, 33 USPQ 504, 506 (C.C.P.A. 1937)

[W]hile workers in the art approached, to some extent, a solution of the problem, the problem was not solved until this appellant conceived the fortunate combination of elements which converted these failures into a success. It is somewhat difficult, sometimes, to say just where invention begins, but it frequently happens, as it seems to have happened here, that someone will conceive of a fortunate combination which produces a great advance in the art, which, perchance, seems to be but a small deviation from the practice and prior knowledge of the art. . . . We are of opinion that the appellant has made an invention, and that he should be given a patent therefor.

14. ***Ex parte Briod***, 41 USPQ 41, 42 (Pat. Off. Bd. App. 1938)

It has frequently been held that the omission of a part or constituent with its function is not a matter of invention but where a part or a constituent is omitted, without sacrifice of function, invention has frequently been found.

15. ***Ex parte Franklin***, 41 USPQ 43, 43 (Pat. Off. Bd. App. 1938)

We do not see how the examiner can conclude without prior art that there is no inventive concept involved. Applicant has certainly provided a new means to accomplish his object.

The affidavit of the Chief Motor Transport Officer establishes prima facie that applicant's invention is responsible for a large increase in motor mileage before engine overhaul was necessary and that since the installation of applicant's invention, the average mileage obtained from truck motors before overhauling was from 30,000 to 60,000 miles. . . .

If it were obvious to install applicant's device to increase the mileage before overhaul from 30,000 to 60,000 miles, the device would have been used years ago.

16. ***In re Atkinson***, 41 USPQ 308, 311 (C.C.P.A. 1939)

It is established law that the difficulty encountered in discovering the defects of existing devices may be taken into consideration in determining the question of invention where the defect has been remedied. This is especially true where the cause of the defect is obscure and discovered only after it had long existed and after much research. The decisions have gone so far as to hold that where the defect of a prior art device had long existed and the cause of the defect was not discovered until after much experimentation, invention might be present, even though the remedy be simple or be suggested by the discovery of the defect or by the prior art.

17. ***Ex parte Levine***, 41 USPQ 411, 412–13 (Pat. Off. Bd. App. 1939)

After appeal was taken the joint applicant Cass filed an affidavit setting forth tests made with seven of the catalysts mentioned in the Jaeger patent. In all of these tests except the one in which stannic chloride was used, a large yield of the higher chlorides was obtained while with stannic chloride the yield of the monochlor cyclohexane was very high. The examiner has criticized this showing as being insufficient. We believe this showing to be sufficient to show the great superiority of stannic chloride over a reasonable number of other catalysts mentioned in the Jaeger patent.

18. ***Ex parte Anderson***, 21 USPQ 2d 1241, 1258 (B.P.A.I. 1991)

In evaluating and assigning weight to the evidence of nonobviousness several factors must be kept in mind. The evidence must represent a comparison with the closer prior art. . . . Merely showing a difference in properties between the prior art and claimed copolymers is not enough. Any difference shown must be such that it should be considered unexpected by one of ordinary skill in the art. . . . The proffered evidence must be commensurate in scope with the claims. . . .

We note that "commercial success is relevant only if it flows from the merits of the *claimed* invention," *Sjolund v. Musland*, 847 F.2d 1573, 1582, 6 USPQ 2d 2020, 2028 (Fed. Cir. 1988) (emphasis in original), i.e., there must be nexus between the claimed invention and the commercial activity relied upon. . . .

Further, merely specifying sales figures alone is not sufficient to establish commercial success. Other evidence such as market share, growth in market share, replacement of earlier products sold by others, etc. need be present.

19. ***Ex parte Anderson***, 30 USPQ 2d 1866, 1869 (B.P.A.I. 1993)

Any *prima facie* case of obviousness established by an examiner is subject to rebuttal, however the burden of rebuttal falls on the patent applicant. What constitutes rebuttal has been broadly set forth in *In re Dillon* . . . as follows:

[R]ebuttal or argument can consist of a comparison of test data showing that the claimed compositions possess unexpectedly improved properties or properties that the prior art does not have (citations omitted), that the prior art is so deficient that there is no motivation to make what might otherwise appear to be obvious changes (citations omitted), or any other argument or presentation of evidence that is pertinent.

20. ***In re Soni***, 34 USPQ 2d 1684, 1687 (Fed. Cir. 1995)

One way for a patent applicant to rebut a prima facie case of obviousness is to make a showing of "unexpected results," i.e., to show that the claimed invention exhibits some superior property or advantage that a person of ordinary skill in the relevant art would have found surprising or unexpected. The basic principle behind this rule is straightforward—that which would have been surprising to a person of ordinary skill in a particular art would not have been obvious. The principle applies most often to the less predictable fields, such as chemistry, where minor changes in a product or process may yield substantially different results.

Consistent with the rule that all evidence of nonobviousness must be considered when assessing patentability, the PTO must consider comparative data in the specification in determining whether the claimed invention provides unexpected results.

21. *In re Soni*, 34 USPQ 2d 1684, 1687–88 (Fed. Cir. 1995)

Here, Soni's specification contains more than mere argument or conclusory statements; it contains specific data indicating improved properties. It also states that the improved properties provided by the claimed compositions "are much greater than would have been predicted given the difference in their molecular weights." . . .

Mere improvement in properties does not always suffice to show unexpected results. In our view, however, when an applicant demonstrates substantially improved results, as Soni did here, and states that the results were unexpected, this should suffice to establish unexpected results in the absence of evidence to the contrary. Soni, who owed the PTO a duty of candor, made such a showing here. The PTO has not provided any persuasive basis to question Soni's comparative data and assertion that the demonstrated results were unexpected. Thus, we are persuaded that the Board's finding that Soni did not establish unexpected results is clearly erroneous.

22. *In re Alton*, 37 USPQ 2d 1578, 1583 (Fed. Cir. 1996)

Dr. Wall's use of the words "it is my opinion" to preface what someone of ordinary skill in the art would have known does not transform the factual statements contained in the declaration into opinion testimony. Consequently, the examiner's dismissal of the declaration on the grounds that "[l]ittle weight is given an opinion affidavit on the ultimate legal question at issue" was error.

23. ***Gambro Lundia AB v. Baxter Health Care Corp.***, 42 USPQ 2d 1378, 1384 (Fed. Cir. 1997)

Additionally, the record contains significant evidence of the commercial success of Gambro's invention. The record shows that Baxter sold over 14,800 dialysis machines allegedly incorporating the Gambro invention since 1987. In fact, Baxter admits that its machines were a commercial success. Of course, the record must show a sufficient nexus between this commercial success and the patented invention. . . . The prominence of the patented technology in Baxter's advertising creates an inference that links the Gambro invention to this success.

24. ***In re Mayne***, 41 USPQ 2d 1451, 1453–54 (Fed. Cir. 1997) (quoting ***In re Soni***, 34 USPQ 2d 1684, 1687 (Fed. Cir. 1995))

With a factual foundation for its prima facie case of obviousness shown, the burden shifts to applicants to demonstrate that their claimed fusion proteins possess an unexpected property over the prior art. . . . An applicant may make this showing with evidence that the claimed invention exhibits some superior property or advantage that a person of ordinary skill in the relevant art would find surprising or unexpected.

> The basic principle behind this rule is straight forward— that which would have been surprising to a person of ordinary skill in a particular art would not have been obvious. The principle applies most often to the less predictable fields, such as chemistry, where minor changes in a product or process may yield substantially different results.

25. ***Arkie Lures, Inc. v. Gene Larew Tackle, Inc.***, 43 USPQ 2d 1294, 1297 (Fed. Cir. 1997)

The so-called "secondary considerations" provide evidence of how the patented device is viewed by the interested public: not the inventor, but persons concerned with the product in the objective arena of the marketplace. In this case the considerations of commercial success, licensing activity, and copying were markedly prevalent, and were not disputed. Such aspects may be highly probative of the issue of nonobviousness. . . . Larew presented evidence of the rapid growth of its business and the numerous licenses granted. Dr. Carver and Mr. Harville testified that Larew's lure "revolutionized" the industry. Ready recognition of the merits of a new product does not establish obviousness. Commercial success and copying are tributes to ingenuity, not evidence of legal obviousness. This rule is no less worthy when the new product narrowly fits into a field already well explored—like the fishing lure art—than when a transcendent scientific breakthrough is launched. The patent law is designed to serve the small inventor as well as the giant research organization.

26. ***Arkie Lures, Inc. v. Gene Larew Tackle, Inc.***, 43 USPQ
2d 1294, 1296 (Fed. Cir. 1997)

It is insufficient to establish obviousness that the separate elements of the invention existed in the prior art, absent some teaching or suggestion, in the prior art, to combine the elements. Indeed, the years of use of salty bait and of plastic lures, without combining their properties, weighs on the side of unobviousness of the combination. Mr. Larew persisted against the accepted wisdom, and succeeded. The evidence that the combination was not viewed as technically feasible must be considered, for conventional wisdom that a combination should not be made is evidence of unobviousness.

27. ***In re Geisler***, 43 USPQ 2d 1362, 1365 (Fed. Cir. 1997)

Addressing a case similar in some respects to this one, the Court of Customs and Patent Appeals stated that a prima facie case of obviousness can be rebutted if the applicant (1) can establish "the existence of unexpected properties in the range claimed" or (2) can show "that the art in any material respect taught away" from the claimed invention. . . . As this court has explained, "[o]ne way for a patent applicant to rebut a prima facie case of obviousness is to make a showing of 'unexpected results,' *i.e.*, to show that the claimed invention exhibits some superior property or advantage that a person of ordinary skill in the relevant art would have found surprising or unexpected." *In re Soni*, 54 F.3d 746, 750, 34 USPQ 2d 1684, 1687 (Fed. Cir. 1995). When an applicant seeks to overcome a prima facie case of obviousness by showing improved performance in a range that is within or overlaps with a range disclosed in the prior art, the applicant must "show that the [claimed] range is *critical*, generally by showing that the claimed range achieves unexpected results relative to the prior art range." *In re Woodruff*, 919 F.2d 1575, 1578, 16 USPQ 2d 1934, 1936 (Fed. Cir. 1990).

Under that standard, "it is not inventive to discover the optimum or workable ranges by routine experimentation." *In re Aller*, 220 F.2d 454, 456, 105 USPQ 233, 235 (CCPA 1955). Only if the "results of optimizing a variable" are "unexpectedly good" can a patent be obtained for the claimed critical range. *In re Antonie*, 559 F.2d 618, 620, 195 USPQ 6, 8 (CCPA 1977); *see also In re Dillon*, 919 F.2d 688, 692, 16 USPQ 2d 1897, 1901 (Fed. Cir. 1990) (in banc). Furthermore, it is well settled that unexpected results must be established by factual evidence. "Mere argument or conclusory statements in the specification does not suffice." *In re De Blauwe*, 736 F.2d 699, 705, 222 USPQ 191, 196 (Fed. Cir. 1994).

28. ***In re Geisler***, 43 USPQ 2d 1362 (Fed. Cir. 1997) (citing ***In re Soni***, 34 USPQ 2d 1684, 1688 (Fed. Cir. 1995))

The court in *Soni* summed up the rule of that case as follows: "[W]hen an applicant demonstrates *substantially* improved results, as Soni did here, and *states* that the results were *unexpected*, this should suffice to establish unexpected results *in the absence of* evidence to the contrary."

29. ***In re Metz***, Civ. App. 97-1263, slip op. at 11–12 (Fed. Cir. Sept. 22, 1998) (unpublished)

[A]ppellant argues that the board did not give sufficient weight to the sales figures provided to demonstrate commercial success. The sales figures appellant provided are essentially meaningless because they do not indicate the size of the market or the market share achieved. They merely demonstrate that Metz sold products and that the volume of those sales increased with time. This could be the result of a wide variety of factors which do not pertain to the merits of the claimed subject matter. Again, there must be some connection between the sales figures and claimed subject matter indicating what impact the claimed subject matter had on the sales volume.

30. ***Brand Management, Inc. v. Menard, Inc.***, Civ. App. 97-1329, slip op. at 22 (Fed. Cir. Jan. 14, 1998) (unpublished), ***cert. denied***, 524 U.S. 927 (1998)

To establish commercial success, the patentee must be armed with evidence of market share, growth in market share, and replacement of prior sales by others. See, e.g., *Kansas Jack, Inc. v. Kuhn*, 719 F.2d 1144, 1150, 219 USPQ 857, 861 (Fed. Cir. 1983). In addition, the patentee must demonstrate a nexus between the claimed sales and the merits of the invention. Id.

31. ***In re Rouffet***, 47 USPQ 2d 1453, 1456 (Fed. Cir. 1998)

The secondary considerations are also essential components of the obviousness determination. *See In re Emert*, 124 F.3d 1458, 1462, 44 USPQ 2d 1149, 1153 (Fed. Cir. 1997) ("Without Emert providing rebuttal evidence, this prima facie case of obviousness must stand."). This objective evidence of nonobviousness includes copying, long felt but unsolved need, failure of others, *see Graham v. John Deere Co.*, 383 U.S. 1, 17–18, 15 L. Ed. 2d 545, 86 S. Ct. 684 (1966), commercial success, *see In re Huang*, 100 F.3d 135, 139–40, 40 USPQ 2d 1685, 1689–90 (Fed. Cir. 1996), unexpected results created by the claimed invention, unexpected properties of the claimed invention, *see In re Mayne*, 104 F.3d 1339, 1342, 41 USPQ 2d 1451, 1454 (Fed. Cir. 1997); *In re Wood-*

ruff, 919 F.2d 1575, 1578, 16 USPQ 2d 1934, 1936–37 (Fed. Cir. 1990), licenses showing industry respect for the invention, *see Arkie Lures, Inc. v. Gene Larew Tackle, Inc.*, 119 F.3d 953, 957, 43 USPQ 2d 1294, 1297 (Fed. Cir. 1997); *Pentec, Inc. v. Graphic Controls Corp.*, 776 F.2d 309, 316, 227 USPQ 766, 771 (Fed. Cir. 1985), and skepticism of skilled artisans before the invention, *see In re Dow Chem. Co.*, 837 F.2d 469, 473, 5 USPQ 2d 1529, 1532 (Fed. Cir. 1988). The Board must consider all of the applicant's evidence.

32. ***Tec Air, Inc. v. Denso Mfg. Mich. Inc.***, 52 USPQ 2d 1294, 1299 (Fed. Cir. 1999)

Although sales figures coupled with market data provide stronger evidence of commercial success, sales figures alone are also evidence of commercial success.

33. ***Demaco Corp. v. F. Von Langsdorff Licensing Ltd.***, 7 USPQ 2d 1222, 1226 (Fed. Cir. 1988)

A prima facie case of nexus is generally made out when the patentee shows both that there is commercial success, and that the thing (product or method) that is commercially successful is the invention disclosed and claimed in the patent.

34. ***In re Case***, Civ. App. No. 98-1531, slip op. at 6 (Fed. Cir. Aug. 31, 1999) (unpublished) (quoting ***In re Baxter Travenol Labs.***, 21 USPQ 2d 1281, 1285 (Fed. Cir. 1991))

A patent applicant can rebut a prima facie case of obviousness by showing "unexpected results," i.e., showing that the claimed invention possesses a superior property or advantage that a person of ordinary skill in the art would have found surprising or unexpected. . . . "When unexpected results are used as evidence of nonobviousness, the results must be shown to be unexpected compared with the closest prior art."

35. ***In re Case***, Civ. App. No. 98-1531, slip op. at 10–13 (Fed. Cir. Aug. 31, 1999) (unpublished)

Because the ranges of magnesium oxide in Cline and the claimed invention at the very least abut each other, some evidence of unexpected results is necessary to show why claims 1 and 17 should be patentable. . . . The closest prior art is that of Cline where the magnesium oxide is used as the sole filler in an amount being as little as 15% by weight of the paper. However, Case selected embodiments of Cline with magnesium oxide in the amounts of 22.2 and 23.0 percent, and embodiments of the claimed invention with magnesium oxide in the amounts of 10.8 and 11.0 percent.

36. ***Carlisle Plastics, Inc. v. Spotless Enters., Inc.***, Civ. App. 98-1170, slip op. at 4 (Fed. Cir. Jan. 26, 1999) (unpublished)

We agree with the district court that the commercial success of the embodiment of the invention and the failure of anyone (including Carlisle's predecessor) to combine the prior art elements before the inventor did so provide significant support for the conclusion that the invention was not obvious, notwithstanding that combining the elements in the prior art would seem, with the considerable benefit of hindsight, to be fairly elementary.

37. ***In re Ductmate Indus., Inc.***, Reexamination Control Number 90/004,369, U.S. Patent 4,584,756, p.3 (Comm'r Feb. 12, 1997)

This document explains Exhibits 1–4 and supplies information concerning these documents which does not appear on the face of the documents. The petition appears to allege that this document is a verified document, but was improperly ignored by the examiner. A review of the document shows that it is not executed under oath, and certainly is not properly authenticated as required with respect to an oath executed abroad, it being noted that Reutlinger is a city in Germany. See MPEP §§ 602.04 and 604. The document lacks a verification clause under 35 USC § 25 and 37 CFR § 1.68.

38. ***In re Ductmate Indus., Inc.***, Reexamination Control Number 90/004,369, U.S. Patent 4,584,756, p.5 (Comm'r Feb. 12, 1997)

Under 28 USC § 1746, a statement under penalty of perjury is acceptable in place of a sworn declaration or oath or affidavit if it is submitted in *substantially* the following form, (emphasis supplied):

[1] If executed without the United States:

"I declare (or certify, verify, or state) under penalty of perjury *under the laws of the United States of America* that the foregoing is true and correct. Executed on (date). (Signature)."

[2] If executed within the United States its territories, possessions or commonwealths:

"I declare (or certify, verify, or state) under penalty of perjury that the foregoing is true and correct Executed on (date). (Signature)." (emphasis supplied)

Clearly, this document does not *substantially* comply with the form permitted under 28 USC § 1746. It omits any reference to the "laws of the United States of America". These very words are the words which Congress chose to require when-

ever a document was executed without the United States, as
opposed to the language required for documents executed
within the United States. Therefore, it cannot be contended
that a statement signed in Germany which omits the words
"under the laws of the United States of America" qualifies as
a statement which is "substantially" in compliance with 28
USC § 1746. Had Congress felt the omitted words to be so unimportant, it would not have taken the trouble to require
them specifically in statements executed abroad.

It appears, therefore, that the statement submitted by
Georg Mez does not qualify as a verified statement under 28
USC § 1746. It is not a verified statement under 35 USC § 25
and is not a verified statement as an oath executed in the
manner of an oath under 35 USC § 115 (when made in a foreign country, must appear before a diplomatic: or consular
office of the United States authorized to administer oaths,
etc.).

39. ***Brown & Williamson Tobacco Corp. v. Philip Morris
Inc.***, 56 USPQ 2d 1456, 1463–64 (Fed. Cir. 2000)

A nexus between commercial success and the claimed features is required. See *J.T. Eaton & Co. v. Atlantic Paste &
Glue Co.*, 106 F.3d 1563, 1571, 41 USPQ 2d 1641, 1647 (Fed.
Cir. 1997); *Demaco Corp. v. F. Von Langsdorff Licensing Ltd.*,
851 F.2d 1387, 1392, 7 USPQ 2d 1222, 1226 (Fed. Cir. 1988).
However, if the marketed product embodies the claimed features, and is coextensive with them, then a nexus is presumed and the burden shifts to the party asserting obviousness to present evidence to rebut the presumed nexus. See
J.T. Eaton, 106 F.3d at 1571, 41 USPQ 2d at 1647; *Demaco*,
851 F.2d at 1392–93, 7 USPQ 2d at 1226. The presumed
nexus cannot be rebutted with mere argument; evidence
must be put forth. . . .

We agree with B&W that the district court erred by not considering the success of the VSSS. Our case law provides that
the success of an infringing product is considered to be evidence of the commercial success of the claimed invention. . . .

B&W argues however, and we agree, that the district
court erred with regard to certain other secondary indica-
tors. Specifically, B&W asserts that the district court erred
as a matter of law in discounting PM's statements of praise
for the Capri, in failing to consider PM's skepticism and
Cundiff's skepticism, and in failing to consider PM's copying
of the Capri. Accordingly, in reaching the ultimate legal determination regarding obviousness, we will accept B&W's
characterization of PM's skepticism, praise, and copying of
the Capri, as well as Cundiff's skepticism.

40. ***Ransomes, Inc. v. Great Dane Power Equipment, Inc.***, Civ. App. No. 98-1504, slip op. at 7–8 (Fed. Cir. Apr. 4, 2000) (unpublished)

Before the district court, GD proferred evidence that a third party, Rich, developed this mower control by 1994, about one year after the filing date of the '678 patent. The district court held that this independent development "strengthened" the conclusion that claim 4 was obvious, because it "was probative of the knowledge of one skilled in the art." Ransomes, slip op. at 16–17. We disagree that this evidence is probative of the knowledge of one skilled in the art because Rich's alleged independent development was simply too late to be probative of whether the invention would have been obvious "at the time the invention was made." 35 U.S.C. § 103 (1994). Put another way, Rich's alleged development of the mower controls of claim 4 approximately one year after the filing date of the '678 patent does not demonstrate that Rich would have known to select and combine the relevant prior art at the time the claimed invention was made, about one year earlier. Although our cases have noted that simultaneous development "may or may not be indicative of obviousness," *Lindemann Maschinenfabrik GMBH v. American Hoist & Derrick Co.*, 730 F.2d 1452, 1460, 221 USPQ 487 (Fed. Cir. 1984), evidence of "contemporaneous development" that occurs after the date of the patented invention will almost never be probative of the ultimate conclusion of obviousness. See *Hybritech Inc. v. Monoclonal Antibodies, Inc.*, 802 F.2d 1367, 1380 n. 4, 231 USPQ 81, 91 n. 4 (Fed. Cir. 1986) (contemporaneous development more than a year after the filing date of patent is "of little probative value"); *Lindemann*, 730 F.2d at 1461, 221 USPQ at 487 (independent development more than five years after the invention was made is not relevant to obviousness determination); see also *Environmental Designs, Ltd v. Union Oil Co. of Cal.*, 713 F.2d 693, 698 n. 7, 218 USPQ 865, 869 n. 7 (Fed. Cir. 1983) ("the virtually simultaneous making of the same invention does not in itself preclude patentability of that invention.").

41. ***Heidelberg Harris, Inc. v. Mitsubishi Heavy Indus., Ltd.***, Civ. App. 1100, slip op. at 22 (Fed. Cir. Sep. 18, 2000) (unpublished)

Accepting as established facts the limited teachings of the prior art, the absence of any motivation to combine the references, and the secondary considerations of non-obviousness, as implicitly found by the jury, we hold that the invention of the asserted claims of the '048 and '981 patents would not have been obvious to one of ordinary skill in the art. We are particularly persuaded of the legal sufficiency of the non-obviousness conclusion by Heidelberg's strong evidence of secondary considerations of non-obviousness, such as the Sunday Press's commercial success, its widespread industry acclaim, and the fact that Mitsubishi heavily relied upon the Heidelberg press in developing its own press. Mitsubishi documents even admit that Heidelberg's design was "unique."

V.H. *Obviousness and Chemical and Biological Inventions*

1. ***In re Bell***, 26 USPQ 2d 1529, 1531 (Fed. Cir. 1993)

     It may be true that, knowing the structure of the protein, one can use the genetic code to hypothesize possible structures for the corresponding gene and that one thus has the potential for obtaining that gene. However, because of the degeneracy of the genetic code, there are a vast number of nucleotide sequences that might code for a specific protein.

2. ***Ex parte D***, 27 USPQ 2d 1067, 1069 (B.P.A.I. 1993)

     While the cited decisions refer to chemical compounds, rather than sequenced DNA, we stress that a gene is a chemical compound, albeit a complex one. . . . Thus, it is manifest that the prior decisions involving chemical compounds are equally applicable to claims directed to the present subject matter.

3. ***Ex parte Obukowicz***, 27 USPQ 2d 1063, 1065 (B.P.A.I. 1992)

     We recognize that given the teachings in appellants' specification regarding incorporation of the gene into the chromosome and utilizing the bacteria in the plant environment, one can theoretically explain the technological rationale for the claimed invention using selected teachings from the references. This approach, however, has been criticized by our reviewing court as hindsight reconstruction.

4. ***In re Grabiak***, 226 USPQ 870, 871 (Fed. Cir. 1985)

   When chemical compounds have "very close" structural similarities and similar utilities, without more a prima facie case may be made. . . . When such "close" structural similarity to prior art compounds is shown, in accordance with these precedents the burden of coming forward shifts to the applicant, and evidence affirmatively supporting unobviousness is required.

5. ***In re Chupp***, 2 USPQ 2d 1437, 1439 (Fed. Cir. 1987)

     To be patentable, a compound need not excel over prior art compounds in all common properties. . . . Evidence that a compound is unexpectedly superior in one of a spectrum of common properties, as here, can be enough to rebut a prima facie case of obviousness.

6. ***In re Baird***, 29 USPQ 2d 1550, 1552 (Fed. Cir. 1994)

The fact that a claimed compound may be encompassed by a disclosed generic formula does not by itself render that compound obvious. *In re Jones*, 958 F.2d 347, 350, 21 USPQ 2d 1941, 1943 (Fed. Cir. 1992) (rejecting Commissioner's argument that "regardless [] how broad, a disclosure of a chemical genus renders obvious any species that happens to fall within it"). *Jones* involved an obviousness rejection of a claim to a specific compound, the 2-(2'-aminoethoxy) ethanol salt of 2-methoxy-3,6-dichlorobenzoic acid (dicamba), as obvious in view of, *inter alia*, a prior art reference disclosing a genus which admittedly encompassed the claimed salt. We reversed the Board's rejection, reasoning that the prior art reference encompassed a "potentially infinite genus" of salts of dicamba and listed several such salts, but that it did not disclose or suggest the claimed salt.

In the instant case, the generic diphenol formula disclosed in Knapp contains a large number of variables, and we estimate that it encompasses more than 100 million different diphenols, only one of which is bisphenol A. While the Knapp formula unquestionably encompasses bisphenol A when specific variables are chosen, there is nothing in the disclosure of Knapp suggesting that one should select such variables. . . .

A disclosure of millions of compounds does not render obvious a claim to three compounds, particularly when that disclosure indicates a preference leading away from the claimed compounds.

7. ***Ex parte Anderson***, 30 USPQ 2d 1866, 1868 (B.P.A.I. 1993)

Obviousness is a question of patent law, not chemistry. . . . Nevertheless, the factual basis for the legal conclusion is often a matter of highly sophisticated chemistry. In the case before us, the examiner has set forth sufficient scientific basis from which one could properly conclude that the primate IL3-like hematopoietic growth factors are part of a family of proteins which are similar in their amino acid sequence but are minor variants or point mutations of each other. This is because as a matter of textbook chemistry, a single variation in the amino acid structure of a protein does not normally change the activity and function of the protein unless the single variation is in a critical region of the protein. Accordingly, the examiner was technologically correct when she stated that the substitution of any one of the amino acids in the protein chain and the similar substitu-

tion of the DNA coding for the amino acid would not normally have been expected to have a significant effect on the
activity of the protein.

8. ***In re Deuel***, 34 USPQ 2d 1210, 1214 (Fed. Cir. 1995)

Because Deuel claims new chemical entities in structural
terms, a prima facie case of unpatentability requires that
the teachings of the prior art suggest the claimed compounds to a person of ordinary skill in the art. Normally a
prima facie case of obviousness is based upon structural similarity, i.e., an established structural relationship between a
prior art compound and the claimed compound. Structural
relationships may provide the requisite motivation or suggestion to modify known compounds to obtain new compounds. . . . In all of these cases, however, the prior art
teaches a specific, structurally-definable compound and the
question becomes whether the prior art would have suggested making the specific molecular modifications necessary to achieve the claimed invention.

9. ***In re Deuel***, 34 USPQ 2d 1210, 1215 (Fed. Cir. 1995)

[W]hile the general idea of the claimed molecules, their function, and their general chemical nature may have been obvious from Bohlen's teachings, and the knowledge that some
gene existed may have been clear, the precise cDNA molecules of claims 5 and 7 would not have been obvious over the
Bohlen reference because Bohlen teaches proteins, not the
claimed or closely related cDNA molecules. The redundancy
of the genetic code precluded contemplation of or focus on
the specific cDNA molecules of claims 5 and 7. Thus, one
could not have conceived the subject matter of claims 5 and
7 based on the teachings in the cited prior art because, until
the claimed molecules were actually isolated and purified, it
would have been highly unlikely for one of ordinary skill in
the art to contemplate what was ultimately obtained. What
cannot be contemplated or conceived cannot be obvious. . . .
A general motivation to search for some gene that exists
does not necessarily make obvious a specifically-defined
gene that is subsequently obtained as a result of that search.

10. ***In re Deuel***, 34 USPQ 2d 1210, 1215 (Fed. Cir. 1995)

A prior art disclosure of the amino acid sequence of a protein
does not necessarily render particular DNA molecules encoding the protein obvious because the redundancy of the genetic code permits one to hypothesize an enormous number
of DNA sequences coding for the protein. No particular one
of these DNAs can be obvious unless there is something in
the prior art to lead to the particular DNA and indicate that

it should be prepared. We recently held in *In re Baird*, 16 F.3d 380, 29 USPQ 2d 1550 (Fed. Cir. 1994), that a broad genus does not necessarily render obvious each compound within its scope. Similarly, knowledge of a protein does not give one a conception of a particular DNA encoding it.

11. ***In re Deuel***, 34 USPQ 2d 1210, 1216 (Fed. Cir. 1995)

[E]ven if, as the examiner stated, the existence of general cloning techniques, coupled with knowledge of a protein's structure, might have provided motivation to prepare a cDNA or made it obvious to prepare a cDNA, that does not necessarily make obvious a particular claimed cDNA. "Obvious to try" has long been held not to constitute obviousness. . . . A general incentive does not make obvious a particular result, nor does the existence of techniques by which those efforts can be carried out.

12. ***In re Deuel***, 34 USPQ 2d 1210, 1215 (Fed. Cir. 1995)

The PTO's focus on known methods for potentially isolating the claimed DNA molecules is also misplaced because the claims at issue define compounds, not methods. *See In re Bell*, 991 F.2d 781, 785, 26 USPQ 2d 1529, 1532 (Fed. Cir. 1993). In *Bell*, the PTO asserted a rejection based upon the combination of a primary reference disclosing a protein (and its complete amino acid sequence) with a secondary reference describing a general method of gene cloning. We reversed the rejection, holding in part that "[t]he PTO's focus on Bell's method is misplaced. Bell does not claim a method. Bell claims compositions, and the issue is the obviousness of the claimed compositions, not of the method by which they are made." *Id.*

We today reaffirm the principle, stated in *Bell*, that the existence of a general method of isolating cDNA or DNA molecules is essentially irrelevant to the question whether the specific molecules themselves would have been obvious, in the absence of other prior art that suggests the claimed DNAs.

13. ***In re Deuel***, 34 USPQ 2d 1210, 1216 (Fed. Cir. 1995)

The fact that one can conceive a general process in advance for preparing an undefined compound does not mean that a claimed specific compound was precisely envisioned and therefore obvious. A substance may indeed be defined by its process of preparation. That occurs, however, when it has already been prepared by that process and one therefore knows that the result of that process is the stated compound. The process is part of the definition of the compound. But that is not possible in advance, especially when the hypothetical process is only a general one. Thus, a conceived method of preparing some undefined DNA does not define it with the precision necessary to render it obvious over the protein it encodes.

14. ***In re Mayne***, 41 USPQ 2d 1451, 1453–54 (Fed. Cir. 1997)

The Patent and Trademark Office (PTO) has the burden of showing a prima facie case of obviousness. . . . Standards for the patenting of chemical entities have evolved. At one time, the PTO focused only on the "structural obviousness" of the chemical entity. Under this standard, the structural formula of the claimed compound was compared for similarity with the structural formulae of known compounds. This regime did not allow evidence of unexpected results to trump the conclusion of obviousness based on structure. Over thirty years ago, courts recognized that unexpected properties can show that a claimed compound that appeared to be obvious on structural grounds was not obvious when looked at as a whole. . . . [T]his court noted the effect of unexpected results in the obviousness determination for chemical entities, but rejected as a requirement for establishing prima facie obviousness that there be an expectation or suggestion in the prior art that the claimed compound will have similar utility as the one newly discovered by applicant. The court held that "structural similarity between claimed and prior art subject matter, proved by combining references or otherwise, where the prior art gives reason or motivation to make the claimed compositions, creates a prima facie case of obviousness." . . . When relying on numerous references or a modification of prior art, it is incumbent upon the examiner to identify some suggestion to combine references or make the modification.

15. ***In re Ivax Indus., Inc.***, Civ. App. 97-1012, slip op. 8–9 (Fed. Cir. Apr. 24, 1998) (unpublished)

The Board's analysis of Novo did not consider at least two questions of fact: (1) whether one of ordinary skill would glean from Novo not only the asserted effects of cellulase (softening and color brightening) but also the method for achieving those effects (microfibril removal) and (2) whether one of ordinary skill would derive from a teaching that cellulase removes microfibrils a suggestion that cellulase could be used to achieve effects in color variation.

Rather than reach these subsidiary factual issues, the Board relied upon its application of *In re Dillon* to invalidate the method claims. The PTO reasons that this court need not consider whether Novo teaches the use of cellulase to achieve effects in color variation; under *Dillon*, it is sufficient that the prior art teaches the use of cellulase for fabric softening, which generates the stonewashed feel. . . . The Board's reliance on *Dillon*—as a way around gaps in the factual inquiry underlying its obviousness analysis—is misplaced.

16. ***In re Case***, Civ. App. No. 98-1531, slip op. at 10–13 (Fed. Cir. Aug. 31, 1999) (unpublished)

   Because the ranges of magnesium oxide in Cline and the claimed invention at the very least abut each other, some evidence of unexpected results is necessary to show why claims 1 and 17 should be patentable. . . . The closest prior art is that of Cline where the magnesium oxide is used as the sole filler in an amount being as little as 15% by weight of the paper. However, Case selected embodiments of Cline with magnesium oxide in the amounts of 22.2 and 23.0 percent, and embodiments of the claimed invention with magnesium oxide in the amounts of 10.8 and 11.0 percent.

V.I. *Obviousness and Dimensional/Range Limitations*

1. ***In re Wertheim***, 191 USPQ 90, 100 (C.C.P.A. 1976)

   Of course, the disclosure in the prior art of any value within a claimed range is an anticipation of the claimed range. We appreciate the arguments . . . to the effect that ranges which overlap or lie inside ranges disclosed by the prior art may be patentable if the applicant can show criticality in the claimed range by evidence of unexpected results. The rejections here are under §103, not §102, which requires us to consider appellants' argument that their invention and Pfluger's disclosure are directed to different purposes and that persons of ordinary skill in the art would not look to Pfluger 1963 for a solution to the problem addressed by appellants.

2. ***In re Russell***, 439 F.2d 1228, 1231, 169 USPQ 426, 428 (C.C.P.A. 1971)

   Appellant's position on the law is sound, for even though part of appellant's range of proportions, and all of his ingredients, are suggested by the broad teaching of Wei, if appellant can establish that his relatively narrow ranges yield unexpectedly superior results as against the broad Wei ranges as a whole, appellant will have established unobviousness of the claimed invention.

3. ***In re Geisler***, 43 USPQ 2d 1362, 1365 (Fed. Cir. 1997)

   Addressing a case similar in some respects to this one, the Court of Customs and Patent Appeals stated that a prima facie case of obviousness can be rebutted if the applicant (1) can establish "the existence of unexpected properties in the range claimed" or (2) can show "that the art in any material respect taught away" from the claimed invention. . . . As this court has explained, "[o]ne way for a patent applicant to rebut a prima facie case of obviousness is to make a showing of 'unexpected results,' *i.e.*, to show that the claimed invention exhibits some superior property or advantage that a person of ordinary skill in the relevant art would have found surprising or unexpected." *In re Soni*, 54 F.3d 746, 750, 34 USPQ 2d 1684, 1687 (Fed. Cir. 1995). When an applicant seeks to overcome a prima facie case of obviousness by showing improved performance in a range that is within or overlaps with a range disclosed in the prior art, the applicant must "show that the [claimed] range is *critical*, generally by showing that the claimed range achieves unexpected results relative to the prior art range." *In re Woodruff*, 919 F.2d 1575, 1578, 16 USPQ 2d 1934, 1936 (Fed. Cir. 1990).

Under that standard, "it is not inventive to discover the optimum or workable ranges by routine experimentation." *In re Aller*, 220 F.2d 454, 456, 105 USPQ 233, 235 (CCPA 1955). Only if the "results of optimizing a variable" are "unexpectedly good" can a patent be obtained for the claimed critical range. *In re Antonie*, 559 F.2d 618, 620, 195 USPQ 6, 8 (CCPA 1977); *see also In re Dillon*, 919 F.2d 688, 692, 16 USPQ 2d 1897, 1901 (Fed. Cir. 1990) (in banc). Furthermore, it is well settled that unexpected results must be established by factual evidence. "Mere argument or conclusory statements in the specification does not suffice." *In re De Blauwe*, 736 F.2d 699, 705, 222 USPQ 191, 196 (Fed. Cir. 1994).

4. *In re Geisler*, 43 USPQ 2d 1362 (Fed. Cir. 1997) (citing *In re Soni*, 34 USPQ 2d 1684, 1688 (Fed. Cir. 1995))

The court in *Soni* summed up the rule of that case as follows: "[W]hen an applicant demonstrates *substantially* improved results, as Soni did here, and *states* that the results were *unexpected*, this should suffice to establish unexpected results *in the absence of* evidence to the contrary."

5. *In re Case*, Civ. App. No. 98-1531, slip op. at 10–13 (Fed. Cir. Aug. 31, 1999) (unpublished)

Because the ranges of magnesium oxide in Cline and the claimed invention at the very least abut each other, some evidence of unexpected results is necessary to show why claims 1 and 17 should be patentable. . . . The closest prior art is that of Cline where the magnesium oxide is used as the sole filler in an amount being as little as 15% by weight of the paper. However, Case selected embodiments of Cline with magnesium oxide in the amounts of 22.2 and 23.0 percent, and embodiments of the claimed invention with magnesium oxide in the amounts of 10.8 and 11.0 percent.

6. ***Hockerson-Halberstadt, Inc. v. Avia Group Int'l, Inc.***, 55 USPQ 2d 1487, 1491 (Fed. Cir. 2000)

Under our precedent, however, it is well established that patent drawings do not define the precise proportions of the elements and may not be relied on to show particular sizes if the specification is completely silent on the issue. *See In re Wright*, 569 F.2d 1124, 1127, 193 USPQ 332, 335 (CCPA 1977) ("Absent any written description in the specification of quantitative values, arguments based on measurement of a drawing are of little value."); *In re Olson*, 212 F.2d 590, 592, 101 USPQ 401, 402 (CCPA 1954); cf. Manual of Patent Examining Procedure Section 2125 (1998). Thus, in the present case, a reasonable competitor, being aware that figures in a patent are not drawn to scale unless otherwise indicated, would understand the arguments in the prosecution history as clearly disclaiming a groove having a width greater than the combined width of the fins.

V.J. Obviousness With Respect to Structural Limitations

1. ***In re Henschell***, 34 USPQ 17, 18 (C.C.P.A. 1937)

The appellant argues that the principal patentable distinction between his particular construction and those of the reference patents lies in the fact that the inner edges of the teeth of his grater are in a plane perpendicular to the plane of the surface of the grater. This is true, and, in our opinion, it is not met by either of the references.

V.K. Patentable Weight of Indefinite Claim Limitations

1. ***Ex parte Anderson***, 21 USPQ 2d 1241, 1255 n.12 (B.P.A.I. 1991)

We do disagree with the language used by the examiner in regard to his consideration of the claim limitations found to be indefinite under 35 U.S.C. §112, second paragraph. Specifically, the examiner stated at pages 14–15 of the Answer that the "comparable" and "superior" limitations are of "no patentable significance" since they are indefinite. However, as set forth in *Steele*, . . . this approach is incorrect.

V.L. Obviousness and Inherency

1. ***Ex parte Levy***, 17 USPQ 2d 1461, 1464 (B.P.A.I. 1990)

[T]he examiner must provide a basis in fact and/or technical reasoning to reasonably support the determination that the allegedly inherent characteristic necessarily flows from the teachings of the applied prior art.

2. ***In re Spormann***, 150 USPQ 449, 452 (C.C.P.A. 1966)

That which may be inherent is not necessarily known. Obviousness cannot be predicated on what is unknown.

3. *In re Gruskin*, 110 USPQ 288, 292 (C.C.P.A. 1956)

We are therefore of the opinion that there is nothing in the references which would have suggested to one skilled in the art that the above teachings could have been combined to give appellant's toothpaste in spite of the fact that the actual substances disclosed in the reference, if combined, inherently gave a toothpaste having the characteristics of appellant's toothpaste.

4. *In re Rinehart*, 189 USPQ 143, 148 (C.C.P.A. 1976)

The view that success would have been "inherent" cannot, in this case, substitute for a showing of reasonable expectation of success.

5. *In re Newell*, 13 USPQ 2d 1248, 1250 (Fed. Cir. 1989)

[A] retrospective view of inherency is not a substitute for some teaching or suggestion which supports the selection and use of the various elements in the particular claimed combination.

6. *In re Adams*, 148 USPQ 742, 746 (C.C.P.A. 1966)

Finally, the solicitor adds the argument that the superiority of Appellant's heat transfer is inherent in the use of foam. Again we observe that, of course, it is. But the art does not suggest that use of foam in heat transfer of any kind and there is not the slightest suggestion that anyone knew of the existence of this inherent superiority until Adams disclosed it.

7. *Ex parte Schricker*, 56 USPQ 2d 1723, 1725 (B.P.A.I. 2000) (unpublished)

[T]he examiner talks in terms of inherency (which is really an anticipation rationale) while on the other hand the examiner talks in terms that it would have been obvious to experiment to divine optimum conditions.

Inherency and obviousness are somewhat like oil and water—they do not mix well. Claimed subject matter can be anticipated because a prior art reference describes a method which inherently meets the limitations of a claimed method. Claimed subject matter can be unpatentable for obviousness when, notwithstanding a difference between that subject matter and a prior art reference, the claimed subject matter, as a whole, would have been obvious. However, when an examiner relies on inherency, it is incumbent on the examiner to point to the "page and line" of the prior art which justifies an inherency theory. *Compare In re Rijckaert*, 9 F.3d 1531, 1533, 28 USPQ 2d 1955, 1957 (Fed. Cir. 1993) (when the PTO asserts that there is an explicit or implicit teaching or suggestion in the prior art, it must indicate where such a teaching or suggestion appears in the prior art) (citing *In re Yates*, 663 F.2d 1054, 1057, 211 USPQ 1149, 1151 (C.C.P.A. 1981).

V.M. Obviousness Reference and Enablement Requirement

1. ***F.B. Leopold Co. v. Roberts Filter Mfg. Co.***, Civ. App. 96-1218, slip op. at 5–6 (Fed. Cir. July 2, 1997) (unpublished)

   [A]lthough our precedent states that a reference must be enabling to be prior art, that precedent simply means that a reference published before a patent's critical date is prior art only for that which the reference enables. The reference does not entirely lose its status as prior art simply because it fails to disclose a device that works as well as the patented device. Rather, if a prior art reference does not disclose or enable the entire claimed invention, we consider that as a factor in the obviousness determination, but we do not disqualify the reference entirely. *See Beckman Instruments, Inc. v. LKB Produkter AB*, 892 F.2d 1547, 1551, 13 USPQ 2d 1301, 1304 (Fed. Cir. 1989) ("Even if a reference discloses an inoperative device, it is prior art for all that it teaches.").

2. ***Ex parte Lemoine***, 46 USPQ 2d 1420, 1426 (B.P.A.I.), ***reconsideration granted in part***, 46 USPQ 2d 1432 (B.P.A.I. 1998) (unpublished)

   It is axiomatic that a reference must be considered in its entirety, and it is well established that the disclosure of a reference is not limited to specific working examples contained therein.

   In re Fracalossi, 681 F.2d 792, 794 n.1, 215 USPQ 569, 570 n.1 (C.C.P.A. 1982). A reference must be considered for everything it teaches by way of technology. *EWP Corp. v. Reliance Universal Inc.*, 755 F.2d 898, 907, 225 USPQ 20, 25 (Fed. Cir.), *cert. denied*, 474 U.S. 843 (1985).

3. ***ATD Corporation v. Lydall, Inc.***, 48 USPQ 2d 1321, 1330–31 (Fed. Cir. 1998)

   Although international search reports may contain information material to patentability if they contain closer prior art than that which was before the United States examiner, it is the reference itself, not the information generated in prosecuting foreign counterparts, that is material to prosecution in the United States. The details of foreign prosecution are not an additional category of material information.

4. ***Rockwell Int'l Corp. v. United States***, 47 USPQ 2d 1027, 1032 (Fed. Cir. 1998)

   That prior art patents may have described failed attempts or attempts that used different elements is not enough. The prior art must be enabling. *See Motorola, Inc. v. Interdigital*

Tech. Corp., 121 F.3d 1461, 1471, 43 USPQ 2d 1481, 1489 (Fed. Cir. 1997) ("In order to render a claimed apparatus or method obvious, the prior art must enable one skilled in the art to make and use the apparatus or method." (quoting *Beckman Instruments, Inc. v. LKB Produkter AB*, 892 F.2d 1547, 1551, 13 USPQ 2d 1301, 1304 (Fed. Cir. 1989))).

V.N. *Obviousness and Claims Drafter Under "Markush" Practice*

1. ***In re Ruff***, 118 USPQ 340, 347–48 (C.C.P.A. 1958)

    That two things are actually equivalents, in the sense that they will both perform the same function, is not enough to bring into play the rule that when one of them is in the prior art the use of the other is obvious and cannot give rise to patentable invention. One need not think very hard to appreciate that the vast majority of patentable inventions perform old functions. In the bearing art, for example, we have progressed through wood blocks, bronze bushings, ball bearings, roller bearings, tapered roller bearings, needle bearings and sintered powdered metal impregnated with lubricant, to name a few. Today they are art-recognized equivalents. But if, in the course of this progress, ball and roll bearings had both been invented by one person and disclosed in one application, and the art had never heard of roller bearings before, on what theory would a patent be denied on the latter when it turned out that another was the first to invent the ball bearing? That the inventor said they would perform the same function? This is not an imaginary problem for patent applicants more often than not invent and disclose and attempt to claim more than turns out to be novel when the art is searched. They should not be penalized merely because of their own industry and the fullness of their disclosures. So far as we have been able to find, this court has never made an intimation to the contrary. . . . To sum it all up, actual equivalence is not enough to justify refusal of a patent on one member of a group when another member is in the prior art. The equivalence must be disclosed in the prior art or be obvious within the terms of Section 103.

2. ***In re Ruff***, 118 USPQ 340, 348 (C.C.P.A. 1958)

    Markush groups—so-called from the title of the case in which they were first permitted, *Ex parte Markush*, 1925 C.D. 126—were originally regarded as an exception . . . and were rigidly restricted to groups of substances belonging to some recognized class. Such was the rule at the time of the decision of *In re Ayres*, 23 C.C.P.A. (Patents) 1118, in 1936. If only equivalents recognized in scientific classification could be included in a Markush group, naturally the mere existence of such a group in an application tended to prove the equivalence of its members and when one of them was anticipated the group was therefore rendered unpatentable, in the absence of some convincing evidence of some degree of nonequivalency of one or more of the remaining members.

However, the original rigid, emergency-engendered restrictions have been progressively relaxed through the years to the point where it is no longer possible to indulge in a presumption that the members of a Markush group are recognized by anyone to be equivalents except as they "possess at least one property in common which is mainly responsible for their function in the claimed relationship."

VI. Judicial Notice/Examiner Personal Knowledge

1. *In re Pardo*, 214 USPQ 673, 677 (C.C.P.A. 1982)

    [T]his court will always construe [the rule permitting judicial notice] narrowly and will regard facts found in such manner with an eye toward narrowing the scope of any conclusions to be drawn therefrom. Assertions of technical facts in areas of esoteric technology must always be supported by citation to some reference work recognized as standard in the pertinent art and the appellant given, in the Patent Office, the opportunity to challenge the correctness of the assertion or the notoriety or repute of the cited reference. . . . Allegations concerning specific "knowledge" of the prior art, which might be peculiar to a particular art should also be supported and the appellant similarly given the opportunity to make a challenge.

2. *In re Rijckaert*, 28 USPQ 2d 1955, 1957 (Fed. Cir. 1993)

    The Commissioner's assertion "that the [analysis discussed in his brief] and Awamoto demonstrate that the relationship was, in fact, well known in the art" is unavailing. While the court appreciates the Commissioner's thorough explanation of the claimed relationship in his brief, the Commissioner's brief is not prior art. The prior art is Awamoto, and it does not indicate that the relationship is well known in the art, nor does it suggest the claimed relationship. *See In re Yates*, 663 F.2d 1054, 211 USPQ 1149, 1151 (C.C.P.A. 1981) (when the PTO asserts that there is an explicit or implicit teaching or suggestion in the prior art, it must indicate where such a teaching or suggestion appears in the reference).

3. *In re Sun*, 31 USPQ 2d 1451, 1454 (Fed. Cir. 1993) (unpublished)

    In making a rejection, however, an examiner may "take notice of facts beyond the record which, while not generally notorious, are capable of such instant and unquestionable demonstration as to defy dispute." *In re Ahlert*, 424 F.2d at 1091, 165 USPQ at 420.

4. ***In re Sun***, 31 USPQ 2d 1451, 1455 (Fed. Cir. 1993) (unpublished)

[T]he PTO points out in its brief, however, the procedures established by 37 C.F.R. § 1.107(b) (1993) expressly entitle an applicant, on mere request, to an examiner affidavit that provides such citations. In this case, appellants admittedly failed to request such an affidavit. Appellants' failure to avail themselves of this procedure entitling them to such citations, without making any showing whatsoever, waived any right thereto under well established rules of law. Accordingly, appellants' challenge on this ground fails due to their procedural default.

5. ***In re Howard***, 157 USPQ 615, 617–18 (C.C.P.A. 1968) (Kirkpatrick, J., concurring)

I do not see how, without any evidence, we can use the doctrine of judicial notice to find that a system exists which anticipates that of the application or is so nearly like it as to make the application an obvious variation. That, it seems to me, is what we would have to do in order to sustain the conclusion reached by the majority. Without some concrete evidence of the prior art (of which there is none) I do not think that it is possible to find that the system of this application is old or that it is obvious under Section 103.

VII. Considering Allowed Claims With Respect to Rejected Claims

1. ***In re Bisley***, 94 USPQ 80, 83 (C.C.P.A. 1952)

Allowability of an appealed claim is not controlled by the fact that similar claims have been allowed in the Patent Office, since an appealed claim must be patentable in its own right in the opinion of this court. However, similar claims allowed by the Patent Office tribunals furnish evidence of what features those tribunals regarded as patentable, and we think it proper, and sometimes necessary, to consider allowed claims in order to fully determine the views of the board and the examiner.

2. ***In re Baker Hughes Inc.***, 55 USPQ 2d 1149, 1153 (Fed. Cir. 2000)

In its reexamination decision, the examiner allowed another claim, claim 37 (added during reexamination), that is identical to claim 1 except that it explicitly recites a "liquid hydrocarbon." . . . Since the examiner concluded that claim 37 would not have been obvious over the Doerges reference, we can safely assume that he would have concluded that claim 1 would not have been obvious over the Doerges reference had he construed the claim as we have.

VIII. Disclosure Under Section 112, First Paragraph

1. ***Atmel Corp. v. Information Storage Devices Inc.***, 53 USPQ 2d 1225, 1230–31 (Fed. Cir. 1999)

Paragraph 1 is, inter alia, an enablement provision requiring that an inventor set forth in the patent specification how to make and use his or her invention. Paragraph 2 requires claims that particularly and distinctly indicate the subject matter that the inventor considers to be his or her invention. Paragraph 6 also addresses claim language, but refers to the specification for its meaning. In doing so, it specifically refers to "structure . . . described in the specification and equivalents thereof." *Id.* § 112, ¶ 6. This provision represents a quid pro quo by permitting inventors to use a generic means expression for a claim limitation provided that the specification indicates what structure(s) constitute(s) the means. See *O.I. Corp. v. Tekmar Co.*, 115 F.3d 1576, 1583, 42 USPQ 2d 1777, 1782 (Fed. Cir. 1997). The language indicates that means-plus-function clauses comprise not only the language of the claims, but also the structure corresponding] to that means that is disclosed in the written description portion of the specification (and equivalents thereof). Thus, in order for a claim to meet the particularity requirement of ¶ 2, the corresponding structure(s) of a means-plus-function limitation must be disclosed in the written description in such a manner that one skilled in the art will know and understand what structure corresponds to the means limitation. Otherwise, one does not know what the claim means.

Fulfillment of the § 112, ¶ 6 trade-off cannot be satisfied when there is a total omission of structure. There must be structure in the specification. This conclusion is not inconsistent with the fact that the knowledge of one skilled in the particular art may be used to understand what structure(s) the specification discloses, or that even a dictionary or other documentary source may be resorted to for such assistance, because such resources may only be employed in relation to structure that is disclosed in the specification. Paragraph 6 does not contemplate the kind of open-ended reference to extrinsic works that ¶ 1, the enablement provision, does.

Paragraph 1 permits resort to material outside of the specification in order to satisfy the enablement portion of the statute because it makes no sense to encumber the specification of a patent with all the knowledge of the past concerning how to make and use the claimed invention. One skilled in the art knows how to make and use a bolt, a wheel, a gear, a transistor, or a known chemical starting material. The specification would be of enormous and unnecessary length if one had to literally reinvent and describe the wheel.

Section 112, ¶ 6, however, does not have the expansive purpose of ¶ 1. It sets forth a simple requirement, a quid pro quo, in order to utilize a generic means expression. All one needs to do in order to obtain the benefit of that claiming device is to recite some structure corresponding to the means in the specification, as the statute states, so that one can readily ascertain what the claim means and comply with the particularity requirement of ¶ 2. The requirement of specific structure in § 112, ¶ 6 thus does not raise the specter of an unending disclosure of what everyone in the field knows that such a requirement in § 112, ¶ 1 would entail. If our interpretation of the statute results in a slight amount of additional written description appearing in patent specifications compared with total omission of structure, that is the trade-off necessitated by an applicant's use of the statute's permissive generic means term.

VIII.A. Enablement

1. ***General Elec. Co. v. Brenner***, 159 USPQ 335, 337 (D.C. Cir. 1968)

[The specification] need only be reasonable with respect to the art involved; they need not inform the layman nor disclose what the skilled already possess. They need not describe the conventional. . . . The intricacies need not be detailed ad absurdum.

2. ***In re Geerdes***, 180 USPQ 789, 793 (C.C.P.A. 1974)

The question thus raised is whether the scope of enablement, provided one of ordinary skill in the art by the disclosure, is commensurate with the scope of protection sought by the claims. . . . The board expressed concern that "experimentation" is involved in the selection of proportions and particle sizes, but this is not determinative of the question of scope of enablement. It is only undue experimentation which is fatal. . . . One skilled in the extruding art would expect variations in proportions and particle sizes to affect the properties of the foamed product. Also, the specification contains a variety of examples showing different proportions and particle sizes.

3. ***In re Angstadt***, 190 USPQ 214, 219 (C.C.P.A. 1976)

We note that the PTO has the burden of giving reasons, supported by the record as a whole, why the specification is not enabling. . . . Showing that the disclosure entails undue experimentation is part of the PTO's initial burden.

4. ***Lindemann Maschinenfabrik GmbH v. American Hoist & Derrick Co.***, 221 USPQ 481, 489 (Fed. Cir. 1984)

The question is whether the disclosure is sufficient to enable those skilled in the art to practice the claimed invention, hence the specification need not disclose what is well known in the art.

5. ***Staehelin v. Secher***, 24 USPQ 2d 1513, 1516 (B.P.A.I. 1992)

It has been consistently held that the first paragraph of 35 USC 112 required nothing more than objective enablement. . . . In satisfying the enablement requirement, an application need not teach, and preferably omits, that which is well-known in the art. . . . How such a teaching is set forth, whether by the use of illustrative examples or by broad descriptive terminology, is of no importance since a specification which teaches how to make and use the invention in terms which correspond in scope to the claims must be taken as complying with the first paragraph of 35 USC 112 unless there is reason to doubt the objective truth of the statements relied upon therein for enabling support. . . .

The error we see in Staehelin's approach to the question before us is that Staehelin would require a patent specification to be a blueprint which, if followed, would unfailingly reproduce exactly an applicant's claimed invention. However, the law does not require a specification to be a blueprint in order to satisfy the requirement for enablement under 35 USC 112, first paragraph.

6. ***In re Wolfensperger***, 133 USPQ 537, 541–42 (C.C.P.A. 1962)

The board's statement that "drawings alone cannot form the basis of a valid claim" is too broad a generalization to be valid and is, furthermore, contrary to well-settled and long established Patent Office practice. . . . For another thing, consider that the only informative and significant disclosure in many electrical and chemical patents is by means of circuit diagrams or graphic formulae, constituting "drawings" in the case.

7. ***In re Howarth***, 210 USPQ 689, 691 (C.C.P.A. 1981)

The starting point under § 112 is that a duty is imposed which must be met by an applicant. In exchange for the patent, he must enable others to practice his invention. An inventor need not, however, explain every detail since he is speaking to those skilled in the art. What is conventional knowledge will be read into the disclosure. Accordingly, an applicant's duty to tell all that is necessary to make or use varies greatly depending upon the art to which the invention pertains.

8. ***In re Howarth***, 210 USPQ 689, 692 (C.C.P.A. 1981)

It is well settled that the disclosure of an application embraces not only what is expressly set forth in words or drawings, but what would be understood by persons skilled in the art. As was said in *Webster Loom Co. v. Higgins et al.,* . . . the applicant "may begin at the point where his invention begins, and describe what he has made that is new and what it replaces of the old. That which is common and well known is as if it were written out in the patent and delineated in the drawings."

9. ***Webster Loom Co. v. Higgins***, 105 U.S. 580, 582–86 (1882)

If a mechanical engineer invents an improvement on any of the appendages of a steam-engine . . . he is not obliged, in order to make himself understood, to describe the engine, nor the particular appendage to which the improvement refers, nor its mode of connection with the principal machine. These are already familiar to others skilled in that kind of machinery. He may begin at the point where his invention begins, and describe what he has made that is new, and what it replaces of the old. That which is common and well known is as if it were written out in the patent and delineated in the drawings.

10. ***In re Wright***, 27 USPQ 2d 1510, 1513 (Fed. Cir. 1993)

When rejecting a claim under the enablement requirement of § 112, the PTO bears an initial burden of setting forth a reasonable explanation as to why it believes that the scope of protection provided by the claim is not adequately enabled by the description of the invention provided in the specification of the application; this includes, of course, providing sufficient reasons for doubting any assertions in the specification as to the scope of enablement.

11. ***Fiers v. Revel***, 25 USPQ 2d 1601, 1607 (Fed. Cir. 1993)

"[A] specification disclosure which contains a teaching of the manner and process of making and using the invention in terms which correspond in scope to those used in describing and defining the subject matter sought to be patented must be taken in as in compliance with the enabling requirement of the first paragraph of § 112 unless there is reason to doubt the objective truth of the statements contained therein which must be relied on for enabling support." *In re*

Marzocchi, 439 F.2d 220, 223, 169 USPQ 367, 369 (C.C.P.A. 1971). "[A]ny party making the assertion that a U.S. patent specification or claims fails, for one reason or another, to comply with § 112 bears the burden of persuasion in showing said lack of compliance." *Weil v. Fritz*, 601 F.2d 551, 555, 202 USPQ 447, 450 (C.C.P.A. 1979).

12. ***Ex parte DeCastro***, 28 USPQ 2d 1391, 1393 (B.P.A.I. 1993)
[U]nder appropriate circumstances an applicant may describe a material used in a claimed invention by referencing materials sold under a particular trade name or trademark.

13. ***In re Fisher***, 166 USPQ 18, 24 (C.C.P.A. 1970)
It is apparent that such an inventor should be allowed to dominate the future patentable inventions of others where those inventions were based in some way on his teachings, are still within his contribution, since the improvement was made possible by his work. It is equally apparent, however, that he must not be permitted to achieve this dominance by claims which are insufficiently supported and hence not in compliance with the first paragraph of 35 U.S.C. 112. That paragraph requires that the scope of the claims must bear a reasonable correlation to the scope of enablement provided by the specification to persons of ordinary skill in the art. In cases involving predictable factors, such as mechanical or electrical elements, a single embodiment provides broad enablement in the sense that, once imagined, other embodiments can be made without difficulty and their performance characteristics predicted by resort to known scientific laws. In cases involving unpredictable factors, such as most chemical reactions and physiological activity, the scope of enablement obviously varies inversely with the degree of unpredictability of the factors involved.

14. ***Gould v. Mossinghoff***, 219 USPQ 393, 396 (D.C. Cir. 1983)
Moreover, even if the claim language may also include laser oscillators, that would not bar appellant from supporting his claim by disclosing only an amplifier. Under the settled rule that a broad mechanical claim can be supported by disclosure of a single embodiment of the claimed invention, a claim can be sustained even if it covers other inoperative or inadequately disclosed forms of the invention. . . . It is thus immaterial that appellant's claims may cover inadequately disclosed oscillators.

15. ***In re Naquin***, 158 USPQ 317, 319 (C.C.P.A. 1968)
The specification need describe the invention only in such detail as to enable a person skilled in the most relevant art

to make and use it. When an invention, in its different aspects, involves distinct arts, that specification is adequate which enables the adepts of each art, those who have the best chance of being enabled, to carry out the aspect proper to their specialty.

16. ***Spectra-Physics, Inc. v. Coherent, Inc.***, 3 USPQ 2d 1737, 1743 (Fed. Cir.), ***cert. denied***, 484 U.S. 954 (1987)

If an invention pertains to an art where the results are predictable, e.g., mechanical as opposed to chemical arts, a broad claim can be enabled by disclosure of a single embodiment, . . . and is not invalid for lack of enablement simply because it reads on another embodiment of the invention which is inadequately disclosed.

17. ***Cedarapids, Inc. v. Nordberg, Inc.***, Civ. App. 95-1529, slip op. 4–5 (Fed. Cir. Aug. 11, 1997) (unpublished)

Rock crusher technology is not in the same category as the chemical arts where a slight variation in a method can yield an unpredictable result or may not work at all.

In cases involving predictable factors, such as mechanical or electrical elements, a single embodiment provides broad enablement in the sense that, once imagined, other embodiments can be made without difficulty and their performance characteristics predicted by resort to known scientific laws. In cases involving unpredictable factors, such as most chemical and physiological activity, the scope of enablement obviously varies inversely with the degree of unpredictability of the factors involved.

In re Fisher, 427 F.2d 833, 839, 166 USPQ 18, 24 (CCPA 1970). . . . Our cases have, therefore, held that in the mechanical as opposed to chemical arts a broad claim can be enabled by disclosure of a single embodiment. . . . It is not invalid for lack of enablement simply because it reads on another embodiment of the invention which is inadequately disclosed.

18. ***Cedarapids, Inc. v. Nordberg, Inc.***, Civ. App. 95-1529, slip op. 5–6 (Fed. Cir. Aug. 11, 1997) (unpublished) (citing ***Christianson v. Colt Indus. Operating Corp.***, 3 USPQ 2d 1016, 1027 (Fed. Cir. 1987), ***vacated on other grounds***, 486 U.S. 800 (1988))

All that is claimed is a method to increase productivity of rock crushers by simultaneously increasing speed and throw. While it may require experimentation to arrive at the optimum level of the simultaneous increases for various size crushers, we have never held that a patent must disclose information sufficient to manufacture a commercial product incorporating the invention.

19. ***Musco Corp. v. Qualite, Inc.***, Civ. App. 96-1212, slip op. 2 (Fed. Cir. Jan. 17, 1997) (unpublished) (quoting ***PPG Indus., Inc. v. Guardian Indus. Corp.***, 37 USPQ 2d 1618, 1623 (Fed. Cir. 1996))

Although some experimentation on the part of the artisan is not fatal, . . . , either the experimentation must be routine, or the specification must give "a reasonable amount of guidance with respect to the direction in which the experimentation should proceed to enable the determination of how to practice a desired embodiment of the invention claimed."

20. ***In re Vickers***, 61 USPQ 122, 127 (C.C.P.A. 1944)

In his statement to the Board of Appeals, the Examiner stated that appellants had not disclosed . . . how such an apparatus could operate; and that appellants had failed to describe such a structure in their application.

In other words, as we understand the Examiner's decision, he held the claims to be too broad because the applicants did not disclose in their application each specific embodiment of the invention covered by the appealed claims. That holding was affirmed by the Board of Appeals.

Obviously, the decision of the Board of Appeals, as well as that of the Primary Examiner, is not in accordance with the rule as stated in the solicitor's brief, that is, "that ordinarily in a mechanical case broad claims may be supported by a disclosure of a single form of the apparatus disclosed in an application." Nor is the board's decision in conformity with the statement contained therein that "in a mechanical case an applicant may generally draw a broad claim on a single construction."

In mechanical cases, such as that here involved, broad claims may be supported by a single form of the apparatus disclosed in an applicant's application.

21. ***Ex parte Goldgaber***, 41 USPQ 2d 1172, 1175 (B.P.A.I. 1996)

If, by that argument, appellants would cast aspersions on the Glenner patent or imply that the patent is non-enabling or otherwise discredit its qualifications as a reference, we disagree. As stated in 35 USC 282, a patent shall be presumed valid and each claim of a patent shall be presumed valid independently of the validity of other claims. Considering that presumption of validity, we presume that Glenner's claims are based on a fully enabling disclosure as required by 35 USC 112, first paragraph.

22. ***In re Cook***, 169 USPQ 298, 302 (C.C.P.A. 1971) (quoting ***In re Skrivan***, 166 USPQ 85, 88 (C.C.P.A. 1970))

[M]any patented claims read on vast numbers of inoperative embodiments in the trivial sense that they can and do omit "factors which must be presumed to be within the level of ordinary skill in the art," . . . and therefore read on embodiments in which such factors may be included in such a manner as to make the embodiments inoperative. There is nothing wrong with this so long as it would be obvious to one of ordinary skill in the relevant art how to include those factors in such manner as to make the embodiment operative rather than inoperative. . . . The word "obvious" as here used means that those skilled in the art would know how to determine utility without having to build and try out the conceived embodiment and could do so without the expenditure of unreasonable effort.

23. ***Applied Medical Resources Corp. v. United States Surgical Corp.***, 47 USPQ 2d 1289, 1291 (Fed. Cir. 1998), ***cert. denied***, 525 U.S. 1104 (1999)

[A]n applicant is obliged to disclose nonclaimed elements necessary to the operation or carrying out of the invention to which the patent is directed. . . . However, where the invention relates only to a part of, or one aspect of, a device, an applicant is not required to disclose a nonclaimed element necessary to the operation of the overall device, but not necessary to the operation of the invention to which the patent is directed.

24. ***Genentech, Inc. v. Novo Nordisk A/S***, 42 USPQ 2d 1001, 1005 (Fed. Cir.), ***cert. denied***, 522 U.S. 963 (1997)

It is true, as Genentech argues, that a specification need not disclose what is well known in the art. . . . However, that general, oft-repeated statement is merely a rule of supplementation, not a substitute for a basic enabling disclosure. It means that the omission of minor details does not cause a specification to fail to meet the enablement requirement. However, when there is no disclosure of any specific starting material or of any of the conditions under which a process can be carried out, undue experimentation is required; there is a failure to meet the enablement requirement that cannot be rectified by asserting that all the disclosure related to the process is within the skill of the art. It is the specification, not the knowledge of one skilled in the art, that must supply the novel aspects of an invention in order to constitute adequate enablement.

25. ***Genentech, Inc. v. Novo Nordisk A/S***, 42 USPQ 2d 1001, 1005 (Fed. Cir.), ***cert. denied***, 522 U.S. 963 (1997)

Tossing out the mere germ of an idea does not constitute enabling disclosure. While every aspect of a generic claim certainly need not have been carried out by an inventor, or exemplified in the specification, reasonable detail must be ·provided in order to enable members of the public to understand and carry out the invention.

26. ***Hyatt v. Boone***, 47 USPQ 2d 1128, 1130 (Fed. Cir. 1998), ***cert. denied***, 525 U.S. 1141 (1999)

The claims as filed are part of the specification, and may provide or contribute to compliance with § 112.

27. ***National Recovery Techs., Inc. v. Magnetic Separation Sys., Inc.***, 49 USPQ 2d 1671, 1675–76 (Fed. Cir. 1999)

The enablement requirement ensures that the public knowledge is enriched by the patent specification to a degree at least commensurate with the scope of the claims. The scope of the claims must be less than or equal to the scope of the enablement. The scope of enablement, in turn, is that which is disclosed in the specification plus the scope of what would be known to one of ordinary skill in the art without undue experimentation. See In re Fisher, 427 F.2d 833, 839, 166 USPQ 18, 24 (C.C.P.A. 1970) ("The scope of the claims must bear a reasonable correlation to the scope of enablement provided by the specification to persons of ordinary skill in the art.")

28. ***National Recovery Techs., Inc. v. Magnetic Separation Sys., Inc.***, 49 USPQ 2d 1671, 1676 (Fed. Cir. 1999)

[A] claim is not invalid for lack of operability simply because the invention does not work perfectly under all conditions. *See Hildreth v. Mastoras*, 257 U.S. 27, 34, 66 L. Ed. 112, 42 S. Ct. 20 (1921) ("The machine patented may be imperfect in its operation; but if it embodies the general principle and works . . . it is enough."); *Decca, Ltd. v. United States*, 210 Ct. Cl. 546, 544 F.2d 1070, 191 USPQ 439 (Ct. Cl. 1976) ("The mere fact that the system has some drawbacks, or that under certain postulated conditions it may not work . . . does not detract from the operability of the disclosed equipment to perform its described function.")

29. ***National Recovery Techs., Inc. v. Magnetic Separation Sys., Inc.***, 49 USPQ 2d 1671, 1676 (Fed. Cir. 1999)

Whether a patented device or process is operable is a different inquiry than whether a particular claim is enabled by the specification. In order to satisfy the enablement requirement of § 112, paragraph 1, the specification must enable one of ordinary skill in the art to practice the claimed invention without undue experimentation. Thus, with respect to enablement the relevant inquiry lies in the relationship between the specification, the claims, and the knowledge of one of ordinary skill in the art. If, by following the steps set forth in the specification, one of ordinary skill in the art is not able to replicate the claimed invention without undue experimentation, the claim has not been enabled as required by § 112, paragraph 1.

30. ***National Recovery Techs., Inc. v. Magnetic Separation Sys., Inc.***, 49 USPQ 2d 1671, 1677 (Fed. Cir. 1999)

While the written description does enable one of ordinary skill in the art to approximate the claimed function, this is not the same as enabling one of ordinary skill in the art to perform the actual selection step of claim 1 for which NRT claims patent protection. The written description does not at all purport to enable one of ordinary skill in the art to determine where irregularities exist in the containers. . . . [C]laim 1 broadly claims exactly this theoretical possibility that NRT admits is not disclosed in the specification of the '576 patent. . . .

The '576 patent therefore recognizes a specific need in the materials sorting field and suggests a theoretical answer to that need. It provides a starting point from which one of skill in the art can perform further research in order to practice the claimed invention, but this is not adequate to constitute enablement. . . . The specification of the '576 patent therefore does not enable one of ordinary skill in the art to practice the full scope of the invention embodied in claim 1 without undue experimentation. The most that NRT can be credited with is promising the ideal result in claim 1, even though the specification does not completely deliver on this promise.

31. ***Process Control Corp. v. HydReclaim Corp.***, 52 USPQ 2d 1029, 1034–35 (Fed. Cir. 1999)

Lack of enablement and absence of utility are closely related grounds of unpatentability. . . . The enablement requirement of 35 U.S.C. § 112, ¶ 1 requires that the specification adequately discloses to one skilled in the relevant art how to make, or in the case of a process, how to carry out, the claimed invention without undue experimentation. . . . The utility requirement of 35 U.S.C. § 101 mandates that any patentable invention be useful and, accordingly, the subject matter of the claim must be operable. . . . If a patent claim fails to meet the utility requirement because it is not useful or operative, then it also fails to meet the how-to-use aspect of the enablement requirement.

32. ***Process Control Corp. v. HydReclaim Corp.***, 52 USPQ 2d 1029, 1035 (Fed. Cir. 1999) (quoting ***Brooktree Corp. v. Advanced Micro Devices, Inc.***, 24 USPQ 2d 1401, 1412 (Fed. Cir. 1992))

[W]hen an impossible limitation, such as a nonsensical method of operation, is clearly embodied within the claim, the claimed invention must be held invalid. While an otherwise valid patent covering a meritorious invention should not be struck down simply because of the patentee's misconceptions about scientific principles concerning the invention, . . . when "the claimed subject matter is inoperable, the patent may indeed be invalid for failure to meet the utility requirement of § 101 and the enablement requirement of § 112."

33. ***Process Control Corp. v. HydReclaim Corp.***, 52 USPQ 2d 1029, 1035 (Fed. Cir. 1999)

In the present case, it is undisputed by both HydReclaim and Process Control that a consistent definition of "discharge rate" in clauses [b] and [d] of claim 1 leads to a nonsensical conclusion. . . . In other words, clause [d] requires determining a quantity from the sum of that exact same quantity and something else, or symbolically, $A = A + B$, which is impossible, where, as here, B is not equal to zero. Accordingly, we hold that the correctly construed claims are invalid because they are inoperative, and thus the claims fail to comply with the utility and enablement requirements of 35 U.S.C. §§ 101 and 112, ¶ 1, respectively.

34. ***In re Cortright***, 49 USPQ 2d 1464, 1466 (Fed. Cir. 1999) (quotations omitted)

A lack of enablement rejection under section 112, ¶ 1 is appropriate where the written description fails to teach those in the art to make and use the invention as broadly as it is claimed without undue experimentation. . . .

This rejection takes several forms. The PTO will make a scope of enablement rejection where the written description enables something within the scope of the claims, but the claims are not limited to that scope. . . . This type of rejection is marked by language stating that the specification does not enable one of ordinary skill to use the invention commensurate with the scope of the claims. On the other hand, if the written description does not enable any subject matter within the scope of the claims, the PTO will make a general enablement rejection, stating that the specification does not teach how to make or use the invention. . . .

If the written description fails to illuminate a credible utility, the PTO will make both a section 112, ¶ 1 rejection for failure to teach how to use the invention and a section 101 rejection for lack of utility. . . . This dual rejection occurs because "the how to use prong of section 112 incorporates as a matter of law the requirement of 35 U.S.C. § 101 that the specification disclose as a matter of fact a practical utility for the invention." . . . Thus, an applicant's failure to disclose how to use an invention may support a rejection under either section 112, ¶ 1 for lack of enablement as a result of "the specification's . . . failure to disclose adequately to one ordinarily skilled in the art 'how to use' the invention without undue experimentation," or section 101 for lack of utility "when there is a complete absence of data supporting the statements which set forth the desired results of the claimed invention." . . .

The PTO cannot make this type of rejection, however, unless it has reason to doubt the objective truth of the statements contained in the written description. . . . The PTO may establish a reason to doubt an invention's asserted utility when the written description "suggests an inherently unbelievable undertaking or involves implausible scientific principles."

35. *In re Cortright*, 49 USPQ 2d 1464, 1469 (Fed. Cir. 1999) (quoting *Newman v. Quigg*, 11 USPQ 2d 1340, 1345 (Fed. Cir. 1989))

"It is not a requirement of patentability that an inventor correctly set forth, or even know, how or why the invention works." . . . Furthermore, statements that a physiological phenomenon was observed are not inherently suspect simply because the underlying basis for the observation cannot be predicted or explained. Therefore, the board erred in suggesting that Cortright was required to prove the cause of the resultant hair growth.

36. *In re Cortright*, 49 USPQ 2d 1464, 1468 (Fed. Cir. 1999)

In light of these disclosures, one of ordinary skill would not construe "restoring hair growth" to mean "returning the user's hair to its original state," as the board required. To the contrary, consistent with Cortright's disclosure and that of other references, one of ordinary skill would construe this phrase as meaning that the claimed method increases the amount of hair grown on the scalp but does not necessarily produce a full head of hair. Properly construed, claim 1 is amply supported by the written description because Example 1 discloses the amount of Bag Balm (R) to apply (about one teaspoon daily) and the amount of time (about one month) in which to expect results. These dosing instructions enable one of ordinary skill to practice the claimed invention without the need for any experimentation. Therefore, we reverse the board's rejection of claim 1.

37. ***Enzo Biochem, Inc. v. Calgene, Inc.***, 52 USPQ 2d 1129, 1135 (Fed. Cir. 1999)

Whether claims are sufficiently enabled by a disclosure in a specification is determined as of the date that the patent application was first filed.

38. ***Enzo Biochem, Inc. v. Calgene, Inc.***, 52 USPQ 2d 1129, 1135–36 (Fed. Cir. 1999)

We have held that a patent specification complies with the statute even if a "reasonable" amount of routine experimentation is required in order to practice a claimed invention, but that such experimentation must not be "undue." . . . [W]e set forth a number of factors which a court may consider in determining whether a disclosure would require undue experimentation. These factors were set forth as follows:

> (1) the quantity of experimentation necessary, (2) the amount of direction or guidance presented, (3) the presence or absence of working examples, (4) the nature of the invention, (5) the state of the prior art, (6) the relative skill of those in the art, (7) the predictability or unpredictability of the art, and (8) the breadth of the claims.

. . . We have also noted that all of the factors need not be reviewed when determining whether a disclosure is enabling.

39. ***Johns Hopkins Univ. v. Cellpro, Inc.***, 47 USPQ 2d 1705, 1713 (Fed. Cir. 1998)

A party who wishes to prove that the claims of a patent are not enabled by means of a failed attempt to make the disclosed invention must show that the patent's disclosure was followed.

40. ***Enzo Biochem, Inc. v. Calgene, Inc.***, 52 USPQ 2d 1129, 1138–39 (Fed. Cir. 1999)

Outside of the three genes regulated in E. coli, virtually no guidance, direction, or working examples were provided for practicing the invention in eukaryotes, or even any prokaryote other than E. coli. . . . Here, however, the teachings set forth in the specifications provide no more than a "plan" or "invitation" for those of skill in the art to experiment practicing antisense in eukaryotic cells; they do not provide sufficient guidance or specificity as to how to execute that plan. . . . We thus conclude that the district court did not clearly err in finding that the specifications provided little guidance or direction as to the practice of antisense in cells other than E. coli, and that such minimal disclosure as there was constituted no more than a plan or invitation to practice antisense in those cells. . . . However, we agree with Calgene that Inouye has provided only the mere "germ of the idea" for exploiting antisense in eukaryotes. . . . What is glaringly "missing" from the specifications is the disclosure of any direction or examples of how such an idea might be implemented in any cell other than E. coli. Inouye's disclosure of practicing antisense in E. coli does not suffice to enable the practice of antisense in all categories of living matter.

41. ***Enzo Biochem, Inc. v. Calgene, Inc.***, 52 USPQ 2d 1129, 1138 n.10 (Fed. Cir. 1999)

In view of the rapid advances in science, we recognize that what may be unpredictable at one point in time may become predictable at a later time.

42. ***In re Vaeck***, 20 USPQ 2d 1438, 1445 (Fed. Cir. 1991)

We do not imply that patent applicants in art areas currently denominated as "unpredictable" must never be allowed generic claims encompassing more than the particular species disclosed in their specification.

VIII.B. *Written Description*

1. ***Orthokinetics Inc. v. Safety Travel Chairs Inc.***, 1 USPQ 2d 1081, 1088 (Fed. Cir. 1986)

The foregoing statement employs two measures impermissible in law: (1) it requires that claim 1 "describe" the invention, which is the role of the disclosure portion of the specification, not the role of the claims; and (2) it applied the "full, clear, concise, and exact" requirement of the first paragraph of §112 to the claim, when that paragraph applies only to the disclosure portion of the specification, not to the claims.

2. ***Forssmann v. Matsuo***, 23 USPQ 2d 1548, 1550 (B.P.A.I. 1992), ***aff'd***, 991 F.2d 809 (Fed. Cir. 1993)

[T]o comply with the description requirement of 35 U.S.C. 112, first paragraph . . .; all that is required is that the application reasonably convey to persons skilled in the art that, as of the filing date thereof, the inventor had possession of the subject matter later claimed by him.

3. ***Vas-Cath, Inc. v. Mahurkar***, 19 USPQ 2d 1111, 1117 (Fed. Cir. 1991)

35 USC 112, first paragraph, requires a "written description of the invention" which is separate and distinct from the en-

ablement requirement. The purpose of the "written description" requirement is broader than to merely explain how to "make and use"; the applicant must also convey with reasonable clarity to those skilled in the art that, as of the filing date sought, he or she was in possession of the invention. The invention is, for purposes of the "written description" inquiry, whatever is now claimed.

4. ***Staehelin v. Secher***, 24 USPQ 2d 1513, 1519 (B.P.A.I. 1992)

The written description requirement of 35 USC 112, first paragraph, is separate from the enablement requirement found in the same provision of 35 USC 112. . . . Satisfaction of the "written description" requirement does not require in haec verba antecedence in the originally filed application.

5. ***Vas-Cath, Inc. v. Mahurkar***, 19 USPQ 2d 1111, 1118 (Fed. Cir. 1991)

[U]nder proper circumstances, drawings alone may provide a "written description" of an invention as required by § 112.

6. ***In re Gardner***, 178 USPQ 149, 149 (C.C.P.A. 1973)

Under these circumstances, we consider the original claim in itself adequate "written description" of the claimed invention. It was equally a "written description" whether located among the original claims or in the descriptive part of the specification.

7. ***Amgen Inc. v. Chugai Pharm. Co.***, 18 USPQ 2d 1016, 1027 (Fed. Cir.), ***cert. denied***, 502 U.S. 856 (1991)

It is well established that a patent applicant is entitled to claim his invention generically, when he describes it sufficiently to meet the requirements of Section 112. See *Utter v. Hiraga*, 845 F.2d 993, 998, 6 USPQ 2d 1709, 1714 (Fed. Cir. 1988) ("A specification may, within the meaning of 35 U.S.C. § 112 ¶ 1, contain a written description of a broadly claimed invention without describing all species that claim encompasses."); *In re Robins*, 429 F.2d 452, 456–57, 166 USPQ 552, 555 (C.C.P.A. 1970) ("[R]epresentative samples are not required by the statute and are not an end in themselves.").

8. ***Ex parte Maizel***, 27 USPQ 2d 1662, 1669 (B.P.A.I. 1992)

In *Amgen Inc. v. Chugai Pharmaceutical Co.*, 927 F.2d 1200, 18 USPQ 2d 1016 [(Fed. Cir.), *cert. denied*, 502 U.S. 856] (1991), the Federal Circuit set forth practical guidelines for determining "conception." These guidelines are applicable to the specifications of patent applications directed to biological subject matter. The court stated:

A gene is a chemical compound, albeit a complex one, and it is well established in our law that conception of a chemical compound requires that the inventor be able to define it so as to distinguish it from other materials, and to describe how to obtain it. . . . Conception does not occur unless one has a mental picture of the structure of the chemical, or is able to define it by its method of preparation, its physical or chemical properties, or whatever characteristics sufficiently distinguish it. It is not sufficient to define it solely by its principal biological property, e.g., encoding human erythropoietin, because an alleged conception having no more specificity than that is simply a wish to know the identity of any material with that biological property. 927 F.2d at 1206, 18 USPQ 2d at 1021.

9. ***In re Wertheim***, 191 USPQ 90, 96 (C.C.P.A. 1976)

It is not necessary that the application describe the claim limitations exactly, . . . but only so clearly that persons of ordinary skill in the art will recognize from the disclosure that appellants invented processes including those limitations.

10. ***Jacobs v. Lawson***, 214 USPQ 907, 910 (B.P.A.I. 1982)

It is well settled that "the invention claimed [in the later application] does not have to be described [in the parent] in ipsis verbis in order to satisfy the description requirement of §112." *Wagoner v. Barger*, 463 F.2d 1377, 175 USPQ 85 (C.C.P.A. 1972).

11. ***Ex parte Parks***, 30 USPQ 2d 1234, 1236–37 (B.P.A.I. 1993)

Adequate description under the first paragraph of 35 U.S.C. 112 does not require literal support for the claimed invention. . . . Rather, it is sufficient if the originally-filed disclosure would have conveyed to one having ordinary skill in the art that an appellant had possession of the concept of what is claimed.

12. ***In re Eickmeyer***, 202 USPQ 655, 662 (C.C.P.A. 1979)

To satisfy the description requirement of section 112, first paragraph, an application must contain sufficient disclosure, expressly or inherently, to make it clear to one skilled in the art that the appellant was in possession of the subject matter claimed. . . . "[A] statement of appellant's invention [in his specification] which is as broad as appellant's broadest claims" is sufficient to meet this requirement.

13. ***Fujikawa v. Wattanasin***, 39 USPQ 2d 1895, 1904 (Fed. Cir. 1996)

[I]psis verbis disclosure is not necessary to satisfy the written description requirement of section 112. Instead, the disclosure need only reasonably convey to persons skilled in the art

that the inventor had possession of the subject matter in question. *In re Edwards*, 568 F.2d 1349, 1351–52, 196 USPQ 465, 467 (CCPA 1978). In other words, the question is whether [the] "application provides adequate direction which reasonably [would lead] persons skilled in the art" to the subgenus of the proposed count. *Id.* at 1352, 196 USPQ at 467.

14. **In re Alton**, 37 USPQ 2d 1578, 1583 (Fed. Cir. 1996)

The examiner (or the Board, if the Board is the first body to raise a particular ground for rejection) "bears the initial burden . . . of presenting a prima facie case of unpatentability." *In re Oetiker*, 977 F.2d 1443, 1445, 24 USPQ2d 1443, 1444 (Fed. Cir. 1992). Insofar as the written description requirement is concerned, that burden is discharged by "presenting evidence or reasons why persons skilled in the art would not recognize in the disclosure a description of the invention defined by the claims." *Wertheim*, 541 F.2d at 263, 191 USPQ at 97. Thus, the burden placed on the examiner varies, depending upon what the applicant claims. If the applicant claims embodiments of the invention that are completely outside the scope of the specification, then the examiner or Board need only establish this fact to make out a prima facie case. *Id.* at 263–64, 191 USPQ at 97. If, on the other hand, the specification contains a description of the claimed invention, albeit not *in ipsis verbis* (in the identical words), then the examiner or Board, in order to meet the burden of proof, must provide reasons why one of ordinary skill in the art would not consider the description sufficient. *Id.* at 264, 191 USPQ at 98.

15. **In re Alton**, 37 USPQ 2d 1578, 1584 (Fed. Cir. 1996)

If a person of ordinary skill in the art would have understood the inventor to have been in possession of the claimed invention at the time of filing, even if every nuance of the claims is not explicitly described in the specification, then the adequate written description requirement is met.

16. **Regents of Univ. of Cal. v. Eli Lilly & Co.**, 43 USPQ 2d 1398, 1404 (Fed. Cir. 1997) (quoting **Lockwood v. American Airlines, Inc.**, 41 USPQ 2d 1961, 1966 (1997))

To fulfill the written description requirement, a patent specification must describe an invention and do so in sufficient detail that one skilled in the art can clearly conclude that "the inventor invented the claimed invention." . . . ; Thus, an applicant complies with the written description requirement "by describing the invention, with all its claimed limitations, not that which makes it obvious," and by using "such descriptive means as words, structures, figures, diagrams, formulas, etc., that set forth the claimed invention."

17. ***Regents of Univ. of Cal. v. Eli Lilly & Co.***, 43 USPQ 2d 1398, 1405 (Fed. Cir. 1997)

Recently, we held that a description which renders obvious a claimed invention is not sufficient to satisfy the written description requirement of that invention. . . . Thus, *a fortiori*, a description that does *not* render a claimed invention obvious does not sufficiently describe that invention for purposes of § 112, ¶ 1.

18. ***Lockwood v. American Airlines, Inc.***, 41 USPQ 2d 1961, 1966 (Fed. Cir. 1997)

It is not sufficient for purposes of the written description requirement of § 112 that the disclosure, when combined with the knowledge in the art, would lead one to speculate as to modifications that the inventor might have envisioned, but failed to disclose. Each application in the chain must describe the claimed features.

19. ***In re Driscoll***, 195 USPQ 434, 438 (C.C.P.A. 1977) (quoting ***Engineering Dev. Labs. v. Radio Corp. of Am.***, 68 USPQ 238, 241–42 (2d Cir. 1946))

This record presents yet another instance of the sort of "hypertechnical application" of the written description requirement of §112 which was recently criticized . . . Were the board's decision permitted to stand, future applicants, particularly in cases of this nature, would in all likelihood find themselves in the predicament reflected in the following observation by Judge Learned Hand:

> If, when [applicants] yield any part of what they originally believed to be their due, they substitute a new "invention," only two courses will be open to them; they must at the outset either prophetically divine what the art contains, or they must lay down a barrage of claims, starting with the widest and proceeding by the successive incorporation of more and more detail, until all combinations have been exhausted which can by any possibility succeed. The first is an impossible task; the second is a custom already more honored in the breach than in the observance, and its extension would only increase that surfeit of verbiage which has for long been the curse of patent practice, and has done much to discredit it. It is impossible to imagine any public purpose which it would serve.

20. ***Tronzo v. Biomet, Inc.***, 47 USPQ 2d 1829, 1832 (Fed. Cir. 1998)

A disclosure in a parent application that merely renders the later-claimed invention obvious is not sufficient to meet the written description requirement; the disclosure must describe the claimed invention with all its limitations. *See Lockwood*, 107 F.3d at 1572, 41 USPQ 2d at 1966

21. ***In re Lakic***, Civ. App. 98-1248, slip op. at 3 (Fed. Cir. Dec. 17, 1998) (unpublished)

Lakic has not proved that his written description discloses "a bladder at least a portion of which is associated with said flexible tongue." The affidavit does not state that one of ordinary skill would "necessarily comprehend" that the bladder of Figure 32 would be associated with the tongue.

22. ***Hyatt v. Boone***, 47 USPQ 2d 1128, 1133 (Fed. Cir. 1998), ***cert. denied***, 525 U.S. 1141 (1999)

We also take note, as held in *Weil v. Fritz*, 572 F.2d 856, 863, 196 USPQ 600, 606 (C.C.P.A. 1978), that the "applicant's oath is not a requirement of § 112, first paragraph, but of 35 U.S.C. § 115; therefore, the sufficiency of [the prior] oath is not material under § 120."

23. ***Hyatt v. Boone***, 47 USPQ 2d 1128, 1130 (Fed. Cir. 1998), ***cert. denied***, 525 U.S. 1141 (1999)

The claims as filed are part of the specification, and may provide or contribute to compliance with § 112.

24. ***In re Cortright***, 49 USPQ 2d 1464, 1469 (Fed. Cir. 1999)

Nevertheless, we must affirm the rejection of claim 15 because the written description fails to disclose that the active ingredient reaches the papilla or that offsetting occurs. . . . Here, although the written description states that people observed hair growth after applying Bag Balm (R) to the scalp, it does not disclose that anyone observed the active ingredient reach the papilla and offset the effects of lower levels of male hormones. It states, rather, that "it is believed that the rubbed-in ointment offsets the effects of lower levels of male hormones in the papilla and/or provides an antimicrobial effect on infection," and that "Applicant surmises that the active antimicrobial agent, 8-hydroxy-quinoline sulfate, reaches the papilla, and is effective to off-set the male hormones such as testosterone and/or androsterone, and/or kill or seriously weaken any bacteria about or in the papilla . . . ." These statements reflect no actual observations. Moreover, we have not been shown that one of ordinary skill would necessarily conclude from the information expressly disclosed by the written description that the active ingredient reaches the papilla or that off-setting occurs.

25. ***Purdue Pharma L.P. v. Faulding Inc.***, 56 USPQ 2d 1481, 1483 (Fed. Cir. 2000)

In order to satisfy the written description requirement, the disclosure as originally filed does not have to provide in haec verba support for the claimed subject matter at issue. See *Fujikawa v. Wattanasin*, 93 F.3d 1559, 1570, 39 USPQ 2d 1895, 1904 (Fed. Cir. 1996). Nonetheless, the disclosure "must . . . convey with reasonable clarity to those skilled in the art that . . . [the inventor] was in possession of the invention." *Vas-Cath Inc. v. Mahurkar*, 935 F.2d 1555, 1563–64, 19 USPQ 2d 1111, 1117 (Fed. Cir. 1991). Put another way, one skilled in the art, reading the original disclosure, must "immediately discern the limitation at issue" in the claims. *Waldemar Link GmbH & Co. v. Osteonics Corp.*, 32 F.3d 556, 558, 31 USPQ 2d 1855, 1857 (Fed. Cir. 1994). That inquiry is a factual one and must be assessed on a case-by-case basis. See *Vas-Cath*, 935 F.2d at 1561, 19 USPQ 2d at 1116 ("Precisely how close the original description must come to comply with the description requirement of § 112 must be determined on a case-by-case basis.").

VIII.C. *Best Mode*

1. ***Dana Corp. v. IPC Ltd. P'ship***, 8 USPQ 2d 1692, 1695 (Fed. Cir. 1988), ***cert. denied***, 490 U.S. 1067 (1989)

   Whether or not a specific disclosure is adequate for best mode purposes is determined by comparing the disclosure with the facts concerning the invention known to the inventor at the time the application was filed. *Spectra-Physics, Inc. v. Coherent, Inc.*, 827 F.2d 1524, 1535, 3 USPQ 2d 1737, 1745 (Fed. Cir. 1987) [*cert. denied*, 484 U.S. 954 (1987)]. Since "there is no objective standard by which to judge the adequacy of a best mode disclosure, . . . only evidence of 'concealment', whether accidental or intentional, is considered." *Id.*

2. ***Dana Corp. v. IPC Ltd. P'ship***, 8 USPQ 2d 1692, 1695 (Fed. Cir. 1988), ***cert. denied***, 490 U.S. 1067 (1989)

   The best mode requirement is not satisfied by reference to the level of skill in the art, but entails a comparison of the facts known to the inventor regarding the invention at the time the application was filed and the disclosure in the specification. . . . Indeed, in expressing this requirement 35 USC § 112 states explicitly that disclosure must be made of the best mode "contemplated by the inventor." Accordingly, Dana's argument that the best mode requirement may be met solely by reference to what was known in the prior art is incorrect.

3. ***Glaxo, Inc. v. Novopharm Ltd.***, 34 USPQ 2d 1565, 1570–71 (Fed. Cir. 1995), ***petition for cert. filed*** (U.S. Sept. 19, 1995)

   However, the practical reality is that inventors in most every corporate scenario cannot know all of the technology in which their employers are engaged. Therefore, whether intentionally or not, inventors will be effectively isolated from research no matter how relevant it is to the field in which they are working. Separating scenarios in which employers unintentionally isolate inventors from relevant research from instances in which employers deliberately set out to screen inventors from research, and finding a best mode violation in the latter case, would ignore the very words of § 112, first paragraph, and the case law as it has developed, which consistently has analyzed the best mode requirement in terms of knowledge of and concealment by the inventor. Congress was aware of the differences between inventors and assignees, *see* 35 U.S.C. §§ 100(d) and 152, and it specifically limited the best mode required to that contemplated by the inventor. We have no authority to extend the requirement beyond the limits set by Congress.

4. ***Transco Prods., Inc. v. Performance Contracting***, 32 USPQ 2d 1077, 1084 (Fed. Cir. 1994), ***cert. denied***, 513 U.S. 1151 (1995)

In *Chemcast Corp. v. Arco Industrial Corp.*, 913 F.2d 923, 16 USPQ 2d 1033 (Fed. Cir. 1990), this court described the analysis to be employed in determining compliance with the best mode requirement as involving two steps. The first, which is wholly subjective, involves determining whether the inventor knew of a mode of practicing the claimed invention that he considered to be better than any other at the time he filed his application. If the inventor contemplated such a preferred mode, the second step is to compare what he knew with what he disclosed to determine whether the disclosure is adequate to enable one skilled in the art to practice the best mode. The second step, which involves assessing the adequacy of the disclosure, is largely an objective inquiry that depends upon the scope of the claimed invention and the level of skill in the art. . . . Even where there is a general reference to the best mode of practicing the claimed invention, the quality of the disclosure may be so poor as to effectively conceal it. . . .

However, the best mode requirement does not require an inventor to disclose production details so long as the means to carry out the invention are disclosed. . . . This includes providing supplier/trade name information where it is not needed, i.e., where such information would be "mere surplusage—an addition to the generic description." *Randomex*, 849 F.2d at 590, 7 USPQ 2d at 1054. Such supplier/trade name information must be provided only when a skilled artisan could not practice the best mode of the claimed invention absent this information.

5. ***Transco Prods., Inc. v. Performance Contracting***, 32 USPQ 2d 1077, 1084 (Fed. Cir. 1994), ***cert. denied***, 513 U.S. 1151 (1995)

Section 120 thus does not exempt the best mode requirement from its reach, and therefore this court must accept the plain and precise language of section 120 as encompassing the same. Accordingly, the date for evaluating a best mode disclosure in a continuing application is the date of the earlier application with respect to common subject matter.

6. ***Transco Prods., Inc. v. Performance Contracting***, 32 USPQ 2d 1077, 1084 (Fed. Cir. 1994), ***cert. denied***, 513 U.S. 1151 (1995)

It has been held that the appropriate date for determining compliance with the best mode requirement for a reissue application is the filing date of the original application and not that of the reissue application. . . . In a similar vein, it has been held that, in the context of a priority claim under 35 U.S.C. § 119, one looks to the foreign application and its filing date to determine the adequacy of the best mode disclosure and not to the filing date of the corresponding U.S. application.

7. ***United States Gypsum Co. v. National Gypsum Co.***, 37 USPQ 2d 1388, 1390 (Fed. Cir. 1996)

Determining whether a patent complies with the best mode requirement involves two underlying factual inquiries. First, it must be determined whether, at the time the patent application was filed, the inventor had a best mode of practicing the claimed invention. *Chemcast Corp. v. Arco Indus. Corp.*, 913 F.2d 923, 927–28, 16 USPQ2d 1033, 1036 (Fed. Cir. 1990). This inquiry is wholly subjective and addresses whether the inventor must disclose any facts in addition to those sufficient for enablement. *Id.* at 928, 16 USPQ2d at 1036. Second, if the inventor had a best mode of practicing the claimed invention, it must be determined whether the specification adequately disclosed what the inventor contemplated as the best mode so that those having ordinary skill in the art could practice it. *Id.* at 928, 16 USPQ2d at 1036–37. The latter question "is largely an objective inquiry that depends upon the scope of the claimed invention and the level of skill in the art." *Id.* at 928, 16 USPQ2d at 1037.

8. ***Wahl Instruments, Inc. v. Acvious, Inc.***, 21 USPQ 2d 1123, 1128 (Fed. Cir. 1991)

Any process of manufacture requires the selection of specific steps and materials over others. The best mode does not necessarily cover each of these selections. To so hold would turn a patent specification into a detailed production schedule, which is not its function. Moreover, a requirement for routine details to be disclosed because they were selected as the "best" for manufacturing or fabrication would lay a trap for patentees whenever a device has been made prior to filing for the patent. . . . A step or material or source or technique considered "best" in a manufacturing circumstance may have been selected for a non-"best mode" reason, such as the manufacturing equipment was on hand, certain materials were available, prior relationship with supplier was satisfactory, or other reasons having nothing to do with development of the invention.

9. ***Transco Prods., Inc. v. Performance Contracting***, 32 USPQ 2d 1077, 1084 (Fed. Cir. 1994), ***cert. denied***, 513 U.S. 1151 (1995)

[S]upplier/trade name information must be provided only when a skilled artisan could not practice the best mode of the claimed invention absent this information.

10. ***United States Gypsum Co. v. National Gypsum Co.***, 37 USPQ 2d 1388, 1393 (Fed. Cir. 1996)

Although it has been said that "[i]nvalidity for violation of the best mode requires intentional concealment of a better mode than was disclosed," *Brooktree Corp. v. Advanced Micro Devices, Inc.*, 977 F.2d 1555, 1575, 24 USPQ2d 1401, 1415 (Fed. Cir. 1992), the rule is not so limited. . . . A best mode violation may occur if the disclosure of the best mode is so objectively inadequate as to *effectively* conceal the best mode from the public. . . . Subsequently, the CCPA clarified that "only evidence of concealment (whether accidental or intentional) is to be considered. That evidence, in order to result in affirmance of a best mode rejection, must tend to show that the *quality* of an applicant's best mode disclosure is so poor as to effectively result in concealment." *In re Sherwood*, 613 F.2d 809, 816, 204 USPQ 537, 544 (CCPA 1980), *cert. denied*, 450 U.S. 994 (1981) . . . We consider *Sherwood* to be binding precedent, and that, by its reference to "accidental" concealment, it holds that failure to find intentional concealment does not preclude a finding that the best mode requirement has been violated.

11. ***Zygo Corp. v. Wyko Corp.***, 38 USPQ 2d 1281, 1284 (Fed. Cir. 1996)

The failure to disclose the commercial mode, however, does not ipso facto result in a section 112 violation. The focus of a section 112 inquiry is not what a particular user decides to make and sell or even in what field the invention is most likely to find success. Rather, in keeping with the statutory mandate, our precedent is clear that the parameters of a section 112 inquiry are set by the claims.

12. ***Thomcast A.G. v. Continental Elecs. Corp.***, Civ. App. 97-1038, slip op. at 5–6 (Fed. Cir. Nov. 5, 1997) (unpublished)

Section 112 of Title 35 requires, *inter alia*, that a patent specification "set forth the best mode contemplated by the inventor of carrying out his invention." This requirement restrains an inventor from applying for a patent while at the same time concealing from the public preferred embodiments which the inventor has, in fact, conceived. . . . To establish invalidity for failure to disclose the best mode, the party seeking to invalidate the patent must present clear and convincing evidence that the inventor both knew of and concealed a better mode of carrying out the claimed invention than was set forth in the specification. . . . The best mode inquiry is directed to what the applicant regards as his invention, which in turn is measured by the claims.

13. ***Thomcast A.G. v. Continental Elecs. Corp.***, Civ. App. 97-1038, slip op. at 13–14 (Fed. Cir. Nov. 5, 1997) (unpublished)

It is not enough merely to say that the amplifier will not "work" without fine modulation, as the district court did, because that conclusion presupposes that a "working" amplifier is supposed to achieve human discernible output. Many claimed inventions are components of a much larger system and, as components, are commercially feckless unless integrated into an operational system. Nonetheless, the components work as they are intended to work even if they do not produce an output that is immediately useful to the user. Although fine modulation may be necessary for the satisfactory performance of a broadcast transmitter or for the performance of an amplifier as viewed by the consumer, it is not necessary for the performance of the claimed amplifier. The claimed amplifier "works" even if its output is stepped. . . .

[T]he lack of disclosure regarding fine modulation in the '944 patent indicates that fine modulation is not part of the claimed amplifier. Nor is fine modulation necessary to the operation of Furrer's claimed amplifier. To read such a limit into the claim would extend the best mode requirement beyond what our case law mandates. Because Furrer was not required to disclose any mode of fine modulation that he may have considered to be the best mode, we reverse the district court's order granting summary judgment of invalidity and remand for further proceedings.

14. ***Chemcast Corp. v. Arco Indus. Corp.***, 16 USPQ 2d 1033, 1036–37 (Fed. Cir. 1990)

   [A] proper best mode analysis has two components. The first is whether, at the time the inventor filed his patent application, he knew of a mode of practicing his claimed invention that he considered to be better than any other. This part of the inquiry is wholly subjective, and resolves whether the inventor must disclose any facts in addition to those sufficient for enablement. If the inventor in fact contemplated such a preferred mode, the second part of the analysis compares what he knew with what he disclosed—is the disclosure adequate to enable one skilled in the art to practice the best mode or, in other words, has the inventor "concealed" his preferred mode from the "public"? Assessing the *adequacy* of the disclosure, as opposed to its *necessity*, is largely an objective inquiry that depends upon the scope of the claimed invention and the level of skill in the art.

15. ***Lenzing Aktiengesellschaft v. Courtaulds Fibers, Inc.***, Civ. App. 96-1155, slip op. 11 (Fed. Cir. July 14, 1997) (unpublished) (quoting ***Spectra-Physics, Inc. v. Coherent, Inc.***, 3 USPQ 2d 1737, 1743 (Fed. Cir.), ***cert. denied***, 484 U.S. 954 (1987))

   As described above, the best mode analysis specifically contemplates the adequacy of the disclosure in light of what one of ordinary skill in the art would conclude from reading such disclosure. If one of skill in the art would recognize, because it is standard operating procedure in the industry, to use the specialized steel or the two pumps with the claimed invention of the '690 patent, then the best mode requirement is satisfied. As we have stated, "[a] patent need not teach, and preferably omits, what is well known in the art," as long as the best mode is adequately disclosed to one of skill in the art.

16. ***Lenzing Aktiengesellschaft v. Courtaulds Fibers, Inc.***, Civ. App. 96-1155, slip op. 6 (Fed. Cir. July 14, 1997) (unpublished) (citing ***Transco Prods. Inc. v. Performance Contracting, Inc.***, 32 USPQ 2d 1077, 1082 (Fed. Cir. 1994))

   The point in time at which we measure the adequacy of the disclosure for a best mode inquiry in the context of a patent with a priority claim under 35 U.S.C. § 119 is the filing date of the foreign application.

17. ***Young Dental Mfg. Co. v. Q3 Special Prods., Inc.***, 42 USPQ 2d 1589, 1594 (Fed. Cir. 1997) (quoting ***Chemcast Corp. v. Arco Indus.***, 16 USPQ 2d 1033, 1037 (Fed. Cir. 1990))

   Two factual inquiries underlie the determination of whether a patent complies with the best mode requirement.

Under the first inquiry, which is entirely subjective, one must ask whether, at the time the patent application was filed, the inventor knew of a mode of practicing the claimed invention that he considered to be better than any other. . . . If the inventor had a best mode of practicing the claimed invention, one proceeds to the second inquiry. That inquiry involves determining whether the specification adequately disclosed what the inventor contemplated as the best mode so that those having ordinary skill in the art could practice it. . . . This latter inquiry is "largely an objective inquiry that depends upon the scope of the claimed invention and the level of skill in the art."

18. ***Young Dental Mfg. Co. v. Q3 Special Prods., Inc.***, 42 USPQ 2d 1589, 1594–95 (Fed. Cir. 1997)

The best mode requirement does not apply to "production details." . . . Our precedent has applied the term "production details" in two senses, only one of which truly refers to production details as such. In the first sense, *i.e.,* that of "true" production details, we have referred to commercial considerations that do not relate to the quality or nature of the invention, such as equipment on hand or prior relationships with suppliers. . . . In the second sense, under the rubric of production details, we have referred to what more properly are considered routine details. Routine details are details that are apparent to one of ordinary skill in the art. . . . They are appropriately discussed separately from production details because routine details *do* relate to the quality or nature of the invention. Nevertheless, they need not be disclosed because, by definition, their disclosure is not required under the second inquiry of the best mode determination. In other words, to satisfy the second inquiry of the best mode test, an inventor need only disclose information about the best mode that would not have been apparent to one of ordinary skill in the art. Because routine details are apparent to one of ordinary skill, they need not be disclosed.

19. ***Wahl Instruments, Inc. v. Acvious, Inc.***, 21 USPQ2d 1123, 1127 (Fed. Cir. 1991)

A description of particular materials or sources or of a particular method or technique selected for manufacture may or may not be required as part of a best mode disclosure respecting a device.

20. ***Applied Med. Resources Corp. v. United States Surgical Corp.***, 47 USPQ 2d 1289, 1291 (Fed. Cir. 1998), ***cert. denied***, 525 U.S. 1104 (1999)

[A]n applicant is obliged to disclose nonclaimed elements necessary to the operation or carrying out of the invention to which the patent is directed. . . . However, where the invention relates only to a part of, or one aspect of, a device, an applicant is not required to disclose a nonclaimed element necessary to the operation of the overall device, but not necessary to the operation of the invention to which the patent is directed.

21. ***Ricoh Co., Ltd. v. Nashua Corp.***, Civ. App. No. 97-1344, slip op. at 10–11 (Fed. Cir. Feb. 18, 1999) (unpublished), ***cert. denied***, 120 S. Ct. 580 (1999) (quoting *Wahl Instruments, Inc. v. Acvious, Inc.*, 21 USPQ 2d 1123, 1128 (Fed. Cir. 1991))

The inventor's unrebutted testimony was that the preferred method of practicing the invention was to use a face seal only. The inventors further testified that a foam gasket was used only to reduce the manufacturing cost of carefully molding the cartridge at lower tolerances. The best mode requirement does not require that every mode for producing the patented invention be disclosed. Nor does it require disclosure of the best method of mass producing the invention. . . . The inventor is only required to disclose his or her own best mode contemplated of practicing the claimed invention at the time the application for the patent was filed. . . . To require disclosure of methods of mass production as advocated by Nashua would "turn a patent specification into a detailed production schedule, which is not its function." . . . We therefore cannot say that the district court's finding that the inventors contemplated the best mode of the invention to operate with a face seal rather than a foam gasket constitutes clear error.

22. ***Eli Lilly & Co. v. Barr Laboratories***, 55 USPQ 2d 1609, 1614 (Fed. Cir. 2000)

Our case law explicating the best mode requirement focuses on a two-prong inquiry. See *Chemcast Corp. v. Arco Indus. Corp.*, 913 F.2d 923, 927–28, 16 USPQ 2d 1033, 1036–37 (Fed. Cir. 1990). First, the factfinder must determine whether, at the time of filing the application, the inventor possessed a best mode for practicing the invention. See *Fonar Corp. v. General Elec. Co.*, 107 F.3d 1543, 1548, 41 USPQ 2d 1801, 1804 (Fed. Cir. 1997); *United States Gypsum Co. v. National Gypsum Co.*, 74 F.3d 1209, 1212, 37 USPQ 2d 1388, 1390 (Fed. Cir. 1996). Second, if the inventor possessed a best mode, the factfinder must determine whether the written description disclosed the best mode such that one reasonably skilled in the art could practice it. See *Fonar*, 107 F.3d at 1548, 41 USPQ 2d at 1804; *U.S. Gypsum*, 74 F.3d at 1212, 37 USPQ 2d at 1390. The first prong involves a subjective inquiry, focusing on the inventor's state of mind at the time of filing. See *U.S. Gypsum*, 74 F.3d at 1212, 37 USPQ 2d at 1390; *Chemcast*, 913 F.2d at 928, 16 USPQ 2d at 1036. The second prong involves an objective inquiry, focusing on the scope of the claimed invention and the level of skill in the art. See *U.S. Gypsum*, 74 F.3d at 1212, 37 USPQ 2d at 1390; *Chemcast*, 913 F.2d at 928, 16 USPQ 2d at 1036–37.

With respect to the second prong of the best mode requirement, the extent of information that an inventor must disclose depends on the scope of the claimed invention. See *Engel Indus. v. Lockformer Co.*, 946 F.2d 1528, 1531, 20 USPQ 2d 1300, 1302 (Fed. Cir. 1991). Accordingly, an inventor need not disclose a mode for obtaining unclaimed subject matter unless the subject matter is novel and essential for carrying out the best mode of the invention. See *Applied Med. Resources Corp. v. United States Surgical Corp.*, 147 F.3d 1374, 1377, 47 USPQ 2d 1289, 1291 (Fed. Cir. 1998). Furthermore, the best mode requirement does not extend to production details or routine details. See *Young Dental Mfg. Co., Inc. v. Q3 Special Prods., Inc.*, 112 F.3d 1137, 1143, 42 USPQ 2d 1589, 1594–95 (Fed. Cir. 1997). Production details, which do not concern the "quality or nature of the [claimed] invention," see *Id.* at 1143, 42 USPQ 2d at 1595, relate to commercial and manufacturing considerations such as equipment on hand, certain available materials, prior relationships with suppliers, expected volume of production, and costs, see *Wahl Instruments, Inc. v. Acvious, Inc.*, 950 F.2d 1575, 1581, 21 USPQ 2d 1123, 1128 (Fed. Cir. 1991) (explaining that a "step or source or technique considered 'best' in a manufacturing circumstance may have been selected for a non-'best mode' reason"). Routine details, on the other hand, implicate the quality and nature of invention, but their disclosure is unnecessary because they are readily apparent to one of ordinary skill in the art. See *Young Dental*, 112 F.3d at 1143, 42 USPQ 2d at 1595.

23. ***Eli Lilly & Co. v. Barr Labs.***, 55 USPQ 2d 1609, 1615 (Fed. Cir. 2000)

Thus, while the best mode for developing fluoxetine hydrochloride involves use of p-trifluoromethylphenol, the claimed inventions do not cover p-trifluoromethylphenol and the patents do not accord Lilly the right to exclude others from practicing Molloy's method for synthesizing p-trifluoromethylphenol. As a result, the best mode requirement does not compel disclosure of Molloy's unclaimed method for synthesizing p-trifluoromethylphenol. . . . In the present case, Molloy disclosed his preference for using p-trifluoromethylphenol when making fluoxetine hydrochloride. What he did not disclose, nor was he required to do so, was the unclaimed method for synthesizing p-trifluoromethylphenol.

24. ***Eli Lilly & Co. v. Barr Labs.***, 55 USPQ 2d 1609, 1615 (Fed. Cir. 2000)

To be sure, if the best mode for carrying out a claimed invention involves novel subject matter, then an inventor must disclose a method for obtaining that subject matter even if it is unclaimed.

25. ***Eli Lilly & Co. v. Barr Labs.***, 55 USPQ 2d 1609, 1616 (Fed. Cir. 2000)

Here, the patents disclose that the best mode of the claimed invention is fluoxetine hydrochloride that is purified through recrystallization. The patents, however, do not claim a process for purifying fluoxetine hydrochloride through recrystallization or a solvent for performing the recrystallization. Thus, failure to disclose a preferred solvent does not equate to a best mode violation because the patents simply do not claim a recrystallization process or a recrystallization solvent.

26. ***Eli Lilly & Co. v. Barr Labs.***, 55 USPQ 2d 1609, 1616–17 (Fed. Cir. 2000)

Further, section 112 requires only "an adequate disclosure of the best mode." *Amgen, Inc. v. Chugai Pharm. Co., Ltd.*, 927 F.2d 1200, 1212, 18 USPQ 2d 1016, 1025–26 (Fed. Cir. 1991). It logically follows that a patentee's failure to disclose an unclaimed, preferred mode for accomplishing a routine detail does not violate the best mode requirement because one skilled in the art is aware of alternative means for accomplishing the routine detail that would still produce the best mode of the claimed invention. Indeed, here, Barr and other companies are able to recrystallize fluoxetine hydrochloride by using solvents different from the one Molloy used. In addition, our cases hold that a patentee complies with section 112 even though some experimentation is necessary to practice the best mode.

27. ***Northern Telecom Ltd. v. Samsung Elecs. Co., Ltd.***, 55 USPQ 2d 1065, 1068–69 (Fed. Cir. 2000)

As we have repeatedly held, the contours of the best mode requirement are defined by the scope of the claimed invention. See *Engel Indus., Inc. v. Lockformer Co.*, 946 F.2d 1528, 1531, 20 USPQ 2d 1300, 1302 (Fed. Cir. 1991) ("The best mode inquiry is directed to what the applicant regards as the invention, which in turn is measured by the claims. Unclaimed subject matter is not subject to the disclosure requirements of § 112."); see also *Chemcast*, 913 F.2d at 927, 16 USPQ 2d at 1037 (an "objective limitation on the extent of the disclosure required to comply with the best mode requirement is, of course, the scope of the claimed invention"); *Randomex, Inc. v. Scopus Corp.*, 849 F.2d 585, 588, 7 USPQ 2d 1050, 1053 (Fed. Cir. 1988) ("It is concealment of the best mode of practicing the *claimed invention* that section 112 P 1 is designed to prohibit" (emphasis in original).); *Zygo Corp. v. Wyko Corp.*, 79 F.3d 1563, 1567, 38 USPQ 2d 1281, 1284 (Fed. Cir. 1996) ("The focus of a section 112 inquiry is not what a particular user decides to make and sell or even in what field the invention is most likely to find success. Rather, in keeping with the statutory mandate, our precedent is clear that the parameters of a section 112 inquiry are set by the *claims*" (emphasis in original).).

This consistent body of law postulates that the first task in any best mode analysis is to define the invention at hand. The definition of the invention, like the interpretation of the patent claims, is a legal exercise, wherein the ordinary principles of claim construction apply. See, e.g., *Johnson Worldwide*, 175 F.3d at 989, 50 USPQ 2d at 1610; *Vitronics Corp. v. Conceptronic, Inc.*, 90 F.3d 1576, 1582, 39 USPQ 2d 1573, 1576–77 (Fed. Cir. 1996). We begin, as always, with the language of the claim itself. See *Johnson Worldwide*, 175 F.3d at 989, 50 USPQ 2d at 1610. Claim language is given its ordinary and accustomed meaning except where a different meaning is clearly set forth in the specification or where the accustomed meaning would deprive the claim of clarity. See *Id.* at 989–90, 50 USPQ 2d at 1610; *Renishaw PLC v. Marposs Societa per Azioni*, 158 F.3d 1243, 1249, 48 USPQ 2d 1117, 1121 (Fed. Cir. 1998).

When the invention is defined, the best mode inquiry moves to determining whether a best mode of carrying out that invention was held by the inventor. If so, that best mode must be disclosed.

28. ***Magnivision, Inc. v. The Bonneau Company***, Civ. App. No. 99-1093, slip op. at 17–18 (Fed. Cir. July 24, 2000) (unpublished)

If the material in a continuation application is "common subject matter" with that of the original application, the inventor need not have updated his best mode disclosure in the continuation application. See *Transco v. Performance Contracting*, 38 F.3d 551, 557, 32 USPQ 2d 1077, 1082 (Fed. Cir. 1994). An inventor only has the obligation to disclose a best mode in a continuation application if the claim feature associated with that best mode first appeared or first received adequate written description in the continuation. See

Id. at 557 n. 6 (quoting Manual of Patent Examining Procedures, § 201.11).

VIII.D.   *Range Limitations—Support in Specification*

1. ***In re Blaser****, 194 USPQ 122, 125 (C.C.P.A. 1977)*

    The question presented is whether the disclosed range of 60°C to 200°C in SN 159,159 supports the recitation of 80°C to 200°C in the claims on appeal.

    Appellants rely on the rationale of *In re Wertheim,* supra, as "clearly applicable here." Appellants urge that if a disclosure of 25–60% solids content taught those skilled in the art that 35–60% was part of the invention in *Wertheim,* although the latter range was not expressly mentioned therein, then appellants' disclosure of 60°C to 200°C in SN 159,159 would likewise teach 80°C to 200°C as part of appellants' invention. We agree with appellants that *Wertheim* is controlling on this point.

2. ***Helene Curtis Indus. v. Sales Affiliates,*** *101 USPQ 220, 231 (D.N.Y. 1954),* ***aff'd****, 109 USPQ 159 (2d Cir.),* ***cert. denied****, 352 U.S. 879 (1956)*

    The master found that amendments of the specification as to concentration and pH ranges did not contain invalidating new matter. I am convinced, after careful examination of the relevant exhibits, that the master's conclusion is correct. . . . But these amendment limitations constituted only a narrowing of the range originally disclosed. They were not contrary to the original teachings, and no reason was shown why defendant should be prohibited from so limiting the original teaching.

3. ***Ex parte Luaces****, 68 USPQ 154, 155 (Pat. Off. Bd. App. 1944)*

    The claims give a temperature range of "above 65°C., but not above 70°C." which is within the range of 50° to 70°C., originally disclosed. We see nothing in the nature of new matter in the 65°–70° temperature range particularly where it appears to have been previously known that around 65°C., the CS_2 would be liberated.

4. ***In re Wertheim****, 191 USPQ 90, 97–98 (C.C.P.A. 1976)*

    Broadly articulated rules are particularly inappropriate in this area. . . . Mere comparison of ranges is not enough, nor are mechanical rules a substitute for an analysis of each case on its facts to determine whether an application conveys to those skilled in the art the information that the applicant invented the subject matter of the claims. In other words, we must decide whether the invention appellants seek to protect by their claims is part of the invention that

appellants have described as theirs in the specification. . . .
In the context of this invention, in light of the description of
the invention as employing solids contents within the range
of 25–60% along with specific embodiments of 36% and 50%,
we are of the opinion that, as a factual matter, persons
skilled in the art would consider processes employing a
35–60% solids content range to be part of appellants' invention and would be led by the Swiss disclosure so to conclude.

VIII.E. *Chemical and Biological Inventions*

1. ***Petisi v. Rennhard***, 150 USPQ 669, 672 (C.C.P.A. 1966)

[W]e turn to another consideration dealing with the adequacy of disclosure in the parent application and which appears to be the crux of the position taken by the board and
argued by the appellees. This position is that the parent Petisi application fails to specify unequivocally, or to "positively identify," [the compound] . . . [W]e think the conclusion derived therefrom is not valid, simply because the
proposition rests upon the false assumption that such positive identification is required for a constructive reduction to
practice. The reason it is not required is simply that we are
concerned only with what has been taught by the parent
specification to those "skilled in the art to which it pertains,"
35 U.S.C. 112, and, as to them, a compound may well be disclosed without positive identification. . . . The product, not
the formula or name, is the invention, and it is as to this that
priority has been shown.

2. ***In re Nathan***, 140 USPQ 601, 603–04 (C.C.P.A. 1964)

It seems to us that the issue here is whether appellants'
identification of their 2-halo steroids in their original disclosure is adequate to identify the claimed subject matter and
whether there is sufficient evidence in the record to show
the alpha orientation to be an inherent characteristic of the
subject matter so identified. If the answers are in the affirmative then appellants' amendment specifying the alpha orientation for the 2-halo substituent is not new matter but
rather is merely a statement of an inherent property of the
steroids as disclosed in appellants' original disclosure.

. . .

We think appellants' identification of their 2-halo steroids
in their original disclosure sufficiently identifies the claimed
subject matter. Appellants' original disclosure was specifically directed to a generic class of 2-halo steroids which steroids were chemically named, no question being presented as
to their nomenclature aside from the orientation of the halogen at the 2-position of the steroid nucleus. . . . Thus, we

consider that the amendatory material of June 15, 1959 is concerned with an inherent characteristic of an illustrative product of appellants' original disclosure as filed. Such amendment is not prohibited by the statute.

3. ***In re Fisher***, 166 USPQ 18, 21 (C.C.P.A. 1970)

[S]ince the parent application lacked any structural description of the ACTH extracts therein disclosed, the board concluded that it could not be determined whether those products would meet the terms of claim 4, which recites a specific sequence of the first 24 amino acids. Appellant contended that the parent application inherently disclosed products meeting the terms of claim 4, even though appellant did not know the chemical structure of those products when the parent application was filed. Appellant cited several cases in support of the proposition that inherent disclosure is sufficient under 35 U.S.C. 112. . . . The board did not dispute the correctness of this proposition, but found that "it has not been established that the parent disclosures inherently produce the claimed products * * *." We agree with the appellant that this finding was erroneous. The parent application discloses treatment of hog pituitary extracts. The Li (J.A.C.S.) article discloses the amino acid sequence for beef ACTH and states that the first 24 amino acids in the sequence are the same for porcine (hog) ACTH, namely, the sequence recited in claim 4. The hog-extracted products disclosed in appellant's parent application must therefore have had the recited sequence.

4. ***In re Angstadt***, 190 USPQ 214, 218 (C.C.P.A. 1976)

We note that many chemical processes, and catalytic processes particularly, are unpredictable, . . . and that the scope of enablement varies inversely with the degree of unpredictability involved.

5. ***Ex parte C***, 27 USPQ 2d 1492, 1495 (B.P.A.I. 1992)

There is no question that one having seeds . . . available through the ATCC depository would be enabled to grow a . . . plant and produce additional seeds therefrom. The procedure to be used by appellant to deposit seeds of the plant does not differ from that used to deposit a culture of microorganism as sanctioned by the Court of Customs and Patent Appeals . . . and accepted by the Patent and Trademark Office in Section 608.01(p) of the M.P.E.P. as an alternative procedure for meeting the requirements of 35 U.S.C. § 112 for "biological material." . . . We are in agreement with appellant that upon deposit of the seeds in the ATCC the specification satisfies the enablement and best mode requirements of 35 U.S.C. § 112.

6. ***Ex parte C***, 27 USPQ 2d 1492, 1495 (B.P.A.I. 1992)

We are in agreement with appellant that there is nothing in 35 U.S.C. § 112 which supports a rejection on the ground that the specification does not provide enough information for the examiner to formulate a search and examine the application.

The examiner has pointed to no case law which indicates that a disclosure which describes an invention and enables the practice of that invention in accord with 35 U.S.C. § 112, in this case by depositing in a public depository the seed necessary for the practice of the invention, must also include additional information to assist in the examination process and make easier the examiner's search and patentability determination.

7. ***Regents of Univ. of Cal. v. Eli Lilly & Co.***, 43 USPQ 2d 1398, 1404–05 (Fed. Cir. 1997) (quoting ***Fiers v. Revel***, 25 USPQ 2d 1601, 1606 (Fed. Cir. 1993))

An adequate written description of a DNA, such as the cDNA of the recombinant plasmids and microorganisms of the '525 patent, "requires a precise definition, such as by structure, formula, chemical name, or physical properties," not a mere wish or plan for obtaining the claimed chemical invention. . . . Accordingly, "an adequate written description of a DNA requires more than a mere statement that it is part of the invention and reference to a potential method for isolating it; what is required is a description of the DNA itself." . . . Describing a method of preparing a cDNA or even describing the protein that the cDNA encodes, as the example does, does not necessarily describe the cDNA itself.

8. ***Regents of Univ. of Cal. v. Eli Lilly & Co.***, 43 USPQ 2d 1398, 1405 (Fed. Cir. 1997) (quoting ***Fiers v. Revel***, 25 USPQ 2d 1601, 1606 (Fed. Cir. 1993))

A written description of an invention involving a chemical genus, like a description of a chemical species, "requires a precise definition, such as by structure, formula, [or] chemical name," of the claimed subject matter sufficient to distinguish it from other materials.

9. ***Regents of Univ. of Cal. v. Eli Lilly & Co.***, 43 USPQ 2d 1398, 1406 (Fed. Cir. 1997)

In claims involving chemical materials, generic formulae usually indicate with specificity what the generic claims encompass. One skilled in the art can distinguish such a formula from others and can identify many of the species that the claims encompass. Accordingly, such a formula is normally an adequate description of the claimed genus. In claims to genetic material, however, a generic statement such as "vertebrate insulin cDNA" or "mammalian insulin cDNA," without more, is not an adequate written description of the genus because it does not distinguish the claimed genus from others, except by function. It does not specifically define any of the genes that fall within its definition. It does not define any structural features commonly possessed by members of the genus that distinguish them from others. One skilled in the art therefore cannot, as one can do with a fully described genus, visualize or recognize the identity of the members of the genus. A definition by function, as we have previously indicated, does not suffice to define the genus because it is only an indication of what the gene does, rather than what it is. . . . The description requirement of the patent statute requires a description of an invention, not an indication of a result that one might achieve if one made that invention. . . . Accordingly, naming a type of material generally known to exist, in the absence of knowledge as to what that material consists of, is not a description of that material.

10. ***Regents of Univ. of Cal. v. Eli Lilly & Co.***, 43 USPQ 2d 1398, 1406 (Fed. Cir. 1997)

A description of a genus of cDNAs may be achieved by means of a recitation of a representative number of cDNAs, defined by nucleotide sequence, falling within the scope of the genus or of a recitation of structural features common to the members of the genus, which features constitute a substantial portion of the genus. This is analogous to enablement of a genus under § 112, ¶ 1, by showing the enablement of a representative number of species within the genus.

11. ***Ex parte Goldgaber***, 41 USPQ 2d 1172, 1176 (B.P.A.I. 1996)

We are mindful of the holding in *Bell*, and the recently issued opinion *In re Deuel*, 51 F.3d 1552, 34 USPQ 2d 1210 (Fed. Cir. 1995), citing *Bell* with approval and reaffirming the principle that a general method of isolating cDNA or DNA molecules is essentially irrelevant to the question whether the specific molecules themselves would have been obvious, in the absence of other prior art that suggests the claimed DNAs. . . . Here, unlike the situation presented in *Bell* or *Deuel*, "there is something in the prior art to lead to the particular DNA and indicate that it should be prepared". *In re Deuel*, 51 F.3d at 1558, 34 USPQ 2d at 1215.

12. ***Ex parte Goldgaber***, 41 USPQ 2d 1172, 1176–77 (B.P.A.I. 1996)

Furthermore, precedent indicates that it is perfectly acceptable to consider the method by which a compound is made in evaluating the obviousness of the compound. *See In re Burt*, 356 F.2d 115, 119, 148 USPQ 548, 551–552 (CCPA 1966) (in determining obviousness, it is appropriate to consider such matters as (1) the manner of preparation of the composition vis-a-vis the prior art, (2) the structural similarities as well as differences between the claimed composition and that of the prior art, and (3) the presence or absence of properties which would be unobvious in view of the prior art).

13. ***In re Johnson***, 194 USPQ 187, 196 (C.C.P.A. 1977)

The notion that one who fully discloses and teaches those skilled in the art how to make and use a genus and numerous species therewithin, has somehow failed to disclose, and teach those skilled in the art how to make and use, that genus minus two of those species, and has thus failed to satisfy the requirements of § 112, first paragraph, appears to result in hypertechnical application of legalistic prose relating to that provision of the statute.

14. ***Ex parte Bhide***, 42 USPQ 2d 1441, 1447 (B.P.A.I. 1996)

A claim is not unpatentable under 35 U.S.C. Section 101 or 35 U.S.C. Section 112, first paragraph, merely because compounds within its scope have different reactivities.

VIII.F. *Computer and Electrical Inventions*

1. ***Ex parte Billottet***, 192 USPQ 413, 415 (B.P.A.I. 1976)

Even if the specification does not particularly identify each of the elements represented by the blocks or the relationships therebetween, and even if the specification does not specify particular apparatus intended to carry out each function, we believe that these functional-type block diagrams, together with their accompanying description, are sufficient to enable a person skilled in this art to practice the claimed invention. Functional-type block diagrams may be acceptable and, in fact, preferable in cases of this nature when they serve in conjunction with the rest of the specification to enable a person skilled in the art to practice the claimed invention with only a reasonable degree of routine operation. . . .

Drawings and descriptions of circuits that are conventional would, in a complex systems disclosure such as is here involved, tend to obscure the claimed invention. Here we feel that practice of the claimed invention could be achieved without the necessity of further experimentation itself of an inventive nature. Since we believe that one skilled in the art would be enabled by the specification to practice the invention without undue experimentation, we will not sustain the rejection of claims 1, 2, 4, 6 and 8–12 under 35 U.S.C. § 112, first paragraph.

2. ***In re Brandstadter***, 179 USPQ 286, 295 (C.C.P.A. 1973)

Without some indication of the amount of time and effort which one of ordinary skill might have to expend to develop the program necessary to practice the invention, or a disclosure of the program from which the examiner and the board, perhaps through the shorthand expression of a flow diagram, could determine these, we think the board reasonably determined that the examiner was correct in holding that appellants have not proved that one skilled in the art would have been able to practice their invention without undue experimentation and delays.

3. ***Northern Telecom, Inc. v. Datapoint Corp.***, 15 USPQ 2d 1321, 1329–30 (Fed. Cir.), ***cert. denied***, 498 U.S. 920 (1990)

In assessing any computer-related invention, it must be remembered that the programming is done in a computer language. The computer language is not a conjuration of some black art, it is simply a highly structured language. . . . [T]he conversion of a complete thought (as expressed in English and mathematics, i.e. the known input, the desired output, the mathematical expressions needed and the methods of using those expressions) into a language a machine understands is necessarily a mere clerical function to a skilled programmer.

4. ***In re Ghiron***, 169 USPQ 723, 727 (C.C.P.A. 1971)

These drawings are in the form of what have been characterized as "block diagrams", i.e., a group of rectangles representing the elements of the system, functionally labelled and interconnected by lines. . . . This disclosure, stated the board, amounts to "no more than a direction to select apparatus from the prior art that will produce the results required to practice the process."

The rejection could not be sustained if this were the sole reasoning of the board with regard thereto. As urged by appellants, if such a selection would be "well within the skill of persons of ordinary skill in the art", such functional-type block diagrams may be acceptable and, in fact, preferable if they serve in conjunction with the rest of the specification to enable a person skilled in the art to make such a selection and practice the claimed invention with only a reasonable degree of routine experimentation.

5. ***In re Hayes Microcomputer Prods., Inc. Patent Litig.***, 25 USPQ 2d 1241, 1246 (Fed. Cir. 1992)

One skilled in the art would know how to program a microprocessor to perform the necessary steps described in the specification. Thus, an inventor is not required to describe every detail of his invention. An applicant's disclosure obligation varies according to the art to which the invention pertains. Disclosing a microprocessor capable of performing certain functions is sufficient to satisfy the requirement of section 112, first paragraph, when one skilled in the relevant art would understand what is intended and know how to carry it out.

6. *In re Gunn*, 190 USPQ 402, 405 (C.C.P.A. 1976)

This court has stated that disclosure of apparatus with diagrams describing the function but not the structure of the apparatus is not, per se, fatal under the enablement requirement of 35 USC 112, paragraph 1, as long as the structure is conventional and can be determined without an undue amount of experimentation.

7. *Fonar Corp. v. General Elec. Co.*, 41 USPQ 2d 1801, 1805 (Fed. Cir.), *cert. denied*, 522 U.S. 908 (1997)

As a general rule, where software constitutes part of a best mode of carrying out an invention, description of such a best mode is satisfied by a disclosure of the functions of the software. This is because, normally, writing code for such software is within the skill of the art, not requiring undue experimentation, once its functions have been disclosed. It is well established that what is within the skill of the art need not be disclosed to satisfy the best mode requirement as long as that mode is described. Stating the functions of the best mode software satisfies that description test. We have so held previously and we so hold today. . . . Thus, flow charts or source code listings are not a requirement for adequately disclosing the functions of software.

8. *Robotic Vision Sys., Inc. v. View Eng'g, Inc.*, 42 USPQ 2d 1619, 1622 (Fed. Cir. 1997)

[T]he inventors in this case disclosed a device for carrying out their method, and it is plainly apparent that a computer, operating under software control, is to be interfaced to the device for controlling the movement of the sensor. Something must be connected to the device for providing control signals to the motors and for receiving information from the linear encoders concerning a position of the sensor, and there is no dispute that that something is a computer. . . . [I]t is clear that a software program was involved in the carrying out of the invention and that no other mode existed. . . . Thus, one cannot conclude that a person skilled in the art would not have known that software was the best mode of carrying out the invention and how to implement it. The patent cannot be held to fail to comply with the best mode requirement for lack of the word "software," the use of which was plainly apparent to one skilled in the art. Such a disclosure was implicit in the specification.

9. ***In re Dossel***, 42 USPQ 2d 1881, 1885 (Fed. Cir. 1997)

Neither the written description nor the claims uses the magic word "computer," nor do they quote computer code that may be used in the invention. Nevertheless, when the written description is combined with claims 8 and 9, the disclosure satisfies the requirements of § 112 ¶ 2. As the written description discloses, the clauses in question claim a device that receives digital data words from a memory and data input from a user. The device then computes, from the received data, the current distribution by mathematical operations including a matrix inversion or pseudo inversion, and then outputs the result to a display. While the written description does not disclose exactly what mathematical algorithm will be used to compute the end result, it does state that "known algorithms" can be used to solve standard equations which are known in the art.

Clearly, a unit which receives digital data, performs complex mathematical computations and outputs the results to a display must be implemented by or on a general or special purpose computer (although it is not clear why the written description does not simply state "computer" or some equivalent phrase). To bolster this result we note that, in the medical imaging field, it is well within the realm of common experience that computers are used to generate images for display by mathematically processing digital input. Therefore, because of the specific facts in this case, the structure underlying the function recited in Claims 8 and 9 is adequate for us to hold that the requirements of § 112 ¶ 2, that the invention be particularly pointed out and distinctly claimed, are satisfied.

VIII.G. *Effect of Disclosure (Narrow or Broad) to Support Claims*

1. ***Tronzo v. Biomet, Inc.***, 47 USPQ 2d 1829, 1833 (Fed. Cir. 1998)

Instead of suggesting that the '589 patent encompasses additional shapes, the specification specifically distinguishes the prior art as inferior and touts the advantages of the conical shape of the '589 cup. *See, e.g.*, id. at col. 3, ll. 63 ("Another extremely important aspect of the present device resides in the configuration of the acetabular cup as a trapezoid or a portion of a truncated cone."). Such statements make clear that the '589 patent discloses only conical shaped cups and nothing broader. The disclosure in the '589 specification, therefore, does not support the later-claimed, generic subject matter in claims 1 and 9 of the '262 patent.

2. ***Tronzo v. Biomet, Inc.***, 47 USPQ 2d 1829, 1834 (Fed. Cir. 1998)

In order for a disclosure to be inherent, however, the missing descriptive matter must necessarily be present in the parent application's specification such that one skilled in the art would recognize such a disclosure. *See Continental Can Co. USA v. Monsanto Co.*, 948 F.2d 1264, 1268, 20 USPQ 2d 1746, 1749 (Fed. Cir. 1991). There is nothing in the '589 specification to suggest that shapes other than conical are necessarily a part of the disclosure. Indeed, as discussed above, the specification clearly suggests the contrary by asserting advantages of the conical shape over prior art shapes. . . .

Accordingly, because the specification of the '589 patent fails to meet the written description necessary to support claims 1 and 9 of the '262 patent, these claims are not entitled to the filing date of the parent application and are invalid as anticipated by the intervening prior art.

3. ***Laitram Corp. v. Morehouse Indus., Inc.***, 46 USPQ 2d 1609, 1614–15 (Fed. Cir. 1998)

Here, the asserted claims will bear only one interpretation: that the "driving surface" limitation is limited to flat driving surfaces. While claims are not necessarily limited by the written description, it is relevant that nothing in the written description suggests that the driving surfaces can be anything but flat. Indeed, the benefits of having flat driving surfaces are stated in the "Summary of the Invention" portion of the written description. These observations warrant a conclusion that the "driving surface" limitation, "extending downwardly . . . and in the direction of intended travel," requires flat driving surfaces.

4. ***Gentry Gallery, Inc. v. Berkline Corp.***, 45 USPQ 2d 1498, 1503 (Fed. Cir. 1998)

In sum, the cases on which Gentry relies do not stand for the proposition that an applicant can broaden his claims to the extent that they are effectively bounded only by the prior art. Rather, they make clear that claims may be no broader than the supporting disclosure, and therefore that a narrow disclosure will limit claim breadth.

5. ***Digital Biometrics, Inc. v. Identix, Inc.***, 47 USPQ 2d 1418, 1424 (Fed. Cir. 1998)

Because the applicant has the burden to "particularly point[] out and distinctly claim[] the subject matter which the applicant regards as his invention," 35 U.S.C. § 112, ¶ 2 (1994), if the claim is susceptible to a broader and a narrower meaning, and the narrower one is clearly supported by the intrinsic evidence while the broader one raises questions of enablement under § 112, ¶ 1, we will adopt the narrower of the two.

6. *Northern Telecom Ltd. v. Samsung Elecs. Co., Ltd.*, 55 USPQ 2d 1065, 1075 (Fed. Cir. 2000)

Samsung next argues that ambiguity in the prosecution history places this case within the ambit of our holding in *Athletic Alternatives, Inc. v. Prince Mfg., Inc.*, 73 F.3d 1573, 37 USPQ 2d 1365 (Fed. Cir. 1996). Samsung suggests that *Athletic Alternatives* established a rule that when the prosecution history presents an unclear choice between a broader and narrower meaning of a claim term, then the narrower meaning controls. Accordingly, Samsung asserts that the confusing language from the prosecution history noted above requires that a narrower meaning of "plasma etching"—that which specifically excludes ion bombardment—applies. This is a misreading of *Athletic Alternatives*. . . . Samsung appears to read *Athletic Alternatives* as requiring that courts choose a narrow definition of a claim limitation whenever there is a dispute over meaning and ambiguity in the intrinsic evidence. This is incorrect. The plain and ordinary meaning of claim language controls, unless that meaning renders the claim unclear or is overcome by a special definition that appears in the intrinsic record with reasonable clarity and precision. See, e.g., *Johnson Worldwide*, 175 F.3d at 990–91, 50 USPQ 2d at 1610. Vagueness and inference cannot overcome an ordinary meaning of a claim term; nor can it serve to invoke the rule of *Athletic Alternatives*. Under Samsung's reading, *Athletic Alternatives* would substitute for reasoned analysis. To the contrary, *Athletic Alternatives* considers the case where reasoned analysis leads to two clear and distinct definitions of claim language. It does not apply here, where confusing statements in the prosecution history simply fail to overcome the ordinary meaning of the "plasma etching" limitation.

7. *Watts v. XL Systems Inc.*, 56 USPQ 2d 1836, 1839 (Fed. Cir. 2000)

While limitations contained in the specification are not ordinarily read into the claims, see *Intervet Am., Inc. v. Kee-Vet Lab., Inc.*, 887 F.2d 1050, 1053, 12 USPQ 2d 1474, 1476 (Fed. Cir. 1989), it is important to examine the specification. See *Markman v. Westview Instruments, Inc.*, 52 F.3d 967, 979, 34 USPQ2d 1321, 1329 (Fed. Cir. 1995) ("Claims must be read in view of the specification, of which they are a part."), aff'd, 517 U.S. 370, 134 L. Ed. 2d 577, 116 S. Ct. 1384

(1996). One purpose for examining the specification is to determine if the patentee has limited the scope of the claims. See *O.I. Corp. v. Tekmar Co.*, 115 F.3d 1576, 1581, 42 USPQ 2d 1777, 1781 (Fed. Cir. 1997) (limiting claims because the specification described only non-smooth or conical passages and distinguished over the prior art based on these characteristics); *Wang Lab., Inc. v. America Online, Inc.*, 197 F.3d 1377, 1382–83, 53 USPQ 2d 1161, 1164–65 (Fed. Cir. 1999) (limiting claims to the only embodiment described, a character-based protocol, and specifically not encompassing a bit-mapped protocol); *Modine Mfg. Co. v. United States Int'l Trade Comm'n*, 75 F.3d 1545, 1551, 37 USPQ 2d 1609, 1612 (Fed. Cir. 1996) ("When the preferred embodiment is described in the specification as the invention itself, the claims are not necessarily entitled to a scope broader than that embodiment.").

8. ***Space Systems/Loral, Inc. v. Lockheed Martin Corp.***, Civ. App. No. 99-1255, slip op. at 11 n.1 (Fed. Cir. Aug. 23, 2000) (unpublished)

Although SSL argues that it was improper for the district court to rely on the abstract in construing the claim, we have previously stated that in determining the scope of a claim, the abstract of a patent is a potentially useful source of intrinsic evidence as to the meaning of a disputed claim term. See *Hill-Rom Co. v. Kinetic Concepts, Inc.*, 209 F.3d 1337, 1341 n.,* 54 USPQ 2d 1437, 1440 n. 1 (Fed.Cir. 2000).

IX. Incorporation by Reference Requirements and Section 112, First Paragraph

1. ***In re Howarth***, 210 USPQ 689, 692–93 (C.C.P.A. 1981)

When an applicant seeks to add necessary information to a specification by incorporating a source for the information by reference, public accessibility of that source alone may be the controlling factor. On the other hand, when no guide at all has been given, as here, an applicant must show that anyone skilled in the art would have actually possessed the requisite knowledge . . . or would reasonably be expected to check the source which the applicant relies upon to complete his disclosure and would be able to locate the information with no more than reasonable diligence.

2. ***Ex parte Maziere***, 27 USPQ 2d 1705, 1706–07 (B.P.A.I. 1993)

Indeed, the present specification and claims are those of Serial No. 07/071,944 which was incorporated by reference in parent Serial No. 07/072,090. This disclosure was present in Serial No. 07/072,090 albeit in a compressed form via the statement of incorporation by reference of Serial No. 07/071,944. In filing this application, appellants in effect "expanded" the compressed file of 07/071,944 which was present in the first paragraph of Serial No. 07/072,090 and "compressed" the remaining disclosure of 07/072,090 into a statement of incorporation by reference.

3. ***In re Howarth***, 210 USPQ 689, 692 (C.C.P.A. 1981)

With respect to matters necessary for an enabling disclosure and which are not common or well known, an applicant may, in the interests of economy of time and space, incorporate certain types of documents by specific reference in his application to such source materials. After ruling that prior U.S. patents may be so incorporated, ... this court extended the doctrine of incorporation by reference stating as a general guideline ... that "any reference to a disclosure which is available to the public is permissible."

4. ***Ultradent Prods., Inc. v. Life-Like Cosmetics, Inc.***, 44 USPQ 2d 1336, 1339–40 (Fed. Cir. 1997)

The error in the district court's summary judgment order related to the nature of the disclosure in the prior art. The Munro patent incorporates by reference the entire contents of the Rosenthal disclosure. Ultradent's assertion that Munro "says nothing" about the Rosenthal compositions and merely discloses using the commercial embodiment of the Rosenthal patent is contrary to the rules of practice, which permit incorporation of prior art by reference. *See* United States Department of Commerce, Patent and Trademark Office, *Manual of Patent Examining Procedures* § 608.01(p) (6th ed. 1996) (discussing incorporation-by-reference procedures). Because the Rosenthal disclosure is not as limited as the district court found, and because the court's conclusion as to the scope of the Rosenthal disclosure was critical to the court's summary judgment ruling, we reverse the court's ruling on the issue of anticipation with respect to the '303 and '342 patents.

5. ***In re Goodwin***, 43 USPQ 2d 1856, 1857 (Comm'r 1997) (unpublished)

The purpose of the incorporation by reference policy of the PTO is to balance the convenience of ready access, by both the Office and the public, to the information per se incorporated into a U.S. Patent, with the offsetting inconvenience that all details which have been already set forth elsewhere, must be tediously repeated in yet another document. However, it is only necessary that the incorporated information

that is relied upon be available to the public pursuant to 35
USC Section 112, in order for that incorporation to be acceptable.

6. ***In re Goodwin***, 43 USPQ 2d 1856, 1857 (Comm'r 1997) (unpublished)

There is no dispute that, as filed, original application No.
07/167,347 properly incorporated Crabb. That is, the incorporation statement identified the Crabb application by both
its application No., and it filing date, which is a sufficiently
specific identification of the Crabb application to have effectuated incorporation of the entire Crabb disclosure into the
above-captioned application. . . .

   Incorporation by reference has the same effect as if the
host specification had set forth the entire text of the incorporated application. . . . Thus, the incorporation by reference
of Crabb set forth in original application No. 07/167,347, and
the resultant above-captioned patent, is equivalent to the
bodily incorporation of Crabb that is set forth herein.

7. ***In re Goodwin***, 43 USPQ 2d 1856, 1857–58 & n.3 (Comm'r
1997) (unpublished)

Furthermore, as petitioners correctly observe, since Crabb
issued prior to the above-captioned patent, there can be no
doubt that Crabb was publicly available within the meaning
of 35 USC 112, when the above-captioned patent issued. As
such, Crabb continued to be properly incorporated by reference at the time original application No. 07/167,374 was
passed to issue by the examiner. . . . That the examiner updated, at that time, the annotation of the referenced Crabb
application, to include the patent No., was in accordance
with the practice set forth in MPEP 1302.04 item No. 5. . . .
Indeed, such would have been acceptable, even if the Crabb
application became abandoned, as referenced abandoned applications become publicly available upon issuance of a patent to the host specification.

8. ***In re Goodwin***, 43 USPQ 2d 1856, 1858 (Comm'r 1997) (unpublished)

Since the totality of the Crabb application was incorporated
by reference, any lack of particular direction to a specific
portion(s) of the subject matter being bodily incorporated
cannot negate the fact that the aforementioned subject matter was already incorporated, in application No. 07/167,347
as filed. Rather, MPEP 608.01(p) merely indicates that "particular attention should" be directed, not that such "must"
be directed to the specific portions of the referenced document, in order to obtain a proper incorporation by reference.

n4 Clearly, such is a matter of form which facilitates the identification and location of the incorporated subject matter, and does not go to the heart of the effectiveness of the incorporation per se.

9. ***In re Goodwin***, 43 USPQ 2d 1856, 1858 n.4 (Comm'r 1997) (unpublished)

It is of no consequence that the original application incorporated by reference the Crabb material, whereas the instant application for reissue bodily incorporates that same subject matter. . . . Put simply, expanding the instant disclosure to specifically set forth referenced material does not introduce new matter. . . . Petitioners correctly further note that it would be illogical to hold the instant bodily incorporation improper, merely because Crabb also incorporates other information not relevant to the situation in hand. *See Ex Parte Maziere*, 27 USPQ 2d 1705, 1707 (B.P.A.I. 1993) (Incorporation by reference is acceptable, and fulfills the requirements of 35 USC 112, Section 1, even where the referenced application itself incorporates essential subject matter).

10. ***In re Goodwin***, 43 USPQ 2d 1856, 1858 n.4 (Comm'r 1997) (unpublished)

Even assuming, arguendo, that the original incorporation by reference of essential subject matter from Crabb was improper, it is well settled that such essential material improperly incorporated by reference can be subsequently bodily incorporated into that specification. . . . Furthermore, that subsequent bodily incorporation does not constitute the insertion of new matter.

11. ***Advanced Display Systems, Inc. v. Kent State University***, 54 USPQ 2d 1673, 1679 (Fed. Cir. 2000), ***cert. denied***, 121 S.Ct. 1226 (Mar. 5, 2001) (citing *General Elec. Co. v. Brenner*, 407 F.2d 1258, 1261–62, 159 USPQ 335, 337 (D.C. Cir. 1968); *In re Lund*, 376 F.2d 982, 989, 153 USPQ 625, 631 (C.C.P.A. 1967)).

Incorporation by reference provides a method for integrating material from various documents into a host document—a patent or printed publication in an anticipation determination—by citing such material in a manner that makes clear that the material is effectively part of the host document as if it were explicitly contained therein. . . . To incorporate material by reference for anticipation, the host document must identify with detailed particularity what specific material it incorporates and clearly indicate where that material is found in the various documents.

12. ***Advanced Display Systems, Inc. v. Kent State University***, 54 USPQ 2d 1673, 1680 (Fed. Cir. 2000), *cert. denied*, 121 S.Ct. 1226 (Mar 05, 2001)

[T]he standard of one reasonably skilled in the art should be used to determine whether the host document describes the material to be incorporated by reference with sufficient particularity.

X. Rule 132 Affidavits Overcoming Rejections Under Section 112, First Paragraph

1. ***In re Naquin***, 158 USPQ 317, 319 (C.C.P.A. 1968)

[W]e think that statements of fact, however commingled with inadmissible assertions, ought to be considered. . . . Here, one of the affidavits contains a sworn statement, made of the affiant's own knowledge, that the average computer programmer is familiar with subroutines for running integration, addition, etc. If this statement is true, the examiner's rejection is, of course, baseless.

2. ***In re Sun***, 31 USPQ 2d 1451, 1455 (Fed. Cir. 1993) (unpublished)

That certain information is missing does not by itself establish that one skilled in the art would not be enabled to practice an invention. After all, they have independent knowledge. Moreover, much information was included in the abstracts.

3. ***Ex parte Parks***, 30 USPQ 2d 1234, 1236–37 (B.P.A.I. 1993)

The examiner contends that the rejected claims lack adequate descriptive support because there is "no literal basis for the" claim limitation "in the absence of a catalyst." Clearly, the observation of a lack of literal support does not, in and of itself, establish a prima facie case for lack of adequate descriptive support under the first paragraph of 35 U.S.C. 112. . . .

Moreover, according to two declarations by Wentworth, a professor of chemistry at the University of Houston, whose expertise in this particular art has not been challenged, one having ordinary skill in the art would have recognized that the reaction generating nitric oxide, according to the equation disclosed in the '562 patent, is conducted without a catalyst. . . . Thus it cannot be said that the originally-filed disclosure would not have conveyed to one having ordinary skill in the art the concept of effecting decomposition at an elevated temperature in the absence of a catalyst.

4. ***In re Alton***, 37 USPQ 2d 1578, 1583 (Fed. Cir. 1996)

Dr. Wall's use of the words "it is my opinion" to preface what someone of ordinary skill in the art would have known does not transform the factual statements contained in the declaration into opinion testimony. Consequently, the examiner's dismissal of the declaration on the grounds that "[l]ittle weight is given an opinion affidavit on the ultimate legal question at issue" was error.

5. ***In re Ductmate Indus., Inc.***, Reexamination Control Number 90/004,369, U.S. Patent 4,584,756, p.3 (Comm'r Feb. 12, 1997)

This document explains Exhibits 1–4 and supplies information concerning these documents which does not appear on the face of the documents. The petition appears to allege that this document is a verified document, but was improperly ignored by the examiner. A review of the document shows that it is not executed under oath, and certainly is not properly authenticated as required with respect to an oath executed abroad, it being noted that Reutlinger is a city in Germany. See MPEP §§ 602.04 and 604. The document lacks a verification clause under 35 USC § 25 and 37 CFR § 1.68.

6. ***In re Ductmate Indus., Inc.***, Reexamination Control Number 90/004,369, U.S. Patent 4,584,756, p.5 (Comm'r Feb. 12, 1997)

Under 28 USC § 1746, a statement under penalty of perjury is acceptable in place of a sworn declaration or oath or affidavit if it is submitted in *substantially* the following form, (emphasis supplied):

[1] If executed without the United States:

"I declare (or certify, verify, or state) under penalty of perjury *under the laws of the United States of America* that the foregoing is true and correct. Executed on (date). (Signature)."

[2] If executed within the United States its territories, possessions or commonwealths:

"I declare (or certify, verify, or state) under penalty of perjury that the foregoing is true and correct Executed on (date). (Signature)." (emphasis supplied)

Clearly, this document does not *substantially* comply with the form permitted under 28 USC § 1746. It omits any reference to the "laws of the United States of America". These very words are the words which Congress chose to require whenever a document was executed without the United States, as opposed to the language required for documents executed within the United States. Therefore, it cannot be contended that a statement signed in Germany which omits the words "under the laws of the United States of America" qualifies as a statement which is "substantially" in compliance with 28 USC § 1746. Had Congress felt the omitted words to be so unimportant, it would not have taken the trouble to require them specifically in statements executed abroad.

It appears, therefore, that the statement submitted by Georg Mez does not qualify as a verified statement under 28 USC § 1746. It is not a verified statement under 35 USC § 25 and is not a verified statement as an oath executed in the manner of an oath under 35 USC § 115 (when made in a foreign country, must appear before a diplomatic: or consular office of the United States authorized to administer oaths, etc.).

XI. Distinctly Claiming Under Section 112, Second Paragraph

1. *Ex parte Wu*, 10 USPQ 2d 2031, 2033 (B.P.A.I. 1989)

   In rejecting a claim under the second paragraph of 35 USC 112, it is incumbent on the examiner to establish that one of ordinary skill in the pertinent art, when reading the claims in light of the supporting specification, would not have been able to ascertain with a reasonable degree of precision and particularity the particular area set out and circumscribed by the claims.

2. *Lear Siegler, Inc. v. Aeroquip Corp.*, 221 USPQ 1025, 1031 (Fed. Cir. 1984)

   It is the inventor applying for a patent who is permitted to be his own lexicographer. . . .

3. *United States v. Telectronics, Inc.*, 8 USPQ 2d 1217, 1220 (Fed. Cir. 1988), *cert. denied*, 490 U.S. 1046 (1989)

   Patent law allows the inventor to be his own lexicographer. . . . [T]he specification aids in ascertaining the scope and meaning of the language employed in the claims inasmuch as words must be used in the same way in both the claims and the specification.

4. *Stiftung v. Renishaw plc*, 20 USPQ 2d 1094, 1101 (Fed. Cir. 1991)

   It has long been held, and we today reaffirm, that it is entirely consistent with the claim definiteness requirement of the second paragraph of section 112, to present "subcombination" claims, drawn to only one aspect or combination of elements of an invention that has separate utility and apart from other aspects of the invention. . . . [I]t is not necessary that a claim recite each and every element needed for the practical utilization of the claimed subject matter.

5. *In re Angstadt*, 190 USPQ 214, 217 (C.C.P.A. 1976)

It is here where the definiteness of the language employed must be analyzed—not in a vacuum, but always in light of the teachings of the prior art and of the particular application disclosure as it would be interpreted by one possessing the ordinary level of skill in the pertinent art.

6. *Fromson v. Advance Offset Plate, Inc.*, 219 USPQ 1137, 1140 (Fed. Cir. 1983)

In *Autogiro Co. of America v. United States*, 384 F.2d 391, 397, 155 USPQ 697, 702 (Ct. Cl. 1967), our predecessor court recognized that patentees are not confined to normal dictionary meanings:

> The dictionary does not always keep abreast of the inventor. It cannot. Things are not made for the sake of words but words for things. To overcome this lag, patent law allows the inventor to be his own lexicographer. (Citation omitted.)

A patentee's verbal license "augments the difficulty of understanding the claims," and to understand their meaning, they must be construed "in connection with the other parts of the patent instrument and with the circumstances surrounding the inception of the patent application."

7. *Fromson v. Advance Offset Plate, Inc.*, 219 USPQ 1137, 1142 (Fed. Cir. 1983)

Claims are normally construed as they would be by those of ordinary skill in the art.

8. *Raytheon Co. v. Roper Corp.*, 220 USPQ 592, 597 (Fed. Cir. 1983), *cert. denied*, 469 U.S. 835 (1984)

That claims are interpreted in light of the specification does not mean that everything expressed in the specification must be read into all the claims. On the contrary, as was said in *Environmental Designs*, supra, 713 F.2d at 699, 218 USPQ at 871:

> [T]he specification must be sufficiently explicit and complete to enable one skilled in the art to practice the invention, while a claim defines only that which the patentee regards as his invention. 35 U.S.C. §112. The claim, not the specification, measures the invention. (Case cited). The argument that claim 1 must include a limitation found in the specification is thus legally unsound.

9. ***Ex parte Holt***, 19 USPQ 2d 1211, 1213 (B.P.A.I. 1991)

It is well established that the invention claimed need not be described *ipsis verbis* in order to satisfy the disclosure requirement of §112.

10. ***In re Pilkington***, 162 USPQ 145, 148 (C.C.P.A. 1969) (quoting ***In re Steppan***, 156 USPQ 143, 148 (C.C.P.A. 1968))

By statute, 35 U.S.C. 112, Congress has placed no limitations on how an applicant claims his invention, so long as the specification concludes with claims which particularly point out and distinctly claim that invention.

11. ***Bocciarelli v. Huffman***, 109 USPQ 385, 388 (C.C.P.A. 1956)

Moreover, it is not the normal function of a claim to disclose the invention, but to point out the features of novelty in the invention as disclosed in the specification and drawing of the application.

12. ***In re Rasmussen***, 211 USPQ 323, 326 (C.C.P.A. 1981)

An applicant is entitled to claims as broad as the prior art and his disclosure will allow.

13. ***In re Rasmussen***, 211 USPQ 323, 326 (C.C.P.A. 1981)

As above indicated, that a claim may be broader than the specific embodiment disclosed in a specification is in itself of no moment.

14. ***In re Zletz***, 13 USPQ 2d 1320, 1322 (Fed. Cir. 1989)

When the applicant states the meaning that the claim terms are intended to have, the claims are examined with that meaning, in order to achieve a complete exploration of the applicant's invention and its relation to the prior art.

15. ***Jonsson v. Stanley Works***, 14 USPQ 2d 1863, 1871 (Fed. Cir. 1990)

In determining the meaning of patent claims, "[w]ords in a claim" will be given their ordinary and accustomed meaning, unless it appears that the inventor used them differently.

16. ***Ex parte Wu***, 10 USPQ 2d 2031, 2033 (B.P.A.I. 1989)

In rejecting a claim under the second paragraph of 35 USC 112, it is incumbent on the examiner to establish that one of ordinary skill in the pertinent art, when reading the claims in light of the supporting specification, would not have been able to ascertain with a reasonable degree of precision and particularity the particular area set out and circumscribed by the claims.

17. ***Ex parte Saceman***, 27 USPQ 2d 1472, 1473–74 (B.P.A.I. 1993)

     In so holding, we point out that the term "mineral carbon" is a salient feature in the claims, i.e., an essential claim limitation relied on by appellant in distinguishing over the prior art which has been cited by the examiner. In our view therefore, it is particularly important that the meaning of this term be reasonably precise and definite.

18. ***North Am. Vaccine, Inc. v. American Cyanamid Co.***, 28 USPQ 2d 1333, 1336 (Fed. Cir. 1993), ***cert. denied***, 511 U.S. 1069 (1994)

     While it is generally accepted in patent parlance that "a" can mean one or more, *see* Robert C. Faber *Landis on Mechanics of Patent Claim Drafting* 531 (3d ed. 1990) ("In a claim, the indefinite article A or AN connotes 'one or more.'"), there is no indication in the patent specification that the inventors here intended it to have other than its normal singular meaning.

19. ***North Am. Vaccine, Inc. v. American Cyanamid Co.***, 28 USPQ 2d 1333, 1339 (Fed. Cir. 1993), ***cert. denied***, 511 U.S. 1069 (1994)

     Specifically, NRC asserts that Cyanamid failed to meet its burden of proving that the claims are indefinite, and that the parties' stipulation was an insufficient basis for the court's holding that the claims are invalid. We agree with NRC that the parties' stipulation of possible inoperativeness of some species does not constitute an admission that those skilled in the art would not be reasonably apprised of the scope of the claims. . . . Whether a claim is invalid for indefiniteness depends on whether those skilled in the art would understand the scope of the claim when the claim is read in light of the specification.

20. ***North Am. Vaccine, Inc. v. American Cyanamid Co.***, 28 USPQ 2d 1333, 1339 (Fed. Cir. 1993), ***cert. denied***, 511 U.S. 1069 (1994)

     The law is clear that "[i]f the claims, read in the light of the specification[s], reasonably apprise those skilled in the art both of the utilization and scope of the invention, and if the language is as precise as the subject matter permits, the courts can demand no more."

21. ***Gargoyles, Inc. v. United States***, 28 USPQ 2d 1715, 1716–17 (Fed. Cir. 1993) (unpublished)

     The terms of a claim carry "their ordinary meaning, unless it appears that the inventor used them differently." *ZMI*

Corp., 844 F.2d at 1579. To determine if the patent uses a term differently than its ordinary meaning, the court should consider the specification and prosecution history. . . .

In this case neither the term "zero power" nor any reference to ANSI standards appear in the specification or the prosecution history. Therefore, "zero power" should carry its ordinary meaning.

22. ***In re Miskinyar***, 28 USPQ 2d 1789, 1790 (Fed. Cir. 1993) (unpublished)

[T]he drawings may be used like the written specification to provide evidence relevant to claim interpretation. *See Autogiro Co. of America v. United States*, 384 F.2d 391, 398, 155 USPQ 697, 703 (Ct. Cl. 1967) ("[I]n those instances where a visual representation can flesh out words, drawings may be used in the same manner and with the same limitations as the specification." (Citations omitted)). Thus, in a proceeding in the PTO the claims must be given their broadest reasonable interpretation consistent with the drawings as well as the specification.

23. ***In re Wertheim***, 191 USPQ 90, 97 (C.C.P.A. 1976)

That what appellants claim as patentable to them is less than what they describe as their invention is not conclusive if their specification also reasonably describes that which they do claim. Inventions are constantly made which turn out not to be patentable, and applicants frequently discover during the course of prosecution that only a part of what they invented and originally claimed is patentable. As we said in a different context in *In re Saunders*, 58 C.C.P.A. 1316, 1327, 444 F.2d 599, 607, 170 USPQ 213, 220 (1971):

. . .

Since the patent law provides for the amendment during prosecution of claims, as well as the specification supporting claims, 35 USC 132, it is clear that the reference to "particularly pointing out and distinctly claiming the subject matter which the applicant regards as his invention" in the second paragraph of 35 USC 112 does not prohibit the applicant from changing what he "regards as his invention" (i.e., the subject matter on which he seeks patent protection) during the pendency of his application.

24. ***In re Fisher***, 166 USPQ 18, 23 (C.C.P.A. 1970)

We recognize a problem in determining differences over the prior art where the claim uses language which is now accepted and precise but which was not used in the art at the time the prior-art references were published. However, were we to require that claims speak in the language of the prior art, we would be prohibiting the use of the newer and frequently more precise language of the present art. We think that the proper solution to this problem is to allow the use of new expressions when they are definite, ...

25. ***In re Fisher***, 166 USPQ 18, 23 (C.C.P.A. 1970)

The absence of the limitation has a precise meaning. . . . This principle is the very basis of this court's consistent refusal to read limitations of the specification into the claims. . . . In our recent decision in *In re Wakefield*, . . . we considered an indefiniteness rejection involving the absence of a limitation. We reversed the rejection, stating . . . : "The scope of the claim is still definite, however, because each recited limitation is definite."

26. ***Burke, Inc. v. Everest & Jennings, Inc.***, 29 USPQ 2d 1393, 1395–96 (Fed. Cir. 1993) (unpublished)

Contrary to the district court's statement, the patent specification shows that a purpose of the patented vehicle is to enable users with limited dexterity to easily separate the vehicle's various modular components. The specification describes a bayonet locking pin used to separate the drive unit from the floor pan. The specification also discloses other connections allowing the connected components to be readily separated. . . . "The patent law does not require that all possible [connections] be listed in the patent, let alone that they be listed in the claims." *Orthokinetics, Inc.*, 806 F.2d at 1576, 1 USPQ 2d at 1088. We therefore disagree with the district court that the patent fails as a matter of law to adequately disclose a definite meaning for the term "removably connecting."

27. ***In re Ehrreich***, 200 USPQ 504, 508 (C.C.P.A. 1979)

The second paragraph of § 112 pertains only to claims. . . . Agreement or lack thereof, between the claims and the specification is properly considered only with respect to the first paragraph of § 112; it is irrelevant to compliance with the second paragraph of that section.

28. ***In re Borkowski***, 164 USPQ 642, 645–46 (C.C.P.A. 1970)

The examiner's approach to determining whether appellants' claims satisfy the requirement of § 112 appears to have been to study appellants' disclosure to formulate a conclusion as to what he (the examiner) regards as the broadest invention supported by the disclosure, and then to determine whether appellants' claims are broader than the examiner's conception of what "the invention" is. We cannot agree that § 112 permits of such an approach to claims. The first sentence of the second paragraph of § 112 is essentially a requirement for precision and definiteness of claim language. If the scope of subject matter embraced by a claim is clear, and if the applicant has not otherwise indicated that he intends the claim to be of a different scope, then the claim does particularly point out and distinctly claim the subject matter which the applicant regards as his invention. . . . What we do suggest is that it should be made clear exactly which of the several requirements of § 112 are thought not to have been met. Is the claim unclear or is the specification's disclosure inadequate to support it?

29. ***Beachcombers Int'l, Inc. v. Wildewood Creative Prods., Inc.***, 31 USPQ 2d 1653, 1656 (Fed. Cir. 1994)

The relevant statute, 35 U.S.C. § 112 ¶ 2 (1988), requires that the claims "particularly [point] out and distinctly [claim] the subject matter which the applicant regards as his invention." The operative standard for determining whether this requirement has been met is "whether those skilled in the art would understand what is claimed when the claim is read in light of the specification." *Orthokinetics Inc. v. Safety Travel Chairs Inc.*, 806 F.2d 1565, 1576, 1 USPQ 2d 1081, 1088 (Fed. Cir. 1986).

The background section of the '046 specification begins with the conventional definition of the phrase "object cell": the chamber at the end of the kaleidoscope barrel opposite to the end containing the eyepiece containing movable objects such as pieces of colored glass or the like. However, the remainder of the specification clarifies that MacCarthy intended the phrase to mean something different in the context of his invention. That is perfectly acceptable. As we have repeatedly said, a patentee can be his own lexicographer provided the patentee's definition, to the extent it differs from the conventional definition, is clearly set forth in the specification.

30. ***Wolverine World Wide, Inc. v. Nike, Inc.***, 32 USPQ 2d 1338, 1340 (Fed. Cir. 1994)

Although the patentee is free to define his claim terms in a manner inconsistent with their ordinary meaning, "he must set out his uncommon definition in some manner within the patent disclosure." *Intellicall, Inc. v. Phonometrics, Inc.*, 952 F.2d 1384, 1387–88, 21 USPQ 2d 1383, 1386 (Fed. Cir. 1992).

31. ***In re Tanksley***, 37 USPQ 2d 1382, 1386 (B.P.A.I. 1994)

The examiner takes the position that appellants' specification and claims do not provide adequate information so that the examiner may readily search and examine the application. We disagree with this line of reasoning. . . . The § 112 rejection amounts to a requirement, imposed by the examiner, that appellants amend their claims in a specified manner to "facilitate a complete search of the prior art." Again, see the Answer, page 13. We find no language in the statute or case law which would support that requirement.

32. ***In re Tanksley***, 37 USPQ 2d 1382, 1386 (B.P.A.I. 1994)

In our judgment, a patent applicant is entitled to a reasonable degree of latitude in complying with the second paragraph of 35 U.S.C. § 112 and the examiner may not dictate the literal terms of the claims . . . Stated another way, a patent applicant must comply with 35 U.S.C. § 112, second paragraph, but just how the applicant does so, within reason, is within applicant's discretion.

33. ***York Prods., Inc. v. Central Tractor Farm & Family Ctr.***, 40 USPQ 2d 1619, 1622 (Fed. Cir. 1996)

Without an express intent to impart a novel meaning to claim terms, an inventor's claim terms take on their ordinary meaning.

34. ***Ex parte Lemoine***, 46 USPQ 2d 1420, 1424 (B.P.A.I.), ***reconsideration granted in part***, 46 USPQ 2d 1432 (B.P.A.I. 1998) (unpublished)

The examiner has rejected claims 24–25, 31–52, 54 and 55 under 35 U.S.C. § 112, second paragraph as indefinite. The examiner indicates that these claims only positively and distinctly claim the interconnection of one binding leaving the positive interconnection of the other safety binding unknown.

We reverse this rejection. At the outset we note that the examiner has apparently interpreted the claims as requiring a binding or bindings. However, none of the claims positively require that bindings be attached to the intermediate support plate. For example, claim 54 recites that the intermediate support plates is "for" having a binding secured thereon.

In any event, we fail to see how lack of a reference to a second binding makes the claim indefinite. . . . The fact that only one binding is recited does not obscure the boundary line between the claimed and unclaimed subject matter or otherwise make the claimed subject matter unclear. The ordinary person working in this art would not, in our view, have any problem ascertaining the scope of the claimed subject matter. In order to fall within the literal scope of the claim, the intermediate support plate need only be "for" securing a single binding.

35. ***Personalized Media Communications, L.L.C. v. International Trade Comm'n***, 48 USPQ 2d 1880, 1888–89 (Fed. Cir. 1998)

We agree with PMC and conclude that the Commission erred in holding the asserted claims to be indefinite. Here, the written description of the specification is sufficient to inform one skilled in the art of the meaning of the claim language "digital detector." It explicitly defines a "digital detector" as a device that "acts to detect the digital signal information" in another stream of information. . . . The Commission makes much of the fact that the specification is otherwise silent concerning the structure of a "digital detector," and it notes that the "digital detectors" of the circuit diagrams do not reveal circuit elements constituting such a device, but only portray these devices as mere functional blocks. . . . We conclude that the evidence relied upon by the Commission does not indicate imprecision of the claims. . . . The invention's operability may say nothing about a skilled artisan's understanding of the bounds of the claim.

36. ***K-2 Corp. v. Salomon S.A.***, 191 F.3d 1356, 52 USPQ 2d 1001, 1006 (Fed. Cir. 1999)

We, of course, recognize that the "ordinary and accustomed" meaning of a claim term will often be in dispute, irrespective of the clarity of the terms used. . . . But a dispute over the ordinary and accustomed meaning does not imply that such a meaning does not exist. Here, for example, we recognize that the term "permanently" has what can be said to be the flavor of infiniteness about its meaning, which might raise questions about the use of the term in this claim: even the most permanent of "permanently affixed" connections between the bootie and the base of the skate can, after all, be undone upon the total destruction of the skate itself. This, however, does not mean that because no connection between the bootie and skate can be "infinitely" permanent, there can be no ordinary and accustomed meaning for the claim term. Indeed, we would be hard pressed to describe anything as "permanent" if that term is understood to require an infinite duration. But claim construction is not philosophy; we need not wring our hands when considering the implications of a metaphysical analysis of claim terms. Instead, we need only recognize that claim construction is firmly anchored in reality by the understanding of those of ordinary skill in the art.

37. ***Atmel Corp. v. Information Storage Devices Inc.***, 53 USPQ 2d 1225, 1230–31 (Fed. Cir. 1999)

Paragraph 1 is, inter alia, an enablement provision requiring that an inventor set forth in the patent specification how to make and use his or her invention. Paragraph 2 requires claims that particularly and distinctly indicate the subject matter that the inventor considers to be his or her invention. Paragraph 6 also addresses claim language, but refers to the specification for its meaning. In doing so, it specifically refers to "structure . . . described in the specification and equivalents thereof." *Id.* § 112, ¶ 6. This provision represents a quid pro quo by permitting inventors to use a generic means expression for a claim limitation provided that the specification indicates what structure(s) constitute(s) the means. See *O.I. Corp. v. Tekmar Co.*, 115 F.3d 1576, 1583, 42 USPQ 2d 1777, 1782 (Fed. Cir. 1997). The language indicates that means-plus-function clauses comprise not only the language of the claims, but also the structure corresponding] to that means that is disclosed in the written description portion of the specification (and equivalents thereof). Thus, in order for a claim to meet the particularity requirement of ¶ 2, the corresponding structure(s) of a means-plus-function limitation must be disclosed in the written description in such a manner that one skilled in the art will know and understand what structure corresponds to the means limitation. Otherwise, one does not know what the claim means.

Fulfillment of the § 112, ¶ 6 trade-off cannot be satisfied when there is a total omission of structure. There must be structure in the specification. This conclusion is not inconsistent with the fact that the knowledge of one skilled in the particular art may be used to understand what structure(s) the specification discloses, or that even a dictionary or other documentary source may be resorted to for such assistance, because such resources may only be employed in relation to structure that is disclosed in the specification. Paragraph 6 does not contemplate the kind of open-ended reference to extrinsic works that ¶ 1, the enablement provision, does.

Paragraph 1 permits resort to material outside of the specification in order to satisfy the enablement portion of the statute because it makes no sense to encumber the specification of a patent with all the knowledge of the past concerning how to make and use the claimed invention. One skilled in the art knows how to make and use a bolt, a wheel, a gear, a transistor, or a known chemical starting material. The specification would be of enormous and unnecessary length if one had to literally reinvent and describe the wheel.

Section 112, ¶ 6, however, does not have the expansive purpose of ¶ 1. It sets forth a simple requirement, a quid pro quo, in order to utilize a generic means expression. All one needs to do in order to obtain the benefit of that claiming device is to recite some structure corresponding to the means in the specification, as the statute states, so that one can readily ascertain what the claim means and comply with the particularity requirement of ¶ 2. The requirement of specific structure in § 112, ¶ 6 thus does not raise the specter of an unending disclosure of what everyone in the field knows that such a requirement in § 112, ¶ 1 would entail. If our interpretation of the statute results in a slight amount of additional written description appearing in patent specifications compared with total omission of structure, that is the trade-off necessitated by an applicant's use of the statute's permissive generic means term.

38. ***Solomon v. Kimberly-Clark Corp.***, 55 USPQ 2d 1279, 1282 (Fed. Cir. 2000)

During the prosecution of a patent application, a claim's compliance with both portions of section 112, paragraph 2, may be analyzed by consideration of evidence beyond the patent specification, including an inventor's statements to the Patent and Trademark Office ("PTO"). See *In re Conley*, 490 F.2d 972, 976, 180 USPQ 454, 456–57 (C.C.P.A. 1974) (noting that the phrase "which the applicant regards as his invention" in the second portion of section 112, paragraph 2, "has been relied upon in cases where some material submitted by applicant, other than his specification, shows that a claim does not correspond in scope with what he regards as his invention."); *In re Moore*, 439 F.2d 1232, 1235, 169 USPQ 236, 238 (C.C.P.A. 1971) (" [T]he definiteness of the language employed must be analyzed—not in a vacuum, but always in light of the teachings of the prior art and of the particular application disclosure as it would be interpreted by one possessing the ordinary level of skill in the pertinent art.").

It is not inappropriate for the PTO or a reviewing tribunal to consider such evidence extrinsic to the patent application in light of the goals of the examination process and the fact that pending claims can be freely amended to comport with those goals. As we explained in *In re Zletz*:

> During patent examination the pending claims must be interpreted as broadly as their terms reasonably allow. When the applicant states the meaning that the claim terms are intended to have, the claims are examined with that meaning, in order to achieve a complete exploration of the applicant's invention and its relation to the prior art. The reason is simply that during patent prosecution when claims can be amended, ambiguities should be recognized, scope and breadth of language explored, and clarification imposed. . . . An essential purpose of patent examination is to fashion claims that are precise, clear, correct, and unam-

biguous. Only in this way can uncertainties of claim scope be removed, as much as possible, during the administrative process.

In re Zletz, 893 F.2d 319, 321–22, 13 USPQ 2d 1320, 1322 (Fed. Cir. 1989) (citation omitted); see *In re Prater*, 415 F.2d 1393, 1404–05, 162 USPQ 541, 550–51 (C.C.P.A. 1969). Thus, in the more fluid environment of patent examination, an inventor's statements are relevant to determining compliance with the statute.

39. ***Solomon v. Kimberly-Clark Corp.***, 55 USPQ 2d 1279, 1283–84 (Fed. Cir. 2000)

On the other hand, when a court analyzes whether issued claims comply with section 112, paragraph 2, the evidence considered in that analysis should be more limited. As for the "definiteness" portion of section 112, paragraph 2, our precedent is well-settled that a court will typically limit its inquiry to the way one of skill in the art would interpret the claims in view of the written description portion of the specification. . . .

A more limited range of evidence should be considered in evaluating validity as opposed to patentability under either portion of section 112, paragraph 2, because the language of issued claims is generally fixed (subject to the limited possibilities of reissue and reexamination), the claims are no longer construed as broadly as is reasonably possible, and what the patentee subjectively intended his claims to mean is largely irrelevant to the claim's objective meaning and scope, see *Markman v. Westview Instruments, Inc.*, 52 F.3d 967, 985–86, 34 USPQ 2d 1321, 1334–35 (Fed. Cir. 1995) (en banc), aff'd, 517 U.S. 370, 38 USPQ 2d 1461 (1996). As has been noted in the context of definiteness, the inquiry under section 112, paragraph 2, now focuses on whether the claims, as interpreted in view of the written description, adequately perform their function of notifying the public of the patentee's right to exclude. See *United Carbon Co. v. Binney & Smith Co.*, 317 U.S. 228, 233, 55 USPQ 381, 384 (1942) ("To sustain claims so indefinite as not to give the notice required by the statute would be in direct contravention of the public interest which Congress therein recognized and sought to protect."); see also 3 Chisum, supra, Section 8.03, at 8–14. ("The primary purpose of this requirement of definiteness in claims is to provide clear warning to others as to what constitutes infringement of the patent.").

It is particularly inappropriate to consider inventor testimony obtained in the context of litigation in assessing validity under section 112, paragraph 2, in view of the absence of probative value of such testimony. . . . [W]e conclude that inventor testimony, obtained in the context of litigation, should not be used to invalidate issued claims under section 112, paragraph 2.

40. *Jeneric/Pentron, Inc. v. Dillon Co., Inc.*, 54 USPQ 2d 1086, 1089 (Fed. Cir. 2000)

Claim 1 contains a mixture of imprecise and precise claim limitations. Specifically, claim 1 uses the word "about" to qualify the values of many variables: the range of the maturing temperature, the coefficient of thermal expansion, the leucite crystallite sizes, and the weight percentage of leucite crystals. In contrast, the claim recites precise ranges for the weight of dental compositions. Under these circumstances, the district court correctly limited the weight ranges to those recited precisely in the table of claim 1.

41. *KCJ Corp. v. Kinetic Concepts, Inc.*, 55 USPQ 2d 1835, 1839 (Fed. Cir. 2000)

This court has repeatedly emphasized that an indefinite article "a" or "an" in patent parlance carries the meaning of "one or more" in open-ended claims containing the transitional phrase "comprising." See *Elkay Mfg. Co. v. Ebco Mfg. Co.*, 192 F.3d 973, 977, 52 USPQ 2d 1109, 1112 (Fed. Cir. 1999); *AbTox, Inc. v. Exitron Corp.*, 122 F.3d 1019, 1023, 43 USPQ 2d 1545, 1548 (Fed. Cir. 1997); *North Am. Vaccine, Inc. v. American Cyanamid Co.*, 7 F.3d 1571, 1575–76, 28 USPQ 2d 1333, 1336 (Fed. Cir. 1993); see also Robert C. Faber, Landis on Mechanics of Patent Claim Drafting 531 (3d ed. 1990). Unless the claim is specific as to the number of elements, the article "a" receives a singular interpretation only in rare circumstances when the patentee evinces a clear intent to so limit the article. See *AbTox*, 122 F.3d at 1023, 43 USPQ 2d at 1548. Under this conventional rule, the claim limitation "a," without more, requires at least one.

42. *Ex parte Bivens*, 53 USPQ 2d 1045, 1046–47 (B.P.A.I. 1999)

It is not apparent, nor has the examiner cogently explained, why the inclusion in a claim of the sort of charts and diagrams at issue here necessarily runs afoul of this standard. As for the content of the particular charts and diagrams contained in the appealed claims, it again is not apparent, nor has the examiner cogently explained, why the timing characteristics embodied therein are unclear. Although these timing characteristics are functional in nature in that they define the prior art engine and the appellant's engine by what they do rather than by what they are, it is well settled that there is nothing intrinsically wrong with the use of such a technique in drafting patent claims. See *In re Swinehart*, 439 F.2d 210, 213, 169 USPQ 226, 228 (C.C.P.A. 1971). Also, the limitations in claims 10 and 12 drawn to the chart and diagram relating to the prior art engine amount to product-by-process limitations used to define the appellant's engine. Such product-by-process limitations do not inherently conflict with the second paragraph of Section 112. See *In re Brown*, 459 F.2d 531, 535, 173 USPQ 685, 688 (C.C.P.A. 1972). The corresponding limitations in method claims 11 and 13 merely present a starting point for the processes recited therein.

In light of the foregoing, and notwithstanding the somewhat unconventional claim format employed by the appellant, the examiner has not made out a prima facie case that claims 10 through 13 fail to set out and circumscribe a particular area with a reasonable degree of precision and particularity. Therefore, we shall not sustain the standing 35 U.S.C. Section 112, second paragraph, rejection of these claims.

43. ***Ex parte Bivens***, 53 USPQ 2d 1045, 1046 (B.P.A.I. 1999)

Also, the limitations in claims 10 and 12 drawn to the chart and diagram relating to the prior art engine amount to product-by-process limitations used to define the appellant's engine. Such product-by-process limitations do not inherently conflict with the second paragraph of Section 112. See *In re Brown*, 459 F.2d 531, 535, 173 USPQ 685, 688 (C.C.P.A. 1972). The corresponding limitations in method claims 11 and 13 merely present a starting point for the processes recited therein.

XI.A. *Aggregation*

1. ***In re Worrest***, 96 USPQ 381, 385 (C.C.P.A. 1953)

The term "aggregation" appears to be used by the courts in either one of two ways. It is applied in one sense to a device having two or more unrelated, independent units or elements, each of which performs its function separately, uninfluenced by and indifferent to the action of the other units. There is no essential or inherent correlation, or cooperation, or coordination of elements which mutually contribute to a common purpose or result, other than mere convenience due to juxtaposition or collection of the units in a common setting. It is applied in another sense (almost invariably preceded by a deprecating adjective as, for example, "mere aggregation") to devices which really appear to be a combination of two or more units coacting or cooperating in the full sense of the term, but which the court regarded as not displaying the exercise of invention because no new or unexpected result was produced by the combination. It seems to us that the former is the correct use

of the term. In the latter case, such a device should, in our
opinion, properly be regarded as an unpatentable combination, and not as an aggregation.

In applying the doctrine of aggregation, the courts have
generally, until relatively recent years, emphasized the necessity for coaction between the component elements or
units of a device. The fallacy of the coaction test is readily
apparent when we consider typewriters, adding machines,
variable speed transmission devices having selective gear
trains, multipurpose machine tools having selective controls, such as automatic screw machines, etc. For this reason, we agree with those courts which have concluded that
strict adherence to the requirement of coaction between elements in order to have a patentable combination is unrealistic and illogical.

2. ***In re Worrest***, 96 USPQ 381, 386 (C.C.P.A. 1953)

We have before us a particular aspect of the aggregation doctrine involving elements which are alternatively and interchangeably attached to a common operating mechanism on
the machine. . . .

While as a general proposition, the claiming of elements
which are only alternatively used may render a claim aggregative, there are certain classes of mechanism which require
for the fulfillment of their purpose parts which are intended
to be used alternatively. In an ordinary typewriter, for instance, only one type can be used at a time and the capitals
and numerals are used alternatively to the small letters.
Moreover, in some typewriters, provision is made for shifting the ribbon so that the record may be printed in either of
two colors of ink.

. . .

A similar situation arises in the case of variable speed
transmission mechanism, such as is employed on automo-
biles or in similar situations. In devices of this character, no
two gear ratios can be in use at the same time but an automobile without a change speed and reverse transmission
would be a device without great utility.

In all of the situations referred to, the unitary result involved may be somewhat complex but we think the alternatively used parts can be held to contribute to a unitary result, and hence that their inclusion in a claim does not
render the same aggregative.

3. ***Ex parte Christensen***, 6 USPQ 161, 161–62 (Pat. Off. Bd.
App. 1930)

The examiner has rejected the claims as drawn to an aggregation, his view being that since there is no cooperation
between the detachable parts which are not being used and

the rest of the mechanism, there is no patentable combination. We do not agree with the examiner.

The claims call for apparatus having unit needle heads and unit work arms and means for interchangeably connecting the needle heads and work arms to the supporting frame. The examiner has not raised any question as to the novelty and utility of the structure, and in our opinion there is no reason why a patent should be denied merely because certain parts of the structure are not utilized while others are employed.

Patents are constantly being allowed in which all of the parts of the apparatus are not utilized at the same time. . . . [T]he mechanism carried by the unit needle head and the unit work arm which is not in use is peculiarly adapted to be interchangeably mounted on the supporting frame.

4. ***In re Worrest***, 96 USPQ 381, 385 (C.C.P.A. 1953)

In applying the doctrine of aggregation, the courts have generally, until relatively recent years, emphasized the necessity for coaction between the component elements or units of a device. . . . [W]e agree with those courts which have concluded that strict adherence to the requirement of coaction between elements in order to have a patentable combination is unrealistic and illogical.

5. ***In re Worrest***, 96 USPQ 381, 385–86 (C.C.P.A. 1953) (quoting ***Sachs v. Hartford Elec. Supply Co.***, 8 USPQ 302, 306–07 (2d Cir. 1931))

The notion that the parts of an invention must co-operate is certainly very persisting in the patent law, and it must correspond to some underlying idea. So far as it means that the whole complex claimed must be a unit in use, each part of which shall be necessary to the common result, we can understand it. So far as it rests upon an implied reference to mechanics, that is, that each part must give or take a strain, it seems to us a false lead. . . . The co-operation of the means necessary to create an invention is to be measured by the purpose to be fulfilled, not by the interaction of the parts. Each factor must indeed be a condition to that result, but the whole may be a mere assemblage; the co-operation between them all may be no more than their necessary presence in a unit which shall answer a single purpose.

XI.B. Dimensional Limitations

1. ***Gardner v. TEC Sys., Inc.***, 220 USPQ 777, 783 (Fed. Cir.), ***cert. denied***, 469 U.S. 830 (1984)

The [District] Court further concludes that the balance of elements of plaintiff's Claim 1 represent limitations that do not really differentiate Gardner '447 from the Vits teachings and do not affect the utilization of the principles of fluid dynamics taught by Vits. * * * [T]he Court views [these limitations] as artificial dimensional limitations that add nothing to the claims, that are of not constructive significance, and are essentially meaningless. The evidence at trial never showed that departing from these formulae would necessarily cause an air bar to function or fail. In other words, these claims [sic, claim limitations] are irrelevant.

2. ***Gardner v. TEC Sys., Inc.***, 220 USPQ 777, 786 (Fed. Cir. 1984), ***cert. denied***, 469 U.S. 830 (1984)

The trial court would not have been clearly erroneous in concluding that the dimensional limitations did not specify a device which performed and operated any differently from the prior art. Its decision therefore stands.

3. ***Shatterproof Glass Corp. v. Libbey-Owens Ford Co.***, 225 USPQ 634, 641 (Fed. Cir. 1985)

The specifications of both patents state that the thickness of the coating is in the range of 50 to 400 angstroms, and that a thicker coating would impair the transmission of visible light and thinner coatings would not significantly reduce solar radiation transmittance. Concerning the size of the glass sheets, the specifications state that "the products of primary concern are architectural glass, vehicle windows, and oven windows. . . ." The amount of detail required to be included in claims depends on the particular invention and the prior art, and is not to be viewed in the abstract but in conjunction with whether the specification is in compliance with the first paragraph of section 112: "If the claims, read in the light of the specifications, reasonably apprise those skilled in the art both of the utilization and scope of the invention, and if the language is as precise as the subject matter permits, the courts can demand no more." *Georgia-Pacific Corp. v. United States Plywood Corp.*, 258 F.2d 124, 136, 118 USPQ 122, 132 (2d Cir.), *cert. denied*, 358 U.S. 884 (1958).

4. ***Cedarapids, Inc. v. Nordberg, Inc.***, Civ. App. 95-1529, slip op. 8 (Fed. Cir. Aug. 11, 1997) (unpublished)

The district court also found claim 1 indefinite because it did not indicate how much the speed or throw should be increased. While the claim is broad and would cover all sizes of rock crushers and in theory any increases in speed and throw, we do not agree that this breadth renders it indefinite. Claim 1 covers a method of increasing crusher performance by simultaneously increasing the speed and throw. The language itself requiring "simultaneously increasing" is not ambiguous except as to the amounts of the required increases. Those, of course, will vary with the size of the crusher involved and with the point of optimum performance. In the specification, the amount of increase for a seven foot crusher is shown, and, with some experimentation, the amounts for other size crushers are determinable by those skilled in the art. . . . The absence of parameters for increasing speed and throw for other size crushers is not an indefiniteness issue.

5. ***Cedarapids, Inc. v. Nordberg, Inc.***, Civ. App. 95-1529, slip op. 9 (Fed. Cir. Aug. 11, 1997) (unpublished)

Failing to provide in the claims the optimal amount of increase of speed and throw for crushers of various sizes does not render the claim indefinite.

XI.C. Antecedent Basis

1. ***Ex parte Moelands***, 3 USPQ 2d 1474, 1476 (B.P.A.I. 1987)

We see a sufficient difference between a situation where the language "said lever" appears in a dependent claim where no such "lever" has been previously recited in a parent claim to that dependent claim, and the situation presented here where the language "the stations" appears in a dependent claim where at least one station was previously recited in a parent claim. The situation presented here is not the same as a situation where no stations have been previously recited, since a station is previously recited.

2. ***Ex parte Porter***, 25 USPQ 2d 1144, 1146 (B.P.A.I. 1992)

The term "the controlled fluid", appearing in claim 7, finds reasonable antecedent basis in the previously recited "controlled stream of fluid," in our opinion. Stated differently, the scope of claim 7 would be reasonably ascertainable by those skilled in the art.

3. ***Ex parte Binda***, 54 USPQ 35, 36 (Pat. Off. Bd. App. 1941)

The examiner objects to these claims because he states that they contain no antecedent for the expression "all curved surfaces". Applicant argues that a lens necessarily has curved surfaces and therefore that the reference made to the lens is sufficient to overcome the examiner's objection. Applicant, however, offers to insert a statement in the claim which will include a specific antecedent for the expression "all curved surfaces". We believe that the examiner's position is well taken and that the claims should be amended to be more definite. If applicant will submit a formal amendment which is satisfactory to the examiner and which over-

comes the objection raised, we recommend that the amendment be entered.

4. ***Ex parte Porter***, 25 USPQ 2d 1144, 1146 (B.P.A.I. 1992)

[W]e do not agree with the examiner's stated reasons that
the claims are indefinite. The term "the controlled fluid", appearing in claim 7, finds reasonable antecedent basis in the
previously recited "controlled stream of fluid," in our opinion. Stated differently, the scope of claim 7 would be reasonably ascertainable by those skilled in the art.

XI.D.   *Functional Limitations and Definiteness*

1. ***In re Swinehart***, 169 USPQ 226, 228 (C.C.P.A. 1971)

On the record produced in the Patent Office, therefore, it
would appear that the single issue before us is whether the
disputed language is in fact "functional". . . . [W]e find that
issue to be not only not determinative of whether claim 24
satisfies the requirements of 35 U.S.C. 112 but also irrelevant in the analysis leading up to that determination. . . .
We take the characterization "functional", as used by the
Patent Office and argued by the parties, to indicate nothing
more than the fact that an attempt is being made to define
something (in this case, a composition) by what it *does*
rather than by what it *is* (as evidenced by specific structure
or material, for example). In our view, there is nothing intrinsically wrong with the use of such a technique in drafting patent claims. Indeed we have even recognized in the
past the practical *necessity* for the use of functional language.

2. ***In re Swinehart***, 169 USPQ 226, 229 (C.C.P.A. 1971)

We are convinced that there is no support, either in the actual holdings of prior cases or in the statute, for the proposition, put forward here, that "functional" language, in and
of itself, renders a claim improper. . . . Assuming that an applicant is claiming what he regards as his invention, there
are in reality only two basic grounds for rejecting a claim
under § 112. The first is that the language used is not precise and definite enough to provide a clear-cut indication of
the scope of subject matter embraced by the claim. . . . The
second is that the language is so broad that it causes the
claim to have a potential scope of protection beyond that
which is justified by the specification disclosure. . . . This
[second] ground of rejection is now recognized as stemming
from the requirements of the first paragraph of 35 U.S.C.
112. . . . The merits of the "functional" language in the claim
before us must be tested in the light of these two requirements alone.

3. ***Cedarapids, Inc. v. Nordberg, Inc.***, Civ. App. 95-1529, slip op. 8 (Fed. Cir. Aug. 11, 1997) (unpublished)

The district court also found claim 1 indefinite because it did not indicate how much the speed or throw should be increased. While the claim is broad and would cover all sizes of rock crushers and in theory any increases in speed and throw, we do not agree that this breadth renders it indefinite. Claim 1 covers a method of increasing crusher performance by simultaneously increasing the speed and throw. The language itself requiring "simultaneously increasing" is not ambiguous except as to the amounts of the required increases. Those, of course, will vary with the size of the crusher involved and with the point of optimum performance. In the specification, the amount of increase for a seven foot crusher is shown, and, with some experimentation, the amounts for other size crushers are determinable by those skilled in the art. . . . The absence of parameters for increasing speed and throw for other size crushers is not an indefiniteness issue.

4. ***Cedarapids, Inc. v. Nordberg, Inc.***, Civ. App. 95-1529, slip op. 9 (Fed. Cir. Aug. 11, 1997) (unpublished)

Failing to provide in the claims the optimal amount of increase of speed and throw for crushers of various sizes does not render the claim indefinite.

5. ***Musco Corp. v. Qualite, Inc.***, Civ. App. 96-1212, slip op. 3–5 (Fed. Cir. Jan. 17, 1997) (unpublished)

Musco avers that its claimed invention comprises neither the apparatus used in the method nor the determining steps cited in the claims, when used alone or in combinations. Instead, it asserts that the essence of its claimed invention is the method of "selectively utilizing" one or more of the various apparatus to solve the problems identified by the determining steps. Qualite responds that Musco's claims include impermissible mental process steps, such as determining the lighting problems and selectively utilizing the accessories. . . . The existence of mental steps in the claims or specifications of a patent do not, in and of themselves, invalidate the patent. . . . [T]he claimed subject matter—the selective utilization process—is composed *solely* of mental steps, at the very least, some aspect of these mental steps must be nonobvious, and the specification must describe this same aspect so as to enable the skilled artisan to practice the invention.

6. ***Rodime PLC v. Seagate Tech., Inc.***, 50 USPQ 2d 1429, 1435 (Fed. Cir. 1999)

A claim need not claim every function of a working device. Rather, a claim may specify improvements in one function without claiming the entire machine with its many functions.

242   *Patent Prosecution Case Digest*

7. ***K-2 Corp. v. Salomon S.A.***, 52 USPQ 2d 1001, 1004 (Fed. Cir. 1999) (citing ***Wright Med. Tech., Inc. v. Osteonics Corp.***, 43 USPQ 2d 1837, 1840 (Fed. Cir. 1997))

The functional language is, of course, an additional limitation in the claim.

8. ***WMS Gaming Inc. v. International Game Tech.***, 51 USPQ 2d 1385, 1393 (Fed. Cir. 1999)

Because the structure recited in the Telnaes patent is limited by the disclosed algorithm, our analysis of structural equivalence necessarily discusses the disclosed algorithm, which includes functional-type elements.

9. ***Moore U.S.A. Inc. v. Standard Register Co.***, 56 USPQ 2d 1225 (Fed. Cir. 2000), ***cert. filed***, (Feb 26, 2001) (No. 00-1346).

The prosecution history further informs our analysis. The examiner's indefiniteness rejection with respect to the "distance sufficient" limitation reveals the examiner's belief that the limitation was not restricted to any particular printer. The applicant's responses to these rejections clearly demonstrate a similar understanding on his part. That the examiner yielded to the applicant's arguments by allowing the claims does not, as the district court suggested, establish that the "distance sufficient" limitation must be limited to the particular specifications of the IBM 3800 printer. On the contrary, the examiner's acquiescence indicates his acceptance of the "distance sufficient" limitation as functionally claimed and as properly definite under 35 U.S.C. § 112, ¶ 2. We note that there is nothing wrong with defining the dimensions of a device in terms of the environment in which it is to be used. See *Orthokinetics, Inc. v. Safety Travel Chairs, Inc.*, 806 F.2d 1565, 1575–76, 1 USPQ 2d 1081, 1087–88 (Fed. Cir. 1986) (holding that the limitation that the claimed wheelchair have a "front leg portion . . . so dimensioned as to be insertable through the space between the doorframe of an automobile and one of the seats thereof" was not indefinite).

XI.E. *Incorporating One Claim Into Another Under Section 112, Fourth Paragraph*

1. ***Ex parte Moelands***, 3 USPQ 2d 1474, 1475 (B.P.A.I. 1987)

11. A data transmission system comprising: at least two of the data transmission stations of claim 10; . . . .

This language in 35 U.S.C. 112, fourth paragraph, encompasses the situation presented here, where a dependent claim makes plural what is already set forth in that dependent claim's parent claim or claims. . . . No element of any respective parent claim is deleted or replaced by any other element in claims 9, 11 and 20.

2. ***Ex parte Porter***, 25 USPQ 2d 1144, 1145–47 (B.P.A.I. 1992)

> 6. A method for unloading non-packed, non-bridging and packed, bridging flowable particle catalyst and bead material from the opened end of a reactor tube which comprises utilizing the nozzle of claim 7. . . .

> The manner in which claim 6 has been drafted has been an acceptable format for years. . . . Contrary to the examiner's assertion that claim 6 has no method step, the claim clearly recites the step of "utilizing." . . . Our decision herein, when considered with *Ex parte Moelands*, . . . should make it clear that we do regard a claim that incorporates by reference all of the subject matter of another claim, that is, the claim is not broader in any respect, to be in compliance with the fourth paragraph of 35 USC § 112.

XI.F. *Adjectives/Words of Degree/Relative Size Limitations*

1. ***In re Oetiker***, 23 USPQ 2d 1661, 1662 (Fed. Cir. 1991) (unpublished)

> The board relied on *Seattle Box Co., Inc. v. Industrial Crating & Packing, Inc.*, . . . which explained that when a word of degree is used in a claim, the specification must provide some standard for measuring that degree.

> The board looked to the specification for the necessary guidance. It found nothing that would reasonably apprise one skilled in the art as to the claimed invention's scope, because the specification essentially uses the same words of degree as are used in the claims. . . .

2. ***Syntex (U.S.A.), Inc. v. Paragon Optical, Inc.***, 7 USPQ 2d 1001, 1038 (D. Ariz. 1987)

> Under 35 U.S.C. §112 the term "about" entitles the patentee to a broad interpretation of any range claimed in the patent.

> "About" is not broad or arbitrary but rather is a flexible term with a meaning similar to "approximately."

3. ***Ex parte George***, 230 USPQ 575, 577 (B.P.A.I. 1984)

> Accordingly, we consider the recitation of "substantial pressure contact" of claim 19 to be supported by the original disclosure; the word substantial being construed as a relative term denoting a desired degree of pressure contact for effecting the gravure printing function.

4. ***In re Corr***, 146 USPQ 69, 70–71 (C.C.P.A. 1965)

The board upheld the examiner's rejection of all claims reciting "high styrene resin" as "indefinite or unduly broad". . . . If only the term "high styrene resin" were used in the specification with no additional disclosure, we would be inclined to agree with the board. However, recourse to appellant's specification indicates that the "high styrene resin" is a resin such as PLIOLITE S-6B. . . . The solicitor has suggested no reason, and we can think of none, why "high styrene resin" as defined by the specification would be so indefinite that one skilled in the art would be unable to practice the invention. . . . Appellant's specification taken with the prior art clearly indicates that the styrene resin component of his composition is conventional and that many equivalents are known to the art. Although some routine experimentation might be necessary to determine whether a particular sytrene resin would perform adequately in the claimed composition, it would not be an unreasonable burden in view of the disclosure given by appellant of the considerations in choosing a resin and the indicated knowledge of the art.

5. ***United States v. Telectronics, Inc.***, 8 USPQ 2d 1217, 1223 (Fed. Cir. 1984), ***cert. denied***, 490 U.S. 1046 (1989)

The district court also held that if claim 1 is read to mean that the current must be applied so as to minimize fibrous tissue formation then it would be invalid under 35 U.S.C. 112 (1982) because it would be "impossible to determine when sufficient minimization takes place to determine what current range is involved." 658 F.Supp. at 589, 3 USPQ 2d at 1578. The district court erred as a matter of law in this holding. . . . Section 112, Paragraph 2, requires only reasonable precision in delineating the bounds of the claimed invention. Adjusting current so as to minimize fibrous tissue formation in other parts of the living being reasonably apprises those skilled in the art of the bounds of the claimed invention and is as precise as the subject matter permits.

6. ***In re Hutchison***, 42 USPQ 90, 93 (C.C.P.A. 1939)

It is realized that "substantial distance" is a relative and somewhat indefinite term, or phrase, but terms and phrases of this character are not uncommon in patents in cases where, according to the art involved, the meaning can be determined with reasonable clearness.

7. ***Ex parte Mallory***, 52 USPQ 297, 297 (Pat. Off. Bd. App. 1941)

The examiner has held that most of the claims are inaccurate because apparently the laminar film will not be entirely eliminated. The claims specify that the film is "substantially" eliminated and for the intended purpose, it is believed that the slight portion of the film which may remain is negligible. We are of the view, therefore, that the claims may be regarded as sufficiently accurate.

8. ***Shatterproof Glass Corp. v. Libbey-Owens Ford Co.***, 225 USPQ 634, 641 (Fed. Cir. 1985)

LOF argues that the Method and Apparatus patent claims are indefinite and thus invalid for failure to comply with the second paragraph of 35 U.S.C. § 112, in that they do not recite the size of the glass sheets or the quantity or quality of the coating, and that the words "freely supporting" in the method claims are vague and indefinite. . . .

The specifications of both patents state that the thickness of the coating is in the range of 50 to 400 angstroms, and that a thicker coating would impair the transmission of visible light and thinner coatings would not significantly reduce solar radiation transmittance. Concerning the size of the glass sheets, the specifications state that "the products of primary concern are architectural glass, vehicle windows, and oven windows. . . ." LOF's assertions that the claims are vague and indefinite in the term "freely supported" was also controverted by reference to the specifications. The amount of detail required to be included in claims depends on the particular invention and the prior art, and is not to be viewed in the abstract but in conjunction with whether the specification is in compliance with the first paragraph of section 112.

9. ***Burke, Inc. v. Everest & Jennings, Inc.***, 29 USPQ 2d 1393, 1395 n.5 (Fed. Cir. 1993) (unpublished)

Contrast this with *In re Certain Convertible Rowing Exercisers*, . . . in which the United States International Trade Commission viewed as definite the plain meaning of "removably coupled" derived from Webster's New Collegiate Dictionary: joined in such a manner as to be readily separable.

10. ***Total Containment, Inc. v. Environ Prods., Inc.***, Civ. App. 96-1138, slip op. at 7 (Fed. Cir. Jan. 17, 1997) (unpublished)

The ordinary meaning of the term "surround" is to "encircle" or "enclose." In a three-dimensional setting, a surrounding object is normally considered to be co-planar with the surrounded object. Thus, for example, a basketball rim would not ordinarily be said to "surround" the net, and a coaster would not ordinarily be said to "surround" a glass that rests on it.

11. ***Energy Absorption Sys., Inc. v. Roadway Safety Servs., Inc.***, Civ. App. 96-1264, slip op. at 10 (Fed. Cir. July 3, 1997) (unpublished)

Claims need only "reasonably apprise those skilled in the art" as to their scope to satisfy the definiteness requirement. *Hybridtech v. Monoclonal Antibodies, Inc.*, 802 F.2d 1367, 1385, 231 USPQ 81, 94 (Fed. Cir. 1986), *cert. denied*, 480 U.S. 947 (1987). In addition, the use of modifiers in the claim, like "generally" and "substantial," does not by itself render the claims indefinite. *See Seattle Box Co. v. Industrial Crating & Packing, Inc.*, 731 F.2d 818 828–29, 221 USPQ 568, 575–76 (Fed. Cir. 1984).

XI.G. *Alternative Expressions*

1. ***Ex parte Holt***, 19 USPQ 2d 1211, 1213–14 (B.P.A.I. 1991)

In the Examiner's opinion, the language "which may in-clude-" and "said optional substitution if present" recited in claim 9, lines 5–6 and line 16 respectively and in claim 10, lines 5–6 and line 10 respectively render the claims vague and indefinite.

The last portion of claim 9, for example, defines what those optional substituents are "if present". The metes and bounds of claims 9 and 10 are not rendered unclear merely because of the presence of the alternative language.

2. ***Ex parte Wu***, 10 USPQ 2d 2031, 2033 (B.P.A.I. 1989)

The examiner bases his request on the prior decisions *Ex parte Steigerwald* . . . and *Ex parte Grundy* . . . , wherein the term "such as" was found to render the claims indefinite. We do not consider the term "optionally" to always result in the same degree of variability or indefiniteness as might result from the use of the phrase "such as". . . . The use of the term "such as" can render a claim indefinite by raising a question of doubt as to whether the feature introduced by such lan-guage is (a) merely exemplary of the remainder of the claim, and therefore not required, or (b) a required feature of the claim. We see no similar question or doubt arising from the present use of the term "optionally."

3. ***Ex parte Cordova***, 10 USPQ 2d 1949, 1952 (B.P.A.I. 1987)

Situations may arise in which the expressions "such as" and "particularly" render a claim indefinite as to whether such expressions introduce exemplary or limiting detail. However, the use of the term "optionally," as employed in claim 1, is akin to expressions such as "up to" and "0 to . . . ." Such alternative language does not normally render claims indefinite under the second paragraph of 35 U.S.C. 112.

4. ***Ex parte Head***, 214 USPQ 551, 553 (B.P.A.I. 1981)

We will not sustain the rejection of the claims at bar as failing to particularly point out and distinctly claim that which appellant [claims] to be his invention as required by the second paragraph of 35 U.S.C. 112. Although we agree with the examiner that the first means clause of independent claim 2 includes an alternative expression as to the form of calculation to be used, which is not in the format of a recognized exception to the general prohibition against the use of alternative expressions in a claim, namely, Markush expressions, the mere use of an alternative expression in a claim is not fatal. . . . In our view, the scope of independent claim 2, for example, is sufficiently clear in specifying that any one of three methods of calculation may be used to determine specified parameters. As such, the artisan reading the claim would not be confused as to what the claim, considered as a whole, would preclude others from doing. Accordingly, we conclude that the mere use of an alternative expression in claim 2 does not render the claim vague and indefinite under 35 U.S.C. 112, second paragraph.

XI.H.   *General Structural Expressions*

1. ***Ex parte Rodgers***, 27 USPQ 2d 1738, 1742–43 (B.P.A.I. 1992)

The language of claim 15 which requires that the bottom camber surface is "located below and extends generally parallel with respect to said chord line" is neither vague nor indefinite, in our view. It is clear from this language precisely what the appellant intends his claim language to cover: an airfoil body having a bottom surface below and parallel to the chord line, and possessing all the other characteristics recited in claim 15. Like the appellant (main brief, page 32), we think that this claim language adequately provides notice as to the metes and bounds of claimed protection.

2. ***Ex parte Olsson***, 65 USPQ 52, 54 (Pat. Off. Bd. App. 1944)

We find no error in examiner's conclusion that this situation clearly falls within a long established rule that if a submechanism really performs two independent functions there is no objection to including it twice in a claim under each separate function.

3. ***Ex parte Hendrickson***, 42 USPQ 634, 635 (Pat. Off. Bd. App. 1939)

On examination of the claims, we are convinced that the examiner's holding of indefiniteness as to claim 1 is merely a matter of scope of the claim. This applies to the expression, "guides associated with the sides of the diaphragm." This is not believed to be indefinite but merely broad. We find the elements set forth in terms which we regard as clear in meaning but admittedly of relatively broad scope. Since no prior art is relied upon, it is presumed that this scope of claim is and should be allowed as a patentable improvement over the state of the art.

4. ***Warminster Fiberglass Co., Inc. v. Delta Fiberglass Structures, Inc.***, 42 USPQ 2d 1154, 1156 (Fed. Cir. 1996) (unpublished)

In this case, the inventors specifically claimed a scum baffle that was integral with the hood. Because we interpret the term integral to mean "structurally related," we cannot consider the accused device, in which the scum baffle and hood are physically separated, to be the equivalent of the claimed invention without reading out the term "integral."

5. ***In re Deters***, 185 USPQ 644, 648 (C.C.P.A. 1975)

We agree, however, with the PTO that the difference between "at least one" and a "plurality" is a de minimus, obvious variation.

6. ***Abtox, Inc. v. Exitron Corp.***, 43 USPQ 2d 1545, 1548 (Fed. Cir.), ***amended on rehearing***, 131 F.3d 1009 (Fed. Cir. 1997)

The claim specifies "a metallic gas-confining chamber." Of particular relevance for the claim dispute before this court, the article "a" suggests a single chamber. However, patent claim parlance also recognizes that an article can carry the meaning of "one or more," for example in a claim using the transitional phrase "comprising."

7. ***Kegel Co. v. AMF Bowling, Inc.***, 44 USPQ 2d 1123, 1127 (Fed. Cir. 1997)

The scope of the three-part improvement is defined by the word "assembly." Without an express intent to impart a novel meaning to a claim term, the term takes on its ordinary meaning. . . . The '290 patent discloses no novel meaning for the term "assembly." When used in the context in which it appears in claim 7, "assembly" ordinarily means "a collection of parts so assembled as to form a complete machine, structure, or unit of a machine." *Webster's Third New International Dictionary* 131 (1986). Thus, the use of the word "assembly" indicates that, in claim 7, the inventors intended to claim a physical structure.

8. ***Young Dental Mfg. Co. v. Q3 Special Prods., Inc.***, 42 USPQ 2d 1589, 1593 (Fed. Cir. 1997)

The plain English meaning of bore is "[a]n internal cylindrical cavity, as of a pipe or tube," which is the definition applied by the district court. *See Webster's New International Dictionary* 255 (3d ed. 1968).

9. ***Strattec Sec. Corp. v. General Automotive Specialty Co.***, 44 USPQ 2d 1030, 1035 (Fed. Cir. 1997)

A review of the '482 patent and its prosecution history reveals that the terms "sheet" and "sheet-like" do not have any special meanings in the art and that the '482 inventors used these terms in their ordinary, everyday sense, i.e., to describe something flat with a fairly broad surface relative to its thickness. The claims thus include within their literal scope only devices with conductive material that comprises a fairly broad surface relative to its thickness.

10. ***MHB Industries Corp. v. Dennis Garberg & Assocs., Inc.***, Civ. App. 96-1539, slip op. 7–8 (Fed. Cir. July 29, 1997) (unpublished) (quoting *Webster's Third New International Dictionary*, 162 (1971))

Claim 1 . . . uses the specific term "bag," which is used in the specification in its ordinary sense, *i.e.*, to mean "a container . . . closed on all sides except for an opening that may be closed."

11. ***Genentech, Inc. v. Chiron Corp.***, 42 USPQ 2d 1608, 1613 (Fed. Cir. 1997) (emphasis in original)

To be joined or connected does not necessitate a *direct* joining or connection.

12. ***Instance v. On Serts Sys., Inc.***, Civ. App. 96-1112, slip op. 5–6 (Fed. Cir. Feb. 21, 1997) (unpublished)

In this case, "operable in response to" has a definite meaning without recourse to the specification for clarification. This claim term is not so amorphous a term that the court can only reconcile the claim language with the inventor's disclosure by recourse to the specification. . . . In this case, the term "operable in response to" defines broadly the relationship between the various components of the claimed device. Broad terms, however, are not necessarily indefinite. Contrary to On Serts's assertion, this drafter did not choose either of the more limiting phrases "directly operable in response to" or "immediately operable in response to."

13. ***Johansson v. Rose Displays Ltd., Inc.***, Civ. App. 96-1410, slip op. at 6 (Fed. Cir. Aug. 5, 1997) (unpublished)

Deformation is a "change in either shape or size of a material body or of a geometrical figure," while destruction is "demolition or complete ruin [or] killing or annihilation." *Webster's Third New Int'l Dictionary* 593, 615 (1966).

14. ***In re Morris***, 44 USPQ 2d 1023, 1027–29 (Fed. Cir. 1997)

According to the Board, "the term 'integral' is a relatively broad term inclusive of means for maintaining parts in a fixed relationship as a single unit." . . . As the cases cited above demonstrate, our predecessor court had on several prior occasions interpreted the term "integral" to cover more that a unitary construction.

15. ***American Permahedge, Inc. v. Barcana, Inc.***, 41 USPQ 2d 1614, 1616–17 (Fed. Cir. 1997)

As the district court properly found in reference to The American Heritage Dictionary (2d ed. 1976), the term "lateral" in its usual dictionary usage means "coming from the side." The court properly noted that there is nothing in the dictionary definition that would limit the term "lateral" to "perpendicular." . . . We therefore conclude that the "extending laterally" limitation simply means extending from the side, with no limitations on the angle.

16. ***Johnstown Am. Corp. v. Trinity Industries, Inc.***, Civ. App. 97-1070, slip op. 6 (Fed. Cir. May 28, 1997) (unpublished)

Whereas the district court's definition implicitly requires that the body through which the axis penetrates be symmetrical, the dictionary definition of "longitudinal axis" conveys no such requirement. Instead, the definition, which defines "longitudinal axis" as "[a]n axis along the lengthwise direction of the figure or body, usually passing through its center of gravity," only requires an ascertainable lengthwise direction in which the longitudinal axis can be drawn.

17. ***MHB Indus. Corp. v. Dennis Garberg & Assocs., Inc.***, Civ. App. 96-1539, slip op. 6–7 (Fed. Cir. July 29, 1997) (unpublished)

Consistent with this depiction of the method in the specification, a common definition of "across" is "from one side to the opposite side of: over." . . . The district court also determined that this was the proper meaning of across but went on to state that the claim required that a bag be transferred "across and over" the header, apparently distinguishing the situation in which the bags are transferred under the header. We agree with MHB that the claim does not require a distinction between over, as in above, and under the header. Simply, the claim requires that the bag be transferred across or, in other words, from one side of the header to the other. Given the other differences in the accused method, however, this error is harmless.

18. ***Trilogy Communications, Inc. v. Times Fiber Communications, Inc.***, 42 USPQ 2d 1129, 1131–33 (Fed. Cir. 1997)

Relying on *The American Heritage Dictionary of the English Language* (1969), the district court stated that the term "fusion" ordinarily means "the act or procedure of liquefying or melting together by heat." . . . Properly construed, the terms "fusion-bonded" and "fusion-bonding" in the asserted claims require the foam to melt and thereby form a bond with the sheath.

19. ***Ekchian v. Home Depot, Inc.***, 41 USPQ 2d 1364, 1367–69 (Fed. Cir. 1997)

Because the specification does not use the term "conductive" in a special or unique way, its ordinary meaning to one skilled in the art controls. . . .

Ekchian contends that those skilled in the art would recognize that the term "conductive liquid-like medium" in the context of the claimed invention refers to any material that is sufficiently more conductive than the dielectric so that a capacitor is formed. We agree. . . . Both Lucas and Ekchian agree that the term "conductive" ordinarily means the ability to transport electric charge. . . . Within the context of this patent, "conductive liquid-like medium" means a medium sufficiently conductive to perform its function as a variable capacitor plate. . . .

The patent claims, specification, and prosecution history uniformly indicate that the patentee intended the term "conductive" to take on its ordinary and accustomed meaning. Therefore, the claim term "conductive liquid-like medium" requires a liquid-like medium that acts as a capacitor plate by storing electric charge.

20. ***Ullstrand v. Coons***, 64 USPQ 580, 581 (C.C.P.A. 1945)

The term "connect" is defined in Webster's New International Dictionary, Second Edition, 1939, as follows:

> connect . . . v. Transitive: 1. To join, or fasten together, as by something intervening, whether physically or logically; as to connect towns by a railroad; to unite or link together, as in an electrical circuit.

The derivative of the term "connect" is defined in the same dictionary as follows:

> connected . . . adj. Joined or linked together.

The above definition of the term "connect" is plain and unambiguous and is identical with the meaning of the term as defined in other authoritative sources. See Funk & Wagnalls New Standard Dictionary.

It is clear that the accepted definition of the term "connected" is restricted to neither a direct nor an indirect connection, and the term is therefore applicable to an indirect connection.

21. ***Foster v. Hallco Mfg. Co.,*** Civ. App. 96-1399, slip op. 13 (Fed. Cir. July 14, 1997) (unpublished)

As the district court correctly noted, the claim does not require "secured" to mean a direct connection. Rather, the term "secured" means "to make tight or firm: FASTEN." Webster's II New Riverside University Dictionary 1055 (2d ed. 1988). Neither the specification nor the prosecution history discloses a more specialized or different meaning. . . . Although the connection is indirect, the claim requires no more than a secure fastening of the fixed opposite end portions to the mounting frame members.

22. ***Foster v. Hallco Mfg. Co.***, Civ. App. 96-1399, slip op. 13–14 (Fed. Cir. July 14, 1997) (unpublished)

Next, the district court construed the claim language "in," "within," and "between." . . . The word "in" does not require that something be completely and continuously inside of something else. The word "within" does not require that something be completely and continuously within something else. Further, as discussed above in more detail, the word "between" does not require that something be completely and continuously between two things. . . . [T]he "between" requirement may be satisfied even if a component extends beyond the specified boundaries. In the same way, the "in" requirement may be met by a component which is located, at least in relevant part, in the defined space, as the "within" requirement may be met by a component which located, at least in relevant part, within the defined area.

23. ***Bailey v. Dunkin Donuts, Inc.***, 45 USPQ 2d 1683, 1687 (Fed. Cir. 1998) (unpublished)

We agree with the magistrate judge's claim construction ("essentially vertical" means "vertical or a few degrees from vertical") and therefore uphold his infringement decision with respect to this limitation. Giving the claim language its ordinary meaning, walls deviating 22 and 28 degrees from vertical would not be "essentially vertical."

24. ***Action Techs., Inc. v. Novell Sys., Inc.***, Civ. App. 97-1460, 97-1481, slip op. at 8 (Fed. Cir. May 27, 1998)

In our view, "type" should be given its ordinary meaning, which is "a kind, class, or group having distinguishing characteristics in common." Webster's New World Dictionary 1446 (3d College ed. 1994). Accordingly, we construe the term "conversation type" in claim 1 to mean an exchange of communications possessing a shared set of distinguishing characteristics.

25. ***Micro Chem., Inc. v. Lextron, Inc.***, Civ. App. 97-1589, slip op. at 6 (Fed. Cir. June 17, 1998) (unpublished)

Representative claim 1 requires a step of "in response to entry of a selected drug treatment requiring a withdrawal period, calculating in the computer means, for the selected drug treatment, when the animal may be released from the feedlot." Although the term "when" is subject to different shades of meaning, the context of its use in this case does not support the district court's construction. In the phrase "when the animal may be released," the word "when" identifies the point in time at which a discrete act (the animal's release) is permitted. In that context, the term "when" is best understood to refer to the point in time at which release is first permitted, although it does not specify whether that point in time must be identified by hour, day, week, or other temporal reference. By analogy, in the phrase "when the prisoner is in prison," the term "when" would be understood to refer to the entire period of the prisoner's incarceration. But in the phrase "when the prisoner may be released," the term "when" would be understood as referring to the point in time at which the prisoner will be set free, whether it be the day, month, or year of release.

26. ***Marquip, Inc. v. Fosber Am., Inc.***, Civ. App. 97-1441, slip op. at 8 (Fed. Cir. May 19, 1998)

Nor does it matter, as Marquip argues, that the Fosber interrupt mechanism is always downstream from the end of the first conveyor. "In response to" does not mean "anytime after." The claim requires the conveyor speed to slow "in response to" passage of the last sheet past the end of the conveyor, not "in response to" passage past an interrupt mechanism.

27. ***Cybor Corp. v. FAS Techs., Inc.***, 46 USPQ 2d 1169, 1177 (Fed. Cir. 1998)

We also agree with the district court's interpretation that the "to" limitation requires only that the liquid move from the filter "in a pathway with a destination of the second pumping means" and does not preclude the fluid from passing through intervening components.

28. ***Gentry Gallery, Inc. v. Berkline Corp.***, 45 USPQ 2d 1498, 1501 (Fed. Cir. 1998)

We agree with Gentry that the term "fixed" requires only that the console be rigidly secured to its two adjacent recliners. The term "fixed" and the explanatory clause "with the console and reclining seats together comprising a unitary structure" were added during prosecution to overcome a rejection based on a sectional sofa in which the seats were not rigidly attached. Thus, because the term "console" clearly refers to the complete section between the recliners, the term "fixed" merely requires that the console be rigidly attached to the recliners.

29. ***Personalized Media Communications, L.L.C. v. International Trade Comm'n***, 48 USPQ 2d 1880, 1888–89 (Fed. Cir. 1998)

We agree with PMC and conclude that the Commission erred in holding the asserted claims to be indefinite. Here, the written description of the specification is sufficient to inform one skilled in the art of the meaning of the claim language "digital detector." It explicitly defines a "digital detector" as a device that "acts to detect the digital signal information" in another stream of information. . . . The Commission makes much of the fact that the specification is otherwise silent concerning the structure of a "digital detector," and it notes that the "digital detectors" of the circuit diagrams do not reveal circuit elements constituting such a device, but only portray these devices as mere functional blocks. . . . We conclude that the evidence relied upon by the Commission does not indicate imprecision of the claims. . . . The invention's operability may say nothing about a skilled artisan's understanding of the bounds of the claim.

30. ***KCJ Corp. v. Kinetic Concepts, Inc.***, 55 USPQ 2d 1835, 1839 (Fed. Cir. 2000)

This court has repeatedly emphasized that an indefinite article "a" or "an" in patent parlance carries the meaning of "one or more" in open-ended claims containing the transitional phrase "comprising." See *Elkay Mfg. Co. v. Ebco Mfg. Co.*, 192 F.3d 973, 977, 52 USPQ 2d 1109, 1112 (Fed. Cir. 1999); *AbTox, Inc. v. Exitron Corp.*, 122 F.3d 1019, 1023, 43 USPQ 2d 1545, 1548 (Fed. Cir. 1997); *North Am. Vaccine, Inc. v. American Cyanamid Co.*, 7 F.3d 1571, 1575–76, 28 USPQ 2d 1333, 1336 (Fed. Cir. 1993); see also Robert C. Faber, Landis on Mechanics of Patent Claim Drafting 531 (3d ed. 1990). Unless the claim is specific as to the number of elements, the article "a" receives a singular interpretation only in rare circumstances when the patentee evinces a clear intent to so limit the article. See *AbTox*, 122 F.3d at 1023, 43 USPQ 2d at 1548. Under this conventional rule, the claim limitation "a," without more, requires at least one.

XI.I. *Chemical Structure/Terminology*

1. ***In re Sus***, 134 USPQ 301, 304 (C.C.P.A. 1962)

While the term "aryl and substituted aryl radicals" is a broad term, it is not objectionable for this reason alone if the term is (1) supported by the specification, and (2) if it properly defines the novel subject matter described in the specification. The public purpose on which the patent law rests requires the granting of claims commensurate in scope with the invention disclosed. This requires as much the granting of broad claims on broad inventions as it does the granting of more specific claims on more specific inventions. It is neither contemplated by the public purpose of the patent laws nor required by the statute that an inventor shall be forced to accept claims narrower than his invention in order to secure allowance of his patent.

2. ***Ex parte Saceman***, 27 USPQ 2d 1472, 1473–74 (B.P.A.I. 1993)

In this case, however, appellant does not define the term "mineral carbon" in the specification or the claims.

. . .

On this record, it is unclear whether appellant's expression "mineral carbon" is intended to cover graphite or natural graphite or fusain. For these reasons, we hold that the term "mineral carbon" and all of the claims on appeal are indefinite.

In so holding, we point out that the term "mineral carbon" is a salient feature in the claims, i.e., an essential claim limitation relied on by appellant in distinguishing over the prior art which has been cited by the examiner. In our view therefore, it is particularly important that the meaning of this term be reasonably precise and definite.

3. ***In re Fisher***, 166 USPQ 18, 23 (C.C.P.A. 1970)

Here the examiner and the board have viewed the absence of a limitation as to amino acids beyond the 24th position as rendering the claim indefinite. While the absence of such a limitation obviously broadens the claim and raises questions of sufficiency of disclosure, it does not render the claim indefinite. The absence of the limitation has a precise meaning. Regardless of the specification, the claimed subject matter is in no way limited by the presence, absence or sequence of amino acids beyond the 24th position. This principle is the very basis of this court's consistent refusal to read limitations of the specification into the claims. In our recent decision in *In re Wakefield*, . . . , we considered an indefiniteness rejection involving the absence of a limitation. We reversed the rejection, stating . . . : "The scope of the claim is still definite, however, because each recited limitation is definite."

4. ***In re Wilson***, 165 USPQ 494, 496 (C.C.P.A. 1970)

The board has disregarded the term "incompatible," as used in the claims, because it is "too relative" to distinguish over the compositions of the references. Appellant contends this limitation is essential in defining his invention. . . . The board said, in effect, that since we do not know what "incompatible" means, and the rest of the claim defines obvious subject matter, there is no basis for concluding unobviousness. This reasoning is incorrect. All words in a claim must be considered in judging the patentability of that claim against the prior art. If no reasonably definite meaning can be ascribed to certain terms in the claim, the subject matter does not become obvious—the claim becomes indefinite. In the present case, we think the term "incompatible" is defined with reasonable definiteness in the specification. While it is true that the word is not perfectly precise, under the circumstances of the present case there appears to be no other way for appellant to describe his discovery. In any event, the ignoring of this term by the board renders its conclusion of obviousness unsupported.

XI.J. *Indefiniteness and Multiplicity of Claims*

1. ***In re Savage***, 45 USPQ 155, 160 (C.C.P.A. 1940)

We think it proper to observe, however, that the mere fact that a larger number of claims are made than are necessary to cover the invention is not sufficient to warrant rejection upon the ground of undue multiplicity of claims. In addition, to warrant a rejection upon that ground, the claims must be not only of greater number than necessary to protect an invention, but they must be of a character "the net result of which is to confuse, rather than to clarify, the issues relative to an alleged improvement, which, it is claimed, involves invention." . . .

If claims are unnecessarily multiplied, but are definite and clear as to the invention claimed, differing only in phraseology that cannot confuse the issue involved, then . . . action should be had upon their merits, and such claims as, in effect, are merely duplicates of other claims should be rejected for that reason, but not upon the ground of undue multiplicity.

XI.K. *Indefiniteness and Negative Expressions*

1. ***Ex parte Williams***, 39 USPQ 125, 127 (Pat. Off. Bd. App. 1938)

Objection has also been made to the negative expression ["being otherwise free of"] with which the claims conclude. While this limitation on the protection sought is expressed in terms not to be found in the original disclosure, we see no valid objection to the appellants' thus eliminating from the scope of the protection sought certain materials which may

possibly have been included in the original disclosure. In
other words, the limitation has a narrowing effect rather
than a broadening one and, under the circumstances, we
think it permissible.

XI.L. *Indefiniteness and Human Intervention*

1. ***In re Johnston***, 183 USPQ 172, 176 (C.C.P.A. 1974), *rev'd
   on other grounds*, 425 U.S. 219 (1976)

   In essence, the "failure to particularly point out and distinctly claim" rejection is based upon the board's conclusion
   that the "relationship of a bank and its customers, not any
   particular configuration of business machinery", is being
   claimed. Upon reading the appealed *apparatus* claims we
   cannot perceive how any such "relationship" is being claimed.
   In typical means-plus-function language, which is expressly
   sanctioned by the [sixth] paragraph of §112, the appealed *apparatus* claims are clearly drawn to a "record-keeping *machine* system for financial accounts" (emphasis added). Accordingly, we cannot sustain the board's rejection on its
   stated grounds.

2. ***Musco Corp. v. Qualite, Inc.***, Civ. App. 96-1212, slip op.
   3–5 (Fed. Cir. Jan. 17, 1997) (unpublished)

   Musco avers that its claimed invention comprises neither
   the apparatus used in the method nor the determining steps
   cited in the claims, when used alone or in combinations. Instead, it asserts that the essence of its claimed invention is
   the method of "selectively utilizing" one or more of the various apparatus to solve the problems identified by the determining steps. Qualite responds that Musco's claims include
   impermissible mental process steps, such as determining
   the lighting problems and selectively utilizing the accessories. . . . The existence of mental steps in the claims or specifications of a patent do not, in and of themselves, invalidate
   the patent. . . . [T]he claimed subject matter—the selective
   utilization process—is composed *solely* of mental steps, at
   the very least, some aspect of these mental steps must be
   nonobvious, and the specification must describe this same
   aspect so as to enable the skilled artisan to practice the invention.

3. ***Ex parte Nassim***, Appeal No. 91-2486 (B.P.A.I. 1991) (unpublished)

   Just because the court in Prater held, in the particular fact
   situation there involved, that the method claimed therein
   was drawn to statutory subject matter because all the steps
   recited therein could be performed by a machine, it does not

follow that a method is drawn to non-statutory subject matter simply because one or more of the method steps recited therein are "mental" steps which cannot be performed by a machine. . . . It is not important whether the claims contain mental steps or not if the process is within the technological or useful arts. *See In re Foster*, 438 F.2d 1011, 169 USPQ 99 (C.C.P.A. 1971). Here, the process defined by independent claim 30 which includes the steps of "supplying . . .," "testing . . ." "storing . . ." and "reading . . ." clearly set forth a process that is within the technological arts and, therefore, the claims here involved are clearly drawn to statutory subject matter under §101. . . .

XI.M. *Indefiniteness and Interpreting Claims Under Section 112, Sixth Paragraph*

1. ***In re Donaldson Co.***, 29 USPQ 2d 1845, 1850 (Fed. Cir. 1994) (in banc)

[I]f one employs means-plus-function language in a claim, one must set forth in the specification an adequate disclosure showing what is meant by that language. If an applicant fails to set forth an adequate disclosure, the applicant has in effect failed to particularly point out and distinctly claim the invention as required by the second paragraph of section 112.

2. ***In re Dossel***, 42 USPQ 2d 1881, 1885 (Fed. Cir. 1997)

Neither the written description nor the claims uses the magic word "computer," nor do they quote computer code that may be used in the invention. Nevertheless, when the written description is combined with claims 8 and 9, the disclosure satisfies the requirements of § 112 ¶ 2. As the written description discloses, the clauses in question claim a device that receives digital data words from a memory and data input from a user. The device then computes, from the received data, the current distribution by mathematical operations including a matrix inversion or pseudo inversion, and then outputs the result to a display. While the written description does not disclose exactly what mathematical algorithm will be used to compute the end result, it does state that "known algorithms" can be used to solve standard equations which are known in the art.

Clearly, a unit which receives digital data, performs complex mathematical computations and outputs the results to a display must be implemented by or on a general or special purpose computer (although it is not clear why the written description does not simply state "computer" or some equivalent phrase). To bolster this result we note that, in the med-

ical imaging field, it is well within the realm of common experience that computers are used to generate images for display by mathematically processing digital input. Therefore,
because of the specific facts in this case, the structure underlying the function recited in Claims 8 and 9 is adequate for
us to hold that the requirements of § 112 ¶ 2, that the invention be particularly pointed out and distinctly claimed, are
satisfied.

3. ***In re Knowlton***, 178 USPQ 486, 494 (C.C.P.A. 1973)

As to the second rationale, it appears to us to be based on
the premise that each means-plus-function element in a
claim can only be read on a single, complete mechanical element of the invention, which performs the recited function
without aid from other elements of the invention. Thus the
board and the examiner considered that the means-plus-
function recitations in the claims were not supported by the
disclosure because some of the hardware disclosed, for example index register 4, will perform or assist in performing
several of the functions listed in those means-plus-function
recitations. . . .

As appellant points out, the board's complaint that "there
never exists at the same time a means for performing both
successive functions" is inconsistent with the fact that when
appellant's program is fully loaded into the computer the
stored pattern of signals transforms the unprogramed machine into a new structure, with all the necessary hardware
elements being physically interrelated so as to enable them
to perform their specified functions. . . .

4. ***Essilor Int'l v. Nidek Co., Ltd.***, Civ. App. No. 98-1558, slip
op. at 8–9 (Fed. Cir. Oct. 29, 1999) (unpublished)

Patentees may express claim elements in "means-plus-
function" format. . . . In a means-plus-function claim, the
claim element is expressed as a means for performing a
specified function and the claim is construed as covering the
corresponding structure described in the specification and
equivalents thereof. . . .

35 U.S.C. § 112, ¶ 2 requires that all claims, including
means-plus-function claims, particularly point out and distinctly claim the subject matter which the applicant regards
as his invention. For a means-plus-function claim to satisfy
the section 112, ¶ 2 requirement, the specification must adequately describe the structure which performs the specified
function. . . .

The specification does not have to describe the structure
corresponding to a means-plus-function limitation in explicit detail. For example, in *In re Dossel*, 115 F.3d 942,

946–47, 42 USPQ 2d 1881, 1885 (Fed. Cir. 1997), we held that the specification adequately described the structure corresponding to the means for reconstructing data when it recited a device that receives digital data from memory and from a user. The fact that the specification did not recite the term "computer" nor quote computer code that may be used in the invention, did not render the means clause invalid under section 112, ¶ 2.

In our case, the patent discloses a "control unit" as the structure that performs the function of storing, comparing and selecting the bevel path. . . . The patent further states that the control unit is composed of a central storage and computation unit and that the construction of a control unit is within the capabilities of a person skilled in the art. . . . The district court found that it would have been clear to one of ordinary skill what structure must perform the function recited in the means-plus-function limitation. The district court found that the necessary elements of the control unit which would perform these functions were described in the patent and that the functions described in the specification could be accomplished using computer programs. We agree with the district court.

5. ***Rodime PLC v. Seagate Tech., Inc.***, 50 USPQ 2d 1429, 1436 (Fed. Cir. 1999)

In reaching the opposite conclusion, the special master seemed concerned that the claim did not recite every last detail of structure disclosed in the specification for performing the claimed moving function. This court's case law, however, does not require such an exhaustive recitation to avoid § 112, ¶ 6. Instead, the claim need only recite "sufficient" structure to perform entirely the claimed function. . . . Based on the structure disclosed in the specification for performing the moving function, these claims recite nearly all (if not all) of the structural components of the positioning mechanism. In any case, they clearly recite more than sufficient structure for moving the transducer from track to track.

6. ***WMS Gaming Inc. v. Int'l Game Tech.***, 51 USPQ 2d 1385, 1391 (Fed. Cir. 1999) (quoting *In re Alappat*, 31 USPQ 2d 1545, 1558 (Fed. Cir. 1994) (en banc))

The structure of a microprocessor programmed to carry out an algorithm is limited by the disclosed algorithm. A general purpose computer, or microprocessor, programmed to carry out an algorithm creates "a new machine, because a general purpose computer in effect becomes a special purpose computer once it is programmed to perform particular functions pursuant to instructions from program software." . . . The instructions of the software program that carry out the algorithm electrically change the general purpose computer by creating electrical paths within the device. These electrical paths create a special purpose machine for carrying out the particular algorithm.

In a means-plus-function claim in which the disclosed structure is a computer, or microprocessor, programmed to carry out an algorithm, the disclosed structure is not the general purpose computer, but rather the special purpose computer programmed to perform the disclosed algorithm.

7. ***Micro Chem., Inc. v. Great Plains Chem. Co.***, 52 USPQ 2d 1258, 1264 (Fed. Cir. 1999)

[I]f the . . . method claim elements fall within § 112, ¶ 6, under that statute, this court looks to the specification for acts corresponding to the step-plus-function element which are necessary to perform the recited function. In this case, these corresponding acts include all acts described in the specification for dispensing microingredient quantities measured by weight. These acts include the cumulative weigh method of the preferred embodiment and the loss of weight method of the alternative embodiment, as well as the weigh dump method of the prior art. . . . In sum, the patent specification describes each of these methods as a way to accomplish the desired function of dispensing predetermined weights of microingredients without substantial intermixing prior to entry into the liquid.

8. ***Atmel Corp. v. Information Storage Devices Inc.***, 53 USPQ 2d 1225, 1230–31 (Fed. Cir. 1999)

Paragraph 1 is, inter alia, an enablement provision requiring that an inventor set forth in the patent specification how to make and use his or her invention. Paragraph 2 requires claims that particularly and distinctly indicate the subject matter that the inventor considers to be his or her invention. Paragraph 6 also addresses claim language, but refers to the specification for its meaning. In doing so, it specifically refers to "structure . . . described in the specification and equivalents thereof." *Id.* § 112, ¶ 6. This provision represents a quid pro quo by permitting inventors to use a generic means expression for a claim limitation provided that the specification indicates what structure(s) constitute(s) the means. See *O.I. Corp. v. Tekmar Co.*, 115 F.3d 1576, 1583, 42 USPQ 2d 1777, 1782 (Fed. Cir. 1997). The language indicates that means-plus-function clauses comprise not only the language of the claims, but also the structure corresponding] to that means that is disclosed in the written description portion of the specification (and equivalents thereof). Thus, in order for a claim to meet the particularity requirement of ¶ 2, the corresponding structure(s) of a means-plus-function limitation must be disclosed in the written description in such a manner that one skilled in the art will know and understand what structure corresponds to the means limitation. Otherwise, one does not know what the claim means.

Fulfillment of the § 112, ¶ 6 trade-off cannot be satisfied when there is a total omission of structure. There must be structure in the specification. This conclusion is not inconsistent with the fact that the knowledge of one skilled in the particular art may be used to understand what structure(s) the specification discloses, or that even a dictionary or other documentary source may be resorted to for such assistance, because such resources may only be employed in relation to structure that is disclosed in the specification. Paragraph 6 does not contemplate the kind of open-ended reference to extrinsic works that ¶ 1, the enablement provision, does.

Paragraph 1 permits resort to material outside of the specification in order to satisfy the enablement portion of the statute because it makes no sense to encumber the specification of a patent with all the knowledge of the past concerning how to make and use the claimed invention. One skilled in the art knows how to make and use a bolt, a wheel, a gear, a transistor, or a known chemical starting material. The specification would be of enormous and unnecessary length if one had to literally reinvent and describe the wheel.

Section 112, ¶ 6, however, does not have the expansive purpose of ¶ 1. It sets forth a simple requirement, a quid pro quo, in order to utilize a generic means expression. All one needs to do in order to obtain the benefit of that claiming device is to recite some structure corresponding to the means in the specification, as the statute states, so that one can readily ascertain what the claim means and comply with the particularity requirement of ¶ 2. The requirement of specific structure in § 112, ¶ 6 thus does not raise the specter of an unending disclosure of what everyone in the field knows that such a requirement in § 112, ¶ 1 would entail. If our interpretation of the statute results in a slight amount of additional written description appearing in patent specifications compared with total omission of structure, that is the trade-off necessitated by an applicant's use of the statute's permissive generic means term.

9. ***Kemco Sales, Inc. v. Control Papers Co., Inc.***, 54 USPQ 2d 1308, 1313 (Fed. Cir. 2000)

35 U.S.C. section 112, paragraph 6 provides that a patentee may define the structure for performing a particular function

generically through the use of a means expression, provided
that it discloses specific structure(s) corresponding to that
means in the patent specification. See 35 U.S.C. § 112, ¶ 6
(1994); *Atmel*, 198 F.3d at 1380–82, 53 USPQ 2d at 1229–31
(holding that the structure supporting a means-plus-function
limitation must be disclosed in the specification); *Valmont
Indus., Inc. v. Reinke Mfg. Co.*, 983 F.2d 1039, 1042, 25 USPQ
2d 1451, 1454 (Fed. Cir. 1993) ("The applicant must describe
in the patent specification some structure which performs the
specified function."). As such, we have referred to 35 U.S.C.
section 112, paragraph 6 as embodying a statutory quid pro
quo. See, e.g., *Atmel*, 198 F.3d at 1381, 53 USPQ 2d at 1230;
see also *B. Braun Med., Inc. v. Abbott Lab.*, 124 F.3d 1419,
1424, 43 USPQ 2d 1896, 1900 (Fed. Cir. 1997) ("The duty to
link or associate structure to function is the quid pro quo for
the convenience of employing § 112, ¶ 6."). If a patentee fails
to satisfy the bargain because of a failure to disclose adequate
structure, the claim will be rendered invalid as indefinite
under 35 U.S.C. section 112, paragraph 2. See *In re Donaldson Co.*, 16 F.3d 1189, 1195, 29 USPQ 2d 1845, 1850 (Fed. Cir.
1994) (en banc).

10. ***Atmel Corp. v. Information Storage Devices Inc.***, 53
    USPQ 2d 1225, 1228 (Fed. Cir. 1999)

    As a general matter, it is well-established that the determi-
    nation whether a claim is invalid as indefinite "depends on
    whether those skilled in the art would understand the scope
    of the claim when the claim is read in light of the specifica-
    tion." *North Am. Vaccine, Inc. v. American Cyanamid Co.*, 7
    F.3d 1571, 1579, 28 USPQ 2d 1333, 1339 (Fed. Cir. 1993); see
    Miles Lab., Inc. v. Shandon, Inc., 997 F.2d 870, 875, 27
    USPQ 2d 1123, 1126 (Fed. Cir. 1993). For purposes of § 112
    ¶ 2, it is the disclosure in the specification itself, not the
    technical form of the disclosure that counts. In *In re Donald-
    son Co., Inc.*, we explained how § 112, ¶ 2 applies in the spe-
    cific context of a § 112, ¶ 6 means-plus-function claim limi-
    tation:

    > Although [§ 112, ¶ 6] statutorily provides that one may
    > use means-plus-function language in a claim, one is still
    > subject to the requirement that a claim "particularly point
    > out and distinctly claim" the invention [§ 112, ¶ 2]. There-
    > fore, if one employs means-plus-function language in a
    > claim, one must set forth in the specification an adequate
    > disclosure showing what is meant by the claim language.
    > If an applicant fails to set forth an adequate disclosure,
    > the applicant has in effect failed to particularly point out
    > and distinctly claim the invention as required by the sec-
    > ond paragraph of section 112.

Donaldson, 16 F.3d 1189, 1195, 29 USPQ 2d 1845, 1850 (Fed. Cir. 1994). . . . As it is well-established that claims are to be construed in view of the understanding of one skilled in the art, see, e.g., *K-2 Corp. v. Salomon S.A.*, 191 F.3d 1356, 1365, 52 USPQ 2d 1001, 1006 (Fed. Cir. 1999) (noting that "claim construction is firmly anchored in reality by the understanding of those of ordinary skill in the art"), the closely related issue concerning whether sufficient structure has in fact been disclosed to support a means-plus-function limitation should be analyzed under the same standard.

11. ***Atmel Corp. v. Information Storage Devices Inc.***, 53 USPQ 2d 1225, 1231 (Fed. Cir. 1999)

While we do agree with ISD that the district court properly held that the Dickson article may not take the place of structure that does not appear in the specification, the specification plainly states that "known Circuit techniques are used to implement high-voltage circuit 34. See On-Chip High Voltage Generation in NMOS Integrated Circuits Using an Improved Voltage Multiplier Technique, IEEE Journal of Solid State Circuits. . . ." '811 patent, col. 4, ll. 58–62. Atmel's expert, Callahan, testified that this title alone was sufficient to indicate to one skilled in the art the precise structure of the means recited in the specification.

XII. Interpreting Preamble

1. ***DeGeorge v. Bernier***, 226 USPQ 758, 761 n.3 (Fed. Cir. 1985)

Generally, and in this case, the preamble does not limit the claims. This case is unlike *Perkin-Elmer Corp. v. Computervision Corp.*, . . . where preamble limitations were "necessary to give meaning to the claim and properly define the invention."

2. ***Perkin-Elmer Corp. v. Computervision Corp.***, 221 USPQ 669, 675–76 (Fed. Cir.), ***cert. denied***, 469 U.S. 857 (1984)

The system of claim 1 is one of unity magnification and is image forming. Those limitations appear in the preamble, but are necessary to give meaning to the claim and properly define the invention.

3. ***Corning Glass Works v. Sumitomo Elec. U.S.A. Inc.***, 9 USPQ 2d 1962, 1966 (Fed. Cir. 1989)

No litmus test can be given with respect to when the introductory words of a claim, the preamble, constitute a statement of purpose for a device or are, in themselves, additional structural limitations of a claim. To say that a preamble is a limitation if it gives "meaning to the claim" may merely state the problem rather than lead one to the answer.

The effect preamble language should be given can be resolved only on review of the entirety of the patent to gain an understanding of what the inventors actually invented and intended to encompass by the claim. Here, the 915 specification makes clear that the inventors were working on the particular problem of an effective optical communication system not on general improvements in conventional optical fibers.

4. *In re Wertheim*, 191 USPQ 90, 102 (C.C.P.A. 1976)

Appellants contend that this preamble gives "life and meaning" to the claims, serving to define the interrelationship of the mechanical elements recited in the body of the claims. This argument appears to be based on *Kropa v. Robie*, 38 C.C.P.A. 858, 187 F.2d 150, 88 USPQ 478 (1951), the classic case in this court on the construction of claim preambles. In *Kropa* the court surveyed prior cases and said 38 C.C.P.A. at 861, 187 F.2d at 152, 88 USPQ at 480–81:

> [I]t appears that the preamble has been denied the effect of a limitation where the claim or count was drawn to a structure and the portion of the claim following the preamble was a self-contained description of the structure not depending for completeness upon the introductory clause * * *. In those cases, the claim or count apart from the introductory clause completely defined the subject matter, and the preamble merely stated a purpose or intended use of that subject matter.

5. *In re Gold*, Civ. App. No. 94-1038, slip op. at 5–6 (Fed. Cir. May 31, 1994) (unpublished)

Nevertheless, the somewhat circular, and oft-repeated rule is that language in the preamble further limits the claim if such is "necessary to give meaning to the claim[s] and properly define the invention." *In re Fritch*, 972 F.2d 1260, 1262, 23 USPQ 2d 1780, 1781 (Fed. Cir. 1992).... Whether preamble language is "necessary" or "essential" is a matter to be determined on the facts of each case in view of the claimed invention as a whole.

6. *In re Gold*, Civ. App. No. 94-1038, slip op. at 7 (Fed. Cir. May 31, 1994) (unpublished)

The specification of the patent application makes clear that Gold was working on the particular problem of underwater signaling devices for human skin divers, and not on general improvements to rattling devices. To construe claim 1 as covering every device having loose parts inside that rattle when manually displaced "would be divorced from reality." ... Rather, given the broad language of the claims at issue, we agree with Gold that the limitations appearing in the preamble are essential to point out the invention as defined by the claims. Thus, the preamble language does give "life and meaning," and thereby provides further limitations that must be disclosed in the prior art for the claims to be anticipated.

7. *In re Paulsen*, 31 USPQ 2d 1671, 1673–74 (Fed. Cir. 1994)

The preamble of a claim does not limit the scope of the claim when it merely states a purpose or intended use of the invention. . . . However, terms appearing in a preamble may be deemed limitations of a claim when they "give meaning to the claim and properly define the invention." *Gerber Garment Technology, Inc. v. Lectra Sys., Inc.*, 916 F.2d 683, 688, 16 USPQ 2d 1436, 1441 (Fed. Cir. 1990) (quoting *Perkin-Elmer Corp. v. Computervision Corp.*, 732 F.2d 888, 896, 221 USPQ 669, 675 (Fed. Cir.), *cert. denied*, 469 U.S. 857 (1984)). Although no "litmus test" exists as to what effect should be accorded to words contained in a preamble, review of a patent in its entirety should be made to determine whether the inventors intended such language to represent an additional structural limitation or mere introductory language.

8. *Derman v. PC Guardian*, 37 USPQ 2d 1733, 1734 (Fed. Cir. 1995) (unpublished) (per curiam)

The preamble of a claim does not limit the scope of a claim when it simply states a purpose or intended use of the invention. *Loctite Corp. v. Ultraseal Ltd.*, 781 F.2d 861, 868, 228 U.S.P.Q. (BNA) 90, 94 (Fed. Cir. 1985). However, if it says more, it may limit the scope of the claim because the determination as to whether a preamble imposes a limitation is determined on a case by case basis. *In re Stencel*, 828 F.2d 751, 754, 4 U.S.P.Q.2D (BNA) 1071, 1073 (Fed. Cir. 1987). "[A] claim preamble has the import that the claim as a whole suggests for it. In other words, when the claim drafter chooses to use both the preamble and the body to define the subject matter of the claimed invention, the invention so defined, and not some other, is the one the patent protects." *Bell Communications Research, Inc. v. Vitalink Communications Corp.*, 55 F.3d 615, 620, 34 U.S.P.Q.2D (BNA) 1816, 1820 (Fed. Cir. 1995).

9. *Applied Materials, Inc. v. Advanced Semiconductor Materials Am., Inc.*, 40 USPQ 2d 1481, 1488 (Fed. Cir. 1996), *cert. denied*, 520 U.S. 1230 (1997)

Whether a preamble stating the purpose and context of the invention constitutes a limitation of the claimed process is determined on the facts of each case in light of the overall form of the claim, and the invention as described in the specification and illuminated in the prosecution history. . . . It is thus appropriate to determine whether the term in the preamble serves to define the invention that is claimed, or is simply a description of the prior art.

10. ***Row v. Dror***, 42 USPQ 2d 1550, 1553 (Fed. Cir. 1997)
Where a patentee uses the claim preamble to recite structural limitations of his claimed invention, the PTO and courts give effect to that usage. . . . Conversely, where a patentee defines a structurally complete invention in the claim body and uses the preamble only to state a purpose or intended use for the invention, the preamble is not a claim limitation.

11. ***C.R. Bard, Inc. v. M3 Sys., Inc.***, 48 USPQ 2d 1225, 1230–31 (Fed. Cir. 1998)
A preamble may serve a variety of purposes, depending on its content. It may limit the scope of the claim, for example when patentability depends on limitations stated in the preamble, as in *In re Stencel*, 828 F.2d 751, 754, 4 USPQ 2d 1071, 1073 (Fed. Cir. 1987), or when the preamble contributes to the definition of the claimed invention, as in *Bell Communications Research, Inc. v. Vitalink Communications Corp.*, 55 F.3d 615, 620, 34 USPQ 2d 1816, 1820 (Fed. Cir. 1995). In this case, however, the preamble simply states the intended use or purpose of the invention, as in *Loctite Corp. v. Ultraseal Ltd.*, 781 F.2d 861, 868, 228 USPQ 90, 94 (Fed. Cir. 1985). Such a preamble usually does not limit the scope of the claim unless the preamble provides antecedents for ensuing claim terms and limits the claim accordingly.

12. ***Pitney Bowes Inc. v. Hewlett-Packard Co.***, 51 USPQ 2d 1161, 1165–66 (Fed. Cir. 1999) (quoting ***Bell Communications Research, Inc. v. Vitalink Communications Corp.***, 34 USPQ 2d 1816, 1820 (Fed. Cir. 1995))
"[A] claim preamble has the import that the claim as a whole suggests for it." . . . If the claim preamble, when read in the context of the entire claim, recites limitations of the claim, or, if the claim preamble is "necessary to give life, meaning, and vitality" to the claim, then the claim preamble should be construed as if in the balance of the claim. . . . Indeed, when discussing the "claim" in such a circumstance, there is no meaningful distinction to be drawn between the claim preamble and the rest of the claim, for only together do they comprise the "claim". If, however, the body of the claim fully and intrinsically sets forth the complete invention, including all of its limitations, and the preamble offers no distinct definition of any of the claimed invention's limitations, but rather merely states, for example, the purpose or intended

use of the invention, then the preamble is of no significance to claim construction because it cannot be said to constitute or explain a claim limitation.

13. ***General Elec. Co. v. Nintendo Co., Ltd.***, 50 USPQ 2d 1910, 1918 (Fed. Cir. 1999)

We must, thus, determine whether the preamble breathes life and meaning into the claim, and is incorporated by reference because of language appearing later in the claim, making it a limitation of the claim.

14. ***Heidelberg Harris, Inc. v. Mitsubishi Heavy Indus., Ltd.***, Civ. App. 1100, slip op. at 12–13 (Fed. Cir. Sep. 18, 2000) (unpublished)

The determination of the effect of preamble language is but a part of the broader task of claim construction. . . . While the phrase "for reducing vibrations and slippage" was originally added to the body of the '048 claims in the context of means-plus-function language, which indisputably would have acted to limit the claimed inventions, its movement to the preamble of the newly-added claims did not create a similar effect. The only relevance of the phrase "reducing vibrations and slippage" is to illustrate the intended purpose of the invention. See *Bowes, Inc. v. Hewlett-Packard Co.*, 182 F.3d 1298, 1305, 51 USPQ 2d 1161, 1165–66 (Fed. Cir. 1999). The phrase is plainly not "necessary to give life, meaning, and vitality to the claim." *Kropa v. Robie*, 187 F.2d 150, 152, 88 USPQ 478, 480–81 (C.C.P.A. 1951). It does not, for example, provide an antecedent basis for terms later used in the body of the claim. See *Gerber Garment Tech., Inc. v. Lectra Sys., Inc.*, 916 F.2d 683, 688–89, 16 USPQ 2d 1436, 1441 (Fed. Cir. 1990). Nor could such an expression of the intended use and function of the offset press have distinguished over the prior art. See *In re Lechene*, 277 F.2d 173, 176, 125 USPQ 396, 399 (C.C.P.A. 1960). Consequently, we hold that the phrase "reducing vibrations and slippage" is not a claim limitation.

XIII. Interpreting Claims/Giving Effect to Claim Limitations

1. ***Ex parte Forsyth***, 151 USPQ 55, 56 (Pat. Off. Bd. App. 1965)

A claim such as those before us cannot be both method and apparatus. It must be clear by its wording that it is drawn to one or the other of these two mutually exclusive statutory classes of invention. A method or process, as indicated above, is an act or a series of acts and from the standpoint of patentability must distinguish over the prior art in terms of steps, whereas a claim drawn to apparatus must distinguish in terms of structure. This is so elemental as not to require citation of authorities.

2. ***In re Angstadt***, 190 USPQ 214, 217 (C.C.P.A. 1976)

We note at the outset that the claim limitation . . . must be given effect since we must give effect to all claim limitations.

3. ***In re Worrest***, 96 USPQ 381, 387 (C.C.P.A. 1953)

Moreover, assuming the office tribunals regarded the physical embodiment as inventive, it is essential that the claims adequately recite the features upon which appellant predicates patentability.

4. ***In re Kathawala***, 28 USPQ 2d 1785, 1789 n.3 (Fed. Cir. 1993)

Similarly, in *In re Pleuddemann*, 910 F.2d 823, 15 USPQ 2d 1738 (Fed. Cir. 1990), we recognized that in the context of an obviousness determination under 35 U.S.C. § 103 that

> [w]hen a new and useful compound or group of compounds is invented or discovered having a particular use it is often the case that what is really a single invention may be viewed legally as having three or more different aspects permitting it to be claimed in different ways, for example: (1) the compound themselves; (2) the method or process of making the compounds; and (3) the method or process of using the compounds for their intended purpose.

Id. at 825–26, 15 USPQ 2d at 1740 (emphases omitted).

5. ***Eastman Kodak Co. v. Goodyear Tire & Rubber Co.***, 42 USPQ 2d 1737, 1740 (Fed. Cir. 1997)

Claim interpretation proceeds under the guidelines set forth by the *Markman* case. *Markman*, 116 S. Ct. 1384; *Markman* 52 F.3d at 979. This court, speaking *in banc*, restated familiar principles of claim interpretation:

> To ascertain the meaning of claims, we consider three sources: The claims, the specification, and the prosecution history. . . . Expert testimony, including evidence of how those skilled in the art would interpret the claims, may also be used.

Markman, 52 F.3d at 979 (citations omitted). The claim language itself defines the scope of the claim. *See York Prods., Inc. v. Central Tractor Farm & Family Center*, 99 F.3d 1568, 1572, 40 USPQ 2d 1619, 1622 (Fed. Cir. 1996). To learn the necessary context for understanding the claim language, however, a construing court may consult other sources, including the patent specification, the administrative record of patent acquisition, expert commentary from those of skill in the art, and other relevant extrinsic evidence. *Markman*, 52 F.3d at 979. In other words, a construing court does not accord the specification, prosecution history, and other relevant evidence the same weight as the claims themselves, but consults these sources to give the necessary context to the claim language.

6. ***Eastman Kodak Co. v. Goodyear Tire & Rubber Co.***, 42 USPQ 2d 1737, 1741 (Fed. Cir. 1997)

The specification, of which the claims are part, teaches about the problems solved by the claimed invention, the way the claimed invention solves those problems, and the prior art that relates to the invention. These teachings provide valuable context for the meaning of the claim language.

7. ***Brand Management, Inc. v. Pro Shop Plans Co.***, slip op. at 7, Civ. App. 96-1523 (Fed. Cir. June 25, 1997) (unpublished)

We have, on a number of occasions, expressed our inclination to interpret narrowly claims that are otherwise ambiguous. . . . The term "sides" is ambiguous to the extent that it could be interpreted to refer to either internal sides or both internal and external sides. Therefore, we rely upon the specification and the prosecution history to provide the meaning the inventors ascribed to the term.

8. ***Sage Prods., Inc. v. Devon Indus.***, 44 USPQ 2d 1103, 1107 (Fed. Cir. 1997)

The claim at issue defines a relatively simple structural device. A skilled patent drafter would foresee the limiting potential of the "over said slot" limitation. No subtlety of language or complexity of the technology, nor any subsequent change in the state of the art, such as later-developed technology, obfuscated the significance of this limitation at the time of its incorporation into the claim. . . . If Sage desired broad patent protection for any container that performed a function similar to its claimed container, it could have sought claims with fewer structural encumbrances. Had Sage done so, then the Patent and Trademark Office (PTO) could have fulfilled its statutory role in helping to ensure that exclusive rights issue only to those who have, in fact, contributed something new, useful, and unobvious. Instead, Sage left the PTO with manifestly limited claims that it now seeks to expand through the doctrine of equivalents. However, as between the patentee who had a clear opportunity to negotiate broader claims but did not do so, and the public at large, it is the patentee who must bear the cost of its failure to seek protection for this foreseeable alteration of its claimed structure. . . . This court recognizes that such reasoning places a premium on forethought in patent drafting. Indeed this premium may lead to higher costs of patent prosecution. However, the alternative rule—allowing broad play for the doctrine of equivalents to encompass foreseeable variations, not just of a claim element, but of a patent claim—also leads to higher costs. Society at large would bear these latter costs in the form of virtual foreclosure of competitive activity within the penumbra of each issued patent claim.

9. ***Abtox, Inc. v. Exitron Corp.***, 43 USPQ 2d 1545, 1548 (Fed. Cir.), ***amended on rehearing***, 131 F.3d 1009 (Fed. Cir. 1997)

Claim interpretation is the process of giving proper meaning to the claim language. Claim language, after all, defines claim scope. . . . Therefore, the language of the claim frames and ultimately resolves all issues of claim interpretation. In determining the meaning of disputed claim terms, however, a construing court considers the descriptions in the rest of the patent specification, the prosecution history, and relevant extrinsic evidence.

10. ***Multiform Desiccants, Inc. v. Medzam, Ltd.***, 45 USPQ 2d 1429, 1432 (Fed. Cir. 1998)

It is the person of ordinary skill in the field of the invention through whose eyes the claims are construed. Such person is deemed to read the words used in the patent documents with an understanding of their meaning in the field, and to have knowledge of any special meaning and usage in the field. The inventor's words that are used to describe the invention—the inventor's lexicography—must be understood and interpreted by the court as they would be understood and interpreted by a person in that field of technology. Thus the court starts the decisionmaking process by reviewing the same resources as would that person, *viz.*, the patent specification and the prosecution history. These documents have legal as well as technological content, for they show not only the framework of the invention as viewed by the inventor, but also the issues of patentability as viewed by the patent examiner.

11. ***Multiform Desiccants, Inc. v. Medzam, Ltd.***, 45 USPQ 2d 1429, 1432 (Fed. Cir. 1998)

When the meaning of a term is sufficiently clear in the patent specification, that meaning shall apply. . . . This rule of construction recognizes that the inventor may have imparted a special meaning to a term in order to convey a character or property or nuance relevant to the particular invention. Such special meaning, however, must be sufficiently clear in the specification that any departure from common usage would be so understood by a person of experience in the field of the invention.

12. ***Multiform Desiccants, Inc. v. Medzam, Ltd.***, 45 USPQ 2d 1429, 1433 (Fed. Cir. 1998)

Courts must exercise caution lest dictionary definitions, usually the least controversial source of extrinsic evidence, be converted into technical terms of art having legal, not linguistic, significance. The best source for understanding a technical term is the specification from which it arose, informed, as needed, by the prosecution history. The evolution of restrictions in the claims, in the course of examination in the PTO, reveals how those closest to the patenting process—the inventor and the patent examiner—viewed the subject matter. . . . When the specification explains and defines a term used in the claims, without ambiguity or incompleteness, there is no need to search further for the meaning of the term.

13. ***York Prods., Inc. v. Central Tractor Farm & Family Ctr.***, 40 USPQ 2d 1619, 1622 (Fed. Cir. 1996)

Without an express intent to impart a novel meaning to claim terms, an inventor's claims take on their ordinary meaning.

14. ***Manchak, Jr. v. Chemical Waste Mgt., Inc.***, Civ. App. 98-1530, slip op. at 10 (Fed. Cir. Dec. 6, 1999) (unpublished) (citing ***Laitram Corp. v. Morehouse Indus.***, 46 USPQ 2d 1609, 1614 (Fed. Cir. 1993))

As Sevenson properly notes, accepting Manchak's expansive construction of "confined space" would yield the anomaly of a specification that nowhere describes or depicts a single embodiment illustrating such breadth of interpretation.

15. ***Pall Corp. v. Hemasure Inc.***, 50 USPQ 2d 1947, 1949 (Fed. Cir. 1999)

A patent claim is construed by examining the claim in the context of the specification, drawing on the specification for an understanding of what is covered by the claim, and looking to the rejections, explanations, and revisions that comprise the record of the patent examination. . . . The subject matter of the invention and its delineation in the claims is construed as it would be understood by persons knowledgeable in the field of the invention. . . . Thus a technical term is taken to have the meaning that it would ordinarily have in the field of the invention, unless it is shown that the inventor used the term with a special meaning and that persons of skill in the field would so understand the usage.

16. ***Pitney Bowes Inc. v. Hewlett-Packard Co.***, 51 USPQ 2d 1161, 1169 (Fed. Cir. 1999) (quoting ***Digital Biometrics, Inc. v. Identix, Inc.***, 47 USPQ 2d 1418, 1425 (Fed. Cir. 1998))

As a general principle, we agree with the district court's "logic". Certainly, "the same word appearing in the same claim should be interpreted consistently." . . . Indeed, our conclusion that the district court's claim construction was erroneous because it would assign a different meaning to the term "spot" in the preamble from that in the rest of the claims is broadly based upon this very principle. Nevertheless, we have also recognized that a patent's written description can set forth more than one definition of a claim term.

17. ***Pitney Bowes Inc. v. Hewlett-Packard Co.***, 51 USPQ 2d 1161, 1170 (Fed. Cir. 1999)

In circumstances such as this, where the language of the written description is sufficient to put a reader on notice of the different uses of a term, and where those uses are further apparent from publicly-available documents referenced in the patent file, it is appropriate to depart from the normal rule of construing seemingly identical terms in the same manner. This entirely accords with the public notice function of claims. . . . The prosecution history indicates to a reviewing member of the public that the '272 patent was one of several patents to be issued based upon the same written description disclosure. Parsing the written description, in the context of the prosecution history, puts the reader on notice that the term "spot" has different meanings in the written description depending on its context. . . . [T]herefore, the term must be read to correspond to the only plausible meaning in each context.

18. ***Johnson Worldwide Assocs., Inc. v. Zebco Corp.***, 50 USPQ 2d 1607, 1610–11 (Fed. Cir. 1999)

We begin, as with all claim interpretation analyses, with the language of the claims. [*Renishaw PLC v. Marposs Societa' Per Azioni*, 158 F.3d 1243, 1248, 48 USPQ 2d 1117, 1120 (Fed. Cir. 1998)]; *Abtox, Inc. v. Exitron Corp.*, 122 F.3d 1019, 1023, 43 USPQ 2d 1545, 1548 (Fed. Cir. 1997); *Bell Communications Research, Inc. v. Vitalink Communications Corp.*, 55 F.3d 615, 619–20, 34 USPQ 2d 1816, 1819 (Fed. Cir. 1995). The general rule is, of course, that terms in the claim are to be given their ordinary and accustomed meaning. *See Renishaw*, 158 F.3d at 1249, 48 USPQ 2d at 1121; *York Prods., Inc. v. Central Tractor Farm & Family Ctr.*, 99 F.3d

1568, 1572, 40 USPQ 2d 1619, 1622 (Fed. Cir. 1996). General descriptive terms will ordinarily be given their full meaning; modifiers will not be added to broad terms standing alone. *See, e.g., Virginia Panel Corp. v. MAC Panel Co.*, 133 F.3d 860, 865–66, 45 USPQ 2d 1225, 1229 (Fed. Cir. 1997) (unmodified term "reciprocating" not limited to linear reciprocation); *Bell Communications*, 55 F.3d at 621–22, 34 USPQ 2d at 1821 (unmodified term "associating" not limited to explicit association); *Specialty Composites v. Cabot Corp.*, 845 F.2d 981, 987, 6 USPQ 2d 1601, 1606 (Fed. Cir. 1988) (unmodified term "plasticizer" given full range of ordinary and accustomed meaning). In short, a court must presume that the terms in the claim mean what they say, and, unless otherwise compelled, give full effect to the ordinary and accustomed meaning of claim terms. *See, e.g., Nike Inc. v. Wolverine World Wide, Inc.*, 43 F.3d 644, 646, 33 USPQ 2d 1038, 1039 (Fed. Cir. 1994); *E.I. Du Pont De Nemours & Co. v. Phillips Petroleum*, 849 F.2d 1430, 1433, 7 USPQ 2d 1129, 1131 (Fed. Cir. 1988); *Envirotech Corp. v. Al George, Inc.*, 730 F.2d 753, 759, 221 USPQ 473, 477 (Fed. Cir. 1984).

In order to overcome this heavy presumption in favor of the ordinary meaning of claim language, it is clear that "a party wishing to use statements in the written description to confine or otherwise affect a patent's scope must, at the very least, point to a term or terms in the claim with which to draw in those statements." *Renishaw*, 158 F.3d at 1248, 48 USPQ 2d at 1121. That is, claim terms cannot be narrowed by reference to the written description or prosecution history unless the language of the claims invites reference to those sources. *See, e.g., McCarty v. Lehigh Valley R.R.*, 160 U.S. 110, 116, 40 L. Ed. 358, 16 S. Ct. 240 (1895) ("If we once begin to include elements not mentioned in the claim in order to limit such claim . . ., we should never know where to stop."); *Renishaw*, 158 F.3d at 1249, 48 USPQ 2d at 1121. In other words, there must be a textual reference in the actual language of the claim with which to associate a proffered claim construction.

Our case law demonstrates two situations where a sufficient reason exists to require the entry of a definition of a claim term other than its ordinary and accustomed meaning. The first arises if the patentee has chosen to be his or her own lexicographer by clearly setting forth an explicit definition for a claim term. *See In re Paulsen*, 30 F.3d 1475, 1480, 31 USPQ 2d 1671, 1674 (Fed. Cir. 1994); *Intellicall, Inc. v. Phonometrics, Inc.*, 952 F.2d 1384, 1387–88, 21 USPQ 2d 1383, 1386 (Fed. Cir. 1992); *Lear Siegler, Inc. v. Aeroquip Corp.*, 733 F.2d 881, 888–89, 221 USPQ 1025, 1031 (Fed. Cir. 1984). The second is where the term or terms chosen by the patentee so deprive the claim of clarity that there is no means by which the scope of the claim may be ascertained from the language used. *See Eastman Kodak Co. v. Goodyear Tire & Rubber Co.*, 114 F.3d 1547, 1554, 42 USPQ 2d 1737, 1741 (Fed. Cir. 1997) (looking past claim language because of lack of clarity), *overruled on other grounds by Cybor Corp. v. FAS Techs., Inc.*, 138 F.3d 1448, 46 USPQ 2d 1169 (Fed. Cir. 1998) (en banc); *J.T. Eaton & Co. v. Atlantic Paste & Glue Co.*, 106 F.3d 1563, 1568, 41 USPQ 2d 1641, 1646 (Fed. Cir. 1997) (Because "[the disputed claim term] is a term with no previous meaning to those of ordinary skill in the prior art[,] its meaning, then, must be found [elsewhere] in the patent."); *North Am. Vaccine, Inc. v. American Cyanamid Co.*, 7 F.3d 1571, 1576, 28 USPQ 2d 1333, 1336 (Fed. Cir. 1993) (using the specification for guidance "when the meaning of a claim term is in doubt"); *E.I. Du Pont De Nemours*, 849 F.2d at 1433, 7 USPQ 2d at 1131 (Fed. Cir. 1988) (the written description can supply understanding of unclear claim terms, but should never trump the clear meaning of claim terms). *Cf. Comark Communications, Inc. v. Harris Corp.*, 156 F.3d 1182, 1187, 48 USPQ 2d 1001, 1005 (Fed. Cir. 1998) ("In this case, the [disputed term] has a clear and well-defined meaning. This term is not so amorphous that one of skill in the art can only reconcile the claim language with the inventor's disclosure by recourse to the specification."). In these two circumstances, a term or terms used in the claim invites—or indeed, requires—reference to intrinsic, or in some cases, extrinsic, evidence, *see Vitronics Corp. v. Conceptronic, Inc.*, 90 F.3d 1576, 1583, 39 USPQ 2d 1573, 1577 (Fed. Cir. 1996) (reference to extrinsic evidence is proper when intrinsic evidence cannot resolve ambiguity in claim language), to determine the scope of the claim language.

19. ***Spectrum Int'l, Inc. v. Sterilite Corp.***, 49 USPQ 2d 1065, 1068–69 (Fed. Cir. 1998)

In determining the proper meaning of the claims, "we first consider the so-called intrinsic evidence, i.e., the claims, the written description, and, if in evidence, the prosecution history." *Digital Biometrics, Inc. v. Identix, Inc.*, 149 F.3d 1335, 1347, 47 USPQ 2d 1418, 1424 (Fed. Cir. 1998). Moreover, "if upon examination of this intrinsic evidence the meaning of the claim language is sufficiently clear, resort to extrinsic evidence, such as treatises and technical references, as well as expert testimony when appropriate, should not be necessary." *Id.*

Unambiguous intrinsic evidence in turn provides sufficient input to the rules of claim construction, in particular in this case, the rule that explicit statements made by a patent applicant during prosecution to distinguish a claimed invention over prior art may serve to narrow the scope of a claim. *See Southwall Techs. Inc. v. Cardinal IG Co.*, 54 F.3d 1570, 1576, 34 USPQ 2d 1673, 1676 (Fed. Cir. 1995) ("The prosecution history limits the interpretation of claim terms so as to exclude any interpretation that was disclaimed during prosecution."); *Standard Oil Co. v. American Cyanamid Co.*, 774 F.2d 448, 452, 227 USPQ 293, 296 (Fed. Cir. 1985) (stating that the prosecution history, which includes "all express representations made by or on behalf of the applicant to the examiner to induce a patent grant," limits the interpretation of the claims "so as to exclude any interpretation that may have been disclaimed or disavowed during prosecution in order to obtain claim allowance").

That explicit arguments made during prosecution to overcome prior art can lead to narrow claim interpretations makes sense, because "the public has a right to rely on such definitive statements made during prosecution." *Digital Biometrics*, 149 F.3d at 1347, 47 USPQ 2d at 1427 (pointing to "notice [as] an important function of the patent prosecution process, as reflected by the [patent] statute itself"). Indeed, "by distinguishing the claimed invention over the prior art, an applicant is indicating what the claims do not cover." [*Ekchian v. Home Depot, Inc.*, 104 F.3d 1299, 1304, 41 USPQ 2d 1364, 1368 (Fed. Cir. 1997)]. Therefore, a patentee, after relinquishing subject matter to distinguish a prior art reference asserted by the PTO during prosecution, "cannot during subsequent litigation escape reliance [by the defendant] upon this unambiguous surrender of subject matter." *Southwall*, 54 F.3d at 1581, 34 USPQ 2d at 1681; *Ekchian*, 104 F.3d at 1304, 41 USPQ 2d at 1368 (citing *Southwall*). Accordingly, "claims may not be construed one way in order to obtain their allowance and in a different way against accused infringers." *Southwall*, 54 F.3d at 1576 (citing *Unique Concepts, Inc. v. Brown*, 939 F.2d 1558, 1562, 19 USPQ 2d 1500, 1504 (Fed. Cir. 1991)).

20. ***Jeneric/Pentron, Inc. v. Dillon Co., Inc.***, 54 USPQ 2d 1086, 1089 (Fed. Cir. 2000)

Claim 1 contains a mixture of imprecise and precise claim limitations. Specifically, claim 1 uses the word "about" to qualify the values of many variables: the range of the maturing temperature, the coefficient of thermal expansion, the leucite crystallite sizes, and the weight percentage of leucite crystals. In contrast, the claim recites precise ranges for the weight of dental compositions. Under these circumstances, the district court correctly limited the weight ranges to those recited precisely in the table of claim 1.

21. ***Watts v. XL Sys. Inc.***, 56 USPQ 2d 1836, 1839 (Fed. Cir. 2000)

While limitations contained in the specification are not ordinarily read into the claims, see *Intervet Am., Inc. v. Kee-Vet Lab., Inc.*, 887 F.2d 1050, 1053, 12 USPQ 2d 1474, 1476 (Fed. Cir. 1989), it is important to examine the specification. See *Markman v. Westview Instruments, Inc.*, 52 F.3d 967, 979, 34 USPQ2d 1321, 1329 (Fed. Cir. 1995) ("Claims must be read in view of the specification, of which they are a part."), aff'd, 517 U.S. 370, 134 L. Ed. 2d 577, 116 S. Ct. 1384 (1996). One purpose for examining the specification is to determine if the patentee has limited the scope of the claims. See *O.I. Corp. v. Tekmar Co.*, 115 F.3d 1576, 1581, 42 USPQ 2d 1777, 1781 (Fed. Cir. 1997) (limiting claims because the specification described only non-smooth or conical passages and distinguished over the prior art based on these characteristics); *Wang Lab., Inc. v. America Online, Inc.*, 197 F.3d 1377, 1382–83, 53 USPQ 2d 1161, 1164–65 (Fed. Cir. 1999) (limiting claims to the only embodiment described, a character-based protocol, and specifically not encompassing a bit-mapped protocol); *Modine Mfg. Co. v. United States Int'l Trade Comm'n*, 75 F.3d 1545, 1551, 37 USPQ 2d 1609, 1612 (Fed. Cir. 1996) ("When the preferred embodiment is described in the specification as the invention itself, the claims are not necessarily entitled to a scope broader than that embodiment.").

22. ***Clearstream Wastewater Sys., Inc. v. Hydro-Action, Inc.***, 54 USPQ 2d 1185, 1189 (Fed. Cir. 2000)

In construing the disputed claim limitations, it must be kept in mind that the claims at issue in this case are combination claims. Combination claims can consist of new combinations of old elements or combinations of new and old elements. See *Intel Corp. v. U.S. Int'l Trade Comm.*, 946 F.2d 821, 842, 20 USPQ 2d 1161, 1179 (Fed. Cir. 1991); *Panduit Corp. v. Dennison Mfg.*, 810 F.2d 1561, 1575, 1 USPQ 2d 1593, 1603 (Fed. Cir. 1987). Because old elements are part of these combination claims, claim limitations may, and often do, read on the prior art. . . . It is well established in patent law that a claim may consist of all old elements, such as the rigid-conduit system, for it may be that the combination of the old elements is novel and patentable. Similarly, it is well established that a claim may consist of all old elements and one new element, thereby being patentable.

XIII.A. *Process/Method Claims*

1. ***Ex parte Ochiai***, 24 USPQ 2d 1265, 1268 (B.P.A.I. 1992)

When the process claimed was considered to be one of "using" a novel material, patentability of the process was linked to the patentability of the material used. However, when the process claimed was considered to be directed to a "method of making" a novel material, patentability of the process was determined based on the inventiveness of the process steps themselves. Selection of a novel starting material was not considered dispositive of patentability if, indeed, an element of the process.

2. *In re Dillon*, 16 USPQ 2d 1897, 1903 (Fed. Cir. 1990) (en banc), *cert. denied*, 500 U.S. 904 (1991)

Suffice it to say that we do not regard *Durden* as authority to reject as obvious every method claim reading on an old *type of process*, such as mixing, reacting, reducing, etc.

Durden did not hold that all methods involving old process steps are obvious; the court in that case concluded that the particularly claimed process was obvious; it refused to adopt an unvarying rule that the fact that nonobvious starting materials and nonobvious products are involved *ipso facto* makes the process nonobvious. Such an invariant rule always leading to the opposite conclusion is also not the law.

3. *In re Kuehl*, 177 USPQ 250, 253 (C.C.P.A. 1973)

Appellant states as a broad proposition that the allowance of the composition claims here necessarily entitles him to claims in the same application directed to the method of using the zeolite, which the Patent Office found to be a new and unobvious composition of matter. We think this proposition is too broadly stated. . . . The unobviousness of the herein claimed method of cracking hydrocarbons using ZK-22 must be judged by applying to the facts of this case the statutory standard for unobviousness of § 103.

4. *In re Kuehl*, 177 USPQ 250, 253–54 (C.C.P.A. 1973)

To the extent, therefore, that the examiner and the board held appellant's process-of-use invention to a more stringent standard of unobviousness by requiring appellant to show unexpected results in the use of ZK-22, as compared to the use of other zeolites in cracking hydrocarbons, in order to be "entitled to the use claims," we consider that they erred. . . .

Not only are the zeolites of series "A" structurally different from appellant's ZK-22, but the test is not whether one "would expect it to have the same catalytic effect that the known [series "A"] zeolites have," but whether it would have been obvious to one skilled in the art to *use* ZK-22 to crack hydrocarbons.

5. *In re Kuehl*, 177 USPQ 250, 255 (C.C.P.A. 1973)

The obviousness of the process of cracking hydrocarbons with ZK-22 as a catalyst must be determined without reference to knowledge of ZK-22 and its properties. So judged, the process of the appealed claims would not have been obvious.

While there may be some distinction between the *Larsen* line of cases which deal with the obviousness of a process of making a composition and the *Saunders* case, the principal opinion in *Larsen* also appears to have erroneously approached the § 103 obviousness question by asking whether "*given* the idea of the compound" (our emphasis) the process for making it is obvious (see MPEP §706.03(q)). To this extent, at least, *Larsen* and its progeny, *Hoeksema* and *Albertson*, are inconsistent with the statutory standards of § 103.

6. *In re Pleuddenmann* 15 USPQ 2d 1738, 1740 (Fed. Cir. 1990)

In essence, appellant contends that in addition to the claims on the new class of coupling agents which the PTO has granted, and the allowed claims on the articles made by using said agents in the usual way, he is also entitled to the appealed claims on the process or method of using those agents—in the usual way—for bonding or priming. It is contended that such method of use claims should be allowed because the articles made by using the new bonding agents have superior moisture resistant properties.

The shibboleth which appellant hopes will get the claims at bar into the golden realm of patentability, notwithstanding precedents cited by the PTO, is that they are "method of use" rather than "method of making" claims.

When a new and useful compound or group of compounds is invented or discovered having a particular use it is often the case that what is really a single invention may be viewed legally as having three or more different aspects permitting it to be claimed in different ways, for example: (1) the compounds themselves; (2) the method or process of making compounds; and (3) the method or process of using the compounds for their intended purpose.

7. *In re Pleuddemann*, 15 USPQ 2d 1738, 1740 (Fed. Cir. 1990)

We are of the opinion that each statutory class of claims should be considered independently on its own merits. . . . The fact that the starting materials and the final product are the subject matter of allowed claims does not *necessarily* indicate that the *process* employed [to *make* the compounds] is patentable. [Emphasis ours.]

8. *In re Pleuddemann*, 15 USPQ 2d 1738, 1741 (Fed. Cir. 1990)

As stated above, the compounds and their use are but different aspects of, or ways of looking at, the same invention and consequently that invention is capable of being claimed both as new compounds or as a new method or process of bonding/priming. On the other hand, a process or method of making the compounds is a quite different thing; they may have been made by a process which was new or old, obvious or nonobvious. In this respect, therefore, there is a real difference between a process of making and a process of using and the cases dealing with one involve different problems from the cases dealing with the other.

9. ***In re Mancy***, 182 USPQ 303, 306 (C.C.P.A. 1974)

In *Kuehl*, . . . we there stated our disagreement with the proposition of the solicitor "that claims calling for a process using an unobvious composition ought to be treated identically with claims calling for the process of making an unobvious composition." We do so again, reiterating that under § 103 neither a novel product made by, nor a novel starting material used in, the process can be treated as prior art. In the method-of-use cases, such as *Kuehl*, the novelty of the starting material may lend unobviousness to the process. In the cases where the invention is a process for making a new product, however novel the product may be, the claimed process steps and starting materials may themselves still be old and the process therefore obvious.

However, it is not required for unobviousness of the method-of-use claims that the new starting material be patentable . . . .

10. ***Fromson v. Advance Offset Plate, Inc.***, 225 USPQ 26, 32 (Fed. Cir. 1985)

Where, as here, nothing of record plainly indicates that it would have been obvious to combine previously separate process steps into one process, it is legal error to conclude that a claim to that process in invalid under §103.

11. ***Ex parte Hogg***, 121 USPQ 96, 98 (Pat. Off. Bd. App. 1958)

Appellants contend that the references do not disclose the application of the specific steps to the particular compounds claimed and that the invention in these process claims resides in the particular combination in order to produce the final product. . . . While it is evident that the individual steps, as procedural operations applicable individually, would be known to the art, we are inclined to agree with appellants herein that there is no teaching of the combination of the individual steps for the production of the final product which is relied upon and which have been found patentable herein. As stated by the appellants in the brief, the process involved is a part of the inventive concept and the mere fact that elements which may be old are combined in a combination does not render such combination unpatentable where the final result is inventive.

12. ***Moleculon Research Corp. v. CBS, Inc.***, 229 USPQ 805, 812 (Fed. Cir. 1986), ***cert. denied***, 479 U.S. 1030 (1987)

We note decisions where structural recitation in a method claim step was construed as a limitation on the claim. . . . Whether structural recitation limits a claim depends on the language of the claim, the specification, prosecution history, and other claims.

13. ***Ex parte Macy***, 132 USPQ 545, 546 (Pat. Off. Bd. App. 1960)

There is no statutory prohibition against single-step method claims, and we see no reasons why such claims should not be patentable if they satisfy the statutory prerequisites to patentability, in the same manner as multiple step methods.

14. ***Ex parte Macy***, 132 USPQ 545, 546 (Pat. Off. Bd. App. 1960)

[T]he material employed by appellant in carrying out his sealing process cannot be ignored in resolving the question of patentability of the process claims. The question before us is, as we see it, whether the use of a core of ductile material covered with a relatively soft material as claimed, which is in substance conceded by the examiner as not being disclosed by the single reference relied upon, is productive of a useful or advantageous result. As the answer must be in the affirmative, the rejection of the claims on the basis of the Gill patent is not sustained.

15. ***Ex parte Stanley***, 121 USPQ 621, 627 (Pat. Off. Bd. App. 1958)

Claims 1 and 2 are further rejected by the examiner as being improper method claims, it being his position that the method set forth therein involves nothing more than the inherent and necessary function of the particular apparatus disclosed. We will not sustain this rejection for the reasons we have given above in refusing to sustain the rejection of these claims on the ground of res judicata. The apparatus, when idling or taxiing, is performing its inherent and necessary function but is not practicing the method claimed. It is only the intervention of the pilot to control the apparatus in a particular way will the process claimed be practiced. The rejection will, therefore, not be sustained.

XIII.B. *Product, Composition, Apparatus Claims*

1. ***In re Luck***, 177 USPQ 523, 525 (C.C.P.A. 1973)

As for the method of application, it is well established that product claims may include process steps to wholly or partially define the claimed product. *See In re Brown*, and the cases cited therein. To the extent these process limitations distinguish the product over the prior art, they must be given the same consideration as traditional product characteristics.

2. *In re Bell*, 26 USPQ 2d 1529, 1532 (Fed. Cir. 1993)

Finally, the PTO emphasizes the similarities between the method by which Bell made the claimed sequences and the method taught by Weissman. The PTO's focus on Bell's method is misplaced. Bell does not claim a method. Bell claims compositions, and the issue is the obviousness of the claimed compositions, not of the method by which they are made. *See In re Thorpe*, 777 F.2d 695, 697, 227 USPQ 964, 966 (Fed. Cir. 1985) ("The patentability of a product does not depend on its method of production.").

3. *In re Naylor*, 152 USPQ 106, 108 (C.C.P.A. 1966)

We cannot ignore the particular product unexpectedly produced by the claimed process, as the Patent Office apparently has done, in determining whether the claimed subject matter *as a whole* is obvious. . . . Here we are concerned with the unexpectedness of the product resulting from a combination of known process steps not suggested by the prior art as suitable for producing such a product.

4. *In re Thorpe*, 227 USPQ 964, 965–66 (Fed. Cir. 1985)

The patentability of a product does not depend on its method of production. . . . If the product in a product-by-process claim is the same as or obvious from a product of the prior art, the claim is unpatentable even though the prior product was made by a different process.

5. *In re Johnson*, 157 USPQ 620, 622 (C.C.P.A. 1968)

We note at the outset that neither the examiner nor the board considered that the mere presence of process limitations was sufficient in itself to justify rejection of the claims. In fact the examiner in his answer correctly conceded that process limitations are not foreclosed in article claims under proper circumstances.

6. *In re Garnero*, 162 USPQ 221, 223 (C.C.P.A. 1969)

However, it seems to us that the recitation of the particles as "interbonded one to another by interfusion between the surfaces of the perlite particles" is as capable of being construed as a structural limitation as "intermixed," "ground in place," "press fitted," "etched," and "welded," all of which at one time or another have been separately held capable of construction as structural, rather than process limitations. . . . Neither Thomas nor Pierce disclose expanded perlite particles interbonded one to another by interfusion between the surfaces thereof.

7. ***Zenith Labs., Inc. v. Bristol-Myers Squibb Co.***, 30 USPQ 2d 1285, 1288 (Fed. Cir. 1994), ***cert. denied***, 513 U.S. 995 (1994)

The '657 claim is a claim for a compound. Its patentability thus derives from the *structure* of the claimed compound in relation to prior compounds. . . . The relevance to patentability of the properties or characteristics exhibited by the compound is limited to assessing the significance of the structural distinctions of the claimed compound over the prior art.

8. ***R.A.C.C. Indus., Inc. v. Stun-Tech, Inc.***, Civ. App. 98-1186, slip op. at 6–8 (Fed. Cir. Dec. 2, 1998) (unpublished)

Stun-Tech argues that claims one and four should be construed as hybrid apparatus and method of use claims. Stun-Tech further contends that these claims, when properly construed, cannot be infringed unless the accused device is used according to method of use limitations in the claims. Stun-Tech cites *In re Benson*, 57 C.C.P.A. 797, 418 F.2d 1251, 164 USPQ 22 (C.C.P.A. 1969), *In re Swinehart*, 58 C.C.P.A. 1027, 439 F.2d 210, 169 USPQ 226 (C.C.P.A. 1971), and *ZMI Corp. v. Cardiac Resuscitator Corp.*, 844 F.2d 1576, 6 USPQ 2d 1557 (Fed. Cir. 1988) in support of its unique hybrid claim argument. These cases, however, do not authorize this court to transform an apparatus claim into a hybrid apparatus and method of use claim. Rather, these cases merely acknowledge that an apparatus claim may include functional limitations. Similarly, in *Intel Corp. v. U.S. International Trade Commission*, 946 F.2d 821, 832, 20 USPQ 2d 1161, 1171 (Fed. Cir. 1991), this court interpreted functional language in an apparatus claim as requiring that an accused apparatus possess the capability of performing the recited function. This court has never determined that functional language in a claim converts an apparatus claim into a method of use or hybrid claim. . . . This prosecution history shows that RACC was unable to distinguish its invention from the prior art based solely on intended use. Only by adding the structural limitation requiring torso mounting did RACC successfully overcome the prior art. Accordingly, the district court correctly decided that the functional language in claims one and four does not convert them into method of use or hybrid claims.

9. ***Armament Sys. & Procedures, Inc. v. Monadnock Lifetime Prods., Inc.***, Civ. App. 97-1174, slip op. at 6 (Fed. Cir. Aug. 7, 1998) (unpublished)

To be sure, the prosecution history makes clear that the product claims have process limitations. But the process limitations referred to are those explicitly found in the claims, i.e., that the baton must be made of annealed material and subsequently heat treated after forming.

XIII.C. *Product-by-Process Claims*

1. ***Atlantic Thermoplastics Co. v. Faytex Corp.***, 23 USPQ 2d 1481, 1488 (Fed. Cir. 1992)

   A "product-by-process" claim is one in which the product is defined at least in part in terms of the method or process by which it is made.

2. ***Atlantic Thermoplastics Co. v. Faytex Corp.***, 23 USPQ 2d 1481, 1490 (Fed. Cir. 1992)

   Product-by-process claims are not specifically discussed in the patent statute. The practice and governing law have developed in response to the need to enable an applicant to claim an otherwise patentable product that resists definition by other than the process by which it is made. For this reason, even though product-by-process claims are limited by and defined by the process, determination of patentability is based on the product itself.

3. ***Atlantic Thermoplastics Co. v. Faytex Corp.***, 23 USPQ 2d 1481, 1491 (Fed. Cir. 1992)

   This court recognizes that product-by-process claims will receive different treatment for administrative patentability determinations than for judicial infringement determinations. This difference originated with the Supreme Court's BASF rules—a difference this court endorsed as recently as 1985.

4. ***Atlantic Thermoplastics Co. v. Faytex Corp.***, Civ. App. Nos. 91-1076, 91-1095, slip op. at 8 (Fed. Cir. Aug. 14, 1992) (request for rehearing en banc denied; Newman, J., dissenting)

   As the cases illustrate, claims that contain both product and process terms appear in an assortment of factual situations, of which the most common are:
   (1) when the product is new and unobvious, but is not capable of independent definition;
   (2) when the product is old or obvious, but the process is new;
   (3) when the product is new and unobvious, but has a process-based limitation (e.g., a 'molded' product).
   Type (2) includes the *Atlantic* class of claim; such claims are examined as process claims, their validity depends on the novelty and unobviousness of the process, and they are infringed only when the process is used. Type (1) is the *Scripps*

class of claim; such claims are examined as product claims, their validity depends on the novelty and unobviousness of the product, and they are infringed by the product however made.

5. ***Fromson v. Advance Offset Plate, Inc.***, 219 USPQ 1137, 1141 (Fed. Cir. 1983)

That a process limitation appears in a claim does not convert it to a product by process claim.

6. ***Atlantic Thermoplastics Co. v. Faytex Corp.***, 23 USPQ 2d 1481, 1489 n.9 (Fed. Cir. 1992)

Product-by-process claims, on the other hand, define the invention solely or primarily in terms of process.

7. ***In re Brown***, 173 USPQ 685, 688 (C.C.P.A. 1972)

In order to be patentable, a product must be novel, useful and unobvious. In our law, this is true whether the product is claimed by describing it, or by listing the process steps used to obtain it. This latter type of claim, usually called a product-by-process claim, does not inherently conflict with the second paragraph of 35 U.S.C. 112. . . . It must be admitted, however, that the lack of physical description in a product-by-process claim makes determination of the patentability of the claim more difficult, since in spite of the fact that the claim may recite only process limitations, it is the patentability of the product claimed and not of the recited process steps which must be established.

8. ***In re Hughes***, 182 USPQ 106, 108 (C.C.P.A. 1974)

We cannot agree with the solicitor that defining a product in terms of process makes the language of the claims imprecise or indefinite. Their scope, if anything, is more definite in reciting a novel product made by a specific process, assuming, of course, that the process is clearly defined.

While we recognize that several structural or characterizing terms derive from processes or methods and that their use in a claim will not prevent it from being considered to be a true product claim, we do not believe that the emphasized language in claim 8 can be considered to be anything other than a description of the shake in terms of the process by which it was made. . . . [H]e is entitled to product-by-process claims that recite his novel process of manufacture as a hedge against the possibility that his broader product claims might be invalidated.

9. ***In re Bridgeford***, 149 USPQ 55, 57–58 (C.C.P.A. 1966)

The rationale stated in the above decisions which permit the product-by-process type claim in ex parte prosecution before the Patent Office is clear: the right to a patent on an invention is not to be denied because of the limitations of the English language, and, in a proper case, a product may be defined by the process of making it. However, the invention so defined is a product and not a process. To this we would add that, similarly, the limitations of known technology concerning the subject matter sought to be patented should not arbitrarily defeat the right to a patent on an invention. Whether the invention be defined in terms of the structure of the compound, or its novel physical characteristics, or by defining it in terms of the process by which it is produced or in a proper case, by employing more than one of these methods of defining the invention, the right to a patent on the invention is the ultimate consideration . . . .

10. *In re Moore*, 169 USPQ 236, 239 (C.C.P.A. 1971)

We must conclude that the board's position cannot stand. We simply cannot understand why it is felt that process parameters are important here. Appellants clearly disclose that it is not the type of fluorination process which is important but the fact that the products are fluorinated and fluorinated to a specific minimum degree (spelled out by all the claims). . . . The board's further comment that fluorination processes also yield undesired degradation products would be pertinent . . . if the word "fluorinated" had to be considered as a "product-by-process" limitation . . . . In any event, since we have found that these claims are not product-by-process claims, such a contention, even if it were true would be irrelevant . . . since it is quite clear that appellants wish to claim only the highly fluorinated alkyl adamantanes which are not degraded.

11. *In re Thorpe*, 227 USPQ 964, 965–66 (Fed. Cir. 1985)

Product-by-process claims are not specifically discussed in the patent statute. The practice and governing law have developed in response to the need to enable an applicant to claim an otherwise patentable product that resists definition by other than the process by which it is made. For this reason, even though product-by-process claims are limited by and defined by the process, determination of patentability is based upon the product itself.

12. *Mentor Corp. v. Coloplast, Inc.*, 27 USPQ 2d 1521, 1526 (Fed. Cir. 1993)

Mentor argues that claims 1–4 are product-by-process claims and that, under *Scripps Clinic & Research Foundation v. Genentech, Inc.*, . . . the process limitations do not prevent the claims from encompassing an identical product made by a different process. Mentor's argument, however, is inapplicable to the present case. The claims in issue here are not in fact product-by-process claims; product-by-process claims recite how a product is made, not how it is used.

13. *In re Johnson*, 157 USPQ 620, 623 (C.C.P.A. 1968)

This group of claims is characterized by being devoid of significant structural description of the final article, but relies upon process recitations to describe the ultimate article. The claims are thus product-by-process claims as that term is generally used.

14. *Fromson v. Advance Offset Plate, Inc.*, 219 USPQ 1137, 1141 (Fed. Cir. 1983)

That a process limitation appears in a claim does not convert it to a product by process claim.

15. *In re Wertheim*, 191 USPQ 90, 103–04 (C.C.P.A. 1976)

These claims are cast in product-by-process form. Although appellants argue, successfully we have found, that the Pfluger 1963 disclosure does not suggest the control of bulk density afforded by appellants' process, the patentability of the products defined by the claims, rather than the processes for making them, is what we must gauge in light of the prior art.

16. *Tri-Wall Containers, Inc. v. United States*, 161 USPQ 116, 118 (Ct. Cl.), *cert. denied*, 396 U.S. 828 (1969)

It is well established that a product claimed as made by a new process is not patentable unless the product itself is new. . . . In the earlier case the plaintiff sued for paper pulp described as produced by a new process. The Supreme Court held the patent claim invalid because paper pulp was itself an old product, stating:

> Paper-pulp obtained from various vegetable substances was in common use before the original patent was granted to Watt & Burgess, and whatever may be said of their process for obtaining it, the product was in no sense new. . . . 90 U.S. (23 Wall.), p. 596.

17. *Hazani v. U.S. Int'l Trade Comm'n*, 44 USPQ 2d 1358, 1363 (Fed. Cir. 1997)

Hazani argues that the "chemically engraved" claims are product-by-process claims. We agree with the respondents, however, that those claims are best characterized as pure product claims, since the "chemically engraved" limitation, read in context, describes the product more by its structure than by the process used to obtain it.

18. ***In re Brown***, 173 USPQ 685, 688 (C.C.P.A. 1972)

In order to be patentable, a product must be novel, useful and unobvious. In our law, this is true whether the product is claimed by describing it, or by listing the process steps used to obtain it. This latter type of claim, usually called a product-by-process claim, does not inherently conflict with the second paragraph of 35 USC 112. *In re Steppan*, 55 CCPA 791, 394 F.2d 1013, 156 USPQ 143 (1967). That method of claiming is therefore a perfectly acceptable one so long as the claims particularly point out and distinctly claim the product or genus of products for which protection is sought and satisfy the other requirements of the statute. It must be admitted, however, that the lack of physical description in a product-by-process claim makes determination of the patentability of the claim more difficult, since in spite of the fact that the claim may recite only process limitations, it is the patentability of the product claimed and not of the recited process steps which must be established.

19. ***In re Brown***, 173 USPQ 685, 688 (C.C.P.A. 1972)

[W]hen the prior art discloses a product which reasonably appears to be either identical with or only slightly different than a product claimed in a product-by-process claim, a rejection based alternatively on either section 102 or section 103 of the statute is eminently fair and acceptable. As a practical matter, the Patent Office is not equipped to manufacture products by the myriad of processes put before it and then obtain prior art products and make physical comparisons therewith.

20. ***Ex parte Bivens***, 53 USPQ 2d 1045, 1046 (B.P.A.I. 1999)

Also, the limitations in claims 10 and 12 drawn to the chart and diagram relating to the prior art engine amount to product-by-process limitations used to define the appellant's engine. Such product-by-process limitations do not inherently conflict with the second paragraph of Section 112. See *In re Brown*, 459 F.2d 531, 535, 173 USPQ 685, 688 (C.C.P.A. 1972). The corresponding limitations in method claims 11 and 13 merely present a starting point for the processes recited therein.

XIII.D. *Functional Limitations*

1. ***Ex parte Skinner***, 2 USPQ 2d 1788, 1789 (B.P.A.I. 1986)

We are mindful that there is a line of cases represented by *In re Swinehart* . . . which indicates that where an examiner has reason to believe that a functional limitation asserted to be critical for establishing novelty in the claimed subject matter may, in fact, be an inherent characteristic of the prior art, the examiner possesses the authority to require an applicant to prove that the subject matter shown to be in the prior art does not possess the characteristic relied on. Nevertheless, before an applicant can be put to this burdensome task, the examiner must provide some evidence or scientific reasoning to establish the reasonableness of the examiner's belief that the functional limitation is an inherent characteristic of the prior art.

2. ***In re Bisley***, 94 USPQ 80, 83 (C.C.P.A. 1952)

It appears to us that, as pointed out by counsel for appellant, the precise degree of angularity of the pivot pin may vary depending on relative size and position of various elements of the mixer as, for example, position of the beater axes, motor unit, pivot pin, and axis of the bowl support, and size and position of the bowl. In view of this, we think that in this particular case appellant may properly recite this feature in geometrical language, and such claims may be allowable if they adequately define over the prior art in accordance with the above-discussed rules.

3. ***In re Bisley***, 94 USPQ 80, 83 (C.C.P.A. 1952)

It appears to us that these claims define the angle of the pivot pin with respect to component elements of the mixer, albeit by geometrical language, in such a manner that the pin is structurally located, by the terms of these claims, at a substantial angle with respect to identified horizontal and vertical datum planes and within that range of angularity which will achieve appellant's desired novel result. Definite limitations in a claim should not be ignored or construed out of the claim. . . . Therefore, we think that claims 20 and 39 patentably define over Kochner et al. and that the board erred in rejecting these claims on that reference.

4. ***In re Attwood***, 148 USPQ 203, 210 (C.C.P.A. 1966)

The *Dalton* case was relied upon apparently for some rather sweeping statement it contains to the effect that "Properties, functions, uses, and results" may not be solely relied upon for patentability and the court in that case was relying heavily on the binding effect of *Halliburton v. Walker.* . . . All this as prior to the Patent Act of 1952 which introduced a new statute with respect to "functional" claims in the last paragraph of 35 U.S.C. 112. One of the purposes of this statute was modification of the *Halliburton* rule. As stated in Federico's Commentary on the New Patent Act, 35 U.S.C.A., at p. 25:

> It is unquestionable that some measure of greater liberality in the use of functional expressions in combination

claims is authorized than had been permitted by some court decisions, and that decisions such as that in *Halliburton Oil Well Cementing Co. v. Walker* * * * are modified or rendered obsolete, but the exact limits of the enlargement remain to be determined.

We have here a combination claim and the limitations ignored by the board as use limitations we think are functional expressions which must be given weight. We consider that 35 U.S.C. 112 has rendered much if not most of what was said in *Dalton* on this point obsolete.

5. ***In re Ludtke***, 169 USPQ 563, 566 (1971)

We agree with the Patent Office that the spatial separation between the panels is recited [in the claim] in functional language; however, as we said recently *In re Swinehart*, . . . there is nothing intrinsically wrong with the use of such claim language.

6. ***In re Land***, 151 USPQ 621, 635–36 (C.C.P.A. 1966)

It is true that the italicized portions [in claim 70, i.e., "adapted to be rendered diffusible"] are "functional" but we do not regard that as good ground to give them "no weight" in view of the third paragraph of 35 U.S.C. 112. We give them weight and with this limitation we think claims 70 and 71 are limited to deferred diffusion *built into the structure recited*, thereby being limited to the actual invention disclosed and hence allowable for the same reasons given by the board.

7. ***In re Weiss***, 26 USPQ 2d 1885 (Fed. Cir. 1993) (unpublished)

Here, applicant has chosen the phrase "preselected level of force" as a specific limitation in the break-away means plus function element to indicate a specific level of force, determined in advance, at which the cleat will break-away. This term is further described in the specification to mean that level of force at which the cleat must break off in order to prevent injury to the wearer without breaking off during athletics involving noninjurious force levels.

The Board incorrectly interpreted this break-away means limitation, giving no effect to the term "preselected level of force," to require only that the cleat break away from the sole at some unknown large level of force not predetermined in advance.

8. ***Rodime PLC v. Seagate Tech., Inc.***, 50 USPQ 2d 1429, 1435 (Fed. Cir. 1999)

A claim need not claim every function of a working device. Rather, a claim may specify improvements in one function without claiming the entire machine with its many functions.

9. **K-2 Corp. v. Salomon S.A.**, 52 USPQ 2d 1001, 1004 (Fed. Cir. 1999) (citing **Wright Med. Tech., Inc. v. Osteonics Corp.**, 43 USPQ 2d 1837, 1840 (Fed. Cir. 1997))

   The functional language is, of course, an additional limitation in the claim.

10. **WMS Gaming Inc. v. Int'l Game Tech.**, 51 USPQ 2d 1385, 1393 (Fed. Cir. 1999)

    Because the structure recited in the Telnaes patent is limited by the disclosed algorithm, our analysis of structural equivalence necessarily discusses the disclosed algorithm, which includes functional-type elements.

XIII.E. Jepson *Format Claims*

1. **In re Simmons**, 136 USPQ 450, 451 (C.C.P.A. 1963)

   Moreover, we find full correspondence in the claims of the Simmons patent with everything recited in the claims on appeal before the word "improvement." By using the so-called "Jepson" form, employed in *Ex parte Jepson*, . . . appellant is relying on the subject matter following "improvement" for novelty. The subject matter after the word "improvement" in claim 16 is not present in the Simmons patent disclosure and, of course, is not included in the patented Simmons claims.

2. **Ethicon Endo-Surgery, Inc. v. Ethicon, Inc.**, 40 USPQ 2d 1019, 1022–23 (Fed. Cir. 1996)

   Initially, we note that claim 6 is a *Jepson* claim. *See Ex parte Jepson*, 243 O.G. 525 (Ass't Comm'r Pat. 1917). Consequently, the inventive portion of the claim must lie in the clause beginning: "the improvement comprising." *See In re Simmons*, 312 F.2d 821, 824 [, 136 USPQ 450] (C.C.P.A. 1963).

3. **Row v. Dror**, 42 USPQ 2d 1550, 1553 (Fed. Cir. 1997)

   [T]he form of the claim itself, the so-called "Jepson" form, suggests the structural importance of the recitations found in the preamble. The Jepson form allows a patentee to use the preamble to recite "elements or steps of the claimed invention which are conventional or known." . . . When this form is employed, the claim preamble defines not only the context of the claimed invention, but also its scope.

4. **Pentec, Inc. v. Graphic Controls Corp.**, 227 USPQ 766, 770 (Fed. Cir. 1985)

   Although a preamble is impliedly admitted to be prior art when a Jepson claim is used, . . . the claimed invention consists of the preamble in combination with the improvement.

5. ***Kegel Co. v. AMF Bowling, Inc.***, 44 USPQ 2d 1123, 1127 (Fed. Cir. 1997)

Jepson form allows a patentee to use the preamble to recite "elements or steps of the claimed invention which are conventional or known." . . . [T]he fact that the patentee has chosen the Jepson form of the claim evidences the intention to use the preamble to define, in part, the structural elements of his claimed invention.

XIII.F. *"Whereby" Clauses*

1. ***Texas Instruments, Inc. v. United States Int'l Trade Comm'n***, 26 USPQ 2d 1018, 1023 (Fed. Cir. 1993)

A "whereby" clause that merely states the result of the limitations in the claim adds nothing to the patentability or substance of the claim.

2. ***Curtis Mfg. Co. v. Plasti-Clip Corp.***, Civ. App. 96-1048, -1055, -1059, slip op. at 23 n.5 (Fed. Cir. Feb. 6, 1998) (unpublished)

We need not address the issue of whether the whereby clause requiring dual functionality of the spring finger is a limitation of claim 1 of the '863 patent or simply a recitation of the resulting function of a structural limitation adding nothing to the claim. *Compare Texas Instruments, Inc. v. U.S. Internat'l Trade Comm.*, 988 F.2d 1165, 1172, 26 USPQ 2d 1018, 1023 (Fed. Cir. 1993) ("A 'whereby' clause that merely states the result of the limitations in the claim adds nothing to the patentability or substance of the claim."), with *Scheinman v. Zalkind*, 112 F.2d 1017, 1019, 27 C.C.P.A. 1354, 1357 (C.C.P.A. 1940) (whereby clause that sets forth a structural limitation and not merely the results achieved by the claimed structure is a positive limitation of the claim).

XIII.G. *Prosecution History Statements/Estoppel and Interpreting Claims*

1. ***Hoganas AB v. Dresser Indus.***, 28 USPQ 2d 1936, 1939 (Fed. Cir. 1993)

The essence of prosecution history estoppel is that patentee should not be able to obtain, through the doctrine of equivalents, coverage of subject matter that was relinquished during prosecution to procure issuance of the patent. . . . The legal standard for determining what subject matter was relinquished is an objective one, measured from the vantage point of what a competitor was reasonably entitled to conclude, from the prosecution history, that the applicant gave up to produce issuance of the patent. . . .

For all the foregoing reasons, we conclude one of skill in the art, the vantage point from which the proper interpretation of the claim is ultimately determined, would not have been put on notice that the term meant other than what it says. Such a one would be perfectly justified in giving the term its ordinary meaning. If Hoganas, who was responsible for drafting and prosecuting the patent, intended something different, it could have prevented this result through clearer drafting. For example, as discussed at the hearing, the phrases "cylindrically-shaped" or "rod-shaped" could have been used. It would not be appropriate for us now to interpret the claim differently just to cure a drafting error made by Hoganas. That would unduly interfere with the function of claims in putting competitors on notice of the scope of the claimed invention.

2. ***Hoganas AB v. Dresser Indus.***, 28 USPQ 2d 1936, 1939 n.15 (Fed. Cir. 1993)

Ordinarily, the test for determining the meaning of a claim term is from the vantage point of one skilled in the art. . . . This test would seem equally appropriate for determining what subject matter was relinquished in the context of prosecution history estoppel. Our precedent dealing with this specific question recites that the test is measured from the vantage point of a reasonable competitor. . . . We do not see these formulations as necessarily inconsistent—the point is the knowledge of one reasonably skilled in the art who views the question from the perspective of a competitor in the marketplace.

3. ***E.I. du Pont de Nemours & Co. v. Phillips Petroleum Co.***, 7 USPQ 2d 1129, 1135–36 (Fed. Cir.), ***cert. denied***, 488 U.S. 986 (1988)

We agree with Phillips that arguments made during the prosecution history are relevant in determining the meaning of the terms at issue. Those arguments, and other aspects of the prosecution history, as well as the specification and other claims, must be examined to ascertain the true meaning of what the inventor intended to convey in the claims. . . . Using the prosecution history in that manner is different from prosecution history estoppel, which is applied as a limitation upon the doctrine of equivalents after the claims have been properly interpreted. . . .

Regardless of the examiner's motives, arguments made during prosecution shed light on what the applicant meant by its various terms.

4. ***Arachnid, Inc. v. Valley Recreation Prods., Inc.***, 29 USPQ 2d 1457, 1459 (Fed. Cir. 1993)

Prosecution history estoppel involves a review of amendments to a claim and the reasons for those amendments in light of the prior art. It does not directly involve an analysis of the accused device.

5. ***Burke, Inc. v. Everest & Jennings, Inc.***, 29 USPQ 2d 1393, 1397 (Fed. Cir. 1993) (unpublished)

As a general rule, "comprising" and "including" are open-ended terms which cover the structural elements recited plus additional elements. See 2 D. Chisum, Patents §8.06[1] (1992). To ascertain the intended meaning of claim language, the court may, among other things, look to the patent prosecution history. . . . The prosecution history before us does not indicate that the claim words "comprising . . . a battery unit including a battery member" should be construed narrowly to exclude additional elements.

6. ***Devon Indus. v. American Med. Mfg.***, Civ. App. 93-1307, slip op. at 7–10 (Fed. Cir. Feb. 3, 1994) (unpublished)

The second limitation of claim 10 at issue is "thin walled impervious plastic [sic] or rubber like material cover body." . . . According to AMMI, the meaning of thin walled cover should be limited by the specification and prosecution history to a cover having a flange that is comprised of a collapsible, thin walled material, whereas the AMMI assembly has a flange comprised instead of a rigid plastic.

. . .

[T]he court must consider the patentees' own interpretation of their claims made during prosecution. . . . When that is done, it becomes clear that, whatever the patentees intended to claim when they drafted their specification, they subsequently limited the scope of their claims in order to obtain allowance. Specifically, in an attempt to distinguish the claimed invention from the prior art and to persuade the examiner of the invention's patentability, the patentees, by their description of "thin walled," argued against an interpretation of their claim that would permit it to read on a cover flange that is not provided in the form of a collapsible, thin walled material, one that has sufficient body to it to prevent a sharp glass edge from protruding or penetrating through it. Such an interpretation has been disclaimed. . . . We therefore hold that claim 10 is limited to a collapsible, thin walled cover that lacks sufficient body to prevent a sharp glass edge from protruding or penetrating through it. The court erred in concluding otherwise.

7. ***Surgical Laser Techs. v. Laser Indus.***, 32 USPQ 2d 1798 (Fed. Cir. 1994) (quoting ***United States v. Telectronics, Inc.***, 8 USPQ 2d 1217, 1221 (Fed. Cir. 1988), ***cert. denied***, 490 U.S. 1046 (1989))

While prosecution history limits the scope of claims by excluding any interpretation of the claim language that may have been disclaimed or disavowed during prosecution in order to obtain claim allowance, . . . where a claim issues that is clearly broader in scope than that which was rejected during prosecution, we "are not permitted to read [those removed limitations] back into the claims."

8. ***Tanabe Seiyaku Co., Ltd. v. International Trade Comm'n***, 41 USPQ 2d 1976, 1982–83 (Fed. Cir.), ***cert. denied***, 522 U.S. 1027 (1997) (quoting ***Caterpillar Tractor Co. v. Berco, S.p.A.***, 219 USPQ 185, 188 (Fed. Cir. 1983))

[I]n evaluating infringement under the doctrine of equivalents, "representation[s] to foreign patent offices should be considered . . . when [they] comprise relevant evidence."

9. ***Brand Management, Inc. v. Pro Shop Plans Co.***, Civ. App. 96-1523, slip op. at 8 (Fed. Cir. June 25, 1997) (unpublished)

The statement in the prosecution history that the claims are directed only at Figures 1–12 could convey to one of ordinary skill in the art that the patentee considers his invention to cover only devices with zig-zagged outer sides. This reading is supported by the fact that Figures 13–15 differ from Figures 1–12 in two major respects: (1) Figures 13–15 contain two-way as opposed to four-way recesses and, importantly, (2) Figures 13–15 do not contain zig-zagged outer sides. . . . Faced with two competing interpretations that are equally tenable, we choose to reinforce the notice requirement by construing claim 1 narrowly. Thus, we hold "sides" to mean both internal and external sides. The Camden molds do not literally infringe because they do not contain zig-zagged outer sides.

10. ***Wang Labs., Inc. v. Mitsubishi Elecs. Am., Inc.***, 41 USPQ 2d 1263, 1269 (Fed. Cir.), ***cert. denied***, 522 U.S. 818 (1997)

Application of the doctrine of equivalents may allow a patentee to recover for infringement though the accused device falls outside the literal scope of the claims if the differences between the claimed invention and the device are insubstantial. . . . Prosecution history estoppel acts as one check on application of the doctrine of equivalents, . . . by precluding a patentee from regaining, through litigation, coverage of subject matter relinquished during prosecution of the application for the patent. . . . We examine the statements and actions of the patentee before the PTO during prosecution, . . . and ask what a competitor reasonably may conclude the patentee surrendered to gain issuance of the patent. . . . Arguments and amendments made to secure allowance of a claim, especially those distinguishing prior art, presumably give rise to prosecution history estoppel. . . .

Once prosecution history estoppel limits the scope of a patent, the patentee may not recover for infringement where infringement would require an equivalence between a claim element and an aspect of the accused item that falls within the estoppel.

11. ***Sage Prods., Inc. v. Devon Indus.***, 44 USPQ 2d 1103, 1113 (Fed. Cir. 1997)

A patentee is not free to retrade or renege on a deal struck with the PTO during patent prosecution. . . . When an applicant distinguishes prior art by surrendering some previously-claimed subject matter, the patentee may not later seek to recover that surrendered subject matter by the doctrine of equivalents.

12. ***Warner-Jenkinson Co. v. Hilton Davis Chem. Co.***, 520 U.S. 17, 117 S. Ct. 1040, 41 USPQ 2d 1865, 1872 (1997)

Our prior cases have consistently applied prosecution history estoppel only where claims have been amended for a limited set of reasons, and we see no substantial cause for requiring a more rigid rule invoking an estoppel regardless of the reasons for a change. . . . Where the reason for the change was not related to avoiding the prior art, the change may introduce a new element, but it does not necessarily preclude infringement by equivalents of that element.

13. ***Warner-Jenkinson Co. v. Hilton Davis Chem. Co.***, 520 U.S. 17, 117 S. Ct. 1040, 41 USPQ 2d 1865, 1873 (1997)

[W]e think the better rule is to place the burden on the patent-holder to establish the reason for an amendment required during patent prosecution. The court then would decide whether that reason is sufficient to overcome prosecution history estoppel as a bar to application of the doctrine of equivalents to the element added by that amendment. Where no explanation is established, however, the court should presume that the PTO had a substantial reason related to patentability for including the limiting element added by amendment. In those circumstances, prosecution history estoppel would bar the application of the doctrine of equivalents as to that element.

14. ***Abtox, Inc. v. Exitron Corp.***, 43 USPQ 2d 1545, 1551 (Fed. Cir.), ***amended on reh'g***, 131 F.3d 1009 (Fed. Cir. 1997)

The prosecution history relevant to this dispute includes not only the two distinct Jacob patent applications, but also the parent application. *See Jonsson v. Stanley Works*, 903 F.2d 812, 818, 14 USPQ2d 1863, 1869 (Fed. Cir. 1990)

15. ***EMI Group N. Am., Inc. v. Intel Corp.***, 48 USPQ 2d 1181, 1189 (Fed. Cir. 1998)

Cancellation of a claim that is written broadly does not always generate an estoppel to narrower subject matter. The particular facts must be considered. *See, e.g., Modine Mfg. Co. v. United States Int'l Trade Comm'n*, 75 F.3d 1545, 1555–56, 37 USPQ 2d 1609, 1616 (Fed. Cir. 1996) (Determination "is based on the reasonable reading, by a person of skill in the field of the invention, of the entire prosecution history."); *Pall Corp. v. Micron Separations, Inc.*, 66 F.3d 1211, 1218–19, 36 USPQ 2d 1225, 1230 (Fed. Cir. 1995) (expert evidence of the significance of terms of art as used in the patent).

16. ***Bai v. L & L Wings, Inc.***, 48 USPQ 2d 1674, 1677–78 (Fed. Cir. 1998)

When determining whether prosecution history estoppel applies to limit the doctrine of equivalents, a court must examine the reason why an applicant amended a claim. *See Warner-Jenkinson*, . . . 117 S. Ct. at 1049, 41 USPQ 2d at 1872. If such examination indicates that a patent applicant has made a substantive change to his claim that clearly responds to an examiner's rejection of that claim as unpatentable over prior art, prosecution history estoppel applies to that claim; only the question of the scope of the estoppel remains. No presumption needs to be applied in such a case because the reason for the amendment is clear. *Warner-Jenkinson* did not change this aspect of prosecution history estoppel. *See Warner-Jenkinson*, . . . 117 S. Ct. at 1049–50, 41 USPQ 2d at 1871–72 (citing with approval five Supreme Court cases invoking prosecution history estoppel where the applicant narrowed his claims in order to overcome a prior art rejection).

What *Warner-Jenkinson* did address was the situation in which the prosecution history fails to disclose a reason for a claim amendment. In that case, the patent applicant responded to a prior art rejection by adding a pH range to his claim. Because the examiner cited prior art relevant to the higher, but not the lower, end of the range, the addition of the upper pH limit clearly responded to the prior art rejection, but the addition of the lower pH limit did not. Thus, the record did not disclose the reason for the addition of the lower pH limit. *See Warner-Jenkinson*, . . . 117 S. Ct. at 1050, 41 USPQ 2d at 1872. The Court held that even in the absence of such a disclosed reason, it nonetheless should be presumed that the lower pH limit was included for a reason related to patentability and thus that prosecution history estoppel applied to that claim limitation unless the patentee could establish that the amendment was not related to patentability. *See id.*, . . . 117 S. Ct. at 1051, 41 USPQ 2d at 1873.

17. ***Bai v. L & L Wings, Inc.***, 48 USPQ 2d 1674, 1678 (Fed. Cir. 1998)

Bai's boilerplate remark to the examiner that he amended his claims to "specifically and expressly recite the structural details" of his invention does not affect our conclusion. Bai's assertion that this language somehow conveys to the examiner his intent to add the term "hemispherical" for clarity purposes is unpersuasive. There is no evidence, and Bai does not argue that there is such evidence, that clarity was a problem with his claims. There was no lack of clarity, and no rejection under Section 112. Prior art was the problem.

18. ***Bai v. L & L Wings, Inc.***, 48 USPQ 2d 1674, 1678–79 (Fed. Cir. 1998)

Bai also argues that the amendment could not have been made to overcome prior art because it was not necessary to overcome the prior art rejection. We disagree. It is now too late in the game for us to analyze whether Bai's addition of the term "hemispherical" was necessary to gain allowance of his claim. When an applicant disagrees with the examiner's prior art rejection and fails to prevail by argument, he has two choices: either to amend the claim or to appeal the rejection. He may not both make the amendment and then challenge its necessity in a subsequent infringement action on the allowed claim. Bai made his choice and amended the claim. . . . A patentee does not have a second chance to relitigate the merits of a prior art rejection that caused an amendment to be made to gain allowance of the claims. We therefore refuse to speculate as to whether the examiner would have found claim 1 to be allowable over the prior art if Bai had not added the term "hemispherical" to the claim. Whether or not the "hemispherical" limitation was superfluous, the prosecution record clearly reveals that Bai made this amendment to overcome prior art. *See American Permahedge v. Barcana*, 105 F.3d 1441, 1446, 41 USPQ 2d 1614, 1618 (Fed. Cir. 1997) ("Clear assertions made during prosecution in support of patentability, whether or not actually required to secure allowance, may create an estoppel.").

19. ***Cybor Corp. v. FAS Techs., Inc.***, 46 USPQ 2d 1169, 1175 (Fed. Cir. 1998)

Under § 112, ¶ 6, an accused device with structure not identical to the structure described in the patent will literally infringe the patent if the device performs the identical function required by the claim with a structure equivalent to that described in the patent. . . . Prosecution history is relevant to the construction of a claim written in means-plus-function form. . . . Indeed, "just as prosecution history estoppel may act to estop an equivalence argument under the doctrine of equivalents, positions taken before the PTO may bar an inconsistent position on claim construction under § 112, ¶ 6." Alpex, 102 F.3d at 1221, 40 USPQ 2d at 1673. Clear assertions made in support of patentability thus may affect the range of equivalents under § 112, ¶ 6. . . . The relevant inquiry is whether a competitor would reasonably believe that the applicant had surrendered the relevant subject matter.

20. ***Digital Biometrics, Inc. v. Identix, Inc.***, 47 USPQ 2d 1418, 1424 (Fed. Cir. 1998)

Because the applicant has the burden to "particularly point[] out and distinctly claim[] the subject matter which the applicant regards as his invention," 35 U.S.C. § 112, ¶ 2 (1994), if the claim is susceptible to a broader and a narrower meaning, and the narrower one is clearly supported by the intrinsic evidence while the broader one raises questions of enablement under § 112, ¶ 1, we will adopt the narrower of the two.

21. ***Digital Biometrics, Inc. v. Identix, Inc.***, 47 USPQ 2d 1418, 1427 (Fed. Cir. 1998)

The remarks contained in the block quote recited above were made without reference to a particular claim. Instead, the remarks were made with respect to "all of the pending claims [that] stand rejected under 35 USC 102(b) or 35 USC 103 over the Ruell German Patent 3,432,886." While it is true that the applicants went on to specifically distinguish each claim, or group of claims, including claim 19, from Ruell on more narrow grounds, that does not eliminate global comments made to distinguish the applicants' "claimed invention" from the prior art.

The public has a right to rely on such definitive statements made during prosecution. Notice is an important function of the patent prosecution process, as reflected by the statute itself, see 35 U.S.C. § 112, ¶ 2, and recently confirmed by the Supreme Court, *see Warner-Jenkinson Co. v. Hilton Davis Chem. Co.*, 520 U.S. 17, 117 S. Ct. 1040, 41 USPQ 2d 1865, 137 L. Ed. 2d 146 (1997). Absent qualifying language in the remarks, arguments made to obtain the allowance of one claim are relevant to interpreting other claims in the same patent.

22. ***Laitram Corp. v. Morehouse Indus., Inc.***, 46 USPQ 2d 1609, 1614 (Fed. Cir. 1998)

Laitram's second argument, that applicant's statement which attempted to distinguish his invention over prior art disclosing curved driving surfaces was not relied upon by the examiner and is therefore irrelevant to claim construction, is not sustainable under our case law. "Regardless of the examiner's motives, arguments made during prosecution shed light on what the applicant meant by its various terms." *E.I. du Pont de Nemours & Co. v. Phillips Petroleum Co.*, 849 F.2d 1430, 1438, 7 USPQ 2d 1129, 1136 (Fed. Cir. 1988). The fact that an examiner placed no reliance on an applicant's statement distinguishing prior art does not mean that the statement is inconsequential for purposes of claim construction. *See id.*, 7 USPQ 2d at 1136.

23. ***Pall Corp. v. Hemasure Inc.***, 50 USPQ 2d 1947, 1951 (Fed. Cir. 1999)

That the added claim was not amended during prosecution but was granted as filed does not preclude the application of prosecution history estoppel. When a claim limitation is added in order to overcome a specific cited reference, estoppel as to that limitation is generated whether the limitation is added by amendment to pending claims, or by the submission of new claims containing the limitation.

24. ***Read Corp. v. Portec, Inc.***, 23 USPQ 2d 1426, 1433 (Fed. Cir. 1992)

Every statement made by a patentee during prosecution to distinguish a prior art reference does not create a separate estoppel. Arguments must be viewed in context. . . . Read pointed out differences not only respecting the wheels, including that they were not collapsible and were in a different location (on the side, not the end) but also marked differences in other parts of the structure. Thus, any estoppel created by Portec's argument encompasses all of these combined distinctions of Deister and not an estoppel respecting each of the individual differences, e.g., that any device with non-movable wheels cannot infringe. . . . Thus, there is no basis for an assertion that Read is seeking to recapture anything which was surrendered to obtain the patent, the essence of the prosecution history estoppel.

25. ***Read Corp. v. Portec, Inc.***, 23 USPQ 2d 1426, 1433 n.4 (Fed. Cir. 1992)

Acceptance of Portec's argument respecting estoppel for each item in a patentee's list of distinctions between the invention and a prior art reference would mean that the less material a prior art reference, the more the estoppel merely by a patentee's pointing out numerous differences. This turns an equitable doctrine into an illogical mechanical rule and would allow easily distinguishable prior art, here Deister, to emasculate the doctrine of equivalents.

26. ***Cybor Corp. v. FAS Techs., Inc.***, 46 USPQ 2d 1169, 1177–78 (Fed. Cir. 1998) (en banc)

An accused device that does not literally infringe a claim may still infringe under the doctrine of equivalents if each limitation of the claim is met in the accused device either literally or equivalently. Prosecution history estoppel provides a legal limitation on the application of the doctrine of equivalents by excluding from the range of equivalents subject matter surrendered during prosecution of the application for the patent. The estoppel may arise from matter surrendered as a result of amendments to overcome patentability rejections, or as a result of argument to secure allowance of a claim. Prosecution history estoppel is a legal question subject to de novo review on appeal.

27. ***Sextant Avionique, S.A. v. Analog Devices, Inc.***, 49 USPQ 2d 1865, 1871 (Fed. Cir. 1999)

If Analog were practicing the prior art, it would have had a complete defense to Sextant's infringement charge, and prosecution history would be irrelevant. Case law has established that the prior art and prosecution history estoppel provide independent policy oriented limitations on the doctrine of equivalents.

28. ***Litton Sys., Inc. v. Honeywell, Inc.***, 46 USPQ 2d 1321, 1327 (Fed. Cir. 1998)

Even arguments made during prosecution without amendments to claim language if sufficient to evince a clear and unmistakable surrender of subject matter may estop an applicant from recapturing that surrendered matter under the doctrine of equivalents. . . . Estoppel by clear and unmistakable surrender without claim amendments may arise even when the arguments to the examiner were not necessary to distinguish prior art. . . . This principle presupposes that the applicant has made the surrender unmistakable enough that the public may reasonably rely on it.

29. ***Sextant Avionique, S.A. v. Analog Devices, Inc.***, 49 USPQ 2d 1865, 1875 (Fed. Cir. 1999)

Moreover, and as a practical matter, anyone desiring to assess the possible scope of an estoppel arising from the operation of the *Warner-Jenkinson* presumption faces a difficult task. . . . Unguided by the prosecution history, the prior art, applicant's argument during prosecution, and sufficient evidence in rebuttal to the presumption, we have no way to set reasonable limits on how far beyond the literal scope of the term . . . the estoppel will allow the doctrine of equivalents to reach. We can expect reasonable competitors assessing the file history . . . to be equally puzzled as to the scope of any potential estoppel. Thus, it is logical and fair that prosecution history estoppel arising from the operation of the *Warner-Jenkinson* presumption allows the doctrine of equivalents no room to operate. Finding the Supreme Court's language clear, we hold that in circumstances in which the *Warner-Jenkinson* presumption is applicable, i.e., where the reason for an amendment is unclear from an analysis of the prosecution history record, and unrebutted by the patentee, the prosecution history estoppel arising therefrom is total and completely "bars" the application of the doctrine of equivalents as to the amended limitation.

30. ***Al-Site Corp. v. VSI Int'l, Inc.***, 50 USPQ 2d 1161, 1170 (Fed. Cir. 1999)

While in some cases, the prosecution history of a related application may limit application of the doctrine of equivalents in a later filed patent, in this case the specific limitation added in the claims of an earlier issued patent is not present in the claims of the later issued patents. . . . The specific limitations added to gain allowance of the . . . patent are not included in and are therefore not relevant to determining the scope of the claims of the later issued patents.

31. ***Georgia-Pacific Corp. v. United States Gypsum Co.***, 52 USPQ 2d 1590, 1599 (Fed. Cir. 1999)

We also note that for Georgia-Pacific to be bound by the statement made to the PTO in connection with a later prosecution of a different patent, the statement would have to be one that the examiner relied upon in allowing the claims in the patent at issue.

32. ***Elkay Mfg. Co. v. Ebco Mfg. Co.***, 52 USPQ 2d 1109, 1114 (Fed. Cir. 1999)

When multiple patents derive from the same initial application, the prosecution history regarding a claim limitation in any patent that has issued applies with equal force to subsequently issued patents that contain the same claim limitation.

33. ***Augustine Med., Inc. v. Gaymar Indus., Inc.***, 50 USPQ 2d 1900, 1907 (Fed. Cir. 1999)

Because the prosecution history of a parent application may limit the scope of a later application using the same claim term, . . . these claim amendments and arguments restrict the scope of the claims in each of the later issued patents containing the "self-erecting" limitation.

34. ***Princeton Biochemicals, Inc. v. Beckman Instruments, Inc.***, Civ. App. 98-1525, slip op. at 10–11 (Fed. Cir. Aug. 19, 1999) (unpublished)

The examiner thus allowed the combined claim to issue as claim 32 without any amendment being made or any argument being espoused that would limit the holder limitation to the embodiment where the holder/capillary is vertically moving in relation to a stationary sample cup/table.

We hold that the prosecution history does not limit the holder limitation of claim 32 to only vertically movable holders. Although the applicant amended claim 1 to include a vertical movement requirement of the holder in the original application, the subsequent filing of the CIP application and the return of claim 1 to its original, unamended form, counsels against applying the usual rule that the entire prosecution history, including parent and grandparent applications, be analyzed in interpreting a claim. . . .

We also hold that the applicant did not limit claim 32 to a vertically moving holder during prosecution as the amendments and arguments cited by the district court were directed to claims other than those that were combined as issued claim 32. . . . Those amendments and remarks were directed primarily at application claim 8, a picture claim containing numerous other limitations and directed to the specific embodiment of a vertically moving holder, and not to the broader holder limitation in claim 1 that eventually resulted in issued claim 32.

35. *Sash Controls, Inc. v. Talon, L.L.C.*, Civ. App. No. 98-1152, slip op. at 6–7 (Fed. Cir. Jan. 27, 1999) (unpublished) (quoting *Quad Envtl. Techs. Corp. v. Union Sanitary Dist.*, 20 USPQ 2d 1392, 1394 (Fed. Cir. 1991))

The district court erred in applying an estoppel to Sash's arguments concerning obviousness. In *Quad Environmental Technologies Corp. v. Union Sanitary District*, we held that a terminal disclaimer "is not an admission of obviousness of the later-filed claimed invention in light of the earlier-filed disclosure." . . . "In legal principle, the filing of a terminal disclaimer simply serves the statutory function of removing the rejection of double patenting, and raises neither presumption nor estoppel on the merits of the rejection."

36. *Antonious v. Spalding & Evenflo Cos., Inc.*, Civ. App. No. 98-1478, slip op. at 8–9 (Fed. Cir. Aug. 31, 1999) (unpublished)

As part of his office action response, Antonious added the "attached solely to said rear wall" language. Antonious referred to this limitation only in distinguishing Sugioka, and argues now that an interpretation of this language to exclude irons where the weight member is attached to the rear wall and peripheral mass is therefore unjustified. This argument is not persuasive.

We do not disagree with Antonious's suggestion that the addition of this claim language may not have been needed in order to distinguish Sugioka. However, an applicant is free to give up more claim scope than is necessary to overcome a reference. . . . We are satisfied that, whether he needed to or not, Antonious gave up a claim scope that could include a weight bar attached to the peripheral mass and the rear wall when he added the "attached solely to said rear wall" limitation.

37. *In re Cortright*, 49 USPQ 2d 1464, 1467 (Fed. Cir. 1999) (quoting *Vitronics Corp. v. Conceptronic, Inc.*, 39 USPQ 2d 1573, 1578–79 (Fed. Cir. 1996))

Prior art references may be "indicative of what all those skilled in the art generally believe a certain term means . . . [and] can often help to demonstrate how a disputed term is used by those skilled in the art." . . . Accordingly, the PTO's interpretation of claim terms should not be so broad that it conflicts with the meaning given to identical terms in other patents from analogous art.

38. *Vermeer Mfg. Co. v. The Charles Mach. Works, Inc.*, Civ. App. No. 00-1119, slip op. at 4 (Fed. Cir. Nov. 27, 2000) (unpublished)

[P]rosecution history estoppel does not bar this claim interpretation because issued Claim 1 was never rejected and was only rewritten in independent form and amended to correct an antecedent basis problem.

39. *Festo Corp. v. Shoketsu Kinzoku Kogyo Kabushiki Co.*, 234 F.3d 558, 56 USPQ 2d 1865, 1870 (Fed. Cir. 2000) (en banc)

For the purposes of determining whether an amendment gives rise to prosecution history estoppel, a 'substantial reason related to patentability' is not limited to overcoming or avoiding prior art but instead includes any reason which relates to the statutory requirements for a patent. Therefore, a narrowing amendment made for any reason related to the statutory requirements for a patent will give rise to prosecution history estoppel with respect to the amended claim element.

40. *Festo Corp. v. Shoketsu Kinzoku Kogyo Kabushiki Co.*, 234 F.3d 558, 56 USPQ 2d 1865, 1871 (Fed. Cir. 2000) (en banc)

In view of the functions of prosecution history estoppel—preserving the notice function of the claims and preventing patent holders from recapturing under the doctrine of equivalents subject matter that was surrendered before the Patent Office—we see no reason why prosecution history estoppel should not also arise from amendments made for other reasons related to patentability, as described above. Indeed, the functions of prosecution history estoppel cannot be fully satisfied if substantial reasons related to patentability are limited to a narrow subset of patentability issues. Rather, substantial reasons related to patentability include 35 U.S.C. §§ 101 and 112 issues, as well as 35 U.S.C. §§ 102 and 103 issues.

41. ***Festo Corp. v. Shoketsu Kinzoku Kogyo Kabushiki Co.**,* 234 F.3d 558, 56 USPQ 2d 1865, 1871 (Fed. Cir. 2000) (en banc)

Voluntary claim amendments are treated the same as other amendments. Therefore, a voluntary amendment that narrows the scope of a claim for a reason related to the statutory requirements for a patent will give rise to prosecution history estoppel as to the amended claim element.

42. ***Festo Corp. v. Shoketsu Kinzoku Kogyo Kabushiki Co.**,* 234 F.3d 558, 56 USPQ 2d 1865, 1872 (Fed. Cir. 2000) (en banc)

When a claim amendment creates prosecution history estoppel with regard to a claim element, there is no range of equivalents available for the amended claim element. Application of the doctrine of equivalents to the claim element is completely barred (a "complete bar").

43. ***Festo Corp. v. Shoketsu Kinzoku Kogyo Kabushiki Co.**,* 234 F.3d 558, 56 USPQ 2d 1865, 1880 (Fed. Cir. 2000) (en banc)

When no explanation for a claim amendment is established, no range of equivalents is available for the claim element so amended.

44. ***Moore U.S.A. Inc. v. Standard Register Co.**,* 56 USPQ 2d 1225 (Fed. Cir. 2000), ***cert. filed**,* (Feb 26, 2001) (No. 00-1346).

The prosecution history further informs our analysis. The examiner's indefiniteness rejection with respect to the "distance sufficient" limitation reveals the examiner's belief that the limitation was not restricted to any particular printer. The applicant's responses to these rejections clearly demonstrate a similar understanding on his part. That the examiner yielded to the applicant's arguments by allowing the claims does not, as the district court suggested, establish that the "distance sufficient" limitation must be limited to the particular specifications of the IBM 3800 printer. On the contrary, the examiner's acquiescence indicates his acceptance of the "distance sufficient" limitation as functionally claimed and as properly definite under 35 U.S.C. § 112, ¶ 2. We note that there is nothing wrong with defining the dimensions of a device in terms of the environment in which it is to be used. See *Orthokinetics, Inc. v. Safety Travel Chairs, Inc.*, 806 F.2d 1565, 1575–76, 1 USPQ 2d 1081, 1087–88 (Fed. Cir. 1986) (holding that the limitation that the claimed wheelchair have a "front leg portion . . . so dimensioned as to be insertable through the space between the doorframe of an automobile and one of the seats thereof" was not indefinite).

45. ***Northern Telecom Ltd. v. Samsung Elecs. Co., Ltd.***, 55 USPQ 2d 1065, 1075 (Fed. Cir. 2000)

Samsung next argues that ambiguity in the prosecution history places this case within the ambit of our holding in *Athletic Alternatives, Inc. v. Prince Mfg., Inc.*, 73 F.3d 1573, 37 USPQ 2d 1365 (Fed. Cir. 1996). Samsung suggests that *Athletic Alternatives* established a rule that when the prosecution history presents an unclear choice between a broader and narrower meaning of a claim term, then the narrower meaning controls. Accordingly, Samsung asserts that the confusing language from the prosecution history noted above requires that a narrower meaning of "plasma etching"—that which specifically excludes ion bombardment—applies. This is a misreading of *Athletic Alternatives*. . . . Samsung appears to read *Athletic Alternatives* as requiring that courts choose a narrow definition of a claim limitation whenever there is a dispute over meaning and ambiguity in the intrinsic evidence. This is incorrect. The plain and ordinary meaning of claim language controls, unless that meaning renders the claim unclear or is overcome by a special definition that appears in the intrinsic record with reasonable clarity and precision. See, e.g., *Johnson Worldwide*, 175 F.3d at 990–91, 50 USPQ 2d at 1610. Vagueness and inference cannot overcome an ordinary meaning of a claim term; nor can it serve to invoke the rule of *Athletic Alternatives*. Under Samsung's reading, *Athletic Alternatives* would substitute for reasoned analysis. To the contrary, *Athletic Alternatives* considers the case where reasoned analysis leads to two clear and distinct definitions of claim language. It does not apply here, where confusing statements in the prosecution history simply fail to overcome the ordinary meaning of the "plasma etching" limitation.

XIII.H. *Doctrine of Equivalents and Section 112, Sixth Paragraph Equivalents*

1. ***E.I. du Pont de Nemours & Co. v. Phillips Petroleum Co.***, 849 F.2d 1430, 1439, 7 USPQ 2d 1129, 1136 (Fed. Cir.), ***cert. denied***, 488 U.S. 986 (1988)

As indicated in *Loctite Corp. v. Ultraseal Ltd.*, 781 F.2d 861, 871, 228 USPQ 90, 96 (Fed. Cir. 1985), merely because certain prosecution history is used to define the claims more narrowly, there still *may* be—even in light of that same prosecution history—an appropriate range of equivalents under the doctrine of equivalents.

2. ***Conroy v. Reebok Int'l Ltd.***, 29 USPQ 2d 1373, 1378 (Fed. Cir. 1994)

Nonetheless, irrespective of the type of analysis chosen to determine the extent to which the prior art limits the application of the doctrine of equivalents, the fundamental purpose of all such evaluations must be to prevent the patentee from "obtaining" under the doctrine of equivalents, coverage which [the patentee] could not lawfully have obtained from the [Patent and Trademark Office] by literal claims." *Wilson*, 904 F.2d at 684, 14 USPQ 2d at 1948. In purporting to follow *Wilson*, however, the district court here concluded that the *mere existence of element* in the prior art automatically precludes Mr. Conroy from asserting a scope of equivalency sufficient to encompass the corresponding element in the accused device. In so doing, the district court applied an improper test of permissible patent scope under the doctrine of equivalents, and thus contravened the rationale of *Wilson*.

3. ***Corning Glass Works v. Sumitomo Elec. U.S.A., Inc.***, 9 USPQ 2d 1962, 1968 (Fed. Cir. 1989)

"Element" may be used to mean a single limitation, but it has also been used to mean a series of limitations which, taken together, make up a component of the claimed invention. In the [*Pennwalt*] All Elements rule, "element" is used in the sense of a *limitation* of a claim. . . . An equivalent must be found for every limitation of the claim somewhere in an accused device, but not necessarily in a corresponding component, although that is generally the case.

4. ***Dolly, Inc. v. Spalding & Evenflo Co.***, 29 USPQ 2d 1767, 1769 (Fed. Cir. 1994)

An accused device may infringe a claim under the doctrine of equivalents if it performs substantially the same overall function or work, in substantially the same way, to produce substantially the same overall result as the claimed invention. . . . "To be a[n] . . . 'equivalent,' the element substituted in the accused device for the element set forth in the claim must not be such as would substantially change the way in which the function of the claimed invention is performed." *Perkin-Elmer Corp. v. Westinghouse Elec. Corp.*, 822 F.2d 1528, 1533, 3 USPQ 2d 1321, 1325 (Fed. Cir. 1987).

5. ***Dolly, Inc. v. Spalding & Evenflo Co.***, 29 USPQ 2d 1767, 1769 (Fed. Cir. 1994)

"Under the doctrine of equivalents, the accused device and the claimed invention cannot work in 'substantially the same way' if a limitation (including its equivalent) is missing." *Valmont Indus. v. Reinke Mfg.*, 983 F.2d 1039, 1043 n.2, 25 USPQ 2d 1451, 1455 n.2 (Fed. Cir. 1993).

6. ***Dolly, Inc. v. Spalding & Evenflo Co.***, 29 USPQ 2d 1767, 1769–70 (Fed. Cir. 1994)

The doctrine of equivalents does not require a one-to-one correspondence between components of the accused device and the claimed invention. . . . An accused device may infringe under the doctrine of equivalents even though a combination of its components performs a function performed by a single element in the patented invention. . . . The accused device must nevertheless contain *every* limitation or its equivalent. . . .

Equivalency can also exist when separate claim limitations are combined into a single component of the accused device. . . . "One-to-one correspondence of components is not required, and elements or steps may be combined without *ipso facto* loss of equivalency. Each case must be decided in light of the nature and extent of the differences between the accused device and the claimed invention, on the equitable principles of the doctrine of equivalents."

7. ***Dolly, Inc. v. Spalding & Evenflo Co.***, 29 USPQ 2d 1767, 1770 (Fed. Cir. 1994)

An "equivalent" of a claim limitation cannot substantially alter the manner of performing the claimed function. . . . Where an accused device performs substantially the same function to achieve substantially the same result but in a substantially different manner, there is no infringement under the doctrine of equivalents.

8. ***Minnesota Mining & Mfg. Co. v. International Biophysics Corp.***, Civ. App. 96-1371, slip op. at 14–15 (Fed. Cir. Jan. 15, 1997) (unpublished)

That a component in the accused product was already in the prior art does not limit the range of equivalents under § 112(6) or under the doctrine of equivalents. . . . Similarly, a feature that is readily available from the prior art may constitute an equivalent under § 112(6). *See Data Line Corp. v. Micro Techs., Inc.*, 813 F.2d 1196, 1202, 1 USPQ 2d 2052, 2055 (Fed. Cir. 1987) (known interchangeability of the structure disclosed in the specification and the structure in the accused device is a factor favoring a finding of equivalence under § 112(6)).

9. ***Endress + Hauser, Inc. v. Hawk Measurement Sys. Pty. Ltd.***, 43 USPQ 2d 1849, 1852 (Fed. Cir. 1997)

Though it is well understood that "equivalents" under § 112 ¶ 6 is a different concept from "equivalents" under the judicially created doctrine of equivalents, the district judge correctly recognized that the statutorily required construction under § 112 ¶ 6 must proceed on a limitation-by-limitation basis, not dissimilar to the analysis under the doctrine of equivalents.

10. ***Sage Prods., Inc. v. Devon Indus.***, 44 USPQ 2d 1103, 1111 (Fed. Cir. 1997)

An accused element cannot perform substantially the same function, in substantially the same way, to achieve substantially the same result as the claimed element if it does not perform at least a function equivalent to that expressly recited in the claimed element. . . . Where a patent claim recites a specific function for an element of the claim and the written description reiterates the importance of that particular function, a patentee may not later argue, during the course of litigation, that an accused device lacking that functionality is equivalent. . . . To hold otherwise would be to frustrate the important definitional and public-notice functions of the statutory claiming requirement.

11. ***Graver Tank & Mfg. Co. v. Linde Air Prods. Co.***, 339 U.S. 605, 609, 85 USPQ 328 (1950)

What constitutes equivalency must be determined against the context of the patent, the prior art, and the particular circumstances of the case. Equivalence, in the patent law, is not the prisoner of a formula and is not an absolute to be considered in a vacuum. It does not require complete identity for every purpose and in every respect. In determining equivalents, things equal to the same thing may not be equal to each other and, by the same token, things for most purposes different may sometimes be equivalents. Consideration must be given to the purpose for which an ingredient is used in a patent, the qualities it has when combined with the other ingredients, and the function which it is intended to perform. An important factor is whether persons reasonably skilled in the art would have known of the interchangeability of an ingredient not contained in the patent with one that was.

12. ***Warner-Jenkinson Co. v. Hilton Davis Chem. Co.***, 520 U.S. 17, 117 S. Ct. 1040, 41 USPQ 2d 1865, 1871 (1997)

We concur with this apt reconciliation of our two lines of precedent. Each element contained in a patent claim is deemed material to defining the scope of the patented invention, and thus the doctrine of equivalents must be applied to individual elements of the claim, not to the invention as a whole. It is important to ensure that the application of the doctrine, even as to an individual element, is not allowed such broad play as to effectively eliminate that element in its entirety.

13. ***Warner-Jenkinson Co. v. Hilton Davis Chem. Co.***, 520 U.S. 17, 117 S. Ct. 1040, 41 USPQ 2d 1865, 1874 (1997)
The known interchangeability of substitutes for an element of a patent is one of the express objective factors noted by Graver Tank as bearing upon whether the accused device is substantially the same as the patented invention.

14. ***Warner-Jenkinson Co. v. Hilton Davis Chem. Co.***, 520 U.S. 17, 117 S. Ct. 1040, 41 USPQ 2d 1865, 1874 (1997)
The better view, and the one consistent with Graver Tank's predecessors and the objective approach to infringement, is that intent plays no role in the application of the doctrine of equivalents.

15. ***Warner-Jenkinson Co. v. Hilton Davis Chem. Co.***, 520 U.S. 17, 117 S. Ct. 1040, 41 USPQ 2d 1865, 1874 (1997)
Insofar as the question under the doctrine of equivalents is whether an accused element is equivalent to a claimed element, the proper time for evaluating equivalency—and thus knowledge of interchangeability between elements is at the time of infringement, not at the time the patent was issued.

16. ***EMI Group N. Am., Inc. v. Intel Corp.***, 48 USPQ 2d 1181, 1188 (Fed. Cir. 1998)
Equivalency is not defeated by using an additional step to achieve what the patentee does in one step. *See, e.g., Intel Corp. v. United States Int'l Trade Comm'n*, 946 F.2d 821, 832, 20 USPQ 2d 1161, 1171 (Fed. Cir. 1991) (infringement under the doctrine of equivalents when a combination of components performed the function of a single element of the patented invention).

17. ***Litton Sys., Inc. v. Honeywell, Inc.***, 46 USPQ 2d 1321, 1324 (Fed. Cir. 1998)
In reconciling the uncertainty surrounding application of the doctrine of equivalents with the definitional and public-notice functions of the statutory claiming requirement, the Supreme Court endorsed an element-by-element analytical framework for infringement. *See Warner-Jenkinson*, 117 S. Ct. at 1049; see also *Pennwalt Corp. v. Durand-Wayland, Inc.*, 833 F.2d 931, 935, 4 USPQ 2d 1737, 1741 (Fed. Cir.

1987) (*in banc*). In this framework, "each element contained in a patent claim is deemed material to defining the scope of the patented invention, and thus the doctrine of equivalents must be applied to individual elements of the claim, not to the invention as a whole." *Warner-Jenkinson*, 117 S. Ct. at 1049. In applying this method, the Court cautioned against a range of equivalents with "such broad play as to effectively eliminate that element in its entirety." *Id.* The essential inquiry is whether "the accused product or process contains elements identical or equivalent to each claimed element of the patented invention." *Id.* at 1054.

18. ***YBM Magnex, Inc. v. International Trade Comm'n***, 46 USPQ 2d 1843, 1847 (Fed. Cir. 1998)

In a great variety of situations the courts have applied the criteria of equivalency to the particular facts, sometimes finding equivalency and sometimes not. The doctrine of equivalents seeks to establish a just balance between the purpose of claims to define and give notice of what is patented, and the judicial responsibility to avoid a "fraud on the patent" based on insubstantial changes from the patented invention.

19. ***Ethicon Endo-Surgery Inc. v. United States Surgical Corp.***, 47 USPQ 2d 1272, 1276 (Fed. Cir. 1998)

Under the doctrine of equivalents, "a product or process that does not literally infringe upon [sic] the express terms of a patent claim may nonetheless be found to infringe if there is 'equivalence' between the elements of the accused product or process and the claimed elements of the patented invention." *Warner-Jenkinson*, 117 S. Ct. at 1045, 41 USPQ 2d at 1868. Infringement may be found under the doctrine of equivalents if every limitation of the asserted claim, or its "equivalent," is found in the accused subject matter, where an "equivalent" differs from the claimed limitation only insubstantially. Whether a component in the accused subject matter performs substantially the same function as the claimed limitation in substantially the same way to achieve substantially the same result may be relevant to this determination. . . . [I]nfringement under the doctrine of equivalents remains a viable basis for a finding of infringement, . . . as long as a court properly applies (1) the so-called "All Elements" rule, . . ., and (2) the doctrine of prosecution history estoppel . . . .

20. ***Corning Glass Works v. Sumitomo Elec. U.S.A., Inc.***, 9 USPQ 2d 1962, 1968 (Fed. Cir. 1989)

An equivalent must be found for every limitation of the claim somewhere in an accused device, but not necessarily in a corresponding component, although that is generally the case.

21. ***Ethicon Endo-Surgery Inc. v. United States Surgical Corp.***, 47 USPQ 2d 1272, 1280 (Fed. Cir. 1998)

We have stated that "one-to-one correspondence of components is not required, and elements or steps may be combined without ipso facto loss of equivalency." *Sun Studs, Inc. v. ATA Equip. Leasing Inc.*, 872 F.2d 978, 989, 10 USPQ 2d 1338, 1347 (Fed. Cir. 1989), *overruled on other grounds, A.C. Aukerman Co. v. R.L. Chaides Constr. Co.*, 960 F.2d 1020, 1038–39, 22 USPQ 2d 1321, 1333 (Fed. Cir. 1992). In other words, two physical components of an accused device may be viewed in combination to serve as an equivalent of one element of a claimed invention, as long as no claim limitation is thereby wholly vitiated.

22. ***Chiuminatta Concrete Concepts, Inc. v. Cardinal Indus., Inc.***, 46 USPQ 2d 1752, 1758 (Fed. Cir. 1998)

Both § 112, ¶ 6, and the doctrine of equivalents protect the substance of a patentee's right to exclude by preventing mere colorable differences or slight improvements from escaping infringement, the former, by incorporating equivalents of disclosed structures into the literal scope of a functional claim limitation, and the latter, by holding as infringements equivalents that are beyond the literal scope of the claim. They do so by applying similar analyses of insubstantiality of the differences. Thus, a finding of a lack of literal infringement for lack of equivalent structure under a means-plus-function limitation may preclude a finding of equivalence under the doctrine of equivalents.

There is an important difference, however, between the doctrine of equivalents and § 112, ¶ 6. The doctrine of equivalents is necessary because one cannot predict the future. Due to technological advances, a variant of an invention may be developed after the patent is granted, and that variant may constitute so insubstantial a change from what is claimed in the patent that it should be held to be an infringement. Such a variant, based on after-developed technology, could not have been disclosed in the patent. Even if such an element is found not to be a § 112, ¶ 6, equivalent because it is not equivalent to the structure disclosed in the patent, this analysis should not foreclose it from being an equivalent under the doctrine of equivalents.

That is not the case here, where the equivalence issue does not involve later-developed technologies, but rather involves technology that predates the invention itself. In such a case, a finding of non-equivalence for § 112, ¶ 6, purposes should preclude a contrary finding under the doctrine of equivalents. This is because, as we have already determined, the structure of the accused device differs substantially from the disclosed structure, and given the prior knowledge of the technology asserted to be equivalent, it could readily have been disclosed in the patent. There is no policy-based reason why a patentee should get two bites at the apple. If he or she could have included in the patent what is now alleged to be equivalent, and did not, leading to a conclusion that an accused device lacks an equivalent to the disclosed structure, why should the issue of equivalence have to be litigated a second time? As indicated, this consideration does not necessarily apply regarding variants of the invention based on after-developed technologies.

23. ***Streamfeeder, LLC v. Sure-Feed Sys., Inc.***, 50 USPQ 2d 1515, 1520 n.1 (Fed. Cir. 1999)

In *Wilson*, we observed that the doctrine of equivalents does not "expand" or "broaden" claims, but instead expands the right to exclude.

24. ***Streamfeeder, LLC v. Sure-Feed Sys., Inc.***, 50 USPQ 2d 1515, 1520 (Fed. Cir. 1999)

In *Wilson*, we set forth a hypothetical claim methodology to aid in determining whether a particular claim may be infringed under the doctrine of equivalents. . . . Under that methodology, the patentee may propose a hypothetical claim which is broad enough in scope to literally read on the accused device. . . . If the hypothetical claim could have been allowed by the Patent and Trademark Office (PTO) in view of the prior art, then the prior art does not preclude the application of the doctrine of equivalents and infringement may be found. See id. On the other hand, as in the PTO's examination process, references may be combined to prove that the hypothetical claim would have been obvious to one of ordinary skill in the art and thus would not have been allowed. . . . A hypothetical claim analysis is not an opportunity to freely redraft granted claims. That opportunity existed in the PTO, where the submitted claims were examined for patentability. Other statutorily prescribed procedures exist for post-grant modification of claims in the PTO in appropriate circumstances. . . . While use of a hypothetical claim may permit a minor extension of a claim to cover subject matter that is substantially equivalent to that literally claimed, one cannot, in the course of litigation and outside of the PTO, cut and trim, expanding here, and narrowing there, to arrive at a claim that encompasses an accused device, but avoids the prior art. Slight broadening is permitted at that point, but not narrowing. . . . Wholesale redrafting of granted claims during litigation by narrowing and expanding the claims at the same time in creating a hypothetical claim is not supported by our case law and it avoids the examination process. It is contrary to the statutory requirement that an applicant "particularly point[] out and distinctly claim[] the subject matter which the applicant regards as his [or her] invention," 35 U.S.C. § 112 (1994), a requirement that presupposes a PTO examination, which does not occur with a hypothetical claim. Hypothetical claim analysis thus cannot be used to redraft granted claims in litigation by narrowing and broadening a claim at the same time.

25. ***Streamfeeder, LLC v. Sure-Feed Sys., Inc.***, 50 USPQ 2d 1515, 1522 (Fed. Cir. 1999)

In *Wilson*, we noted a narrow, counterintuitive exception to the general principle that, when one does not infringe a broader claim, one cannot infringe a dependent claim containing all of that broader claim's limitations plus more:

> While this proposition is no doubt generally correct, it does not apply in the circumstances of this case. Here, we have reversed the judgment of infringement of independent claim 1 solely because the asserted range of equivalents of the claim limitations would encompass the prior art Uniroyal ball. The dependent claims, of course, are narrower than claim 1; therefore, it does not automatically follow that the ranges of equivalents of these narrower claims would encompass the prior art, because of their added limitations.

26. ***Read Corp. v. Portec, Inc.***, 23 USPQ 2d 1426, 1431 (Fed. Cir. 1992) (quoting ***Malta v. Schulmerich Carillons, Inc.***, 21 USPQ 2d 1161, 1164–65 (Fed. Cir. 1991), ***cert. denied***, 504 U.S. 974 (1992))

Under the doctrine of equivalents, a patentee must show that the accused device performs substantially the same function, in substantially the same way, to achieve substantially the same result. . . . "The 'substantially the same way' prong of the test may be met if an equivalent of a recited limitation has been substituted in the accused device." . . . Thus, infringement requires that each limitation of a claim be met exactly or by a substantial equivalent.

27. ***Al-Site Corp. v. VSI Int'l, Inc.***, 50 USPQ 2d 1161, 1168 (Fed. Cir. 1999)

Section 112, ¶ 6 recites a mandatory procedure for interpreting the meaning of a means- or step-plus-function claim element. These claim limitations "shall be construed to cover the corresponding structure, material, or acts described in the specification and equivalents thereof." 35 U.S.C. § 112,

¶ 6. Thus, § 112, ¶ 6 procedures restrict a functional claim element's "broad literal language . . . to those means that are 'equivalent' to the actual means shown in the patent specification." . . . Section 112, ¶ 6 restricts the scope of a functional claim limitation as part of a literal infringement analysis. . . . Thus, an equivalent under § 112, ¶ 6 informs the claim meaning for a literal infringement analysis. The doctrine of equivalents, on the other hand, extends enforcement of claim terms beyond their literal reach in the event "there is 'equivalence' between the elements of the accused product or process and the claimed elements of the patented invention."

One important difference between § 112, ¶ 6 and the doctrine of equivalents involves the timing of the separate analyses for an "insubstantial change." As this court has recently clarified, a structural equivalent under § 112 must have been available at the time of the issuance of the claim. . . . An equivalent structure or act under § 112 cannot embrace technology developed after the issuance of the patent because the literal meaning of a claim is fixed upon its issuance. An "after arising equivalent" infringes, if at all, under the doctrine of equivalents. . . . In other words, an equivalent structure or act under § 112 for literal infringement must have been available at the time of patent issuance while an equivalent under the doctrine of equivalents may arise after patent issuance and before the time of infringement.

28. ***K-2 Corp. v. Salomon S.A.***, 52 USPQ 2d 1001, 1007 (Fed. Cir. 1999) (quoting ***Warner-Jenkinson Co. v. Hilton Davis Chem. Co.***, 520 U.S. 17, 29, 41 USPQ 2d 1865, 1871 (1997), and ***Royal Typewriter Co. v. Remington Rand***, 77 USPQ 517, 518 (2d Cir. 1948) (Hand, J.))

[W]hile unquestionably retaining vitality, the doctrine of equivalents exists in some tension with other core tenets of the patent law, perhaps most notably the requirement that the patentee "particularly point[] out and distinctly claim[] the subject matter which the applicant regards as his invention," 35 U.S.C. § 112 ¶ 2 (1994), and the function of patent claims to provide notice to competitors regarding the scope of the patent grant . . . .

The courts have responded to such concerns by developing an array of legal limitations, formulations, and tests regarding the application of the doctrine of equivalents. These efforts reflect two animating concepts. The first is that the doctrine of equivalents is limited. It cannot allow a patent claim to encompass subject matter that could not have been patented; nor can it be used to ignore the actual language of the patent. Thus, we have held that the doctrine of equivalents cannot allow a patent to encompass subject matter ex-

isting in the prior art. . . . It is also fundamental that the text
of the claim must be closely followed: "each element contained in a patent claim is deemed material to defining the
scope of the patented invention, and thus the doctrine of
equivalents must be applied to individual elements of the
claim, not to the invention as a whole." . . . Therefore, the
doctrine of equivalents cannot be used to vitiate an element
from the claim in its entirety. . . .

The second conceptual limitation on the doctrine of equivalents is the idea that the patentee may not use the doctrine to
recover subject matter that has been surrendered. For example, prosecution history estoppel will exclude from the doctrine of equivalents any subject matter that was, by amendment or argument during prosecution, relinquished. . . .
Where these limitations are inapplicable, the doctrine of
equivalents operates to "prevent an infringer from steal-
ing the benefit of an invention." To have this effect, however,
the doctrine of equivalents must, as noted above, remain
within the boundaries established by the prior art, the scope
of the patent claims themselves, and any surrendered subject
matter.

29. ***WMS Gaming Inc. v. International Game Tech.***, 51
USPQ 2d 1385, 1393 (Fed. Cir. 1999)

The two structures are not identical because the microprocessor disclosed in the Telnaes patent is programmed differently from the microprocessor disclosed in the Durham
patent. Put another way, the two disclosed machines are different, i.e., not identical.

30. ***WMS Gaming Inc. v. International Game Tech.***, 51
USPQ 2d 1385, 1393 (Fed. Cir. 1999)

Because the structure recited in the Telnaes patent is limited by the disclosed algorithm, our analysis of structural
equivalence necessarily discusses the disclosed algorithm,
which includes functional-type elements.

31. ***Overhead Door Corp. v. Chamberlain Group, Inc.***, 52
USPQ 2d 1321, 1326–27 (Fed. Cir. 1999)

In operation of a mechanical switch, a human operator
would indeed set the memory selection switch to one of five
positions. This "user operated" characteristic of a mechanical switch, however, would not necessarily preclude a finding that software performs equivalently without human operation. Indeed in other contexts, this court has noted the
interchangeability of hardware and software. . . . Moreover
the Supreme Court has acknowledged that interchangeability can be one of the hallmarks of an equivalent.

32. ***Overhead Door Corp. v. Chamberlain Group, Inc.***, 52 USPQ 2d 1321, 1329 (Fed. Cir. 1999)

The differences in claim language, bolstered by the patentees' statements during the reissue proceedings, cause this court to reach a broader construction for claim 5 than for claim 1. . . . The district court erred in ruling that only the mechanical switch in Figure 2 is "corresponding structure" for the claimed "switch means." "Switch means," when properly construed, also covers the software-based embodiment described in Figure 3.

33. ***Evans Med. Ltd. v. American Cyanamid Co.***, 52 USPQ 2d 1455 (Fed. Cir. 1999) (unpublished)

It is equally clear that under the circumstances there can be no infringement under the doctrine of equivalents, for a product cannot be found to be insubstantially different from a claimed one if arriving at such a finding would require vitiation of an essential claim element. *See Warner-Jenkinson Co. v. Hilton Davis Chem. Co.*, 520 U.S. 17, 39 n.8, 41 USPQ 2d 1865, 1875 n.8 (1997) ("if a theory of equivalence would entirely vitiate a particular claim element, partial or complete judgment should be rendered by the court, as there would be no further material issue for the jury to resolve").

34. ***Kraft Foods, Inc. v. International Trading Co.***, 203 F.3d 1362, 53 USPQ 2d 1814, 1822 (Fed. Cir. 2000)

[P]reclusion of a finding of infringement under the doctrine of equivalents for pre-existing technology after an adverse holding of no literal infringement for the same technology applies only to means-plus-function claim limitations. Where the patentee does not use the means-plus-function format, the resolution of infringement under the doctrine of equivalents would not allow the patentee "two bites at the apple," since the resolution of the literal infringement question would not address the issue of equivalence in a claim drawn to structure rather than to a means-plus-function. Thus, for a claim limitation not drafted in means-plus-function language, the mere fact that the asserted equivalent structure was pre-existing technology does not foreclose a finding of infringement under the doctrine of equivalents.

35. ***Kemco Sales, Inc. v. Control Papers Co., Inc.***, 54 USPQ 2d 1308, 1315–16 (Fed. Cir. 2000)

In order for an accused structure to literally meet a 35 U.S.C. section 112, paragraph 6 means-plus-function limitation, the accused structure must either be the same as the disclosed structure or be a 35 U.S.C. section 112, paragraph 6 "equivalent," i.e., (1) perform the identical function and (2)

be otherwise insubstantially different with respect to structure. See *Odetics, Inc. v. Storage Tech. Corp.*, 185 F.3d 1259,
1267, 51 USPQ 2d 1225 (Fed. Cir. 1999); *Pennwalt Corp. v.
Durand-Wayland, Inc.*, 833 F.2d 931, 934, 4 USPQ 2d 1737,
1739 (Fed. Cir. 1987) (en banc). Under a modified version of
the function-way-result methodology described in *Graver
Tank & Manufacturing Co. v. Linde Air Products Co.*, 339
U.S. 605, 608, 85 USPQ 328, 330, 94 L. Ed. 1097, 70 S. Ct.
854 (1950), two structures may be "equivalent" for purposes
of 35 U.S.C. section 112, paragraph 6 if they perform the
identical function, in substantially the same way, with substantially the same result. See *Odetics*, 185 F.3d at 1267, 51
USPQ 2d at 1229–30 (setting forth a modified function-way-
result analysis, acknowledging that "this tripartite test developed for the doctrine of equivalents is not wholly trans-
ferable to the § 112, ¶ 6 statutory equivalence context" due
to the functional identity requirement).

If an accused structure is not a 35 U.S.C. section 112,
paragraph 6 equivalent of the disclosed structure because it
does not perform the identical function of that disclosed
structure and hence does not literally infringe, it may nevertheless still be an "equivalent" under the doctrine of equivalents. Thus, if one applies the traditional function-way-result test, the accused structure must perform substantially
the same function, in substantially the same way, to achieve
substantially the same result, as the disclosed structure. See
Dawn Equip. Co. v. Kentucky Farms Inc., 140 F.3d 1009,
1016, 46 USPQ 2d 1109, 1113 (Fed. Cir. 1998). A key feature
that distinguishes "equivalents" under 35 U.S.C. section
112, paragraph 6 and "equivalents" under the doctrine of
equivalents is that 35 U.S.C. section 112, paragraph 6 equivalents must perform the identical function of the disclosed
structure, see *Odetics*, 185 F.3d at 1267, 51 USPQ 2d at
1229; *Pennwalt*, 833 F.2d at 934, 4 USPQ 2d at 1739, while
equivalents under the doctrine of equivalents need only perform a substantially similar function, see *Al-Site Corp. v.
VSI Int'l, Inc.*, 174 F.3d 1308, 1320–21, 50 USPQ 2d 1161,
1168 (Fed. Cir. 1999).

Because the "way" and "result" prongs are the same under
both the 35 U.S.C. section 112, paragraph 6 and doctrine of
equivalents tests, a structure failing the 35 U.S.C. section
112, paragraph 6 test under either or both prongs must fail
the doctrine of equivalents test for the same reason(s). That
was the case in *Chiuminatta*, in which the "way" was determined to be substantially different under a 35 U.S.C. section
112, paragraph 6 analysis. See *Chiuminatta*, 145 F.3d at
1309, 46 USPQ 2d at 1757. Accordingly, we concluded that
the accused structure did not infringe under the doctrine of

equivalents for precisely the same reason. See *Id.* at 1311, 46 USPQ 2d at 1758. . . . When a court determines that the "way" and/or "result" is/are substantially different under a 35 U.S.C. section 112, paragraph 6 equivalents analysis, a patentee cannot prevail under the doctrine of equivalents for the same reason(s).

36. ***IMS Technology, Inc. v. Haas Automation, Inc.***, 54 USPQ 2d 1129, 1138 & n.3 (Fed. Cir.), ***cert. dismissed***, 530 U.S. 1299 (2000)

This court has on several occasions compared statutory equivalence under § 112, ¶ 6 and the judicial doctrine of equivalents. . . . While acknowledging that there are differences between § 112, ¶ 6 and the doctrine of equivalents, this court on several occasions has indicated that the tests for equivalence under § 112, ¶ 6 and the doctrine of equivalents are "closely related," involving "similar analyses of insubstantiality of the differences." *Chiuminatta*, 145 F.3d at 1310, 46 USPQ 2d at 1757–58; see also *Warner-Jenkinson Co. v. Hilton Davis Chem. Co.*, 520 U.S. 17, 28, 41 USPQ 2d 1865, 1870, 137 L. Ed. 2d 146, 117 S. Ct. 1040 (1997) (stating that application of § 112, ¶ 6 "is an application of the doctrine of equivalents in a restrictive role . . . ."); *Valmont*, 983 F.2d at 1043, 25 USPQ 2d at 1455 ("The word 'equivalent' in section 112 invokes the familiar concept of an insubstantial change which adds nothing of significance."). Thus, a reduced version of the well-known tripartite test for the doctrine of equivalents has been applied in the § 112, ¶ 6 context to determine if the differences are insubstantial, i.e., after determining that the accused device performs the identical function, as required by statute, whether it performs the function in substantially the same way to achieve substantially the same result. . . . Evidence of known interchangeability between structure in the accused device and the disclosed structure has also been considered an important factor. . . .

In light of the similarity of the tests for equivalence under § 112, ¶ 6 and the doctrine of equivalents, the context of the invention should be considered when performing a § 112, ¶ 6 equivalence analysis just as it is in a doctrine of equivalents determination. . . . As a result, two structures that are equivalent in one environment may not be equivalent in another. More particularly, when in a claimed "means" limitation the disclosed physical structure is of little or no importance to the claimed invention, there may be a broader range of equivalent structures than if the physical characteristics of the structure are critical in performing the claimed function in the context of the claimed invention. Thus, a rigid comparison of physical structures in a vacuum may be inappropriate in a particular case. Indeed, the statute requires two structures to be equivalent, but it does not require them to be "structurally equivalent, " i.e., it does not mandate an equivalency comparison that necessarily focuses heavily or exclusively on physical structure.

In some cases, an analysis of insubstantial differences in the context of the invention results in a finding of equivalence under § 112, ¶ 6 even though two structures arguably would not be considered equivalent structures in other contexts, e.g., if performing functions other than the claimed function. . . . In other cases, in which the specific physical features of the structure corresponding to the "means" limitation may have more relevance to the claimed invention, a finding of noninfringement results. . . .

The difference between "equivalent structures" and "structural equivalents" can be demonstrated with a simple example borrowed from the late Judge Rich. A claim includes part A, part B, and "means for securing parts A and B together in a fixed relationship." The written description discloses that parts A and B are made of wood and are secured together by nails. For purposes of the invention, it does not matter how parts A and B are secured; nails are not a critical part of the invention. A screw is not a nail, but for purposes of § 112, ¶ 6, it is equivalent structure in the context of the invention, though it is not the "structural equivalent" of a nail.

XIII.I. *Interpreting Claims Under Section 112, Sixth Paragraph*

1. ***Waterloo Furniture Components Ltd. v. Haworth, Inc.,*** 25 USPQ 2d 1138, 1142 (N.D. Ill. 1992)

   Consequently, we hold that the use of the word "means" in a claim does not as a matter of law refer to an element expressed in means-plus-function form. Whether the bare use of the term "means" renders a claim indefinite depends on the interpretation of that claim.

2. ***In re Hyatt***, 218 USPQ 195, 197 (Fed. Cir. 1983)

   A mere recital of a multitude of elements or steps in a claim is not determinative of the invention it defines. A claim must be read in accordance with the precepts of English grammar. In claim 35, the invention defined is what follows the word "comprising." . . . The proper statutory rejection of a single means claim is the requirement of the first paragraph of § 112 that the enabling disclosure of the specification be commensurate in scope with the claim under consideration.

The long-recognized problem with a single means claim is that it covers every conceivable means for achieving the stated result, while the specification discloses at most only those means known to the inventor. *See O'Reilly v. Morse*, 56 U.S. (15 How.) 62, 112 (1854). Thus, the claim is properly rejected for what used to be known as "undue breadth," but has since been appreciated as being, more accurately, based on the first paragraph of §112. . . .

The final paragraph of §112 saves combination claims drafted using means-plus-function format from this problem by providing a construction of that format narrow enough to avoid the problem of undue breadth as forbidden by the first paragraph. But no provision saves a claim drafted in means-plus-function format which is not drawn to a combination, i.e., a single means claim.

An apparatus claim reciting both of the functions of the involved element or circuit in means-plus-function language is adequately supported if the apparatus is adequately described.

3. ***Ex parte Freborg***, 49 USPQ 213, 214 (Pat. Off. Bd. App. 1940)

In respect to the first point above, we believe the clause following the term "means" is clear when taken in connection with the disclosure. While it is true that it does not describe specifically where the means are located or in detail how they are capable of cooperating with a record to move it, we regard this as being merely a matter of scope of the clause.

4. ***Ex parte Freborg***, 49 USPQ 213, 214 (Pat. Off. Bd. App. 1940)

The term "means" may ordinarily properly include more than one specific detail. Most machine elements or subcombinations properly termed "means" may be divided up into several parts depending on how specific or to what extent the division is carried.

5. ***Ex parte Olsson***, 65 USPQ 52, 54 (Pat. Off. Bd. App. 1944)

We find no error in examiner's conclusion that this situation clearly falls within a long established rule that if a submechanism really performs two independent functions there is no objection to including it twice in a claim under each separate function.

6. ***Ex parte Anderson***, 52 USPQ 552, 555 (Pat. Off. Bd. App. 1941)

It is well settled that the term "means" may be used in either a singular or a plural sense. So far as we know, there is no particular limit on the degree of plurality to which the term is applicable. If an attempt were made in machines of the complicated character here involved to define the various elements and their relationships by separate expressions, the lengths of the resulting claims would render them extremely confusing, to say the least. While some of the expressions used by appellant are doubtless extremely comprehensive, as the examiner contends, we do not believe that the claims are subject to rejection on this account.

7. ***Ex parte Sherman***, 45 USPQ 532, 534 (Pat. Off. Bd. App. 1940)

While the claims contain numerous functional statements, these statements seem to be used for the purpose of clearly defining or differentiating elements which have been positively included in the claims. We see no objection to the use of the functional statement to define an element, even where the element may be set forth by the term "means."

8. ***In re Donaldson Co.***, 29 USPQ 2d 1845, 1848–50 (Fed. Cir. 1994) (en banc)

The plain and unambiguous meaning of paragraph six is that one construing means-plus-function language in a claim must look to the specification and interpret that language in light of the corresponding structure, material, or acts described therein, and equivalents thereof, to the extent that the specification provides such disclosure. Paragraph six does not state or even suggest that the PTO is exempt from this mandate . . . .

Per our holding, the "broadest reasonable interpretation" that an examiner may give means-plus-function language is that statutorily mandated in paragraph six. Accordingly, the PTO may not disregard the structure disclosed in the specification corresponding to such language when rendering a patentability determination.

9. ***In re Donaldson Co.***, 29 USPQ 2d 1845, 1852 (Fed. Cir. 1994) (en banc)

Nevertheless, as explained previously, section 112, paragraph six, requires us and the PTO to construe the "means, responsive to pressure" language recited in claim 1 as limited to a flexible-wall, diaphragm-like structure as disclosed in *Schuler's* specification, or an "equivalent" thereof. In this regard, the Commissioner has failed to establish the existence in conventional hopper structures like Swift's of any inherent vibrations resulting from pulse-jet cleaning sufficient to loosen hardened dust that gathers on hopper walls. Thus, because the Commissioner's unsupported assertion that Swift's hopper walls would vibrate in response to pressure increases caused by pulse-jet cleaning is mere speculation unsupported by any rational basis for believing it might be true, the burden clearly did not shift to Schuler to establish non-equivalence. Furthermore, the Commissioner has failed to persuade us that such vibration, even if it did occur, should be viewed as making Swift's hopper structure an "equivalent" of Schuler's flexible-wall, diaphragm-like structure.

10. ***Carroll Touch, Inc. v. Electro Mechanical Sys., Inc.***, 27 USPQ 2d 1836, 1840 (Fed. Cir. 1993)

In order to meet a means-plus-function limitation, an accused device must (1) perform the identical function recited in the means limitation and (2) perform that function using the structure disclosed in the specification or an equivalent structure.

11. ***Johnston v. IVAC Corp.***, 12 USPQ 2d 1382, 1386 (Fed. Cir. 1989)

That part of a claim contains means-plus-function language does not make section 112 paragraph 6 applicable to the entirety of the claim.

12. ***In re Roberts***, 176 USPQ 313, 315 (C.C.P.A. 1973)

We have also concluded that the board's other views of the claims under § 112 are not well taken. The [sixth] paragraph of that section specifically allows the use of functional language to define claim limitations. . . .

Neither the examiner nor the board framed the rejection under § 112 in a manner that indicates it was based upon anything but an objection to the "functional" language employed. At most, the board's rejection suggests that the language objected to might not comport with the requirements of the second paragraph since "reducing the coefficient of friction" is regarded as "not a step but the result of an unstated step" in the words of the board.

We do not agree with this characterization of the language of claim 5. It calls for an affirmative treatment of the film in a manner not stated in the claim, as the specification clearly indicates that untreated PET film has a coefficient of friction of 0.80 or higher. However, the absence in the claim of specific steps which would bring about the desired friction property is no defect. The claims define the limits of the claimed invention, and it is the function of the specification to detail how this invention is to be practiced. In our view these requirements are met.

13. ***Zygo Corp. v. Wyko Corp.***, 38 USPQ 2d 1281, 1286 (Fed. Cir. 1996)

A finding of equivalency just because the same result is achieved is "a flagrant abuse of the term 'equivalent'." *Burr v. Duryee*, 68 U.S. (1 Wall.) 531, 573 (1864).

14. ***York Prods., Inc. v. Central Tractor Farm & Family Ctr.***,
40 USPQ 2d 1619, 1623 (Fed. Cir. 1996)

In determining whether to apply the statutory procedures of section 112, ¶ 6, the use of the word "means" triggers a presumption that the inventor used this term advisedly to invoke the statutory mandates for means-plus-function clauses. . . . Nonetheless, mere incantation of the word "means" in a clause reciting predominantly structure cannot evoke section 112, ¶ 6. . . . Conversely, "[t]he recitation of some structure in a means plus function element does not preclude the applicability of section 112(6)." . . . Without an identified function, the term "means" in this claim cannot invoke 35 U.S.C. § 112, ¶ 6. Without a "means" sufficiently connected to a recited function, the presumption in use of the word "means" does not operate.

15. ***Engel Indus., Inc. v. Lockformer Co.***, 40 USPQ 2d 1161,
1166 (Fed. Cir. 1996)

It is not enough if both devices perform the same function when it is apparent from the patent drawings that the devices are differently constructed and perform that function in different ways.

16. ***Graver Tank & Mfg. Co. v. Linde Air Prods. Co.***, 339
U.S. 605, 609 (1950)

Equivalence, in the patent law, is not the prisoner of a formula and is not an absolute to be considered in a vacuum . . . . An important factor is whether persons reasonably skilled in the art would have known of the interchangeability of an ingredient not contained in the patent with one that was.

17. ***Cole v. Kimberly-Clark Corp.***, 41 USPQ 2d 1001, 1006
(Fed. Cir. 1996)

To invoke this statute, the alleged means-plus-function claim element must not recite a definite structure which performs the described function. Patent drafters conventionally achieved this by using only the words "means for" followed by a recitation of the function performed. Merely because a named element of a patent claim is followed by the word "means," however, does not automatically make that element a "means-plus-function" element under 35 U.S.C. § 112, ¶ 6. . . . The converse is also true; merely because an element does *not* include the word "means" does not automatically prevent that element from being construed as a means-plus-function element.

18. ***Greenburg v. Ethicon Endo-Surgery, Inc.***, 39 USPQ 2d
1783, 1786–87 (Fed. Cir. 1996)

We do not mean to suggest that section 112(6) is triggered only if the claim uses the word "means." The Patent and

Trademark Office has rejected the argument that only the term "means" will invoke section 112(6), . . . and we agree . . . Nonetheless, the use of the term "means" has come to be so closely associated with "means-plus-function" claiming that it is fair to say that the use of the term "means" (particularly as used in the phrase "means for") generally invokes section 112(6) and that the use of a different formulation generally does not.

19. ***O.I. Corp. v. Tekmar Co.***, 42 USPQ 2d 1777, 1781–82 (Fed. Cir. 1997)

The statute of course uses terms that might be viewed as having a similar meaning, namely, steps and acts. It refers to means and steps, which must be supported by structure, material, or acts. It does not state which goes with which. The word "means" clearly refers to the generic description of an apparatus element, and the implementation of such a concept is obviously by structure or material. We interpret the term "steps" to refer to the generic description of elements of a process, and the term "acts" to refer to the implementation of such steps. This interpretation is consistent with the established correlation between means and structure. In this paragraph, structure and material go with means, acts go with steps. Of course, as we have indicated, section 112, ¶ 6, is implicated only when means *plus function* without definite structure are present, and that is similarly true with respect to steps, that the paragraph is implicated only when steps *plus function* without acts are present. The statute thus in effect provides that an element in a combination method or process claim may be recited as a step for performing a specified function without the recital of acts in support of the function. Being drafted with the permissive "may," the statute does not require that steps in a method claim be drafted in step-plus-function form but rather allows for that form.

20. ***Sage Prods., Inc. v. Devon Indus.***, 44 USPQ 2d 1103, 1109 (Fed. Cir. 1997)

The use of the word "means," which is part of the classic template for functional claim elements, gives rise to "a presumption that the inventor used the term advisedly to invoke the statutory mandates for means-plus-function clauses." . . . However, the presumption is not conclusive. For example, where a claim uses the word "means," but specifies no corresponding function for the "means," it does not implicate section 112. . . . Likewise, where a claim recites a function, but then goes on to elaborate sufficient structure, material, or acts within the claim itself to perform entirely the recited function, the claim is not in means-plus-function format.

21. ***In re Morris***, 44 USPQ 2d 1023, 1028 (Fed. Cir. 1997)

In *Donaldson*, this court considered the question of how the PTO was required to interpret claims drafted pursuant to 35 U.S.C. §112 ¶ 6, claims in so-called "means-plus-function" language. . . . The PTO argued that they were permitted to interpret the claims as broadly as the claim language permitted without the constraint of the written description contained in the specification. The *Donaldson* court, *in banc*, held that claims written in means-plus-function language are interpreted in the same manner during prosecution as they are during litigation. . . . The statute requires that claims so written "shall be construed to cover the corresponding structure, material, or acts described in the specification and equivalents thereof." . . . The court found no basis in the statute or legislative history for exempting the PTO from this statutory mandate. Therefore the PTO is required to consult the specification during examination in order to determine the permissible scope of the claim.

22. ***Ex parte Lemoine***, 46 USPQ 2d 1432, 1435 (B.P.A.I. 1998) (unpublished)

After reviewing the specification, we find that the specification describes two structures corresponding to the "means of longitudinally displacing . . ." and "means of immobilizing . . ." of claim 54 and "means for selectively adjusting . . ." and "means of immobilizing . . ." of claim 55. . . .

According to 35 U.S.C. § 112, ¶ 6, as construed by our reviewing court, the means clauses are limited to these two structures and equivalent structures. . . . A structure is an "equivalent" if it differs from the disclosed structure by an insubstantial change which adds nothing of significance. . . . We recognize that applicant's specification indicates that the specific structures disclosed are "non-limiting examples." . . . However, the language of paragraph 6, is unequivocal in mandating that means plus function "shall be construed to cover the corresponding structure, materials or acts described in the specification and equivalents thereof." Our reviewing court has instructed that means claims are limited to the structures disclosed by the specification and equivalents. . . .

We must now compare the structures disclosed in the specification with the reference disclosures.

23. ***Mas-Hamilton Group v. LaGard, Inc.***, 48 USPQ 2d 1010, 1015 (Fed. Cir. 1998)

For literal infringement of a section 112, ¶ 6 limitation, the fact-finder must determine whether the accused device performs an identical function to the one recited in the means-

plus-function clause. *See Pennwalt*, 833 F.2d at 934, 4 USPQ
2d at 1739 (holding that if the identical function is not performed, literal infringement is not possible). If the identical
function is performed, the fact-finder must then determine
whether the accused device utilizes the same structure or
materials as described in the specification, or their equivalents. *See Cybor*, 138 F.3d at 1467, 46 USPQ 2d at 1184.

Determination of infringement under the doctrine of equivalents requires the fact-finder to determine whether the
structural differences between the particular elements of the
accused device and the asserted claim's limitations as recited
in the claim and as shown in the corresponding means structures in the specification are insubstantial. *See Warner-Jenkinson Co. v. Hilton Davis Chem. Co.*, 520 U.S. 17, 137 L. Ed.
2d 146, 117 S. Ct. 1040, 1046 (1997) . . . One way to determine
if substantial differences exist is to apply the function-way-
result analysis of *Graver Tank*, as sanctioned by *Warner-
Jenkinson*.

24. ***Personalized Media Communications, L.L.C. v. International Trade Comm'n***, 48 USPQ 2d 1880, 1886–87 (Fed.
Cir. 1998)

We also made clear that use of the term "means" is central
to the analysis: "the use of the term 'means' has come to be
so closely associated with 'means-plus-function' claiming
that it is fair to say that the use of the term 'means' (particularly as used in the phrase 'means for') generally invokes
[Section 112, Para. 6] and that the use of a different formulation generally does not." Id. at 1584, 39 USPQ2d at 1787 .

Subsequent cases have clarified that use of the word "means"
creates a presumption that Section 112, Para. 6 applies . . .
and that the failure to use the word "means" creates a presumption that Section 112, Para. 6 does not apply, . . . In
deciding whether either presumption has been rebutted,
the focus remains on whether the claim as properly construed
recites sufficiently definite structure to avoid the ambit of
§ 112, ¶ 6.

25. ***Signtech USA, Ltd. v. Vutek, Inc.***, 50 USPQ 2d 1372, 1374
(Fed. Cir. 1999)

Typically, if the word "means" appears in a claim element in
combination with a function, it is presumed to be a
means-plus-function element to which § 112, ¶ 6 applies.

26. ***Signtech USA, Ltd. v. Vutek, Inc.***, 50 USPQ 2d 1372, 1375
(Fed. Cir. 1999)

Although patentees are not necessarily limited to their preferred embodiment, . . . interpretation of a means-plus-func-

tion element requires this court to consult the structure disclosed in the specification, which often, as in this case, describes little more than the preferred embodiment.

27. ***Signtech USA, Ltd. v. Vutek, Inc.***, 50 USPQ 2d 1372, 1376 (Fed. Cir. 1999)

Thus, this decision, like many others emanating from this court, . . . emphasizes the importance of careful language choices in the specification and, particularly, in the claims. To avoid having its claims limited to exclude the embodiments disclaimed in the specification, the claim drafter for this patent might have chosen language to avoid application of 35 U.S.C. § 112, ¶ 6. Otherwise, assuming that no intervening statutory bars had arisen, Signtech could have filed a new application . . . without limitation in the specification or claims to the dual air sources. It did neither. Therefore, because of the statutory limitations governing the meaning of means-plus-function elements, courts must limit the scope of these claim elements to the corresponding structure disclosed in the specification and its equivalents. Signtech's arguments are therefore unavailing.

28. ***Rodime PLC v. Seagate Tech., Inc.***, 50 USPQ 2d 1429, 1434 (Fed. Cir. 1999)

The word "means" is "part of the classic template for functional claim elements." *Sage Prods. Inc. v. Devon Indus., Inc.*, 126 F.3d 1420, 1427, 44 USPQ 2d 1103, 1109 (Fed. Cir. 1997). Accordingly, in determining whether a claim element falls within § 112, ¶ 6, this court has presumed an applicant advisedly used the word "means" to invoke the statutory mandates for means-plus-function clauses. *See id.* Two specific rules, however, overcome this presumption. First, a claim element that uses the word "means" but recites no function corresponding to the means does not invoke § 112, ¶ 6. *See id.* at 1427. Second, even if the claim element specifies a function, if it also recites sufficient structure or material for performing that function, § 112, ¶ 6 does not apply. *See id.* at 1427–28 ("Where a claim recites a function, but then goes on to elaborate sufficient structure, material, or acts within the claim itself to perform entirely the recited function, the claim is not in means-plus-function format.").

29. ***Rodime PLC v. Seagate Tech., Inc.***, 50 USPQ 2d 1429, 1435 (Fed. Cir. 1999)

A claim need not claim every function of a working device. Rather, a claim may specify improvements in one function without claiming the entire machine with its many functions.

30. ***Rodime PLC v. Seagate Tech., Inc.***, 50 USPQ 2d 1429, 1436 (Fed. Cir. 1999)

In reaching the opposite conclusion, the special master seemed concerned that the claim did not recite every last detail of structure disclosed in the specification for performing the claimed moving function. This court's case law, however, does not require such an exhaustive recitation to avoid § 112, ¶ 6. Instead, the claim need only recite "sufficient" structure to perform entirely the claimed function. . . . Based on the structure disclosed in the specification for performing the moving function, these claims recite nearly all (if not all) of the structural components of the positioning mechanism. In any case, they clearly recite more than sufficient structure for moving the transducer from track to track.

31. ***Essilor Int'l v. Nidek Co., Ltd.***, Civ. App. No. 98-1558, slip op. at 8–9 (Fed. Cir. Oct. 29, 1999) (unpublished)

Patentees may express claim elements in "means-plus-function" format. . . . In a means-plus-function claim, the claim element is expressed as a means for performing a specified function and the claim is construed as covering the corresponding structure described in the specification and equivalents thereof. . . .

35 U.S.C. § 112, ¶ 2 requires that all claims, including means-plus-function claims, particularly point out and distinctly claim the subject matter which the applicant regards as his invention. For a means-plus-function claim to satisfy the section 112, ¶ 2 requirement, the specification must adequately describe the structure which performs the specified function. . . .

The specification does not have to describe the structure corresponding to a means-plus-function limitation in explicit detail. For example, in *In re Dossel*, 115 F.3d 942, 946–47, 42 USPQ 2d 1881, 1885 (Fed. Cir. 1997), we held that the specification adequately described the structure corresponding to the means for reconstructing data when it recited a device that receives digital data from memory and from a user. The fact that the specification did not recite the term "computer" nor quote computer code that may be used in the invention, did not render the means clause invalid under section 112, ¶ 2.

In our case, the patent discloses a "control unit" as the structure that performs the function of storing, comparing and selecting the bevel path. . . . The patent further states that the control unit is composed of a central storage and computation unit and that the construction of a control unit is within the capabilities of a person skilled in the art. . . . The district court found that it would have been clear to one of ordinary skill what structure must perform the function recited in the means-plus-function limitation. The district court found that the necessary elements of the control unit which would perform these functions were described in the patent and that the functions described in the specification could be accomplished using computer programs. We agree with the district court.

32. ***WMS Gaming Inc. v. International Game Tech.***, 51 USPQ 2d 1385, 1391 (Fed. Cir. 1999) (quoting ***In re Alappat***, 31 USPQ 2d 1545, 1558 (Fed. Cir. 1994) (en banc))

The structure of a microprocessor programmed to carry out an algorithm is limited by the disclosed algorithm. A general purpose computer, or microprocessor, programmed to carry out an algorithm creates "a new machine, because a general purpose computer in effect becomes a special purpose computer once it is programmed to perform particular functions pursuant to instructions from program software." . . . The instructions of the software program that carry out the algorithm electrically change the general purpose computer by creating electrical paths within the device. These electrical paths create a special purpose machine for carrying out the particular algorithm.

In a means-plus-function claim in which the disclosed structure is a computer, or microprocessor, programmed to carry out an algorithm, the disclosed structure is not the general purpose computer, but rather the special purpose computer programmed to perform the disclosed algorithm.

33. ***WMS Gaming Inc. v. International Game Tech.***, 51 USPQ 2d 1385, 1393 (Fed. Cir. 1999)

The two structures are not identical because the microprocessor disclosed in the Telnaes patent is programmed differently from the microprocessor disclosed in the Durham patent. Put another way, the two disclosed machines are different, i.e., not identical.

34. ***WMS Gaming Inc. v. International Game Tech.***, 51 USPQ 2d 1385, 1393 (Fed. Cir. 1999)

Because the structure recited in the Telnaes patent is limited by the disclosed algorithm, our analysis of structural equivalence necessarily discusses the disclosed algorithm, which includes functional-type elements.

35. ***Micro Chem., Inc. v. Great Plains Chem. Co.***, 52 USPQ 2d 1258, 1263–64 (Fed. Cir. 1999)

Application of § 112, ¶ 6 requires identification of the structure in the specification which performs the recited function. . . . Therefore, § 112, ¶ 6 requires both identification of the claimed function and identification of the structure in the written description necessary to perform that function. The statute does not permit limitation of a means-plus-function claim by adopting a function different from that explicitly recited in the claim. Nor does the statute permit incorporation of structure from the written description beyond that necessary to perform the claimed function. . . .

After identifying the function of the means-plus-function element, this court looks to the written description to identify the structure corresponding to that function. Identification of corresponding structure may embrace more than the preferred embodiment. A means-plus-function claim encompasses all structure in the specification corresponding to that element and equivalent structures. . . .

When multiple embodiments in the specification correspond to the claimed function, proper application of § 112, ¶ 6 generally reads the claim element to embrace each of those embodiments.

36. ***Micro Chem., Inc. v. Great Plains Chem. Co.***, 52 USPQ 2d 1258, 1264 (Fed. Cir. 1999)

[I]f the . . . method claim elements fall within § 112, ¶ 6, under that statute, this court looks to the specification for acts corresponding to the step-plus-function element which are necessary to perform the recited function. In this case, these corresponding acts include all acts described in the specification for dispensing microingredient quantities measured by weight. These acts include the cumulative weigh method of the preferred embodiment and the loss of weight method of the alternative embodiment, as well as the weigh dump method of the prior art. . . . In sum, the patent specification describes each of these methods as a way to accomplish the desired function of dispensing predetermined weights of microingredients without substantial intermixing prior to entry into the liquid.

37. ***Micro Chem., Inc. v. Great Plains Chem. Co.***, 52 USPQ 2d 1258, 1265 (Fed. Cir. 1999)

Claim treatment outside of the requirements of § 112, ¶ 6 generally gives the claims a broader scope. If the meaning of these claim elements is not limited to the specific acts described in the specification and their equivalents through operation of § 112, ¶ 6, then they will be given their ordinarily understood meanings in the art.

38. ***Nagle Indus., Inc. v. Ford Motor Co.***, Civ. App. 97-1449, slip op. at 9–10 (Fed. Cir. June 22, 1999) (unpublished)

The proper construction of a means-plus-function claim limitation requires interpretation of the limitation in light of the corresponding structure or material described in the written description, and equivalents thereof, to the extent that the written description provides such disclosure. . . . Structure disclosed in the written description is "corresponding" to the claimed means under § 112, ¶ 6 only if the structure is clearly linked by the written description or the prosecution history to the function recited in the claim.

39. ***Al-Site Corp. v. VSI Int'l, Inc.***, 50 USPQ 2d 1161, 1166 (Fed. Cir. 1999)

This court has delineated several rules for claim drafters to invoke the strictures of 35 U.S.C. § 112, ¶ 6. Specifically, if the word "means" appears in a claim element in combination with a function, it is presumed to be a means-plus-function element to which § 112, ¶ 6 applies. . . . Nevertheless, according to its express terms, § 112, ¶ 6 governs only claim elements that do not recite sufficient structural limitations. . . . Therefore, the presumption that § 112, ¶ 6 applies is overcome if the claim itself recites sufficient structure or material for performing the claimed function. . . .

Although use of the phrase "means for" (or "step for") is not the only way to invoke § 112, ¶ 6, that terminology typically invokes § 112, ¶ 6 while other formulations generally do not. . . . Therefore, when an element of a claim does not use the term "means," treatment as a means-plus-function claim element is generally not appropriate. . . . However, when it is apparent that the element invokes purely functional terms, without the additional recital of specific structure or material for performing that function, the claim element may be a means-plus-function element despite the lack of express means-plus-function language.

40. ***Watts v. XL Systems Inc.***, 56 USPQ 2d 1836, 1838 (Fed. Cir. 2000)

In *Personalized Media Communications, LLC v. Int'l Trade Comm'n*, 161 F.3d 696, 48 USPQ 2d 1880 (Fed. Cir. 1998), building upon a line of cases interpreting 35 U.S.C. § 112, paragraph 6, we stated that the failure to use the word "means" in a claim element created a rebuttable presumption that 35 U.S.C. § 112, paragraph 6 did not apply. See *Personalized Media*, 161 F.3d at 703–04, 48 USPQ 2d at 1886–87. We also reiterated that in determining whether a presumption is rebutted, "the focus remains on whether the claim . . . recites sufficiently definite structure." *Id.* at 704, 48 USPQ 2d at 1887. We noted, however, that the claim limitation need not "connote a precise physical structure." *Id.* at 705, 48 USPQ 2d at 1888. The following year, we further clarified that the presumption that § 112, paragraph 6 did not apply could be rebutted by showing that the claim element recited a function without reciting sufficient structure for performing that function. See *Rodime PLC v. Seagate Tech., Inc.*, 174 F.3d 1294, 1302, 50 USPQ 2d 1429, 1434 (Fed. Cir. 1999) (explaining the converse rules for rebutting a presumption that § 112, paragraph 6 does apply). As an aid in determining whether sufficient structure is in fact recited by a term used in a claim limitation, this court has inquired into whether the "term, as the name for structure, has a reasonably well understood meaning in the art." *Greenberg*, 91 F.3d at 1583, 39 USPQ 2d at 1786 (applying this test to the term "detent mechanism"). If § 112, paragraph 6 applies, then we follow the guidelines to claim construction specified in the statute: "such claim shall be construed to cover the corresponding structure, material, or acts described in the specification and equivalents thereof." 35 U.S.C. § 112, para. 6.

41. ***Eisenberg v. Alimed, Inc.***, Civ. App. No. 98-1317, slip op. at 5 (Fed. Cir. Aug. 8, 2000) (unpublished)

[W]hen multiple embodiments in the specification correspond to the claimed function, proper application of § 112, ¶ 6 generally reads the claim limitation to embrace each of those embodiments. See *Micro Chem., Inc. v. Great Plains Chem. Co., Inc.*, 194 F.3d 1250, 1258, 52 USPQ2d 1258, 1264 (Fed.Cir. 1999).

42. ***Clearstream Wastewater Systems, Inc. v. Hydro-Action, Inc.***, 54 USPQ 2d 1185, 1189 (Fed. Cir. 2000)

It is not disputed that both corresponding structures are adequately described in the written description. The only issue in dispute is whether, for purposes of claim construction, both structures should be considered corresponding structures for the disputed means-plus-function language. . . . There are certain situations in which a means-plus-function limitation in a combination claim will be construed to cover only new elements. Hydro-Action argued and the district court concluded that this was such a case in which claim limitations could not read on the prior art because the written description taught away from the prior art. . . . In Sofamor, the means-plus-function element was the only new element in the claim for a non-novel combination. Because the combination was not novel and none of the other elements of the claim were novel, it was proper for the claim to be construed such that the means-plus-function element covered only the novel corresponding structure in the written description.

In contrast, in the case at hand, the means-plus-function elements for the aerating system are not the only points of novelty. The new filtering system is also novel. In fact, all

the asserted claims contain an element covering the new filtering system. Essentially, when read in their entirety,
claims 1 and 4 cover a wastewater treatment plant that has
a new filtering system and that may or may not have the
new, flexible-hose system. Thus, it was error for the district
court to conclude that the means limitations for the aerating system could only cover new elements of the preferred
embodiment.

XIII.J.   *Examples When Claim Is/Is Not Interpreted Under Section 112, Sixth Paragraph*

1. **Serrano v. Tellular Corp.**, 42 USPQ 2d 1538, 1542 (Fed. Cir. 1997)

   We next address method claim 1 of the '997 patent. It includes a determining step rather than a determination
means, but it is not drafted in "step plus function" form.
That is because it does not recite a function. *See* 35 U.S.C.
§ 112, ¶ 6 (1994). Rather, it recites only the act of determining a last-dialed digit. Therefore, we must simply apply the
claim language to the accused devices free from the limiting
requirements of section 112, ¶ 6. It is clear from the specification that the determining step determines *when* a last
digit is dialed.

2. **O.I. Corp. v. Tekmar Co.**, 42 USPQ 2d 1777, 1780 (Fed. Cir. 1997)

   However, the court erroneously concluded that the word
"passage" recited in the claim is part of a means-plus-function clause and hence subject to the limitations of section
112, ¶ 6. . . . Although the passage may act upon the slug by
channeling it while it is being passed, it is not the means
that causes the passing. Rather, it is the place where the
function occurs, not the structure that accomplishes it.
Thus, although claim 17 is a means-plus-function claim subject to section 112, ¶ 6, it is not so in respect of the word "passage." . . . We will consider only whether the court ultimately
interpreted the meaning of the word "passage" correctly in
light of our conclusion that it is not a part of the recited
"means . . . for performing a specified function" for purposes
of section 112, ¶ 6, and is therefore itself not subject to the
construction called for by that statutory provision.

3. **Greenburg v. Ethicon Endo-Surgery, Inc.**, 39 USPQ 2d 1783, 1786 (Fed. Cir. 1996)

   First, the fact that a particular mechanism—here "detent
mechanism"—is defined in functional terms is not sufficient
to convert a claim element containing that term into a

"means for performing a specified function" within the meaning of section 112(6). Many devices take their names from the functions they perform. The examples are innumerable, such as "filter," "brake," "clamp," "screwdriver," or "lock." Indeed, several of the devices at issue in this case have names that describe their functions, such as "graspers," "cutters," and "suture applicators." . . . What is important is not simply that a "detent" or "detent mechanism" is defined in terms of what it does, but that the term, as the name for structure, has a reasonably well understood meaning in the art.

4. ***Cole v. Kimberly-Clark Corp.***, 41 USPQ 2d 1001, 1006 (Fed. Cir. 1996)

The district court correctly ruled that the claimed "perforation means . . . for tearing" is not a means-plus-function element under § 112, ¶ 6 . . . For example, the "perforation means . . . . for tearing" element of Cole's claim fails to satisfy the statute because it describes the structure supporting the tearing function (i.e., perforations). The claim describes not only the structure that supports the tearing function, but also its location (extending from the leg band to the waist band) and extent (extending through the outer impermeable layer). An element with such a detailed recitation of its structure, as opposed to its function, cannot meet the requirements of the statute. Here, the claim drafter's perfunctory addition of the word "means" did nothing to diminish the precise structural character of this element. It definitely did not somehow magically transform this element into a § 112, ¶ 6, "means-plus-function" element.

5. ***Lehman v. Dunham's Athleisure Corp.***, Civ. App. 96-1381, slip op. at 5 (Fed. Cir. Oct. 11, 1996) (unpublished)

Here, the limitations in issue recite structure—battery and lamp—and not functions. A battery and a lamp are not functions, and the addition of the word "means" does not convert the structure to a means or a step for performing a specific function. Consequently, the limitations fail the test of § 112, para. 6, and must be construed as ordinary limitations.

6. ***Ex parte Klumb***, 159 USPQ 694, 695 (Pat. Off. Bd. App. 1967)

The terms "plate" and "wing", if used in the normal sense, particularly when predicated on the instant specification and drawings, may well be proper structural definitions of elements of appellant's combination but the use thereof in the adjective or modifier sense as "plate means" or "wing means" departs from a structural definition of that element of the invention by reliance on a "structureless" term, "means" as the nounal element. Only where such structureless terms specify a function performed by the corresponding element of the invention does section 112 sanction the claiming of that which otherwise would be a self-contradiction of purporting to define a structure by the use of structureless terms.

Hence, we must turn to the instant claim to ascertain what, if any, functions are specified therein by the terms "plate means" and "wing means" thereof.

Although the [sixth] paragraph of section 112 suggests the use of a prepositional phrase as the modifier of the structureless term "means", we see no necessity for construing the statute to require a particular grammatic construction, so long as the modifier of that term specifies a function to be performed. Thus, expressions, such as "means for printing" or "printing means", would have the same connotations and both would be in conformity with the statute.

However, the terms "plate" and "wing", as modifiers of the structureless term "means", specify no function to be performed as is self-evident if one attempts to recast into the alternative grammatical form of "means for plating" or "means for winging", which of course are obviously not pertinent to the instant disclosure.

Thus, it is apparent that whatever functions are to be performed by the "plate" and "wing" means of the instant claim, they have not been specified in the claim, as is required by statute.

7. ***Ex parte Stanley***, 121 USPQ 621, 627–28 (Pat. Off. Bd. App. 1958)

We will not sustain this latter ground of rejection. The examiner apparently accepts as being proper a "means" coupled with a function. Under the particular circumstances of the present case the term "device" with respect to its significance and coverage is synonymous with the term "means", in these claims to the apparatus. Accordingly, the term "device" coupled with a function is a proper definition of structure and is therefore within the requirements of 35 USC 112, last paragraph. The addition of the words "jet driving" to the term "device" merely renders the latter term more definite and specific.

8. ***Fairchild Semiconductor Corp. v. Nintendo Co.***, 30 USPQ 2d 1657, 1660 (W.D. Wash.), ***aff'd***, 39 F.3d 1197 (Fed. Cir. 1994) (unpublished, table)

Claim language can be written as a "means plus function" element or a "structural" element. A means plus function element is written to describe what an element of the invention does. A structural element refers to what the element is. . . . A "locking means" is a way for a device to lock. Fairchild contends that "locking means" should be interpreted as a structural description that uses non-means language, yet the very language of the claim includes "means."

Fairchild further contends that not all limitations that contain the word "means" necessarily refer to function. *Quantum Corp. v. Mountain Computer*, 5 USPQ 2d 1103 (N.D. Cal. 1987) ("correction signal generator means" not a means element because corrector signal generator is a structure). While Fairchild correctly states a rule of claim construction, the case for which its proposition stands is distinguishable from this case on its facts. "Locking means" is unintelligible without referring to a function because the term "locking" is too broad a referent. In *Quantum Corp.*, in contrast, a "correction signal generator" refers to a structure that does not require a functional description. . . .

9. ***Fairchild Semiconductor Corp. v. Nintendo Co.***, 30 USPQ 2d 1657, 1659 (W.D. Wash.), ***aff'd***, 39 F.3d 1197 (Fed. Cir. 1994) (unpublished, table)

Fairchild maintains that because the locking means element and the connector means element contain some structural limitations, they are not subject to the infringement test set forth in 35 U.S.C. § 112(6). However, the Federal Circuit has expressly held that "[t]he recitation of some structure in a means plus function element does not preclude the applicability of Section 112(6)." *Laitram Corp. v. Rexnord, Inc.*, 939 F.2d 1533, 1536 [19 USPQ 2d 1367] (Fed. Cir. 1991). The inclusion of some descriptive structural terms does not remove the claim from the ambit of § 112(6). *Intellicall, Inc. v. Phonometrics, Inc.*, 952 F.2d 1384 [21 USPQ 2d 1383] (Fed. Cir. 1992) (*cost register* means including a digital display); *Texas Instruments Inc. v. U.S. Int'l Trade Comm'n*, 805 F.2d 1558 [231 USPQ 833] (Fed. Cir. 1986) ("display means", "memory means", and "input means including a keyboard"). The "locking means" and "connector means" elements of the '791 patent therefore are construed as means plus function elements for the purposes of claim interpretation.

10. ***Haney v. Timesavers, Inc.***, Civ. App. No. 94-1287, slip op. at 5–6 (Fed. Cir. Feb. 10, 1995) (unpublished)

[W]e do not view the double-drive-mechanism limitation of claim 20 as subject to § 112, paragraph 6. The clause "a double-drive mechanism interposed between and connecting the platen and frame" recites structure. This recitation of structure in concert with accompanying function—"where the double-drive mechanism imparts at least one translational orbital movement superimposed on another movement to the platen relative to the frame"—removes the claim from the purview of § 112, paragraph 6. . . . [C]laim 20 is limited to a double-drive mechanism which functions to impart the two described motions "to the platen relative to the frame," and is not limited to the structures described in the specification and equivalents thereof under Section 112, paragraph 6.

11. ***Ex parte Zimmerley***, 153 USPQ 367, 369 (Pat. Off. Bd. App. 1966)

Under the particular facts of this case, it is our opinion that this rejection is improper. 35 USC 112, [sixth] paragraph, sanctions functionally defined steps in claims drawn to a combination of steps. The decision of *In re Stack*, . . . cited by the examiner, was in 1937, which is prior to the effective date of 35 USC 112 (Jan. 1, 1953). The step of "raising the pH", in our opinion, is properly functional as this is a common industrial expedient, and almost always means merely adding any alkali that does not interfere with the process reactions.

12. ***In re Weiss***, 26 USPQ 2d 1885, 1887 (Fed. Cir. 1993) (unpublished)

The specification clearly indicates that the break-away means is an actual structural element which responds at a specific preselected level of force by causing the separation of the cleat from the sole of the shoe when that level of force is applied. The specification further defines that preselected level of force as that level of force at which the breaking away will prevent injury to the wearer during athletic exertion. Our interpretation does not improperly read limitations from the specification into the claim, because the limitation already exists in the claim and we resort to the specification only to interpret this limitation. To do otherwise would be to improperly expand the meaning of a claim term beyond that intended by the inventor as described in the disclosure.

13. ***Mas-Hamilton Group v. LaGard, Inc.***, 48 USPQ 2d 1010, 1015–16 (Fed. Cir. 1998)

La Gard asserts that the "lever moving element" should not be construed as claimed in means-plus-function format because it does not employ the catch phrase "means for." . . . Although such a presumption is helpful in beginning the claim construction analysis, it is not the end of the inquiry. In the instant case, even though the catch phrase is not used, the limitation's language does not provide any structure. The limitation is drafted as a function to be performed rather than definite structure or materials. . . . In the instant case, the claimed "lever moving element" is described in terms of its function not its mechanical structure. If we accepted La Gard's argument that we should not apply section 112, ¶ 6, a "moving element" could be any device that can cause the lever to move.

14. ***Mas-Hamilton Group v. LaGard, Inc.***, 48 USPQ 2d 1010, 1016 (Fed. Cir. 1998)

According to La Gard, the district court erred by considering the claim term "movable" to invoke section 112, ¶ 6. We agree with La Gard that the claim term "movable" alone does not cause the claim to be read in means-plus-function format. However, we note that the subsequent functional language requires two functions: (1) "for holding the lever out of engagement with the cam surface before entry of a combination," and (2) "for releasing the lever after entry of the combination." Such language is precisely what was intended by the statutory phrase in section 112, ¶ 6 requiring that means-plus-function limitations provide "a specified function." 35 U.S.C. § 112, ¶ 6.

15. ***Ranpak Corp. v. Storopack, Inc.***, Civ. App. 98-1009, slip op. at 4–5 (Fed. Cir. July 15, 1998) (unpublished)

Initially, Ranpak argues the term "settable control module" unlike the term "settable control means" is not a means-plus-function term and that the district court erred in treating them alike. Neither term recites definite structure to perform its particular function. *See, e.g., Cole v. Kimberly-Clark Corp.*, 102 F.3d 524, 531, 41 USPQ 2d 1001, 1006 (Fed. Cir. 1996) ("To invoke [35 U.S.C. section 112 paragraph 6], the alleged means-plus-function claim element must not recite a definite structure which performs the described function."). Clearly, "settable control means" invokes section 112 paragraph 6 by not reciting a definite structure to perform a particular function; namely "selectively programming said motor for actuation thereof for a selected one period of time of a predetermined plurality of periods of time." '635 patent, col. 8, ll. 39–41. Likewise, the use of the term "settable control module" invokes section 112 paragraph 6, because it merely sets forth the same black box without recitation of structure for providing the same specified function. *See* '635 patent, col. 10, ll. 7–10 (omitting word "predetermined" from the function of claim 1's "settable control means"). Therefore, both "settable control means" and "settable control module" require the same means-plus-function analysis.

16. ***Personalized Media Communications, L.L.C. v. International Trade Comm'n***, 48 USPQ 2d 1880, 1886 (Fed. Cir. 1998)

We have had several recent opportunities to assess whether certain claim language has invoked § 112, ¶ 6. In

Greenberg v. Ethicon Endo-Surgery, Inc., 91 F.3d 1580, 39 USPQ 2d 1783 (Fed. Cir. 1996), we were presented with the claim language "detent mechanism defining conjoint rotation of said shafts." In deciding that § 112, ¶ 6 was not invoked, we stated

> [T]he fact that a particular mechanism—here "detent mechanism"—is defined in functional terms is not sufficient to convert a claim element containing that term into a "means for performing a specified function" within the meaning of [§ 112, ¶ 6]. Many devices take their names from the functions they perform. The examples are innumerable, such as "filter," "brake," "clamp," "screwdriver," or "lock." . . . .

> "Detent" (or its equivalent "detent mechanism") is just such a term. Dictionary definitions make clear that the noun "detent" denotes a type of device with a generally understood meaning in the mechanical arts, even though the definitions are expressed in functional terms. It is true that "detent" does not call to mind a single well-defined structure, but the same could be said of other commonplace structural terms such as "clamp" or "container." What is important is not simply that a "detent" or "detent mechanism" is defined in terms of what it does, but that the term, as the name for structure, has a reasonably well understood meaning in the art.

Greenberg , 91 F.3d at 1583, 39 USPQ2d at 1786 (citations omitted).

17. ***Personalized Media Communications, L.L.C. v. International Trade Comm'n***, 48 USPQ 2d 1880, 1887–88 (Fed. Cir. 1998)

[W]e agree with PMC that the Commission erred in construing the term "digital detector" as a means-plus-function limitation. The "digital detector" limitation does not use the word "means," and therefore this limitation is presumed not to invoke § 112, ¶ 6. Neither intrinsic nor extrinsic evidence rebuts this presumption because the term "detector" is a sufficient recitation of structure. "Detector" is not a generic structural term such as "means," "element," or "device"; nor is it a coined term lacking a clear meaning, such as "widget" or "ram-a-fram." Instead, as noted by the ALJ by reference to dictionary definitions, "detector" had a well-known meaning to those of skill in the electrical arts connotative of structure, including a rectifier or demodulator. . . . [A]n adjectival qualification ("digital") placed upon otherwise sufficiently definite structure ("detector") does not make the sufficiency of that structure any less sufficient for purposes of § 112, ¶ 6.

Instead, it further narrows the scope of those structures covered by the claim and makes the term more definite. The use of the word "digital" in conjunction with the word "detector" merely places an additional functional constraint (extraction of digital information) on a structure (detector) otherwise adequately defined.

18. ***Personalized Media Communications, L.L.C. v. International Trade Comm'n***, 48 USPQ 2d 1880, 1887 n.9 (Fed. Cir. 1998)

Cases holding Section 112, paragraph six applies when the claim language uses the phrase "means for", include:

> *Unidynamics Corp. v. Automatic Prods. Int'l, Ltd.*, 157 F.3d 1311, 1319, 48 USPQ 2d 1099, 1104 (Fed. Cir. 1998) (holding that the claim language "spring means tending to keep the door closed" invokes § 112, ¶ 6: "the recitation of 'spring,' which is structural language, [does not take] the limitation out of the ambit of the construction dictate of § 112, ¶ 6."); *Serrano v. Tellular Corp.*, 111 F.3d 1578, 1582, 42 USPQ 2d 1538, 1541 (Fed. Cir. 1997) (holding that the claim language "determination means . . . for determining" invokes § 112, ¶ 6); *Laitram Corp. v. Rexnord, Inc.*, 939 F.2d 1533, 1536, 19 USPQ 2d 1367, 1369 (Fed. Cir. 1991) (holding that the claim language "means for joining said pluralities [of link ends] to one another so that the axes of [certain holes are arranged in certain configurations]" invokes § 112, ¶ 6: "The recitation of some structure in a means-plus-function element does not preclude the applicability of [§ 112, ¶ 6 when it] merely serves to further specify the function of the means. The recited structure tells only what the means-for-joining does, not what it is structurally.").

19. ***Personalized Media Communications, L.L.C. v. International Trade Comm'n***, 48 USPQ 2d 1880, 1887 n.10 (Fed. Cir. 1998)

Cases holding Section 112, paragraph six applies even when the phrase "means for" was not recited, include:

> *Mas-Hamilton*, 156 F.3d at 1214, 48 USPQ 2d at 1017 (holding that the claim language "lever moving element for moving the lever" invokes § 112, ¶ 6: "even though the catch phrase ['means for'] is not used, the limitation's language does not provide any structure. The limitation is drafted as a function to be performed rather than definite structure or materials."); *id.* at 1215, 48 USPQ 2d at 1017 (holding that the claim language "a movable link member for . . . " invokes § 112, ¶ 6).

20. ***Personalized Media Communications, L.L.C. v. International Trade Comm'n***, 48 USPQ 2d 1880, 1887 n.10 (Fed. Cir. 1998)

Cases holding Section 112, paragraph six did not apply even when the phrase "means for" was recited, include:

> *York*, 99 F.3d at 1573–75, 40 USPQ 2d at 1623–24 (holding that the claim language "means formed on the . . . sidewall portions including a plurality of spaced apart . . . members protruding from the . . . sidewall portions and forming load lock . . ." did not invoke § 112, ¶ 6: "The claim language does not link the term means to a function . . . Instead, the claim recites structure. . . . Without a 'means' sufficiently connected to a recited function, the presumption in use of the word 'means' does not operate."); *Cole v. Kimberly-Clark Corp.*, 102 F.3d at 524, 531, 41 USPQ 2d 1001, 1006–07 (Fed. Cir. 1996) (holding that the claim language "perforation means extending from the leg band means to the waist band means through the outer impermeable layer means" did not invoke § 112, ¶ 6: this language "describes the structure supporting the tearing function (i.e., perforations). The claim describes not only the structure that supports the tearing function, but also its location (extending from the leg band to the waist band). An element with such a detailed recitation of structure, as opposed to its function, cannot meet the requirements of [§ 112, ¶ 6].").

21. ***Storz Instrument Co. v. Alcon Labs., Inc.***, Civ. App. 97-1149, slip op. at 6 (Fed. Cir. Jan. 26, 1998) (unpublished)

The district judge correctly determined that "procedure control means [for defining and providing a plurality of predetermined and selectable ophthalmic surgical procedures]" is a means-plus-function limitation in accordance with 35 U.S.C. § 112, ¶ 6 (1994), because it sets forth a means for performing a specific function, defining and providing a plurality of predetermined and selectable ophthalmic surgical procedures, without reciting any specific structure for performing that function.

22. ***Trimedyne, Inc. v. Surgical Laser Techs., Inc.***, Civ. App. 96-1538, slip op. at 18 (Fed. Cir. July 10, 1998) (unpublished)

The district judge correctly determined that "beam-splitting means [, disposed entirely within said cavity, for receiving laser energy transmitted through said conduit and for directed . . .]" in claim 1 is a means-plus-function limitation in accordance with 35 U.S.C. § 112, ¶ 6, because it sets forth a means for performing a specific function without reciting any specific structure for performing that function.

23. ***Signtech USA, Ltd. v. Vutek, Inc.***, 50 USPQ 2d 1372, 1374–75 (Fed. Cir. 1999)

In this case, the claim element "ink delivery means" uses the term "means" in association with a function, namely "ink delivery." Although the phrase "means for" is not used, the phrase "ink delivery means" is equivalent to the phrase "means for ink delivery," because "ink delivery" is purely functional language. Furthermore, the claim does not recite disqualifying structure which would prevent application of § 112, ¶ 6.

24. ***Nagle Indus., Inc. v. Ford Motor Co.***, Civ. App. 97-1449, slip op. at 9 (Fed. Cir. June 22, 1999) (unpublished) (quoting ***Rodime PLC v. Seagate Tech., Inc.***, 50 USPQ 2d 1429, 1436 (Fed. Cir. 1999))

The exact wording of the claim limitation is "slack adjustment means attached to said ends of said strand means for adjusting slack in said strand means."

The claim phrase "slack adjustment means" is defined by the functional language "for adjusting slack in said strand means." The only structural recitation of attaching the slack adjustment means to the end of the strand means involves the placement of the slack adjustment means within the claimed cable assembly. This recitation of structure does not specify what the slack adjustment means is structurally. . . . Therefore, the claim does not recite "sufficient structure to perform entirely the claimed function." . . . We agree with the district court that the claim limitation "slack adjusting means" is written in means-plus-function language because it recites a means for performing a specified function without the recital of specific structure to carry out that function.

25. ***Al-Site Corp. v. VSI Int'l, Inc.***, 50 USPQ 2d 1161, 1166–67 (Fed. Cir. 1999)

Under this established analytical framework, the "eyeglass hanger member" elements in the claims . . . do not invoke § 112, ¶ 6. In the first place, these elements are not in traditional means-plus-function format. The word "means" does not appear within these elements. Moreover, although these claim elements include a function, namely, "mounting a pair of eyeglasses," the claims themselves contain sufficient structural limitations for performing those functions. As noted above, claim 1 . . . describes the eyeglass hanger member as "made from flat sheet material" with an "open-

ing means formed . . . below [its] upper edge." This structure
removes this claim from the purview of § 112, ¶ 6.

XIII.K. *Examples of Equivalents/Non-Equivalents Under Section 112, Sixth Paragraph and Doctrine of Equivalents*

1. ***Alpex Computer Corp. v. Nintendo Co. Ltd.***, 40 USPQ 2d 1667, 1674 (Fed. Cir. 1996), ***petition for cert. filed*** (Apr. 15, 1997)

   In this case, using shift registers, instead of RAM, to process data for video display, is not merely an unimportant and insubstantial change.

2. ***Microsoft Corp. v. IQ Techs., Inc.***, 28 USPQ 2d 1477, 1479 (Fed. Cir. 1993)

   The '698 patent claims "connector means for electrical connection." It is impermissible to define "connector means" solely by the claimed function—*viz.*, any structure for electrical connection. The only structure actually described in the patent corresponding to connector means is male-female type plus. We therefore reject IQ Technologies' overbroad definition of connector means, and conclude that, as described in the specification and claimed, "connector means" literally are male-female type plugs and equivalents thereof for electrical connection.

3. ***Total Containment, Inc. v. Environ Prods., Inc.***, Civ. App. 96-1138, slip op. at 4–5 (Fed. Cir. Jan. 17, 1997) (unpublished)

   Like the district court, we reject TCI's contention that a removable cover is an equivalent structure to the access lids disclosed in the specification of the '509 patent. Of course, a removable cover that has an access lid is, in a sense, interchangeable with a removable cover that lacks an access lid, in that either design permits access to and observation of the inside of the sump. But the cover with an access lid is capable of the additional function of permitting such access without the need to remove the cover altogether, a function that obviously cannot be performed by a removable cover that lacks an access lid.

4. ***View Eng'g, Inc. v. Robotic Vision Sys.***, Civ. App. 97-1001, slip op. at 3–4 (Fed. Cir. July 3, 1997) (unpublished)

   The district court further concluded that View's method is not equivalent to RVSI's claimed method, and we agree. Under the claimed method, a disagreement between the two values computed for the target point results in rejection of both values. Under View's method, that does not happen. Instead, a disagreement between the two values results in one of the two being retained and passed along to the second stage. In the second stage, all values that were passed along from the first stage are tested for consistency with the values obtained for neighboring points, and outlier values are rejected. The two methods are similar to the extent that both perform two computations for each target point and then filter out suspect data. Each method, however, follows a distinctly different path to achieve that general goal.

5. ***PSC Inc. v. Accu-Sort Sys., Inc.***, Civ. App. 96-1092, slip op. at 7 (Fed. Cir. Jan. 17, 1997) (unpublished)

The district court also found that the mirrors used in Accu-Sort's Model 20 and 22 devices are the equivalent of the beamsplitters described in the '750 patent. We conclude that this finding of fact is not clearly erroneous.

6. ***Monroe Eng.g Prods., Inc. v. J. W. Winco, Inc.***, Civ. App. 97-1134, slip op. at 5–6 (Fed. Cir. Aug. 13, 1997) (unpublished)

A reasonable juror could certainly conclude that an octagon with a circular hole in the center is substantially ring-like. An octagon will roll (although not smoothly), and the outer periphery follows the general contours of a circle (that is, it is continuously convex). Although these may not establish annularity in all cases, they certainly are enough to support this jury verdict under the substantial evidence standard. Likewise, a reasonable juror could certainly conclude that the arrangement of the anchoring projections here is substantially uniform. There are two groups of three anchoring projections arranged symmetrically around the octagonal perimeter of the coupling element with one projection on each of three adjacent sides, then a blank side, then again one per side for three consecutive sides and a final blank side. It was certainly reasonable for the jury to conclude that "no significant portion of the outer periphery [was] lacking or treated differently" in the arrangement of the anchoring projections, despite the absence of an anchoring projection on two opposing sides of the octagon. These two sides each only constitute one-eighth of the periphery. It was not unreasonable for the jury to conclude that these projection-less sides were not "significant portion[s] of the outer periphery.

7. ***Monroe Eng'g Prods., Inc. v. J. W. Winco, Inc.***, Civ. App. 97-1134, slip op. at 9 (Fed. Cir. Aug. 13, 1997) (unpublished)

Examining the arrangement of the projections on the trapezoidal coupler, we conclude that there is not substantial evidence to support the jury's finding that they are substantially uniformly arranged. There are four projections grouped rather tightly at the top of the coupler, with two more, somewhat more widely spaced pairs of projections in each of the two lower quadrants. There are three substantial areas completely lacking projections. We therefore conclude that the trapezoidal coupler is lacking the element of uniformly arranged projections, and we reverse the jury's finding that the trapezoidal coupler equivalently infringes the '614 patent.

8. ***Atlanta Motoring Accessories, Inc. v. Saratoga Techs.,*** 31 USPQ 2d 1929, 1932 (Fed. Cir. 1994)

We find ourselves in disagreement with the trial court's conclusions respecting the separable legs of the two devices and their connection to the vertical support member. While they serve, of course, to perform the same function of supporting the vertical member when separated and the *function* of being foldable to reduce the floor space occupied by the rack when not in use, that is not enough, as we have already pointed out, and as the trial court seems to have appreciated. Our point of disagreement is that we find they perform these functions in very *different ways* because they are differently constructed, as mere perusal of the drawings shows. . . . They are not shaped, supported, moved, or positioned as are the horizontal frame members of the patent and do not meet the "same way" requirement of the Graver tripartite test. The doctrine of equivalents is therefore not to be applied because they are not equivalents even if they do perform the same function.

9. ***Conopco, Inc. v. May Dep't Stores Co.,*** 32 USPQ 2d 1225, 1228 (Fed. Cir. 1994), ***cert. denied***, 514 U.S. 1078 (1995)

The doctrine of equivalents cannot be used to erase "meaningful structural and functional limitations of the claim on which the public is entitled to rely in avoiding infringement." *Pennwalt Corp. v. Durand-Wayland, Inc.*, 833 F.2d 931, 935, 4 USPQ 2d 1737, 1739 (Fed. Cir. 1987) (*en banc*), *cert. denied*, 485 U.S. 1009 (1988) (quoting *Perkin-Elmer Corp. v. Westinghouse Elec. Corp.*, 822 F.2d 1528, 1532, 3 USPQ 2d 1321, 1324 (Fed. Cir. 1987)); *see also Graver Tank*, 339 U.S. at 610 (doctrine of equivalents inapplicable in the case of a substantial change between limitation recited in claim and corresponding element in accused product). That would be the effect of concluding that the 162.9:1 formulation infringes under the doctrine of equivalents. As noted, the "about 40:1" limitation is a meaningful limitation in the claim. A conclusion that the 162.9:1 formulation infringes under the doctrine of equivalents would eviscerate the plain meaning of that limitation.

10. ***Valley Recreation Prods., Inc. v. Arachnid, Inc.***, 35 USPQ 2d 1218, 1221 (Fed. Cir. 1994) (unpublished)

The '461 patent requires human computation and entry of scores in all of its disclosed embodiments. The Arachnid games require no human computation or entry, but automatically score the games based on the dart landings. Arachnid's game is far more than a mere insubstantial change from the claimed invention. The score entering structure in the Arachnid device works in a substantially different way from the score entry means recited in claim 1, as properly constructed in light of the '461 patent specification. . . . Therefore, Arachnid did not infringe under the doctrine of equivalents either.

11. ***In re Ruff***, 118 USPQ 340, 347–48 (C.C.P.A. 1958)

That two things are actually equivalents, in the sense that they will both perform the same function, is not enough to bring into play the rule that when one of them is in the prior art the use of the other is obvious and cannot give rise to patentable invention. One need not think very hard to appreciate that the vast majority of patentable inventions perform old functions. In the bearing art, for example, we have progressed through wood blocks, bronze bushings, ball bearings, roller bearings, tapered roller bearings, needle bearings and sintered powdered metal impregnated with lubricant, to name a few. Today they are art-recognized equivalents. But if, in the course of this progress, ball and roll bearings had both been invented by one person and disclosed in one application, and the art had never heard of roller bearings before, on what theory would a patent be denied on the latter when it turned out that another was the first to invent the ball bearing? That the inventor said they would perform the same function? This is not an imaginary problem for patent applicants more often than not invent and disclose and attempt to claim more than turns out to be novel when the art is searched. They should not be penalized merely because of their own industry and the fullness of their disclosures. So far as we have been able to find, this court has never made an intimation to the contrary. . . . To sum it all up, actual equivalence is not enough to justify refusal of a patent on one member of a group when another member is in the prior art. The equivalence must be disclosed in the prior art or be obvious within the terms of Section 103.

12. ***Mas-Hamilton Group v. LaGard, Inc.***, 48 USPQ 2d 1010, 1015–16 (Fed. Cir. 1998)

The accused X-07 lock does not use a solenoid to provide power to move the lever. It uses, instead, a stepper motor. A stepper motor is an electric motor that rotates in short and essentially uniform angular movements rather than continuously. See *McGraw-Hill*, ante, at 1918. As the district court aptly pointed out in its section 112, ¶ 6 analysis, the solenoid is continuously operated and hence requires considerable power. *Mas-Hamilton*, slip op. at 59. "In contrast, the stepper motor used in the X-07 lock is actuated by a short electrical pulse, remains in its second state without application of power, [and] is returned manually to its original state." Id. In addition, the stepper motor translates its power into rotational motion, whereas the claimed solenoid uses linear motion. Hence, we hold that the district court did not clearly err in determining that the stepper motor of the accused X-07 lock is not a structural equivalent under section 112 to the claimed solenoid. The "lever operating means" limitation, therefore, is not literally met by the accused device which substitutes a stepper motor; and hence, the accused X-07 lock does not literally infringe claim 1.

13. ***Mas-Hamilton Group v. LaGard, Inc.***, 48 USPQ 2d 1010, 1015 (Fed. Cir. 1998)

Although the solenoid and the stepper motor both function to provide power to other components in the lock and hence the lever, as discussed with respect to literal infringement under section 112, ¶ 6, the solenoid draws continuous power and translates its power into linear motion. The stepper motor, however, draws intermittent power and translates its power into rotational motion. The solenoid inside the solenoid housing automatically returns to its original position whereas the stepper motor of the accused device must be manually returned to its original state. We affirm, therefore, the district court's determination of no equivalent infringement, for the district court did not clearly err in holding that the solenoid and the stepper motor provide power to the lever to operate the lock in substantially different ways.

14. ***Tronzo v. Biomet, Inc.***, 47 USPQ 2d 1829, 1834 (Fed. Cir. 1998)

Biomet argues that infringement of claims 2 and 10 under the doctrine of equivalents by a hemispherical cup would vitiate the limitation requiring that the cup have a "generally conical outer surface." Tronzo responds that substantial evidence supports the jury's conclusion that a hemispherical shape is equivalent to a generally conical shape.

We are convinced that the evidence offered did not adequately establish legal equivalency of the hemispherical shape.

15. ***Laitram Corp. v. Morehouse Indus., Inc.***, 46 USPQ 2d 1609, 1616 (Fed. Cir. 1998)

Laitram cannot successfully argue that the single bar of the "All-In-One" module is equivalent to the "sprocket recess" limitation. Using a single bar rather than opposing trans-verse elements creates a module that produces a different result, *i.e.*, a module capable of moving in only one direction rather than two. No reasonable fact finder could conclude that such a difference is an insubstantial difference.

16. ***Ethicon Endo-Surgery Inc. v. United States Surgical Corp.***, 47 USPQ 2d 1272, 1277–78 (Fed. Cir. 1998)

In *Dolly*, . . . this court noted that it had previously con-strued the claim limitation "a stable rigid frame . . . which along with said seat panel and said back" as requiring "that the stable rigid frame must be formed independently of the seat and back panels." *Dolly*, 16 F.3d at 397, 29 USPQ 2d at 1768. . . . The court reasoned that "[a] stable rigid frame as-sembled from the seat and back panels is not the equivalent of a separate stable rigid frame . . . exclusive of seat and back panels." *Id.* at 400. There was no question that the ac-cused device's seat and back panels were fully attached to the frame; the frame clearly and unambiguously included seat and back panels. Thus, given the marked differences between the allegedly infringing device and the claim limi-tation, no reasonable fact finder could have found equiva-lence.

17. ***Ethicon Endo-Surgery Inc. v. United States Surgical Corp.***, 47 USPQ 2d 1272, 1278 (Fed. Cir. 1998)

[I]n *Weiner*, . . . this court determined that there was no in-fringement by equivalents as a matter of law. We first con-strued the claim term "columns" to mean those columns lo-cated within the "data matrix," also known as a "memory array." *Weiner*, 102 F.3d at 540, 41 USPQ 2d at 1029. The patentee argued that the allegedly infringing "VRAM" had columns equivalent to those of the asserted claims, even though the VRAM's columns were located in a data register, not in a memory array. *See id.* at 541, 41 USPQ 2d at 1029. Because the VRAM "disconnects the gates and latches to electronically isolate the data register from the memory array" at the relevant time, *id.* at 537, 41 USPQ 2d at 1025, we concluded that the difference between the claim limita-tion and the VRAM was "not insubstantial." *Id.* at 541, 41 USPQ 2d at 1029. Given the clear demarcation and physical separation between the memory array and the data register in the VRAM, no reasonable fact finder could have found in-fringement by equivalents.

18. ***Ethicon Endo-Surgery Inc. v. United States Surgical Corp.***, 47 USPQ 2d 1272, 1278 (Fed. Cir. 1998)

In *Sage*, . . . this court affirmed a grant of summary judg-ment of non-infringement by equivalents. Specifically, regarding the "top of the container" limitation, we stated that "the district court properly rejected all four of Sage's theories of infringement by equivalents. . . . Sage's first three theories place the location of the 'elongated slot' in this accused device far enough within the container body that, as a matter of law, no reasonable juror could find that it is located at substantially the 'top of the container.'" *Sage*, 126 F.3d at 1424, 44 USPQ 2d at 1106.

19. ***Ethicon Endo-Surgery Inc. v. United States Surgical Corp.***, 47 USPQ 2d 1272, 1278 (Fed. Cir. 1998)

[T]he district court properly granted summary judgment with respect to claim 6. The district court observed that the "connected to said longitudinal slots" limitation "ties the lockout to a specific place." *Ethicon III, slip op.* at 12. The court then rejected Ethicon's theory of infringement by equivalents because USSC's lockout "is located at the distal end of the [DLU] nowhere near the longitudinal slots which are located in the staple cartridge at the front end of the stapler." We agree with this reasoning; it is consistent with our case law. . . . Because the rear of the stapler is opposite the longitudinal slots, no reasonable jury could have found that the USSC lockout was substantially "connected to said longitudinal slots."

20. ***Multiform Desiccants, Inc. v. Medzam, Ltd.***, 45 USPQ 2d 1429, 1435 (Fed. Cir. 1998)

Applying *Graver Tank* and *Warner-Jenkinson*, we review whether the Medzam porous envelope performs substantially the same function as that of the dissolving envelope of the '266 patent and, if so, whether it is performed in substantially the same way to achieve substantially the same result. . . .

The district court found that the Medzam envelope performs the function of releasing its contents in a substantially different way than does the envelope of the '266 patent, in that the Medzam envelope is not soluble in and does not degrade in the liquid. Although Multiform argues that the Medzam packet functions in a way that is "consistent" with the '266 invention, for the Medzam porous envelope releases its contents upon contact with liquid, the district court found a porous envelope that bursts with inner pressure to be substantially different from a degradable envelope that dissolves. This finding has not been shown to be clearly erroneous.

Multiform argues that the interchangeability of the envelopes weighs heavily on the side of equivalency. . . . The modes of dissolving and bursting are not clearly interchangeable, and we do not discern clear error in the district court's finding that they were not interchangeable.

21. ***Technical Chems. & Prods., Inc. v. Home Diagnostics, Inc.***, Civ. App. 97-1068, 97-1075, slip op. at 18 (Fed. Cir. Apr. 9, 1998) (unpublished)

   We conclude that the Ultra+ Blood Glucose Color Chart, when coupled with HDI's Ultra+ test strips, does not infringe claim 1 of the '580 patent, either literally or under the doctrine of equivalents, because it does not satisfy the means-for-positioning claim limitation. See *Strattec Sec. Corp.*, 126 F.3d at 1418, 44 USPQ 2d at 1036 (literal infringement requires that the accused device possess every limitation of the claim); *Warner-Jenkinson*, 117 S. Ct. at 1049, 41 USPQ 2d at 1871 (the doctrine of equivalents may not be used to eliminate a claim element in its entirety). The human action of placing the Ultra+ test strip behind the Ultra+ color chart is not identical to the corresponding folder or bottle label structures described in the specification of the '580 patent, nor is it equivalent structure. The district court's conclusion that "holding the Ultra+ test strip behind the Ultra+ Blood Glucose Color chart constitutes 'the means for positioning said test strip relative to the aperture of each of said color fields so as to mask from view the inert support'" was clearly erroneous.

22. ***Fromson v. Anitec Printing Plates, Inc.***, 45 USPQ 2d 1269, 1275 (Fed. Cir. 1997), ***cert. denied***, 525 U.S. 817 (1998)

   The court considered all of the evidence concerning the patented and the accused oxide coatings, and determined that the Anitec oxide formed in the phosphoric cell did not have the same properties as the Fromson oxide formed in the sulfuric cell, and did not serve the same purpose and solve the same problem. The court found that the primary function of the phosphoric cell in Anitec's process was to clean and condition the aluminum, not to provide an anodized layer to protect the web from surges or burning at high current densities. The court found that the thin barrier oxide coating initially formed on the Anitec web did not provide such protection, unlike Fromson's thicker porous coating. Thus the court found that there was not equivalency between the initial Anitec oxide and the "anodized coating" required by the '754 claims, in that the functions were not substantially the same. This finding has not been shown to be clearly erroneous.

23. ***Chiuminatta Concrete Concepts, Inc. v. Cardinal Indus., Inc.***, 46 USPQ 2d 1752, 1757 (Fed. Cir. 1998)

   The fundamental flaw in Chiuminatta's argument is that "flattened planes" are not structure. The undisputed struc-

ture that produces the concededly identical function of supporting the concrete consists of soft round wheels that are
rotatably mounted onto the saw. The assertedly equivalent
structures are wheels, and the differences between the
wheels and the skid plate are not insubstantial. The former
support the surface of the concrete by rolling over the concrete while the latter skids. The former are soft, compressible, and round; the latter is hard and predominantly flat
(albeit with rounded edges to prevent gouging of the concrete). Additionally, the wheels rotate as opposed to skid as
the saw moves across the concrete and thus have a different
impact on the concrete. Since the wheels and the skid plate
are substantially different from each other, they cannot be
equivalent, and no reasonable jury could so find.

24. ***Chiuminatta Concrete Concepts, Inc. v. Cardinal
    Indus., Inc.***, 46 USPQ 2d 1752, 1757 (Fed. Cir. 1998)

   Chiuminatta also argues that the wheels are equivalent to
the skid plate because they are interchangeable; the alleged
infringer's saw may be outfitted with a skid plate and the
patentee's saw may be outfitted with the accused wheels.
This argument is not persuasive. Almost by definition, two
structures that perform the same function may be substituted for one another. The question of known interchangeability is not whether both structures serve the same function, but whether it was known that one structure was an
equivalent of another. Moreover, a finding of known interchangeability, while an important factor in determining
equivalence, is certainly not dispositive.

25. ***Chiuminatta Concrete Concepts, Inc. v. Cardinal
    Indus., Inc.***, 46 USPQ 2d 1752, 1758 (Fed. Cir. 1998)

   In this case there can also be no doctrine of equivalents infringement because, as we have explained, the structure in
the accused device, the wheels, operates in a substantially
different way compared with the structure of the claimed device, the skid plate. The former support the surface of the
concrete by rolling over the concrete while the latter skids.
The former are soft, compressible, and round; the latter is
hard and predominantly flat (albeit with rounded edges to
prevent gouging of the concrete). Additionally, the wheels rotate as opposed to skid as the saw moves across the concrete
and thus have a different impact on the concrete. The wheels
flatten slightly, applying more localized pressure against the
concrete than that produced by a hard flat skid plate. Accordingly, for this additional reason, it cannot be an equivalent under the doctrine of equivalents and the district court
is directed to enter summary judgment of non-infringement.

26. ***Digital Biometrics, Inc. v. Identix, Inc.***, 47 USPQ 2d 1418, 1429 (Fed. Cir. 1998)

The TP-600 is too different from the patented invention to support a verdict of infringement under the doctrine of equivalents; no reasonable jury could find otherwise. In the TP-600, each digital data value produced by the A/D converter is temporarily held in a register while that value is processed. These values are not accumulated and then stored in memory, as in the claimed invention. The data value produced by the A/D converter is not filtered to eliminate the blue-sky data from the non-blue-sky data, as in the claimed invention. The prosecution history, as discussed above, confirms the significance of the slice data to the invention. DBI distinguished the Ruell reference, inter alia, on the ground that "Ruell does not teach a system which identifies active portions of the image." The A/D converter generates only a single value; therefore, it does not and can not differentiate between individual values, as in the claimed invention. In light of these significant differences, no reasonable jury could find that the TP-600 infringes either claim 1 or 16 under the doctrine of equivalents.

27. ***Bailey v. Dunkin Donuts, Inc.***, 45 USPQ 2d 1683, 1687 (Fed. Cir. 1998) (unpublished)

We agree with the magistrate judge's claim construction ("essentially vertical" means "vertical or a few degrees from vertical") and therefore uphold his infringement decision with respect to this limitation. Giving the claim language its ordinary meaning, walls deviating 22 and 28 degrees from vertical would not be "essentially vertical."

28. ***In re Bernhart***, 163 USPQ 611, 615 (C.C.P.A. 1969)

The specification here mentions only mechanical drafting machines. The claims therefore cover, under section 112, only such mechanical drafting machines and their equivalents. We know of no authority for holding that a human being, such as a draftsman, could ever be the equivalent of a machine disclosed in a patent application, and we are not prepared to so hold in this case.

29. ***Moore U.S.A. Inc. v. Standard Register Co.***, 56 USPQ 2d 1225, 1235–36 (Fed. Cir. 2000), ***cert. filed***, (Feb 26, 2001) (No. 00-1346)

In this case, we hold that the applicant's use of the term "majority" is not entitled to a scope of equivalents covering a minority for at least two reasons. First, to allow what is undisputedly a minority (i.e., 47.8%) to be equivalent to a majority would vitiate the requirement that the "first and second longitudinal strips of adhesive . . . extend the majority of the lengths of said longitudinal marginal portions." '464 patent, col. 10, ll. 56–60. If a minority could be equivalent to a majority, this limitation would hardly be necessary, since the immediately preceding requirement of a "first and second longitudinal strips of adhesive disposed in said first and second longitudinal marginal portions, respectively, of said first face" would suffice. Second, it would defy logic to conclude that a minority—the very antithesis of a majority—could be insubstantially different from a claim limitation requiring a majority, and no reasonable juror could find otherwise.

30. ***Moore U.S.A. Inc. v. Standard Register Co.***, 56 USPQ 2d 1225, 1236 (Fed. Cir. 2000), ***cert. filed***, (Feb 26, 2001) (No. 00-1346)

Likewise, while Moore argues that the written description's teaching that the length of the first and second strips may be about "half of the length" of the longitudinal marginal portions gives rise to a scope of equivalents that would cover a "minority," our case law reveals that Moore is mistaken. In *Maxwell v. J. Baker, Inc.*, 86 F.3d 1098, 39 USPQ 2d 1001 (Fed. Cir. 1996), we explained the contrary principle that "subject matter disclosed in the specification, but not claimed, is dedicated to the public" in determining infringement under the doctrine of equivalents. *Id.* at 1107, 39 USPQ 2d at 1007. Having fully disclosed two distinct embodiments, one in which the first and second longitudinal strips extend a majority of the length of the longitudinal marginal portions, and one in which they do not, Moore is not entitled to "enforce the unclaimed embodiment as an equivalent of the one that was claimed." *YBM Magnex, Inc. v. International Trade Comm'n*, 145 F.3d 1317, 1320, 46 USPQ 2d 1843, 1845 (Fed. Cir. 1998).

31. ***Space Systems/Loral, Inc. v. Lockheed Martin Corp.***, Civ. App. No. 99-1255, slip op. at 12 (Fed. Cir. Aug. 23, 2000) (unpublished)

SSL argues that claim 1 does not preclude manual initiation of simultaneous stationkeeping and desaturation maneuvers. However, we agree with Lockheed that manual initiation is antithetical to the concept of being automatic. Moreover, examination of the specification shows that manual initiation of such maneuvers is neither disclosed nor contemplated by the Chan patent.

32. ***Stairmaster Sports/Medical Products, Inc. v. Groupe Procycle, Inc.***, Civ. App. No. 99-1149, slip op. at 6 (Fed. Cir. Mar. 15, 2000) (unpublished)

Put another way, no reasonable jury could find that the "connections" within a single piece of metal perform substantially the same function as an engagement between two separate pieces.

33. ***Toro Co. v. White Consol. Indus., Inc.***, 53 USPQ 2d 1065, 1068 (Fed. Cir. 1999)

Applying §112 ¶ 6, the district court did not clearly err in ruling that the hinge and latch of the accused device is equivalent to the tab-and-detent illustrated in the '528 patent. The use of a latch with a hinged cover is shown in the prior art, performing the identical function of securing the cover to the air inlet during use as a blower, using known interchangeable structures. *Cf. Rite-Hite Corp. v. Kelley Co.*, 819 F.2d 1120, 1124, 2 USPQ 2d 1915, 1918 (Fed. Cir. 1987) (equivalence of rack-and-pinion with ratchet-and-pawl). Although White argues that section 112 ¶ 6 requires that the asserted equivalent is described in the specification, that is an incorrect statutory interpretation, for such a requirement would render the statutory provision meaningless.

XIII.L. *Interpreting Claims With Respect to Subject Matter Disclosed But Not Claimed*

1. ***Maxwell v. J. Baker, Inc.***, 39 USPQ 2d 1001, 1006 (Fed. Cir. 1996), ***cert. denied***, 520 U.S. 1115 (1997)

In *Unique Concepts, Inc. v. Brown*, 939 F.2d 1558, 19 USPQ 2d 1500 (Fed. Cir. 1991), we reiterated the well-established rule that "subject matter disclosed but not claimed in a patent application is dedicated to the public." 939 F.2d at 1562–63, 19 USPQ 2d at 1504. *See also Miller v. Bridgeport Brass Co.*, 104 U.S. 350, 352 (1881) ("[T])he claim of a specific device or combination, and an omission to claim other devices or combinations apparent on the face of the patent, are, in law, a dedication to the public of that which is not claimed."). We have frequently applied this rule to prohibit a finding of literal infringement when an accused infringer practices disclosed but unclaimed subject matter. *E.g., Environmental Instructions, Inc. v. Sutron Corp.*, 877 F.2d 1561, 1564, 11 USPQ 2d 1132, 1134 (Fed. Cir. 1989). This rule, however, applies equally to prevent a finding of infringement under the doctrine of equivalents. A patentee may not narrowly claim his invention and then, in the course of an infringement suit, argue that the doctrine of equivalents should permit a finding of infringement because the specification discloses the equivalents. Such a result would merely encourage a patent applicant to present a broad disclosure in the specification of the application and file narrow claims, avoiding examination of broader claims that the applicant could have filed consistent with the specification.

2. ***Genentech, Inc. v. Wellcome Found., Ltd.***, 31 USPQ 2d 1161, 1167 (Fed. Cir. 1994)

An Applicant should not be able deliberately to narrow the scope of examination to avoid during prosecution scrutiny by the PTO of subject matter . . . and then, obtain in court, either literally or under the doctrine of equivalents, a scope of protection which encompasses that subject matter.

3. ***Maxwell v. J. Baker, Inc.***, 39 USPQ 2d 1001, 1007 (Fed. Cir. 1996), ***cert. denied***, 520 U.S. 1115 (1997)

Here, Maxwell limited her claims to fastening tabs attached between the inner and outer soles. She disclosed in the specification, without claiming them, alternatives in which the fastening tabs could be "stitched into the lining seam of the shoes." Col. 2, l. 42. By failing to claim these alternatives, the Patent and Trademark Office was deprived of the opportunity to consider whether these alternatives were patentable. n3 A person of ordinary skill in the shoe industry, reading the specification and prosecution history, and interpreting the claims, would conclude that Maxwell, by failing to claim the alternate shoe attachment systems in which the tabs were attached to the inside shoe lining, dedicated the use of such systems to the public. As a matter of law, J. Baker could not infringe by using an alternate shoe attachment system that Maxwell dedicated to the public.

4. ***YBM Magnex, Inc. v. International Trade Comm'n***, 46 USPQ 2d 1843, 1846 (Fed. Cir. 1998)

Indeed, the facts in *Maxwell* are not the routine facts of an equivalency determination. *Maxwell* disclosed two distinct alternative ways in which pairs of shoes are attached for sale, and claimed only one of them. Both embodiments were fully described in the patent. The court in its opinion observed that by this action *Maxwell* avoided examination of the unclaimed alternative, which was distinct from the claimed alternative. In view of the distinctness of the two embodiments, both of which were fully described in the specification, the Federal Circuit denied *Maxwell* the opportunity to enforce the unclaimed embodiment as an equivalent of the one that was claimed. . . .

The Supreme Court's guidance in *Warner-Jenkinson Co. v. Hilton Davis Chemical Co.*, 520 U.S. 17, 117 S. Ct. 1040, 41 USPQ 2d 1865, 137 L. Ed. 2d 146 (1997) and *Graver Tank & Mfg. Co. v. Linde Air Products Co.*, 339 U.S. 605, 85 USPQ 328, 94 L. Ed. 1097, 70 S. Ct. 854 (1950) does not permit the blanket rule that everything disclosed but not claimed is barred from access to the doctrine of equivalents, whatever the facts, circumstances, and evidence. *Maxwell* accords with the Court's precedent only when its decision is understood and applied in light of its particular facts.

5. ***Northern Telecom Ltd. v. Samsung Elecs. Co., Ltd.***, 55 USPQ 2d 1065, 1070 (Fed. Cir. 2000)

In *Dana*, 860 F.2d at 419, 8 USPQ 2d at 1695, we held that the failure to disclose an unclaimed fluoride treatment, which was necessary for satisfactory performance of the claimed seal, was a violation of the best mode requirement. Similarly, in *Northern Telecom, Inc. v. Datapoint Corp.*, 908 F.2d 931, 940–41, 15 USPQ 2d 1321, 1328 (Fed. Cir. 1990), we held that the failure to disclose special audio tapes for capturing data, which the inventors preferred to conventional audio cassettes, was a violation of the best mode requirement, where the claim included the use of magnetic tapes. See *Id.* at 940, 15 USPQ 2d at 1323.

Dana and *Datapoint* are different from the present case because each involved a situation in which the omitted best mode related directly to the claimed invention. For instance, the disputed claim in *Dana* included, inter alia, "a valve stem seal for sealing between said valve stem and said valve guide." 860 F.2d at 416, 8 USPQ 2d at 1694. The claim stated that the invention was for use "in an internal combustion engine." *Id.* We held that the inventor's failure to disclose an unclaimed fluoride treatment violated the best mode requirement because the treatment was necessary for satisfactory performance of the valve stem seal. See *Id.* at 419, 8 USPQ 2d at 1695. Thus, the asserted best mode in *Dana* directly related not only to the claimed utility of the invention (sealing poppet valve stems in an internal combustion engine), but also to a specific claim limitation (a valve stem seal).

Likewise, in *Datapoint*, the disputed claims were directed to a method of capturing source data comprising, inter alia, storing data on magnetic tape. We affirmed the district court's finding that the inventors violated the best mode requirement by not disclosing a specially designed magnetic tape that was preferred to ordinary audio tape cassettes. See *Datapoint*, 908 F.2d at 940–41, 15 USPQ 2d at 1328. Again, the asserted best mode in *Datapoint* directly related both to the claimed utility (capturing source data) and a specific claim limitation (storing data on magnetic tape). *Accord Spectra-Physics*, 827 F.2d 1524, 1536, 3 USPQ 2d 1737, 1746 (Fed. Cir. 1987) (failure to disclose a six-stage braze cycle violated best mode requirement, where a claim limitation required a means for attaching two components).

Dana and *Datapoint* are consistent with other decisions of this court in which we have held that unclaimed matter that is unrelated to the operation of the claimed invention does not trigger the best mode requirement. . . .

In the present case, the best mode alleged by Samsung is the use of aluminum silicon alloy—instead of pure aluminum—as the interconnect layer in manufacturing integrated circuits with conductive lines of less than 2 microns. However, as we have discussed above, claim 1 is not limited to the use of gas plasma etching to produce semiconductor devices with fine conductive lines. Instead, the claim is directed to a general process for plasma etching of aluminum and aluminum oxide in the presence of a gaseous trihalide. Accordingly, the inventors of the process were not required, under 35 U.S.C. § 112, to disclose the best mode of achieving fine line etching—only the best mode of carrying out the claimed method of plasma etching aluminum and aluminum oxide with a gaseous trihalide. It is undisputed that this requirement was satisfied in the specification.

XIII.M. Linking Between Claims and Specification Under Section 112, Sixth Paragraph

1. **B. Braun Med., Inc. v. Abbott Labs.**, 43 USPQ 2d 1896, 1900 (Fed. Cir. 1997)

Section 112, paragraph 6 states that a means-plus-function claim "shall be construed to cover the *corresponding* structure . . . described in the specification." (emphasis added). We hold that, pursuant to this provision, structure disclosed in the specification is "corresponding" structure only if the specification or prosecution history clearly links or associates that structure to the function recited in the claim. This duty to link or associate structure to function is the *quid pro quo* for the convenience of employing § 112, ¶ 6.

2. **Storer v. Hayes Microcomputer Prods., Inc.**, 46 USPQ 2d 1083, 1086–87 (D. Mass. 1998)

Not only is it possible for a prior art reference in the specification to supply the missing structure in a means-plus-function claim, but Claim 18 recites an update means that is entirely distinct from the AP heuristic that the specification distinguishes from prior art.

As a preliminary matter, it is well established that prior art references can serve as elements in a patent claim. See, e.g., *Intel Corp. v. United States Int'l Trade Commission*, 946 F.2d 821, 842 (Fed. Cir. 1991) ("Claims limitations may, and often do, read on the prior art, particularly in combination patents."); *Panduit Corp. v. Dennison Mfg. Co.*, 810 F.2d 1561, 1575 (Fed. Cir. 1987) ("Virtually all inventions are necessarily combinations of old elements."); *Medtronic, Inc. v.*

Cardiac Pacemakers, Inc., 721 F.2d 1563, 1566 (Fed. Cir. 1983) (same).

3. ***Kemco Sales, Inc. v. Control Papers Co., Inc.***, 54 USPQ 2d 1308, 1313 (Fed. Cir. 2000)

35 U.S.C. section 112, paragraph 6 provides that a patentee may define the structure for performing a particular function generically through the use of a means expression, provided that it discloses specific structure(s) corresponding to that means in the patent specification. See 35 U.S.C. § 112, ¶ 6 (1994); *Atmel*, 198 F.3d at 1380–82, 53 USPQ 2d at 1229–31 (holding that the structure supporting a means-plus-function limitation must be disclosed in the specification); *Valmont Indus., Inc. v. Reinke Mfg. Co.*, 983 F.2d 1039, 1042, 25 USPQ 2d 1451, 1454 (Fed. Cir. 1993) ("The applicant must describe in the patent specification some structure which performs the specified function."). As such, we have referred to 35 U.S.C. section 112, paragraph 6 as embodying a statutory quid pro quo. See, e.g., *Atmel*, 198 F.3d at 1381, 53 USPQ 2d at 1230; see also *B. Braun Med., Inc. v. Abbott Lab.*, 124 F.3d 1419, 1424, 43 USPQ 2d 1896, 1900 (Fed. Cir. 1997) ("The duty to link or associate structure to function is the quid pro quo for the convenience of employing § 112, ¶ 6."). If a patentee fails to satisfy the bargain because of a failure to disclose adequate structure, the claim will be rendered invalid as indefinite under 35 U.S.C. section 112, paragraph 2. See *In re Donaldson Co.*, 16 F.3d 1189, 1195, 29 USPQ 2d 1845, 1850 (Fed. Cir. 1994) (en banc).

XIII.N. *Interpreting Claims in View of Embodiments Disclosed in Specification*

1. ***Personalized Media Communications, L.L.C. v. International Trade Comm'n***, Civ. App. 97-1532, slip op. at 7 (Fed. Cir. Jan. 7, 1999) (unpublished) (citing ***Electro Med. Sys. S.A. v. Cooper Life Sciences, Inc.***, 34 F.3d 1048, 1054, 32 USPQ 2D 1017, 1021 (Fed. Cir. 1994))

While examples disclosed in the preferred embodiments may aid in the proper interpretation of a claim term, the particular embodiments appearing in the written description will not be read into the claims when the claim language is broader than such embodiments.

2. ***Electro Med. Sys. S.A. v. Cooper Life Sciences***, 32 USPQ 2d 1017, 1021 (Fed. Cir. 1994)

[C]laims are not to be interpreted by adding limitations appearing only in the specification. . . . Although the specification may well indicate that certain embodiments are preferred, particular embodiments appearing in [the] specification will not be read into the claims when the claim language is broader than such embodiments.

3. ***Karlin Tech. Inc. v. Surgical Dynamics, Inc.***, 50 USPQ 2d 1465, 1469 (Fed. Cir. 1999)

Although Figure 4 is expressly stated to show the "present invention," and Figures 4A and 4B refer to "one preferred embodiment," the same spinal implant is shown in each of the figures. The remainder of the written description has similarly mixed references to "present invention" and "preferred embodiment." We therefore conclude that the written description uses the terms "present invention" and "preferred embodiment" interchangeably. Given this, it is clear that only the preferred embodiment is described as having highly specialized threads. The general rule, of course, is that the claims of a patent are not limited to the preferred embodiment, unless by their own language. . . . There is nothing in this case that warrants departing from the general rule. Thus, the written description does not narrow the ordinary meaning of "series of threads."

4. ***Virginia Panel Corp. v. Mac Panel Co.***, 45 USPQ 2d 1225, 1229 (Fed. Cir. 1997), ***cert. denied***, 525 U.S. 815 (1998)

It is well settled that device claims are not limited to devices which operate precisely as the embodiments described in detail in the patent.

5. ***K-2 Corp. v. Salomon S.A.***, 191 F.3d 1356, 52 USPQ 2d 1001, 1006 (Fed. Cir. 1999)

We, of course, recognize that the "ordinary and accustomed" meaning of a claim term will often be in dispute, irrespective of the clarity of the terms used. . . . But a dispute over the ordinary and accustomed meaning does not imply that such a meaning does not exist. Here, for example, we recognize that the term "permanently" has what can be said to be the flavor of infiniteness about its meaning, which might raise questions about the use of the term in this claim: even the most permanent of "permanently affixed" connections between the bootie and the base of the skate can, after all, be undone upon the total destruction of the skate itself. This, however, does not mean that because no connection between the bootie and skate can be "infinitely" permanent, there can be no ordinary and accustomed meaning for the claim term. Indeed, we would be hard pressed to describe anything as "permanent" if that term is understood to require an infinite duration. But claim construction is not philosophy; we need not wring our hands when considering the implications of a metaphysical analysis of claim terms. Instead, we need only recognize that claim construction is firmly anchored in reality by the understanding of those of ordinary skill in the art.

6. ***Total Containment, Inc. v. Intelpro Corp.***, Civ. App. No. 99-1059, slip op. at 17–18 (Fed. Cir. Sept. 15, 1999) (unpublished), ***petition for cert. filed***, (Feb. 7, 2000)

Environ principally argues that the '981 specification describes the invention as having a removable inner pipe and that even if the claim does not specify the removability of the inner pipe, each and every embodiment provided in the specification requires the inner pipe to be removable. We have held that "when the preferred embodiment is described in the specification as the invention itself, the claims are not necessarily entitled to a scope broader than that embodiment." *Modine Mfg. Co. v. U.S. Int'l Trade Comm'n*, 75 F.3d 1545, 1551, 37 USPQ 2d 1609, 1612 (Fed. Cir. 1996) . . . . We agree with Environ that if the specification only described the invention as having a removable inner pipe, then we would have to analyze this case under *Modine*. However, we do not agree with Environ that the '981 specification is limited to removable inner pipe systems. The Summary of the Invention states that "the present invention provides a piping system for conveying fluid from the outlet port of a pump to the inlet port of a fluid dispenser." '981 Pat., Col 1, ll. 30–32. The system is further described in the specification as having a "primary pipe of flexible material" and a "secondary pipe of flexible material generally surrounding the primary pipe." '981 Pat., Col. 1, ll. 32–24. We note that the specification does state that an advantage of the invention is that "the piping can be replaced without excavating or breaking ground at the installed tank site." We will not, however, in the absence of any other support, read a limitation into a claim, particularly when the claim has no verbal hook upon which to hang the limitation, simply because the inventor stated that it was an advantage.

XIV. Transitional Phrases (*Comprising*, Etc.)

1. ***Atlas Powder Co. v. E.I. du Pont de Nemours & Co.***, 224 USPQ 409, 411 (Fed Cir. 1984)

Though Egly teaches the presence of solid ammonium nitrate prills as an essential ingredient, Du Pont argues that the '978 claims, because of the phrase "consisting essentially of", does not exclude the presence of those prills. . . . Du Pont is correct.

2. ***Ex parte Hoffman***, 12 USPQ 2d 1061, 1063 (B.P.A.I. 1989)

The language "consisting essentially of", which is typically applied to compositions of matter, is defined in *Ex parte Davis*, . . . as follows:

> . . . recital of "essentially" along with "consisting of" [is regarded] as rendering the claim open only for the inclusion of unspecified ingredients which do not materially affect the basic and novel characteristics of the composition.

3. ***Moleculon Research Corp. v. CBS, Inc.***, 229 USPQ 805, 812 (Fed. Cir. 1986), ***cert. denied***, 479 U.S. 1030 (1987)

The transitional phrase, which joins the preamble of a claim with the body of a claim, is a term of art and as such affects the legal scope of a claim. While a transitional term such as "comprising" or, as in the present case, "which comprises," does not exclude additional unrecited elements, or steps (in the case of a method claim), we conclude that the transitional phrase does not, in the present case, affect the scope of the particular structure recited within the method claim's step.

4. ***In re Garnero***, 162 USPQ 221, 223 (C.C.P.A. 1969)

Moreover, the "consisting essentially of * * *" terminology would, as the board pointed out, exclude additional unspecified ingredients which would affect the basic and novel characteristics of the product defined in the balance of the claim.

5. ***In re Bertsch***, 56 USPQ 379, 384 (C.C.P.A. 1942)

With respect to claim 5 which contains the language "a composition of matter comprising essentially a sulfuric acid," while it is true that the word "comprising" is usually in patent law held to be synonymous with the word "including" we think that the use of the two words "comprising essentially" should receive a different interpretation, especially in view of the above quotation from appellant's brief.

It is our opinion the combination of the two words "comprising essentially" should, under the circumstances, be held to mean as in claims 1 to 4 that the composition claimed is "free from other sulfate and sulfonic acid groups."

In the case *Pittsburgh Iron & Steel Foundries Co. v. Seaman-Sleeth Co.*, . . . the court held that the word "essentially" in a patent claim which contained the words "comprising essentially" is not a synonym for "substantially" and when used in a patent claim means indispensably necessary; important in the highest degree.

6. ***Ex parte Rawles***, 3 USPQ 199, 199 (Pat. Off. Bd. App. 1929)

This application discloses a composition for polishing. It is described as consisting of paraffin, kerosene and grease such as cup grease. The claims on appeal are, however, broadened in scope by the use of the word "comprising" instead of "consisting of." As a result any reference showing the three ingredients named anticipates them even though the reference shows additional ingredients.

7. ***Ex parte Glycofrides***, 63 USPQ 242, 243 (Pat. Off. Bd. App. 1944)

[E]ach of the claims employs terms such as "comprises" or "consisting substantially" which the examiner holds to be not exclusive of other constituents. It has been established in patent practice that the terms "comprise" or "contain" are not exclusive of other materials in contrast with "consisting of" or "composed of."

8. ***Burke, Inc. v. Everest & Jennings, Inc.***, 29 USPQ 2d 1393, 1397 (Fed. Cir. 1993) (unpublished)

As a general rule, "comprising" and "including" are open-ended terms which cover the structural elements recited plus additional elements.

9. ***In re Bertsch***, 56 USPQ 379, 384 (C.C.P.A. 1942)

[W]e hold that the words "composed of" should be regarded as synonymous with "consisting of."

In the case of *Hopkins Mfg. Co. v. General Electric Co.*, . . . there was before the court the construction to be given the words "composed of," "formed of," and "comprising" in certain patent claims. The court said "Now 'formed of' and 'composed of' are the same; they both mean consisting of."

While the words "composed of" may under certain circumstances be given, in patent law, a broader meaning than "consisting of," we believe that in the case at bar . . . the claims should not be given a broader interpretation than the Patent Office tribunals gave to claims 1 to 4.

10. ***Ex parte Davis***, 80 USPQ 448, 449 (Pat. Off. Bd. App. 1948)

The word "comprising" alone [is] synonymous with "including".

11. ***Ex parte Davis***, 80 USPQ 448, 450 (Pat. Off. Bd. App. 1948)

It may now be stated that search was made for some authoritative decision construing the term "consisting essentially of." While decisions were found in which it was mentioned . . ., none was construed.

It has come to our attention that a group of the Primary Examiners of the Patent Office, for their own guidance, adopted a code of terms for use in compositions to aid uniformity of practice, which regarded:

(1) "comprising" and "comprising essentially" as leaving the claim open for the inclusion of unspecified ingredients even in major amounts;

(2) "consisting of" as closing the claim to the inclusion of materials other than those recited except for impurities ordinarily associated therewith, and

(3) recital of "essentially" along with "consisting of" as rendering the claim open only for the inclusion of unspecified ingredients which do not materially affect the basic and novel characteristics of the composition.

We regard the meaning of the terms "comprising" and "consisting of" to be well settled by numerous decisions of which *In re Gray* and *In re Bertsch* are typical. It is also clear that the expression "comprising essentially" was considered in *In re Bertsch* . . . with quotations from earlier court decisions. In particular, it was pointed out that "essentially" imposed the meaning of—indispensably necessary; important in the highest degree. . . .

In the present case where the claims recite three ingredients and the reference discloses four, the important question is whether the term "consisting essentially of" excludes that fourth ingredient. We think that it does, since the "modifier" materially changes the fundamental character of the three-ingredient composition of claims 13, 14 and 16. We therefore hold that these claims are patentably distinguished in substance from Abrams et al., and withdraw the recommendation made in our former decision that "consisting essentially of" be changed to "comprising essentially." In so doing, we are influenced by the facts that the construction of the term "consisting essentially of" quoted hereinbefore from the code of the Primary Examiners suits the situation in this case and also that numerous patents have issued using the term in reliance upon the meaning given it in the said code.

12. ***Moleculon Research Corp. v. CBS, Inc.***, 229 USPQ 805, 812 n.8 (Fed. Cir. 1986), ***cert. denied***, 479 U.S. 1030 (1987)

During the oral argument, Moleculon argued that the word "comprising" in step (b) ("rotating a first set of cube pieces comprising four cubes about a first axis") means that the step covers four cubes *or more*. "Comprising" is not used here as a transitional phrase and has no special legal effect as such. Hence, it should be interpreted according to the normal rules of claim interpretation. No analogous word precedes the structural recitation of the number of cube pieces in steps (a) and (c). "Comprising" in step (c) reasonably interpreted means "having" but not "having at least."

13. ***Genentech, Inc. v. Chiron Corp.***, 42 USPQ 2d 1608, 1613 (Fed. Cir. 1997)

"Comprising" is a term of art used in claim language which means that the named elements are essential, but other elements may be added and still form a construct within the scope of the claim.

14. ***Kress Corp. v. Alexander Servs., Inc.***, Civ. App. 97-1309, slip op. at 13 n.2 (Fed. Cir. June 15, 1998) (unpublished)

Kress' argument that claim 1 is written in comprising format and therefore can be infringed by carriers that have two pairs of actuators performing the lifting and dumping function is without merit. When a claim is written in comprising format, the claim includes the recited elements, but does not exclude additional elements. *See Stiftung v. Renishaw PLC*, 945 F.2d 1173, 1178, 20 USPQ 2d 1094, 1098 (Fed. Cir. 1991).

15. ***PPG Indus. Inc. v. Guardian Indus. Corp.***, 48 USPQ 2d 1351, 1353–54 (Fed. Cir. 1998)

"Consisting essentially of" is a transition phrase commonly used to signal a partially open claim in a patent. Typically, "consisting essentially of" precedes a list of ingredients in a composition claim or a series of steps in a process claim. By using the term "consisting essentially of," the drafter signals that the invention necessarily includes the listed ingredients and is open to unlisted ingredients that do not materially affect the basic and novel properties of the invention. A "consisting essentially of" claim occupies a middle ground between closed claims that are written in a "consisting of" format and fully open claims that are drafted in a "comprising" format.

16. ***Georgia-Pacific Corp. v. United States Gypsum Co.***, 52 USPQ 2d 1590, 1596 (Fed. Cir. 1999)

The use of the term "comprising" in the '569 patent and "consisting of" in the '989 patent renders the scope of the two claims different, but the difference is not sufficient to render claim 17 of the '989 patent nonobvious in light of claim 1 of the '569 patent, because it would have been obvious to construct the mat only out of glass fibers and adhesive, rather than out of glass fibers and adhesive and other unspecified substances.

17. ***Vehicular Techs. Corp. v. Titan Wheel Int'l, Inc.***, 54 USPQ 2d 1841, 1844 (Fed. Cir. 2000)

The phrase "consisting of" is a term of art in patent law signifying restriction and exclusion, while, in contrast, the term "comprising" indicates an open-ended construction. *See Parmelee Pharm. Co. v. Zink*, 285 F.2d 465, 469, 128 USPQ 271, 275 (8th Cir. 1961); John Landis, Mechanics of Patent Claim Drafting 11–13 (1974). In simple terms, a drafter uses the phrase "consisting of" to mean "I claim what follows and nothing else." A drafter uses the term "comprising" to mean "I claim at least what follows and potentially more." In this case, the drafter limited the claim to two concentric springs and nothing else.

As this court noted in Vehicular, the drafter's choice of the phrase "consisting of" does not foreclose infringement under the doctrine of equivalents.

18. ***KCJ Corp. v. Kinetic Concepts, Inc.***, 55 USPQ 2d 1835, 1839 (Fed. Cir. 2000)

This court has repeatedly emphasized that an indefinite article "a" or "an" in patent parlance carries the meaning of "one or more" in open-ended claims containing the transitional phrase "comprising." See *Elkay Mfg. Co. v. Ebco Mfg. Co.*, 192 F.3d 973, 977, 52 USPQ 2d 1109, 1112 (Fed. Cir. 1999); *AbTox, Inc. v. Exitron Corp.*, 122 F.3d 1019, 1023, 43 USPQ 2d 1545, 1548 (Fed. Cir. 1997); *North Am. Vaccine, Inc. v. American Cyanamid Co.*, 7 F.3d 1571, 1575–76, 28 USPQ 2d 1333, 1336 (Fed. Cir. 1993); see also Robert C. Faber, Landis on Mechanics of Patent Claim Drafting 531 (3d ed. 1990). Unless the claim is specific as to the number of elements, the article "a" receives a singular interpretation only in rare circumstances when the patentee evinces a clear intent to so limit the article. See *AbTox*, 122 F.3d at 1023, 43 USPQ 2d at 1548. Under this conventional rule, the claim limitation "a," without more, requires at least one.

19. ***Vivid Techs., Inc. v. American Science & Eng'g, Inc.***, 53 USPQ 2d 1289, 1301 (Fed. Cir. 1999)

[T]he signal "comprising," . . . is generally understood to signify that the claims do not exclude the presence in the accused apparatus or method of factors in addition to those explicitly recited. See *Stiftung v. Renishaw PLC*, 945 F.2d 1173, 1178, 20 USPQ 2d 1094, 1098 (Fed. Cir. 1991) (a claim "which uses the term 'comprising' is an 'open' claim which will read on devices which add additional elements"); *Moleculon Research Corp. v. CBS, Inc.*, 793 F.2d 1261, 1271, 229 USPQ 805, 812 (Fed. Cir. 1986) ("comprising" opens a method claim to the inclusion of steps in addition to those stated in the claim). The signal "comprising" implements the general rule that absent some special circumstance or estoppel which excludes the additional factor, infringement is not avoided by the presence of elements or steps in addition to those specifically recited in the claim. . . . [T]he signal "comprising" accommodates additional variables, provided that all of the elements stated in the claim are present.

XV. Priority/Date of Invention With Respect to Related Applications

1. ***Innovative Scuba Concepts Inc. v. Feder Indus. Inc.***, 27 USPQ 2d 1254, 1264 (D. Colo. 1993), ***rev'd on other grounds***, 31 USPQ 2d 1132 (Fed. Cir. 1994)

    A general rule of patent law is that the date of invention is presumed to be the date the applicant or patentee files a complete patent application in the PTO disclosing the invention.

2. ***Cooper v. Goldfarb***, 47 USPQ 2d 1896, 1900–01 (Fed. Cir. 1998)

    In determining priority of invention, the Board must consider "not only the respective dates of conception and reduction to practice of the invention, but also the reasonable diligence of one who was first to conceive and last to reduce to practice, from a time prior to conception by the other." 35 U.S.C. § 102(g) (1994). Accordingly, priority of invention goes to the first party to reduce an invention to practice unless the other party can show that it was the first to conceive of the invention and that it exercised reasonable diligence in later reducing that invention to practice. . . . Priority therefore depends upon conception and reduction to practice. Priority, conception, and reduction to practice are questions of law which are based on subsidiary factual findings.

3. ***Kawai v. Metlesics***, 178 USPQ 158, 162 (C.C.P.A. 1973)

    Under our law, an applicant for a patent, with one exception not relevant here, cannot establish a date of invention by proving acts done in a foreign country except as provided for in section 119. This prohibition is found in 35 U.S.C. 104. The only act done abroad that is referred to in section 119 is the filing of an application for patent in a foreign country. Therefore, the net effect of sections 104 and 119 is to restrict a foreign inventor, for purposes of United States law, to a date of invention which corresponds to the date when his United States application was filed unless there was an earlier filing of a foreign application. In this respect, the act of filing the United States application has the legal effect of being, constructively at least, a simultaneous conception and reduction to practice of the invention.

4. ***Burroughs Wellcome Co. v. Barr Labs., Inc.***, 32 USPQ 2d 1915, 1919 (Fed. Cir. 1994), ***cert. denied***, 515 U.S. 1130 (1995)

Conception is the touchstone of inventorship, the completion of the mental part of invention. . . . It is "the formation in the mind of the inventor, of a definite and permanent idea of the complete and operative invention, as it is hereafter to be applied in practice." *Hybritech Inc. v. Monoclonal Antibodies, Inc.*, 802 F.2d 1367, 1376, 231 USPQ 81, 87 (Fed. Cir. 1986) [*cert. denied*, 480 U.S. 947 (1987)] (citation omitted). Conception is complete only when the idea is so clearly defined in the inventor's mind that only ordinary skill would be necessary to reduce the invention to practice, without extensive research or experimentation. . . . An idea is definite and permanent when the inventor has a specific, settled idea, a particular solution to the problem at hand, not just a general goal or research plan he hopes to pursue. . . . But an inventor need not know that his invention will work for conception to be complete. . . . He need only show that he had the idea; the discovery that an invention actually works is part of its reduction to practice.

5. ***Hyatt v. Boone***, 47 USPQ 2d 1128, 1129 (Fed. Cir. 1998), ***cert. denied***, 525 U.S. 1141 (1999)

Determination of priority of invention invokes a complex body of procedural and substantive law, applied in the first instance in administrative proceedings in accordance with 35 U.S.C. § 135(a) ("The Board of Patent Appeals and Interferences shall determine questions of priority of the inventions and may determine questions of patentability.") . . .

The general rule is that the first person to conceive the invention is the first inventor, . . . provided that when the first to conceive the invention is the last to reduce it to practice, the person who was first to conceive must have exercised reasonable diligence to his own actual or constructive reduction to practice, "from a time prior to conception by the other." 35 U.S.C. § 102(g).

XV.A. Claiming Benefit of Foreign Priority Under Section 119

1. ***Forssmann v. Matsuo***, 23 USPQ 2d 1548, 1550 (B.P.A.I. 1992), ***aff'd***, 991 F.2d 809 (Fed. Cir. 1993)

An applicant may antedate prior art by relying on the benefit of a previously filed foreign application to establish an effective filing date earlier than that of the reference. 35 U.S.C. 119. Under 35 U.S.C. 119, the claims set forth in a United States application are entitled to the benefit of a foreign priority date if the corresponding foreign application meets the requirements of 35 U.S.C. 112, first paragraph, for those claims.

2. ***Staehelin v. Secher***, 24 USPQ 2d 1513, 1516 (B.P.A.I. 1992)

The question of whether or not references which "intervened" between the filing date of Secher's British applications whose benefit had been sought under 35 USC 119 and the filing date of Secher's later filed U.S. application depends on whether Secher's earlier filed British applications support, within the meaning of section 112, first paragraph, what is claimed in Secher's U.S. application.

3. ***In re Wertheim***, 191 USPQ 90, 95 (C.C.P.A. 1976)

The dispositive issue under this heading is whether appellants' parent and Swiss applications comply with 35 USC 112, first paragraph, including the description requirement, as to the subject matter of these claims. If they do, these claims are entitled to the filing dates of the parent application under 35 USC 120, . . . and the Swiss application under 35 USC 119.

4. ***In re Gosteli***, 872 F.2d 1008, 1010, 10 USPQ 2d 1614, 1616 (Fed. Cir. 1989)

Generally, an applicant may antedate prior art by relying on the benefit of a previously filed foreign application to establish an effective date earlier than that of the reference. . . . Under section 119, the claims set forth in a United States application are entitled to the benefit of a foreign priority date if the corresponding foreign application supports the claims in the manner required by section 112, ¶ 1.

5. ***Kawai v. Metlesics***, 178 USPQ 158, 162–63 (C.C.P.A. 1973)

It is our opinion that this "right to prove" a date of invention corresponding to the date of filing in the foreign country requires that the act of filing the foreign application be regarded for purposes of United States law as a constructive reduction to practice of the invention in the same way that a filing of a United States application can be so regarded. . . . Therefore, we are of the opinion that the foreign application must meet the requirements of the first paragraph of section 112 if the act of filing it is to be regarded as a reduction to practice of the invention.

6. ***Kawai v. Metlesics***, 178 USPQ 158, 163 (C.C.P.A. 1973)

[A] constructive reduction to practice, as opposed to an actual reduction to practice, is not proven unless the specification relied upon discloses a practical utility for the invention where one would not be obvious. We also think that proof of a constructive reduction to practice would also require that there be sufficient disclosure in the specification to enable any person skilled in the art to take advantage of that utility where it would not be obvious how this is done. This latter requirement is, of course, the so-called "how to use" requirement of section 112. It goes without saying that proof of a constructive reduction to practice would also require that the specification be sufficient to enable anyone skilled in the art to make the invention, i.e., the "how to make" requirement of section 112 should also be met by the specification.

If these are requirements which a United States specification must meet if it is to be adequate to support a reduction to practice by the act of filing the application, it follows that a foreign application must meet the same requirements if it is to be used to prove a date of invention.

7. ***Reitz v. Inoue***, 39 USPQ 2d 1838, 1840 (B.P.A.I. 1995)

[W]here the inventive entity differs in the foreign and in the United States application, the examiner should refuse to recognize the priority date *until* the inconsistency or disagreement is resolved. . . . Here, the apparent inconsistency between inventive entities has been satisfactorily resolved/explained by Inoue's reliance upon the amended version of 35 U.S.C. § 116, the corresponding revised MPEP guidelines, and the declarations of Inoue and Suzuki which indicate that Inoue is the sole inventor with respect to subject matter embraced by at least some of Inoue's claims corresponding to the count.

8. ***Reitz v. Inoue***, 39 USPQ 2d 1838, 1840 (B.P.A.I. 1995)

[T]he proposition that the inventive entity must be the same in both the foreign and the corresponding U.S. application in order to obtain benefit can no longer be accepted, if it ever was, as a hard and fast rule in view of the liberalization of the requirements for filing a U.S. application as joint inventors wrought by the 1984 amendment of 35 U.S.C. § 116.

9. ***Reitz v. Inoue***, 39 USPQ 2d 1838, 1840 (B.P.A.I. 1996)
(quoting MPEP §605.07)

Where two or more foreign applications are combined to take advantage of the changes to 35 U.S.C. 103 or 35 U.S.C. 116, benefit as to each foreign application may be claimed if each complies with 35 U.S.C. 119 and the U.S. application inventors are the inventors of the subject matter of the foreign applications. For example, if foreign applicant A invents X; and files a foreign application. Applicant B invents

Y and files a separate foreign application. A + B combine inventions X + Y and file U.S. application to X + Y and claim 35 U.S.C. 119 benefit for both foreign applications: then 35 U.S.C. 119 benefit will be accorded for each foreign application if 35 U.S.C. 119 requirements are met.

10. ***Lenzing Aktiengesellschaft v. Courtaulds Fibers, Inc.***, Civ. App. 96-1155, slip op. 6 (Fed. Cir. July 14, 1997) (unpublished) (citing ***Transco Prods. Inc. v. Performance Contracting, Inc.***, 32 USPQ 2d 1077, 1082 (Fed. Cir. 1994))

The point in time at which we measure the adequacy of the disclosure for a best mode inquiry in the context of a patent with a priority claim under 35 U.S.C. § 119 is the filing date of the foreign application.

11. ***In re Van Esdonk***, 187 USPQ 671, 671 (Comm'r 1975)

35 USC 119 clearly requires that in order to be entitled to the right of priority, there must be a claim therefor filed in the Office before the patent is granted. The question in this case is whether the priority claim made in the parent application, a copy of which was supplied in connection with filing the rule 60 continuation, will satisfy this requirement. . . .

If the oath or declaration filed in the parent application is sufficient to satisfy the statutory requirements of section 115 for the continuation application, the same reasoning would seem to make it unnecessary, so far as section 119 is concerned, to make another claim of priority in the later application which is identical to and filed during the pendency of the parent application. . . .

Accordingly, it is held that applicants' perfection of a priority claim under 35 USC 119 in the parent application will satisfy the statute with respect to their continuation application.

XV.B. Continuation and Continuation-in-Part (CIP) Application Issues Under Section 120

1. ***Litton Sys., Inc. v. Whirlpool Corp.***, 221 USPQ 97, 106 (Fed. Cir. 1984)

If matter added through amendment to a C-I-P application is deemed inherent in whatever the original parent application discloses, however, that matter also is entitled to the filing date of the original, parent application.

2. ***In re Hogan***, 194 USPQ 527, 536 n.13 (C.C.P.A. 1977)

If the present appellants had not filed continuing applications, the only filing date involved would be that of the 1953 application. To judge the 1971 application in isolation would have a chilling effect upon the right of applicants to file continuations. The 24 years of pendency herein may be decried, but a limit upon continuing applications is a matter of policy for the Congress, not for us. . . . As presently constituted, the law as set forth in 35 USC 112 and 120 is the same for all applications, whether of long or short pendency.

3. ***Jonsson v. Stanley Works***, 14 USPQ 2d 1863, 1869 (Fed. Cir. 1990)

Despite Jonsson's contentions it is not disputed that the '912 patent, like the '251 patent, requires the use of "diffuse light." The '912 patent is the result of a continuation-in-part application from the original '008 application, which led to the '251 patent. Hence, the prosecution history of the '251 patent and the construction of the term "diffuse light" contained in that patent, is relevant to an understanding of "diffuse light" as that term is used in the '912 patent. Consequently, as to "diffuse light" in its interpretation of the '912 patent, the district court did not err in relying on "arguments and remarks" made during the prosecution of the '251 patent.

4. ***Ex parte Maziere***, 27 USPQ 2d 1705, 1706–07 (B.P.A.I. 1993)

35 U.S.C. § 120 requires in relevant part that the now claimed invention be disclosed in an earlier application in the manner provided by the first paragraph of § 112. Section 120 of the statute does not place any restrictions or limitation as to how the now claimed invention must be disclosed in the earlier application in that matter. . . . There is no dispute that the present application fully describes and enables the subject matter now claimed. No issue regarding best mode has been raised. Indeed, the present specification and claims are those of Serial No. 07/071,944 which was incorporated by reference in parent Serial No. 07/072,090. *This* disclosure was present in Serial No. 07/072,090 *albeit* in a compressed form via the statement of incorporation by reference of Serial No. 07/071,944. In filing this application, appellants in effect "expanded" the compressed file of 07/071,944 which was present in the first paragraph of Serial No. 07/072,090 and "compressed" the remaining disclosure of 07/072,090 into a statement of incorporation by reference.

5. ***Paperless Accounting, Inc. v. Bay Area Rapid Transit Sys.***, 231 USPQ 649, 652 (Fed. Cir. 1986), ***cert. denied***, 480 U.S. 933 (1987)

The filing of a continuation-in-part, in and of itself, is not an admission of the correctness of a rejection. Law and policy liberally authorize the filing of c-i-p applications for a number of reasons, whether to enlarge the disclosure to include new technological information, thereby providing the public with knowledge of recent developments or improvements; or to enable more extensive prosecution or improved draftsmanship of specification or claims; or to provide a vehicle for prosecution of non-elected claims.

In those cases where a continuation-in-part application contains claims which depend upon an enlarged disclosure for support, that must of course be considered when it is required to establish dates of compliance with 35 U.S.C. § 112. But the mere filing of a continuation-in-part with additional matter or revised claims is not of itself an admission that the matter is "new" or that the original application was legally insufficient to support the claims.

6. ***Eiselstein v. Frank***, 34 USPQ 2d 1467, 1470 n.4 (Fed. Cir. 1995)

In order for the Eiselstein application to be entitled under 35 U.S.C. § 120 to the filing date of an earlier application in the chain of applications of which it is a part, there must also have been a "continuing disclosure through the chain of applications, without hiatus." *Lemelson v. TRW, Inc.*, 760 F.2d 1254, 1266, 225 USPQ 697, 706 (Fed. Cir. 1985)

7. ***Eiselstein v. Frank***, 34 USPQ 2d 1467, 1470–71 (Fed. Cir. 1995)

The grandparent application described "An alloy containing about 15% to 22% chromium, 10% to 28% iron, 6% to 9% molybdenum, 2.5% to 5% columbium, 1% to 2% titanium, up to 1% aluminum, advantageously 0.05 to about 0.1% aluminum, *and balance essentially nickel in a weight proportion of 45% to 55% of the alloy* [emphasis added]." . . . [W]e are of the firm conviction that in his grandparent application, Eiselstein disclosed the invention of an alloy of various elements and the balance nickel, the nickel being an imprecise quantity, i.e., from about 45% to about 55% of said alloy and, on the basis of that disclosure, one skilled in the art reading the grandparent application would readily know that Eiselstein possessed that invention. Eiselstein need not be bound to maximum precision for the nickel content when the whole tenor of his disclosure indicates approximation. The Board clearly erred in finding otherwise.

8. ***Therma-Tru Corp. v. Peachtree Doors, Inc.***, 33 USPQ 2d 1274, 1276 (Fed. Cir. 1995)

A claim in a CIP application is entitled to the filing date of the parent application when the claimed invention is described in the parent specification in a manner that satis-

fies, inter alia, the description requirement of 35 U.S.C.
§112. . . . Therma-Tru testified that the numerical value of
0.005 inch was included in the CIP in order to quantify the
difference from the prior art, and that it did not change the
invention that was disclosed in the parent application.

As discussed in *Kennecott*, the later explicit description of
an inherent property does not deprive the product of the
benefit of the filing date of the earlier application.

9. ***Waldemar Link, GmbH & Co. v. Osteonics Corp.***, 31
   USPQ 2d 1855, 1857 (Fed. Cir. 1994)

   A CIP application can be entitled to different priority
   dates for different claims. Claims containing any matter introduced in the CIP are accorded the filing date of the CIP
   application. However, matter disclosed in the parent application is entitled to the benefit of the filing date of the parent application.

10. ***In re Chu***, 36 USPQ 2d 1089, 1093 (Fed. Cir. 1995)

    The 1984 amendment to § 120 plainly allows continuation,
    divisional, and continuation-in-part applications to be filed
    and afforded the filing date of the parent application even
    though there is not complete identity of inventorship be-
    tween the parent and subsequent applications. D. Chisum,
    Patents § 13.07 (1995). Thus, the Board erred in requiring
    complete identity of inventorship between the Doyle patent
    and the Chu application in order for Chu to have the bene-
    fit of the Doyle patent's filing date. There is overlap in the
    inventive entities of the Doyle patent and the Chu applica-
    tion, which, after the 1984 amendment, is all that is re-
    quired in terms of inventorship or "inventive entity" to have
    the benefit of an earlier filing date. But this does not deter-
    mine whether Chu is entitled to the Doyle date. There is an-
    other requirement.

    It is elementary patent law that a patent application is en-
    titled to the benefit of the filing date of an earlier filed ap-
    plication only if the disclosure of the earlier application pro-
    vides support for the claims of the later application, as
    required by 35 U.S.C. § 112.

11. ***Waldemar Link, GmbH & Co. v. Osteonics Corp.***, 31
    USPQ 2d 1855, 1857 (Fed. Cir. 1994)

    A [continuation-in-part] application can be entitled to differ-
    ent priority dates for different claims. Claims containing any
    matter introduced in the [continuation-in-part] are accorded
    the filing date of the [continuation-in-part] application. How-
    ever, matter disclosed in the parent application is entitled to
    the benefit of the filing date of the parent application.

12. ***Lockwood v. American Airlines, Inc.***, 41 USPQ 2d 1961, 1966 (Fed. Cir. 1997)

It is not sufficient for purposes of the written description requirement of § 112 that the disclosure, when combined with the knowledge in the art, would lead one to speculate as to modifications that the inventor might have envisioned, but failed to disclose. Each application in the chain must describe the claimed features.

13. ***Studiengesellschaft Kohle, M.B.H. v. Shell Oil Co.***, 42 USPQ 2d 1674, 1677 (Fed. Cir.), ***cert. denied***, 522 U.S. 996 (1997)

To qualify for an earlier filing date, section 120 requires, *inter alia*, that the earlier-filed U.S. patent application contain a disclosure which complies with 35 U.S.C. § 112, ¶ 1 (1994) for each claim in the newly filed application. Thus, this benefit only applies to claims that recite subject matter adequately described in an earlier application, and does not extend to claims with subject matter outside the description in the earlier application. . . . In other words, a claim complies with 35 U.S.C. § 120 and acquires an earlier filing date if, and only if, it could have been added to an earlier application without introducing new matter.

14. ***Studiengesellschaft Kohle, M.B.H. v. Shell Oil Co.***, 42 USPQ 2d 1674, 1677 (Fed. Cir.), ***cert. denied***, 522 U.S. 996 (1997) (quoting ***Vas-Cath Inc. v. Mahurkar***, 19 USPQ 2d 1111, 1117 (Fed. Cir. 1991))

Under 35 U.S.C. § 112, ¶ 1, and consequently under 35 U.S.C. § 120 as well, an applicant must "convey with reasonable clarity to those skilled in the art that, as of the filing date sought, he or she was in possession of the invention." . . . An applicant cannot show possession of an invention based upon a combination of several distinct previous applications unless he shows that one of the applications discloses the invention. . . . In other words, a claim that relies upon a combination of previously-filed applications is not be entitled to an earlier filing date because the applicant has not demonstrated possession of the complete invention at the time of an earlier application. . . . In sum, 35 U.S.C. § 120 requires an applicant to meet the disclosure requirement of § 112, ¶ 1 in a single parent application in order to obtain an earlier filing date for individual claims.

15. ***Elkay Mfg. Co. v. Ebco Mfg. Co.***, 52 USPQ 2d 1109, 1114 (Fed. Cir. 1999)

When multiple patents derive from the same initial application, the prosecution history regarding a claim limitation in any patent that has issued applies with equal force to subsequently issued patents that contain the same claim limitation.

16. ***Augustine Med., Inc. v. Gaymar Indus., Inc.***, 50 USPQ 2d 1900, 1907 (Fed. Cir. 1999)

Because the prosecution history of a parent application may limit the scope of a later application using the same claim term, . . . these claim amendments and arguments restrict the scope of the claims in each of the later issued patents containing the "self-erecting" limitation.

17. ***Augustine Med., Inc. v. Gaymar Indus., Inc.***, 50 USPQ 2d 1900, 1908 (Fed. Cir. 1999) (quoting ***Waldemar Link v. Osteonics Corp.***, 31 USPQ 2d 1855, 1857 (Fed. Cir. 1994))

A CIP application contains subject matter from a prior application and may also contain additional matter not disclosed in the prior application. . . . Different claims of such an application may therefore receive different effective filing dates. See id. Subject matter that arises for the first time in the CIP application does not receive the benefit of the filing date of the parent application. . . . Thus, the decision on the proper priority date—the parent application date or the CIP application date—for subject matter claimed in a CIP application depends on when that subject matter first appeared in the patent disclosures. To decide this question, a court must examine whether the "disclosure of the application relied upon reasonably conveys to the artisan that the inventor had possession at that time of the later claimed subject matter."

18. ***Princeton Biochemicals, Inc. v. Beckman Instruments, Inc.***, Civ. App. 98-1525, slip op. at 10–11 (Fed. Cir. Aug. 19, 1999) (unpublished)

The examiner thus allowed the combined claim to issue as claim 32 without any amendment being made or any argument being espoused that would limit the holder limitation to the embodiment where the holder/capillary is vertically moving in relation to a stationary sample cup/table.

We hold that the prosecution history does not limit the holder limitation of claim 32 to only vertically movable holders. Although the applicant amended claim 1 to include a vertical movement requirement of the holder in the original application, the subsequent filing of the CIP application and the return of claim 1 to its original, unamended form, counsels against applying the usual rule that the entire prosecution history, including parent and grandparent applications, be analyzed in interpreting a claim. . . .

We also hold that the applicant did not limit claim 32 to a vertically moving holder during prosecution as the amendments and arguments cited by the district court were directed to claims other than those that were combined as issued claim 32. . . . Those amendments and remarks were directed primarily at application claim 8, a picture claim containing numerous other limitations and directed to the specific embodiment of a vertically moving holder, and not to the broader holder limitation in claim 1 that eventually resulted in issued claim 32.

19. ***Reiffin v. Microsoft Corp.***, 54 USPQ 2d 1915, 1917 (Fed. Cir. 2000)

We conclude that the district court erred in looking to the text of the original 1982 application to determine whether the '603 and '604 patents, filed in 1990 and 1994, comply with the written description requirement. For purposes of Section 112 Para.1, the relevant specifications are those of the '603 and '604 patents; earlier specifications are relevant only when the benefit of an earlier filing date is sought under 35 U.S.C. Section 120. . . .

Compliance of the '603 and '604 patents with the written description requirement requires that the specifications of these patents describe the inventions claimed in these patents.

20. ***Reiffin v. Microsoft Corp.***, 54 USPQ 2d 1915, 1918 (Fed. Cir. 2000)

Analysis of the disclosure in ancestor applications is appropriate when benefit of an earlier filing is sought under 35 U.S.C. Section 120:

> 35 U.S.C. Section 120. An application for patent for an invention disclosed in the manner provided by the first paragraph of section 112 of this title in an application previously filed in the United States . . . shall have the same effect, as to such invention, as though filed on the date of the prior application . . . .

Although Section 120 incorporates the requirements of Section 112 Para.1, these requirements and the statutory mechanism allowing the benefit of an earlier filing date are separate provisions with distinct consequences. In accordance with Section 120, claims to subject matter in a later-filed application not supported by an ancestor application in terms of Section 112 Para.1 are not invalidated; they simply do not receive the benefit of the earlier application's filing date. See, e.g., *Hyatt v. Boone*, 146 F.3d 1348, 1352, 47 USPQ2d 1128, 1130 (Fed. Cir. 1998).

21. ***In re Van Esdonk***, 187 USPQ 671, 671 (Comm'r 1975)

35 USC 119 clearly requires that in order to be entitled to the right of priority, there must be a claim therefor filed in the Office before the patent is granted. The question in this case is whether the priority claim made in the parent application, a copy of which was supplied in connection with filing the rule 60 continuation, will satisfy this requirement. . . .

If the oath or declaration filed in the parent application is sufficient to satisfy the statutory requirements of section 115 for the continuation application, the same reasoning would seem to make it unnecessary, so far as section 119 is concerned, to make another claim of priority in the later application which is identical to and filed during the pendency of the parent application. . . .

Accordingly, it is held that applicants' perfection of a priority claim under 35 USC 119 in the parent application will satisfy the statute with respect to their continuation application.

XV.C. *Overcoming Prior Art Based on Priority and Rule 131*

1. ***In re Gosteli***, 10 USPQ 2d 1614, 1617 (Fed. Cir. 1989) (***but see*** 35 U.S.C. § 104 (Supp. 1995))

As an alternative position, Gosteli contends that they can swear behind Menard, under Rule 131, by establishing a constructive reduction to practice in this country based on their foreign priority date of the two species disclosed by Menard.

. . . Rule 131 requirements are quite specific. To antedate a prior art reference, the applicant submits an oath or declaration alleging acts that establish a completion of the *invention in this country* before the effective date of the prior art. 37 C.F.R. § 1.131(a).

The requirements and operation of section 119 differ from those of Rule 131. . . . Rule 131 provides a mechanism for removing specific prior art references, whereas section 119 is concerned only with an applicant's effective filing date. Because section 119, unlike Rule 131, operates independently of the prior art, it is appropriate that the showing required under section 119 differs from that required under Rule 131.

2. ***In re Stempel***, 113 USPQ 77, 81 (C.C.P.A. 1957)

We are convinced that under the law all the applicant can be required to show is priority with respect to so much of the claimed invention as the references happen to show. When he has done that he has disposed of the reference. . . . In the case of a reference, it is fundamental that it is valid only for what it discloses and if the applicant establishes priority with respect to that disclosure, and there is no statutory bar, it is of no effect at all.

What is a "reference"? It is nothing more than a patent or publication cited to show that all or part of the invention for which a patent is sought was in the prior art, either more than a year before the filing date to which the applicant is entitled, in which case it is "statutory bar" and cannot be sworn back of, or before the applicant's date of invention. When a reference is not a statutory bar, Rule 131 provides a procedure by which the applicant is permitted to show, if he can, that his date of invention was earlier than the date of reference. The rule must be construed in accordance with the rights given to inventors by statute and this excludes a construction permitting the further use of a reference as a ground of rejection after all pertinent subject matter in it has been antedated to the satisfaction of the Patent Office.

3. *In re Tanczyn*, 146 USPQ 298, 300 (C.C.P.A. 1965)

A different situation may prevail when the rejection is based upon 35 U.S.C. 103. In such a case the purpose of an affidavit is to establish that the claimed invention was made by the applicant before the effective date of a reference relied upon to show that the invention was obvious. By so doing, the applicant may prove, by eliminating a reference, that at the time the invention was made "subject matter as a whole would [not] have been obvious * * *."

4. *In re Costello*, 219 USPQ 389, 390–91 (Fed. Cir. 1983)

In section 120, Congress set forth two requirements that an applicant must satisfy in order for a later filed application to be accorded the same effect as if it were filed on the same date as an earlier application by the same inventor disclosing the same invention. Those conditions are (1) copendency of the applications, and (2) reference in the later filed to the earlier filed application.

Even if an applicant is unable to secure an effective filing date previous to the effective date of a prior art reference under section 120, the applicant may overcome a reference by evidence of prior invention. A prior art reference that is not a statutory bar may be overcome by two generally recognized methods. "The most common way to 'antedate' a reference is to submit an affidavit satisfying the requirements of Rule 131." (Footnotes omitted.) Rule 131, however, is only one way of overcoming a reference that is not a statutory bar. An applicant may also overcome a reference by showing that the relevant disclosure is a description of the applicant's own work. The pertinent inquiry is under 35 U.S.C.

§102(e). Appellants can overcome a reference by showing that they were in possession of their invention prior to the effective date of the reference.

5. *In re Costello*, 219 USPQ 389, 391 (Fed. Cir. 1983)

Rule 131 governs whether an applicant has proved a date of invention "before" the effective date of the reference. . . . In order to overcome Cereijo appellants must either (1) comply with the substantive requirements of Rule 131, or (2) establish that the relevant disclosure is of their own work. . . .

Appellants' principal contention is that the filing of the later abandoned original application constitutes a constructive reduction to practice of the invention. Appellants cite no authority, nor can they, to support their argument. It has long been settled, and we continue to approve the rule, that an abandoned application, with which no subsequent application was copending, cannot be considered a constructive reduction to practice. It is inoperative for any purpose, save as evidence of conception.

6. *In re Wilkinson*, 134 USPQ 171, 172 (C.C.P.A. 1962)

Since the Stephens reference does not allege or disclose a use, nor is a use alleged to be obvious, the issue is whether, under such circumstances, appellant can properly be required to show an actual reduction to practice, including a showing of use, to overcome the reference. In other words, if Stephens shows A, can appellant be compelled to show A plus B before he can overcome Stephens? We do not think so, nor do we find any authority for such a requirement in cases relied on below.

. . . Since appellants have satisfactorily shown they did everything done by Stephens prior to the latter's publication date, they have overcome Stephens as a valid ground rejection.

7. *In re Facius*, 161 USPQ 294, 297 n. 4 (C.C.P.A. 1969)

Although it seems clear that appellant's characterization of the affidavits as "Affidavits under Rule 131" was a misnomer, we said in *In re Land*, . . .: "[T]he proper subject of inquiry [is] not compliance with Rule 131 but what the *evidence* [shows] as to who invented the subject matter disclosed by [the reference] which was relied on to support the rejection" and "[e]vidence of such a state of facts, whatever its form, must be considered." [Emphasis supplied.] Even though the affidavits fail to satisfy the requirements of Rule 131, they are "affidavits traversing grounds of rejection," which are permitted under Rule 132, and may be considered as evidence.

8. ***In re Facius***, 161 USPQ 294, 301 (C.C.P.A. 1969)

Moreover, appellants further showed that they themselves had made the inventions upon which the relevant disclosures in the patent had been based. This is a significant fact. If all the appellants had done was to bring the invention of another to the attention of the patentees, then that disclosure in the patent would have been the invention of another and still available as prior art, albeit it was appellants' "contribution" to the disclosure. In both *Blout* and *Mathews*, the appellants had claimed the inventions disclosed in the patents and had made oaths that they were the inventors of everything both described and claimed. The claims and appended oath evidenced the fact of inventorship by the appellants. Thus, the appellants had made a satisfactory showing that the disclosure relied upon was a description of and based upon their own inventions.

9. ***In re Asahi/Am., Inc.***, 37 USPQ 2d 1204, 1206 (Fed. Cir. 1995)

The purpose of filing a 131 declaration is to demonstrate that the applicant's date of invention is prior to the effective date of the reference cited in support of a rejection. *In re Eickmeyer*, 602 F.2d 974, 202 U.S.P.Q. 655 (C.C.P.A. 1979). Where the reference cited in support of a rejection "substantially shows or describes but does not claim" the subject matter of the invention in question, § 131 allows the patent owner to overcome the reference by showing that the invention in question was reduced to practice prior to the filing date of the reference.

XVI. Restricting One Application Into Multiple Applications

1. ***Caterpillar Tractor Co. v. Commissioner of Patents and Trademarks***, 231 USPQ 590, 590–91 (E.D. Va. 1986) (quoting MPEP § 806.05(e))

The PTO interprets this regulation [37 CFR 1.141(b)(2)] to mean:

> Process and apparatus for its practice can be shown to be distinct inventions, if either or both of the following can be shown: (1) that the process as claimed can be practiced by another materially different apparatus or by hand, or (2) that the apparatus as claimed can be used to practice another and materially different process.
>
> . . . .
>
> An example, while not completely analogous, may help to illustrate the issue. If the process was the removal of a man's

beard from his face, and a safety razor was the apparatus, the PTO rule and interpretation would hold that, because the razor could also be used to scrape paint from a pane of glass it was not "specifically designed" for removal of the beard. It would also hold that because the process could be performed with the use of a straight razor the safety razor was not "specifically designed" for the removal of the beard.

2. **MPEP § 1850** (6th ed., rev. 1, 1995)

The decision in *Caterpillar Tractor Company v. Commissioner of Patents and Trademarks* ... held that the Patent and Trademark Office interpretation of 37 CFR 1.141(b)(2) as applied to unity of invention determinations in international applications was not in accordance with the Patent Cooperation Treaty and its implementing regulations. In the *Caterpillar International* application, the USPTO acting as an International Searching Authority, had held lack of unity of invention between a set of claims directed to a process for forming a sprocket and a set of claims drawn to an apparatus (die) for forging a sprocket. The court stated that it was an unreasonable interpretation to say that the expression "specifically designed" as found in the PCT Rule 13.2(ii) means that the process and apparatus have unity of invention if they can only be used with each other, as set forth in the Manual of Patent Examining Procedure (MPEP) § 806.05(e).

3. ***Ex parte Binda***, 54 USPQ 35, 36 (Pat. Off. Bd. App. 1941)

Comparing the process claims, such as allowed claim 21, with the article claims, it is believed that the process of claim 21 when carried out will necessarily produce the article defined by the article claims. Applicant so contends. He states that there is serious doubt that a Court would sustain separate patents on the process and the article. He argues that the inventions claimed here are so closely related that they should be claimed in a single patent. We believe that applicant in the present case has presented a well founded argument for not dividing the process claims from the article claims. They are no doubt so closely related that if separate patents be taken out on them the question of double patenting might be likely to arise.

4. ***Helifix Ltd. v. Blok-Lok, Ltd.***, 54 USPQ 2d 1299, 1305 (Fed. Cir. 2000)

The Patent Office can issue a restriction requirement if it finds that two or more inventions claimed in a patent application are "independent and distinct." 35 U.S.C. Section 121 (1994). A process and apparatus (tool) for its practice can be restricted if either "the process as claimed can be practiced by another materially different apparatus or by hand" or "the apparatus as claimed can be used to practice another and materially different process." Man. Pat. Examining Proc. Section 806.05(e) (7th ed. 1998). In response to a restriction requirement, an applicant must elect one invention for examination. See 37 C.F.R. Section 1.142(a) (1999). Claims to the non-elected invention(s) are withdrawn from consideration and must be canceled before the application is allowed to issue as a patent. See 37 C.F.R. Section 1.142(b) (1999).

5. ***Helifix Ltd. v. Blok-Lok, Ltd.***, 54 USPQ 2d 1299, 1305 (Fed. Cir. 2000)

Both Block-Lok and the district court, however, have read too much into the restriction requirements in this case. The restriction requirements at issue merely reflect the Patent Office's conclusions that claim 1, by its terms, is not limited to a method using the tool recited in claim 2. Accordingly, the restriction requirements between the method claimed in the [Helifix] patent and the specific tool described in the specification in no way bear on the enablement of a different tool.

XVI.A.   Recitation of Alternatives Under Markush Practice

1. ***In re Schechter***, 98 USPQ 144, 149 (C.C.P.A. 1953)

If on examination of a generic Markush type claim, it be found that the applicant has included one or more members known to be old in the art for the same purpose as in the applicant's invention, the group in its entirety must fail of recognition in exactly the same manner as would have been the case had the group of elements of the claim been identified by a single term. In such contingency, a formula of lesser scope may be invoked, provided that the remaining members of the group have a common quality which is distinctive from the characteristics of the major group, and which itself imparts patentable merit to the subgroup over the generic group.

2. ***Ex parte Brouard***, 201 USPQ 538, 540 (Pat. Off. Bd. App. 1976)

Claim 24 has been rejected under 35 U.S.C. 121 on the ground that radical "B" misjoins independent and distinct inventions and, hence, is drawn to an improper markush group. . . .

We will not sustain this rejection. We agree with appellants that the compounds as a whole must be considered, rather than the "B" substituent alone. . . .

When we consider the compounds as a whole encompassed by claim 24, we agree with appellants that there is unity of invention based upon the cinnamonitrile radical common to all of the compounds included in claim 24. Appellants have

presented more than 60 examples of compounds corresponding to the different "B" groupings and have shown that
all of them dye polyester fibers. Hence, we conclude from the
record before us that compounds corresponding to claim 24
belong to a recognized genus (cinnamonitrile derivatives)
and have a community of properties; *i.e.*, the capability of
dyeing polyester fibers.

3. ***Ex parte Brouard***, 201 USPQ 538, 540 (Pat. Off. Bd. App.
1976)

The fact that the various groups of compounds corresponding to claim 24 are classified in different subclasses does not
mean that it would be repugnant to accepted principles of
scientific classification to associate them together as a
genus; on the contrary, the fact that all of the claimed compounds share a common cinnamonitrile group and have the
capability to dye polyester fibers suggests that it would not
be repugnant to scientific classification to associate them together as a genus.

4. ***Ex parte Brouard***, 201 USPQ 538, 540 (Pat. Off. Bd. App.
1976)

We appreciate the fact that different fields of search are involved for the six groups listed by the examiner at pages 2
to 4 of his answer. However, the fact that different fields of
search are involved does not establish that the Markush
group is improper. We might point out that the examiner
has, in fact, searched most of the subclasses involved.

5. ***In re Jones***, 74 USPQ 149, 151 (C.C.P.A. 1947)

It is evident that in any Markush group, the compounds
which are included will differ from each other in certain respects. In determining the propriety of the grouping, these
differences must, to some extent, be weighed against the
similarities and, as hereinbefore noted, the board pointed
out in its decision that "whether a group is proper must be
decided in view of the facts of each particular case." The inclusion in Markush groups of compounds which differed
widely in some respects, has been permitted. Thus in *Ex
parte Clarke and Malm*, 1931 C.D. 6, 11 USPQ 52, the Commissioner of Patents permitted the inclusion of aliphatic,
aromatic and aralkyl compounds in a single group. In *Ex
parte Kendall*, 56 USPQ 119, the Board of Appeals permitted the grouping of substances which varied "in the character of the connecting chain," and in *Ex parte Dahlen et al.*,
1934 C.D. 9, 42 USPQ 208, the board permitted the grouping of compounds having nuclei and side chains, despite the
fact that the allowed claims covered a wide variation in the
composition of the side chains.

6. ***In re Jones***, 74 USPQ 149, 151 (C.C.P.A. 1947)

[A]ll the claimed compounds belong to the genus of tetralyl compounds having a substituted methyl group at position 6, but it is not established that all members of this genus would be suitable for appellant's purposes. Accordingly, appellant could not properly claim this entire genus and it was necessary to limit his claims to the individual compounds which were known to possess the desired property.

We have carefully considered the views expressed by the Patent Office tribunals, but are of opinion that, under all the circumstances of this case, the substances grouped have "a community of chemical or physical characteristics" which justify their inclusion in a common group, and that such inclusion is not repugnant to principles of scientific classification.

8. ***In re Schechter***, 98 USPQ 144, 149 (C.C.P.A. 1953)

A Markush grouping is proper where the substances grouped have a community of chemical and physical characteristics which justify their inclusion in a common group, and such inclusion is not repugnant to the principles of scientific classification.

9. ***In re Schechter***, 98 USPQ 144, 149 (C.C.P.A. 1953)

[A]ppellants' new synthesized cyclopentenolone intermediates are affirmatively recited in the claim and the exclusion of the known prior compounds results merely from claiming a subgroup of lesser scope having a common quality which is distinctive from the characteristics of the major group. This common distinctive quality is that the compounds recited are novel synthesized intermediates produced by a novel process from a novel synthesized starting material for use in a novel method of providing by synthesis the novel desired pyrethrinlike insecticides. We therefore think claim 48 presents a subgroup meeting the first of the two requirements for such subgroups. . . . In the peculiar facts of this case, we think the recitation of the italicized compound in specific form, whereas the others are recited in broad form so as to include dextro and levo isomers and racemic mixtures, does not, ipso facto, make the claim an improper Markush claim.

10. ***In re Harnisch***, 206 USPQ 300, 303–04 (C.C.P.A. 1980)

We will first express our views concerning the PTO's reliance on "judicially created doctrine" in its rejection of claims for "improper Markush grouping." Appellant injected this point into the case by contending that the PTO had no right to rely on doctrine because a statutory basis for rejection must be stated. He also seems to contend that there is no "doctrine" and that while this court could create one it should not do

so. . . . Upon reflection and consideration of the cases cited by
the board, the discussion of those and others by the solicitor,
and the recorded history of Markush practice, it appears to us
that all of the discussion of "doctrine" is beside the point because there is no "Markush doctrine." . . . In summary, there
is no "doctrine" to be considered but only a body of case law,
emanating from both "higher" and "lower" authority, not altogether consistent, the latest decisions tending to carry the
most weight as precedent.

11. ***In re Harnisch***, 206 USPQ 300, 303 (C.C.P.A. 1980)

"Markush" was the name of an applicant for patent (Eu-
gene A. Markush) who happened to use in a claim a type of
definition of a genus or subgenus by enumeration of species,
which he did not devise and which had been used before in
patent claims. The examiner considered the claim to be "alternative" in form, objected to it, and Markush petitioned
the Commissioner. Assistant Commissioner Kinnan, in *Ex
parte Markush*, 1925 CD 126 (Com. Pat. 1924), approved the
form of claim and granted the petition, thus requiring the
examiner to examine it for patentability. Thus the name
"Markush" became attached to a type of claim expression,
and that is all it connotes. As others rang changes on the
type of expression used by Markush and approved by Assistant Commissioner Kinnan, further decisions and opinions
on petitions and in appeals ensued and a considerable body
of case law evolved, approving and disapproving various
forms of Markush-type expression, from which cases a number of rules can be deduced.

12. ***In re Harnisch***, 206 USPQ 300, 305 (C.C.P.A. 1980)

Over thirty years ago this court decided *In re Jones*, 34
CCPA 1150, 162 F.2d 479, 74 USPQ 149 (1947), reversing an
"improper Markush group" rejection of claims to chemical
compounds which were growth-regulating compositions for
plants, fungicides, and insecticides. Notwithstanding their
various properties, the court found all of the compounds included in the claims were plant growth stimulants, thus
having a common function. The court noted that in any
Markush group the compounds "will differ from each other
in certain respects." It laid down the proposition, with which
the PTO agrees in its MPEP, that in determining the propriety of a Markush grouping the compounds must be considered as wholes and not broken down into elements or
other components.

13. ***In re Harnisch***, 206 USPQ 300, 305 (C.C.P.A. 1980)

Citing *Ex parte Clark*, 11 USPQ 52 (Com. Pat. 1931), a case
decided by the author of the original *Markush* opinion, it

noted that "the inclusion in Markush groups of compounds which differed widely in some respects," namely, aliphatic, aromatic, and aralkyl compounds, had been permitted. [The Board] cited *Ex parte Dahlen*, 42 USPQ 208 (Bd. App. 1938) as permitting the grouping of compounds having the same nuclei but side chains wherein there was a wide variation. It found the claims before it to cover compounds all belonging to a genus of tetralyl compounds having a substituted methyl group at position 6 and ruled that they had a community of properties justifying their grouping which was not repugnant to principles of scientific classification.

14. ***In re Harnisch***, 206 USPQ 300, 306 (C.C.P.A. 1980)

The board's reliance on its notion that some of the claimed compounds are "no more than intermediates" overlooked the now admitted fact that they are dyes as well. Clearly, they are all coumarin compounds which the board admitted to be "a single structural similarity." We hold, therefore, that the claimed compounds all belong to a subgenus, as defined by appellant, which is not repugnant to scientific classification. Under these circumstances we consider the claimed compounds to be part of a single invention so that there is unity of invention.

15. ***In re Swenson***, 56 USPQ 180, 183 (C.C.P.A. 1942)

In the instant case it was held by the tribunals below that an improper Markush grouping resided in the phrase "a reducing agent selected from the group consisting of sulfur, coal, carbon, charcoal, starch, wood flour, sugar and glycerine." Applying the Markush doctrine to the claims containing such grouping it is at once apparent that sulfur, which is an element, cannot possibly have any common characteristic with the other seven reducing agents except that it will perform the same function as the other agents. This is not sufficient. . . . [E]ach of the said seven agents can be included in the coined expression "carbonaceous reducing agent". But sulfur is not to be found classifiable as a member of such a kind or class of reducing agents, and therefore its inclusion with carbonaceous reducing agents vitiates all of the claims in which it appears, and under the Markush doctrine those claims were properly rejected.

16. ***In re Swenson***, 56 USPQ 180, 182 (C.C.P.A. 1942)

An exception to the long established practice in the Patent Office rejecting claims which in form are alternative, for the reason they do not definitely set out the invention but only state that the invention may reside in any one of several specified alternatives . . . is the [rule] first enunciated by the

Commissioner of Patents in the case of *Ex parte Markush*,
340 O.G. 839, 1925 C.D. 126. Hence the term "Markush"
claim. In that case a petition was filed with the Commissioner challenging the action of the examiner objecting to
the form of certain claims as being alternative. The applicant in his application had stated he discovered that the coupling of a diazo compound of aniline or its homologues or the
halogen substitutes thereof with halogen substituted pyra-
zolones would produce dyes of exceptional fastness. The examiner objected to the form of the claims, holding them to
be alternative in that they included a diazotized solution of
aniline or its homologues or hologen substitutes. Thereupon,
to avoid the objection as to alternativeness the term "mono-
amine" was substituted. The examiner held that term to be
too broad for the reason that it would include compounds
that which would not work in the combination set out in the
application and also that only aniline and its homologues
had been disclosed. To meet this objection, the applicant
substituted for "mono-amine" in the same claims the phrase
"material selected from the group consisting of aniline, homologues of aniline and halogen substitutes of aniline." The
examiner objected to the use of that phrase for the reason
that in his opinion it evaded the alternative form without in
fact avoiding alternativeness, and he also stated that that
the phrase was not the expression of a generic term. From
the objection the petition to the Commissioner was filed.

The Commissioner in his decision noted the examiner had
admitted the expression "mono-amine" to be truly generic
but held that it was an example of a generic term which included a number of substances not all of which could be used
in the combination stated, instancing aliphatic monoamines and pyridine monoamines. The Commissioner then
held, that if there were a true subgeneric term, which would
include the elements which the applicant found useful and
exclude those which are not, that the use of such term is
proper and does make the claim in which it is used alternative. He also held that if there be no known subgeneric term
then the applicant might employ a generic term limited to
the elements found to be operative.

XVII. New Matter Rejections

1. *In re Wolfensperger*, 133 USPQ 537, 542 (C.C.P.A. 1962)

The practical, legitimate inquiry in each case of this kind
is what the drawing in fact discloses to one skilled in the art.
Whatever it does disclose may be added to the specification
in words without violation of the statute and rule which pro-

hibit "new matter," 35 U.S.C. 132, Rule 118, for the simple reason that what is originally disclosed cannot be "new matter" within the meaning of this law. If the drawing, then, contains the necessary disclosure, it can "form the basis of a valid claim."

2. ***In re Rasmussen***, 211 USPQ 323, 326 (C.C.P.A. 1981)

Broadening a claim does not add new matter to the disclosure. Disclosure is that which is taught, not that which is claimed. An applicant is entitled to claims as broad as the prior art and his disclosure will allow.

The proper basis for rejection of a claim amended to recite elements thought to be without support in the original disclosure, therefore, is § 112, first paragraph, not § 132. The latter section prohibits addition of new matter to the original disclosure. It is properly employed as a basis for objection to amendments to the abstract, specifications, or drawings attempting to add new disclosure to that originally presented.

3. ***In re Oda***, 170 USPQ 268, 270–71 (C.C.P.A. 1971)

"New matter" is a technical legal term in patent law—a term of art. Its meaning has never been clearly defined for it cannot be. The term is on a par with such terms as infringement, obviousness, priority, abandonment, and the like which express ultimate legal conclusions and are in the nature of labels attached to results after they have been reached by processes of reasoning grounded on analyses of factual situations. In other words, the statute gives us no help in determining what is or is not "new matter." We have to decide on a case-by-case basis what changes are prohibited as "new matter" and what changes are not.

In a sense, anything inserted in a specification that was not here before is new to the specification but that does not necessarily mean it is prohibited as "new matter."

4. ***In re Smythe***, 178 USPQ 279, 285 (C.C.P.A. 1973)

By disclosing in a patent application a device that inherently performs a function, operates according to a theory, or has an advantage, a patent applicant necessarily discloses that function, theory or advantage even though he says nothing concerning it. The application may later be amended to recite the function, theory or advantage without introducing prohibited new matter.

5. ***In re Rasmussen***, 211 USPQ 323, 326 n.5 (C.C.P.A. 1981)

An original claim is part of the disclosure at the time of filing.

6. ***In re Oda***, 170 USPQ 268, 272 (C.C.P.A. 1971)

Once the translator decided, incorrectly, that what the Japanese application said was "nitrous" it was only reasonable that he should be consistent; we are considering a translation error, not a typographical error. . . . On all the evidence, we conclude that one skilled in the art would appreciate not only the existence of error in the specification but what the error is. As a corollary, it follows that when the nature of this error is known it is also known how to correct it. We therefore disagree with the board's first conclusion that the change of "nitrous" to "nitric" is "new matter". . . . The Patent Office complains that there is no certified copy of the Japanese application on file and no sworn translation. While no doubt the best evidence of translation error would be, in part, a copy of the Japanese application or patent, its absence is not fatal since we find the evidence of record sufficient.

7. ***In re Oda***, 170 USPQ 268, 273 (C.C.P.A. 1971)

We do not agree with the "new matter" rejection under these circumstances. The mere fact that a change deprives a phrase of a needed antecedent so that a reader might be somewhat perplexed or confused does not result in the injection into a specification of prohibited "new matter" within the meaning of § 251.

8. ***Ex parte Brodbeck***, 199 USPQ 230, 231 (Pat. Off. Bd. App. 1977)

A change of wording to correct an error is not new matter if one skilled in the art would appreciate not only the existence of the error in the specification but what the error is. . . . Insofar as these uncontradicted declarations appear to establish a prima facie case that one skilled in the art would recognize both that the original patent is in error and what the erroneous expression should be, we are obliged to reverse the rejection.

9. ***Ex parte Porter***, 25 USPQ 2d 1144, 1146 (B.P.A.I. 1992)

As to the number of openings in the claimed nozzle, we note that such recitations of the number of nozzle openings were present in original claims 2 and 3. Since original claims constitute part of the original disclosure, . . . the examiner's rejection of claims 2 and 3 under 35 USC § 112, first paragraph, as lacking descriptive support is clear legal error.

10. ***Bocciarelli v. Huffman***, 109 USPQ 385, 388 (C.C.P.A. 1956)

It is well settled that the specification of an application may be corrected or implemented by matter contained in an original claim, and that such matter may form as much a part of the disclosure of an application as if it had appeared in the body of the specification.

11. ***In re Benno***, 226 USPQ 683, 686–87 (Fed. Cir. 1985)

While it is true . . . that "a claim is part of the disclosure," that point is of significance principally in the situation where a patent application as filed contains a claim which specifically discloses something not disclosed in the descriptive part of the specification (claims being technically part of the "specification," 35 USC 112, 2d par.), in which case the applicant may amend the specification without being charged with adding "new matter," within the meaning of Section 132.

XVII. A. New Matter and Range Limitations

1. ***In re Wertheim***, 191 USPQ 90, 99 (C.C.P.A. 1976)

The issue to be decided here is whether the limitation appearing in claim 6, carried forward into the other claims affected by this rejection, that the frozen foam be ground "to a particle size of at least 0.25 mm" before it is dried, was added to the instant application in violation of 35 USC 132. This new matter rejection rests on a finding by the PTO that the application as filed did not describe this limitation. Thus, the . . . new matter rejection is tantamount to a rejection of the claims on the description requirement of 35 USC 112, first paragraph.

. . .

The examples speak of drying frozen ground particles of sizes between 0.1 and 2 mm. While the specification indicates that the 0.25 to 2.0 mm range is preferred, we think it clearly indicates that, as an alternative embodiment of appellants' invention, the foam may be dried in limps or plates of undisclosed size, which are reduced to the obviously smaller preferred particle size by grinding only after being dried. The solicitor argues that the claimed "range" has no upper limit, wherefore it is not disclosed. The clear implication of this disclosed modification is that appellants' specification does describe as their invention processes in which particle size is "at least 0.25 mm," without upper limit, as delineated by the rejected claims.

XVIII. Incomplete Rejections

1. ***In re Piasecki***, 223 USPQ 785, 788 (Fed. Cir. 1984)

Regardless of whether the prima facie case would have been characterized as strong or weak, the examiner must consider all of the evidence anew. The process is as stated in

In re Rinehart, 531 F.2d 1048, 1052, 189 USPQ 143, 147 (C.C.P.A. 1976):

> When prima facie obviousness is established and evidence is submitted in rebuttal, the decision-maker must start over. . . . An earlier decision should not, as it was here, be considered as set in concrete, and applicant's rebuttal evidence then be evaluated only on its knockdown ability.

2. **In re Warner**, 154 USPQ 173, 178 (C.C.P.A. 1967), **cert. denied**, 389 U.S. 1057 (1968)

The Patent Office has the initial duty of supplying the factual basis for its rejection. It may not, because it may doubt that the invention is patentable, resort to speculation, unfounded assumptions or hindsight reconstruction to supply deficiencies in its factual basis.

3. **Ex parte Blanc**, 13 USPQ 2d 1383, 1384–85 (B.P.A.I. 1989)

As we see it, the examiner's statement of rejection includes no fewer than 40 separate rejections of the appealed claims. By setting forth such a broad-brush statement and by failing to explain with a reasonable degree of specificity any one rejection, the examiner has failed, procedurally, to establish a prima facie case of obviousness. As the court said in *Herrick*, "[a] rejection so stated defeats the intent and purpose of 35 U.S.C. 132". Accordingly, we shall reverse the examiner's rejections.

4. **Paperless Accounting, Inc. v. Bay Area Rapid Transit Sys.**, 231 USPQ 649, 652 (Fed. Cir. 1986), **cert. denied**, 480 U.S. 933 (1987)

As stated in *Ex parte Martin*, 104 USPQ 124, 128 (Supr. Exmr. 1952):

> When an examiner fails to mention a rejection in his final action, it has been dropped by the examiner and needs no further response by the applicant. On appeal, on those grounds of rejection which have been made in the final rejection and commented upon in the examiner's answer to brief are considered by the Board. All rejections previously made and not continued in the final rejection are considered as withdrawn. It is not necessary for the examiner to make any specific statement to that effect.

5. **In re Oetiker**, 24 USPQ 2d 1443, 1447 (Fed. Cir. 1992) (Plager, J., concurring)

The examiner cannot sit mum, leaving the applicant to shoot arrows in the dark hoping to somehow hit a secret objection harbored by the examiner. The "prima facie" case notion, the exact origin of which appears obscure . . ., seemingly was intended to leave no doubt among examiners that they must state clearly and specifically any objections (the prima facie case) to patentability, and give the applicant fair opportunity to meet those objections with evidence and argument. To that extent the concept serves to level the playing field and reduces the likelihood of administrative arbitrariness.

6. ***In re Gustafson***, 141 USPQ 585, 590 (C.C.P.A. 1964)

[A] recent address by the new Commissioner of Patents to the Patent Office professional staff on April 6, 1964, wherein he said . . . :

> The main operations of the Patent Office are, of course, the examination of patent applications and the granting of patents on patentable inventions. Promptness of examination is an important element of our work. Further, in addition to our responsibility of protecting the public by refusing to grant patents on unpatentable inventions, we should also make it our job to assist the inventor or his attorney in a positive manner to arrive at proper claims covering his invention where the invention is patentable, and I wish to request that we give greater emphasis in the future towards fulfilling this key function.

7. ***Gechter v. Davidson***, 43 USPQ 2d 1030, 1035 (Fed. Cir. 1997)

In the present case, the Board's opinion lacks a claim construction, makes conclusory findings relating to anticipation, and omits any analysis on several limitations. For example, the Board opinion does not separately construe the term "agent status messages" before finding that Canale discloses just such "agent status messages." In addition, the Board never construed the scope of the structures disclosed in the specification for the claimed "receiving means," nor did the Board expressly find that the "receiving means" disclosed in the specification was structurally equivalent to that embodied in Canale. Moreover, the Board's opinion also failed to define the exact function of the receiving means, as well as to find that Canale disclosed the *identical* function.

8. ***Gechter v. Davidson***, 43 USPQ 2d 1030, 1035 (Fed. Cir. 1997)

In sum, we hold that the Board is required to set forth in its opinions specific findings of fact and conclusions of law adequate to form a basis for our review. In particular, we expect that the Board's anticipation analysis be conducted on a limitation by limitation basis, with specific fact findings for each contested limitation and satisfactory explanations for such findings. Claim construction must also be explicit, at least as to any construction disputed by parties to the interference (or an applicant or patentee in an ex parte proceeding).

9. ***Ex parte Schricker***, 56 USPQ 2d 1723, 1725 (B.P.A.I. 2000) (unpublished)

There are two Komourdjian documents, but the examiner talks in terms of "[t]he Komourdjian system." One Komourdjian document deals with administering porcine somatotropin to salmon to improve survival when transferred from fresh to salt water; the other deals with administering porcine somatotropin to trout to increase the rate at which trout put on weight and grow. When articulating his rationale in the examiner's answer, the examiner fails to distinguish between the two Komourdjian documents. What "system" is being discussed by the examiner?

10. ***Ex parte Schricker***, 56 USPQ 2d 1723, 1725 (B.P.A.I. 2000) (unpublished)

Thus, the rationale in the examiner's answer seems to assume a difference between the claims and the prior art and purports to justify why the claimed subject matter, as a whole, would have been obvious notwithstanding the difference. The examiner's shifting rationale in support of his rejections gives us pause as to the precise basis upon which the examiner has bottomed the rejections. Moreover, the examiner's actions have made it difficult for us to decide what issues are on appeal and how those issues might be resolved on the merits.

First, the examiner does not individually address either of the Komourdjian documents. Each should be addressed separately and the examiner should state why each supports a rejection.

Second, the examiner does not address individual claims despite the fact that applicant has singled out numerous claims for separate consideration. . . .

The examiner has left applicant and the board to guess as to the basis of the rejection and after having us guess would have us figure out (i.e., further guess) what part of which Komourdjian document supports the rejection. We are not good at guessing; hence, we decline to guess.

XIX. Final Rejections/Appeal to Board

1. **MPEP §§714.12–.13** (6th ed., rev. 1, 1995)

Any amendment that will place the case either in a condition for allowance or in better form for appeal may be entered. . . . Except where an amendment . . . adopts examiner suggestions, removes issues for appeal, or in some other way requires only a cursory review by the examiner, compliance with the requirement of a showing under 37 C.F.R. §1.116(b) is expected in all amendments after final rejection.

2. **MPEP §714.13** (6th ed., rev. 1, 1995)

An amendment filed at any time after final rejection but before an appeal brief is filed, may be entered upon or after filing of an appeal provided the total effect of the amendment is to (1) remove issues for appeal, and/or (2) adopt examiner suggestions.

3. ***Ex parte Binda***, 54 USPQ 35, 36 (Pat. Off. Bd. App. 1941)

The examiner objects to these claims because he states that they contain no antecedent for the expression "all curved surfaces". . . . Applicant, however, offers to insert a statement in the claim which will include a specific antecedent for the expression "all curved surfaces". We believe that the examiner's position is well taken and that the claims should be amended to be more definite. If applicant will submit a formal amendment which is satisfactory to the examiner and which overcomes the objection raised, we recommend that the amendment be entered.

XX.   New Grounds of Rejection by Board

1. ***In re Kronig***, 190 USPQ 425, 426–27 (C.C.P.A. 1976)

Appellants urge that the ultimate criterion of whether a rejection is considered "new" in a decision by the board is whether appellants have had fair opportunity to react to the thrust of the rejection. We agree with this general proposition, for otherwise appellants could be deprived of the administrative due process rights established by 37 C.F.R. §1.196(b) of the Patent and Trademark Office. . . .

2. ***In re Doebel***, 174 USPQ 158, 160 (C.C.P.A. 1972)

While the board did not consider that it was actually making a new ground of rejection, even assuming that it did so, it is well established that the board may make a new ground of rejection and that it need not necessarily label the new rejection as such under Rule 196(b). . . .

If in fact a new ground of rejection was set forth, appellants may submit new arguments and evidence in accordance with Rule 196(b).

3. ***Ex parte GPAC, Inc.***, 29 USPQ 2d 1401, 1414 (B.P.A.I. 1993), ***aff'd***, 35 USPQ 2d 1116 (Fed. Cir. 1995)

This dissent questions whether our affirmance of the examiner's decision amounts to a new ground of rejection in that we gave further reasons why patent owner's rebuttal evidence was insufficient. We disagree. Here, in contrast to the circumstances in *In re DeBaluwe*, . . . both the examiner and the Board considered the evidence of record. Patent owner was apprised by the examiner's actions that the evidence of record was not a sufficient rebuttal of the obviousness rejections of record.

XXI. Appealing Issues to Board

1. ***Ex parte Holt***, 19 USPQ 2d 1211, 1214 (B.P.A.I. 1991)

   In those relatively rare cases where the Federal Circuit has not addressed an issue, but there is "authorized published" Board precedent, that published Board precedent is binding on panels of the Board and Examiners in the patent Examining Corps. . . .

   Unpublished Board opinions, except as they may be the "law of the case", may not be binding precedent, since the opinions are often fact driven by the specific facts present in the appeal before the Board. Unless the facts in a succeeding case are "on all fours" with or substantially the same as the facts in the preceding appeal, generally, the opinion in the preceding unpublished appeal decision may not be controlling in a succeeding appeal.

2. ***In re Gosteli***, 10 USPQ 2d 1614, 1617 (Fed. Cir. 1989)

   The CCPA's later decisions control because that court always sat en banc. Accordingly, we conclude that no conflict currently exists.

3. ***In re Epstein***, 31 USPQ 2d 1817, 1821 (Fed. Cir. 1994)

   The general rule is that administrative agencies like the PTO are not bound by the rules of evidence that govern judicial proceedings. . . . Agencies may provide for the application of evidence rules, as the PTO has so provided in patent interference proceedings, 37 C.F.R. § 1.671(b) (1993), and patent public use proceedings, id. § 1.292(a), both of which are inter partes in nature. The PTO has not, however, provided for the application of evidence rules during ex parte examination.

   The inapplicability of hearsay evidence rules in ex parte PTO examination is appropriate in light of the purpose and reason for the hearsay rule.

4. ***In re Epstein***, 31 USPQ 2d 1817, 1821 (Fed. Cir. 1994)

   During ex parte PTO examination, applicants are free to investigate hearsay assertions relied upon by an examiner during the three to six month period available to respond to

an office action. They also have the right to introduce rebuttal evidence under 37 C.F.R. § 1.132 (1993). Moreover, if
applicants wish to cross-examine the authors of written
hearsay assertions, under 35 U.S.C. § 145 (1988) they may
bring a civil action in the United States District Court for
the District of Columbia seeking adjudication that they are
entitled to receive a patent. In such an action, testimony
could be compelled by subpoena under Federal Civil Procedure Rule 45. . . . Accordingly, we reject appellant's argument that the PTO can never rely upon hearsay evidence in
making rejections.

5. ***In re Zurko***, 46 USPQ 2d 1691, 1696–99 (Fed. Cir.) (*en
   banc*), ***rev'd on other grounds***, ***Dickinson v. Zurko***, 50
   USPQ 2d 1930, 1931–32 (U.S. 1999)

The first patent act gave the Secretary of State, the Secretary of War, and the Attorney General the authority to examine and issue patents. *See* Act of April 10, 1790, ch. 7, § 1,
1 Stat. 109, 109–10. There was no provision for an appeal
from the decision of these Commissioners for the Promotion
of Useful Arts. In 1793, Congress eliminated the examination of patents and directed that they be issued when the formal technical requirements, which were enumerated by
statute, had been met. *See* Act of Feb. 21, 1793, ch. 11, §§ 3,
12, 1 Stat. 318–23. Congress gave the district courts responsibility for striking down invalid patents. *See id.* at 323
(§ 10). The act also provided for a three-member panel to ar-
bitrate interfering applications, with one member suggested
by each party and the third by the Secretary of State. *See id.*
at 322–23 (§ 9). However, the act provided no standards or
processes by which an applicant could secure review when
the application was determined not to meet the formal technical requirements.

By the Act of July 4, 1836, Congress created an examination system for issuing patents. *See* Act of July 4, 1836, ch.
357, 5 Stat. 117. This act established a Patent Office, which it
attached to the Department of State. *See id.* at 117–18 (§ 1).
The act also created a presidentially appointed Commissioner of Patents to decide, inter alia, questions of patentability, and a three-member board of examiners appointed by the
Secretary of State to hear ex parte appeals from those whose
applications the Commissioner denied. *See id.* at 119–20 (§ 7).
A party aggrieved by the outcome of an interference proceeding could "have remedy by bill in equity" in a United States
court. *Id.* at 123–24 (§ 16). However, there was no appeal
available from the decision of the board of examiners. In
1839, Congress first provided for review of patentability determinations of the Commissioner through a bill in equity to

the Chief Justice of the District of Columbia, instead of review by the board of examiners. *See* Act of March 3, 1839, ch. 88, §§ 10, 11, 5 Stat. 353, 354.

In 1861, Congress provided for presidential appointment of three examiners-in-chief to consider appeals from an examiner's denial of a patent "for the purpose of securing greater uniformity of action in the grant and refusal of letters-patent." Act of March 2, 1861, ch. 88, § 2, 12 Stat. 246. The Commissioner of Patents heard appeals from this board, and then, as provided by the 1839 Act, the Chief Justice of the District of Columbia heard appeals from the Commissioner. *See id.* If unsuccessful in either venue, an applicant could still bring an action in equity in a federal district court. However, neither the 1839 nor the 1861 acts articulated the standard of review to be used by these courts.

The Act of July 8, 1870, ch. 230 § 1, 16 Stat. 198, attached the Patent Office to the Department of the Interior. This act directed review of the examiners' patentability determinations to the examiners-in-chief (§ 46), from there to the Commissioner (§ 47), and then to the supreme court of the District of Columbia, sitting in banc (§ 48). If the Commissioner or the supreme court of the District of Columbia refused to grant a patent, applicant could seek a remedy by bill in equity. *See id.* (§ 52). This act also provided for review of the supreme court of the District of Columbia in the Supreme Court of the United States for any action "touching patent rights." *Id.* (§ 56). However, despite this elaborate review ladder, the act set out no standard for reviewing patentability determinations. . . .

In 1925, Congress moved the Patent Office to the Department of Commerce, *see* Act of March 4, 1925, ch. 1, § 1, 44 Stat. 1165, and in 1927, conjoined the review functions of the examiners-in-chief and the adjudicatory authority of the Commissioner, thereby eliminating appeals from the former to the latter, *see* Act of March 2, 1927, ch. 273, § 3, 44 Stat. 1335, 1335–36. The 1927 act gave the Commissioner authority to choose the three-member board, called the Board of Appeals, that would review patentability decisions. *See id.* It also provided dissatisfied applicants with appeal rights to the Court of Appeals of the District of Columbia, in which case the applicants could not seek remedy by bill in equity under section 4915 of the Revised Statutes. *See id.* at 1336 (§ 8). Two years later, Congress created the Court of Customs and Patent Appeals (CCPA), splicing jurisdiction from the Court of Appeals for the District of Columbia over patent and trademark appeals from the Patent Office together with the jurisdiction of the Court of Customs Appeals over customs cases. *See* Act of March 2, 1929, ch. 488, §§ 1, 2, 45 Stat. 1475, 1475–76. . . .

Congress changed the name of the Patent Office to the Patent and Trademark Office, see Act of January 2, 1975, Pub. L. No. 93-596, § 1, 88 Stat. 1949, and passed the Federal Courts Improvement Act of 1982, which in part merged the CCPA with the United States Court of Claims to create this court and what is now the Court of Federal Claims, *see* Act of April 2, 1982, Pub. L. No. 97-164, 96 Stat. 25. The 1982 act combined, inter alia, nationwide jurisdiction over appeals from district courts in cases arising under the patent laws, 28 U.S.C. § 1295(a)(1), with jurisdiction over direct appeals from the Patent and Trademark Office's Board of Appeals and its Board of Patent Interferences, *id.* § 1295(a)(4). An expressed purpose for doing so, similar to the purpose expressed in the Act of March 2, 1861, was to increase uniformity of decisionmaking in patent cases. . . . In 1984, Congress merged the Board of Appeals and the Board of Patent Interferences into the Board of Patent Appeals and Interferences. *See* Act of November 8, 1984, Pub. L. No. 98-622, § 201, 98 Stat. 3383, 3386. Thus, after more than two hundred years of evolution, the board is composed of members including the Commissioner, deputy and assistant commissioners, and examiners-in-chief. *See* 35 U.S.C. § 7(a). Panels of at least three board members selected by the Commissioner review twice-rejected or final decisions of a primary examiner, *see* 37 C.F.R. § 1.191 (1997), and can affirm or reverse on the grounds specified by the examiner, or remand to the examiner for further consideration with or without a new ground for rejection, or permit amendments. *See id.* § 1.196(a)-(b). The board's ex parte proceedings involving patentability are not recorded, nor are they "hearings on the record" within the meaning of 5 U.S.C. § 554 (requiring trial-type procedures and a reliance on a closed record). . . .

The proceedings rely on the technical expertise of board members, *see* 37 C.F.R. § 1.196(b) (1997), they provide the option of an oral hearing, *see id.* § 1.194(c) (twenty minutes for appellant and fifteen for primary examiner) though no live testimony is taken, they are conducted largely in confidence, *see* 35 U.S.C. § 122, they do not prohibit consideration of materials beyond the record, *see* 37 C.F.R. § 1.196(b), and they are conducted under considerable time constraints. The examiners-in-chief operate under their authority as experienced patent examiners, with "competent legal knowledge and scientific ability," 35 U.S.C. § 7, rather than under the discretionary adjudicatory authority delegated to the Commissioner.

6. **Schulze v. Green**, 45 USPQ 2d 1770, 1772–73 (Fed. Cir. 1998)

Prior to the 1984 Amendments to the patent statute (the "1984 Amendments"), the Board of Patent Interferences decided questions of priority, but not of patentability. Issues of patentability over the prior art were decided only by the Board of Appeals. . . . Under the old statute and its implementing regulations, if issues of patentability were raised during an interference, the interference would be stayed, examination would resume ex parte to resolve the patentability issue, and thereafter the interference proceeding would resume. If other issues of patentability were still pending at the conclusion of the interference, as was often the case, the application was once again returned to ex parte examination for resolution of those issues. . . .

Congress became dissatisfied with the inefficiency of this "start-and-stop" process in which a case could "ping-pong" back and forth between interference and examination proceedings. Therefore, in 1984, Congress combined the Board of Patent Interferences with the Board of Patent Appeals to create the current Board of Patent Appeals and Interferences, and also amended 35 U.S.C. Section 135(a) to include the following provision: "The Board of Patent Appeals and Interferences shall determine questions of priority of the inventions and *may determine questions of patentability.*" Patent Law Amendments Act of 1984, Pub. L. No. 98-622, Sections 201–207, 98 Stat. 3383, 3386–89 (1984) (codified as amended at 35 U.S.C. Section 135(a) (1994)) (emphasis added). Consolidation of the two boards into one, with authority to consider questions both of patentability and of priority in a unified proceeding, was intended to streamline such proceedings before the PTO. *See* 130 Cong. Rec. 28,065, 28,072 (1984), reprinted in 1984 U.S.C.C.A.N. 5827, 5836–37.

7. **Ex parte Lemoine**, 46 USPQ 2d 1432, 1434 (B.P.A.I. 1998) (unpublished)

To decide whether we have statutory jurisdiction, we must determine whether the appellant is an applicant "any of whose claims have been twice rejected." 35 U.S.C. § 134. On the matter of the jurisdiction placed on this Board by statute, the decision of a Group Director, while worthy of serious consideration, is not, and can not be, binding. The effect of the Group Director's decision, in this case, was merely to overrule the examiner's decision not to transmit the application to the Board because the application was abandoned.

We recognize that 37 C.F.R. § 1.191(e) provides that jurisdiction over an application vests in the Board when the application is transmitted to the Board. However, this provision does not create jurisdiction, it merely specifies timing. Normally, jurisdiction over a matter transfers to an appellate tribunal upon the filing of an appeal. Our jurisdiction does not attach until the examining corps has finished its job and transfers the application file to the Board. This permits, inter alia, examiners to allow the application to issue or enter new grounds of rejection without requesting a remand from the Board. While under appropriate circumstances, an examiner or a Group Director may refuse to transmit an application to the Board (see, 37 C.F.R. § 1.193(a)), they can not create jurisdiction where none exists.

8. ***Ex parte Lemoine***, 46 USPQ 2d 1420, 1423 (B.P.A.I.), ***reconsideration granted in part***, 46 USPQ 2d 1432 (B.P.A.I. 1998)(unpublished)

Section 134 is part of Chapter 12 of Title 35. Chapter 12 is titled "Examination of Application" and sets forth the general procedures to be followed in the Office for examination. Sections 131 to 134 provide the general procedures relating to ex parte examination. In relevant part, these sections specify that (1) an examination shall be made (§ 131); (2) if "any claim for a patent" is rejected, the applicant shall be informed of the bases of the rejection (§ 132); (3) if the applicant persists in the "claim for a patent, with or without amendment," the application shall be reexamined (§ 132); and (4) if applicant's claims have been twice rejected, the applicant may appeal (§ 134). Considering these sections together, we conclude that the "claims" as used in § 134 is a reference to the repeated "claim for a patent" as used in § 132 rather than a reference to a particular claim "of an application." Under our interpretation, so long as the applicant has twice been denied a patent, an appeal may be filed. So construing the statute, we conclude that applicant's claims for a patent have been twice rejected. Applicant has been denied a patent three times. Applicant, therefore, had the right to appeal and we, accordingly, have jurisdiction.

9. ***Ex parte Lemoine***, 46 USPQ 2d 1420, 1424 (B.P.A.I.), ***reconsideration granted in part***, 46 USPQ 2d 1432 (B.P.A.I. 1998)(unpublished)

In presenting the appeal, applicant has separately addressed each rejection, but has not separately asserted the patentability of the claims within each group. Accordingly, the claims in each group stand or fall together. . . . Where an applicant does not "point out what relevance the additional limitations have to the patentability of the narrower claims," the claims will stand or fall together even if applicant asserts that the claims do not stand or fall together. *In re Herbert*, 461 F.2d 1390, 1391, 174 USPQ 259, 260 (C.C.P.A. 1972).

10. ***In re Schechter***, 98 USPQ 144, 150 (C.C.P.A. 1953)

Allowability of an appealed claim is not controlled by the fact that similar claims have been allowed in the Patent Office, since an appealed claim must be patentable in its own right in the opinion of this court. However, similar claims allowed by the Patent Office tribunals furnish evidence of what features those tribunals regard as patentable, and we think it proper, and sometimes necessary, to consider allowed claims in order to fully determine the views of the board and the examiner.

11. ***In re Duve***, Civ. App. 97-1095, slip op. at 5 n. 1 (Fed. Cir. Feb. 26, 1999)

Mr. Duve had requested reconsideration of the Board decision as to claim 8. The Board objected that because he had not argued claim 8 separately in his initial argument, he was precluded from requesting reconsideration of claim 8. We do not believe that such legalistic rigidity is appropriate in the proceeding before the Board, particularly when appeal to the Board was taken to all the rejected claims.

12. ***Gustavsson v. Valentini***, 25 USPQ 2d 1401, 1405 (B.P.A.I. 1992)

Congress "may leave it to administrative officials to establish rules within the prescribed limits of the statute." *Ethicon v. Quigg*, 849 F.2d 1422, 1425, 7 USPQ2d 1152, 1154 (Fed. Cir. 1988) (quoting *Patlex Corp. v. Mossinghoff*, 758 F. 2d 594, 605, 225 USPQ 243, 251 (Fed. Cir. 1985)). In the patent field, Congress has done precisely that by providing that the Director "may, subject to the approval of the Secretary of Commerce, establish regulations, not inconsistent with law, for the conduct of proceedings in the Patent and Trademark Office." 35 U.S.C. § 6(a) (1994). In this type of situation, "the validity of a regulation promulgated thereunder will be sustained so long as it is 'reasonably related to the enabling legislation.'" *Mourning v. Family Publications Service, Inc.*, 411 U.S. 356, 369 (1973) (quoting *Thorpe v. Housing Authority of Durham*, 393 U.S. 268, 280 (1969)).

13. ***Teacherson v. Patent and Trademark Office***, Civ. App. No. 99-1465, slip op. at 4 (Fed. Cir. Mar. 10, 2000) (unpublished), ***cert. denied***, 531 U.S. 997 (2000)

The Patent Act has mandated the appeal route for rejections of patent applications:

An applicant for a patent, any of whose claims has been twice rejected, may appeal from the decision of the primary examiner to the Board of Patent Appeals and Interferences, having once paid the fee for such appeal.

35 U.S.C. § 134 (1994).

An applicant dissatisfied with the decision in an appeal to the Board of Patent Appeals and Interferences under section 134 of this title may appeal the decision to the United States Court of Appeals for the Federal Circuit.

35 U.S.C. § 141 (1994). Alternatively, an applicant dissatisfied with a decision of the Board of Patent Appeals and Interferences may also file a civil suit against the Commissioner of Patents and Trademarks in United States District Court for the District of Columbia. 35 U.S.C. § 145 (1994). . . . The Patent Act created the PTO review process, imposing the duty to follow a specified appeal process on both applicant and PTO. The Act does not create jurisdiction to circumvent these statutory appeal routes.

14. ***In re Baker Hughes Inc.***, 55 USPQ 2d 1149, 1153 (Fed. Cir. 2000)

In its reexamination decision, the examiner allowed another claim, claim 37 (added during reexamination), that is identical to claim 1 except that it explicitly recites a "liquid hydrocarbon." . . . Since the examiner concluded that claim 37 would not have been obvious over the Doerges reference, we can safely assume that he would have concluded that claim 1 would not have been obvious over the Doerges reference had he construed the claim as we have.

XXI.A. *Collateral Estoppel From Board Decisions*

1. ***Gould v. Mossinghoff***, 219 USPQ 393, 395 (D.C. Cir. 1983)

However, the doctrine of collateral estoppel bars relitigation only of issues actually determined in prior litigation. . . . Fundamental to any application of the doctrine is that the issue or issues previously determined be identical to the issue or issues presently barred. . . . As this requirement has been interpreted in patent litigation involving continuation application under 35 U.S.C. §120, reviewing courts will apply collateral estoppel only after determining, based on a comparison of the prior adjudicated claims and the appealed claims, that the invention claimed in both prior and present proceedings is the same. The application rule was succinctly stated by the Court of Customs and Patent Appeals in *In re Szwarc*, 319 F.2d 277, 138 USPQ 208 (C.C.P.A. 1963), *overruled in part on other grounds*, *In re Kirk*, 376 F.2d 936, 946,

153 USPQ 56 (C.C.P.A. 1967), where, as here, the PTO argued that a prior finding of inadequate disclosure in a parent application had collateral estoppel effect:

> [We must] determine, by comparing the appealed claims and the claims rejected in the parent case, whether the "invention" of the appealed claims is the same or is different from "the invention" in the prior rejected claims. Only after such a comparison can it be decided if estoppel by judgment or collateral estoppel prevents us from making a determination of whether, under 35 U.S.C. §120, the appealed claims are entitled to the benefit of the filing date of the earlier parent application.

2. ***Gould v. Mossinghoff***, 219 USPQ 393, 396 (D.C. Cir. 1983)
Absent substantial identity of inventions, we would rather err on the side of granting a hearing on the merits than summarily deny patent rights to which an applicant may be statutorily entitled.

The issue identity requirement is plainly unsatisfied here. The Javan interference proceeding bars appellant from attempting to disclose a gas discharge laser oscillator. Appellant, however, advances a different claim that principally concerns a gas discharge laser amplifier.

3. ***Arachnid, Inc. v. Valley Recreation Prods., Inc.***, 29 USPQ 2d 1457, 1459 (Fed. Cir. 1993) (unpublished)
Collateral estoppel precludes a party from relitigating issues previously decided in other actions where the following criteria are met: "(1) the issue is identical to one decided in the first action; (2) the issue was actually litigated in the first action; (3) resolution of the issue was essential to a final judgment in the first action; and (4) plaintiff had a full and fair opportunity to litigate the issue in the first action."

XXII. Practice and Procedure for Rejections/Objections

1. ***Ex parte C***, 27 USPQ 2d 1492, 1494 (B.P.A.I. 1992)
There are significant legal and procedural distinctions between an "objection" and a "rejection". An "objection" to the specification indicates that the specification is not satisfactory to the examiner because it does not conform to certain criteria established by (a) the patent statute, (b) the Patent and Trademark Office rules of practice, or (c) conventions and customary practices which have evolved over the years. A "rejection" constitutes an adverse decision by the examiner denying the grant of a patent for the subject matter claimed

on the ground that the invention as set forth in the claims does not meet the requirements imposed by Congress in the patent statute.

In this case, that part of the examiner's "objection" which centers on description, enablement and best mode concerns the correspondence of the specification to the statutory requirements set forth in 35 U.S.C. § 112 and is within the jurisdiction of this Board. However, that part of the "objection" which relates . . . [to the] examiner's desire for information concerning (a) an explanation of the "gist" of the invention, (b) the phenotypic characteristics of the parent plants and the inheritability thereof, and (c) the goals sought to be achieved by the inventors, relates solely to the ease and accuracy of the examination process and the ability of the examiner to obtain sufficient information therefrom to effectively examine the application. It concerns either the rules of practice or established customs and practices. It is outside the jurisdiction of this Board.

2. ***Ex parte C***, 27 USPQ 2d 1492, 1494 n.3 (B.P.A.I. 1992)

35 U.S.C. § 134, which provides the right to appeal, refers only to the appeal of rejections of claims and, accordingly, restricts the jurisdiction of the Board of Patent Appeals and Interferences to considering the propriety of "rejections". The propriety of "objections" and other procedural requirements is solely within the jurisdiction of the Commissioner of Patents.

3. ***In re Gustafson***, 141 USPQ 585, 589 (C.C.P.A. 1964)

When claims have not been rejected for want of novelty or utility, the principal remaining questions are whether they define subject matter which would not have been obvious, at the time the invention was made, to one of ordinary skill in the art, and whether they define it in such manner as to comply with 35 U.S.C. 112.

4. ***Magnivision, Inc. v. Bonneau Co.***, 42 USPQ 2d 1925, 1927 (Fed. Cir. 1997), ***cert. denied***, 522 U.S. 1090 (1998)

The patent examining process is conducted by way of a series of exchanges between patent examiner and patent applicant. To facilitate and speed the process, the Rules of the Patent and Trademark Office authorize personal and telephone interviews. The rules require that all interviews be recorded by the patent applicant, in accordance with 37 C.F.R. §1.133:

> (b) . . . In every instance where reconsideration is requested in view of an interview with an examiner, a complete written statement of the reasons presented at the in-

terview as warranting favorable action must be filed by the applicant.

The Manual of Patent Examining Procedure at §713.04 elaborates, requiring the applicant to record the substance of the interview unless the examiner does so:

> ... It is the responsibility of the applicant or the attorney or agent to make the substance of an interview of record in the application file, unless the examiner indicates that he or she will do so. It is the examiner's responsibility to see that such a record is made and to correct material inaccuracies which bear directly on the question of patentability.

5. ***Magnivision, Inc. v. Bonneau Co.***, 42 USPQ 2d 1925, 1929 (Fed. Cir. 1997), ***cert. denied***, 522 U.S. 1090 (1998)

Imperfection in patent examination, whether by the examiner or the applicant, does not create a new defense called "prosecution irregularities" ...

The validity of a patent is always subject to plenary challenge on its merits. A court may invalidate a patent on any substantive ground, whether or not that ground was considered by the patent examiner. Procedural lapses during examination, should they occur, do not provide grounds of invalidity. Absent proof of inequitable conduct, the examiner's or the applicant's absolute compliance with the internal rules of patent examination becomes irrelevant after the patent has issued.

6. ***Baxter Int'l, Inc. v. McGaw, Inc.***, 47 USPQ 2d 1225, 1234 (Fed. Cir. 1998)

The sole question before this court, then, is whether the submission of a set of claims, accompanied by instructions to the PTO to cancel those claims, satisfies the requirement of 35 U.S.C. § 120 that the applicant submit "an application for patent" where the term "application" is defined by 35 U.S.C. § 111. . . . We conclude that where the applicant has submitted a set of claims with an accompanying instruction to the PTO to cancel all of those claims, without the substitution of new claims, the applicant has not fulfilled the requirements of 35 U.S.C. § 112, paragraph 2, and is not entitled to a filing date until at least one claim has been submitted.

7. ***Hyatt v. Boone***, 47 USPQ 2d 1128, 1133 (Fed. Cir. 1998), ***cert. denied***, 525 U.S. 1141 (1999)

The issue here raised is not one of substantive continuity of disclosure, but solely of whether a photocopy of the prior oath, instead of a new oath, was acceptable for filing, when

it was in fact accepted for filing. Any technical deficiency in
meeting the formal requirements of Rule 60 must be viewed
in light of the agency's acceptance of the applications as in
compliance with the Rule. Regularity of routine administrative procedures is presumed, and departure therefrom,
should such have occurred, is not grounds of collateral attack. Courts should not readily intervene in the day-to-day
operations of an administrative agency, especially when the
agency practice is in straightforward implementation of the
statute.

8. ***Hyatt v. Boone***, 47 USPQ 2d 1128, 1133 (Fed. Cir. 1998),
cert. denied, 525 U.S. 1141 (1999)
We also take note, as held in *Weil v. Fritz*, 572 F.2d 856, 863,
196 USPQ 600, 606 (C.C.P.A. 1978), that the "applicant's
oath is not a requirement of § 112, first paragraph, but of 35
U.S.C. § 115; therefore, the sufficiency of [the prior] oath is
not material under § 120."

9. ***In re Ductmate Indus., Inc.***, Reexamination Control Number 90/004,369, U.S. Patent 4,584,756, p.3 (Comm'r Feb. 12,
1997)
This document explains Exhibits 1–4 and supplies information concerning these documents which does not appear on
the face of the documents. The petition appears to allege
that this document is a verified document, but was improperly ignored by the examiner. A review of the document
shows that it is not executed under oath, and certainly is not
properly authenticated as required with respect to an oath
executed abroad, it being noted that Reutlinger is a city in
Germany. See MPEP §§ 602.04 and 604. The document lacks
a verification clause under 35 USC § 25 and 37 CFR § 1.68.

10. ***In re Ductmate Indus., Inc.***, Reexamination Control Number 90/004,369, U.S. Patent 4,584,756, p.5 (Comm'r Feb. 12,
1997)
Under 28 USC § 1746, a statement under penalty of perjury
is acceptable in place of a sworn declaration or oath or affidavit if it is submitted in *substantially* the following form,
(emphasis supplied):
[1] If executed without the United States:

"I declare (or certify, verify, or state) under penalty of
perjury *under the laws of the United States of America*
that the foregoing is true and correct. Executed on (date).
(Signature)."

[2] If executed within the United States its territories,
possessions or commonwealths:

"I declare (or certify, verify, or state) under penalty of perjury that the foregoing is true and correct Executed on (date). (Signature)." (emphasis supplied)

Clearly, this document does not *substantially* comply with the form permitted under 28 USC § 1746. It omits any reference to the "laws of the United States of America". These very words are the words which Congress chose to require whenever a document was executed without the United States, as opposed to the language required for documents executed within the United States. Therefore, it cannot be contended that a statement signed in Germany which omits the words "under the laws of the United States of America" qualifies as a statement which is "substantially" in compliance with 28 USC § 1746. Had Congress felt the omitted words to be so unimportant, it would not have taken the trouble to require them specifically in statements executed abroad.

It appears, therefore, that the statement submitted by Georg Mez does not qualify as a verified statement under 28 USC § 1746. It is not a verified statement under 35 USC § 25 and is not a verified statement as an oath executed in the manner of an oath under 35 USC § 115 (when made in a foreign country, must appear before a diplomatic: or consular office of the United States authorized to administer oaths, etc.).

11. ***Li Second Family Ltd. P'ship v. Toshiba Corp.***, 231 F.3d 1373, 56 USPQ 2d 1681, 1685 (Fed. Cir. 2000)

The PTO requires all business before it to be conducted, or at least documented, in writing. *Litton Sys., Inc. v. Whirlpool Corp.*, 728 F.2d 1423, 1439, 221 USPQ 97, 106 (Fed. Cir. 1984) (citing 37 C.F.R. § 1.2). It is the responsibility of the applicant to ensure that the substance of any interview with the examiner is included in the written record of the application, unless the examiner indicates that he will do so. See id. (citing Manual of Patent Examining Procedure § 713.04).

XXII.A. *Arguing Invention Recited in Patent Claims*

1. ***In re Bisley***, 94 USPQ 80, 83 (C.C.P.A. 1952)

The right of an applicant to patent claims, however, depends not only on what new and unobvious results his disclosed device will produce but also on whether the claims adequately recite the feature which produces these results and upon which applicant predicates patentability. . . . If the claims fail to adequately define such feature by proper limitations, they are not allowable even though the device as disclosed would support patentable claims.

2. ***In re Crowell***, 84 F.2d 206, 208 (C.C.P.A. 1936)

We do not find in the specification at bar any use of the phrase "a by-pass through the plug" nor any use of the term "by-pass," but the drawings seem to disclose such a feature. However, whatever the specification and drawings may show in that respect, the claims themselves do not contain the feature in any form, and it would seem that appellant is insisting that a limitation which he did not himself express in the claims shall be read into them by the Patent Office or by this court. This court, following the principle announced by the Supreme Court of the United States in the case of *McCarty v. Lehigh Valley Railroad Co.*, . . . has again and again held that limitations not in the claims need not be considered. In the case of *In re Buckwalter*, . . . we said: "As has been so often said, the claim is the measure of the invention, and, if appellant's claims were so broadly drawn as to read upon the prior art, we know of no rule which would authorize the tribunals of the Patent Office, or the courts to read limitations, based upon extraneous arguments, into them."

3. ***In re Deutsch***, 193 USPQ 645, 649 (C.C.P.A. 1977)

A determination of the presence or absence of statutory subject matter must rest upon the claimed invention considered as a whole, not upon selected unclaimed portions of the specification. It was error, therefore, for the board to focus upon one of Deutsch's disclosed optimization techniques and to transpose it from the specification to the claims as though the optimization technique were being claimed and preempted.

4. ***In re Henschell***, 34 USPQ 17, 18 (C.C.P.A. 1937)

The difficulty with appellant's position is, however, that this particular limitation is not disclosed in any of the claims. . . . The particular feature, therefore, upon which the appellant so strongly relies, although disclosed by him in his specification, is not claimed in this application, and hence he can have no benefit from it here. The right to appellant to a patent depends not only upon what his devices will do, but what he claims for it.

XXIII. Double Patenting

1. ***Studiengesellschaft Kohle mbH v. Northern Petrochemical Co.***, 228 USPQ 837, 844 (Fed. Cir. 1986) (Newman, J., concurring)

Since the 1952 Patent Act, § 121 has protected patentees from the need to prove, before the PTO or the courts, that the claims of the divisional application are to an independent and distinct invention, when the patent examiner had determined during examination that the inventions were independent and distinct, and by requiring restriction had refused to examine the claims to any non-elected claims in a new patent application, or to abandon them. Section 121 effects a form of estoppel that shields the applicant from having to prove the correctness of the restriction requirement in order to preserve the validity of the second patent.

2. ***In re Land***, 151 USPQ 621, 624 (C.C.P.A. 1966)

We here make the observation that "double patenting" is normally applied as a ground of rejection when the patent used to support the double patenting rejection is not available as a reference to show "prior art" under 35 U.S.C. 102 or 103.

3. ***In re Lonardo***, 43 USPQ 2d 1262, 1266 (Fed. Cir. 1997), ***cert. denied***, 522 U.S. 1147 (1998)

The doctrine of double patenting is intended to prevent a patentee from obtaining a time-wise extension of patent for the same invention or an obvious modification thereof. *E.g.*, *In re Longi*, 759 F.2d 887, 892, 225 USPQ 645, 648 (Fed. Cir. 1985). "Same invention" double patenting is based upon 35 U.S.C. § 101 (1994), which states that an inventor may obtain "a patent" for an invention. The statute thus permits only one patent to be obtained for a single invention, and the phrase "same invention" refers to an invention drawn to substantially identical subject matter. *Id.* Obviousness-type double patenting, on the other hand, is judicially created and prohibits an inventor from obtaining a second patent for claims that are not patentably distinct from the claims of the first patent. *Id.* With obviousness-type double patenting, however, a terminal disclaimer may overcome that basis for unpatentability, assuming that the first patent has not expired.

4. ***Ex parte Davis***, 56 USPQ 2d 1434, 1435 (B.P.A.I. 2000) (unpublished)

Double patenting is a legal doctrine that forbids an inventor from obtaining a second valid patent for either the same invention or an obvious modification of the same invention claimed in that inventor' s first patent. See *In re Longi*, 759 F.2d 887, 892, 225 USPQ 645, 648 (Fed. Cir. 1985). The basic concept of double patenting is that the same invention cannot be patented more than once since to do so would result in a second patent that would expire some time after the first patent expired and extend the protection timewise. *General Foods Corp. v. Studiengesellschaft Kohle mbH*, 972 F.2d 1272, 1279–80, 23 USPQ2d 1839, 1845 (Fed. Cir. 1992); *In re Kaplan*, 789 F.2d 1574, 1579–80, 229 USPQ 678, 683 (Fed. Cir. 1986).

35 U.S.C. § 101 states "Whoever invents or discovers any new and useful process, machine, manufacture, or composition of matter, or any new and useful improvement thereof, may obtain a patent therefor . . . ." The prohibition of double patenting of the same invention is based on 35 U.S.C. § 101. *In re Goodman*, 11 F.3d 1046, 1052, 29 USPQ2d 2010, 2015 (Fed. Cir. 1993); *Longi*, 759 F.2d at 892, 225 USPQ at 648. By "same invention," the court means "identical subject matter," *Longi*, 759 F.2d at 892, 225 USPQ at 648; *In re Vogel*, 422 F.2d 438, 441, 164 USPQ 619, 621 (CCPA 1970). A good test, and probably the only objective test, for "same invention," is whether one of the claims would be literally infringed without literally infringing the other. If it could be, the claims do not define identically the same invention. *Vogel*, 422 F.2d at 441, 164 USPQ at 621–22 (halogen is not the "same" as chlorine; meat is not the "same" as pork). All types of double patenting which are not "same invention" double patenting have come to be referred to as "obviousness-type" double patenting. See *In re Van Ornum*, 686 F.2d 937, 942–43, 214 USPQ 761, 766 (CCPA 1982), which states in discussing cases leading to *Vogel's* restatement of the law of double patenting,

> numerous cases were considered in which application claims were directed to mere obvious modifications of, or improvements on, inventions defined in the claims of patents already issued to the same inventors, or to common assignees, and it had been decided that they might be allowed to go to patent if the applicants filed terminal disclaimers. We classified these as "obviousness type double patenting." This latter classification has, in the course of time, come, somewhat loosely, to indicate any "double patenting" situation other than one of the "same invention" type.

See also *General Foods*, 972 F.2d at 1279–80, 23 USPQ2d at 1844–45.

"Obviousness-type" double patenting extends the fundamental legal doctrine to preclude "obvious variants" of what has already been patented. See *In re Berg*, 140 F.3d 1428, 1432, 46 USPQ2d 1226, 1229 (Fed. Cir. 1998); *Goodman*, 11 F.3d at 1052, 29 USPQ2d at 2015 and *General Foods*, 972 F.2d at 1280, 23 USPQ2d at 1845. "Obviousness-type" double patenting precludes issuance where there is no "patentable difference" or no "patentable distinction" between the two claims. *Goodman*, 11 F.3d at 1052, 29 USPQ2d at 2015; *Gen-*

eral Foods, 972 F.2d at 1278–79, 23 USPQ2d at 1844. This allows the public to practice obvious variations of the first patented invention after the first patent expires. See *Longi*, 759 F.2d at 892–93, 225 USPQ at 648. The courts adopted the doctrine out of necessity where claims in two applications by the same inventor were so much alike that to allow the latter would effectively extend the life of the first patent. See *Gerber Garment Technology, Inc. v. Lectra Sys.*, 916 F.2d 683, 686, 16 USPQ2d 1436, 1439 (Fed. Cir. 1990); *In re Thorington*, 418 F.2d 528, 534, 163 USPQ 644, 648 (CCPA 1969), cert. denied, 397 U.S. 1038, 165 USPQ 290 (1970).

In summary, "obviousness-type" double patenting is a judge-made doctrine that prevents an unjustified extension of the patent right beyond the statutory time limit. It requires rejection of an application claim when the claimed subject matter is not patentably distinct from the subject matter claimed in a commonly owned patent when the issuance of a second patent would provide an unjustified extension of the term of the right to exclude granted by a patent. In order to overcome an "obviousness-type" double patenting rejection, an applicant may file a "terminal disclaimer," foregoing that portion of the term of the second patent that extends beyond the term of *Berg*, 140 F.3d at 1431–32, 46 USPQ2d at 1229.

Thus, if a claim sought in the application is not identical to yet not patentably distinct from a claim in an inventor's earlier patent, then the claim must be rejected under "obviousness-type" double patenting rejection. See *Berg*, 140 F.3d at 1431, 46 USPQ2d at 1229; *In re Braat*, 937 F.2d 589, 592, 19 USPQ2d 1289, 1291–92 (Fed. Cir. 1991); *Goodman*, 11 F.3d at 1052, 29 USPQ2d at 2015; *Vogel*, 422 F.2d at 441, 164 USPQ at 622. In determining whether a claim sought in the application is patentably distinct from the claims in an inventor's earlier patent a variety of tests have been utilized. In *Berg*, 140 F.3d at 1433–34, 46 USPQ2d at 1230–31 and *In re Emert*, 124 F.3d 1458, 1461–62, 44 USPQ2d 1149, 1152 (Fed. Cir. 1997), a "one-way" test was applied. Under this "one-way" test, the examiner asks whether the application claims are obvious over the patent claims. In *Goodman*, 11 F.3d at 1052–53, 29 USPQ2d at 2015–16 and *Van Ornum*, 686 F.2d at 942–43, 214 USPQ at 766–67, a test similar to the "one-way" test was applied. Under this test, the examiner asks whether the application claims are generic to any species set forth in the patent claims. In *In re Dembiczak*, 175 F.3d 994, 1002, 50 USPQ2d 1614, 1619–20 (Fed. Cir. 1999) and *Braat*, 937 F.2d at 593–94, 19 USPQ2d at 1292–93, a "two-way" test was applied. Under this "two-way" test, the examiner asks whether the application claims are obvious over the patent claims and also asks whether the patent claims are obvious over the application claims.

5. ***Eli Lilly & Co. v. Barr Labs.***, 55 USPQ 2d 1609, 1618 (Fed. Cir. 2000)

[D]ouble patenting is not "concerned with what one skilled in the art would be aware [of] from reading the claims but with what inventions the claims define." *In re Sarett*, 51 C.C.P.A. 1180, 327 F.2d 1005, 1013, 140 USPQ 474, 481 (C.C.P.A. 1964). Here, claim 1 of the '895 patent, when properly construed, already covered the administration of fluoxetine hydrochloride for treating depression. Further, Lilly's reliance on *In re Baird*, 16 F.3d 380, 29 USPQ 2d 1550 (Fed. Cir. 1994), and *In re Jones*, 958 F.2d 347, 21 USPQ 2d 1941 (Fed. Cir. 1992), is unavailing. In those cases, we held that a species claim is not necessarily obvious in light of a prior art disclosure of a genus. See *Baird*, 16 F.3d at 382, 29 USPQ 2d at 1552; *Jones*, 958 F.2d at 350, 21 USPQ 2d at 1943. The present case, however, in which the same party claims a genus in an earlier patent and then claims a species in a later patent is entirely different from cases such as *Baird* and *Jones*, in which the prior art merely discloses a genus and a later patent claims a species.

XXIII.A.   *Same Invention Double Patenting*

1. ***Studiengesellschaft Kohle mbH v. Northern Petrochemical Co.***, 228 USPQ 837, 840 (Fed. Cir. 1986) (per curiam)

We agree with SGK, and hold that because the two patents claim different statutory classes of subject matter, composition and process, they are not the same invention. The Court of Customs and Patent Appeals held that this alone is sufficient to avoid same invention-type double patenting.

2. ***Studiengesellschaft Kohle mbH v. Northern Petrochemical Co.***, 228 USPQ 837, 840 (Fed. Cir. 1986) (per curiam) (quoting ***In re Vogel***, 422 F.2d 438, 441, 164 USPQ 619, 621–22 (C.C.P.A. 1970))

By "same invention" we mean identical subject matter. Thus the invention defined by a claim reciting "halogen" is not the same as that defined by a claim reciting "chlorine," because the former is broader than the latter. . . . A good test, and probably the only objective test, for "same invention," is whether one of the claims would be literally infringed without literally infringing the other. If it could be, the claims do not define identically the same invention.

Patent Prosecution Case Digest

3. ***Studiengesellschaft Kohle mbH v. Northern Petro-chemical Co.***, 228 USPQ 837, 840 (Fed. Cir. 1986) (per curiam)

This body of CCPA law as represented in *Boylan, Walles, Taylor, Vogel*, and other cases, dealt with the "same invention" issue. Our predecessor court refused to find double patenting based, variously, on differences in claimed subject matter on different statutory classes; on the existence of non-infringing uses; on differences in the breadth of the claims; and on the absence of "cross-reading" (whether the claims of one patent can be infringed without infringing the other).

4. ***In re Baird***, 146 USPQ 579, 582–83 (C.C.P.A. 1965)

In our view, the patent and the application do not claim the same invention. They claim two different inventions. The patent claims a method comprising, in claim 6, six steps, step (c) being irradiation. The other patent claims are similar and need not be separately analyzed. They all include irradiation. The application claims omit the irradiation step, whatever other similarities may exist, and hence the claimed method is different. It cannot be said that the method of steps ABCD is the same method or invention as one consisting only of steps ACD or ABD. So much for the solicitor's argument that the inventions claimed are the same.

5. ***In re Longi***, 225 USPQ 645, 648 (Fed. Cir. 1985)

A double patenting rejection precludes one person from obtaining more than one valid patent for either (a) the "same invention," or (b) an "obvious" modification of the "same invention. A rejection based on double patenting of the same invention" type finds its support in the language of 35 U.S.C. § 101 which states that "Whoever invents or discovers any new and useful process * * * may obtain a patent therefor . . ." (Emphasis added.) Thus, the term "same invention," in this context means an invention drawn to identical subject matter.

XXIII.B. Obviousness-Type Double Patenting

1. ***In re Baird***, 146 USPQ 579, 583 (C.C.P.A. 1965)

The next question we must consider is whether the difference, due to the inclusion or omission of irradiation, is a difference adequate to warrant the issue of a second patent or, as it may otherwise be stated, whether the application claims are patentable over the claims of the patent. This problem may also be stated to be whether it would have been obvious to one of ordinary skill to modify the process of the patent claims by eliminating the irradiation step. In considering this question it must be carefully remembered that by reason of the copendency of the application at bar and the application for the patent, the patent disclosure is not "prior art" and cannot be looked to for what it teaches. Under the Greenlee case it may be looked to to find out what the terms of the claims mean but that is all.

2. ***In re Zickendraht***, 138 USPQ 22, 24 (C.C.P.A. 1963)

The sole issue is whether the instant claim defines a patently distinct invention over that claimed in applicants' patent. The doctrine is well established that claims in different applications need be more than merely different in form or content; and that a patentable distinction must exist to entitle applicants to a second patent.

3. ***In re Simmons***, 136 USPQ 450, 452 (C.C.P.A. 1963)

Where, as here, two applications of the same applicant for closely related subject matter are copending, a patent can properly be granted on each of them only if there is a patentable distinction between their respective claims. *In re Greenlee*, supra. If two patents are to be granted, there must be two separate patentable inventions.

4. ***Ex parte Malcom***, 47 USPQ 395, 396 (Pat. Off. Bd. App. 1940)

The examiner states that if these claims are considered as combination claims, they are subject to rejection on the ground of double patenting over applicant's allowed case, Serial No. 10,018 [issued as Patent No. 2,222,970, see 47 USPQ 395]. He states that the specified claims in the allowed case are directed to the combination of a plate of a specified structure anchored in a paving section and combined with a joint strip in a stated manner. It is understood that applicant desires to claim here an element of the combination claimed in the other application as an article of manufacture separate from the combination. It is believed that he is entitled to claim an element of the combination in this manner adapted to function in the combination.

5. ***Ex parte Sturm***, 49 USPQ 149, 151 (Pat. Off. Bd. App. 1940)

After review of the claims on appeal and claims 67–72 of the patent, we are not convinced that all these claims are directed to the same subject matter even if it be assumed that the essential novelty is in the carrying mechanism common to all of the accumulators. But with appellant's showing that the carrying mechanism common to all the accumulators required more elements when a total is to be transferred from one accumulator to another, and therefore the expression employed in claims of the patent inferentially calls for a different set of elements than in the claims involved on appeal, we believe the holding of the examiner should not be sustained. There is no question that the combination recited in the claims on appeal differentiates from the combination recited in the claims of the patent.

6. ***In re McKee***, 27 USPQ 353, 355 (C.C.P.A. 1935)

From the various authorities considered we think the rule is well settled that under circumstances like those at bar, if the method of the claims can be performed by any other apparatus or by hand, it cannot be said that the claims recite the mere function of a machine, so that their allowance would be double patenting. . . .

The important inquiry in determining the issue presented, therefore, is whether or not the method claims call for steps which can be performed only by the apparatus for which appellant was allowed said claim 1 of the patent.

7. ***In re Cady***, 25 USPQ 345, 348 (C.C.P.A. 1935)

We are in agreement with the contention of appellant that the legal precedents are uniformly to the effect that "double patenting is not sustainable when the product can be fabricated by processes other than that secured by the issued process patent".

8. ***In re Carlton***, 25 USPQ 390, 391 (C.C.P.A. 1935)

We deem it unnecessary to cite authorities in support of the proposition that a party might be entitled to a patent for "a combination," because of the cooperation of the elements contained therein, and at the same time be entitled to a separate patent for one of the elements of the combination. Such, we think, is the situation confronting us here.

We are of opinion, therefore, that the mere fact that appellant included in his patented combination the element or composition of matter here involved, does not preclude him from receiving a patent for the composition of matter defined by the appealed claims.

9. ***Ex parte Harold***, 44 USPQ 84, 85 (Pat. Off. Bd. App. 1938)

The fact that claims to a species have been granted in a patent is no bar to the grant of generic claims in a subsequent patent, provided other species are disclosed therein.

10. ***Ex parte Lippert***, 40 USPQ 579, 579 (Pat. Off. Bd. App. 1939)

As a general proposition, where an applicant has copending applications directed to different species of a generic invention, he may have the generic claims in either application, provided they are not inserted in the application last to issue long after the first application becomes a patent. In the present case, the application seems to have been directed to the generic invention from its filing and while the present claims may be supported by the issued patent, we do not feel that it is fatal to their allowance here that a patent, which may be considered an improvement patent, has already been granted.

11. ***Ex parte Adam***, 51 USPQ 534, 535 (Pat. Off. Bd. App. 1941)

The claims on appeal are directed to locking mechanism particularly designed for use on jail doors. . . .

It is the examiner's view that the allowance of the claims here on appeal would involve double patenting. Some of the claims of the patent include, as an element thereof, the specific locking mechanism which is here claimed, but all of the claims of the patent are directed to a door-controlling system which includes a series of doors. It is the examiner's view that the allowance of the present claims would prolong the monopoly on the specific locking mechanism embodied in the combination claims of the patent beyond the statutory term of 17 years.

Inasmuch as the claims of the patent are all combination claims which involve a series of doors, appellant now has no monopoly on the specific lock mechanism and it cannot, therefore, be held that the allowance of lock mechanism claims would prolong such monopoly. . . . The examiner's action is reversed.

12. ***Ex parte Berlin***, 48 USPQ 140, 140–41 (Pat. Off. Bd. App. 1940)

The reference relied on is applicant's copending design patent and the claims here on appeal read squarely on the design of the patent, but it is contended that the claims on appeal would read on many other designs than the exact one of the design patent, which is one specific form.

The claims on appeal do not exclude the use of more than one wing or more than two power plant nacelles. Claims 4 and 5 are not limited to symmetrically disposed nacelles and the brief refers to other variations from the design of the patent possible under the claims on appeal.

It often happens that a specific patent is the first to issue but this does not necessarily invalidate a subsequently issued patent with broad claims.

13. ***Ex parte Johnson***, 45 USPQ 233, 234 (Pat. Off. Bd. App. 1940)

It is a general rule that design patents and mechanical patents are distinct entities and may be supported, even where based on the same disclosure. It is only when it would be practically impossible to produce the structure claimed in a mechanical patent without infringing the design, and vice versa, that double patenting is involved. In the present case, this situation does not exist. We think it would be easily possible to construct a mechanical device within the terms of the present claim without infringing the design and obviously the design would not infringe the present claim as it would lack many of the mechanical features and relationships therein set forth.

14. ***In re Barber***, 28 USPQ 187, 188 (C.C.P.A. 1936)

It is well established that the mere fact that a design sought to be patented may involve some mechanical or utilitarian function does not render it unpatentable, but the "invention must relate to the design, and be distinguishable from the mechanical function involved." *In re La Montagne, . . .*

It is also well established that while, as a matter of law, one may have a mechanical patent and a design patent upon the same subject-matter, there must be a clear patentable distinction between the two; or, in other words, they must involve different inventions.

15. ***In re Land***, 151 USPQ 621, 626 (C.C.P.A. 1966)

As we view it, the board deemed Rogers '606, insofar as it had value as a reference, to be available as prior art and therefore saw no reason to utilize that patent under a "double patenting" theory, which is "narrower" in the sense that one cannot thus reject on the disclosure, as the board preferred to do, but must reject on the claims, or what has already been patented, plus other art if desired. Thus viewed, it is reasonable to assume that the board's view was that on any theory, including "double patenting," claim 56 distinguished from the references, including the claimed subject matter in Rogers '606, by defining an unobvious process. It should be remembered that Rogers '606 was used to support an obviousness type of "double patenting" rejection.

16. ***In re Goodman***, 29 USPQ 2d 2010, 2015–16 (Fed. Cir. 1993)

To prevent extension of the patent right beyond statutory limits, the doctrine of obviousness-type double patenting rejects application claims to subject matter different but not patentably distinct from the subject matter claimed in a prior patent. . . .

The double patenting determination involves two inquiries. First, is the same invention claimed twice? . . . This

inquiry hinges upon the scope of the claims in question. . . .
If the claimed inventions are identical in scope, the proper
rejection is under 35 U.S.C. § 101 because an inventor is entitled to a single patent for an invention. . . .

If one claimed invention has a broader scope than the
other, the court must proceed to a second inquiry: whether
one claim defines merely an obvious variation of the other
patent claim. . . . Without a patentable distinction—because
the pending claim defines merely an obvious variation of the
patented claim—the patentee may overcome the double
patenting rejection by filing a terminal disclaimer.

17. ***In re Goodman***, 29 USPQ 2d 2010, 2016 (Fed. Cir. 1993)

In *In re Braat*, . . . this court required in certain circumstances, an additional inquiry to support the double patenting obviousness rejection. Under these circumstances, a
double patenting obviousness rejection will only be sustained if the application claims are not patentably distinct
from the prior patent claims, and the prior patent claims are
also not patentably distinct from the application claims.
This "two-way" analysis is necessary because a later-filed
improvement patent may issue before an earlier-filed basic
invention. . . .

In *Braat*, the later-filed application contained claims to a
patentable combination that included a subcombination
which was the subject of an independent prior application.
Although the later-filed application became a patent first,
this court did not reduce the term of the earlier-filed, but
later-issued, patent. This court did not require a terminal
disclaimer because Braat's application was held up not by
the applicant, but by "the rate of progress of the application
through the PTO, over which the applicant does not have
complete control." . . .

This case requires no "two-way" analysis. Although application claims 12 and 13 form the genus containing the
species of patent claim 3, PTO actions did not dictate the
rate of prosecution. Rather, appellant chose to file a continuation and seek early issuance of the narrow species claims.
The appellant also chose to forego an immediate appeal to
this court on its broader claims when it filed a continuation
application.

18. ***In re Longi***, 225 USPQ 645, 648 (Fed. Cir. 1985)

Under that facet of the doctrine of double patenting, we
must direct our inquiry to whether the claimed invention in
the application for the second patent would have been obvious from the subject matter of the claims in the first patent,
in light of the prior art.

19. ***In re Longi***, 225 USPQ 645, 649 (Fed. Cir. 1985)

It is well-established that a common assignee is entitled to proceed with a terminal disclaimer to overcome a rejection based on double patenting of the obviousness type. . . . Since the second patent would expire simultaneously with the first, this use of a terminal disclaimer is consistent with the policy that the public should be free to use the invention as well as any obvious modifications at the end of the patent's term.

20. ***Applied Materials, Inc. v. Advanced Semiconductor Materials Am., Inc.***, 40 USPQ 2d 1481, 1484 (Fed. Cir. 1996), ***cert. denied,*** 520 U.S. 1230 (1997)

[W]hen the existence of multiple patents is due to the administrative requirements imposed by the Patent and Trademark Office, 35 U.S.C. §121 provides that the inventor shall not be prejudiced by having complied with those requirements. Thus when two or more patents result from a PTO restriction requirement, whereby aspects of the original application must be divided into separate applications, §121 insulates the ensuing patents from the charge of double patenting. . . . A restriction requirement does not prohibit subsequent amendments to the claims. As discussed in *Texas Instruments, Inc. v. U.S. Int'l Trade Comm'n*, 988 F.2d 1165, 1179, 26 USPQ2d 1018, 1029 (Fed. Cir. 1993), the examiner's demarcation among the separate inventions should be preserved. However, even if such consonance is lost, double patenting does not follow if the requirements of §121 are met or if the claims are in fact patentably distinct. *See id.* at 1179, 26 USPQ2d at 1029–30. In this case consonance was not violated, for the process claims remained in separate patents from the apparatus claims although the scope of the process claims was modified.

21. ***Ex parte Michno***, 38 USPQ 2d 1211, 1212 (B.P.A.I. 1993) (unpublished)

We are unaware of any judicial precedent which stands for the proposition that an obviousness-type double patenting situation automatically arises when a patent on a narrow invention issues during pendency of an application for a claimed invention which encompasses or dominates the narrow invention. The notion that a pending claim to a generic invention is necessarily patentably indistinct, in the sense of double patenting of the obviousness type, from a narrower patented claim encompassed by the pending generic claim was scotched by *In re Braat*, 937 F.2d 589 at 594, 19 USPQ2d 1289 at 1293 (Fed. Cir. 1991).

22. ***In re Butera***, 28 USPQ 2d 1399, 1400 (Fed. Cir. 1993) (unpublished)

[A] mere genus-species or broad-narrow relationship between pending and patented claims is not a litmus test for resolving the question of double patenting of the obviousness type.

23. ***In re Robeson***, 141 USPQ 485, 488 (C.C.P.A. 1964)

Where, as here, the claimed subject matter is an obvious modification of what has already been claimed, a second patent is contrary to one of the fundamental principles underlying the patent system, namely, that when the right to exclude granted by a patent expires at the end of the patent term, the public shall be free to use the invention as well as obvious modifications thereof or obvious improvements thereon. Thus, to grant a second patent for an obvious variation deprives the public of those rights. If, however, the second patent expires simultaneously with the first, the right to fully utilize the patented discovery at the expiration date remains unimpaired. Thus the terminal disclaimer here precludes any extension of monopoly.

24. ***In re Deters***, 185 USPQ 644, 648 (C.C.P.A. 1975)

We agree, however, with the PTO that the difference between "at least one" and a "plurality" is a de minimus, obvious variation.

25. ***In re Emert***, 44 USPQ 2d 1149, 1152 (Fed. Cir. 1997) (quoting ***In re Braat***, 19 USPQ 2d 1289, 1292 (Fed. Cir. 1991) and citing ***In re Goodman***, 29 USPQ 2d 2010, 2015 (Fed. Cir. 1993))

This court has set forth two tests for obviousness-type double patenting rejections. In *In re Braat,* . . . the court applied a "two-way" patentability test. In that case, the applicant filed two applications, the second of which issued first due to the PTO's unjustified delays in the prosecution of the earlier filed application. This court also noted that the assignee could not have included the claims of the later-filed Dil application in the Braat application. . . . Because "applications for basic and improvement patents should not be penalized by the rate of progress of the applications through the PTO, a matter over which the applicant does not have complete control," this court applied a two-way obviousness analysis. . . . Under the two-way analysis, this court examined each claim to determine whether it was an obvious variant of the other, rather than just examining the application claim for patentable distinctiveness from the patent claim. . . .

In *Goodman*, this court set forth the "one-way" test for obviousness-type double patenting. In that case, the applicant chose to file a continuation for a broad claim while seeking early issuance of a narrow species claim. . . . Therefore, because PTO action did not dictate the rate of prosecution, this court looked only to see if the pending application claims were patentably distinct from the issued patent.

26. ***In re Berg***, 46 USPQ 2d 1226, 1229 (Fed. Cir. 1998)

Obviousness-type double patenting is a judge-made doctrine that prevents an extension of the patent right beyond the statutory time limit. It requires rejection of an application claim when the claimed subject matter is not patentably distinct from the subject matter claimed in a commonly owned patent. *See In re Braat*, 937 F.2d 589, 592, 19 USPQ 2d 1289, 1291–92 (Fed. Cir. 1991). Its purpose is to prevent an unjustified extension of the term of the right to exclude granted by a patent by allowing a second patent claiming an obvious variant of the same invention to issue to the same owner later. *See In re Goodman*, 11 F.3d 1046, 1052, 29 USPQ 2d 2010, 2015 (Fed. Cir. 1993). . . .

Generally, a "one-way" test has been applied to determine obviousness-type double patenting. Under that test, the examiner asks whether the application claims are obvious over the patent claims. . . . Under the one-way test, if the scope of the application and the patent claims is not identical, the court must ask whether the former defines merely an obvious variation of the latter. . . . If the application claim is not patentably distinct, in order to overcome the double patenting rejection, the applicant must file a "terminal disclaimer," foregoing that portion of the term of the second patent that extends beyond the term of the first. . . .

Under special circumstances, however, this court and the Court of Customs and Patent Appeals have both made an exception and instead have applied a two-way test. Specifically, in *Braat*, this court examined the application claim and the patent claim to determine whether each was obvious in view of the other, rather than considering only whether the application claim was patentably distinct from the patent claim.

27. ***In re Berg***, 46 USPQ 2d 1226, 1230–31 (Fed. Cir. 1998)

Berg relies on *Braat* to support application of the two-way test. *Braat* was an unusual case; moreover, its factual situation is not likely to be repeated since the 1984 Act went into effect. Even assuming that *Braat* retains some vitality, it is, nevertheless, distinguishable. In *Braat* the common assignee could not have filed both sets of claims together because the inventive entity named in the application did not invent the subject matter of all the patent claims and vice-versa. *See Braat*, 937 F.2d at 594, 19 USPQ 2d at 1293. In addition, in *Braat* the "patent invention . . . [was] totally separate from that of [the application], and could conceivably have been developed earlier rather than later." *Id.* at 593, 19 USPQ 2d at 1292. The court in *Braat*, however, emphasized the more typical scenario in which, despite common inventive entities, the two-way test applied: "when a *later-filed improvement* patent issues before an *earlier filed basic* invention." *Id.* (emphasis added); *accord Borah*, 354 F.2d at 1009, 148 USPQ at 214 (allowing the earlier filed but later allowed basic patent application to issue without a terminal disclaimer because the two applications could not have been filed as one since the improvements were not made until after the application on the basic invention was filed); *see also Calvert*, 97 F.2d at 640, 38 USPQ at 185 (allowing an earlier filed patent application for generic invention to issue without a terminal disclaimer after a later filed improvement patent).

28. ***In re Berg***, 46 USPQ 2d 1226, 1231 (Fed. Cir. 1998)

Contrary to Berg's assertions, the facts of the present case are close to those in *Goodman*, a case in which we applied the standard one-way test. In *Goodman*, the applicant filed both species and genus claims in the same application. The examiner allowed the species claims but rejected the genus claims. Rather than appealing the rejection of the genus claims, the applicant permitted the species claims to issue upon allowance and continued to prosecute the genus claims in a continuation application. The genus claims were subsequently rejected for obviousness-type double patenting in light of the now issued species claims. Rather than file a terminal disclaimer, the applicant appealed to the Board and then to this court. *See Goodman*, 11 F.3d at 1049, 29 USPQ 2d at 2013. This court held that "although application claims 12 and 13 form the genus containing the species of patent claim 3, PTO actions did not *dictate the rate of prosecution.* Rather, appellant chose to file a continuation and seek early issuance of the narrow species claims." *Id.* at 1053, 29 USPQ 2d at 2016 (emphasis added).

29. ***In re Berg***, 46 USPQ 2d 1226, 1231 n.6 (Fed. Cir. 1998)

[E]ven in a case where the inventions could not have been filed in a single application, if the applicant thereafter controlled the respective rates of prosecution to cause the species or improvement claims to issue prior to the genus or basic invention claims as could have been done by, e.g., filing the genus claims long after the species claims even though the two were invented at nearly the same time or the genus claims were invented first, or by filing numerous continuations in the genus application while failing to respond substantively to PTO Office actions, such applicant seems not to be entitled to the two-way test under settled case law.

30. ***In re Berg***, 46 USPQ 2d 1226, 1233 (Fed. Cir. 1998)

If an applicant could have filed both sets of claims in a single application because the disclosure of the first application supports the second set of claims, then pursuant to this case and *Goodman*, the one-way test is appropriate to determine if a rejection for obviousness-type double patenting should be sustained.

If, on the other hand, an applicant could not have filed both sets of claims in one application—for example, because the second application claimed an invention that was not adequately disclosed in the first application—but the first application was delayed in prosecution causing the second application to issue as a patent first, then one would expect that the "control test" as discussed in *Borah* would be applied to determine whether the applicant or the PTO is responsible for the delay. Under this scenario, the one-way test is appropriate to determine whether a rejection for obviousness-type double patenting will be sustained if the applicant is found responsible for the delay in prosecution of the first-filed application. The two-way test may be appropriate, however, in the unusual circumstance that the PTO is solely responsible for the delay in causing the second-filed application to issue prior to the first.

31. ***In re Dembiczak***, 50 USPQ 2d 1614, 1619 (Fed. Cir. 1999) (quoting ***Carman Indus., Inc. v. Wahl***, 220 USPQ 481, 487 (Fed. Cir. 1983))

The law provides that, in some very rare cases, obvioustype double patenting may be found between design and utility patents. . . . In these cases, a "two-way" test is applicable. . . . Under this test, the obviousness-type double patenting rejection is appropriate only if the claims of the two patents cross-read, meaning that "the test is whether the subject matter of the claims of the patent sought to be invalidated would have been obvious from the subject matter of the claims of the other patent, and vice versa."

32. ***Georgia-Pacific Corp. v. United States Gypsum Co.***, 52 USPQ 2d 1590, 1596 (Fed. Cir. 1999)

The use of the term "comprising" in the '569 patent and "consisting of" in the '989 patent renders the scope of the two claims different, but the difference is not sufficient to render claim 17 of the '989 patent nonobvious in light of claim 1 of the '569 patent, because it would have been obvious to construct the mat only out of glass fibers and adhesive, rather than out of glass fibers and adhesive and other unspecified substances.

33. ***Sash Controls, Inc. v. Talon, L.L.C.,*** Civ. App. No.
    98-1152, slip op. at 6–7 (Fed. Cir. Jan. 27, 1999) (unpub-
    lished) (quoting ***Quad Envtl. Techs. Corp. v. Union San-
    itary Dist.,*** 20 USPQ 2d 1392, 1394 (Fed. Cir. 1991))

    The district court erred in applying an estoppel to Sash's
    arguments concerning obviousness. In *Quad Environmental
    Technologies Corp. v. Union Sanitary District*, we held that
    a terminal disclaimer "is not an admission of obviousness of
    the later-filed claimed invention in light of the earlier-filed
    disclosure." . . . "In legal principle, the filing of a terminal
    disclaimer simply serves the statutory function of removing
    the rejection of double patenting, and raises neither pre-
    sumption nor estoppel on the merits of the rejection."

34. ***Eli Lilly & Co. v. Barr Labs.,*** 55 USPQ 2d 1609, 1618 (Fed.
    Cir. 2000)

    [D]ouble patenting is not "concerned with what one skilled
    in the art would be aware [of] from reading the claims but
    with what inventions the claims define." *In re Sarett*, 51
    C.C.P.A. 1180, 327 F.2d 1005, 1013, 140 USPQ 474, 481
    (C.C.P.A. 1964). Here, claim 1 of the '895 patent, when prop-
    erly construed, already covered the administration of fluox-
    etine hydrochloride for treating depression. Further, Lilly's
    reliance on *In re Baird*, 16 F.3d 380, 29 USPQ 2d 1550 (Fed.
    Cir. 1994), and *In re Jones*, 958 F.2d 347, 21 USPQ 2d 1941
    (Fed. Cir. 1992), is unavailing. In those cases, we held that
    a species claim is not necessarily obvious in light of a prior
    art disclosure of a genus. See *Baird*, 16 F.3d at 382, 29 USPQ
    2d at 1552; *Jones*, 958 F.2d at 350, 21 USPQ 2d at 1943. The
    present case, however, in which the same party claims a
    genus in an earlier patent and then claims a species in a
    later patent is entirely different from cases such as *Baird*
    and *Jones*, in which the prior art merely discloses a genus
    and a later patent claims a species.

35. ***Eli Lilly & Co. v. Barr Labs.,*** 55 USPQ 2d 1609, 1619 (Fed.
    Cir. 2000)

    The only discernible difference between claim 1 of the '895
    patent and claim 7 of the '549 patent is that the former ad-
    dresses the treatment of depression in humans while the lat-
    ter addresses the treatment of serotonin uptake in animals.
    Humans are a species of the animal genus, and depression
    is a species ailment of the genus of ailments caused by de-
    fective serotonin uptake. Our case law firmly establishes
    that a later genus claim is not patentable over an earlier
    species claim. See *In re Berg*, 140 F.3d 1428, 1437, 46 USPQ

2d 1226, 1233 (Fed. Cir. 1998) (affirming the rejection of genus claims in a later patent application for obviousness-type double patenting in light of species claims in an earlier patent); *In re Lonardo*, 119 F.3d 960, 967, 43 USPQ 2d 1262, 1267 (Fed. Cir. 1997) (invalidating claims in later patent for obviousness-type double patenting when "many of the alleged differences in elements are in species-genus form," with the earlier patent claiming elements more specifically and the later patent claiming elements more generally); *Goodman*, 11 F.3d at 1053, 29 USPQ 2d at 2016; *In re Vogel*, 57 C.C.P.A. 920, 422 F.2d 438, 442, 164 USPQ 619, 622–23 (C.C.P.A. 1970) (affirming a rejection of a claim in a later patent covering a method for packaging meat as obviousness-type double patenting in light of claims in an earlier patent covering a method for packaging pork); see also *Miller v. Eagle Mfg. Co.*, 151 U.S. 186, 198, 38 L. Ed. 121, 14 S. Ct. 310 (1894) (reasoning that a later patent "containing a broader claim, more generical [sic] in its character than the specific claim in the prior patent" is void); *Gosteli*, 872 F.2d at 1010, 10 USPQ 2d at 1616 (holding that earlier species invention anticipates later generic claim); *Titanium Metals Corp. v. Banner*, 778 F.2d 775, 782, 227 USPQ 773, 779 (Fed. Cir. 1985) (holding that an earlier species disclosure in the prior art defeats any generic claim).

36. ***Eli Lilly & Co. v. Barr Labs.***, 55 USPQ 2d 1609, 1617–18 (Fed. Cir. 2000)

Obviousness-type double patenting entails a two-step analysis. First, as a matter of law, the court construes the claim in the earlier patent and the claim in the later patent, and it overlays the later claim on the earlier claim to determine whether the later claim encompasses subject matter previously claimed. See *Georgia-Pacific Corp. v. United States Gypsum Co.*, 195 F.3d 1322, 1326, 52 USPQ 2d 1590, 1593 (Fed. Cir. 1999) (stating that "analysis of the claims is the first step" in an obviousness-type double patenting inquiry); *General Foods Corp. v. Studiengesellschaft Kohle*, 972 F.2d 1272, 1279, 23 USPQ 2d 1839, 1844 (Fed. Cir. 1992). Second, the court determines whether the differences in subject matter between the two claims is such that the claims are patentably distinct. See *Georgia-Pacific*, 195 F.3d at 1327, 52 USPQ 2d at 1595 (proceeding to determine whether differences between the two claims are patentably distinct after construing the claims); *General Foods*, 972 F.2d at 1279, 23 USPQ 2d at 1844 (explaining that the terms "patentably distinguishable," "patentable distinctions," and obvious variations are equivalent for analytical purposes).

37. ***Ex parte Davis***, 56 USPQ 2d 1434, 1434 n.8 (B.P.A.I. 2000) (unpublished)

A first patent or application "dominates" a second patent or application when the first patent or application has a broad or generic claim which fully encompasses or reads on an invention defined in a narrower or more specific claim in the second patent or application.

XXIV. Design Patent Issues

1. ***In re Butera***, 28 USPQ 2d 1399, 1400 (Fed. Cir. 1993) (unpublished)

Our predecessor court determined that "one of ordinary skill in the art to which [the] subject matter pertains" in design cases is a "designer of ordinary capability who designs articles of the type presented in the application." *In re Nalbandian*, 661 F.2d 1214, 1216, 211 USPQ 782, 784 (C.C.P.A. 1981). The "art to which the subject matter pertains" thus consists of articles of the type claimed.

A prior design is of the type claimed if it has the same general use as that claimed in the design patent application. Although Butera and Hodge share a similar scalloped spherical design, Butera's design is for air fresheners and insect repellents, while Hodge's is for metal ball anodes. The design of Hodge involves a different type of article from Utera's design and it is not analogous.

2. ***Keystone Retaining Wall Sys., Inc. v. Westrock, Inc.***, 27 USPQ 2d 1297, 1302 (Fed. Cir. 1993)

A design patent protects the non-functional aspects of an ornamental design as shown in a patent. *See Lee v. Dayton-Hudson Corp.*, 838 F.2d 1186, 1188–89, 5 USPQ 2d 1625, 1627 (Fed. Cir. 1988). "[I]t is the appearance of a design as a whole which is controlling in determining questions of patentability and infringement." *In re Rubinfield*, 270 F.2d 391, 395, 123 USPQ 210, 214 (C.C.P.A. 1959), *cert. denied*, 362 U.S. 903 (1960).

3. ***In re Harvey***, 29 USPQ 2d 1206, 1208 (Fed. Cir. 1993)

In ornamental design cases, a proper obviousness rejection based on a combination of references requires that the visual ornamental features (design characteristics) of the claimed design appear in the prior art in a manner which suggests such features as used in the claimed design. . . . If, however, the combined teachings suggest only components of a claimed design, but not its overall appearance, an obviousness rejection is inappropriate. . . .

As the Board recognized, a primary reference (basic design) must be cited having design characteristics which are "basically the same" as the claimed design. . . . The designs of other references may then properly be relied upon for modification of such basic design when the references are "so related that the appearance of certain ornamental features in one . . . would have suggested application of those features to another."

4. ***Swede Indus. v. Zebco Corp.***, Civ. App. No. 93-1403, slip op. at 4–5 (Fed. Cir. Apr. 12, 1994) (unpublished)

As in utility patent cases, *Graham v. John Deere Co.* . . . governs the determination of obviousness in design patent cases . . . . Thus, a proper obviousness analysis examines the scope and content of the prior art, the differences between the prior art and the claims, the level of ordinary skill in the art, and objective criteria bearing on obviousness. The level of ordinary skill in the design cases is "a designer of ordinary skill who designs articles of the type involved." *In re Carter*, 673 F.2d 1378, 1380, 213 USPQ 625, 626 (C.C.P.A. 1982).

In the context of design patents, an obviousness analysis examines whether the teachings of the prior art suggest the overall appearance of the claimed design. . . . In particular, if the combined teachings of the prior art suggest only components, not the overall appearance, of the claimed design, section 103 does not operate to render the claims obvious. Thus, as for utility patents, the prior art references must motivate one of ordinary skill in the art to make the claimed combination. In determining motivation to combine, the relevant question is whether the prior art designs are so closely related that the appearance of specific ornamental features in one reference actually suggest the application of those features in the other design.

5. ***Swede Indus. v. Zebco Corp.***, Civ. App. No. 93-1403, slip op. at 5 (Fed. Cir. Apr. 12, 1994) (unpublished)

In *Glavas* this court's predecessor reversed a determination of obviousness for a design patent application because, even though the prior art contained all component features of the claimed design, the prior art references did not suggest the combination. . . . A patented ornamental design has use only for its visual appearance. Consequently, "in considering prior art references for purposes of determining patentability of ornamental designs, the focus must be on appearances and not uses." This court also clarified that any modification to the prior art designs in applying the obviousness test cannot be more than *de minimis* in nature. . . . Moreover, any *de minimis* modifications necessary to reach an obviousness conclusion must not relate to the overall aesthetic appearance of the design.

6. ***In re Harvey***, 29 USPQ 2d 1206, 1208 (Fed. Cir. 1993)

Like the examiner, the Board improperly mixed principles of obviousness for utility patents with those for ornamental design patents. Unlike an invention in a utility patent, a patented ornamental design has no use other than its visual appearance, *In re Glavas*, 230 F.2d 447, 450, 109 USPQ 50, 52 (C.C.P.A. 1956), and its scope is "limited to what is shown in the application drawings," *In re Mann*, 861 F.2d 1581, 1582, 8 USPQ 2d 2030, 2031 (Fed. Cir. 1988). Therefore, in considering prior art references for purposes of determining patentability of ornamental designs, the focus must be on appearances and not uses. *In re Glavas*, 230 F.2d at 450, 109 USPQ at 52. Extending the rule in *In re Glavas* and *In re Mann* one step further, we hold that the Board should have focused on the actual appearances, rather than "design concepts."

7. ***In re Schnell***, 8 USPQ 19, 25 (C.C.P.A. 1931)

[A]n inventor may invent, we will say for the purposes of this case, at least three kinds of designs for articles of manufacture. First a design for an ornament, impression, print or picture to be applied to an article of manufacture; second, the design for a shape or configuration for an article of manufacture; third, a combination of the first two, that is, a design which consists of the shape or configuration of an article plus additional ornamentation.

8. ***Ex parte Daniels***, 40 USPQ 2d 1394, 1404 (B.P.A.I. 1996) (quoting ***Racing Strollers Inc. v. TRI Indus. Inc.***, 11 USPQ 2d 1300, 1301 (Fed. Cir. 1989) (en banc))

There is, and can be, no debate that a design patent application may be entitled to the benefit of the filing date of an earlier design application when the earlier design application describes the design claimed in the manner required by the first paragraph of 35 U.S.C. § 112. See 35 U.S.C. § 120. However, we note that the "best mode" provision of the first paragraph of § 112: "is not applicable, as a design has only one 'mode' and it can be described only by illustrations showing what it looks like (though some added description in words may be useful to explain the illustrations)."

9. ***Ex parte Hanback***, 231 USPQ 739, 741 (Pat. Off. Bd. App. 1986)

As stated in 35 USC 171, second paragraph, "[t]he provisions of this title relating to patents for inventions shall

apply to patents for designs, except as otherwise provided."
It follows that a design patent applicant may amend the
claim in his application before final rejection and, moreover,
is entitled to have the amended claim reconsidered and reexamined.

10. ***In re Platner***, 155 USPQ 222, 223 (Comm'r Pat. 1967)

[M]ore than one embodiment of a design may be illustrated
in an application. It cannot, therefore, be properly held that
the claim of a design application is indefinite solely because
more than one embodiment is shown.

11. ***In re Rubinfield***, 123 USPQ 210, 214 (C.C.P.A. 1959)

The fact that it may be permissible, in a proper case, to illustrate more than one embodiment of a design invention
does not require or justify more than one claim. Such embodiments can be presented only if they involve a single inventive concept; and such a concept can be protected by a
single claim.

12. ***Best Lock Corp. v. Ilco Unican Corp.***, 40 USPQ 2d 1048,
1049 (Fed. Cir. 1996)

[I]f the design claimed in a design patent is dictated solely
by the function of the article of manufacture, the patent is
invalid because the design is not ornamental. . . . A design is
not dictated solely by its function when alternative designs
for the article of manufacture are available.

13. ***Durling v. Spectrum Furniture Co.***, 40 USPQ 2d 1788,
1791 (Fed. Cir. 1996)

The error in the district court's approach is that it construed Durling's claimed design too broadly. The district
court's verbal description of Durling's claimed design does
not evoke a visual image consonant with the claimed design.
Instead, the district court's description merely represents
the general concept of a sectional sofa with integrated end
tables. As we have explained in the past, however, the focus
in a design patent obviousness inquiry should be on visual
appearances rather than design concepts. . . . By focusing on
the design concept of Durling's design rather than its visual
appearance, the district court erred.

14. ***Ex parte Pappas***, 23 USPQ 2d 1636, 1638 (B.P.A.I. 1992)

[T]he test for determining obviousness of a claimed design
under § 103 is whether the design would have been obvious
to a designer of ordinary skill who designs articles of the
type involved, not to "an average worker" as asserted by appellant.

15. ***Ex parte Porter***, 39 USPQ 2d 1060, 1061 (B.P.A.I. 1995) (unpublished)

Here, we cannot agree with the examiner that Ortion illustrates a "something in existence" the design characteristics of which are basically "the same as" the claimed design. In our view, a designer of ordinary skill would find the design of Ortion and the appellant's design to be significantly different in concept. The appellant's design includes a handle which resembles a baseball bat and has bristles which extend perpendicularly from the head. On the other hand Ortion, while having a head which is of a shape similar to that of the appellant's design, has a completely different bristle structure and a generally flat, rectangular handle with a necked-down portion on the end which is joined to the head via a rectangular abutment 6. In the final analysis, the only similarity between the design of Ortion and that of the appellant's is in the shape of the head. Because such major modifications would be required to make Ortion's toothbrush look like the claimed design, we are of the opinion that it cannot qualify as a basic design.

16. ***In re Salmon***, 217 USPQ 981, 983–84 (Fed. Cir. 1983) (quoting ***In re Zahn***, 204 USPQ 988, 995 (C.C.P.A. 1980))

The court [in *Zahn*] rejected the Patent and Trademark Office's view that a design patent could not be issued for "a design which is embodied in less than all of an article of manufacture"—in that case, the shank of the drill bit. The court stated:

> Section 171 authorizes patents on ornamental designs for articles of manufacture. While the design must be embodied in some articles, the statute is not limited to designs for complete articles, or "discrete" articles. . . . No sound authority has been cited for any limitation on how a design is to be embodied in an article of manufacture. Here the design is embodied in the shank portion of a drill and a drill is unquestionably an article of manufacture. It is thus applied design as distinguished from abstract design.

17. ***In re Borden***, 39 USPQ 2d 1524, 1526 (Fed. Cir. 1996)

The central inquiry in analyzing an ornamental design for obviousness is whether the design would have been obvious to "a designer of ordinary skill who designs articles of the type involved." *Avia Group,* 853 F.2d at 1564, 7 USPQ2d at 1554; *In re Nalbandian,* 661 F.2d 1214, 1216, 211 USPQ 782, 784–85 (CCPA 1981). That inquiry focuses on the visual impression of the claimed design as a whole and not on selected individual features. . . .

In order for a design to be unpatentable because of obviousness, there must first be a basic design reference in the prior art, "a something in existence, the design characteristics of which are basically the same as the claimed design." *In re Rosen*, 673 F.2d at 391, 213 USPQ at 349; *see In re Harvey*, 12 F.3d 1061, 1063, 29 USPQ2d 1206, 1208 (Fed. Cir. 1993). A finding of obviousness cannot be based on selecting features from the prior art and assembling them to form an article similar in appearance to the claimed design.

18. ***In re Borden***, 39 USPQ 2d 1524, 1526–27 (Fed. Cir. 1996)

If the basic reference alone does not render the claimed design unpatentable, design elements from other references in the prior art can be considered in determining whether the claimed design would have been obvious to one of skill in the art. In order for secondary references to be considered, however, there must be some suggestion in the prior art to modify the basic design with features from the secondary references. . . . That is, the teachings of prior art designs may be combined only when the designs are "so related that the appearance of certain ornamental features in one would suggest the application of those features to the other." *In re Glavas*, 230 F.2d 447, 450, 109 USPQ 50, 52 (CCPA 1956).

19. **Ex parte Michno**, 38 USPQ 2d 1211, 1212 (B.P.A.I. 1993) (unpublished)

Our predecessor court determined that "one of ordinary skill in the art to which [the] subject matter pertains" in design cases is a "designer of ordinary capability who designs articles of the type presented in the application." *In re Nalbandian*, 661 F.2d 1214, 1216, 211 USPQ 782, 784 (CCPA 1981). The "art to which the subject matter pertains" thus consists of articles of the type claimed.

20. ***Ex parte Michno***, 38 USPQ 2d 1211, 1212 (B.P.A.I. 1993) (unpublished)

A prior design is of the type claimed if it has the same general use as that claimed in the design patent application. Although Butera and Hodge share a similar scalloped spherical design, Butera's design is for air fresheners and insect repellents, while Hodge's is for metal ball anodes. The design of Hodge involves a different type of article from Butera's design and it is not analogous. One designing a combined insect repellent and air freshener would therefore not have reason to know of or look to a design for a metal ball anode.

21. ***Hupp v. Siroflex of Am., Inc.***, 43 USPQ 2d 1887, 1890 (Fed. Cir. 1997)

Although the design patent is directed to the ornamental aspect of a useful article, that the design of a particular article is related to the article's use may not defeat patentability. When the design is primarily ornamental, although it also serves a utilitarian purpose, this design patent condition is met. As explained in *Bonito Boats, Inc. v. Thunder Craft Boats, Inc.*, 489 U.S. 141, 148, 9 USPQ2d 1847, 1851 (1989), to qualify for design patent protection, a design must have an ornamental appearance that is not dictated by function alone. . . . [T]he fact that the article of manufacture serves a function is a prerequisite of design patentability, not a defeat thereof. The function of the article itself must not be confused with "functionality" of the design of the article. . . . In determining whether the statutory requirement is met that the design is "ornamental," it is relevant whether functional considerations demand only this particular design or whether other designs could be used, such that the choice of design is made for primarily aesthetic, non-functional purposes.

22. ***Hupp v. Siroflex of Am., Inc.***, 43 USPQ 2d 1887, 1890 (Fed. Cir. 1997)

In determining whether a design patent is invalid based on a description in a printed publication, 35 U.S.C. §102(a), the factual inquiry is the same as that which determines anticipation by prior publication of the subject matter of a utility patent; *see* 35 U.S.C. §171. The publication must show the same subject matter as that of the patent, and must be identical in all material respects.

23. ***Hupp v. Siroflex of Am., Inc.***, 43 USPQ 2d 1887, 1891 (Fed. Cir. 1997)

The determination of the ultimate question of obviousness is made from the viewpoint of a person of ordinary skill in the field of the patented design. . . . The scope of the prior art is not the universe of abstract design and artistic creativity, but designs of the same article of manufacture or of articles sufficiently similar that a person of ordinary skill would look to such articles for their designs.

24. ***Hupp v. Siroflex of Am., Inc.***, 43 USPQ 2d 1887, 1891 (Fed. Cir. 1997) (quoting ***In re Rosen***, 213 USPQ 347, 350 (C.C.P.A. 1982))

The requirement for a "primary reference" is explained . . . as meaning that "there must be a reference, a something in existence, the design characteristics of which are basically the same as the claimed design in order to support a holding of obviousness." The correct application of this analytic approach is to ascertain whether, upon application of the *Graham* factors to the invention viewed as a whole, the same or a substantially similar article of manufacture is known to have design characteristics of which the design of the article as shown in the claim is an obvious variant. . . . Obviousness, in turn, is determined by ascertaining whether the applicable prior art contains any suggestion or motivation for making the modifications in the design of the prior art article in order to produce the claimed design.

25. ***Hupp v. Siroflex of Am., Inc.***, 43 USPQ 2d 1887, 1891–92 (Fed. Cir. 1997)

Hupp argues that a mold design for a concrete walkway of simulated stones is sufficiently different from a flooring of ceramic tiles on a fiber backing that the tile flooring can not be a primary reference. Hupp also argues that . . . there is no teaching or suggestion in the prior art whereby one of ordinary skill would look to flooring designs in designing a mold suitable for making a simulated stone walkway out of concrete. Hupp argues that any similarity of stone shapes in the final products does not make obvious his design of a mold for a concrete walkway. We agree with Hupp that this step is taken only with the hindsight knowledge of Hupp's product. We have been directed to no teaching or suggestion to a person of ordinary skill to look to a floor tile construction and convert it into the design of a mold to make a concrete simulated stone outdoor walkway. That idea came from Hupp, not from the prior art.

26. ***Berry Sterling Corp. v. Prescor Plastics, Inc.***, 43 USPQ 2d 1953, 1956 (Fed. Cir. 1997) (citing ***L.A. Gear, Inc. v. Thom McAn Shoe Co.***, 25 USPQ 2d 1913, 1917 (Fed. Cir. 1993))

While analyzing elements of the design may be appropriate in some circumstances, the determination of whether the patented design is dictated by the function of the article of manufacture must ultimately rest on an analysis of its overall appearance.

27. ***Berry Sterling Corp. v. Prescor Plastics, Inc.***, 43 USPQ 2d 1953, 1956 (Fed. Cir. 1997) (quoting ***L.A. Gear, Inc. v. Thom McAn Shoe Co.***, 25 USPQ 2d 1913, 1917 (Fed. Cir. 1993))

We have held that "[w]hen there are several ways to achieve the function of an article of manufacture, the design of the article is more likely to serve a primarily ornamental purpose." . . . Consideration of alternative designs, if present, is a useful tool that may allow a court to conclude that a challenged design is not invalid for functionality. As such, alternative designs join the list of other appropriate considerations for assessing whether the patented design as a whole—its overall appearance—was dictated by functional

considerations. Other appropriate considerations might include: whether the protected design represents the best design; whether alternative designs would adversely affect the
utility of the specified article; whether there are any con-
comitant utility patents; whether the advertising touts particular features of the design as having specific utility; and
whether there are any elements in the design or an overall
appearance clearly not dictated by function.

28. ***Continental Plastic Containers v. Owens Brockway
Plastic Prods., Inc.***, 46 USPQ 2d 1277, 1280–81 (Fed. Cir.
1998)

In *Tone Bros.* this court held that "public use" under section
102(b) could be negated by experimentation directed at optimizing the functional aspects of an article while not addressing the ornamental aspects of its design. *Tone Bros.*, 28 F.3d
at 1199–1200, 31 USPQ 2d at 1325–26. *Tone Bros.* is a "public
use" case. We see no reason to extend the analysis to the
"on-sale" context. "Public use" and "on-sale" bars, while they
share the same statutory basis, are grounded on different policy emphases. The primary policy underlying the "public use"
case is that of detrimental public reliance, whereas the primary policy underlying an "on-sale" case is that of prohibiting
the commercial exploitation of the design beyond the statutorily prescribed time period. Thus, in *Tone Bros.* the court
merely distinguished between the display of a design to generate public interest versus the display of a design for experimental use. It concluded that the display was not contrary to
the policy of detrimental public reliance because the display
was for the sole purpose of experimentation. In contrast, Continental's agreement with L&A Juice to sell the patented design is an explicit commercial exploitation of the claimed design outside of the generous one year grace period.

29. ***Continental Plastic Containers v. Owens Brockway
Plastic Prods., Inc.***, 46 USPQ 2d 1277, 1279 (Fed. Cir.
1998)

A claimed design is considered to be "on-sale," within the
meaning of section 102(b), when an embodiment of the design was sold or offered for sale in this country more than
one year before a filing date to which the claim is entitled
(the critical date) and the sale or offer to sell was primarily
for profit rather than for experimental purposes.

30. ***Continental Plastic Containers v. Owens Brockway
Plastic Prods., Inc.***, 46 USPQ 2d 1277, 1281 (Fed. Cir. 1998)
The claim is solely directed to the ornamental or appearance
aspects of the article of manufacture as depicted in the

patent drawings. . . . We conclude that it was irrelevant to triggering the "on-sale" bar that Continental had not yet manufactured a "functionally acceptable container." There is no functionality requirement in obtaining a design patent. . . . Since design inventions are reduced to practice as soon as an embodiment is constructed, . . . experimental use negation is virtually inapplicable in the design patent context. Applying experimental use negation in the design patent context would allow entities to increase the life of their design patents merely by tarrying over the production of the article of manufacture.

31. ***Continental Plastic Containers v. Owens Brockway Plastic Prods., Inc.***, 46 USPQ 2d 1277, 1281 (Fed. Cir. 1998)

Continental argues that the "on-sale" status of its patented design before the critical date is negated by experimental use. Experimental use negation applies, in utility patent cases, if there is genuine experimentation directed to perfecting the features of the claimed invention. . . . Continental did not sell the bottles to L&A Juice for any purpose other than commercial exploitation. The fact that it had to make minor modifications to the article is entirely unrelated to the sale. This is not a case in which Continental sold a discrete number of the bottles to L&A Juice so that L&A Juice might experiment on them to ascertain whether they were suitable for a particular purpose. In fact, under the terms of its supply agreement with L&A Juice, Continental was to provide as many bottles of the patented design as L&A Juice required for its retail sales. This is a clear commercial exploitation unaccompanied by any of the indicia of experimentation.

32. ***In re Daniels***, 46 USPQ 2d 1788, 1790 (Fed. Cir. 1998)

The statutory provision governing the effective filing date of the subject matter of continuing applications . . . . It was confirmed in *Racing Strollers* that "there are no 'otherwise provided' statutes to take design patent applications out of the ambit of § 120 which makes no distinction between applications for design patents and applications for utility patents . . . ." 878 F.2d at 1421, 11 USPQ 2d at 1302.

That the law of § 120 applies to design patent applications is illustrated in the court's rulings that design and utility patents are each entitled to claim priority from the other.

33. ***In re Daniels***, 46 USPQ 2d 1788, 1790 (Fed. Cir. 1998)

The test for sufficiency of the written description is the same, whether for a design or a utility patent. This test has been expressed in various ways; for example, "whether the disclosure of the application relied upon 'reasonably conveys to the artisan that the inventor had possession at that time of the later claimed subject matter.'" *Ralston Purina Co. v. Far-Mar-Co, Inc.*, 772 F.2d 1570, 1575, 227 USPQ 177, 179 (Fed. Cir. 1985) (quoting *In re Kaslow*, 707 F.2d 1366, 1375, 217 USPQ 1089, 1096 (Fed. Cir. 1983)).

34. ***In re Daniels***, 46 USPQ 2d 1788, 1790 (Fed. Cir. 1998)

It is the drawings of the design patent that [generally] provide the description of the invention. *In re Klein*, 987 F.2d 1569, 1571, 26 USPQ 2d 1133, 1134 (Fed. Cir. 1993) ("usually in design applications, there is no description other than the drawings"). Although linguists distinguish between a drawing and a writing, the drawings of the design patent are viewed in terms of the "written description" requirement of § 112. Thus when an issue of priority arises under § 120, one looks to the drawings of the earlier application for disclosure of the subject matter claimed in the later application. . . . The inquiry is simply to determine whether the inventor had possession at the earlier date of what was claimed at the later date.

35. ***In re Daniels***, 46 USPQ 2d 1788, 1790–91 (Fed. Cir. 1998)

The leecher as an article of manufacture is clearly visible in the earlier design application, demonstrating to the artisan viewing that application that Mr. Daniels had possession at that time of the later claimed design of that article; . . . The leaf ornamentation did not obscure the design of the leecher, all details of which are visible in the drawings of the earlier application. The leaf design is a mere indicium that does not override the underlying design. The subject matter of the later application is common to that of the earlier application. . . . The leaf ornamentation in the parent application, superimposed upon the design of the leecher itself, does not obscure that design, which is fully shown in the parent application drawings. On the correct law, it must be concluded that Mr. Daniels possessed the invention that is claimed in the continuation application, and that he is entitled to claim priority under § 120.

36. ***Unidynamics Corp. v. Automatic Prods. Int'l Ltd.***, 48 USPQ 2d 1099, 1107 (Fed. Cir. 1998)

Automatic Products asserts that the . . . design patent is invalid because the district court's asserted point of novelty is functional and not ornamental. . . . In applying the ordinary observer test, however, the district court looked only to the point of novelty. The district court ignored other ornamental features . . . This merging of the ordinary observer and the point of novelty tests was legal error.

37. ***In re Butler***, Civ. App. 98-1555, slip op. at 4–5 (Fed. Cir. Mar. 23, 1999) (unpublished)

The Board stated that because both Hutton and Gerszewski are directed toward prefabricated concrete devices used in subterranean environments and Hutton is a known alternative to the shape of the footing of Gerszewski, it would have been obvious to substitute the shape of the Hutton anchor for the footing shape taught by Gerszewski.

We reject this reasoning. Although both anchors and footings are subterranean devices, they serve fundamentally different purposes. An anchor is primarily designed to resist upward (or tension) forces, while a footing is a load-bearing device primarily designed to resist downward (or compression) forces. Gerszewski relates to a footing which is employed as a load-bearing device. Hutton relates to an anchor which is a tension-resisting device designed to provide resistance to the withdrawal of the anchor from the earth. Nowhere in Hutton is there any indication or suggestion that Hutton's frustum shaped anchor can act as a load-bearing device and resist downward forces.

38. ***Seiko Epson Corp. v. Nu-Kote Int'l, Inc.***, 52 USPQ 2d 1011, 1017–18 (Fed. Cir. 1999)

The district court ruled that the D '190 design patent was invalid because the design was "not a matter of concern to consumers." The patent is directed to the design or shape of ink cartridges. The district court reasoned that since the cartridge is not in view after its installation and during use in the printer, the consumer is not concerned with its design and thus that there can not be a valid design patent.

The premise is incorrect. The validity of a design patent does not require that the article be visible throughout its use; it requires only that the design be of an article of manufacture and that the design meets the requirements of Title 35. . . . The district court erred in holding that an article that is not exposed to view during use can not be the subject of a design patent.

Nor need the design be aesthetically pleasing. The "ornamental" requirement of the design statute means that the design must not be governed solely by function, i.e., that this is not the only possible form of the article that could perform its function. . . . A design patent is for a useful article, but patentability is based on the design of the article, not the use. The design may contribute distinctiveness or consumer recognition to the design, but an absence of artistic merit does not mean that the design is purely functional.

39. ***Sash Controls, Inc. v. Talon, L.L.C.***, Civ. App. No. 98-1152, slip op. at 7 (Fed. Cir. Jan. 27, 1999) (unpublished) (citing ***Avia Group Int'l v. L.A. Gear Cal., Inc.***, 7 USPQ 2d 1548, 1553 (Fed. Cir. 1988))

Design patents must meet the same novelty and nonobvious requirements as utility patents.

40. ***Sash Controls, Inc. v. Talon, L.L.C.***, Civ. App. No. 98-1152, slip op. at 8 (Fed. Cir. Jan. 27, 1999) (unpublished) (quoting ***Litton Sys., Inc. v. Whirlpool Corp.***, 221 USPQ 97, 109 (Fed. Cir. 1984))

A person of ordinary skill for § 103 purposes in a design patent case is "the designer of ordinary capability who designs articles of the type presented in the applications."

41. ***Berry Sterling Corp. v. Pescor Plastics, Inc.***, Civ. App. 98-1381, slip op. at 11 (Fed. Cir. Aug. 30, 1999) (unpublished)

A design is functional "when the appearance of the claimed design is 'dictated by' the use or purpose of the article. If the particular design is essential to the use of the article, it can not be the subject of a design patent." *L.A. Gear, Inc. v. Thom McAn Shoe Co.*, 988 F.2d 1117, 1123 (Fed. Cir. 1993) (citations omitted). The proper inquiry for determining functionality of a design is whether the overall appearance of the design is dictated by a utilitarian or ornamental purpose. Id. Such a distinction makes it possible to obtain both a utility patent and a design patent on the same article. *Carman Indus. v. Wahl*, 724 F.2d 932, 938–39 (Fed. Cir. 1983). "When there are several ways to achieve the function of an article of manufacture, the design of the article is more likely to serve a primarily ornamental purpose." *L.A. Gear*, 988 F.2d at 1123.

42. ***Berry Sterling Corp. v. Pescor Plastics, Inc.***, Civ. App. 98-1381, slip op. at 12 (Fed. Cir. Aug. 30, 1999) (unpublished)

In this case, each of the features that create the overall appearance of the design are dictated by functional considerations. The rim, the tapered upper and lower body portions, the transitional shoulder, and the fluted bottom and their arrangement are all dictated by functional considerations. In short, the overall appearance of the design is dictated by the use of the article and is not primarily ornamental.

43. ***Antonious v. Spalding & Evenflo Cos.,*** Civ. App. No.
98-1478, slip op. at 15–16 (Fed. Cir. Aug. 31, 1999) (unpublished)

A design patent may disclose more than one embodiment
of a design. *See In re Rubinfield*, 270 F.2d 391, 395, 123
USPQ 210, 214 (C.C.P.A. 1959) ("We are of the opinion that
it cannot be stated as an invariable rule that a design application cannot disclose more than one embodiment of the
design. Whether such disclosure is improper must depend
upon the particular circumstances of the individual case involved."); *see also In re Klein*, 987 F.2d 1569, 1570 n.1, 26
USPQ 2d 1133, 1134 n.1 (Fed. Cir. 1993) ("The drawings depict three slight variations on a single basic design. . . . No
objection has been made to this not uncommon practice.").
The primary validity issue here, then, is whether the '056
and '308 patents each disclose one embodiment of one design, more than one embodiment of one design, or more than
one design.

44. ***In re Dembiczak***, 50 USPQ 2d 1614, 1619 (Fed. Cir. 1999)
(quoting ***Carman Indus., Inc. v. Wahl***, 220 USPQ 481, 487
(Fed. Cir. 1983))

The law provides that, in some very rare cases, obvioustype double patenting may be found between design and
utility patents. . . . In these cases, a "two-way" test is applicable. . . . Under this test, the obviousness-type double
patenting rejection is appropriate only if the claims of the
two patents cross-read, meaning that "the test is whether
the subject matter of the claims of the patent sought to be
invalidated would have been obvious from the subject matter of the claims of the other patent, and vice versa."

45. ***In re Dembiczak***, 50 USPQ 2d 1614, 1619–20 (Fed. Cir.
1999) (quoting ***In re Borden,*** 39 USPQ 2d 1524, 1526 (Fed.
Cir. 1996))

In order for a design to be unpatentable because of obviousness, there must first be a basic design reference in the prior
art, the design characteristics of which are "basically the
same as the claimed design." . . . The phrase "having facial
indicia thereon" found in the claims of the pending utility
application is not a design reference that is "basically the
same as the claimed design." . . . In fact, it describes precious
little with respect to design characteristics. The Board's suggestion that the design details were simply "a matter of design choice" evinces a misapprehension of the subject matter of design patents. . . . The position adopted by the
Board—that a textual description of facial indicia found in

the claims of the utility patent application makes obvious the specific designs claimed in the (patentably distinct) Dembiczak design patents—would presumably render obvious, or even anticipate, all design patents where a face was depicted on a bag. But this, of course, is not the law; the textual description cannot be said to be a reference "basically the same as the claimed design," of the design patents at issue here.

XXV.   Appealing Issues to Federal Circuit

1. ***Miles Labs,. Inc. v. Shandon, Inc.***, 27 USPQ 2d 1123, 1129 (Fed. Cir. 1993), ***cert. denied***, 510 U.S. 1100 (1994)

   Where the parties stipulate to "representative" claims, however, a validity resolution for the representative claims applies to the other claims as well. . . . This stipulation of the parties made claim 1 a representative for the other claims in the patent. Thus, the parties, their counsel, and the trial court understood that the result the court reached for claim 1 would bind all other claims.

2. ***Ex parte Raske***, 28 USPQ 2d 1304, 1304–05 (B.P.A.I. 1993)

   Initially, we note the examiner's reference to U.S. Patent Number 4,424,330 issued to Raviola and European Patent Number 109,779 issued to Mitsui Petrochemical Industries. See the examiner's Answer, page 4, first paragraph, where these references are cited to "show the general state of the art". This is improper. The examiner does not cite Raviola or Mitsui in the "listing of the prior art of record relied upon in the rejection of claims under appeal", and the examiner expressly states that "[n]o new prior art has been applied in this examiner's Answer". See the examiner's Answer, page 2, sections (7) and (8). We therefore view the reference to Raviola and Mitsui, at page 4 of the Answer, as an improper effort to bring these references in the "back door". . . . Raviola and Mitsui are not positively included in the statement of rejection, and we have considered the issue under 35 USC 103 based solely on the evidence contained in Ishikawa and Billmeyer.

3. ***Preemption Devices, Inc. v. Minnesota Mining & Mfg. Co.***, 221 USPQ 841, 844 (Fed. Cir. 1984)

   It is regrettable that we should have to remind counsel that attacking the judge as lacking in skill or understanding or legal competence, as has repeatedly been done in this case, is improper argument and wholly ineffective, if not counterproductive. It has no tendency to prove anything . . . .

4. ***In re Land***, 151 USPQ 621, 629 (C.C.P.A. 1966)

Generally speaking, we decline to consider questions which could and should have been raised in the Patent Office so that we have the benefit of the views of its trained personnel on matters within their special competence and so that the Patent Office has the opportunity to furnish its position as expert on technical questions, the interpretation of references, applications, and the like. We will nevertheless consider a question of law, such as the availability of a reference, which is necessary to the determination of patentability.

5. ***SGS-Thomson Microelectronics, Inc. v. International Rectifier Corp.***, 32 USPQ 2d 1496, 1504 (Fed. Cir.) (unpublished), ***cert. denied***, 513 U.S. 1052 (1994)

Finally, both SGS and IR cited in their briefs the nonprecedential decision *Katz v. Lear Siegler, Inc.* . . . Not only do the citations of a nonprecedential case constitute clear violations of Federal Circuit Rule 47.6(b), but, as cited by the parties, they are miscitations because they do not acknowledge the nonprecedential status of the case. That is, they omit "(table)." At the very least, this is misleading to the court, and we condemn such behavior.

6. ***Merck & Co. v. Kessler***, 38 USPQ 2d 1347, 1351 (Fed. Cir. 1996), ***cert. denied***, 519 U.S. 1101 (1997)

Commissioners Kessler and Lehman contend that "under the familiar instructions of the Supreme Court in *Chevron*, 467 U.S. at 844, PTO's Final Determination is entitled to controlling weight." The contention is unavailing, based as it is on a mistake as to *Chevron's* breadth. Under *Chevron*, where Congress has authorized an agency to promulgate substantive rules under a statute it is charged with administering, we must uphold the agency's interpretation of an ambiguity or omission in that statute if the interpretation is a reasonable one. *Chevron, U.S.A., Inc. v. Natural Resources Defense Council, Inc.*, 467 U.S. 837, 842–45 (1984). . . .

As we have previously held, the broadest of the PTO's rulemaking powers—35 U.S.C. § 6(a)—authorizes the Commissioner to promulgate regulations directed only to "the conduct of proceedings in the [PTO]"; it does *not* grant the Commissioner the authority to issue substantive rules. *Animal Legal Defense Fund v. Quigg*, 932 F.2d 920, 930, 18 USPQ2d 1677, 1686 (Fed. Cir. 1991). Because Congress has not vested the Commissioner with any general substantive rulemaking power, the "Final Determination" at issue in this case cannot possibly have the "force and effect of law." *Chrysler Corp. v. Brown*, 441 U.S. 281, 302 (1979) . . . . Thus, the rule of controlling deference set forth in *Chevron* does not apply.

7. ***Gechter v. Davidson***, 43 USPQ 2d 1030, 1035 (Fed. Cir. 1997)

In the present case, the Board's opinion lacks a claim construction, makes conclusory findings relating to anticipation, and omits any analysis on several limitations. For example, the Board opinion does not separately construe the term "agent status messages" before finding that Canale discloses just such "agent status messages." In addition, the Board never construed the scope of the structures disclosed in the specification for the claimed "receiving means," nor did the Board expressly find that the "receiving means" disclosed in the specification was structurally equivalent to that embodied in Canale. Moreover, the Board's opinion also failed to define the exact function of the receiving means, as well as to find that Canale disclosed the *identical* function.

8. ***Gechter v. Davidson***, 43 USPQ 2d 1030, 1035 (Fed. Cir. 1997)

In sum, we hold that the Board is required to set forth in its opinions specific findings of fact and conclusions of law adequate to form a basis for our review. In particular, we expect that the Board's anticipation analysis be conducted on a limitation by limitation basis, with specific fact findings for each contested limitation and satisfactory explanations for such findings. Claim construction must also be explicit, at least as to any construction disputed by parties to the interference (or an applicant or patentee in an ex parte proceeding).

9. ***YBM Magnex, Inc. v. International Trade Comm'n***, 46 USPQ 2d 1843, 1845 n.2 (Fed. Cir. 1998)

Even were there an apparent conflict in statements of Federal Circuit law, the earlier statement prevails unless or until it has been overruled in banc. *Newell Cos. v. Kenney Mfg. Co.*, 864 F.2d 757, 765, 9 USPQ 2d 1417, 1423 (Fed. Cir. 1988). Subsequent panel opinions may elaborate and refine and thus advance the evolution of judge-made law, but they can not change the law as established in prior rulings.

10. ***Multiform Desiccants, Inc. v. Medzam, Ltd.***, 45 USPQ 2d 1429, 1432 (Fed. Cir. 1998)

When the meaning of a term is sufficiently clear in the patent specification, that meaning shall apply. . . . This rule of construction recognizes that the inventor may have imparted a special meaning to a term in order to convey a character or property or nuance relevant to the particular invention. Such special meaning, however, must be sufficiently clear in the specification that any departure from common usage would be so understood by a person of experience in the field of the invention.

11. ***Multiform Desiccants, Inc. v. Medzam, Ltd.***, 45 USPQ 2d 1429, 1433 (Fed. Cir. 1998)

Courts must exercise caution lest dictionary definitions, usually the least controversial source of extrinsic evidence, be converted into technical terms of art having legal, not linguistic, significance. The best source for understanding a technical term is the specification from which it arose, informed, as needed, by the prosecution history. The evolution of restrictions in the claims, in the course of examination in the PTO, reveals how those closest to the patenting process—the inventor and the patent examiner—viewed the subject matter. . . . When the specification explains and defines a term used in the claims, without ambiguity or incompleteness, there is no need to search further for the meaning of the term.

12. ***In re Beasley***, Civ. App. 99-1055, slip op. at 4 (Fed. Cir. July 20, 1999) (unpublished)

In reviewing factual determinations by the Board, this court must apply the standard of review provided by the Administrative Procedure Act, codified at 5 U.S.C. § 706.

13. ***Dickinson v. Zurko***, 50 USPQ 2d 1930, 1931–32 (U.S. 1999)

The Administrative Procedure Act (APA) sets forth standards governing judicial review of findings of fact made by federal administrative agencies. 5 U.S.C. § 706. We must decide whether § 706 applies when the Federal Circuit reviews findings of fact made by the Patent and Trademark Office (PTO). We conclude that it does apply, and the Federal Circuit must use the framework set forth in that section.

14. ***Giese v. Pierce Chem. Co.***, 50 USPQ 2d 1810, 1813–14 n.1 (D. Mass. 1999)

This Court recognizes that *Armament Systems* is an unpublished opinion and is "not citable as precedent" under Fed. Cir. Loc. R. 47.6(b). This hardly means, however, that it cannot be cited at all. The Federal Circuit, like the other circuits, not infrequently issues opinions that are officially deemed "unpublished." *See* Kirt Shuldberg, Comment, Digital Influence: Technology and Unpublished Opinions in the Federal Courts of Appeals, 85 Calif. L. Rev. 541, 545–547 (1997) (describing development of circuit rules to limit publication of opinions following 1972 recommendation by the Ju-

dicial Conference of the United States). The nationwide pro-
liferation of this body of "unpublished" opinions—which are,
in fact, promptly published in West's national reporters and
other legal publications—is both confusing and troubling. It
becomes all the more troubling in those circuits which disal-
low or severely restrict citation of "unpublished" opinions,
see 1st Cir. Loc. R. 36.2(b)(6) (citation only in related cases);
7th Cir. Loc. R. 53(b)(2)(iv) (citation only for binding or
preclusive effect); 9th Cir. Loc. R. 36-3 (same); D.C. Cir. Loc.
R. 28(c) (same); Fed. Cir. Loc. R. 47.6(b) (same), especially
when one of the taboo opinions turns out to be highly relevant to a case at bar.

There is sound reasoning behind the practice, however. As
recently explained to the judges within the First Circuit by
the Hon. Bruce Selya, in these days of already crowded federal appellate dockets burgeoning with ever more cases each
month, there is sometimes a need, due to the presentation
of unique factual circumstances or inartful briefing, to resolve an appeal without creating a precedent that would
bind later panels of the same court. Hence the "unpublished"
opinion "not citable as precedent." Informal remarks of
Bruce Selya at the First Circuit Judicial Conference, Oct. 28,
1998 (unpublished); *see also* Shuldberg, 85 Calif. L. Rev. at
547–551 (describing historical justifications for practice of
restricting citation of unpublished opinions). At the same
time, these decisions represent the considered opinions of
sitting judges deciding actual cases so it is little wonder that
the legal reporting services disseminate them and members
of the bar read them. Moreover, where, as here, a body of law
falls under the exclusive jurisdiction of only one federal circuit, the incremental worth of any opinion—even one expressly designated as "unpublished"—is enhanced.

What, then, are the bar and the district courts to do? Quite
simply, take the circuit rules at their word and, when an "unpublished opinion" is persuasive, go ahead and cite it—noting its unpublished status and providing copies to the court
and opposing counsel—not as precedent but as one would
cite a law review article by three respected authors. Many
circuits have already adopted this approach explicitly. *See*
5th Cir. Loc. R. 47.5.4; 8th Cir. Loc. R. 28A(k); 10th Cir. Loc.
R. 36.3; 11th Cir. Loc. R. 36-2 (each affording persuasive authority to unpublished opinions); cf. 4th Cir. Loc. R. 36(c); 6th
Cir. Loc. R. 24(c) (both allowing unpublished opinions to be
cited as precedent in certain circumstances). When a district
court chooses to follow an unpublished opinion, it further ex-
plicates its own analysis—always a desirable result—by reference to legal reasoning it considers persuasive albeit not
binding. That is what the Court has done here.

15. ***Gustavsson v. Valentini***, 25 USPQ 2d 1401, 1405 (B.P.A.I. 1992)

Congress "may leave it to administrative officials to establish rules within the prescribed limits of the statute." *Ethicon v. Quigg*, 849 F.2d 1422, 1425, 7 USPQ2d 1152, 1154 (Fed. Cir. 1988) (quoting *Patlex Corp. v. Mossinghoff*, 758 F. 2d 594, 605, 225 USPQ 243, 251 (Fed. Cir. 1985)). In the patent field, Congress has done precisely that by providing that the Director "may, subject to the approval of the Secretary of Commerce, establish regulations, not inconsistent with law, for the conduct of proceedings in the Patent and Trademark Office." 35 U.S.C. § 6(a) (1994). In this type of situation, "the validity of a regulation promulgated thereunder will be sustained so long as it is 'reasonably related to the enabling legislation.'" *Mourning v. Family Publications Service, Inc.*, 411 U.S. 356, 369 (1973) (quoting *Thorpe v. Housing Authority of Durham*, 393 U.S. 268, 280 (1969)).

16. ***In re Gartside***, 53 USPQ 2d 1769, 1773 (Fed. Cir. 2000)

In *Zurko*, the Supreme Court did not determine whether the correct standard of review for PTO findings of fact is the "arbitrary, capricious" or the "substantial evidence" test. See *Zurko*, 119 S. Ct. at 1821, 50 USPQ 2d at 1934. We feel compelled to decide that question, in order to secure the standard of review through which we will test the decision of the Board in this case. . . . [T]he "substantial evidence" standard asks whether a reasonable fact finder could have arrived at the agency's decision, see *Consolidated Edison Co. v. NLRB*, 305 U.S. 197, 229, 83 L. Ed. 126, 59 S. Ct. 206 (1938); see generally 3 Charles H. Koch, Jr., Administrative Law and Practice § 10.3[1], at 22–26 (2d ed. 1997), and is considered to be a less deferential review standard than "arbitrary, capricious." See *American Paper Inst., Inc. v. American Elec. Power Serv. Corp.*, 461 U.S. 402, 412–13 n.7, 76 L. Ed. 2d 22, 103 S. Ct. 1921 (1983) (characterizing the "arbitrary, capricious" standard as "more lenient" than the "substantial evidence" standard); *Abbott Lab. v. Gardner*, 387 U.S. 136, 143, 18 L. Ed. 2d 681, 87 S. Ct. 1507 (1967) (characterizing "substantial evidence" review as "more generous judicial review" than "arbitrary, capricious" review). The Supreme Court has described "substantial evidence" in the following manner:

> Substantial evidence is more than a mere scintilla. It means such relevant evidence as a reasonable mind might accept as adequate to support a conclusion. . . . Mere uncorroborated hearsay or rumor does not constitute substantial evidence.

Consolidated, 305 U.S. at 229–30 (citations omitted); see also *AK Steel Corp. v. United States*, 192 F.3d 1367, 1371 (Fed. Cir. 1999) (quoting *Consolidated*). The Court has emphasized that "substantial evidence" review involves examination of the record as a whole, taking into account evidence that both justifies and detracts from an agency's decision. See *Universal Camera Corp. v. NLRB*, 340 U.S. 474, 487–88, 95 L. Ed. 456, 71 S. Ct. 456 (1951). The Court has also stated, however, that "the possibility of drawing two inconsistent conclusions from the evidence does not prevent an administrative agency's finding from being supported by substantial evidence." See *Consolo v. Federal Maritime Comm'n*, 383 U.S. 607, 620, 16 L. Ed. 2d 131, 86 S. Ct. 1018 (1966).

17. ***In re Gartside***, 53 USPQ 2d 1769, 1774–75 (Fed. Cir. 2000)

Supreme Court precedent and the law of our sister circuits also indicate that "substantial evidence" review is appropriate in view of the plenary nature of the record before us. The Supreme Court has stated generally that the "basic requirement" for "substantial evidence" review is that the agency hearing produce a record that serves as the foundation for the agency's action. See *Overton Park*, 401 U.S. at 415; *Camp v. Pitts*, 411 U.S. 138, 141, 36 L. Ed. 2d 106, 93 S. Ct. 1241 (1973) (noting that "substantial evidence" review "is appropriate when reviewing findings made on a hearing record"). In *Zurko* the Court echoed these prior decisions when it intimated that "substantial evidence" review is the appropriate standard for our review of Board factfinding. See *Zurko*, 119 S. Ct. at 1823, 50 USPQ 2d at 1936 ("A reviewing court reviews an agency's reasoning to determine whether it is 'arbitrary' or 'capricious,' or, if bound up with a record-based factual conclusion, to determine whether it is supported by 'substantial evidence.'").

18. ***In re Kotzab***, 55 USPQ 2d 1313, 1316 (Fed. Cir. 2000)

The ultimate determination of whether an invention would have been obvious under 35 U.S.C. § 103(a) is a legal conclusion based on underlying findings of fact. See *Dembiczak*, 175 F.3d at 998, 50 USPQ 2d at 1616. We review the Board's ultimate determination of obviousness de novo. See Id. However, we review the Board's underlying factual findings for substantial evidence. See *In re Gartside*, 203 F.3d 1305, 1316, 53 USPQ 2d 1769, 1776 (Fed. Cir. 2000).

Substantial evidence is something less than the weight of the evidence but more than a mere scintilla of evidence. See Id. at 1312, 53 USPQ 2d at 1773 (quoting *Consolidated Edi-*

son Co. v. NLRB, 305 U.S. 197, 229–30, 83 L. Ed. 126, 59 S. Ct. 206 (1938)). In reviewing the record for substantial evidence, we must take into account evidence that both justifies and detracts from the factual determinations. See Id. (citing *Universal Camera Corp. v. NLRB*, 340 U.S. 474, 487–88, 95 L. Ed. 456, 71 S. Ct. 456 (1951)). We note that the possibility of drawing two inconsistent conclusions from the evidence does not prevent the Board's findings from being supported by substantial evidence. See Id. Indeed, if a reasonable mind might accept the evidence as adequate to support the factual conclusions drawn by the Board, then we must uphold the Board's determination.

19. ***Anastasoff v. U.S.***, 56 USPQ 2d 1621, 1627 (8th Cir.), ***opinion vacated on reh'g en banc***, 235 F.3d 1054 (8th Cir. 2000)

Federal courts, in adopting rules, are not free to extend the judicial power of the United States described in Article III of the Constitution. *Willy v. Coastal Corp.*, 503 U.S. 131, 135 (1992). The judicial power of the United States is limited by the doctrine of precedent. Rule 28A(i) allows courts to ignore this limit. If we mark an opinion as unpublished, Rule 28A(i) provides that is not precedent. Though prior decisions may be well-considered and directly on point, Rule 28A(i) allows us to depart from the law set out in such prior decisions without any reason to differentiate the cases. This discretion is completely inconsistent with the doctrine of precedent; even in constitutional cases, courts "have always required a departure from precedent to be supported by some 'special justification.'" *United States v. International Business Machines Corp.*, 517 U.S. 843, 856 (1996), quoting *Payne v. Tennessee*, 501 U.S. 808, 842 (1991) (Souter, J., concurring). Rule 28A(i) expands the judicial power beyond the limits set by Article III by allowing us complete discretion to determine which judicial decisions will bind us and which will not. Insofar as it limits the precedential effect of our prior decisions, the Rule is therefore unconstitutional.

20. ***Teacherson v. Patent and Trademark Office***, Civ. App. No. 99-1465, slip op. at 4 (Fed. Cir. Mar. 10, 2000) (unpublished), ***cert. denied***, 531 U.S. 997 (2000)

The Patent Act has mandated the appeal route for rejections of patent applications:

> An applicant for a patent, any of whose claims has been twice rejected, may appeal from the decision of the primary examiner to the Board of Patent Appeals and Interferences, having once paid the fee for such appeal.

35 U.S.C. § 134 (1994).

An applicant dissatisfied with the decision in an appeal to the Board of Patent Appeals and Interferences under section 134 of this title may appeal the decision to the United States Court of Appeals for the Federal Circuit.

35 U.S.C. § 141 (1994). Alternatively, an applicant dissatisfied with a decision of the Board of Patent Appeals and Interferences may also file a civil suit against the Commissioner of Patents and Trademarks in United States District Court for the District of Columbia. 35 U.S.C. § 145 (1994). . . . The Patent Act created the PTO review process, imposing the duty to follow a specified appeal process on both applicant and PTO. The Act does not create jurisdiction to circumvent these statutory appeal routes.

XXVI. Policy and Purposes of U.S. Patent System

1. ***Pfaff v. Wells Elecs., Inc.***, 525 U.S. 55, 48 USPQ 2d 1641, 1645 (1998)

As we have often explained, most recently in *Bonito Boats, Inc. v. Thunder Craft Boats, Inc.*, 489 U.S. 141, 151, 103 L. Ed. 2d 118, 109 S. Ct. 971 (1989), the patent system represents a carefully crafted bargain that encourages both the creation and the public disclosure of new and useful advances in technology, in return for an exclusive monopoly for a limited period of time. The balance between the interest in motivating innovation and enlightenment by rewarding invention with patent protection on the one hand, and the interest in avoiding monopolies that unnecessarily stifle competition on the other, has been a feature of the federal patent laws since their inception. As this Court explained in 1871:

> "Letters patent are not to be regarded as monopolies . . . but as public franchises granted to the inventors of new and useful improvements for the purpose of securing to them, as such inventors, for the limited term therein mentioned, the exclusive right and liberty to make and use and vend to others to be used their own inventions, as tending to promote the progress of science and the useful arts, and as matter of compensation to the inventors for their labor, toil, and expense in making the inventions, and reducing the same to practice for the public benefit, as contemplated by the Constitution and sanctioned by the laws of Congress." *Seymour v. Osbore*, 78 U.S. 516, 11 Wall. 516, 533–534, 20 L. Ed. 33.

2. ***Pfaff v. Wells Elecs., Inc.***, 525 U.S. 55, 48 USPQ 2d 1641, 1644 (1998)

It is well settled that an invention may be patented before it is reduced to practice. In 1888, this Court upheld a patent issued to Alexander Graham Bell even though he had filed his application before constructing a working telephone. . . .

"The law does not require that a discoverer or inventor, in order to get a patent for a process, must have succeeded in bringing his art to the highest degree of perfection. It is enough if he describes his method with sufficient clearness and precision to enable those skilled in the matter to understand what the process is, and if he points out some practicable way of putting it into operation." *The Telephone Cases*, 126 U.S. 1, 31 L. Ed. 863, 8 S. Ct. 778 (1888).

3. ***Markman v. Westview Instruments, Inc.***, 517 U.S. 370, 38 USPQ 2d 1461, 1463–64 (1996)

The Constitution empowers Congress "to promote the Progress of Science and useful Arts, by securing for limited Times to Authors and Inventors the exclusive Right to their respective Writings and Discoveries." U.S. Const., Art I, § 8, cl. 8. Congress first exercised this authority in 1790, when it provided for the issuance of "letters patent," Act of Apr. 10, 1790, ch. 7, § 1, 1 Stat. 109, which, like their modern counterparts, granted inventors "the right to exclude others from making, using, offering for sale, selling, or importing the patented invention," in exchange for full disclosure of an invention, H. Schwartz, Patent Law and Practice 1, 33 (2d ed. 1995). It has long been understood that a patent must describe the exact scope of an invention and its manufacture to "secure to [the patentee] all to which he is entitled, [and] to apprise the public of what is still open to them." *McClain v. Ortmayer*, 141 U.S. 419, 424, 35 L. Ed. 800, 12 S. Ct. 76 (1891). Under the modern American system, these objectives are served by two distinct elements of a patent document. First, it contains a specification describing the invention "in such full, clear, concise, and exact terms as to enable any person skilled in the art . . . to make and use the same." 35 U.S.C. § 112; *see also* 3 E. Lipscomb, Walker on Patents § 10:1, pp. 183–184 (3d ed. 1985) (Lipscomb) (listing the requirements for a specification). Second, a patent includes one or more "claims," which "particularly point out and distinctly claim the subject matter which the applicant regards as his invention." 35 U.S.C. § 112. "A claim covers and secures a process, a machine, a manufacture, a composition of matter, or a design, but never the function or result of either, nor the scientific explanation of their operation." 6 Lipscomb § 21:17, at 315–316. The claim "defines the scope of a patent grant," 3 *id.*, § 11:1, at 280, and functions to forbid not only exact copies of an invention, but products that go to "the heart of the invention but avoid the literal language of the claim by making a noncritical change," *Schwartz, supra*, at 82. . . .

Characteristically, patent lawsuits charge what is known as infringement, *Schwartz, supra*, at 75, and rest on allegations that the defendant "without authority made, used or [sold the] patented invention, within the United States during the term of the patent therefor . . . ." 35 U.S.C. § 271(a). Victory in an infringement suit requires a finding that the patent claim "covers the alleged infringer's product or process," which in turn necessitates a determination of "what the words in the claim mean." *Schwartz, supra*, at 80.

4. ***Topliff v. Topliff***, 145 U.S. 156, 171 (1892).

The specification and claims of a patent, particularly if the invention be at all complicated, constitute one of the most difficult legal instruments to draw with accuracy, and in view of the fact that valuable inventions are often placed in the hands of inexperienced persons to prepare such specifications and claims, it is no matter of surprise that the latter frequently fail to describe with requisite certainty the exact invention of the patentee, and err either in claiming that which the patentee had not in fact invented, or in omitting some element which was a valuable or essential part of his actual invention. . . . The object of the patent law is to secure to inventors a monopoly of what they have actually invented or discovered, and it ought not to be defeated by a too strict and technical adherence to the letter of the statute, or by the application of artificial rules of interpretation.

5. ***Florida Prepaid Postsecondary Ed. Expense Bd. v. College Savings Bank***, 51 USPQ 2d 1081, 1090–91 (U.S. 1999).

In his commentaries on the Federal Constitution, Justice Story said of the Patent and Copyright Clauses:

"It is beneficial to all parties, that the national government should possess this power; to authors and inventors, because, otherwise, they would be subjected to the varying laws and systems of the different states on this subject, which would impair, and might even destroy the value of their rights; to the public, as it will promote the progress of science and the useful arts, and admit the people at large, after a short interval, to the full possession and enjoyment of all writings and inventions without restraint." J. Story, Commentaries on the Constitution of the United States § 502, p. 402 (R. Rotunda & J. Nowak eds. 1987).

James Madison said of the same Clause, "The utility of this power will scarcely be questioned . . . . The States cannot separately make effectual provision for either [copyrights or patents], and most of them have anticipated the decision of this point, by laws passed at the instance of Congress." The Federalist No. 43, p. 267 (H. Lodge ed. 1908) (J. Madison).

6. *University of Colorado Found., Inc. v. American Cyanamid Co.*, 52 USPQ 2d 1801, 1805 (Fed. Cir. 1999)

A primary purpose of patent law is to reward invention. . . . The law of inventorship, which has heretofore developed solely under federal law, supports this purpose by identifying the actual inventors of an invention eligible for patent protection. With its advent in Article 1 of the Constitution, patent law has developed under federal law to achieve the objective of national uniformity.

7. *Prima Tek II, L.L.C. v. A-Roo Co.*, 55 USPQ 2d 1742, 1747 & n.2 (Fed. Cir. 2000)

A patent represents the legal right to exclude others from making, using, selling, or offering to sell a patented invention in the United States, and from importing the invention into the United States. See 38 U.S.C. § 154 (1994). Implicit in the right to exclude is the ability to waive that right, i.e., to license activities that would otherwise be excluded, such as making, using and selling the patented invention in the United States. Those activities, of course, may be subject to further limitations such as governmental restrictions or "blocking" patents. . . . A "blocking patent" is an earlier patent that must be licensed in order to practice a later patent. This often occurs, for instance, between a pioneer patent and an improvement patent.

8. *Ex parte Davis*, 56 USPQ 2d 1434, 1434 n.8 (B.P.A.I. 2000) (unpublished)

A first patent or application "dominates" a second patent or application when the first patent or application has a broad or generic claim which fully encompasses or reads on an invention defined in a narrower or more specific claim in the second patent or application.

9. *Ajinomoto Co., Inc. v. Archer-Daniels-Midland Co.*, 56 USPQ 2d 1332, 1338 (Fed. Cir. 2000)

Requiring inclusion in the patent of known scientific/technological information would add an imprecise and open-ended criterion to the content of patent specifications, could greatly enlarge the content of patent specifications and unnecessarily increase the cost of preparing and prosecuting patent applications, and could tend to obfuscate rather than highlight the contribution to which the patent is directed. A patent is not a scientific treatise, but a document that that presumes a readership skilled in the field of the invention.

10. ***Northern Telecom Ltd. v. Samsung Elecs. Co., Ltd.***, 55 USPQ 2d 1065, 1068 (Fed. Cir. 2000)

[I]f a patent requires A, and the accused device or process uses A and B, infringement will be avoided only if the patent's definition of A excludes the possibility of B. See, e.g., *Northern Telecom, Inc. v. Datapoint Corp.*, 908 F.2d 931, 945, 15 USPQ 2d 1321, 1332 (Fed. Cir. 1990) ("The addition of features does not avoid infringement, if all the elements of the patent claims have been adopted."); *Uniroyal, Inc. v. Rudkin-Wiley Corp.*, 837 F.2d 1044, 1057, 5 USPQ 2d 1434, 1444 (Fed. Cir. 1988) ("Adding features to an accused device will not result in noninfringement if all the limitations in the claims, or equivalents thereof, are present in the accused device."); *A.B. Dick*, 713 F.2d at 703, 218 USPQ at 967. Statements simply noting a distinction between A and B are thus unhelpful: what matters is not that the patent describes A and B as different, but whether, according to the patent, A and B must be mutually exclusive.

11. ***Solomon v. Kimberly-Clark Corp.***, 55 USPQ 2d 1279, 1283–84 (Fed. Cir. 2000)

[A]n inventor is not competent to construe patent claims for the following reasons:

> [C]ommonly the claims are drafted by the inventor's patent solicitor and they may even be drafted by the patent examiner in an examiner's amendment (subject to the approval of the inventor's solicitor). While presumably the inventor has approved any changes to the claim scope that have occurred via amendment during the prosecution process, it is not unusual for there to be a significant difference between what an inventor thinks his patented invention is and what the ultimate scope of the claims is after allowance by the PTO.

Markman, 52 F.3d at 985, 34 USPQ 2d at 1335 (citation omitted).

XXVII. Information Disclosure Statements and Duty of Disclosure

1. ***In re Schuurs***, 218 USPQ 443, 444 (Comm'r 1983)

The policy of the Office does not require listing on the face of a patent all of the art considered by the examiner prior to issuance of the patent. M.P.E.P. § 1302.12 states:

All references * * * submitted by applicant if they conform to the requirements set forth in §§ 707.05 (b) * * * must be listed on either a form PTO-892 or PTO-1449. All such reference citations will be printed in the patent.

M.P.E.P. § 707.05 states:

However, if the prior art is submitted in a manner which does not comply with the § 609 guidelines, it is not necessary to list all cited prior art on form PTO-892 in order to make the citations of record. This is because the complete listing of applicant's citations will be in the application file and will be available for inspection by the public after issuance of the patent with notations as indicated under item C of § 717.05.

2. ***Demaco Corp. v. F. Von Langsdorff Licensing Ltd.***, 7 USPQ 2d 1222, 1228 (Fed. Cir. 1988)

The concept of inequitable conduct in patent procurement derives from the equitable doctrine of unclean hands: that a person who obtains a patent by intentionally misleading the PTO can not enforce the patent. Inequitable conduct may be held although the common law elements of fraud are absent. To achieve a just application of this penalty in the variety of situations that may arise, this court established a balancing test in *American Hoist & Derrick Co. v. Sowa & Sons, Inc.*, 725 F.2d 1350, 1364, 220 USPQ 763, 774 (Fed. Cir.), *cert. denied*, 469 U.S. 821 [224 USPQ 520] (1984) whereby the materiality of the information that was not provided to the PTO is weighed against the intent of the actor. The court is charged with reaching an equitable result in view of the particular circumstances of the case.

3. ***Demaco Corp. v. F. Von Langsdorff Licensing Ltd.***, 7 USPQ 2d 1222, 1229 (Fed. Cir. 1988)

We note, for example, that Geb. '249 was listed in the German priority document filed with the PTO: this does not support a conclusion of intentional withholding. Indeed, the record contains no evidence of deliberate concealment.

[A]n applicant who knew or should have known of the art or information, and of its materiality, is not automatically precluded thereby from an effort to convince the fact finder that the failure to disclose was nonetheless not due to an intent to mislead the PTO. . . .

Id. at 1416, 5 USPQ2d at 1116.

4. ***Scripps Clinic & Research Found. v. Genentech Inc.***, 18 USPQ 2d 1001, 1008 (Fed. Cir. 1991)

The materiality of a representation, and whether the representation was made with intent to deceive or mislead, are the two essential factual predicates to determination of inequitable conduct. *Modine Mfg. Co. v. Allen Group, Inc.,* 917 F.2d 538, 541, 16 USPQ 2d 1622, 1624 (Fed. Cir. 1990). . . . Notably missing is the element of intent, essential as a matter of law to a ruling of inequitable conduct. *See Kingsdown Medical Consultants, Ltd. v. Hollister, Inc.,* 863 F.2d 867, 876, 9 USPQ 2d 1384, 1392 (Fed. Cir. 1988). Conduct that requires forfeiture of all patent rights must be deliberate, and proved by clear and convincing evidence.

5. ***ATD Corp. v. Lydall, Inc.***, 48 USPQ 2d 1321, 1330–31 (Fed. Cir. 1998)

In view of § 609 it can not be inequitable conduct for an applicant not to resubmit, in the divisional application, the information that was cited or submitted in the parent application. *See Transmatic, Inc. v. Gulton Industries, Inc.,* 849 F. Supp. 526, 31 USPQ 2d 1225 (E.D. Mich. 1994), *aff'd in pertinent part, rev'd in part,* 53 F.3d 1270, 35 USPQ 2d 1035 (Fed. Cir. 1995) (a material reference that is already of record in parent application need not be resubmitted by the applicant in a continuing application). Nor was ATD required to submit the documents relating to Sendzimir in the record of the PCT application, when Sendzimir was already of record in the United States parent application. Although international search reports may contain information material to patentability if they contain closer prior art than that which was before the United States examiner, it is the reference itself, not the information generated in prosecuting foreign counterparts, that is material to prosecution in the United States. The details of foreign prosecution are not an additional category of material information.

XXVIII. Reexamination

1. ***In re Recreative Techs. Corp.***, 38 USPQ 2d 1776, 1777–78 (Fed. Cir. 1996)

The reexamination statute was an important part of a larger effort to revive the United States' competitive vitality by restoring confidence in the validity of patents issued by the PTO. *Patlex Corp. v. Mossinghoff,* 758 F.2d 594, 601, 225 USPQ 243, 248, *aff'd on reh'g* 771 F.2d 480, 226 USPQ 985 (Fed. Cir. 1985). Congressman Robert Kastenmeier described the reexamination proposal as "an effort to reverse the current decline in U.S. productivity by strengthening the patent and copyright systems to improve investor confidence in new technology." 126 Cong. Rec. 29,895 (1980).

The proponents of reexamination anticipated three principal benefits. First, reexamination based on references that were not previously included in the patentability examination could resolve validity disputes more quickly and less expensively than litigation. Second, courts would benefit from the expertise of the PTO for prior art that was not previously of record. Third, reexamination would strengthen confidence in patents whose validity was clouded because pertinent prior art had not previously been considered by the PTO. *Patlex*, 758 F.2d at 602, 225 USPQ at 248–49. These benefits are achieved by authorizing the PTO to correct errors in the prior examination:

> The reexamination statute's purpose is to correct errors made by the government, to remedy defective governmental (not private) action, and if need be to remove patents that never should have been granted. . . . A defectively examined and therefore erroneously granted patent must yield to the reasonable Congressional purpose of facilitating the correction of governmental mistakes.

Patlex, 758 F.2d at 604, 225 USPQ at 250.

However, Congress recognized that this broad purpose must be balanced against the potential for abuse, whereby unwarranted reexaminations can harass the patentee and waste the patent life. The legislative record and the record of the interested public reflect a serious concern that reexamination not create new opportunities for abusive tactics and burdensome procedures. Thus reexamination as enacted was carefully limited to new prior art, that is, "new information about pre-existing technology which may have escaped review at the time of the initial examination of the application." H.R. Rep. No. 96-1307, 96th Cong., 2d Sess. 3 (1980), *reprinted in* 1980 U.S.C.C.A.N. 6460, 6462. No grounds of reexamination were to be permitted other than based on new prior art and sections 102 and 103. As explained in the legislative history, matters that were decided in the original examination would be barred from reexamination:

> This "substantial new question" requirement would protect patentees from having to respond to, or participate in unjustified reexaminations. Further, it would act to bar reconsideration of any argument already decided by the Office, whether during the original examination or an earlier reexamination.

Id. at 7, *reprinted in* 1980 U.S.C.C.A.N. at 6466.

Thus the statute guarded against simply repeating the prior examination on the same issues and arguments. Commissioner Diamond explained the importance of this safeguard:

[The proposed statute] carefully protects patent owners from reexamination proceedings brought for harassment or spite. The possibility of harassing patent holders is a classic criticism of some foreign reexamination systems and we made sure it would not happen here.

Industrial Innovation & Patent & Copyright Law Amendments: Hearings on H.R. 6933, 6934, 3806 & 214 Before the Subcomm. on Courts, Civil Liberties and the Administration of Justice of the House Comm. on the Judiciary, 96th Cong., 2d Sess. 594 (1980) (statement of Sidney Diamond, Cmr. of Patents & Trademarks).

2. ***In re Recreative Techs. Corp.***, 38 USPQ 2d 1776, 1778 (Fed. Cir. 1996)

The Commissioner's argument that reexamination, once begun, can be limited to grounds previously raised and finally decided, can not be accommodated by the statute, and is directly contravened by the legislative history. Although Congress may entrust the administrative agency with administration of a statute, the agency can not depart from the statutory purpose.

3. ***In re Recreative Techs. Corp.***, 38 USPQ 2d 1776, 1779 (Fed. Cir. 1996)

The statutory instruction that a new question of patentability must be raised is explicit in 35 U.S.C. § 303. Reexamination is barred for questions of patentability that were decided in the original examination. That power can not be acquired by internal rule of procedure or practice. The policy balance reflected in the reexamination statute's provisions can not be unilaterally realigned by the agency.

4. ***In re Recreative Techs. Corp.***, 38 USPQ 2d 1776, 1779 (Fed. Cir. 1996)

The question of patentability in view of the Ota reference was decided in the original examination, and thus it can not be a substantial new question. . . . Ota, however, had been cited. It was the subject of extensive prosecution during the original examination, and the rejection had been overcome.

5. ***In re Portola Packaging Inc.***, 42 USPQ 2d 1295, 1298 (Fed. Cir. 1997)

The reexamination statute, Pub. L. 96-517, was enacted with the intent of achieving three principal benefits. Reexamination of patents by the PTO would (i) settle validity disputes more quickly and less expensively than litigation, (ii) allow courts to refer patent validity questions to an agency with expertise in both the patent law and technology, and

(iii) reinforce investor confidence in the certainty of patent rights by affording an opportunity to review patents of doubtful validity. . . .

However, Congress did not authorize the PTO to evaluate patentability anew whenever there existed doubt as to a patent's validity. Rather, the PTO was authorized to reexamine an issued patent only within strictly defined limits. Congress recognized that holdings of patent invalidity by courts were mostly based on prior art that was not before the PTO. . . . Congress also was aware that newly-discovered prior art often is identified only after a patent is issued because a potential infringer generally has greater resources and incentives to search for and find prior art than does the PTO.

6. ***In re Portola Packaging Inc.***, 42 USPQ 2d 1295, 1298–99 (Fed. Cir. 1997)

Thus, Congress provided for reexamination of patents, but it was also concerned about subjecting patentees to repeated examinations on the same prior art. It therefore limited the scope of reexamination. As this court stated in *Recreative Technologies*:

Congress recognized that [the] broad purpose [of reexamination] must be balanced against the potential for abuse, whereby unwarranted reexaminations can harass the patentee and waste the patent life. The legislative record and the record of the interested public reflect a serious concern that reexamination not create new opportunities for abusive tactics and burdensome procedures. *Thus, reexamination as enacted was carefully limited to new prior art, that is, "new information about pre-existing technology which may have escaped review at the time of the initial examination of the patent application."* H.R. Rep. No. 96-1307, [at] 3 (1980) reprinted in 1980 U.S.C.C.A.N. 6460, 6462. *No grounds of reexamination were to be permitted other than on new prior art* and sections 102 and 103. As explained in the legislative history, matters that were decided in the original examination would be barred from reexamination: "This 'substantial new question' requirement would protect patentees from having to respond to, or participate in unjustified reexaminations. Further, it would act to bar reconsideration of any argument already decided by the [PTO], whether during the original examination or an earlier reexamination." *Id.* at 7, *reprinted [in]* 1980 U.S.C.C.A.N. at 6466.

83 F.3d at 1397, 38 USPQ2d at 1778 (emphasis added). . . . Accordingly, reexamination was only intended for those in-

stances in which the examiner did not have all of the relevant prior art at his disposal when he originally considered
the patentability of an invention.

7. ***In re Portola Packaging Inc.***, 42 USPQ 2d 1295, 1299
(Fed. Cir. 1997)

The regulations that prescribe an examiner's conduct indicate that, in conducting an examination, an examiner must
evaluate each cited reference and then determine which of
those references, alone or in combination, provides the most
appropriate statutory ground for rejecting the claims. See 37
C.F.R. § 1.106(b) ("In rejecting claims for want of novelty or
for obviousness, the examiner must cite the best references
at his command."). . . . If the references were in front of the
examiner, it must be assumed that he or she reviewed them.
Accordingly, we reject the Commissioner's suggestion that
the PTO is entitled to conclude during reexamination that
an earlier examination was not conducted properly and to do
it again. Instead, the narrow mandate of the reexamination
statute requires that reexamination proceedings be conducted in light of the presumption that earlier examinations
complied with the applicable statutes and regulations and
that earlier examiners did their work correctly with respect
to the prior art references at their disposal.

8. ***In re Portola Packaging Inc.***, 42 USPQ 2d 1295, 1299
(Fed. Cir. 1997)

Whether the earlier examination was correct or not, reexamination of the same claims in light of the same references
does not raise a substantial new question of patentability,
which is the statutory criterion for reexamination.

9. ***In re Portola Packaging Inc.***, 42 USPQ 2d 1295, 1299
(Fed. Cir. 1997)

Congress intended that on reexamination a patent holder
would not have to argue that claims were valid over the
same references that had been considered by the PTO during the original examination. . . . A reexamination system
that requires a patentee to revisit such arguments on reexamination, by permitting the PTO to redo what it was expected to have done earlier, would lead to the "burdensome
procedures" Congress sought to avoid.

10. ***In re Portola Packaging Inc.***, 42 USPQ 2d 1295, 1299–
1300 (Fed. Cir. 1997)

We also reject the Commissioner's argument that the
amendments made during reexamination created a substantial new question of patentability. That the claims were

amended by Portola does not mean that a new examination of the amended claims involved substantial new issues of patentability. It is clear that the scope of a patent claim may not be enlarged by amendment during reexamination. . . . Thus, after the reexamination amendment, the claim could not cover subject matter broader than the scope of the claim that was originally allowed. . . . It naturally follows then that when the original examiner examined the original claims in light of the cited prior art, the subject matter of the narrower, amended claims was necessarily considered in relation to the cited prior art.

11. ***In re Freeman***, 31 USPQ 2d 1444, 1447 (Fed. Cir. 1994)

35 U.S.C. § 305, entitled "conduct of reexamination proceedings" sets forth in part that "no proposed amendment or new claim enlarging the scope of a claim of the patent will be permitted in a reexamination proceeding." Whether amendments enlarge the scope of a claim is a matter of claim construction. Claim construction is a question of law which we review de novo. . . .

A claim is enlarged if it includes within its scope any subject matter that would not have infringed the original patent.

12. ***In re Freeman***, 31 USPQ 2d 1444, 1447 (Fed. Cir. 1994)

The test for when a new claim enlarges the scope of an original claim under § 305 is the same as that under the two-year limitation for reissue applications adding enlarging claims under 35 U.S.C. § 251, last paragraph. . . . In the reissue context this court has stated that

> a claim of a reissue application is broader in scope than the original claims if it contains within its scope any conceivable apparatus or process which would not have infringed the original patent . . . A claim that is broader in any respect is considered to be broader than the original claims even though it may be narrower in other respects.

Tillotson Ltd. v. Walbro Corp., 831 F.2d 1033, 1037 n.2, 4 USPQ 2d 1450, 1453 n.2 (Fed. Cir. 1987).

13. ***Patlex Corp. v. Quigg***, 6 USPQ 2d 1296, 1298 (D.D.C. 1988)

Under 35 U.S.C. section 301, any person may cite to the PTO prior art, consisting of patents and printed publications, that may affect the patentability of any claim of a patent. 35 U.S.C. section 302 authorizes any person to request reexamination of a patent based on that "prior art." Within three months of receiving such a request, the Commissioner then determines whether the prior art raises a "substantial new question of patentability." *Id.* sec. 303(a). If the Commissioner determines that it does, he must order reexamination of the patent. *Id.* sec. 304. If he determines that the cited prior art raises no substantial new question of patentability, he denies the request for reexamination. The "determination . . . that no substantial new question of patentability has been raised will be final and nonappealable." *Id.* sec. 303(c). The statute contains no provision for appeal or review of a determination that a substantial new question has been raised. . . . The Commissioner's threshold determination merely triggers the reexamination proceeding; it does not affect the validity of the patent. As to the larger question of whether the cited patents and printed publications render the claims of the challenged patent unpatentable on the merits, the statute confers a right of appeal and court review. 35 U.S.C. sec. 306.

It is immediately apparent that a patent owner will ultimately prevail on the merits in all cases in which the Commissioner determines a substantial new question of patentability exists, but erroneously rejects claims on the merits. It is also clear that the patent owner could not avoid reexamination by seeking immediate judicial review, because at this stage there is no final agency action. *See* 5 U.S.C. sec. 704. The Court consequently concludes that the legislative scheme leaves the Commissioner's section 303 determination entirely to his discretion and not subject to judicial review.

14. ***Patlex Corp. v. Quigg***, 6 USPQ 2d 1296, 1299 (D.D.C. 1988)

The reexamination statute limits the scope of the reexamination to patents and printed publications. 35 U.S.C. secs. 301–302. Consequently, the Commissioner may not on reexamination consider whether the specification of a patent being reexamined contains an enabling disclosure for the issued patent claims. . . . Moreover, section 2258 of the PTO's Manual of Patent Examining Procedure captioned "Scope of Reexamination," provides:

> New or amended claims are to be examined for compliance with 35 U.S.C. sec. 112 and . . . consideration of 35 U.S.C. sec. 112 issues should be limited to the amendatory (i.e., new language) matter. For example, a claim which is amended or a new claim which is presented containing a limitation not found in the original patent claim should be considered for compliance under 35 U.S.C. sec. 112 only with respect to that limitation.

15. ***Patlex Corp. v. Quigg***, 6 USPQ 2d 1296, 1299 (D.D.C. 1988)
[T]he reexamination statute does not contemplate a "reexamination" of the sufficiency of a disclosure. Rather, it is limited to reexamination of patentability based on prior art patents and publications. Hence, the Court concludes that the examiner and the Board lacked jurisdiction in this case to "reexamine" the sufficiency of the specification of the "great-grandparent" application.

16. ***Laitram Corp. v. NEC Corp.***, 21 USPQ 2d 1276, 1278 (Fed. Cir. 1991)
Reexamination provides a mechanism for enabling the Patent and Trademark Office to review and correct an initial examination. Thus reexamination is conducted afresh, without the burdens and presumptions that accompany litigation of an issued patent. . . . The Commissioner, having determined that a substantial new question of patentability is raised, may order reexamination of the patent, 35 U.S.C. § 304, and conduct reexamination proceedings using the same procedures as in initial examination.

17. ***Laitram Corp. v. NEC Corp.***, 21 USPQ 2d 1276, 1280 (Fed. Cir. 1991)
We thus answer the certified question as follows: When claims are amended during reexamination following a rejection based on prior art, the claims are not deemed substantively changed as a matter of law. There is no per se rule. To determine whether a claim change is substantive it is necessary to analyze the claims of the original and the reexamined patents in light of the particular facts, including the prior art, the prosecution history, other claims, and any other pertinent information.

18. ***In re Lonardo***, 43 USPQ 2d 1262, 1266 (Fed. Cir. 1997), ***cert. denied***, 522 U.S. 1147 (1998)
Since the statute in other places refers to prior art in relation to reexamination, see id., it seems apparent that Congress intended that the phrases "patents and publications" and "other patents or printed publications" in section 303(a) not be limited to prior art patents or printed publications. . . . A patent is clearly the type of evidence that Congress intended the PTO to consider during reexamination, and the cost of examination is not significantly increased by having the PTO consider the ground of double patenting, as it involves issues of claim identity and obviousness, well within the PTO's everyday expertise. . . . Thus, we conclude that the PTO was authorized during reexamination to consider the question of double patenting based upon the '762 patent.

19. ***Ex parte Obiaya***, 227 USPQ 58, 61 (B.P.A.I. 1985)

Where do "double patenting rejections of the obviousness type" fit in? Are they permissible under the reexamination statute, or are they, like public use and sale rejections, and Section 112 rejections (except as to new and amended claims), excluded? *In re Etter, supra,* states (p. 4): "Patent claims are reexamined only in light of patents and printed publications under 35 U.S.C. PP102, 103 . . . ." Double patenting rejections are analogous to Section 103 rejections and depend on the presence of a prior "patent" as the basis for the rejection. Thus, we take the position that such rejection falls within the ambit of those intended by the statute and are not specifically excluded by the *Etter* case. Further, the *Etter* court focused on the question of presumption of validity with regard to a reexamination patent and its statement as to the scope of proper rejections in the evaluation of a reexamination patent are not the point of the ruling.

20. ***In re Lanham***, 1 USPQ 2d 1877, 1877–78 (Comm'r 1986)

Insofar as the request for the Commissioner to consider the issue of fraud and inequitable conduct is concerned, such issues are not proper for consideration during reexamination. In this regard the issues that are proper for consideration in a reexamination proceeding are set forth in 37 CFR 1.552(a) and (b). As set forth therein, patent claims will be examined on the basis of patents or printed publications and new and amended claims must not enlarge the scope of the claims of the patent. Further, new and amended claims will be examined on the basis of patents or printed publications and also for compliance with the provisions of 35 U.S.C. 112 and the new matter prohibition of 35 U.S.C. 132. Questions other than those indicated in 37 CFR 1.552(a) and (b) will not be resolved in a reexamination proceeding. 37 CFR 1.552(c).

Clearly the issues of fraud and failure of the duty of disclosure are not among those set forth in 37 CFR 1.552(a) and (b) and are therefore, under 37 CFR 1.552(c), improper questions for consideration in a reexamination proceeding.

21. ***Ex parte Chicago Rawhide Mfg. Co.***, 226 USPQ 438, 440 (Pat. Off. Bd. App. 1984)

The mere reliance on a reference to evidence the obviousness of a particular feature of a claim pending during the prosecution of an application prior to the issuance of a patent, which claim is cancelled prior to the granting of the patent, is not sufficient to justify a holding that "a substantial new question of patentability affecting" a claim of a patent has not been raised by the citation of that patent. . . . This is especially true, where, as here, the reference had previously

been considered in a secondary manner for a very limited
purpose. . . . Under the facts here present we find that there
was no reason why the Examiner was here precluded from
bottoming a proper rejection on Baney.

22. ***Ex parte Rodgers***, 27 USPQ 2d 1738, 1742 & n.8 (B.P.A.I.
1992)

[W]e hold that claims added during reexamination proceeding and determined to be patentable therein nevertheless remain "[a]mended or new claims presented during a reexamination proceeding . . . [which] will be examined . . . for
compliance with the requirements of 35 USC 112," as required by 37 CFR 1.552(b), in any later reexamination proceeding. Indeed, there appears to be nothing in the statutory
scheme which would prevent reexamination of even original
patent claims for compliance with 35 USC 112. *See Bowles
Fluidics Corp. v. Mossinghoff*, 620 F. Supp. 1297, 228 USPQ
512 (D.D.C. 1985). 35 USC 305 provides that "reexamination
will be conducted according to the procedures established for
initial reexamination under the provisions of sections 132
and 133 of this title."

23. ***Scripps Clinic & Research Found. v. Genentech Inc.***, 18
USPQ 2d 1001, 1008–09 (Fed. Cir. 1991)

In accordance with 37 C.F.R. §1.175(a)(5) and (a)(3) the
applicant for reissue must "specify[] the errors relied upon,
and how they arose or occurred," and must "distinctly specify[] the excess or insufficiency in the claims"; and in accordance with 37 C.F.R. §1.175(a)(6) the applicant must declare
the absence of deceptive intention.

The principal error that the inventors sought to cure was
the claiming of "less than [they] had a right to claim in the
patent" due to the omission of product claims.

An error of law is not excluded from the class of error subject to correction in accordance with the reissue statute. Although attorney error is not an open invitation to reissue in
every case in which it may appear, *see In re Weiler*, 790 F.2d
1576, 1579, 229 USPQ 673, 675 (Fed. Cir. 1986) ("not every
event or circumstance that might be labeled 'error' is correctable by reissue"), the purpose of the reissue statute is to
avoid forfeiture of substantive rights due to error made
without intent to deceive. *See generally Ball Corp. v. United
States*, 729 F.2d 1429, 1939 n.28, 221 USPQ 289, 296 n.28
(Fed. Cir. 1984) (the reissue statute "is based on fundamental principles of equity and fairness").

When the statutory requirements are met, reissuance of
the patent is not discretionary with the Commissioner; it is
mandatory ("shall"). . . .

24. **Scripps Clinic & Research Found. v. Genentech Inc.**, 18 USPQ 2d 1001, 1008–09 (Fed. Cir. 1991)

The law does not require that no competent attorney or alert inventor could have avoided the error sought to be corrected by reissue. Failure of the attorney to claim the invention sufficiently broadly is "one of the most common sources of defects". *In re Wilder*, 736 F.2d 1516, 222 USPQ 369 (Fed. Cir. 1984), *cert. denied*, 469 U.S. 1209 (1985):

> An attorney's failure to appreciate the full scope of the invention is one of the most common sources of defects in patents. The fact that the error could have been discovered at the time of prosecution with a more thorough patentability search or with improved communication between the inventors and the attorney does not, by itself, preclude a patent owner from correcting defects through reissue.

Id. at 1519, 222 USPQ at 371.

25. **Ex parte GPAC Inc.**, 29 USPQ 2d 1401, 1403 n.1 (B.P.A.I. 1993)

Claims involved in a reexamination proceeding are to be read as broad as reasonably possible, consistent with the supporting specification. *In re Yamamoto*, 740 F.2d 1569, 222 USPQ 234 (Fed. Cir. 1984).

26. **In re Rief,** Reexamination Control No. 90/004,654, p.2 (Comm'r Sept. 19, 1997)

Petitioners' contentions that the examiner should not have tried to equate original prior art with equivalent or similar prior art fail to address the fact that a substantial new question of patentability is shown by pointing out "how any questions of patentability raised are substantially different from those raised in the earlier prosecution of the patent before the Office." MPEP Section 2216. One very logical way to show whether or not such differences exist is to compare the prior art cited or applied in the patent prosecution with the new prior art cited in the reexamination request.

While an order granting or denying a request for reexamination must address that issue, i.e., how any questions of patentability raised are substantially different from those raised in the earlier prosecution, there is no requirement in the reexamination statutes or rules that an examiner must perform a *Graham v. John Deere* type analysis of each piece of prior art cited in a reexamination request, as petitioners contend. The case law cited to support petitioner's contention, *Bausch & Lomb, Inc. v. Barnes-Hind/Hydrocurve*,

Inc., 230 USPQ 416 (Fed. Cir. 1986), dealt with an infringement proceeding, not a reexamination proceeding, and is not relevant here.

27. ***In re Rief***, Reexamination Control No. 90/004,654, p.3 (Comm'r Sept. 19, 1997)

Petitioner's second contention is that in sections 5 through 19 of the order denying reexamination, there is a new patentability standard set forth, i.e., "substantial equivalent" (to other prior art). This contention overlooks the explicit language of the reexamination statutes and rules, i.e., "substantial new question of patentability." To state that certain teachings in newly cited prior art are substantially equivalent to teachings in prior art of record is perfectly logical, reasonable and proper. The use of the term "substantial" is found in the reexamination statutes and rules and its use in a reasoned statement supporting a decision not to order reexamination appears eminently reasonable. To state that something is substantially equivalent to a previously considered prior art teaching is considered reasonably related to the issue of whether a particular question of patentability is or is riot substantially different from an issue raised earlier in the prosecution of the patent for which reexamination is sought.

28. ***In re Ductmate Indus., Inc.***, Reexamination Control No. 90/004,369, U.S. Patent 4,584,756, p.6 (Comm'r Feb. 12, 1997)

The general rule is that administrative agencies are not bound by the rules of evidence which govern judicial proceedings, *In re Epstein*, 31 USPQ2d 1817 (Fed. Cir. 1994). Agencies may provide for the application of evidence rules, as the Office has done in certain *inter partes* proceedings. *Id.* No specific evidentiary rule has been promulgated with respect to the quality of evidence received during the initial phase of a reexamination proceeding. By its nature, reexamination during the period prior to the beginning of ex pane examination under 37 CFR § 1.550(a) can be considered to be *inter partes* in that limited participation by a "third party" Requester is permitted, 37 CFR §§ 1.510, 1.515 and 1.535. It is noted that reexamination is specifically required to be conducted in a manner similar to that in which other *ex parte* "examinations" are conducted, 37 CFR § 1.550(a), following the period in which the granting or denying of the order to reexamination takes place. It is logical that prior to the commencement of the *ex parte* stage of reexamination, the evidence submitted in the reexamination proceeding should be treated in a manner analogous to the manner in which evidence is treated during other Office *inter partes* proceedings. Therefore, it is believed that evidence should be submitted in a manner analogous to the manner in which evidence is received in proceedings such as interferences and public use proceedings. Pursuant to 37 CFR §§ 1.292(a) and 1.671(b), statements of individuals in these proceedings would have to be verified statements. Even with respect to *ex parte* examinations conducted pursuant to 37 CFR §§ 1.104–119, evidence such as a statement submitted by an individual with respect to the status of a document as "prior art", or a statement submitted to establish other relevant factual matters relating to "prior art" such as inoperability of a device described in a document, must be verified statements.

29. ***Patlex Corp. v. Quigg***, 680 F.Supp. 33, 6 USPQ 2d 1296, 1298 (D. D.C. 1988)

Under 35 U.S.C. section 301, any person may cite to the PTO prior art, consisting of patents and printed publications, that may affect the patentability of any claim of a patent. 35 U.S.C. section 302 authorizes any person to request reexamination of a patent based on that "prior art." Within three months of receiving such a request, the Commissioner then determines whether the prior art raises a "substantial new question of patentability." *Id.* sec. 303(a). If the Commissioner determines that it does, he must order reexamination of the patent. *Id.* sec. 304. If he determines that the cited prior art raises no substantial new question of patentability, he denies the request for reexamination. The "determination . . . that no substantial new question of patentability has been raised will be final and nonappealable." *Id.* sec. 303(c). The statute contains no provision for appeal or review of a determination that a substantial new question has been raised. . . . The Court consequently concludes that the legislative scheme leaves the Commissioner's section 303 determination entirely to his discretion and not subject to judicial review.

30. ***Patlex Corp. v. Quigg***, 680 F.Supp. 33, 6 USPQ 2d 1296, 1298 n.1 (D. D.C. 1988)

The Federal Circuit ultimately held that (1) the reexamination statute is constitutional, 758 F.2d at 599–606 [225 USPQ at 246–252], (2) there is no presumption of validity of a patent in reexamination proceedings, 758 F.2d at 605 [225 USPQ at 251], (3) PTO practice which does not permit a patent owner to oppose a request for reexamination prior to the decision to order reexamination is constitutional, 758 F.2d at 607 [225 USPQ at 253], and (4) PTO practice resolv-

ing doubt in favor of ordering reexamination was void, 771
F.2d at 486–87 [226 USPQ at 989–90].

31. ***Patlex Corp. v. Quigg***, 680 F.Supp. 33, 6 USPQ 2d 1296,
1299 (D. D.C. 1988)

The reexamination statute limits the scope of the reexamination to patents and printed publications. 35 U.S.C.
secs. 301–302. Consequently, the Commissioner may not on
reexamination consider whether the specification of a patent
being reexamined contains an enabling disclosure for the issued patent claims. . . . [T]he reexamination statute does not
contemplate a "reexamination" of the sufficiency of a disclosure. Rather, it is limited to reexamination of patentability
based on prior art patents and publications. Hence, the
Court concludes that the examiner and the Board lacked jurisdiction in this case to "reexamine" the sufficiency of the
specification of the "great-grandparent" application.

XXIX. Reissue

1. ***Nupla Corp. v. IXL Mfg. Co.***, 42 USPQ 2d 1711, 1715–16
(Fed. Cir. 1997)

We do note that this is not a case in which the examiner
dictated specific amendments necessary for the reissue application claims to be allowed. In that event, arguably he
would already know what the declaration might tell him.
Nor is this a case in which only small language changes that
do not affect the scope of the claims were suggested by the
applicant. We make no comment, ruling, or intimation on
the need for a supplemental declaration explaining such dictated or non-substantive amendments.

2. ***In re Wilder***, 222 USPQ 369, 371–72 (Fed. Cir. 1984), ***cert.
denied***, 469 U.S. 1209 (1985)

These statements in the declarations accompanying the
reissue application show that the error relied upon is the attorney's failure to appreciate the full scope of the invention.
That error arose because the attorney assumed the presence
of features in the prior art that were not there. The board
concluded this is not error that may be corrected through
reissue because the defect could have been discovered during prosecution of the original patent. The board said, "there
may have been a lack of prescience of the existence of a
genus but such lack of prescience does not constitute an
error in the sense of section 251." . . . An attorney's failure
to appreciate the full scope of the invention is one of the
most common sources of defects in patents. The fact that the
error could have been discovered at the time of prosecution

with a more thorough patentability search or with improved communication between the inventors and the attorney does not, by itself, preclude a patent owner from correcting defects through reissue. . . . Under these circumstances, the attorney's explanation of his error in misunderstanding the scope of the invention is sufficient to satisfy the error requirement of 35 U.S.C. § 251. We accordingly reverse the board's rejection for failure to allege error correctable through reissue.

3. ***In re Clement***, 45 USPQ 2d 1161, 1165 (Fed. Cir. 1997)

[T]he following principles flow: (1) if the reissue claim is as broad as or broader than the canceled or amended claim in all aspects, the recapture rule bars the claim; (2) if it is narrower in all aspects, the recapture rule does not apply, but other rejections are possible; (3) if the reissue claim is broader in some aspects, but narrower in others, then: (a) if the reissue claim is as broad as or broader in an aspect germane to a prior art rejection, but narrower in another aspect completely unrelated to the rejection, the recapture rule bars the claim; (b) if the reissue claim is narrower in an aspect germane to prior art rejection, and broader in an aspect unrelated to the rejection, the recapture rule does not bar the claim, but other rejections are possible.

4. ***In re Clement***, 45 USPQ 2d 1161, 1166 (Fed. Cir. 1997)

In *Ball*, we said that the recapture rule does not apply when the reissue claim is broader than the canceled claim in a manner unrelated to the alleged error supporting reissue, but did not address whether the recapture rule would apply if the broadening did relate to the alleged error. . . . We can envision a scenario in which the patentee intentionally fails to enumerate an error so that he may eliminate a limitation that he argued distinguished the claim from a reference or added in an effort to overcome a reference and claim protection under *Ball*. We, therefore, think *Ball* is limited to its facts: the recapture rule does not apply when the broadening not only relates to an aspect of the claim that was never narrowed to overcome prior art, or argued as distinguishing the claim from the prior art, but also is not materially related to the alleged error.

5. ***In re Weiler***, 229 USPQ 673, 676 (Fed. Cir. 1986)

Moreover, § 251 authorizes reissue for "the" invention disclosed in the original patent, not for just "any" and "every" invention for which one may find some support in the disclosure of the original patent. . . . Here too, the question redounds to one of error, for when an applicant makes some disclosure, as

Weiler did, of as many as five distinct inventions, claims one, and ignores the rest, it is difficult to find error in the failure to claim those ignored on the sole basis that they were disclosed. To so hold would render meaningless the statutory requirement that an applicant point out and distinctly claim subject matter he regards as his invention.

6. ***In re Weiler***, 229 USPQ 673, 676–77 (Fed. Cir. 1986)

References to "intent to claim" in our cases, though occasionally including § 112 considerations, resolve ultimately into the question of error. "Determining what protection [an inventor] intended to secure by [an] original patent for the purposes of § 251 is an essentially factual inquiry confined to the *objective* intent manifested by the original patent." *In re Rowand*, 526 F.2d 558, 560, 187 USPQ 487, 489 (C.C.P.A. 1975) (emphasis in original). As explained in a later decision, Rowand's test of "intent to claim" was not one of "intent" per se, but looked to "objective indicia of intent." *In re Mead*, 581 F.2d 251, 256, 198 USPQ 412, 417 (C.C.P.A. 1978). . . .

This court has recently moved the "intent to claim" approach toward closer conformity with the statute, describing it as merely one factor "that sheds light upon whether the claims of the reissue application are directed to the same invention as the original patent *and the reissue would correct an inadvertent error in the original patent*." *In re Hounsfield*, 699 F.2d 1320, 1323, 216 USPQ 1045, 1048 (Fed. Cir. 1982) (emphasis added).

7. ***Hester Indus. Inc. v. Stein***, 46 USPQ 2d 1641, 1647 (Fed. Cir.), ***cert. denied***, 525 U.S. 947 (1998)

One of the most commonly asserted "errors" in support of a broadening reissue is the failure of the patentee's attorney to appreciate the full scope of the invention during the prosecution of the original patent application. . . . This form of error has generally been accepted as sufficient to satisfy the "error" requirement of § 251.

8. ***Hester Indus. Inc. v. Stein***, 46 USPQ 2d 1641, 1648 (Fed. Cir.), ***cert. denied***, 525 U.S. 947 (1998)

"Under [the recapture] rule, claims that are 'broader than the original patent claims in a manner directly pertinent to the subject matter surrendered during prosecution' are impermissible." *Clement*, 131 F.3d at 1468, 45 USPQ 2d at 1164 (quoting *Mentor*, 998 F.2d at 996, 27 USPQ 2d at 1525). Application of the recapture rule begins with a determination of whether and in what respect the reissue claims are broader than the original patent claims. *See id.* A reissue claim that does not include a limitation present in the original patent claims is broader in that respect. . . . Having determined that the reissue claims are broader in these respects, under the recapture rule we next examine whether these broader aspects relate to surrendered subject matter. *See* 131 F.3d at 1468–69, 45 USPQ 2d at 1164. "To determine whether an applicant surrendered particular subject matter, we look to the prosecution history for *arguments* and changes to the claims made in an effort to overcome a prior art rejection." *Id.* at 1469, 45 USPQ 2d at 1164 (emphasis added).

9. ***Hester Indus. Inc. v. Stein***, 46 USPQ 2d 1641, 1648 (Fed. Cir.), ***cert. denied***, 525 U.S. 947 (1998)

This statement in *Clement* indicates that a surrender can occur by way of arguments or claim changes made during the prosecution of the original patent application. To date, the cases in which this court has found an impermissible recapture have involved claim amendments or cancellations.

10. ***Hester Indus. Inc. v. Stein***, 46 USPQ 2d 1641, 1648 (Fed. Cir.), ***cert. denied***, 525 U.S. 947 (1998)

This court's prior opinions indicate that, as a general proposition, in determining whether there is a surrender, the prosecution history of the original patent should be examined for evidence of an admission by the patent applicant regarding patentability.

11. ***Hester Indus. Inc. v. Stein***, 46 USPQ 2d 1641, 1648 (Fed. Cir.), ***cert. denied***, 525 U.S. 947 (1998)

Arguments made to overcome prior art can equally evidence an admission sufficient to give rise to a finding of surrender. . . . Logically, this is true even when the arguments are made in the absence of any claim amendment. Amendment of a claim is not the only permissible predicate for establishing a surrender.

12. ***Hester Indus. Inc. v. Stein***, 46 USPQ 2d 1641, 1649 (Fed. Cir.), ***cert. denied***, 525 U.S. 947 (1998)

Indeed, the recapture rule is quite similar to prosecution history estoppel, which prevents the application of the doctrine of equivalents in a manner contrary to the patent's prosecution history. . . . Like the recapture rule, prosecution history estoppel prevents a patentee from regaining subject matter surrendered during prosecution in support of patentability.

13. ***Hester Indus. Inc. v. Stein***, 46 USPQ 2d 1641, 1650–51 (Fed. Cir.), ***cert. denied***, 525 U.S. 947 (1998)

No doubt if two patent attorneys are given the task of drafting patent claims for the same invention, the two attorneys will in all likelihood arrive at somewhat different claims of somewhat different scope. And such differences are even more likely when, as here, the second attorney drafts the new claims nearly a decade later and with the distinct advantage of having before him the exact product offered by the now accused infringer. This reality does not justify recapturing surrendered subject matter under the mantra of "failure to appreciate the scope of the invention." The circumstances of the case before us simply do not fit within the concept of "error" as contemplated by the reissue statute.

14. ***Hester Indus. Inc. v. Stein***, 46 USPQ 2d 1641, 1651 (Fed. Cir.), ***cert. denied***, 525 U.S. 947 (1998)

This court squarely addressed the issue in *Amos*, 953 F.2d at 616, 21 USPQ 2d at 1273. The *Amos* court held that § 251 does not include a separate requirement of an objective intent to claim. . . . Rather, the court concluded: "the essential inquiry under the 'original patent' clause of § 251 . . . is whether one skilled in the art, reading the specification, would identify the subject matter of the new claims as invented and disclosed by the patentees." *Id.* at 618, 21 USPQ 2d at 1275. The court noted that this inquiry is analogous to the "written description" requirement of 35 U.S.C. § 112 ¶ 1 (1994). *Id.* The court further stated that, to the extent the construct of an objective intent to claim is useful, it is "only one factor that sheds light" on whether the "original patent" clause of § 251 is satisfied.

15. ***C.R. Bard Inc. v. M3 Sys. Inc.***, 48 USPQ 2d 1225, 1228 (Fed. Cir. 1998), ***cert. denied***, 526 U.S. 1130 (1999)

The United States application was filed on July 30, 1986, naming Dr. Lindgren as the inventor. Corresponding United States Patent No. 4,699,154 (the '154 patent) was issued on October 13, 1987, with claims to the combination of the second generation gun and the new needle assembly. The '154 patent did not claim the needle assembly alone. . . . . Bard applied for reissue of the '154 patent in order to add claims to the needle assembly alone. This reissue patent issued on September 8, 1992, and is the '056 patent in suit.

16. ***C.R. Bard Inc. v. M3 Sys. Inc.***, 48 USPQ 2d 1225, 1234 (Fed. Cir. 1998), ***cert. denied***, 526 U.S. 1130 (1999)

M3 Systems states that since the needles were not claimed originally they were not "intended" to be claimed, and that absence of such intent is not an error correctable by reissue. That too is an incorrect statement of the law. An inventor's failure to appreciate the scope of an invention at the time of the original patent grant, and thus an initial intent not to claim the omitted subject matter, is a remediable error.

17. ***C.R. Bard Inc. v. M3 Sys. Inc.***, 48 USPQ 2d 1225, 1234 (Fed. Cir. 1998), ***cert. denied***, 526 U.S. 1130 (1999)

The reissue statute sets a two-year time limit for filing a broadening reissue application. This requirement was met. . . . There is no requirement that a patentee act earlier rather than later during the two-year window established by statute.

18. ***In re Fotland***, 228 USPQ 193, 194–95 (Fed. Cir. 1985), ***cert. denied***, 476 U.S. 1183 (1986)

In *Doll* the Court of Customs and Patent Appeals held that when a broadening reissue application was on file within the two year period, the claims could be further broadened after the two year period. Appellants argue that this also applies to "no defect" reissue applications that did not seek to enlarge the claims during the two year period. We must reject this position as contrary to precedent, contrary to regulation, and contrary to the plain language of § 251.

19. ***Ball Corp. v. United States***, 221 USPQ 289, 296 (Fed. Cir. 1984)

The CCPA, in *In re Rogoff*, [261 F.2d 601, 603–04, 120 USPQ 185, 186 (C.C.P.A. 1958)] noted that section 251

> contains no exceptions or qualifications as to time or extent of enlargement. The sole issue, therefore, is whether the claims on appeal enlarge, i.e., broaden, the patent claim.
>
> It is well settled that a claim is broadened, so far as the question of right to reissue is concerned, if it is so changed as to bring within its scope any structure which was not within the scope of the original claim. In other words, a claim is broadened if it is broader in any respect than the original claim, even though it may be narrowed in other respects.

Thus, the principle that a claim is broadened if it is broader in any respect than the original claim serves to effect the bar of section 251 against reissue filed later than 2 years after issuance of the original patent.

20. ***Ball Corp. v. United States***, 221 USPQ 289, 296 (Fed. Cir. 1984)

The recapture rule, however, is based on equitable principles. The rigidity of the broader-in-any-respect rule makes it inappropriate in the estoppel situation presented in this appeal.

Hence, we decline to apply that rule here, where the broader feature relates to an aspect of the invention that is not material to the alleged error supporting reissue.

21. ***Mentor Corp. v. Coloplast Inc.***, 27 USPQ 2d 1521, 1524 (Fed. Cir. 1993)

The deliberate cancellation of a claim of an original application in order to secure a patent cannot ordinarily be said to be an "error" and will in most cases prevent the applicant from obtaining the cancelled claim by reissue. The extent to which it may also prevent him from obtaining other claims differing in form or substance from that cancelled necessarily depends upon the facts in each case and particularly on the reasons for the cancellation.

22. ***Mentor Corp. v. Coloplast Inc.***, 27 USPQ 2d 1521, 1525 (Fed. Cir. 1993)

If a patentee tries to recapture what he or she previously surrendered in order to obtain allowance of original patent claims, that "deliberate withdrawal or amendment . . . cannot be said to involve the inadvertence or mistake contemplated by 35 U.S.C. § 251, and is not an error of the kind which will justify the granting of a reissue patent which includes the matter withdrawn." *Haliczer v. United States*, 174 Ct. Cl. 507, 356 F.2d 541, 545, 148 USPQ 565, 569 (Ct. Cl. 1966). "The recapture rule bars the patentee from acquiring, through reissue, claims that are of the same or of broader scope than those claims that were cancelled from the original application." *Ball Corp.*, 729 F.2d at 1436, 221 USPQ at 295 (citations omitted). The recapture rule does not apply where there is no evidence that amendment of the originally filed claims was in any sense an admission that the scope of that claim was not in fact patentable.

23. ***Mentor Corp. v. Coloplast Inc.***, 27 USPQ 2d 1521, 1525 (Fed. Cir. 1993)

Error under the reissue statute does not include a deliberate decision to surrender specific subject matter in order to overcome prior art, a decision which in light of subsequent developments in the marketplace might be regretted. It is precisely because the patentee amended his claims to overcome prior art that a member of the public is entitled to occupy the space abandoned by the patent applicant. Thus, the reissue statute cannot be construed in such a way that competitors, properly relying on prosecution history, become patent infringers when they do so. In this case, Mentor narrowed its claims for the purpose of obtaining allowance in the original prosecution and it is now precluded from recapturing what it earlier conceded.

24. ***Mentor Corp. v. Coloplast Inc.***, 27 USPQ 2d 1521, 1525 (Fed. Cir. 1993)

Reissue claims that are broader in certain respects and narrower in others may avoid the effect of the recapture rule. If a reissue claim is broader in a way that does not attempt to reclaim what was surrendered earlier, the recapture rule may not apply.

25. ***Vectra Fitness Inc. v. TNWK Corp.***, 49 USPQ 2d 1144, 1146 (Fed. Cir. 1998), ***cert. denied***, 526 U.S. 1160 (1999)

[B]oth the current regulation and the regulation in 1990 set forth the requirements for a valid disclaimer and therefore the requirements for the recording of the disclaimer. Moreover, nothing in the statutes or regulations requires any action by the PTO for a disclaimer to be "recorded."

26. ***Vectra Fitness Inc. v. TNWK Corp.***, 49 USPQ 2d 1144, 1147–48 (Fed. Cir. 1998), ***cert. denied***, 526 U.S. 1160 (1999)

TNWK counters that the plain language of 35 U.S.C. § 253 and the pertinent case law indicates that a disclaimer becomes a part of the original patent and that the disclaimed claims are viewed as if they never existed. TNWK asserts that, by filing a disclaimer, Vectra effectively modified the original patent to exclude the disclaimed claims and that any reissue application that enlarged the scope of the non-disclaimed claims must have been applied for within two years of the grant of the original patent. We agree with TNWK.

This court has interpreted the term "considered as part of the original patent" in section 253 to mean that the patent is treated as though the disclaimed claims never existed. *See Guinn v. Kopf*, 96 F.3d 1419, 1422, 40 USPQ 2d 1157, 1160 (Fed. Cir. 1996) ("A statutory disclaimer under 35 U.S.C. § 253 has the effect of canceling the claims from the patent and the patent is viewed as though the disclaimed claims had never existed in the patent.") . . .

In sum, we conclude that the reading of sections 251 and 253 that is urged by Vectra—that in the wake of a disclaimer, subsequent reissue claims are bounded by the claims as originally filed prior to the disclaimer—is contrary to the plain language of the statutes and pertinent case law.

27. ***In re Altenpohl***, 183 USPQ 38, 43 (C.C.P.A. 1974)

Lack of antecedent basis in a claim could render it invalid under 35 USC 112, second paragraph, and correction of such a defect by reissue should not have to depend on difference in scope of the claim. Inasmuch as 35 USC 251 is a remedial provision, which should be liberally construed, a patentee should be allowed to correct an error or ambiguity in a claim without having to rely on implication or litigation.

28. *In re Altenpohl*, 183 USPQ 38, 43 (C.C.P.A. 1974)

That the error was discovered by another (in this case the examiner) does not diminish the assertion in the supplemental reissue declaration that the original patent is wholly or partly inoperative or invalid because of the ambiguity, or the assertion that the error arose without any deceptive intention.

29. *In re Willingham*, 127 USPQ 211, 214 (C.C.P.A. 1960)

This governing principle as long ago as 1832, before there was statutory provision for granting reissues, was stated by Chief Justice Marshall in *Joseph Grant, et al. v. E. & H. Raymond*, 6 Peters 217, as follows:

> . . . The great object and intention of the [Patent] act is, to secure to the public the advantages to be derived from the discoveries of individuals, and the means it employs are the compensation made to those individuals, for the time and labor devoted to these discoveries, by the exclusive right to make, use and sell the things discovered, for a limited time. That which gives complete effect to this object and intention, by employing the same means for the correction of inadvertent error, which are directed in the first instance, cannot, we think, be a departure from the spirit and character of the act.

* * *

> It has been urged, that the public was put into possession of the machine, by the open sale and use of it under the defective specification, and cannot be deprived of it, by the grant of a new patent. The machine is no longer the subject of a patent. This would be perfectly true, if the second patent could be considered as independent of the first. But it is in no respect so considered. The communication of the discovery to the public has been made in pursuance of law, with the intent to exercise a privilege which is the consideration paid by the public for the future use of the machine. If, by an innocent mistake, the instrument introduced to secure this privilege fails in its object, the public ought not to avail itself of this mistake, and to appropriate the discovery, without paying the stipulated consideration. The attempt would be disreputable in an individual, and a court of equity might interpose to restrain him. (P. 240–241.)

30. *Topliff v. Topliff*, 145 U.S. 156, 171 (1891)

To hold that a patent can never be reissued for an enlarged claim would be not only to override the obvious intent of the statute, but would operate in many cases with great hardship upon the patentee. The specification and claims of a patent, particularly if the invention be at all complicated, constitute one of the most difficult legal instruments to draw with accuracy, and in view of the fact that valuable inventions are often placed in the hands of inexperienced persons to prepare such specifications and claims, it is no matter of surprise that the latter frequently fail to describe with requisite certainty the exact invention of the patentee, and err either in claiming that which the patentee had not in fact invented, or in omitting some element which was a valuable or essential part of his actual invention. Under such circumstances, it would be manifestly unjust to deny him the benefit of a reissue to secure to him his actual invention, provided it is evident that there has been a mistake and he had been guilty of no want of reasonable diligence in discovering it, and no third persons have in the meantime acquired the right to manufacture or sell what he had failed to claim. The object of the patent law is to secure to inventors a monopoly of what they have actually invented or discovered, and it ought not to be defeated by a too strict and technical adherence to the letter of the statute, or by the application of artificial rules of interpretation.

31. ***In re Willingham***, 127 USPQ 211, 215 (C.C.P.A. 1960)

Was there a deceptive intention on the part of appellant in requesting the examiner "in his discretion" to make the changes? We think not. Unfortunately the record does not reveal what occurred at the interview between appellant's attorney and the examiner. We think it proper to take judicial notice of the fact that such interviews are common and usually are conducted in the spirit of a free and open discussion as to the merits of the invention, the pertinency of the prior art and the allowability of claims. We feel certain that the interview referred to in the amendment of February 10, 1954, in the original application must have been of this type and that appellant's attorneys must as a result of the interview have been very confident of the competency of the examiner to have permitted him to use his "discretion" in deleting claim 12 and substituting claim 15 therefor. We think this reliance on the examiner's discretion was in good faith and without any deceptive intention. We are, therefore, unable to find in this entire proceeding anything which constitutes any evidence of a "deceptive intention" in the error which resulted in the cancellation of claim 12.

32. ***In re Willingham***, 127 USPQ 211, 215 (C.C.P.A. 1960)

The deliberate cancellation of a claim of an original application in order to secure a patent cannot ordinarily be said to be an "error" and will in most cases prevent the applicant from obtaining the cancelled claim by reissue. The extent to which it may also prevent him from obtaining other claims differing in form or substance from that cancelled necessarily depends upon the facts in each case and particularly on the reasons for the cancellation.

33. *In re Peters*, 221 USPQ 952, 953 (Fed. Cir. 1983)

The broadened claims merely omit an unnecessary limitation that had restricted one element of the invention to the exact and non-critical shape disclosed in the original patent. In sum, nothing in the original disclosure indicates or suggests that the tapered shape of the tips was essential or critical to either the operation or patentability of the invention. Indeed, if the reissue claims had been submitted with the original application, it is difficult to perceive how they could have been properly rejected under § 112.

34. *In re Peters*, 221 USPQ 952, 954 (Fed. Cir. 1983)

In the present case, the board having drawn the unsupported conclusion that the tapered shape of the metal tips was "critical", apparently felt that Peters must be restricted to claims containing a limitation specifying that shape. That was error, for where, as here, the overall disclosure reasonably conveys to one skilled in the art that the inventor had possession of the broad invention at the time the original application was filed, a claim drawn to that invention is available upon compliance with all provisions of § 251.

35. *Ex parte Scudder*, 169 USPQ 814, 815 (Pat. Off. Bd. App. 1971)

In *The State of Israel* case the court held that it was proper to file a reissue application in order to perfect a claim for priority under 35 U.S.C. 119 by filing a certified copy of the foreign application. The court held that the word "claiming" in 35 U.S.C. 251 should be construed as including a claim for priority as well as a claim defining the invention. In view of the liberalization of Section 251 advocated by the courts, we are unable to agree that Section 256 was intended by Congress to be the only avenue for correcting misjoinder of inventors in an issued patent.

36. *Ex parte Scudder*, 169 USPQ 814, 815 (Pat. Off. Bd. App. 1971)

It is our opinion that the reference in Section 251 to "claiming more or less than he had a right to claim in the patent" cannot be restricted to the patentability of the claims over the prior art but must also be interpreted to cover a situation where it is discovered that one of several joint inventors is the sole inventor of some of the claimed subject matter in a patent issued to joint inventors. In this case the joint inventors would be claiming more than they had a right to by asserting that they were the inventors of the subject matter which was invented by only one of them and vice versa.

37. ***In re Graff***, 42 USPQ 2d 1471, 1473 (Fed. Cir. 1997)
§ 251 does not bar multiple reissue patents in appropriate circumstances. Section 251[3] provides that the general rules for patent applications apply also to reissue applications, and § 251[2] expressly recognizes that there may be more than one reissue patent for distinct and separate parts of the thing patented. The statute does not prohibit divisional or continuation reissue applications, and does not place stricter limitations on such applications when they are presented by reissue, provided of course that the statutory requirements specific to reissue applications are met.

38. ***In re Graff***, 42 USPQ 2d 1471, 1473 (Fed. Cir. 1997)
[W]hether § 251[4] is met if there is no broadening reissue application on file within the two-year period. We conclude that it is not. In *In re Fotland*, 779 F.2d 31, 228 USPQ 193 (Fed. Cir. 1985) the Federal Circuit declined to permit the filing of broadened claims in a reissue application that had been filed within two years of patent grant, where the broadened claims were first presented more than two years after patent grant.

39. ***In re Graff***, 42 USPQ 2d 1471, 1474 (Fed. Cir. 1997)
We conclude that the reissue statute requires that proposals to broaden a patented invention must be brought to public notice within two years of patent issuance. The interested public is entitled to rely on the absence of a broadening reissue application within two years of grant of the original patent. Since Mr. Graff's broadened claims were first filed more than two years after patent grant, the Board's rejection of these claims is affirmed on this ground.

40. ***Hewlett-Packard Co. v. Bausch & Lomb Inc.***, 11 USPQ 2d 1750, 1756 n.7 (Fed. Cir. 1989), ***cert denied***, 493 U.S. 1076 (1990)
It is well settled that, in the reverse case of inequitable conduct during prosecution of the original application, reissue is not available to obtain new claims and thereby rehabilitate the patent.

41. ***Hewlett-Packard Co. v. Bausch & Lomb Inc.***, 11 USPQ
2d 1750, 1757 (Fed. Cir. 1989), ***cert denied***, 493 U.S. 1076
(1990)

As explained in *In re Wilder*, 736 F.2d 1516, 222 USPQ 369
(Fed. Cir. 1984), *cert. denied*, 469 U.S. 1209, 84 L. Ed. 2d
323, 105 S. Ct. 1173 (1985):

There are two distinct statutory requirements that a reissue oath or declaration must satisfy. First, it must state
that the patent is defective or partly inoperative or invalid
because of defects in the specification or drawing, or because the patentee has claimed more or less than he is entitled to. Second, the applicant must allege that the defective, inoperative, or invalid patent arose through error
without deceptive intent.

Id. at 1518, 222 USPQ at 370 . . . In sum, the statutorily required "error" of section 251 has two parts: (1) error in the
patent, and (2) error in conduct.

42. ***Hewlett-Packard Co. v. Bausch & Lomb Inc.***, 11 USPQ
2d 1750, 1757 (Fed. Cir. 1989), ***cert denied***, 493 U.S. 1076
(1990)

Although neither "more" nor "less" in the sense of scope of
the claims, the practice of allowing reissue for the purpose
of including narrower claims as a hedge against the possible
invalidation of a broad claim has been tacitly approved, at
least in dicta, in our precedent.

43. ***Hewlett-Packard Co. v. Bausch & Lomb Inc.***, 11 USPQ
2d 1750, 1759 (Fed. Cir. 1989), ***cert denied***, 493 U.S. 1076
(1990)

There is no disagreement with the long-standing proposition that invalidation of a new claim (added during reissue)
on prior art does not invalidate the other claims.

44. ***In re Oda***, 170 USPQ 268, 270 (C.C.P.A. 1971)

This court on previous occasions, particularly since the effective date of the 1952 Patent Act, has observed that the
reissue statute is based on fundamental fairness and that,
as a remedial provision, intended to bail applicants out of
difficult situations into which they get "without any deceptive intention," it should be liberally construed so as to carry
out its purpose to the end that justice may be done to both
patentees and the public.

45. ***In re Oda***, 170 USPQ 268, 273 (C.C.P.A. 1971)

What the 1952 statute says is that when the patent is
deemed "inoperative or invalid"—i.e., it is ineffective to pro-

tect the invention adequately or it is a nullity—and it is so
because of *error*, and the applicant for reissue is not guilty
of "any deceptive intention," then the patent may be reissued, subject to the other provisions of the statute. We are
unable to find in this provision anything pertaining to the
timeliness of an applicant's actions in the prosecution of the
application for the original patent. Neither do we find any
prohibition of reissue on the ground the applicant or his attorney knew of the error at the time the original patent issued.

46. ***In re Oda***, 170 USPQ 268, 273 (C.C.P.A. 1971)
[T]he 1952 reissue statute broadened the term "error" by not
limiting it to "error" that had arisen through "inadvertence,
accident, or mistake."

47. ***In re Oda***, 170 USPQ 268, 273 (C.C.P.A. 1971)
The mere fact that a change deprives a phrase of a needed
antecedent so that a reader might be somewhat perplexed or
confused does not result in the injection into a specification
of prohibited "new matter" within the meaning of § 251.

48. ***State of Israel, Ministry of Defence v. Brenner***, 155
USPQ 486, 488 (D.D.C. 1967)
The purpose of the statute governing reissue of patents is to
provide a remedy and method for correcting errors made by
applicants or their attorneys. The Congressional intent
should be effectuated and should not be defeated or limited
by artificial restrictions. The statute is remedial and should
be liberally construed.

49. ***State of Israel, Ministry of Defence v. Brenner***, 155
USPQ 486, 488 (D.D.C. 1967)
In light of the foregoing discussion, the Court concludes that
the phrase "claim in the patent" as used in Section 251 includes a claim to a right of priority on the basis of a foreign
filing date and is not limited to claims defining the invention; that a patent may be reissued for the purpose of establishing a claim to priority which was not asserted, or which
was not perfected during the prosecution of the original application; and that, accordingly, the plaintiff is entitled to a
reissue of its patent.

50. ***In re Amos***, 21 USPQ 2d 1271, 1273 (Fed. Cir. 1991)
The section requires that the patentee base the application
for reissue upon one of four specified grounds statutorily-
identified as correctable defects. . . . First, an asserted defect
may arise from an error in the specification. . . . Second, the

patentee may correct a defective drawing. The final two reasons for which the patentee may seek reissue concern original claims subsequently discovered to have been either too narrow or too broad.

51. *In re Wilder*, 736 F.2d 1516, 1518, 222 USPQ 369, 370 (Fed. Cir. 1984)

There are two distinct statutory requirements that a reissue oath or declaration must satisfy. First, it must state that the patent is defective or partly inoperative or invalid because of defects in the specification or drawing, or because the patentee has claimed more or less than he is entitled to. Second, the applicant must allege that the defective, inoperative, or invalid patent arose through error without deceptive intent.

52. *In re Amos*, 21 USPQ 2d 1271, 1274 (Fed. Cir. 1991)

Finally, the statute restricts the Commissioner to reissuing the patent only "for the invention disclosed in the original patent" with the proviso that "no new matter shall be introduced into the application." The "original patent" clause of § 251 creates a requirement that precludes reissue, historically styled as a "same invention" rejection, of patents with claims to subject matter that could not have been claimed in the original patent that is submitted for reissue.

53. *In re Mead*, 581 F.2d 251, 256, 198 USPQ 412, 417 (C.C.P.A. 1978)

"[I]ntent to claim" arose from the requirement that the reissue be for the "same invention" as the original, i.e., that it cover what was "intended to have been covered" by the original . . .

Thus, in *Rowand* and similar cases, "intent to claim" has little to do with "intent" *per se*, but rather is analogous to the requirement of § 112, first paragraph that the specification contain a "written description of the invention, and of the manner and process of making and using it." It is, as appellant urges, synonymous with "right to claim."

54. *In re Amos*, 21 USPQ 2d 1271, 1274–75 (Fed. Cir. 1991) (quoting *In re Wilder*, 736 F.2d 1516, 1520, 222 USPQ 369, 372 (Fed. Cir. 1984))

Hence, the purpose of the rubric "intent to claim" is to ask the same question as to whether "new matter" has been "introduced into the application for reissue" thus, perforce, indicating that the new claims are not drawn to the same invention that was originally disclosed. . . . Thus, the inquiry that must be undertaken to determine whether the new claims are "for the invention" originally disclosed, to para-phrase *Rowand*, is to examine the entirety of the original disclosure and decide whether, through the "objective eyes" of the hypothetical person having ordinary skill in the art, an inventor could fairly have claimed the newly submitted subject matter in the original application, given that the requisite error has been averred. We agree with, and, in any event, are bound by, the statement in *Mead*, quoted above, that the inquiry under § 251 as to whether the new claims are for the invention originally disclosed is analogous to the analysis required by § 112 para. 1. Under one aspect of that analysis, a court must ascertain whether "the disclosure originally filed [conveys] to those skilled in the art that applicant had invented the subject matter later claimed."

55. ***In re Amos***, 21 USPQ 2d 1271, 1275 (Fed. Cir. 1991)

We conclude that, under both *Mead* and *Rowand*, a claim submitted in reissue may be rejected under the "original patent" clause if the original specification demonstrates, to one skilled in the art, an absence of disclosure sufficient to indicate that a patentee could have claimed the subject matter. Merely finding that the subject matter was "not originally claimed, not an object of the original patent, and not depicted in the drawing," does not answer the essential inquiry under the "original patent" clause of § 251, which is whether one skilled in the art, reading the specification, would identify the subject matter of the new claims as invented and disclosed by the patentees. In short, the absence of an "intent," even if objectively evident from the earlier claims, the drawings, or the original objects of the invention is simply not enough to establish that the new claims are not drawn to the invention disclosed in the original patent.

56. ***Sampson v. Commissioner of Patents and Trademarks***, 195 USPQ 136, 136–38 (D. D.C. 1976)

During several rounds of litigation it was determined by the courts that plaintiff could not establish a 1959 filing date under the reference requirements of 35 U.S.C. 120, and that, therefore, under 35 U.S.C. 102(b) plaintiff was not entitled to letters patent since he had "published" his invention more than one year prior to the earliest filing date he could establish. Specifically, the co-pending applications plaintiff relied upon to satisfy section 120 contained the serial numbers, titles, and subject matter disclosures but lacked the filing date of prior applications in the chain. Plaintiff's "specific reference" was not specific enough. . . .

The language of the statute and cases under it seem to indicate that plaintiff's predicament is the very type of situation for which the section provides a remedy. Had omissions occurred in the application upon which the patent issued, there is little question that the reissue patent would be granted. But here the omissions occurred in prior intermediate applications which had become abandoned. Plaintiff therefore filed amendments to the abandoned, intermediate applications to insert what he believed to be technical information, i.e., the filing dates of the applications relied upon in his application chain. . . .

35 [U.S.C.] 120 does not bar amendment of intermediate abandoned applications to include technical information when, as in this case, that information would allow a reissuance of letters patent if the amendments were applied to the application upon which the patent originally issued. The legislative history makes it clear that equity shall guide section 251 actions.

57. *Ex parte Larkin*, 9 USPQd 2d 1078, 1079–80 (B.P.A.I. 1988)
The reissue statute is remedial in nature and based upon fundamental principles of equity and fairness. Accordingly, the reissue statute is to be construed liberally. *In re Weiler*, supra; *In re Bennett*, 766 F.2d 524, 226 USPQ 413, 416 (Fed. Cir. 1985) (in banc).

58. *Ex parte Larkin*, 9 USPQd 2d 1078, 1080 (B.P.A.I. 1988)
The requirement for an "intent to claim" has been characterized as a judicial shorthand denoting whether the requirement of the statute for "error" has been established. In order to ascertain whether an appellant had the "intent to claim," it is necessary to look to "objective indicia of intent." *In re Weiler*, supra; *In re Mead*, 581 F.2d 251, 256, 198 USPQ 412, 417 (C.C.P.A. 1978).

59. *Ex parte Larkin*, 9 USPQd 2d 1078, 1080 (B.P.A.I. 1988)
The determination of whether the requisite "error" under 35 U.S.C. 251 has been established must necessarily depend upon the facts of each case. Under the facts of this particular case, it is our opinion that the food grade monoalkyltin stabilizer previously claimed is so inextricably linked to the now claimed packaged foodstuff comprising a food grade vinyl halide polymer stabilized with that particular monoalkyltin compound that appellant's failure to claim the packaged foodstuff in the original application constitutes the "error" capable of being remedied by the reissue statute. The filing of the reissue application before us would appear to be a legitimate attempt by appellant to limit the claims simply as a hedge against possible invalidity of the original claims. *In re Handel*, 312 F.2d 943, 136 USPQ 460 (C.C.P.A. 1963).

60. ***In re Lambrech***, 202 USPQ 620, 622 (Comm'r Pat, 1976)

Omission of a reference to an earlier application on which priority is based is a mistake "of a minor character" which is correctable by Certificate. *In re Van Esdonk et al*, 187 USPQ 671. Correction would not involve the addition of new matter, since the relation between the several cases here involved is a matter of record. No reexamination would be required.

61. ***Brenner v. State of Israel***, 158 USPQ 584, 584–85 (D.C. App. 1968)

It is stipulated that appellee without deceptive intention neglected to file in the Patent Office the "certified copy of the original foreign application" for a patent which Section 119 requires to be filed "before the patent is granted," if the applicant wishes to avail himself of the benefits of the prior application. Less than three weeks after the U.S. patent was issued by the Patent Office, appellee discovered that, due to a clerical error, it had failed to file the required certified copy. It acted immediately to repair its mistake by sending the Patent Office the necessary copy, and by applying for a reissue of its patent with the priority rights included. . . .

Congress placed in the Patent Act another provision, Section 251, which in our view controls the disposition of this case. This section provides that "[w]henever any patent is, through error without any deceptive intention, deemed wholly or partly inoperative or invalid * * * by reason of the patentee claiming more or less than he had a right to claim in the patent," the Commissioner shall grant him the reissue of the patent with the faults corrected. The plain meaning of this section would seem to cover this situation. The patent issued was partly inoperative (insofar as it did not include the priority right), and the patentee (by failing to file the certified copy, although it did inform the Patent Office of its intention to claim the prior right and the existence of the foreign patent appears on the face of its application) did claim less than he had a right to claim. In any event, the purpose of this section is to allow patentees to correct inadvertent errors without penalty other than the payment of a small fee. This was such a case.

XXX. Certificate of Correction

1. ***In re Van Esdonk***, 187 USPQ 671, 672 (Comm'r 1975)

Under the circumstances of the present case, to deny patentees the benefit of their foreign priority, once properly claimed with respect to precisely the same subject matter, would seem to allow formal requirements to interfere undesirably with substantive rights.

Accordingly, it is held that applicants' perfection of a priority claim under 35 USC 119 in the parent application will satisfy the statute with respect to their continuation application. . . . It follows that petitioners properly requested a certificate of correction under 35 USC 255, since the mistake to be corrected cannot be said to be the fault of the Patent and Trademark Office.

2. *In re Schuurs*, 218 USPQ 443, 443–44 (Comm'r 1983)

The associate solicitor's requirement for an "acknowledgment * * * of intervening rights" as a condition for the issuance of a certificate of correction is reversed.

Intervening rights do not arise if a correction makes no change in the scope of a patent. . . . A correction for the purpose of perfecting a claim for priority under 35 USC 120 does not change the scope of a patent.

3. *In re Lambrech*, 202 USPQ 620, 622 (Comm'r 1976)

When the request is treated as based on 37 CFR 1.323, most of the requirements for granting a Certificate appear to be met. Omission of a reference to an earlier application on which priority is based is a mistake "of a minor character" which is correctable by Certificate. In re Van Esdonk et al, 187 USPQ 671. Correction would not involve the addition of new matter, since the relation between the several cases here involved is a matter of record. No reexamination would be required.

4. *Southwest Software Inc. v. Harlequin Inc.*, 56 USPQ 2d 1161, 1172 (Fed. Cir. 2000)

Section 254 provides that "[a] printed copy [of the certificate of correction] shall be attached to each printed copy of the patent, and such certificate shall be considered as part of the original patent." 35 U.S.C. § 254. It also provides that "[e]very such patent, together with such certificate, shall have the same effect and operation in law on the trial of actions for causes thereafter arising as if the same had been originally issued in such corrected form." *Id.* . . . We conclude that this language requires that, for causes arising after the PTO issues a certificate of correction, the certificate of correction is to be treated as part of the original patent—i.e., as if the certificate had been issued along with the original patent. By necessary implication, for causes arising before its issuance, the certificate of correction is not effective.

5. *Southwest Software Inc. v. Harlequin Inc.*, 56 USPQ 2d 1161, 1172–73 (Fed. Cir. 2000)

[A] patent with a single claim in means-plus-function form might, through a PTO mistake, omit from the specification the structure, material, or acts corresponding to the function recited in the claim. Until the PTO issues a certificate of correction pursuant to 35 U.S.C. § 254 adding the corresponding structure, such a claim would appear invalid to the public, and reasonable competitors would be justified in conducting their affairs accordingly. In such a case, where the claim is invalid on its face without the certificate of correction, it strikes us as an illogical result to allow the patent holder, once the certificate of correction has issued, to sue an alleged infringer for activities that occurred before the issuance of the certificate of correction. Moreover, it does not seem to us to be asking too much to expect a patentee to check a patent when it is issued in order to determine whether it contains any errors that require the issuance of a certificate of correction. In this case, the omission of the Program Printout Appendix from the '257 patent resulted in the absence of approximately 330 pages of text from the specification. It would seem that such an error would be readily apparent.

6. ***Southwest Software Inc. v. Harlequin Inc.***, 56 USPQ 2d 1161, 1172 (Fed. Cir. 2000)

Southwest's cause of action against Harlequin and ECRM arose before the certificate of correction was issued. Because the certificate of correction is not effective for purposes of this action, the Program Printout Appendix cannot be considered part of the '257 patent for purposes of this action, because it was added to the patent by the certificate. . . . Put another way, if claim 1 is found to have been invalid without the Program Printout Appendix, the invalidity ceased on April 1, 1997, when the PTO issued the certificate of correction.

7. ***Hallmark Cards Inc. v. Lehman***, 42 USPQ 2d 1134, 1137–38 (D. D.C. 1997)

In the instant action, the Congressional framework precludes the right of third parties to file a civil action in the case of the issuance of a Certificate of Correction; the third party's recourse for the alleged errors made by the PTO is to raise the issue as a defense in an infringement suit. . . . The Court finds that reissue and reexamination proceedings and issuances of Certificates of Correction have many similarities and should therefore be treated similarly with respect to judicial review. First, all three provisions are located within Title 35, Chapter 25 of the United States Code. Second, the Patent Statute makes clear that the effect of a reissued patent, a reexamined patent, and a patent for which a Certificate of Correction has been granted are the same: all have the full force and effect of the original issued patent. Additionally, all three proceedings are conducted, with limited exceptions, ex parte in the PTO.

Since the three types of proceedings are so similar in their purpose and effect, logic dictates the conclusion that Congress intended the same framework for judicial review to apply under all three provisions.

Moreover, it would strain credulity to conclude that Congress did not provide for judicial review by third parties of PTO decisions when the PTO conducts a thorough and comprehensive review of a patent in reissue and reexamination proceedings, but intended that third parties have the right to judicial review when the PTO issues Certificates of Correction, which involves a far less intrusive examination of a patent for minor, typographical, and clerical errors. . . .

[T]he Certificate of Correction section of the Patent Statute is more general and completely silent on the issue of judicial review. Participation by third parties in reissue proceedings is limited to the protest provision, from which there is no appeal. 37 C.F.R. Section 1.291. Participation in reexamination proceedings is limited to a request for reexamination and a reply to the patent owner's statement. 37 C.F.R. Sections 1.510, 1.535. The requester may not actively participate further and may not appeal. 37 C.F.R. Section 1.552(e); *Syntex (U.S.A.) Inc. v. U.S. PTO*, 882 F.2d 1570 [11 USPQ 2d 1866] (Fed. Cir. 1989). . . .

The PTO regulations do not expressly provide for any participation by third parties in requests for Certificates of Correction. See 37 C.F.R. Sections 1.322–323. It therefore is concluded that Congress did not intend that third parties have the right to judicial review of Certificates of Correction issued by the PTO.

8. ***In re Lambrech***, 202 USPQ 620, 622 (Comm'r Pat, 1976)

Omission of a reference to an earlier application on which priority is based is a mistake "of a minor character" which is correctable by Certificate. *In re Van Esdonk et al*, 187 USPQ 671. Correction would not involve the addition of new matter, since the relation between the several cases here involved is a matter of record. No reexamination would be required.

XXXI. Maintenance Fees

1. ***California Med. Prods., Inc. v. Tecnol Med. Prods., Inc.***, 921 F. Supp. 1219, 1260 (D. Del. 1995)

When entering the '219 patent on the docket list, however, Thurber made the mistake of following the usual routine and entering the issue date of the patent in the "issue date" column. This was an error on her part, but it was not an error which Strauss, as a reasonable and prudent person, could have expected, not after the August 12, 1986 letter. . . .

The Court finds that this subsequent reliance upon the docketing system was reasonable. The purpose of a docketing system is to be a readily accessible source of important information. It is not reasonable to expect a docket clerk, or a lawyer, to question and recalculate the information on a docket sheet every time the docket sheet is used, for that would completely negate its effectiveness.

2. ***California Med. Prods., Inc. v. Tecnol Med. Prods., Inc.***, 921 F. Supp. 1219, 1260 (D. Del. 1995)

The Court finds, however, that this failure is not crucial, because the Court finds that a reasonably prudent patent practitioner need not even have a backup system. All that is required is a reliable docketing system. Strauss had such a system, and it failed him on this occasion. Moreover, Strauss did not have any knowledge that the system had failed him until the PTO returned the maintenance fee payment, well after the expiration of the grace period for the maintenance fee payment. . . . Once Strauss learned of the lapse, he promptly sought reinstatement.

3. ***R.R. Donnelley & Sons Co. v. Dickinson***, 57 USPQ 2d 1244, 1248 (N.D. Ill. 2000)

Plaintiff next argues that the PTO has revived patents for lesser cause than that demonstrated in the instant case, such as its decision to revive a patent in *Laerdal*, 877 F.Supp. 255, due to a docketing error. *Laerdal* is distinguished from the instant case, however, since the patentee in that case personally hired a patent attorney to handle matters related to the patent.

XXXII. Terminal Disclaimer

1. ***Vectra Fitness Inc. v. TNWK Corp.***, 49 USPQ 2d 1144, 1146 (Fed. Cir. 1998), ***cert. denied***, 526 U.S. 1160 (1999)

[B]oth the current regulation and the regulation in 1990 set forth the requirements for a valid disclaimer and therefore the requirements for the recording of the disclaimer. Moreover, nothing in the statutes or regulations requires any action by the PTO for a disclaimer to be "recorded."

2. ***Sash Controls, Inc. v. Talon, L.L.C.***, Civ. App. No. 98-1152, slip op. at 6–7 (Fed. Cir. Jan. 27, 1999) (unpublished) (quoting ***Quad Envtl. Techs. Corp. v. Union Sanitary Dist.***, 20 USPQ 2d 1392, 1394 (Fed. Cir. 1991))

The district court erred in applying an estoppel to Sash's arguments concerning obviousness. In *Quad Environmental Technologies Corp. v. Union Sanitary District*, we held that a terminal disclaimer "is not an admission of obviousness of the later-filed claimed invention in light of the earlier-filed disclosure." . . . "In legal principle, the filing of a terminal disclaimer simply serves the statutory function of removing the rejection of double patenting, and raises neither presumption nor estoppel on the merits of the rejection."

3. *In re Lonardo*, 43 USPQ 2d 1262, 1266 (Fed. Cir. 1997), *cert. denied*, 522 U.S. 1147 (1998)

The doctrine of double patenting is intended to prevent a patentee from obtaining a time-wise extension of patent for the same invention or an obvious modification thereof. *E.g.*, *In re Longi*, 759 F.2d 887, 892, 225 USPQ 645, 648 (Fed. Cir. 1985). "Same invention" double patenting is based upon 35 U.S.C. § 101 (1994), which states that an inventor may obtain "a patent" for an invention. The statute thus permits only one patent to be obtained for a single invention, and the phrase "same invention" refers to an invention drawn to substantially identical subject matter. *Id.* Obviousness-type double patenting, on the other hand, is judicially created and prohibits an inventor from obtaining a second patent for claims that are not patentably distinct from the claims of the first patent. *Id.* With obviousness-type double patenting, however, a terminal disclaimer may overcome that basis for unpatentability, assuming that the first patent has not expired.

4. *In re Goodman*, 29 USPQ 2d 2010, 2015–16 (Fed. Cir. 1993)

To prevent extension of the patent right beyond statutory limits, the doctrine of obviousness-type double patenting rejects application claims to subject matter different but not patentably distinct from the subject matter claimed in a prior patent. . . .

The double patenting determination involves two inquiries. First, is the same invention claimed twice? . . . This inquiry hinges upon the scope of the claims in question. . . . If the claimed inventions are identical in scope, the proper rejection is under 35 U.S.C. § 101 because an inventor is entitled to a single patent for an invention. . . .

If one claimed invention has a broader scope than the other, the court must proceed to a second inquiry: whether one claim defines merely an obvious variation of the other patent claim. . . . Without a patentable distinction—because the pending claim defines merely an obvious variation of the patented claim—the patentee may overcome the double patenting rejection by filing a terminal disclaimer.

5. *In re Longi*, 225 USPQ 645, 649 (Fed. Cir. 1985)

It is well-established that a common assignee is entitled to proceed with a terminal disclaimer to overcome a rejection based on double patenting of the obviousness type. . . . Since the second patent would expire simultaneously with the first, this use of a terminal disclaimer is consistent with the policy that the public should be free to use the invention as well as any obvious modifications at the end of the patent's term.

6. ***R.R. Donnelley & Sons Co. v. Dickinson***, 57 USPQ 2d 1244, 1246–47 (N.D. Ill. 2000)

35 U.S.C. § 41(c)(1) gives defendant authority to accept maintenance fee payments (and thus revive patents) that are over 30 months late if "the delay is shown to the satisfaction of [defendant] to have been unavoidable." Whether or not a delay is unavoidable is decided on a case-by-case basis, taking all of the facts and circumstances into account. *Smith v. Mossinghoff*, 671 F.2d 533, 538 [213 USPQ 977] (D.C. Cir. 1982). The burden of showing the cause of the delay is on the person seeking to revive the patent. *Id.* Pursuant to PTO regulations, plaintiff can show that the delay in paying a maintenance fee was unavoidable by making a showing that:

> the delay was unavoidable since reasonable care was taken to ensure that the maintenance fee would be paid timely and that the petition was filed promptly after the patentee was notified of, or otherwise became aware of, the expiration of the patent. The showing must enumerate the steps taken to ensure timely payment of the maintenance fee, the date and the manner in which the patentee became aware of the expiration of the patent, and the steps taken to file the petition promptly.

37 C.F.R. 1.378(b)(3). Decisions on reinstating a lapsed patent are made by applying the "reasonably prudent person" standard. *Ray v. Lehman*, 55 F.3d 606, 608–09 [34 USPQ 2d 1786] (Fed. Cir. 1995).

"The test of whether the delay is unavoidable is applicable to ordinary human affairs, and requires no more or greater care or diligence that is generally used and observed by prudent and careful men in relation to their most important business." *In re Mattullath*, 38 App. D.C. 497 (1912).

Table of Cases

References are to page numbers.

—23 USPQ 2d 1661 (Fed. Cir. 1991) (unpublished) 243
—977 F.2d 1443, 24 USPQ 2d 1443 (Fed. Cir. 1992) 106, 112, 392
O'Farrell, In re, 7 USPQ 2d 1673 (Fed. Cir. 1988) 106
O.I. Corp. v. Tekmar Co., 42 USPQ 2d 1777 (Fed. Cir. 1997) 325, 334
Olsson, Ex parte, 65 USPQ 52 (Pat. Off. Bd. App. 1944) 247, 321
Orfeo, In re, 169 USPQ 487 (C.C.P.A. 1971) 149
Orthokinetics, Inc. v. Safety Travel Chairs, Inc., 806 F.2d 1565, 1 USPQ 2d 1081 (Fed. Cir. 1986) 188
Overhead Door Corp. v. The Chamberlain Group, Inc., 52 USPQ 2d 1321 (Fed. Cir. 1999) 316, 317

P

Paine, Webber, Jackson & Curtis, Inc. v. Merrill Lynch, Pierce, Fenner & Smith, Inc., 218 USPQ 212 (D. Del. 1983) 46
Pall Corp. v. Hemasure Inc., 50 USPQ 2d 1947 (Fed. Cir. 1999) 300
Panduit Corp. v. Dennison Mfg. Co., 1 USPQ 2d 1593 (Fed. Cir.), *cert. denied,* 481 U.S. 1052 (1987) 106, 128
Pannu v. Iolab Corp., 47 USPQ 2d 1657 (Fed. Cir. 1998) 13, 81
Paperless Accounting, Inc. v. Bay Area Rapid Transit Sys., 231 USPQ 649 (Fed. Cir. 1986), *cert. denied,* 480 U.S. 933 (1987) 372, 392
Pappas, Ex parte, 23 USPQ 2d 1636 (B.P.A.I. 1992) 430
Pardo, In re, 214 USPQ 673 (C.C.P.A. 1982) 23, 28, 173
Parks, Ex parte, 30 USPQ 2d 1234 (B.P.A.I. 1993) 190, 220
Patlex Corp. v. Quigg 6 USPQ 2d 1296 (D.D.C. 1988) 460, 461, 462, 467, 468
Patton, In re, 53 USPQ 376 (C.C.P.A. 1942) 47
Paulsen, In re, 31 USPQ 2d 1671 (Fed. Cir. 1994) 266
Pentec, Inc. v. Graphic Controls Corp., 227 USPQ 766 (Fed. Cir. 1985) 291
Perkin-Elmer Corp. v. Computervision Corp., 221 USPQ 669 (Fed. Cir.), *cert. denied,* 469 U.S. 857 (1984) 264
Personalized Media Communications, L.L.C. v. U.S. Int'l Trade Comm'n, 48 USPQ 2d 1880 (Fed. Cir. 1998) 230, 254, 327, 339, 340, 341, 342, 359
Peters, In re, 221 USPQ 952 (Fed. Cir. 1983) 478
Petisi v. Rennhard, 150 USPQ 669 (C.C.P.A. 1966) 206
Pfaff v. Wells Elecs., Inc., 43 USPQ 2d 1928 (Fed. Cir. 1997), *rev'd,* 525 U.S. 55, 48 USPQ 2d 1641 (1998) 64, 94, 95, 449, 450
Piasecki, In re, 223 USPQ 785 (Fed. Cir. 1984) 391
Pilkington, In re, 162 USPQ 145 (C.C.P.A. 1969) 224
Pioneer Hi-Bred Int'l, Inc. v. J.E.M. Ag. Supply, Inc., 53 USPQ 2d 1440 (Fed. Cir. 2000), *cert. granted,* 121 S. Ct. 1077 (Feb. 20, 2001) 22, 50
Pitney Bowes Inc. v. Hewlett-Packard Co., 51 USPQ 2d 1161 (Fed. Cir. 1999) 267, 273
Platner, In re, 155 USPQ 222 (Comm'r. Pat. 1967) 430
Pleuddemann, In re, 910 F.2d 823, 15 USPQ 2d 1738 (Fed. Cir. 1990) 279
Porter, Ex parte
—25 USPQ 2d 1144 (B.P.A.I. 1992) 239, 240, 243, 390
—39 USPQ 2d 1060 (B.P.A.I. 1995) (unpublished) 431
Portola Packaging Inc., 42 USPQ 2d 1295 (Fed. Cir. 1997) 457, 458, 459
PPG Indus., Inc. v. Guardian Indus. Corp.
—37 USPQ 2d 1618 (Fed. Cir. 1996) 63
—48 USPQ 2d 1351 (Fed. Cir. 1998) 365
Prater, In re, 162 USPQ 541 (C.C.P.A. 1969) 24
Preemption Devices, Inc. v. Minnesota Mining & Mfg. Co., 221 USPQ 841 (Fed. Cir. 1984) 441
Prima Tek II, L.L.C. v. A-Roo Co., 222 F.3d 1372, 55 USPQ 2d 1742 (Fed. Cir. 2000) 18, 19, 21, 452
Princeton Biochemicals, Inc. v. Beckman Instruments, Inc., Civ. App. 98-1525 (Fed. Cir. Aug. 19, 1999) (unpublished) 302, 376
Process Control Corp. v. HydReclaim Corp., 52 USPQ 2d 1029 (Fed. Cir. 1999) 38, 39, 184, 185
PSC Inc. v. Accu-Sort Sys., Inc., Civ. App. 96-1092 (Fed. Cir. Jan. 17, 1997) (unpublished) 345
Purdue Pharma L.P. v. Faulding Inc., 56 USPQ 2d 1481 (Fed. Cir. 2000) 193

Trimedyne, Inc. v. Surgical Laser Technologies, Inc., Civ. App. 96-1538 (Fed. Cir. July 10, 1998) (unpublished) 342

Tri-Wall Containers, Inc. v. United States, 161 USPQ 116 (Ct. Cl.), *cert. denied,* 396 U.S. 828 (1969) 287

Tronzo v. Biomet, Inc., 47 USPQ 2d 1829 (Fed. Cir. 1998) 192, 193, 213, 214, 348

U

Ullstrand v. Coons, 64 USPQ 580 (C.C.P.A. 1945) 251

Ultradent Prods., Inc. v. Life-Like Cosmetics, Inc., 44 USPQ 2d 1336 (Fed. Cir. 1997) 86, 217

Unidynamics Corp. v. Automatic Prod. Int'l Ltd., 48 USPQ 2d 1099, (Fed. Cir. 1998) 437

Union Carbide Corp. v. American Can Co., 220 USPQ 584 (Fed. Cir. 1984) 121, 135

United States v. *See name of opposing party*

United States Gypsum Co. v. National Gypsum Co., 37 USPQ 2d 1388 (Fed. Cir. 1996) 196, 197

University of Colo. Found., Inc. v. American Cyanamid Co., 52 USPQ 2d 1801 (Fed. Cir. 1999) 14, 452

V

Vaeck, In re, 20 USPQ 2d 1438 (Fed. Cir. 1991) 188

Valley Recreation Prods., Inc. v. Arachnid, Inc., 35 USPQ 2d 1218 (Fed. Cir. 1994) 347

Van Der Bolt, In re, Civ. App. No. 92-1517 (Fed. Cir. Aug. 10, 1993) (unpublished) 145

Van Esdonk, In re, 187 USPQ 671 (Comm'r 1975) 371, 378, 485

Vanmoor v. Wal-Mart Stores, Inc., 53 USPQ 2d 1377 (Fed. Cir.), *cert. denied,* 531 U.S. 821 (2000) 75

Vas-Cath, Inc. v. Mahurkar, 19 USPQ 2d 1111 (Fed. Cir. 1991) 188, 189

Vectra Fitness Inc. v. TNWK Corp., 49 USPQ 2d 1144 (Fed. Cir. 1998), *cert denied,* 526 U.S. 1160 (1999) 475, 489

Vehicular Techs. Corp. v. Titan Wheel Int'l, Inc., 54 USPQ 2d 1841 (Fed. Cir. 2000) 365

Vermeer Mfg. Co. v. The Charles Mach. Works, Inc., Civ. App. No. 00-1119 (Fed. Cir. Nov. 27, 2000) (unpublished) 304

Vickers, In re, 62 USPQ 122 (C.C.P.A. 1944) 181

View Eng'g, Inc. v. Robotic Vision Sys., Civ. App. 97-1001 (Fed. Cir. July 3, 1997) (unpublished) 344

Virginia Electronic & Lighting Corp. v. National Service Indus., Inc., Civ. App. No. 99-1226 (Fed Cir. Jan. 6, 2000) (unpublished), *cert denied,* 530 U.S. 1275 (2000) 15

Virginia Panel Corp. v. Mac Panel Co., 42 USPQ 2d 1225 (Fed. Cir. 1997), *cert. denied,* 525 U.S. 815 (1998) 360

Vivid Techs., Inc. v. American Science & Eng'g, Inc., 53 USPQ 2d 1289 (Fed. Cir. 1999) 366

W

Wahl Instruments, Inc. v. Acvious, Inc., 21 USPQ 2d 1123 (Fed. Cir. 1991) 196, 200

Waldemar Link, GmbH & Co. v. Osteonics Corp., 31 USPQ 2d 1855 (Fed. Cir. 1994) 374

Walter, In re, 205 USPQ 397 (C.C.P.A. 1980) 23

Wang Labs., Inc.

—v. Mitsubishi Elec. Am., Inc., 41 USPQ 2d 1263 (Fed. Cir.), *cert. denied,* 522 U.S. 818 (1997) 295

—v. Toshiba Corp., 26 USPQ 2d 1767 (Fed. Cir. 1993) 112

Warminster Fiberglass Co. v. Delta Fiberglass Structures, Inc., 42 USPQ 2d 1154 (Fed. Cir. 1996) (unpublished) 248

Warner, In re, 154 USPQ 173 (C.C.P.A. 1967), *cert. denied,* 389 U.S. 1057 (1968) 51, 392

Warner-Jenkinson Co. v. Hilton Davis Chem. Co., 520 U.S. 17, 41 USPQ 2d 1865 (1997) 296, 309, 310

Waterloo Furniture Components, Inc. v. Haworth, Inc., 25 USPQ 2d 1138 (N.D. Ill. 1992) 320

Watter, In re, 64 USPQ 571 (C.C.P.A. 1945) 113

Watts v. XL Sys., Inc., 56 USPQ 2d 1836 (Fed. Cir. 2000) 215, 277, 332

Weatherchem Corp. v. J. L. Clark, Inc., 49 USPQ 2d 1001 (Fed. Cir. 1998) 73, 74

Webster Loom Co. v. Higgins, 105 U.S. 580 (1882) 178